PENTECOSTA
A Theology of Encounter

PENTECOSTAL THEOLOGY
A Theology of Encounter

Keith Warrington

t&t clark

Published by T&T Clark

The Tower Building   80 Maiden Lane
11 York Road   Suite 704, New York
London SE1 7NX   NY 10038

www.continuumbooks.com

British Library Cataloguing-in-Publication Data
A catalogue record for this book is available from the British Library

ISBN-10: HB: 0-567-04442-4
        PB: 0-567-04452-1
ISBN-13: HB: 978-0-567-04442-6
        PB: 978-0-567-04452-5

Typeset by Newgen Imaging Systems Pvt Ltd, Chennai, India
Printed on acid-free paper in Great Britain by Athenaeum Press Ltd, Gateshead, Tyne and Wear

CONTENTS

Preface   vii
Abbreviations   xi

 1 In Pursuit of Pentecostalism   1
 2 The Quest for a Pentecostal Theology   17
 3 God   28
 4 The Church   131
 5 The Bible   180
 6 Spirituality and Ethics   206
 7 Mission   246
 8 Healing, Exorcism and Suffering   265
 9 Eschatology   309
10 Postscript   324

Subject Index   327
Scripture References   329

PREFACE

A number of issues are important to an appreciation of the purposes of this book and its presentation of Pentecostalism in particular. It is not to be viewed as a systematic or historical theology or a comprehensive presentation of all that Pentecostals believe.[1] Such an enterprise would need to cover more topics and there would be a great deal of overlap with other books exploring theology. Many of the beliefs of Pentecostals are also shared by other believers and they have been the cause of reflection and exploration by many other authors. To repeat that which has already been offered elsewhere is of little value, especially when the topics have been covered in depth, quality, objectivity and scholarship. At the same time, it may be concluded that there are already sufficient books exploring theology; one dedicated to Pentecostal theology may be an unnecessary luxury. However, it is the objective of this book to focus on a Pentecostal theology which is defined by distinctive elements of Pentecostal belief and praxis but especially by an undergirding Pentecostal philosophy.[2] This exercise has been based on a desire to explore issues relating to the major emphases of Pentecostals – encapsulated by the framework of Jesus, Saviour, Healer, Baptiser, Sanctifier and Coming King. Topics related to these emphases and others that are of central importance in current Pentecostalism will be the focus of the book. The fundamentally important doctrines of God, the Bible and the Church

---

[1] Similarly, movements associated with some elements of Pentecostalism (including Catholic Charismatics, the Word of Faith and Renewal movements) have also been largely excised because of the limitations of space.

[2] G.B. McGee, '"More than Evangelical": The Challenge of the Evolving Theological Identity of the Assemblies of God', *Pneuma* 25.2 (2003), pp. 289–300; D. Dayton, 'The Limits of Evangelicalism: The Pentecostal Tradition', in D. Dayton, R.K. Johnson (eds), *The Variety of American Evangelicalism* (Downers Grove: InterVarsity Press, 1991), pp. 48–51; W.W. Menzies, 'The Methodology of Pentecostal Theology: An Essay on Hermeneutics', in P. Elbert (ed.), *Essays on Apostolic Themes: Studies in Honor of Howard M. Ervin* (Peabody: Hendrickson, 1985), pp. 1–14; C.T. Thomas, 'Pentecostal Theology in the Twenty-First Century: 1998 Presidential Address to the Society for Pentecostal Studies', *Pneuma* 21 (1998), pp. 3–19.

are inevitable additions to the above topics as are the issues relating to personal spirituality and ethics. The provision of a broader discussion of the Spirit (as compared with the sections referring to Jesus and the Father) is largely due to the volume of literature written by Pentecostals exploring his character and function.

The emphasis of this book is on the formation and ongoing formulation of Pentecostal theology as reflected mainly in more recent literature. In order to ensure that the focus is kept on recent discussion, while at the same time offering an assessment on current theological debates and emphases, the majority of scholarly Pentecostal journal articles, books and theses accessed are from 1990 onwards.[3] Although Pentecostals exist in nearly every country in the world, the language of this resource has been largely restricted to English as the lingua franca of the majority of the potential readers; to include other language-based material to a bibliography that is already very large would have made the project impossible. Pentecostal denominational magazines, of which there are many, have also been largely excluded from this exploration for that would have resulted in an unhelpfully detailed enterprise.[4]

It has been intentional to almost exclusively concentrate on Pentecostal authors to portray Pentecostal theology because despite the apparent arrogance and exclusivity of this process, to understand Pentecostalism, it is a significant advantage to be a Pentecostal. The ethos of this book has been to allow the reader hear Pentecostals reflecting on the Bible and their spirituality. It is intended to be a snapshot of Pentecostal discussions and also a source for developing dialogue; therefore, the footnotes, while not intruding into the text of the book, are in order to encourage further research and interaction with the scholars who have written on the topics under discussion. The Pentecostal authors who have been interacted with may be assumed to speak for a significant proportion, if not a majority, of Pentecostals. Care has been taken to ensure that an objective and evaluative portrayal of Pentecostal theology has been provided, partnering with other Pentecostal scholars who are best able to comment on the history, theology and praxis of Pentecostalism. The purpose has been to thereby offer an authentic and accurate presentation of most of the major elements of that which may be best identified as Pentecostal theology in its global setting. The beliefs of Pentecostals will be presented as well as critiques and suggestions for development offered. The value of the book will be not just in the recording of current Pentecostal theology/praxis but also in the offering of suggestions for (re)direction as well as the identification of changes that have taken

---

[3] Earlier Pentecostal literature is still valuable, exploring earlier and current Pentecostal beliefs.

[4] See www.keithwarrington.co.uk for bibliographies.

place or movements for change that are growing. It is anticipated that a Reader in Pentecostal Theology would be an ideal future partner in this process.

It is appropriate to thank Regents Theological College, Nantwich, Cheshire, England, at which I have the pleasure and privilege to serve and teach, for facilitating my research for this book. My colleagues, Dr. Tim Walsh and Rev. Julian Ward, have taken time to engage with the text and improve it. I am also very indebted to the hundreds of Pentecostal authors whose work I have read, engaged with and learnt from. The motivation for this journey has been my students and others like them whose theological tradition has related most prominently to Pentecostalism in its global context. To them I owe a debt of gratitude for allowing me to be their teacher and also for the opportunity of learning from them much that has developed me as a teacher of others and a follower of Jesus. My wife has been my constant best friend and partner in life, and has provided for all that I have needed to ensure that this enterprise has been completed.

As all authors and research students will know, the more one studies and writes, the less contented one becomes with that which has been achieved; the closer one is acquainted with a finished project, the more its imperfections and the inadequacies of the author are identified. This book is no exception and so I offer it in the knowledge that others could do better and, no doubt, will do so in the future. Nevertheless, in the hope that it will contribute to the development of Pentecostalism, its beliefs and praxis, I present it to you. If God becomes the increased focus of your imagination, the Spirit becomes more valuable to you and Jesus is identified as even more remarkable, then I will feel that at least, to a small degree, I have succeeded in my quest.

ABBREVIATIONS

AfJPS	*African Journal of Pentecostal Studies*
AJPS	*Asian Journal of Pentecostal Studies*
AJT	*Asian Journal of Theology*
AoG	Assemblies of God
CGJ	*Church Growth Journal*
CJT	*Canadian Journal of Theology*
CPCR	*Cyberjournal for Pentecostal-Charismatic Research*
DPCM	*The Dictionary of Pentecostal and Charismatic Movements*
EB	*Epta Bulletin*
EMQ	*Evangelical Missions Quarterly*
EPCC	*Encyclopedia of Pentecostal and Charismatic Christianity*
EPCRA	*European Pentecostal Charismatic Research Association*
EPTA	European Pentecostal Theological Association
ER	*The Ecumenical Review*
ERT	*Evangelical Review of Theology*
GOTR	*Greek Orthodox Theological Review*
HTR	*Harvard Theological Review*
IBMR	*International Bulletin of Missionary Research*
IRB	*Irish Biblical Studies*
IRM	*International Review of Mission*
JACT	*Journal of African Christian Thought*
JAM	*Journal of Asian Mission*
JARA	*Journal of African Religion in Africa*
JAS	*Journal of African Studies*

ABBREVIATIONS

JBV	*Journal of Beliefs and Values*
JEPTA	*Journal of the European Pentecostal Theological Association*
JES	*Journal of Ecumenical Studies*
JETS	*Journal of the Evangelical Theological Society*
JHLT	*Journal of Hispanic/Latino Theology*
JPT	*Journal of Pentecostal Theology*
JRA	*Journal of Religion in Africa*
JSNT	*Journal of the Study of the New Testament*
NIDPCM	*The New International Dictionary of Pentecostal and Charismatic Movements*
NTCG	The New Testament Church of God
NTS	*New Testament Studies*
PR	*The Pneuma Review*
RRR	*Review of Religious Resources*
SC	*The Spirit and the Church*
SJT	*Scottish Journal of Theology*
SPS	Society for Pentecostal Studies
TTR	*Teaching Theology and Religion*
WTJ	*Wesleyan Theological Journal*
ZNTW	*Zeitschrift für die neutesamentliche Wissenschaft*

1

IN PURSUIT OF
PENTECOSTALISM

Introduction

Just over 100 years ago, Pentecostalism was born. Since then, it has grown to be one of the biggest and fastest growing components of Christianity.[1] Its inception in the West is generally identified as being in Azusa Street, Los Angeles, in 1906.[2] So important are the events associated with Azusa Street in Pentecostal history that the AoG journal *Enrichment* dedicated an edition to the history and legacy of the event and its centenary was celebrated in Los Angeles with a week of events attracting thousands of Pentecostals.[3] However, although much of early Pentecostalism received its driving force from the West, some expressions of Pentecostalism in India, China and Chile predated these occurrences[4] while others started spontaneously with little external assistance.[5]

In spite of the romantic suggestion that Pentecostalism had no founding father and that the Spirit was its leader, Pentecostalism did not arise in a vacuum.[6] Nevertheless, Pentecostals have often sought to identify themselves

---

[1] The journal *Heritage* is dedicated to the history of the AoG (www.AGHeritage.org) in association with the Flower Pentecostal Heritage Center; E.A. Wilson, 'They Crossed the Red Sea, Didn't They? Critical History and Pentecostal Beginnings', in M.W. Dempster, B.D. Klaus, D. Petersen (eds), *The Globalization of Pentecostalism: A Religion Made to Travel* (Oxford: Regnum Books, 1999), pp. 85–115; W.W. Menzies, 'The Movers and Shakers', in H.B. Smith (ed.), *Pentecostals from the Inside Out* (Wheaton: Victory, 1990), pp. 29–41; V. Synan, 'An Equal Opportunity Movement', in H.B. Smith (ed.), *Pentecostals from the Inside Out* (Wheaton: Victory, 1990), pp. 43–50; C.H. Mason, *History and Formative Years of the Church of God in Christ with Excerpts from the Life and Works of Its Founder: Bishop C.H. Mason* (Memphis: Church of God in Christ Publishing House, 1973); A.H. Anderson, *An Introduction to Pentecostalism* (Cambridge: Cambridge University Press, 2004), pp. 19–165; A. Clayton, 'The Significance of

as an *organism* rather than an *organization*.[7] Its antecedents and influences
have been identified as Anabaptism,[8] Dispensationalism,[9] Evangelicalism,[10]

William H. Durham for Pentecostal Historiography', *Pneuma* 1.2 (1970), pp. 27–42;
J.R. Goff, *Fields White unto Harvest: Charles F. Parham and the Missionary Origins
of Pentecostalism* (Fayetteville: University of Arkansas Press, 1988); C.M. Robeck Jr,
'Pentecostal Origins from a Global Perspective', in H.D. Hunter, P.D. Hocken (eds), *All
Together in One Place: Theological Papers from the Brighton Conference on World
Evangelization* (Sheffield: Sheffield Academic Press, 1993), pp. 166–80; D. Irvin,
'Pentecostal Historiography and Global Christianity: Rethinking the Question of Ori-
gins', *Pneuma* 27.1 (2005), pp. 35–50; D. Jacobsen, *Thinking in the Spirit: Theologies
of the Early Pentecostal Movement* (Bloomington: University of Indiana Press, 2003);
N. Bloch-Hoell, *The Pentecostal Movement: Its Origin, Development, and Distinctive
Character* (Oslo: Allen and Unwin, 1964); P. Pomerville, 'The Pentecostals and Growth',
in L.G. McClung Jr (ed.), *Azusa Street and Beyond: Pentecostal Missions and Church
Growth in the Twentieth Century* (South Plainfield: Bridge, 1986), pp. 151–55;
E.A. Wilson, *Strategy of the Spirit: J. Philip Hogan and the Growth of the Assemblies of
God Worldwide 1960–1990* (Carlisle: Regnum, 1997); E.L. Blumhofer, *The Assemblies
of God: A Chapter in the Story of American Pentecostalism* (2 vols; Springfield: Gospel
Publishing House, 1989); idem, *Restoring the Faith: The Assemblies of God, Pentecos-
talism and American Culture* (Urbana: University of Illinois Press, 1993); S.M. Burgess,
E.M. van der Maas (eds), *NIDPCM* (Grand Rapids: Zondervan, 2002).

[2] J. Creech, 'Visions of Glory: The Place of Azusa Street Revival in Pentecostal History',
Church History 65 (1996), pp. 405–24; D.J. Nelson, 'For Such a Time as This: The Story
of William J. Seymour and the Azusa Street Revival' (unpublished doctoral dissertation,
University of Birmingham, 1981); J.T. Nichol (*Pentecostalism* (Plainfield: Logos, 1966),
p. 19) offers alternative dates and locations which may function as rivals to this date
(North Carolina, 1896; Topeka, Kansas, 1901); C.M. Robeck Jr, 'Azusa Street Revival',
in Burgess and van der Maas (eds), *NIDPCM*, pp. 344–50; idem, *The Azusa Street
Mission and Revival: The Birth of the Global Pentecostal Mission* (Nashville: Nelson,
2006); A. Cerillo Jr, G. Wacker, 'Bibliography and Historiography', in Burgess and
van der Maas (eds), *NIDPCM*, pp. 382–405 (394); F. Bartleman, *Azusa Street* (South
Plainfield: Bridge Publishing, 1925, 1980).

[3] 11.2 (2006); see S.M. Horton (ed.), *Systematic Theology: A Pentecostal Perspective*
(Springfield: Logion Press, 1994), pp. 9–37; V. Synan, *The Old Time Power: A Centen-
nial History of the International Pentecostal Holiness Church* (Franklin Springs: Life
Springs Resources, 1998); idem, *The Century of the Holy Spirit: 100 Years of Pentecostal
and Charismatic Renewal* (Nashville: Nelson, 2001).

[4] A.H. Anderson, 'Revising Pentecostal History in Global Perspective', in A.H. Anderson,
E. Tang (eds), *Asian and Pentecostal: The Charismatic Face of Christianity in Asia* (Oxford:
Regnum, 2005), pp. 147–73; idem, *An Introduction to Pentecostalism*, pp. 170–76;
M. Ketcham, W. Warner, 'When the Pentecostal Fire Fell in Calcutta' in L.G. McClung Jr
(ed.), *Azusa Street and Beyond: 100 Years of Commentary on the Global Pentecostal/
Charismatic Movement* (Orlando: Bridge-Logos Publishing, 2006), pp. 27–34; Irvin,
'Pentecostal Historiography', pp. 45–6; J.T. Benson, *A History (1898–1915) of the
Pentecostal Mission Incorporated* (Nashville: Trevecca Press, 1977); D.W. Faupel, *The
Everlasting Gospel: The Significance of Eschatology in the Development of Pentecostal
Theology* (Sheffield: Sheffield Academic Press, 1996), pp. 136–85.

[5] D. Petersen, 'The Formation of Popular, National, Autonomous Pentecostal Churches in Central America', *Pneuma* 16.1 (1994), pp. 23–48; P. Pulikottil, 'As East and West Met in God's Own Country: Encounter of Western Pentecostalism with Native Pentecostalism in Kerala', *AJPS* 5.1 (2002), pp. 5–22 (18–19).

[6] Those who have challenged the earlier simplistic view include W.K. Kay, 'Three Generations on: The Methodology of Pentecostal History', *EB* 11.1, 2 (1992), pp. 58–70; T.B. Cargal, 'Beyond the Fundamentalist-Modernist Controversy: Pentecostals and Hermeneutics in a Postmodern Age', *Pneuma* 15.2 (1993), pp. 163–87 (168–71); F.D. Bruner, *A Theology of the Holy Spirit. The Pentecostal Experience and the New Testament Witness* (Grand Rapids: Eerdmans, 1970), pp. 35–55; A.H. Anderson, 'The Pentecostal and Charismatic Movements in Britain: An Historical Overview', *Refleks* 3.1 (2004), pp. 78–90; idem, *An Introduction to Pentecostalism*, 25–38; J.H. Carpenter, 'Genuine Pentecostal Traditioning: Rooting Pentecostalism in Its Evangelical Soil: A Reply to Simon Chan', *AJPS* 6.2 (2003), pp. 303–26; W. César, 'From Babel to Pentecost: A Socio-Historical-Theological Study of the Growth of Pentecostalism' in A. Corten, R. Marshall-Fratani (eds), *Between Babel and Pentecost: Transnational Pentecostalism in Africa and Latin America* (Bloomington: Indiana University Press, 2001), pp. 55–75; A. Cerillo Jr, 'The Origins of American Pentecostalism', *Pneuma* 15.1 (1993), pp. 77–88; B. Klaus, 'The Holy Spirit and Mission in Eschatological Perspective: A Pentecostal Viewpoint', *Pneuma* 27.2 (2005), pp. 322–42 (326–28); G. Wacker, 'Wild Theories and Mad Excitement', in Smith (ed.), *Pentecostals from the Inside Out*, pp. 19–28 (22–3); Faupel, *The Everlasting Gospel*, pp. 28–41; S. Land, *Pentecostal Spirituality: A Passion for the Kingdom* (Sheffield: Sheffield Academic Press, 1993), pp. 47–9; S.M. Burgess, 'Cutting the Taproot: The Modern Pentecostal Movement and Its Traditions', in M.W. Wilson (ed.), *Spirit and Renewal: Essays in Honor of J. Rodman Williams* (Sheffield: Sheffield Academic Press, 1994), pp. 56–68; Robeck, 'Pentecostal Origins from Global Perspective', pp. 166–80.

[7] In the 'Preamble and Resolution of Constitution' (in the *Minutes of the General Council of the Assemblies of God in the United States of America, Canada and Foreign Lands held at Hot Springs, AR, April 2–12, 1914* (Findlay: Gospels Publishing House, 1914), p. 4), the AoG described itself as 'members of said GENERAL ASSEMBLY OF GOD (which is God's organism) and do not believe in identifying ourselves as . . . a human organisation'.

[8] M.S. Clark, 'Pentecostalism's Anabaptist Roots: Hermeneutical Roots', in W. Ma, R.P. Menzies (eds), *The Spirit and Spirituality. Essays in Honour of Russell P. Spittler* (Sheffield: Sheffield Academic Press, 2004), pp. 194–211; Nichol, *Pentecostalism*, pp. 2–3; G. H. Boyd III, 'Pentacostalism's Anabaptist Heritage: The Zofingen Disputation of 1532', *JEPTA* 29.1 (2008), pp. 49–61.

[9] G.T. Sheppard, 'Pentecostals and the Hermeneutics of Dispensationalism: The Anatomy of an Uneasy Relationship', *Pneuma* 6 (1984), pp. 5–33; L.V. Crutchfield, *The Origins of Dispensationalism: The Darby Factor* (Lanham: University Press of America, 1992).

[10] M.C. Dyer, 'An examination of the theology and practice of the Lord's Supper in British Pentecostalism' (unpublished master's dissertation, King's College, London, 2004), pp. 23–65; W.J. Hollenweger, 'From Azusa Street to the Toronto Phenomenon: Historical Roots of the Pentecostal Movement', in J. Moltmann, K-J. Kuschel (eds), *Pentecostal Movements as an Ecumenical Challenge, Concilium* (London: SCM, 1996), pp. 3–14 (8–9); P. Althouse, 'The Influence of Dr. J.E. Purdie's Reformed Anglican Theology on the Formation and Development of the Pentecostal Assemblies of Canada', *Pneuma* 19.1 (1996), pp. 3–28; I.M. Randall, 'Old Time Power: Relationships between Pentecostalism and Evangelical Spirituality in England', *Pneuma* 19.1 (1997), pp. 53–80;

Pietism,[11] Wesleyanism[12] and the following Holiness movement,[13] the teachings associated with Keswick[14] (in which the emphasis was placed on the importance of abiding in Christ (Jn 15:1–11) and the baptism in the Spirit was identified as a post-conversion crisis experience intended to empower believers and act as the gateway to a 'life of overcoming' and service, rather than a means of instantaneous sanctification or sinless perfection) and the Higher Life Movement,[15] the, mainly American and Welsh, healing and revival movements[16] and healing evangelists,[17] the Latter Rain movement[18] (which developed into and was associated with Restorationism, a movement that expected the restoration of apostolic Christianity before the return of Jesus[19]), premillennialism,[20] black spirituality[21] and various individuals.[22]

E.L. Blumhofer, 'The "Overcoming Life": A Study in the Reformed Evangelical Origins of Pentecostalism' (unpublished doctoral dissertation, Harvard University, 1977).

[11] D.D. Bundy, 'European Pietist Roots of Pentecostalism', in Burgess and van der Maas (eds), *NIDPCM*, pp. 610–13.

[12] H.H. Knight III, 'From Aldersgate to Azusa: Wesley and the Renewal of Pentecostal Spirituality', *JPT* 8 (1996), pp. 82–98; D.W. Dayton, *Theological Roots of Pentecostalism* (Metuchen: Scarecrow Press, 1987), pp. 35–84; R.H. Gause, 'Issues in Pentecostalism', in R.P. Spittler (ed.), *Perspectives on the New Pentecostalism* (Grand Rapids: Baker, 1976), pp. 106–16 (108); D. Petersen, *Not by Might nor by Power: A Pentecostal Theology of Social Concern* (Oxford: Regnum, 1996), pp. 16–19; M.E. Dieter, 'The Wesleyan/Holiness and Pentecostal Movements: Commonalities, Confrontation, and Dialogue', *Pneuma* 12.1 (1990), pp. 4–13; W.W. Menzies, 'The Non-Wesleyan Origins of the Pentecostal Movement', in V. Synan (ed.), *Aspects of Pentecostal-Charismatic Origins* (Plainfield: Logos International, 1975), pp. 81–98.

[13] C.E. Jones, 'Holiness Movement', in Burgess and van der Maas (eds), *NIDPCM*, pp. 726–29; Dyer, 'An Examination of Theology', pp. 20–3; S.S. Dupree, 'In the Sanctified Holiness Pentecostal Charismatic Movement', *Pneuma* 23.1 (2001), pp. 97–114; V. Synan, *The Holiness-Pentecostal Tradition: Charismatic Movements in the Twentieth Century* (Grand Rapids: Eerdmans, 1997); Dayton, *Theological Roots of Pentecostalism*, p. 174; A. Cerillo, 'The Beginnings of American Pentecostalism', in E.L. Blumhofer, R.P. Spittler, G.A. Wacker (eds), *Pentecostal Currents in American Pentecostalism* (Urbana: University of Illinois Press, 1999), pp. 229–59.

[14] Keswick is a town in the Lake District in the North West of England at which conventions were held (and still are), dedicated to preaching and the seeking of a closer relationship with God; D.D. Bundy, 'Keswick Higher Life Movement', in Burgess and van der Maas (eds), *NIDPCM*, pp. 820–21; Faupel, *The Everlasting Gospel*, pp. 85–8; Petersen, *Not by Might nor by Power*, pp. 19–21; C.Price, J. Randall, *Transforming Keswick* (Carlisle: Paternoster, 2000).

[15] See Faupel, *The Everlasting Gospel*, pp. 89–90, 96–114.

[16] The Welsh revival (1904–1905) had a significant part to play in the establishing of British Pentecostalism; see Dyer, 'An Examination of Theology', pp. 18–20; Faupel, *The Everlasting Gospel*, p. 190; T.B. Walsh, '"To Meet and Satisfy a Very Hungry People": An Exploration of the Origins, Emergence, and Development of the Pentecostal Movement in England, 1907–1925' (unpublished doctoral dissertation, University of Manchester, 2007).

From the 1960s onwards, the Charismatic Renewal,[23] and its later permutations, have had an increasingly important influence on Pentecostals[24] as has the Full Gospel Business Men's Fellowship International.[25]

---

[17] Including William Branham, Oral Roberts, Smith Wigglesworth (D. Cartwright, 'The Real Wigglesworth', *JEPTA* 17 (1997), pp. 90–96; idem, *The Real Smith Wigglesworth* (Grand Rapids: Chosen Books, 2003), T.L. Osborne, Reinhard Bonnke and D.G.S. Dhinakaran.

[18] Faupel, *The Everlasting Gospel*, pp. 30–43.

[19] W.W. Menzies, *Anointed to Serve. The Story of the Assemblies of God* (Springfield: Gospel Publishing House, 1971), pp. 57–9; G. Wacker, 'Playing for Keeps: The Primitive Impulse of Early Pentecostalism' in R.T. Hughes (ed.), *The American Quest for the Primitive Church* (Urbana: University of Illinois, 1988), pp. 196–219; Blumhofer, *The Assemblies of God*, pp. 18–22.

[20] R.M. Anderson, *Vision of the Disinherited: The Making of American Pentecostalism* (Oxford: Oxford University Press, 1979), p. 97; Walsh, "To Meet and Satisfy", pp. 163–202.

[21] R.I.H. Gerlof, *A Plea for British Black Theologies: The Black Church Movement in Britain in Its Transatlantic Cultural and Theological Interaction* (Frankfurt: Peter Lang, 1992); idem, 'The Holy Spirit and the African Diaspora: Spiritual, Cultural and Social Roots of Black Pentecostal Churches', *EB* 14 (1995), pp. 85–100; L. Lovett, 'Black Origins of the Pentecostal Movement', in Synan (ed.), *The Holiness-Pentecostal Tradition*, pp. 123–42; L. Lovett, 'Aspects of the Spiritual Legacy of the Church of God in Christ: Ecumenical Implications', in D.T. Shannon, G.S. Wilmore (eds), *Black Witness to the Apostolic Faith* (Grand Rapids: Eerdmans, 1985), pp. 41–9; A. Paris, *Black Pentecostalism* (Amherst: University of Massachusetts Press, 1982); C.J. Sanders, *Saints in Exile: The Holiness-Pentecostal Experience in African Religion and Culture* (Oxford: Oxford University Press, 1996); D.W. Cartwright, 'Black Pentecostal Churches in Britain', *JEPTA* 27.2 (2007), pp. 128–37; C.E. Jones, *Black Holiness: A Guide to the Study of Black Participation in Wesleyan Perfectionistic and Glossalalic Pentecostal Movements* (Metuchen: Scarecrow Press, 1987); L. MacRobert, 'The Black Roots of Pentecostalism' in J.A.B. Jongeneel (ed.), *Pentecost, Mission and Ecumenism. Essays on Intercultural Theology* (Frankfurt: Peter Lang, 1992), pp. 73–84; idem, *The Black Roots and White Racism of Early Pentecostalism in the USA* (Basingstoke: Macmillan, 1988); J.S. Tinney, 'Black Origins of the Pentecostal Movement', *Christianity Today* 16.1 (Oct. 8, 1971), pp. 4–6; D. Daniels, 'Dialogue between Some Black and Hispanic Pentecostal Scholars: A Report and Some Personal Reflections', *Pneuma* 17 (1995), pp. 219–28; W. Hollenweger, *Between Black and White* (Belfast: Christian Journals, 1974); idem, 'The Black Roots of Pentecostalism', in A.H. Anderson, W.J. Hollenweger (eds), *Pentecostals after a Century. Global Perspectives on a Movement in Transition* (Sheffield: Sheffield Academic Press, 1999), pp. 33–44; idem, 'From Azusa Street to the Toronto Phenomenon', pp. 4–5.

[22] Including Edward Irving (see D. Allen, 'Regent Square Revisited: Edward Irving – Precursor of the Pentecostal Movement', *JEPTA* 17 (1997), pp. 49–58), John Alexander Dowie, Andrew Murray, A.B. Simpson, A. Torrey, A.A. Boddy, T.B. Barratt, David du Plessis, Dennis Bennett and others; see Anderson, *An Introduction to Pentecostalism*, pp. 146–48; C.M. Robeck Jr, 'Future Trajectories for Pentecostal Research' (*EPCRA* conference paper, University of Uppsala, 2007), pp. 1–38 (6).

Multidenominational

There are now so many different Classical Pentecostal, neo-Pentecostal and independent Pentecostal churches that it takes two dictionaries, one of which has been revised, and a regular supply of books and articles to try to do justice to exploring them.[26] Research is also being carried out exploring Pentecostalism as it is expressed in its various cultural contexts, on a country-by-country basis,[27] or relating to individuals,[28] often in the form of doctoral research projects.[29]

[23] F.D. Macchia, 'God Present in a Confused Situation: The Mixed Influence of the Charismatic Movement on Classical Pentecostalism in the United States', *Pneuma* 18.1 (1996), pp. 33–54; R.A.N. Kydd, 'The Impact of the Charismatic Renewal on Classical Pentecostalism in Canada', *Pneuma* 18.2 (1996), pp. 55–67; R.I.J. Hackett, 'New Directions and Connections for African and Asian Charismatics', *Pneuma* 18.1 (1996), pp. 69–77; the 1994 (16.2) edition of *Pneuma* offered a global survey of the Charismatic movement (pp. 167–274); J.K. Asamoah-Gyadu, *African Charismatics* (Leiden: Brill, 2004); B. Bay, 'Charismatic Renewal and Its Inter-Denominational Dialogue', *The Spirit and the Church* 4.2 (2002), pp. 177–93; R.H. Hughes, 'A Traditional Pentecostal Looks at the New Pentecostals', *Christianity Today* 18 (1974), pp. 6–10; D.N. Hudson, 'You'll Never Know Your Future until You Know Where Your Past Is', *Evangel* 21.2 (2003), pp. 37–40 (38–9).

[24] P.D. Hocken, 'Charismatic Movement', in Burgess and van der Maas (eds), *NIDPCM*, pp. 477–519; E.N. Newberg, 'Charismatic Movement', in S. Burgess (ed.), *EPCC* (London: Routledge, 2006), pp. 89–95; M.W.G. Stibbe, 'The Theology of Renewal and the Renewal of Theology', *JPT* 3 (1993), pp. 71–90; W. Ma, 'A "First Waver" Looks at the "Third Wave": A Pentecostal Reflection on Charles Kraft's Power Encounter Terminology', *Pneuma* 19.2 (1997), pp. 189–206; Anderson, pp. 144–65.

[25] Anderson, *An Introduction to Pentecostalism*, p. 145–46; K. Asamoah-Gyadu, '"Missionaries without Robes": Lay Charismatic Fellowships and the Evangelization of Ghana', *Pneuma* 19.2 (1997), pp. 171–88.

[26] See bibliographies at www.keithwarrington.co.uk; see especially the various articles in Burgess and van der Maas (eds), *NIDPCM*, pp. 3–282, 382–417, 467–72, 530–44, 640, 715–23, 777–83, 791–94, 797–801, 937–46, 961–74, 1157–166; Burgess (ed.), *EPCC*, passim; C.E. Jones, *A Guide to the Study of Pentecostalism* (Metuchen: Scarecrow Press, 1983); Anderson, *An Introduction to Pentecostalism*, pp. 39–165; B.D. Klaus, 'Pentecostalism as a Global Culture: An Introductory Overview', in Dempster, Klaus and Petersen (eds), *The Globalization of Pentecostalism*, pp. 127–30.

[27] **North America** G. Wacker, *Heaven Below: Early Pentecostals and American Culture* (Cambridge: Harvard University Press, 2001); C.W. Conn, *Like a Mighty Army: A History of the Church of God, 1886–1976* (Cleveland: Pathway Press, 1977); M. Crewes, *The Church of God: A Social History* (Knoxville: University of Tennessee Press, 1990); R.M. Mapes, *Vision of the Disinherited: The Making of American Pentecostalism* (Peabody: Hendrickson, 1992); C. Alvarez, 'Hispanic Pentecostals: Azusa Street and Beyond', *Cyberjournal for Pentecostal-Charismatic Research* 5 (1999); Cerillo, 'The Beginnings of American Pentecostalism', pp. 229–59; Faupel, *The Everlasting Gospel*, pp. 44–76, 187–227; S. DuPree, *African-American Holiness Pentecostal Movement: An Annotated Bibliography* (New York: Garland Publishing House, 1996); A. Cerillo Jr,

'Interpretative Approaches to the History of American Pentecostal Origins', *Pneuma* 19.1 (1997), pp. 29–52; T.W. Miller, *Canadian Pentecostals: A History of the Pentecostal Assemblies of Canada* (Mississauga: Full Gospel Publishing House, 1994); N.M. van Cleave, *The Vine and the Branches: A History of the International Church of the Foursquare Gospel* (Los Angeles: International Church of the Foursquare Gospel, 1992); G.B. McGee, *People of the Spirit: The Assemblies of God* (Springfield: Gospel Publishing House, 2004); E. Patterson, E. Rybarczyk, *The Future of Pentacostalism in the United States* (Plymouth: Lexington Books, 2007).

South and Central America and the Caribbean K-W. Westmeier, *Protestant Pentecostalism in Latin America* (London: Associated University Presses, 1999); S. Cruz, *Masked Africanisms: Puerto Rican Pentecostalism* (Dubuque: Hunt Publishing Company, 2005); C.d'E. Lalive, *Haven to the Masses. A Study of the Pentecostal Movement in Chile* (London: Lutterworth, 1969); J.M. Bonino, *Faces of Latin American Protestantism* (Grand Rapids: Eerdmans, 1997); M.J. Gaxiola-Gaxiola, 'Latin American Pentecostalism: A Mosaic within a Mosaic', *Pneuma* 13.2 (1991), pp. 107–29; Corton and Marshall-Fratani (eds), *Between Babel and Pentecost*; S. Solivan, *The Spirit, Pathos and Liberation: Towards a Hispanic Pentecostal Theology* (Sheffield: Sheffield Academic Press, 1998); R.A. Chesnut, *Born Again in Brazil: The Pentecostal Boom and the Pathogens of Poverty* (New Brunswick: Rutgers University Press, 1997); E.L. Cleary, H.W. Stewart-Gambino (eds), *Power, Politics and Pentecostals in Latin America* (Boulder: Westview Press, 1997); E.L. Cleary, 'Latin American Pentecostalism', in Dempster, Klaus and Petersen (eds), *The Globalization of Pentecostalism*, pp. 131–50; E.A. Wilson, 'Passion and Power: A Profile of Latin American Pentecostalism', in M.W. Dempster, B.D. Klaus and D. Petersen (eds), *Called and Empowered. Global Mission in Pentecostal Perspective* (Peabody: Hendrickson, 1991), pp. 67–97; J. Root, *Encountering West Indian Pentecostalism: Its Ministry and Worship* (Bramcote: Grove Books, 1979); W.C. Hoover, *History of the Pentecostal Revival in Chile* (trans. M.G. Hoover; Santiago: Imprenta Eben-Ezer, 2000); CEPLA, *Jubileo. La Fiesta del Espiritu. Idendiad y mission del Pentecostlismo Latinamericano* (Maracaibo: Comision Evangelica Pentecostal Latinamericano, 1999); B. Boudewijnse, A. Droogers, F. Kamsteeg (eds), *Algo mas que opio: Una lelectura antropologica del pentecostalismo latino-americano y caribeno* (San Jose: Departmento Ecumenico de Investigaciones, 1991); Anderson, *An Introduction to Pentecostalism*, pp. 63–82; E.L. Cleary, J. Sepúlveda, 'Chilean Pentecostalism: Coming of Age', in Cleary and Stewart-Gambino (eds), *Power, Politics and Pentecostals*, pp. 98–113; J. Sepùlveda, 'Indigenous Pentecostalism and the Chilean Experience', in Anderson and Hollenweger (eds), *Pentecostals after a Century*, pp. 111–34; D. Martin, *Tongues of Fire: The Explosion of Protestantism in Latin America* (Oxford: Basil Blackwell, 1990); M. Alvarez, 'The South and the Latin American Paradigm of the Pentecostal Movement', *AJPS* 5.1 (2002), pp. 135–53; Petersen, 'The Formation of Popular', pp. 23–48; J.N. Saracco, 'Type of Ministry Adopted by the Pentecostal Churches in Latin America', *IRM* 66 (1977), pp. 64–70; M.D. Litonjua, 'Pentecostalism in Latin America: Scrutinizing a Sign of the Times', *JHLT* 7.4 (2000), pp. 26–49; M. Bergunder, 'The Pentecostal Movement and Basic Ecclesial Communities in Latin America', *IRM* 91 (2002), pp. 163–86.

Europe W.K. Kay, *Pentecostals in Britain* (Carlisle: Paternoster, 2000); idem, 'British Assemblies of God: The War Years', *Pneuma* 11.1 (1989), pp. 51–8; idem, *Inside Story* (Mattersey: Mattersey Hall Publishing, 1990); idem (with Bernhardt), 'Born in Difficult Times: The Founding of the Volksmission and the Work of Karl Fix', *JEPTA* 23 (2003), pp. 72–101; M.J. Calley, *God's People: West Indian Pentecostal Sects in England* (London: Oxford University Press, 1965); G. Lie, 'The Charismatic/Pentecostal

Movement in Norway: The Last 30 Years', *CPCR* 7 (Feb. 2000); V. Teraudkalns, 'Origins of Pentecostalism in Latvia', *CPCR* 6 (August 1999); idem, 'Pentecostalism in the Baltics: Historical Retrospection', *JEPTA* 21 (2001), pp. 91–108; J-D. Pluess, 'Globalization of Pentecostalism or Globalization of Individualism? A European Perspective', in Dempster, Klaus and Petersen (eds), *The Globalization of Pentecostalism*, pp. 170–82; B. Bjelajac, 'Early Pentecostalism in Serbia', *JEPTA* 23 (2003), pp. 129–36; V-M. Kärkkäinen, 'The Pentecostal Movement in Finland', *JEPTA* 23 (2003), pp. 102–28; A.C. Barata, B. Martinez, J.T. Parreira, S.R. Pinheiro, T. Lopes, *Linguas de fogo: Historia da Assembleia de Deus em Lisboa* (Lisbon: Casa Publicadora da Convencao das Assembleia de Deus em Portugal, 1999); D.N. Hudson, 'The Earliest Days of British Pentecostalism', *JEPTA* 21 (2001), pp. 49–67; D.D. Bundy, 'Historical and Theological Analysis of the Pentecostal Church in Norway', *JEPTA* 20 (2000), pp. 66–92; idem, 'The Roumanian Pentecostal Church in Recent Literature', *Pneuma* 7.1 (1985), pp. 19–40; idem, 'Pentecostalism in Belgium', *Pneuma* 8.1 (1986), pp. 41–56; J. Brenkus, 'A Historical and Theological Analysis of the Pentecostal Church in the Czech and Slovak Republics', *JEPTA* 20 (2000), pp. 49–65; W. Gajewski, K. Wawrzeniuk, 'A Historical and Theological Analysis of the Pentecostal Church of Poland', *JEPTA* 20 (2000), pp. 32–48; J. Robinson, *Pentecostal Origins: Early Pentecostalism in Ireland in the Context of the British Isles* (Carlisle: Paternoster Press, 2005); J. Edwards, 'Afro-Caribbean Pentecostalism in Britain', *JEPTA* 17 (1997), pp. 37–48; Ø. Årdval, *Pinsevekkelsen I Norge. En kortfattet historikk* (Oslo: Rex Forlag, 1992); I. Ceuta, 'The Pentecostal Apostolic Church of God in Romania 1944–1990', *EB* 13 (1994), pp. 74–87; R. Dudley, 'History of the Assemblies of God in Portugal', *EB* 12 (1993), pp. 49–63; D. Brandt-Bessire, 'L'Implantation des Assemblées Pentecôtites en Belgique Francaphone', *EB* 11.1–2 (1992), pp. 5–23; F.M. Matre, 'A Synopsis of Norwegian Pentecostal History', *EB* 9.2–3 (1990), pp. 53–62; C. van der Laan, 'Discerning the Body: Analysis of Pentecostalism in the Netherlands', in Jongeneel (ed.), *Pentecost, Mission and Ecumenism*, pp. 123–42; D. Gee, *Wind and Flame* (Croydon: Heath Press, 1941); Anderson, 'The Pentecostal and Charismatic Movements', pp. 78–90; idem, *An Introduction to Pentecostalism*, pp. 83–102; V-M. Kärkkäinen, "From the Ends of the Earth to the Ends of the Earth'– the Expansion of the Finnish Pentecostal Missions from 1927 to 1997', *JEPTA* 20 (2000), pp. 116–31; R. Pandrea, 'A Historical and Theological Analysis of the Pentecostal Church in Romania', *JEPTA* 21 (2001), pp. 109–35.

Africa J.K. Asamoah-Gyadu, 'The Church in the African State: The Pentecostal/ Charismatic Experience in Ghana', *JACT* 1.2 (1998), pp. 51–70; A.H. Anderson, A.H. Tumelo, *The Faith of African Pentecostals in South Africa* (Pretoria: Unisa, 1993); C. Amenyo, 'The Charismatic Renewal Movement in Ghana', *Pneuma* 16.2 (1994), pp. 180–83; O. Adeboye, '"Arrowhead" of Nigerian Pentecostalism: The Redeemed Christian Church of God, 1952–2005', *Pneuma* 29.1 (2007), pp. 24–58; A.H. Anderson, *Moya: The Holy Spirit in an African Context* (Pretoria: Unisa, 1991); idem, *Zion and Pentecost: The Spirituality and Experience of Pentecostal and Zionist/Apostolic Churches in South Africa* (Pretoria: University of South Africa Press, 1992); idem, *Bazalwane: African Pentecostals in South Africa* (Pretoria: University of South Africa Press, 1991); idem, 'The Newer Pentecostal and Charismatic Churches: The Shape of Future Christianity in South Africa', *Pneuma* 24.2 (2002), pp. 167–84; idem, *An Introduction to Pentecostalism*, pp. 103–22; R.W. Wylie, 'Pioneers of Ghanaian Pentecostalism: Peter Amim and James McKeown', *JARA* 6.2 (1974), pp. 109–22; E.K. Larbi, *Pentecostalism: The Eddies of Ghanaian Christianity* (Accra: Centre for Pentecostal and Charismatic Studies, 2001); idem, 'African Pentecostalism in the Context of Global Pentecostal Ecumenical Fraternity: Challenges and Opportunities', *Pneuma* 24.2 (2002), pp. 138–66; idem, 'Ghanaian Pentecostalism in the Context of Global Pentecostal Ecumenical Fraternity: Challenges and Opportunities', *AJPS* 2 (2004), pp. 68–90; D. Maxwell, '"Delivered from the Spirit of Poverty": Pentecostalism, Prosperity and Modernity in Zimbabwe', *JRA* 28.4 (1998), pp. 350–73; M.A. Ojo, 'The Church in the African State: The Charismatic/Pentecostal Experience in Nigeria', *Journal of African Studies* 1.2 (1998), pp. 25–32; C.N. Omenyo, *Pentecost Outside Pentecostalism: A Study of the Development of Charismatic Renewal in the Mainline Churches in Ghana* (Zoetermeer: Boekencentrum, 2002); A.M.B. Rasmussen, *Modern African Spirituality: The Independent Spirit Churches in East Africa, 1902–1976* (London: British Academic Press, 1996); W.A. Saayman, 'Some Reflections on the Development of the Pentecostal Mission Model in South Africa', *Missionalia* 21.1 (1993), pp. 40–56; R.I.H. Gerloff, '"Pentecostals in the African Diaspora', in Anderson and Hollenweger (eds), *Pentecostals after a Century*, pp. 67–86; C.P. Watt, *From Africa's Soil: The Story of the Assemblies of God in Southern Africa* (Cape Town: Struik, 1992); A Koduah, *Christianity in Ghana Today* (Accra: Church of Pentecost, 2004); P. Gifford, *Ghana's New Christianity. Pentecostalism in a Globalizing African Economy* (Bloomington: Indiana University Press, 2004).

Asia, Australasia P. Pulikottil, 'As East and West Met in God's Own Country: Encounter of Western Pentecostalism with Native Pentecostalism in Kerala', *AJPS* 5.1 (2002), pp. 5–22; M. Bergunder, 'Constructing Indian Pentecostalism: On Issues of Methodology and Representation' in Anderson and Tang (eds), *Asian and Pentecostal*, pp. 177–213; H.V. Synan, 'The Yoido Full Gospel Church', *CPCR* 2 (July 1997); S.M. Burgess, 'Pentecostalism in India: An Overview', *AJPS* 4.1 (2001), pp. 85–98; P.T. Shew, 'A Forgotten History: Correcting the Historical Record of the Roots of Pentecostalism in Japan', *AJPS* 5.1 (2002), pp. 23–49; B.K. Sharma, 'A History of the Pentecostal Movement in Nepal', *AJPS* 4.2 (2001), pp. 295–305; Joshua, 'Pentecostalism in Vietnam: A History of the Assemblies of God', *AJPS* 4.2 (2001), pp. 307–26; C.K. Khai, 'Pentecostalism in Myanmar: An Overview', *AJPS* 5.1 (2002), pp. 51–71; idem, *The Cross among Pagodas: A History of the Assemblies of God in Myanmar* (Baguio City: Asia Pacific Theological Seminary, 2003); M. Bergunder, 'Die sudindische Pfingstbewegung im 20. Jahrhundert (*SPS/EPCRA* conference paper, Doncaster, 1995); M. Suzuki, 'A New Look at the Pre-War History of the Japan Assemblies of God', *AJPS* 4.2 (2001), pp. 239–67; I-J. Kim, *History and Theology of Korean Pentecostalism: Sunbogeum (Pure Gospel) Pentecostalism* (Zoetermeer: Boekencentrum Publishing House, 2003); Anderson and Tang (eds), *Asian and Pentecostal*; L. Wesley, *The Church in China: Persecuted, Pentecostal, and Powerful* (Baguio City: AJPS Books, 2004); idem, 'Is the Chinese Church Predominantly Pentecostal?', *AJPS* 7.1 (2004), pp. 225–54; S.H. Kim, 'Global Conquest – The Mission of the Assemblies of God in Korea' (*SPS* conference paper, Cleveland, 2007), pp. 165–72; Anderson, *An Introduction to Pentecostalism*, pp. 123–43; J. Hosack, 'The Arrival of Pentecostals and Charismatics in Thailand', *AJPS* 4.1 (2001), pp. 109–17; H.J. Lee, 'Minjung and Pentecostal Movements in Korea', in Anderson and Hollenweger (eds), *Pentecostals after a Century*, pp. 138–60; G.B. McGee, '"Latter Rain" Falling in the East: Twentieth Century Pentecostalism in India and the Debate over Speaking in Tongues', *Church History* 68.3 (1999), pp. 648–65; M. Nagasaw, 'Makuya Pentecostalism: A Survey', *AJPS* 3.2 (2000), pp. 203–18; R.E. Hedlund, 'Critique of Pentecostal Mission by a Friendly Evangelical (India)', *AJPS* 8.1 (2005), pp. 67–94; E.J.F. Kim, 'Filipino Pentecostalism in a Global Context', *AJPS* 8.2 (2005), pp. 235–54; D.A. Benavidez, 'The Early Years of the Church of God in Northern Luzon (1947-1953): A Historical and Theological Overview', *AJPS* 8.2 (2005), pp. 255–69; T.E. Seleky, 'The Organization of the Philippine Assemblies of God and the Role of Early Missionaries', *AJPS* 8.2 (2005) pp. 272–87; C. Lumahan, 'Facts and Figures: A History of the Growth of the Philippine Assemblies of God', *AJPS* 8.2 (2005), pp. 331–34; S-H. Myung, Y-G. Hong, *Charis and Charisma: David Yonggi Cho and the Growth of Yoido Full Gospel Church* (Carlisle: Regnum, 2003); L.H. Jung, 'Minjung and Pentecostal Movements in Korea', in Anderson and Hollenweger (eds), *Pentecostals after a Century*, pp. 138–60; T. Pagaialii, 'The Pentecostal Movement of Samoa: Reaching the Uttermost', *AJPS* 7.1 (2004), pp. 265–79; B-W. Yoo, 'Pentecostal-ism in Korea', in Jongeneel (ed.), *Pentecost, Mission and Ecumenism*, pp. 169–76; Y-H. Lee, 'Korean Pentecost: The Great Revival of 1907', *AJPS* 4.1 (2001), pp. 73–83; T.E. Seleky, 'Six Filipinos and One American: Pioneers of the Assemblies of God in the Philippines', *AJPS* 4.1 (2001), pp. 119–29; G.B. McGee, 'The Calcutta Revival of 1907 and the Reformulation of Charles F. Partham's "Bible Evidence Doctrine"',*AJPS* 6.1 (2003), pp. 123–43; B. Knowles, *The History of a New Zealand Pentecostal Movement: The New Life Churches of New Zealand from 1946–1979* (Lewiston: Edwin Mellen Press, 2000).

[28] L. Price, *Theology Out of Place: A Theological Biography of Walter J. Hollenweger* (London: Sheffield Academic Press, 2002); M.S. Park, 'David Yonggi Cho and International Pentecostal/Charismatic Movements', *JPT* 12.1 (2003), pp. 107–28; C. Nienkirchen, *A. B. Simpson and the Pentecostal Movement* (Peabody: Hendrickson, 1992); L. Martin, *The Life and Ministry of William J. Seymour* (Joplin: Christian Life Books, 1999); D.E. Harrell Jr, *Oral Roberts: An American Life* (Bloomington: Indiana University Press, 1985); Goff, *Fields White unto Harvest*; Cartwright, *The Real Smith Wigglesworth*; R.G.W. Sanders, *William Joseph Seymour: Black Father of the Twenti-eth Century Pentecostal/Charismatic Movement* (Sandusky: Alexandria Publications, 2001); E.C.W. Boulton, *George Jeffreys* (C. Cartwright (ed.); Tonbridge: Sovereign World, 1999); J. Wilson, *Wigglesworth. The Complete Story* (Milton Keynes: Authen-tic, 2002); D.M. Epstein, *Sister Aimee: The Life of Amy Semple McPherson* (New York: Harcourt, Brace and Jovanovich, 1993); E. Blumhofer, *Aimee Semple McPherson: Everybody's Sister* (Grand Rapids: Eerdmans, 1993); A.H. Anderson, 'The Contribu-tion of David Yonggi Cho to a Contextual Theology of Korea', *JPT* 12.1 (2003), pp. 85–105; J. Robinson, 'Arthur Booth-Clibborn: Pentecostal Patriarch', *JEPTA* 21 (2001), pp. 68–90; R.G. Robins, *A.J. Tomlinson: Plainfolk Modernist* (Oxford; Oxford University Press, 2004); H. Letson, 'Serving His Generation: The Contribution of John Nelson Parr to the Pentecostal Movement', *JEPTA* 26.1 (2006), pp. 7–20; D.D. Bundy, 'Thomas Ball Barratt: From Methodist to Pentecostal', *EB* 13 (1994), pp. 19–49; idem, 'Thomas B. Barratt and *Byposten*: An Early European Pentecostal Leader and His Periodical', in Jongeneel (ed.), *Pentecost, Mission and Ecumenism*, pp. 115–21; M.R. Hathaway, 'The role of William Oliver Hutchinson and the Apostolic Church in the Formation of British Pentecostal Churches', *JEPTA* 16 (1996), pp. 40–57; K. Ekorness, *'Samtaler' Met T.B. Barratt* (Oslo: Filadefiaforlaget, 1991); G. Wakefield, *Alexander Boddy. Pentecostal Anglican Pioneer* (Milton Keynes: Paternoster Press, 2007); V. Teraudkalns, 'William Fetler – Friend of Pentecostalism in Latvia', *JEPTA* 19 (1999), pp. 81–8; W. Ma, W.W. Menzies, H-S, Bae, *David Yonggi Cho. A Close Look at his Theology and Ministry* (Baguio: APTS Press, 2004); S.K.H. Chan, 'The Pneumatology of Paul Yonggi Cho', *AJPS* 7.1 (2004), pp. 779–99; C-s. Kang, 'Resources for Studies of David Yonggi Cho', in Ma, Menzies and Bae, *David Yonggi Cho*, pp. 273–302; E.J. Moodley, 'The Legacy of John Francis Rowlands: Missionary to the Indians of South Africa (1925–1980)' (SPS conference paper, Cleveland), pp. 237–44; C.K. Khai, 'Legacy of Hau Lian Kham (1944–1995): A Revivalist, Equipper, and Transformer for the Zomi-Chin People of Myanmar', *AJPS* 4.1 (2001), pp. 99–107; Author anonymous,

'A History of the Pentecostal Movement in Indonesia', *AJPS* 4.1 (2001), pp. 131–48; J.R. Goff, G. Wacker (eds), *Portraits of a Generation: Early Pentecostal Leaders* (Fayetteville: University of Arkansas Press, 2002); J.R. Colletti, 'Lewi Pethrus: His Influence upon Scandinavian-American Pentecostalism', *Pneuma* 5.2 (1983), pp. 18–29.

[29] **Africa** T.J. Padwick, 'Spirit, Desire and the World: Roho Churches of Western Kenya in the Era of Globalization' (unpublished doctoral dissertation, University of Birmingham, 2003); E.K. Larbi, 'The Development of Ghanaian Pentecostalism' (unpublished doctoral dissertation, University of Edinburgh, 1995); J.K. Asamoah-Gyadu, 'Renewal within African Christianity: A Study of Some Current Historical and Theological Developments within Independent Indigenous Pentecostalism in Ghana' (unpublished doctoral dissertation, University of Birmingham, 2000); R.S. Beckford, 'Towards a Dread Pentecostal Theology: The Context of a Viable Political Theology within Pentecostal Churches in Britain' (unpublished doctoral dissertation, University of Birmingham, 1999); C.R. Clarke, 'Faith in Christ in Post-Missionary Africa: Christology among Akan African Indigenous Churches in Ghana' (unpublished doctoral dissertation, University of Birmingham, 2003); O. Onyinah, 'Akan Witchcraft and the Concept of Exorcism in the Church of Pentecost' (unpublished doctoral dissertation, University of Birmingham, 2002); A.H. Anderson, 'African Pentecostalism in a South African Urban Environment: A Missiological Evaluation' (unpublished doctoral dissertation, University of South Africa, 1992); C. de Wet, 'The Apostolic Faith Mission in Africa, 1908–1980. A Case Study in Church Growth in a Segregated Society' (unpublished doctoral dissertation, University of Cape Town, 1989).

North America R.J. Stephens, '"The Fire Spreads": The Origins of the Southern Holiness and Pentecostal Movements' (unpublished doctoral dissertation, University of Florida, 2003); M.A. Sutton, 'Hollywood Religion: Aimee Semple McPherson, Pentecostalism, and Politics' (unpublished doctoral dissertation, University of California, 2005); M. Robinson, 'To the Ends of the Earth: The Pilgrimage of an Ecumenical Pentecostal, David J. Du Plessis (1905–1987)' (unpublished doctoral dissertation, University of Birmingham, 1987); Nelson, 'For Such a Time as This'.

South America J.N. Saracco, 'Argentine Pentecostalism. Its History and Theology' (unpublished doctoral dissertation, University of Birmingham, 1989); E.D. Filho, 'O Movimento Pentecostal Brasileiro' (unpublished master's dissertation, Fuller Theological Seminary, 1988).

Asia, Australasia C.H. Jeong, 'The Formation and Development of Korean Pentecostalism from the Viewpoint of a Dynamic Contextual Theology' (unpublished doctoral dissertation, University of Birmingham, 2001); J. Jeong, 'Filipino Pentecostal Spirituality: An Investigation into Filipino Indigenous Spirituality and Pentecostalism in the Philippines' (unpublished doctoral dissertation, University of Birmingham, 2001); J.B. Lee, 'Pentecostal Type Distinctives and Korean Pentecostal Church Growth' (unpublished doctoral dissertation, Fuller Theological Seminary, 1986); Y.H. Lee, 'The Holy Spirit Movement in Korea: Its Historical and Doctrinal Development' (unpublished doctoral dissertation, Temple University, 1996); S-Y, Z. Kim, 'Lessons from the Pentecostal Movement in Korea in the Twentieth Century' (unpublished doctoral dissertation, Fuller Theological Seminary, 1990); Y. Boo-Woong, 'Korean Pentecostalism: Its History and Theology' (unpublished doctoral dissertation, University of Birmingham, 1988); J.S. Clifton, 'An Analysis of the Developing Ecclesiology of the Assemblies of God in Australia' (unpublished doctoral dissertation, Australian Catholic University, 2005).

Europe D. Allen, 'Signs and Wonders: The Origins, Growth, Development and Significance of the Assemblies of God in Britain and Ireland, 1900–1980' (unpublished doctoral dissertation, University of London, 1990); Walsh, 'To Meet and Satisfy'.

Multidimensional

Increasingly, it is more accurate to identify Pentecostalism in the plural form (Pentecostalisms) as there is no longer an adequate framework into which all Pentecostals easily fit. Its history has been a journey that has resulted in a number of different racial and doctrinal streams being developed.[30] There are three major groups within Pentecostalism, the first (which also encapsulates apostolic traditions) affirming two main works of grace, salvation and the baptism in the Spirit, the latter often associated with the gift of tongues and understood to be the means of gaining greater power to function as believers. In this group, sanctification is understood to be an ongoing aspect of the life of the believer. A smaller Wesleyan Holiness group affirms much of the above but identifies another crisis experience after conversion resulting in 'entire sanctification'.[31] A further group which holds similar tenets to the former group but has a non-Trinitarian understanding of God also exists in large numbers, often referred to as Oneness Pentecostals.

The increasing variety within Pentecostalism is partially due to its global nature as well as the nuances of its belief and praxis.[32] In 1953, Newbigin identified Pentecostalism as a third stream alongside Protestantism and Catholicism.[33] More recently, Omenyo noted that Pentecostalism is becoming the norm for African Christianity[34] while Espinoza concluded that 'a Pentecostalization process is helping to usher in a period of spiritual renewal throughout the Spanish-speaking Americas'.[35] The latest figures indicate that 523 million Christians (nearly 30% of global Christianity of which about 65 million would be identified as Pentecostals) would subscribe to Pentecostal/Charismatic beliefs; furthermore, it is currently growing rapidly (9 million new members per year (25,000 per day)).[36]

The very diversity of Pentecostalism means that it is less identifiable than it once was, though Larbi describes all Pentecostals as 'drinking from the

---

[30] M.W. Dempster, 'The Search for Pentecostal Identity', *Pneuma* 15.1 (1993), pp. 1–8; Dayton, *Theological Roots of Pentecostalism*, pp. 18–33.

[31] Dayton, *Theological Roots of Pentecostalism*, pp. 87–113.

[32] A.M.S. Walsh, *Latino Pentecostal Identity: Evangelical Faith, Self, and Society* (New York: Columbia University Press, 2003); V. Synan, 'Pentecostalism: Varieties and Contributions', *Pneuma* 9.1 (1987), pp. 31–49; H.W. Greenway, 'The All-Flesh Prophecy', in P.S. Brewster (ed.), *Pentecostal Doctrine* (Cheltenham: Elim, 1976), pp. 293–304; D. Martin, *Pentecostalism: The World Their Parish* (London: Blackwell, 2002), pp. 2–17.

[33] L. Newbigin, *The Household of God* (London: SCM, 1953), p. 30.

[34] Omenyo, *Pentecost Outside Pentecostalism*, p. 306.

[35] G. Espinoza, 'The Pentecostalization of Latin American and U.S Latino Christianity', *Pneuma* 26.2 (2004), p. 291; D. Petersen, 'Latin American Pentecostalism: Social Capital, Networks, and Politics', *Pneuma* 26.2 (2004), pp. 293–306.

same theological melting pot'.[37] Some of its most distinctive beliefs (including glossolalia and its place as the initial evidence of the baptism in the Spirit) are less distinctive in some expressions of Pentecostalism than they were; at the same time, some of the foundational elements of Pentecostalism are now also present in the lives of many non-Pentecostal believers. The rise of renewal movements and neo-Pentecostalism have blurred the dividing lines. Yong concludes, 'It is difficult, if not well nigh impossible, to 'essentialize' Pentecostalism conceptually'.[38] To locate a common ethos that reflects Pentecostalism is increasingly difficult though some have tried.[39] Furthermore, to be Pentecostal varies depending on the continent, tradition, denomination or experience of the Spirit of the individual concerned.[40] Similarly, some practices vary from one part of Pentecostalism to another.[41] Even umbrella organizations, such as the Pentecostal World Conference, do not incorporate all (or even many) of the many Pentecostal groups in the world.[42]

Also, although originally a largely Western movement, it is now increasingly multicultural, being mainly represented by people from the Majority world.[43] 66% of Pentecostals now live in the Majority world, 87% live in

---

[36] D.B. Barrett, T.M. Johnson, 'Global Statistics', in Burgess and van der Maas (eds), *NIDPCM*, pp. 284–302; Hedlund, 'Critique of Pentecostal Mission', p. 71.

[37] Larbi, 'African Pentecostalism', p. 79.

[38] A. Yong, '"Not Knowing Where the Wind Blows . . .", On Envisioning a Pentecostal-Charismatic Theology of Religions', *JPT* 14 (April, 1999), pp. 81–112 (94).

[39] Anderson, *An Introduction to Pentecostalism*, p. 10; Smith (ed.), *Pentecostals from the Inside Out*, pp. 12, 53; C.M. Robeck Jr, 'Making Sense of Pentecostalism in a Global Context' (SPS conference paper, Springfield, 1999) p. 18.

[40] W. Ma, 'Toward an Asian Pentecostal Theology', *CPCR* 1 (1997).

[41] For an exploration of a church stream that that has aberrant and even cultic elements, though still may be defined by some as Pentecostal, see the Universal Church of the Kingdom of God which commenced in Rio Janeiro in 1977 and is now in 80 countries, see B. Furre, 'Crossing Boundaries: The "Universal Church" and the Spirit of Globalization', in S.J. Stålsett (ed.), *Spirits of Globalization. The Growth of Pentecostalism and Experiential Spiritualities in a Global Age* (London: SCM, 2006), pp. 39–51; M.R.G. Esperando, 'Globalization and Subjectivity: A Reflection on the "Universal Church of the Kingdom of God" in a Perspective drawn from the Psychology of Religion', in Stålsett (ed.), *Spirits of Globalization*, pp. 52–64; S.J. Stålsett, 'Offering On-Time Deliverance: The Pathos of Neo-Pentecostalism and the Spirits of Globalization', in Stålsett (ed.), *Spirits of Globalization*, pp. 198– 212.

[42] C.T. Thomas, 'Pentecostal Theology in the Twenty-First Century: 1998 Presidential Address to the Society for Pentecostal Studies', *Pneuma* 21 (1998), pp. 3–19.

[43] J.C. Ma, 'Growing Churches in Manila', *AJT* 11 (1997), pp. 324–42; Larbi, 'African Pentecostalism', pp. 138–66; W. Hollenweger, *The Pentecostals: The Charismatic Movement in the Churches* (Minneapolis: Augsburg, 1972), pp. 1–74; Tinney, 'Black Origins of Pentecostal Movement', pp. 4–6; Jones, *Black Holiness*; Anderson, *An Introduction to Pentecostalism*, pp. 168–70. P. Jenkins, *The Next Christendom: The Coming of Global Christianity* (Oxford: Oxford University Press, 2002), p. 67; Anderson, 'The Newer Pentecostal and Charismatic Churches', pp. 167–84. H. Yung, 'Pentecostalism

poorer areas of the world while 71% are non-white.[44] Ma estimates that by 2025, more than 80% of Pentecostals will reside in Asia.[45] Although the trend is obvious, the picture is complicated because Pentecostal diasporas cross continents, taking their Pentecostal spiritualities with them into their new cultures and countries, sometimes to be assimilated into them though often times maintaining an individual vibrancy and identity.[46]

Self-analytical

To a large degree, Pentecostal denominations were developed because of opposition by other believers, at the time, who rejected some of their doctrines, especially concerning the baptism in the Spirit, speaking in tongues and divine healing.[47] Although Pentecostalism was attacked particularly in its early years (as well as more recently[48]) by other Christians and some of its beliefs were severely critiqued,[49] in its later expressions, it has matured to such an extent that mainstream Christianity has, in general, accepted it as a valid member of the Church. This development and its recognition as a legitimate grouping of believers within the family of God has enabled it to dialogue with other believers as well as to confidently reflect on its own history and theology, resulting in some refinements to the latter. At the same time, the contributions made by Pentecostals to the life and theology of the wider Church have also increasingly been appreciated.[50] This has been the

and the Asian Church', in Anderson and Tang (eds), *Asian and Pentecostal*, pp. 37–57.

[44] J.H. Logan Jr, 'Black Pentecostalism', in Burgess (ed.), *EPCC*, pp. 60–4.

[45] W. Ma, 'Asia, East', in Burgess (ed.), *EPCC*, p. 49.

[46] D. Daniels, 'Transgressing the North-South Divide: The Afro-Pentecostal Factor in Global Pentecostalism' (EPCRA conference paper, University of Uppsala, 2007).

[47] W.L. De Arteaga, *Quenching the Spirit* (Lake Mary: Creation House, 1992), pp. 128–298; G.A. Wacker, 'Travail of a Broken Family: Radical Evangelical Responses to the Emergence of Pentecostalism in America, 1906–1916', in Blumhofer, Spittler and Wacker (eds), *Pentecostal Currents*, pp. 23–49.

[48] L. du Plessis ('A Proprium for Pentecostal Theology', in M.S. Clark, H.I. Lederle (eds), *What Is Distinctive about Pentecostal Theology?* (Pretoria: University of South Africa, 1989), pp. 143–52 (146)) refers to it being identified as a sect by other South African Christians in 1989.

[49] C.M. Robeck Jr, 'Pentecostals and the Apostolic Faith: Implications for Ecumenism', *Pneuma* 9.1 (1987), pp. 61–84 (61–4); see P. Hocken, 'Berlin Declaration', in Burgess and van der Maas (eds), *NIDPCM*, p. 371 issued in 1909, it condemned Pentecostalism.

[50] J. Veenhof, 'The Significance of the Charismatic Renewal for Theology and the Church', in Jongeneel (ed.), *Pentecost, Mission and Ecumenism*, pp. 289–300; C.B. Johns, 'What Can the Mainline Learn from the Pentecostals about Pentecost?', in A. Droogers, C. van der Laan, W. van Laar (eds), *Fruitful in This Land: Pluralism, Dialogue and Healing in Migrant Pentecostalism* (Zoetermeer, Netherlands: Boekencentrum Publishing House, 2006), pp. 93–9; Synan (ed.), *Aspects of Pentecostal-Charismatic Origins*, pp. 99–122.

result, among other considerations, of Pentecostals who have been prepared to maturely reflect on their core values, as well as the influence of the Charismatic Renewal and other associated groups who have allied themselves with, learnt from and mentored their older sibling in ways that have helped modify its teaching and practices. At the same time, this process has been helped by the rise of Pentecostal theological colleges, the increase in Pentecostal scholarship and academic excellence and a growing desire to interact with the Bible in a way that is both authentic and hermeneutically sound.

Pentecostalism is coming of age; it has come through its adolescence and is in the process of maturing.[51] In the last few decades, there has been a plethora of scholarly writings by Pentecostals, reflecting on their history, theology, missiology and ecclesiology among other issues; this has been achieved in the context of a very limited tradition of scholarly work and expression. At the same time, Pentecostals are increasingly prepared to analyse their own history and critique any excesses or inadequacies, as well as articulating a case for the need of a Pentecostal theology, suggestive of a recently felt maturity[52] that is manifested in its readiness to dialogue with others outside its tradition.[53]

Experiential

Pentecostals have always emphasized experiential Christianity rather than doctrinal confession. Rather than describe or explain doctrines in the mode

---

[51] Hollenweger, *The Pentecostals*, p. xvii; C.B. Johns, 'The Adolescence of Pentecostalism: In Search of a Legitimate Sectarian Identity', *Pneuma* 16 (1994), pp. 3–17; V-M. Kärkkäinen, *Toward a Pneumatological Theology: Pentecostal and Ecumenical Perspectives on Ecclesiology, Soteriology, and Theology of Mission* (Lanham: University Press of America, 2002), p. 3; C.H. Pinnock, 'Divine Relationality: A Pentecostal Contribution to the Doctrine of God', *JPT* 16 (2000), pp. 3–26 (3–5).

[52] W.J. Hollenweger, 'The Critical Tradition of Pentecostalism', *JPT* 1 (1992), pp. 7–17; J.K.A. Smith, 'Advice to Pentecostal Philosophers', *JPT* 11.2 (2003), pp. 235–47; T.L. Cross, 'A Proposal to Break the Ice: What Can Pentecostal Theology Offer Evangelical Theology?', *JPT* 10.2 (2002), pp. 44–73; D.W. Faupel, 'Whither Pentecostalism?', *Pneuma* 15.1 (1993), pp. 9–27; C.M. Robeck Jr, 'Taking Stock of Pentecostalism: The Personal Reflections of a Retiring Editor', *Pneuma* 15.1 (1993), pp. 35–60; A. Yong, 'The Spirit and Creation: Possibilities and Challenges for a Dialogue between Pentecostal Theology and Science', *JEPTA* 25 (2005), pp. 82–110; M.S. Clark, 'Questioning Every Consensus: A Plea for a Return to the Radical Roots of Pentecostalism', *AJPS* 5.1 (2002), p. 74.

[53] W.J. Hollenweger, 'Fire from Heaven: A Testimony by Harvey Cox', *Pneuma* 20.2 (1998), pp. 197–204; H.G. Cox, 'Some Personal Reflections on Pentecostalism', *Pneuma* 15.1 (1993), pp. 29–34; A. Yong, 'In Search of Foundations: The Oeuvre of Donald L. Gelpi, SJ, and Its Significance for Pentecostal Theology and Philosophy', *JPT* 11.1 (2002), pp. 3–26; D.L. Gelpi, 'A Response to Amos Yong', *JPT* 11.2 (2002), pp. 27–40.

of systematic or dogmatic theologians associated with the seminary and scholar, they typically explore them in the biblical narrative and by the testimony of those affected by them. Their theology is praxis-oriented and experiential, defined by Johns as 'oral-narrative', where life experiences are valid elements of one's hermeneutic and theology as much as conceptual theologizing, for the former allow for and enable theology 'to become part of the life of the community of faith'.[54]

Pentecostals (traditionally) do not think theologically so much as live out their theology practically. Pentecostalism is not just distinctive because of its belief base but also because of the worldview it owns. The latter is based on a certainty that a religion that does not work is not worth much. Consequently, they look for expressions of life and vitality in their faith. The sense of the immediate, the God of the now, not the distant past, are characteristics that underlie how they do theology. Pentecostal theology tends to be seen through the eyes of people, not theologians; through the faith and worship of their community, not ancient or modern creeds. Thus, Mursell describes Pentecostalism as an 'essentially oral, musical and experimental movement' which renders it 'less susceptible to neat academic assessment'.[55] It is a theology of the dynamic, seen through the lens of experience. It is a functional theology that exists to operate in life and to incorporate an experiential dimension. Pentecostal theology does not operate as other theologies which often only detail a list of beliefs; it does this but also and (more) importantly, it insists on exploring them in the context of praxis.

[54] C.B. Johns, *Pentecostal Formation. A Pedagogy among the Oppressed* (Sheffield: Sheffield Academic Press, 1993), p. 87.
[55] G. Mursell, *English Spirituality: From 1700 to the Present Day* (London: SPCK, 2001), p. 405.

2

THE QUEST FOR
A PENTECOSTAL THEOLOGY

Introduction

Clark observes that Pentecostal theology 'is researched at the researcher's peril'[1] while Ma observes that it is 'simply impossible' to clearly identify what is the best definition of a Pentecostal.[2] Chan is concerned that Pentecostalism may be 'in danger of death by a thousand qualifications'[3] while Hollenweger writes, 'I do not know anybody who could convincingly define what "mainstream Pentecostalism" is', compounded by the fact that despite their differences, 'most Pentecostal denominations believe themselves to be mainstream'.[4] The comments of the latter authors indicate the challenge that many feel in attempting to identify the heartbeat of Pentecostalism.

[1] Clark and Lederle (eds), *What Is Distinctive*, p. 109; T. Cross, 'Can There Be a Pentecostal Systematic Theology? An Essay on Theological Method in a Post-Modern World', in *Teaching to Make Disciples: Education for Pentecostal-Charismatic Spirituality and Life: The Collected Papers of the 30th Annual Meeting of the SPS* (Tulsa: Oral Roberts University, 2001), pp. 145–66; for an interesting but very localized assessment of differences in beliefs by Pentecostals, see R.D. Braswell, 'Passing Down Pentecost', *Paraclete* 28.3 (1994), pp. 1–11.

[2] W. Ma, 'Asian (Classical) Pentecostal Theology in Context', in Anderson and Tang (eds), *Asian and Pentecostal*, p. 73.

[3] S. Chan, 'Whither Pentecostalism?', in Anderson and Tang (eds), *Asian and Pentecostal*, p. 580; D.L. Dabney, 'Saul's Armor: The Problem and the Promise of Pentecostal Theology Today', *Pneuma* 23.1 (2001), pp. 115–46; V-M. Kärkkäinen, 'David's Sling: The Promise and the Problem of Pentecostal Theology Today: A Response to D. Lyle Dabney', *Pneuma* 23.1 (2001), pp. 147–52.

[4] W. J. Hollenweger, 'Pentecostalism, Past, Present and Future', *JEPTA* 21 (2001), pp. 41–8 (46).

Theology

Some have sought to identify Pentecostals on the basis of their beliefs.[5] A way of identifying the core of Pentecostal theology would be to note its main theological loci. Thus, Land identifies the heart of Pentecostal theology as focused on justification, sanctification and Spirit-baptism[6] though most Pentecostals view it as comprising Jesus as Saviour, healer, baptizer and coming king,[7] sometimes to which is added the sanctifying role of Jesus.[8] These beliefs, that are clustered around Jesus, do not encapsulate all that Pentecostalism stands for, but they do represent some of the emphases traditionally maintained by its adherents. Macchia deduces that the 'fourfold gospel is important for understanding the origins and enduring accents of emerging Pentecostal theologies'[9] though Coulter reflects that although this may have represented Pentecostals as they were, it is less valuable as a depiction of their current position which is much more diverse.[10] Complicating the quest for core beliefs is that Pentecostalism is often defined differently in various cultures.[11] Thus, for example, Korean Pentecostal, or Full Gospel, theology comprises salvation, healing, the second coming of Jesus, the fullness of the Spirit and blessing, the latter being a distinctive contribution of Yonggi Cho.[12] In it, he argues that God desires prosperity in all aspects of the life of a believer.[13]

---

[5] Nichol, *Pentecostalism*, pp. 2–3; R.H. Hughes, *What Is Pentecost?* (Cleveland: Pathway Press, 1963); R.H. Hughes, *Church of God Distinctives* (Cleveland: Pathway Press, 1968); Clark and Lederle (eds), *What Is Distinctive*, p. 17; R. Cotton, 'What Does it Mean to Be Pentecostal? Three Perspectives. The Dynamic behind the Doctrine', *Paraclete* 28.3 (1994), pp. 12–17 (12); N.D. Sauls, *Pentecostal Doctrines: A Wesleyan Approach* (Dunn: Heritage Press, 1979).

[6] Land, *Pentecostal Spirituality*, pp. 82–98, 117–19, 125–64, 196–205.

[7] Dayton, *Theological Roots of Pentecostalism*, pp. 21–2; W. Vondey, 'Christian Amnesia: Who in the World Are Pentecostals?', *AJPS* 4.1 (2001), pp. 21–39 (32–4); Wacker, 'Wild Theories', p. 21; F. Macchia, 'Theology, Pentecostal', in Burgess and van der Maas (eds), *NIDPCM*, pp. 1120–141 (1124).

[8] B. Bay, 'The Current Tendencies of the Wesleyan-Holiness Movement and the Growth of Pentecostal-Charismatic Christianity', *AJPS* 7.1 (2004), pp. 255–64; Land, *Pentecostal Spirituality*, p. 18; Thomas, 'Pentecostal Theology', pp. 3–19; for a critique, see Cross, 'Can there be', pp. 145–66.

[9] Macchia, 'Theology, Pentecostal', p. 1124.

[10] D.M. Coulter, 'What Meaneth This? Pentecostals and Theological Inquiry', *JPT* 10.1 (2001), pp. 38–64 (41).

[11] M.L. Tan-Chow, *Pentecostal Theology for the Twenty-First Century: Engaging with Multi-Faith Singapore* (London: Ashgate, 2007).

[12] D.Y. Cho, *Five-Fold Gospel and Three-Fold Blessing* (Seoul: Young San Publishing, 1983).

[13] D.Y. Cho, *Salvation, Health and Prosperity. Our Threefold Blessings in Christ* (Altamonte Springs: Creation House, 1987), pp. 11–18, 55.

That which most distinguishes Pentecostalism is the doctrine relating to the baptism in the Spirit. However, even the baptism in the Spirit has received varied comment by Pentecostals. For example, although many anticipate that a consequence of the baptism of the Spirit will be power, this has various nuances and expectations for different Pentecostals. Many expect to manifest this power in their lives specifically with regard to evangelism. However, the revision to the article defining the baptism in the Spirit as outlined in the AoG Statement of Fundamental Truths also identifies this power as resulting in a greater love for Jesus, while others anticipate that the baptism in the Spirit will result in a greater sense of God's presence or a more consecrated Christian lifestyle, sometimes resulting in a crisis experience of sanctification. In practice, however, this power has been mainly associated with charismatic gifts.

But there are other divisive aspects related to this apparently central belief of Pentecostalism. The subsequent nature of the baptism in the Spirit to conversion has been a topic that has created a great deal of discussion in recent years. For example, while many assume that the baptism in the Spirit is subsequent to conversion, some disagree. Similarly, the distinctive practice of many Pentecostals has been speaking in tongues but its precise significance has been the subject of disagreement. While many Pentecostals associate the gift of speaking in tongues with the baptism in the Spirit, viewing it as the initial evidence of that experience, others do not; while some believe that when combined with the gift of interpretation they are equivalent to prophecy, others maintain that both are Godward expressions of prayer or praise; while some sanction their corporate use without interpretation, others do not.

There has also been a fluidity with regard to other doctrines during the history of Pentecostalism. Lewis identifies major changes, including the early twentieth century move away from the notion of a crisis experience associated with sanctification to a more progressive understanding of sanctification in the life of the believer, and the development of Oneness Pentecostalism. Other changes resulted from a closer relationship with evangelicals from the 1950s onwards, including less emphasis on pacifism, reduced ecumenical dialogue, restrictions on women in leadership, and a stricter understanding of the infallibility and inerrancy of the Bible.[14] It is thus much more difficult to identify Pentecostals now on the basis of their doctrines because of the various nuances of beliefs, some of which are significant. However, and as importantly, this difficulty has been compounded by the fact that many aspects of theology once distinctive to Pentecostalism have now also been embraced by others; Pentecostal perspectives are not as distinct as they once were.

---

[14] P.W. Lewis, 'Reflections of a Hundred Years of Pentecostal Theology', *CPCR* 12 (Jan. 2003).

An alternative emphasis needs to be discovered that best identifies the nucleus of Pentecostalism.

Encounter

A clue in our quest to locate the core of Pentecostalism may be gleaned from the early Pentecostals who were suspicious of creeds and preferred to concentrate on shared experiences. Indeed, Anderson deduces, 'In its beginnings, Pentecostalism in the western world was an ecumenical movement of people claiming a common experience rather than a common doctrine'.[15] Similarly, Hollenweger concludes, 'What unites the Pentecostal churches is not a doctrine but a religious experience'.[16] Indeed, Sepulveda cautions against seeking to identify Pentecostalism on the basis of its doctrinal beliefs for fear of

> running the great risks of forgetting, and thereby mutilating, what is essential, viz. the primacy of experience over doctrine, and of relationship over belief; in other words, the freedom of the Spirit who does not permit himself to be confined by doctrinal categories which are in the end rational.[17]

Similarly, Ellington concludes,

> Doctrines may be challenged and even overturned without striking at the heart of Pentecostal faith because the essential emphasis of Pentecostalism is not a teaching which must be believed or a proof which can be deduced and defended against all challenges, but a God who must be reckoned with in direct encounter.[18]

Although an overstatement, this does signal that which is fundamental to Pentecostalism – a personal, experiential encounter of the Spirit of God.[19] It is this that best identifies the Pentecostal heartbeat.[20]

A more productive route in seeking to identify Pentecostal theology may therefore be to recognize the central Pentecostal expectation of a radical experience of the Spirit, and, in particular, as it relates to their identity as children of God, their perception of God, their worship and service, their

---

[15] Anderson, *An Introduction to Pentecostalism*, p. 60.

[16] Hollenweger, 'From Azusa Street to the Toronto Phenomenon', p. 7.

[17] J. Sepulveda, 'Reflections on the Pentecostal Contribution to the Mission of the Church in Latin America', *JPT* 1 (1992), pp. 93–108 (101).

[18] S.A. Ellington, 'Pentecostalism and the Authority of Scripture', *JPT* 9 (1996), pp. 16–38 (17).

mission and evangelism, their reading and application of the Bible and their relationships with other believers.[21]

That which is central to their faith and practice are the concepts of 'encounter' and 'experience'. They aim to know God experientially, whether it is via an intellectual recognition of his being or an emotional appreciation of his character and it is this that often makes them functionally different within the Christian tradition. Kärkkäinen concludes that 'the essence of Pentecostalism can hardly be captured by any theological formulation; spirituality and spiritual experience is primary'.[22]

For Pentecostals, revelation is not just intended to affect the mind but also the emotions; theology is not explored best in a rationalistic context alone but also with a readiness to encounter the divine and be impacted by one's discoveries in a way that will enlighten the mind but also transform the life. Indeed, Pentecostal theology may be best identified as a theology of encounter – encounter of God, the Bible and the community.

Such encounters are not merely viewed as self-authenticating or self-oriented; they are deemed to be valuable as motivational forces, leading to personal transformation as a result of the Spirit's involvement in their lives. MacDonald, preferring to identify the spirituality of Pentecostals as

[19] V-M. Kärkkäinen, '"The Re-Turn of Religion in the Third Millennium": Pentecostalisms and Postmodernities' (*EPCRA* conference paper, University of Uppsala, 2007) pp. 1–14 (5); H. Zegwaart, 'Christian Experience in Community', *CPCR* 11 (Feb. 2002); D.E. Albrecht, *Rites in the Spirit. A Ritual Approach to Pentecostal/Charismatic Spirituality* (Sheffield: Sheffield Academic Press, 1999), p. 10; D. Gee, *The Pentecostal Movement* (London: Elim, 1949), p. 30; D.J. du Plessis, 'Golden Jubilee of Twentieth Century Pentecostal Movements', *IRM* 47 (April, 1958), pp. 193–201 (194); Nichol, *Pentecostalism*, p. 55; G.L. Anderson, 'Pentecostals Believe in More Than Tongues', in Smith (ed.), *Pentecostals from the Inside Out*, pp. 53–64 (55–6); J.K. Asamoah-Gyadu, 'An African Pentecostal on Mission in Eastern Europe: The Church of the "Embassy of God" in the Ukraine', *Pneuma* 27.2 (2005), pp. 297–321 (314); Cross, 'A Proposal to Break', pp. 49–58. For a non-Pentecostal Roman Catholic enquiry of the relationship between power, experience and the Spirit, see B. Cooke, *Power and the Spirit of God: Toward an Experience-Based Pneumatology* (Oxford: Oxford University Press, 2004). In it, he describes himself as someone who is in search of an experience-based pneumatology.

[20] Anderson, *An Introduction to Pentecostalism*, p. 256; A. Semple McPherson, *This Is That: Personal Experiences, Sermons, and Writings* (Los Angeles: Echo Park Evangelistic Association, 1923) p. 713; R.P. Spittler, 'Spirituality, Pentecostal and Charismatic', in Burgess and van der Maas (eds), *NIDPCM*, pp. 1096–102 (1096–097).

[21] K. Warrington, 'Experience: The *sina qua non* of Pentecostalism' (SPS conference paper, Cleveland, 2007), pp. 331–38.

[22] V-M, Kärkkäinen, 'Pentecostal Theological Education in a Theological and Missiological Perspective' (*EPTA* conference paper, Iso Kirja, Sweden, 2006), p. 13; W.J. Hollenweger, 'Creator Spiritus: The Challenge of Pentecostal Experience to Pentecostal Theology', *Theology* 81 (1978), pp. 32–40.

'fully experienced gospel' or 'Christ-centred, experience-certified theology', concludes that 'any genuine experience with the living God will leave an emotional wake in a man's psyche'.[23] Such encounters are believed to be reflected in the Bible, and Pentecostals fully anticipate an experiential outworking. Thus, where there is sometimes an absence of credal confession and formal ceremony in Pentecostal spirituality, there is the presence of experience, often spontaneous, emotional, heartfelt, intensely personal and life-transforming. Pentecostals embrace a spirituality that expects to touch God and to be touched by him. It may be intensely personal (I-Thou), sometimes has a numinous quality (resulting in a sense of awe) and mystical experiences are also possible.

Pentecostals do not simply affirm a list of biblical beliefs; they have encountered them experientially. Thus, the baptism in the Spirit is not simply to be recognized as a distinctive doctrinal feature of Pentecostal theology but to be understood as reflecting that which is central to Pentecostalism, namely encounter and experience. Thus, Chan identifies the baptism in the Holy Spirit as the matrix in which Pentecostals receive 'a certain kind of spiritual experience of an intense, direct and overwhelming nature centring in the person of Christ',[24] Coulter concluding that 'the experience is more fundamental than the theological metaphor expressing it'.[25]

De Matviuk deduces Latin American Pentecostalism to be characterized by 'a religious experience with the divine'[26] while Urrabazo concludes, 'For Latinos, God is not so much a concept, as an experience'.[27] Christenson describes Pentecostalism as 'Christianity standing on tiptoe, expecting something to happen'.[28] When du Plessis was asked to identify the difference between him and the other Christian ecumenical leaders, he responded, 'You have the truth on ice, and I have it on fire'.[29] McClung defines Pentecostals

---

[23] W.G. MacDonald, 'Pentecostal Theology: A Classical Viewpoint', in Spittler (ed.), *Perspectives on the New Pentecostalism*, pp. 63–5; S.K.H. Chan, *Pentecostal Theology and the Christian Spiritual Tradition* (Sheffield: Sheffield Academic Press, 2000), p. 7; Land, *Pentecostal Spirituality*, p. 184; J.D. Johns, 'Pentecostalism and the Postmodern Worldview', *JPT*, 7 (1995), pp. 73–96 (91).

[24] Chan, *Pentecostal Theology*, p. 7; M.J. Cartledge, 'Pentecostal experience', *JEPTA*, 28.1 (2008), pp. 21–33.

[25] Coulter, 'What Meaneth This?', p. 43.

[26] M.A.C. de Matviuk, 'Latin American Pentecostal Growth: Culture, Orality and the Power of Testimonies', *AJPS* 5.2 (2002), pp. 205–22 (208); M.M. Poloma, *The Assemblies of God at the Crossroads* (Knoxsville: University of Tennessee Press, 1989), p. 213.

[27] R. Urrabazo, 'Therapeutic Sensitivity to the Latino Spiritual Soul', in M. Flores, G. Carey (eds), *Family Therapy with Hispanics: Toward Appreciating Diversity* (Needham Heights: Allyn and Bacon, 2000), pp. 205–28 (213).

[28] L. Christenson, 'Pentecostalism's Forgotten Forerunner', in Synan (ed.), *Aspects of Pentecostal-Charismatic Origins*, pp. 25–31 (27).

[29] D.J. du Plessis, *A Man Called Mr. Pentecost* (South Plainfield: Bridge Publishing, 1977), p. 182.

as understanding God to be the 'One who is there-now'.[30] Pentecostals are less defined by their doctrines and more by their perception that God lives with them in the here and now. They believe that their experience of God is based on the NT kerygma but without the experience, they would argue that the kerygma is lifeless. This provides for a pneumatology that is experientially as well as biblically based, centred in encounter, as well as, and even more than, power. Thus, Lederle concludes, 'there is something unique about the Pentecostal emphasis on experiencing God in the charismatic manifestations of his power'.[31]

It is no surprise to discover that there is sometimes fluidity in Pentecostal praxis and thought as they seek to locate a biblical framework that is sufficiently flexible for their spirituality, a spirituality that is, by definition, dynamic since it is pneumatic. Anderson writes, 'Pentecostals are not unnerved by the search for a theological explanation for a divine act that has been experienced but not understood'.[32] Pragmatism, sometimes used to describe an immature or unstable faith, may be, occasionally, an appropriate response to that which has no precedent or a limited historical context. Indeed, Pentecostals are prepared to accept the dangers of pragmatism rather than miss the opportunity of observing and experiencing a new work of the Spirit.[33] Wacker identifies this feature in the earliest years of Pentecostalism also, noting their remarkable capacity to

> work within the social and cultural expectations of the age. Again and again we see them holding their proverbial finger to the wind, calculating where they were, where they wanted to go and, above all, how to get there . . . the ability to figure the odds and react appropriately made them pragmatists to the bone.[34]

[30] L.G. McClung, 'Truth on Fire: Pentecostals and an Urgent Missiology', in McClung (ed.), *Azusa Street and Beyond*, pp. 47–54 (48); MacDonald, 'Pentecostal Theology', pp. 59–74 (62).

[31] H.I. Lederle, 'An Ecumenical Investigation into the Proprium or Distinctive Elements of Pentecostal Theology', in Clark and Lederle (eds), *What Is Distinctive*, pp. 158–71 (166–67); E.L. Blumhofer, *'Pentecost in My Soul': Explorations in the Meaning of Pentecostal Experience in the Assemblies of God* (Springfield: Gospel Publishing House, 1989); Edwards, 'Afro-Caribbean Pentecostalism', p. 46; J.D. Johns, C.B. Johns, 'Yielding to the Spirit: A Pentecostal Approach to Group Bible Study', *JPT* 1 (1992), pp. 109–34; C.B. Johns, 'Partners in Scandal: Wesleyan and Pentecostal Scholarship', *Pneuma* 21 (1999), pp. 183–97.

[32] Anderson, 'Pentecostals Believe', p. 58.

[33] K. McDonnell, 'The Experiential and the Social: New Models from the Pentecostal/ Roman Catholic Dialogue', *One in Christ* 9 (1972), pp. 43–58 (47).

[34] Wacker, *Heaven Below*, pp. 13–14.

Williams concludes, 'Pentecostals are basically people who have had a certain experience; so they find little use for theology or doctrine that does not recognise and, even more, participate in it'.[35] Although overstating his case, he does identify this central issue that for Pentecostals, defining an encounter with God as less important than encountering God in the first place. The absence of a definition does not necessarily invalidate the experience. Clark writes, 'Pentecostal theology demands more than *belief* in an experience – it demands the *experience* of the experience itself'.[36] For Pentecostals, to know God is to experience him, Bond writing, 'Theology follows experience. First comes the act of God, then follows the attempt to understand it'.[37]

To try to ally all aspects of spirituality with a rigid biblical framework may be unnecessary and assumes that the Spirit's activity is circumscribed by the Bible. Care must be maintained in retaining the belief that the Spirit is dynamic, sometimes radically so. It is thus vital to emphasize the role of the community of believers, who function as the temple of the Spirit (1 Cor. 6.19) and as a mouthpiece for his prophetic voice; they can help to ensure good practice and godly belief and to protect from the inappropriate elevation of individuals and experiences. Nevertheless, the benefits to be gained from affording the dynamic Spirit the opportunity to be creatively engaged in the Church and its mission must not be overlooked. Rather than the relationship between doctrine and experience be viewed as a tension[38] or even a difficulty,[39] it is more appropriate to recognize it as an opportunity to discover the creative mind of the Spirit who may wish to manifest himself in ways that are reflected in the Bible but who may also wish to radiate his presence in innovative and fresh ways. Believers are thus provided with the opportunity to observe their remarkable God working remarkably. Similarly, Hollenweger deduces that Pentecostalism is best expressed as providing an opportunity for believers to engage in 'an adventure in fellowship with the Holy Spirit and each other'.[40] If the Spirit is exalted to his true role as God and, as such, is granted the freedom to be creative and flexible in leading believers, they may be surprised as to where they may go, though it will not be in the absence of his dignity, authenticity and glory.

---

[35] J.R. Williams, 'Pentecostal Spirituality', *One in Christ* 10 (1974), pp. 180–92 (181).

[36] Clark and Lederle (eds), *What Is Distinctive*, p. 40 (italics in original); also pp. 69–75; T. Neuman ('Paul's appeal to the experience of the Spirit in Galatians 3:1–5: Christian experience as defined by the cross and effected by the Spirit', *JPT* 9 (1996), pp. 53–69 (59)) concludes, 'Paul's appeal to experience is crucial to his argument in Galatians'.

[37] J. Bond, 'What Is Distinctive about Pentecostal Theology?', in Clark and Lederle (eds), *What Is Distinctive*, pp. 133–42 (135).

[38] Gause, 'Issues in Pentecostalism', pp. 113–16.

[39] L.D. Hart, 'Problems of Authority in Pentecostalism', *Review and Expositor* 75 (1978), pp. 249–66.

[40] Hollenweger, 'Pentecostalism, Past, Present, and Future', pp. 43–5.

There is thus an increasing readiness by Pentecostals to allow for the possibility of a phenomenon being divinely initiated even where there is no historical precedent for it, as long as its consequence has been to lead the believer concerned closer to God.[41] Pentecostals are prepared to live with tensions, to accept the inexplicable and to acknowledge mystery. They recognize that one can begin to know God but never completely comprehend him. At best, he is imperfectly understood; after all, he is God. They are neither predicated to understand everything nor do they feel disposed to accommodate their spirituality within a framework that is tightly circumscribed by logic or rationality. They are much more prepared to believe that God is dynamic, not static; complex, even mystifying, but one who desires to be encountered. This issue merits a comprehensive and robust theological study that could helpfully result in the provision of a safe framework that would enable the articulation and outworking of a belief that explores the sovereign will of the Spirit as it is facilitated creatively, dynamically and with flexibility in the Church.

It is difficult, on occasions, to articulate a response to that which one perceives God is doing simply by offering theological propositions.[42] One may tell a story easier than one may define what happened. Similarly, prophets in the past have sometimes found it difficult to explain divine encounters to others (John, Rev. 1.17) and, on occasions, have instead fallen silent (Paul, 2 Cor. 12.4). Although Peter defended the encounter with God experienced by those in Jerusalem which resulted in tongues of fire resting on them and their speaking in tongues as a fulfilment of Joel 2.28–32, it is clear that the experience went beyond the prophecy for there is no mention there of speaking in tongues or tongues of fire. Peter offers a biblical framework of sorts in which the experience may be contextualized but it is a pragmatic response rather than a careful, comprehensive treatise. The fact is that the encounter was outside the received norms of how God worked and rather than attempt to completely explain it biblically, Peter offers a minimal biblical validation of the experience. The affirmation of the authenticity of the experience was not achieved by an intellectual rationale but by its effect in causing many to be prepared to listen to Peter who presented them with the possibility of engaging personally with God. The aspiration of some to explain every experience they have with and concerning God has an inbuilt problem. It results in his being restricted from doing that which may not be explained; the Creator would be reduced to the limits of the intellectual permission of the created.

---

[41] This is reflected also by R.A. Knox (*Enthusiasm: A Chapter in the History of Religion* (Oxford: Clarendon Press, 1950), pp. 520–28) who notes that some spiritual experiences common to early Methodists had limited biblical precedent.

[42] M.T. Kelsey, 'Courage, Unity and Theology', in Spittler (ed.), *Perspectives on the New Pentecostalism*, pp. 232–44 (233).

In truth, encountering God via experience is often more challenging than encountering him via the intellect. As Kelsey, who is not Pentecostal, notes,

> It is far easier to deal with ideas about God than with God himself. Ideas about God rarely overwhelm the thinker . . . when a man does encounter God, it is not God who is put under the microscope and examined with reason, but man who finds himself under scrutiny.[43]

One experience with God can be more life changing than an encyclopedic knowledge of God. Rather than view experiencing God as the easier, less authentic and ultimately flawed means of encountering God (when contrasted with a cerebral appreciation of him), it ought to be realized that the former is often the way that God revealed himself in the Bible and can be a powerful transforming influence in the life of a believer. At the same time, an expectation of an experiential encounter with God can provide a guard against a merely cerebral theology.

Thus, Pentecostals value experience-based encounters with God because they have the potential to transform believers. They believe that if God initiates an experience, it must be in order to positively transform the individual concerned; a lack of consequence calls into question the experience or, at least, questions whether the person has benefited fully from the potential that the experience had to offer.

Pentecostals also value experience as potentially providing the impetus for mission. Offering an account of the meetings held at Azusa Street in the beginning of the last century, where many encounters with God were experienced with dramatic consequences, Bartleman writes, 'Missionary enthusiasm ran high . . . Hundreds definitely met with God . . . Many received a call to foreign fields . . . The altars were seldom empty of seekers day and night . . . we determined to fight nothing but sin, and fear nothing but God'.[44] Although this is a snapshot of an extraordinary move of God, nevertheless, it represents that which best reflects the Pentecostal ideal which advocates the value of experience as powerfully instrumental in Pentecostal mission.[45]

None of the above underestimates the dangers associated with encountering God via experience (no more than to assume that an intellectual

---

[43] Kelsey, 'Courage Unity and Theology', pp. 240–41.

[44] Bartleman, *Azusa Street*, p. 107.

[45] P. Pomerville, *The Third Force in Mission: A Pentecostal Contribution to Contemporary Mission Theology* (Peabody: Hendrickson, 1985), p. 104; A.M. Lord, 'The Voluntary Principle in Pentecostal Missiology', *JPT* 17 (Oct. 2000), pp. 81–95 (91); A.A. Ayuk, 'The Pentecostal Transformation of Nigerian Church Life', *AJPS* 5.2 (2002), pp. 189–204 (191); A.H. Anderson, 'Towards a Pentecostal Missiology for the Majority World', *AJPS* 8.1 (2005), pp. 29–47 (43).

appreciation of God does not also have potential drawbacks); meaningless experiences may be little more than vacuous sensations.[46] There is the constant danger for Pentecostals of so desiring authentic experiences with God that the latter may be debased to an expectation and insistence on experience on demand. The dangers of emotionalism, triumphalism and inauthentic, shallow, subjective and unscriptural experiences are to be guarded against by those who seek to encounter God. Dube warns against the danger of attempting to constantly maintain

> an involvement in some active form of transcendence, an identifiable event and moment of ecstasy. The only way to sustain an adequate sense of this tension is to string together as many events of ecstasy as closely together as possible. Essentially, like any other sensational lifestyle, it is the life of addiction'.[47]

Bueno similarly cautions Pentecostals to be aware of the variety of experiences and to remember that they often depend for their significance on historical, social, ethnic and cultural contexts; to attempt to homogenize them is unhelpful.[48] Nevertheless, Pentecostals seek to validate experience as an appropriate channel for an authentic encounter of and with God and it is incumbent on them that they consistently offer careful guidelines to ensure this occurs.

---

[46] C. Dube, 'From Ecstasy to *Ecstasis*: A Reflection on Prophetic and Pentecostal Ecstasy in the Light of John the Baptizer', *JPT* 11.1 (2002), pp. 41–52.

[47] Dube, 'From Ecstasy to *Ecstasis*', p. 48.

[48] R.N. Bueno, 'Listening to the Margins: Re-Historicizing Pentecostal Experiences and Identities', in Dempster, Klaus and Petersen (eds), *The Globalization of Pentecostalism*, pp. 268–88.

3

GOD

Introduction

Pentecostals, along with other evangelical believers, take for granted the existence of God (Rom. 1.20),[1] on occasion apologetically employing natural theology and cosmological, teleological, aesthetic and moral arguments to support their belief.[2] Recognizing that he is creative (Ps. 104.24), transcendent (1 Kgs 8.27), eternal (Isa. 57.15), faithful (Deut. 7.9), wise (Ps. 147.5), truthful (Num. 23.19), patient (Num. 14.18), gracious (Ps. 103.8), righteous (Ps. 145.17), sovereign (1 Tim. 6.15), just (Ps. 19.9), merciful (1 Pet. 1.3), tender (2 Sam. 22.36), love (1 Jn 4.16) and dependable (Jas. 1.17), they also affirm his omnipotence (Jer. 32.17), omnipresence (Jer. 23.23), omniscience (Ps. 139.1–6) and holiness (Isa. 57.15; 1 Pet. 1.15–16).[3] That he is described as being holy is not simply a reference to his sinlessness but rather to his extraordinariness, the word 'holy' (*hagios*) fundamentally meaning 'set apart'. He is unequalled, incomparable, irreplaceable and unimprovable. Despite his 'otherness', Pentecostals also acknowledge his readiness to transmit some of his characteristics to humanity and believers in particular. At the same time, they believe that he has chosen to reveal himself through the Bible, creation, human nature, including the conscience, as well as through Jesus.

---

[1] A. Rowe, *One Lord, One Faith* (Llanelli: Apostolic Publications, 1998), p. 29; R.E. Joyner, 'The One True God', in Horton (ed.), *Systematic Theology*, pp. 117–77.

[2] W.W. Menzies, S.M. Horton, *Bible Doctrines: A Pentecostal Perspective* (Springfield: Logion Press, 1993, 2000), pp. 46–8.

[3] K. Warrington, *God and Us: A Life Changing Adventure* (Milton Keynes: Scripture Union, 2004); J.T. Bradley, 'The Trinity', in Brewster (ed.), *Pentecostal Doctrine*, pp. 319–40 (338); Rowe, *One Lord, One Faith*, pp. 29–35; D.W. Cartwright, 'The Doctrine of Judgements', in Brewster (ed.), *Pentecostal Doctrine*, pp. 273–91.

Their relationship with God and expectations of his work within the world and their lives are based on a belief that he is vibrant, active and able to wisely set his agenda for his world. Such a God can create the unimaginable, initiate the unexpected, institute unique phenomena, surprise the watcher and resurrect the dead. He makes his own rules, acting in conformity to his nature. Pentecostals accept the inexplicable nature of God and they acknowledge his supremacy in determining possibilities and initiating assumed impossibilities. Thus, it is no hardship for Pentecostals to accept that the one who created the universe also created people for relationship with himself. It is a consequence of his unselfishness and willingness to bless that which he creates with his presence. He creates so that his creation can receive his smile and those whom he forms are granted the privilege of feeling his pleasure. That which he causes to come into being is crafted out of his desire to care for his craftsmanship and his creativity is channelled into being because of love alone.

The personal involvement of God in his creation is reflected in the descriptions of how he creates. In picture language, the biblical writers describe him using his fingers (Ps. 8.3), shaping the mountains and creating the wind (Amos 4.13). His intimacy with his creation is demonstrated in that it reflects him (Pss. 8.1; 19.1–2) and praises him (Ps. 145.10). God does not create in order to receive praise as if he needed it. Rather, that which is created by him is described as spontaneously and naturally expressing its pride at being created in such a perfect way by such a perfect Creator.

Trinity

As with many other evangelicals, Pentecostals have traditionally identified themselves as Trinitarian[4] and thus (often unknowingly) affirmed the classical creeds, adopting the orthodox beliefs of the Western Church, as defined by the Council of Nicea.[5] Many Pentecostals, as most other believers, have limited understanding of the complexities of the relationship between the Spirit, the Son and the Father. They are unlikely to explain (or even be aware of)

---

[4] Gen. 1.26; Mt. 28.19; 1 Cor. 12.4–6; 2 Cor. 13.14; Eph. 4.4–6; Col. 2.9; 1 Pet. 1.2.

[5] Menzies and Horton, *Bible Doctrines*, p. 53–7; the Statement of Fundamental Truths (13) of the AoG states, 'The Holy Ghost is from the Father and the Son, proceeding . . .'; G.T. Sheppard, 'Nicean Creed, *Filioque*, and Pentecostal Movements in the United States', *Greek Orthodox Theological Review*, 31.3–4 (1986); K.D. McRoberts, 'The Holy Trinity', in Horton (ed.), *Systematic Theology*, pp. 145–77; Bradley, 'The Trinity', pp. 319–40; Kärkkäinen, *Toward a Pneumatological Theology*, pp. 97–8, 104–08; D.J. Massey, 'Trinitarianism', in Burgess (ed.), *EPCC*, pp. 449–51; A. Somdal, *Tro og Laere. Et forsøk på en samlet presentasjon av pinsevennes tro og laere* (Oslo: Filadelfiaforlaget, 1990), pp. 45–152.

issues relating to the procession of the Spirit. In general, they accept that he proceeds from the Father (Jn 15.26) but also has been sent by Jesus (Jn 16.7).[6] For many, this has inevitably resulted in an assumption that the Spirit is somewhat inferior to Jesus and the Father since he can be sent by them. It is best, however, to acknowledge that any subordinationist language is to be understood as valuable in identifying function, though does not indicate difference in essence.

Most Pentecostals practically relate to the individual members of the Godhead as if they were three different persons. While some may attempt to be technically correct in their address to the Godhead in prayer, most will pray to the one they are most familiar with, either Jesus or the Father, or refer to God as a term that circumvents the problem as it encompasses them all. Theologically, they are Trinitarian though practically, this is less clearly defined. They have often resorted to metaphors to explain how the individual members relate to one another, though without a great deal of success, such attempts resulting in inadequate descriptions of the relationships within the Godhead.

They have wrestled with the concept of hierarchy within the Godhead and have generally identified the Father as being the first or the primary member.[7] Basically, the Father, Son and Spirit are each identified as equally God though none of them are completely God without the others, each functioning separately, though in unity and harmony with each other, and being worthy of worship.[8]

Although they are independent within the Godhead, they are also interdependent, sharing equal honour, Conn offering the notion of 'a Tri-unity, three personalities who constitute one identity of God'.[9] Pentecostals do not believe in three gods (tritheism) though they recognize the difficulty of adequately describing the relationships within the Godhead. The concept of the trinity is not an easy one to understand and the NT does not provide a clear and explicit Trinitarian formula for the Godhead. Indeed, although Paul is clearly Trinitarian, it is not clear that he wished to present a final statement concerning the intricate interrelationship within the Godhead. He does little to

---

[6] R.M. Pruitt, *Fundamentals of the Faith* (Cleveland: White Wing Publishing, 1981), p. 102; see further V-M. Kärkkäinen, 'Trinity as Communion in the Spirit: Koinonia, Trinity, and Filioque in the Roman Catholic-Pentecostal Dialogue', *Pneuma* 22.2 (2000), pp. 209–30; G.P. Duffield, N.M. Van Cleave, *Foundations of Pentecostal Theology* (Los Angeles: LIFE Bible College, 1983), p. 109.

[7] C.W. Conn, *A Balanced Church* (Cleveland: Pathway Press, 1975), p. 21; Rowe, *One Lord, One Faith*, p. 32.

[8] Rowe, *One Lord, One Faith*, p. 33; Menzies and Horton, *Bible Doctrines*, pp. 44–5.

[9] Conn, *A Balanced Church*, p. 23.

help the monotheistic Jewish Christian to transition from a belief in one God to a position in which Jesus, the Spirit and the Father are each viewed as divine, Fee concluding that he is 'too busy being a missionary pastor to have the luxury of purely reflective theology'.[10] To this may be added the fact that the provision of a clear and systematic formulation of the relationships within the Godhead does not appear to be a priority for Paul. Not only is it beyond human comprehension but it may also be deduced that such a task would be to remove the focus from that which is central to Pauline theology – experience with God, rather than a systematic and comprehensive exploration of God (though there are aspects of the latter in his letters). Fee, concludes that Paul is drawn to a wider understanding about God precisely because of his 'experience of the Spirit, as the one who enables believers to confess the risen Christ as exalted Lord'.[11] Similarly, Kärkkäinen concludes, 'the most important thing for Pentecostals is not the doctrine *per se*, but the experience of the Trinity'.[12]

A large Pentecostal constituency is identified as being particularly Christocentric.[13] They are generally referred to as Oneness Pentecostals[14] and although their forebears were expelled from the AoG, there has been some dialogue with Trinitarian Pentecostals, especially through the Society

[10] G.D. Fee, *Paul, the Spirit and the People of God* (Peabody: Hendrickson, 1997), p. 38.

[11] G.D. Fee, *To What End Exegesis? Essays Textual, Exegetical, and Theological* (Grand Rapids: Eerdmans, 2001), p. 332.

[12] Kärkkäinen, *Toward a Pneumatological Theology*, p. 103.

[13] Anderson suggests that they may number up to a quarter of all Pentecostals (*An Introduction to Pentecostalism*, p. 49) and identifies a number of Pentecostal denominations including the United Pentecostal Church (the largest Oneness denomination in North America, founded in 1945), the Pentecostal Assemblies of the World (predominantly African American), the (predominantly black) British Apostolic Church and the True Jesus Church (the largest Chinese Pentecostal church); K.D. Gill, 'The Oneness Doctrine as a Contextualized Doctrine of the Trinity for Mexico', in Jongeneel (ed.), *Pentecost, Mission and Ecumenism*, pp. 107–14; D.A. Reed, 'Origins and Development of the Theology of Oneness Pentecostalism in the United States', *Pneuma* 1.1 (1979), pp. 31–7; idem, 'Aspects of the Origins of Oneness Pentecostalism', in Synan (ed.), *Aspects of Pentecostal-Charismatic Origins*, pp. 143–68; idem, 'Origins and Development of the Theology of Oneness Pentecostalism' (unpublished doctoral dissertation, Boston University, 1978); Faupel, *The Everlasting Gospel*, pp. 275–306; K.J. Archer, 'Early Pentecostal Biblical Interpretation', *JPT* 18 (2001), pp. 32–70 (56–67); McRoberts, 'The Holy Trinity', pp. 171–76.

[14] G. Boyd, *Oneness Pentecostals and the Trinity* (Grand Rapids: Baker, 1992), pp. 10, 227–28; Boyd, an ex-Oneness Pentecostal, estimates that there are 1 million in the USA and 5 million globally; T.L. French, *Our God Is One: The Story of Oneness Pentecostalism* (Indianapolis: Voice and Vision Publications, 1999).

of Pentecostal Studies,[15] though not without some resistance.[16] Fundamentally, Oneness Pentecostals reject the concept that the members of the trinity may be identified as separate and equal. Instead, they believe that Jesus is the revelation of God, Jehovah being identical to Jesus. Furthermore, they believe that God is revealed to humanity in the person of the Son, the whole Godhead existing in Jesus. Thus, Jesus is not viewed as one of the Godhead but the Godhead in one. Since God is essentially one, the terms 'Father', 'Son' and 'Spirit' are identified as manifestations of God for the purposes of revelation but not intended to indicate members of the Godhead. Reed concludes that for Oneness Pentecostals, 'there is only one divine being who is revealed as Father *in* the Son and as Spirit *through* the Son',[17] Col. 2.9 being a key verse for them. Bernard succinctly writes, 'There is no possibility of separating God and Jesus, and there is no God visible outside of Jesus'.[18] Oneness Pentecostals view Jesus and the Father synonymously (Jn 8.19; 10.30; 12.45 being used to support their view), Bernard deducing, 'If there is only one God and that God is the Father, and if Jesus is God, then it logically follows that Jesus is the Father'.[19] The Spirit is also confused with Jesus (Rom. 8.9–11; 2 Cor. 3.17 being used as proof texts) and referred to as the transcendent presence of God as revealed in the Son. Furthermore, their

---

[15] M. Gaxiola-Gaxiola, 'The Unresolved Issue: A Third-World Perspective on the Oneness Question' (SPS conference paper, CBN University, 1987); K.D. Gill, 'The New Issue Reconsidered: A Missiological Analysis of the Oneness Doctrine of the Trinity' (SPS conference paper, Christ for the Nations, Dallas, 1990); D.K. Bernard, 'Dialogue between Trinitarian and Oneness Pentecostals' (SPS conference paper, Evangel University, Springfield, 1999); idem, 'A Response to Ralph Del Colle's "Oneness and Trinity: A Preliminary Proposal for Dialogue with Oneness Pentecostalism"' (SPS conference paper, Toronto, 1996); C.H. Montgomery, D.A. Reed, 'The Experience of Jesus in Baptismal Doctrine: A Third Way in the Trinitarian-Oneness Divide' (SPS conference paper, Cleveland, 2007), pp. 229–36; D.M. Flynn, 'The Oneness-Trinity Debate in the Early Church' (SPS conference paper, Springfield, 1999); R. Del Colle, 'Spirit-Christology: Dogmatic Foundations for Pentecostal-Charismatic Spirituality', *JPT* 3 (1993) pp. 91–114 (93–114); idem, 'Oneness and Trinity: A Preliminary Proposal for Dialogue with Oneness Pentecostalism', *JPT* 10 (1997), pp. 85–110; D. Reed, 'Oneness Pentecostalism: Problems and Possibilities for Pentecostal Theology', *JPT* 11 (1997), pp. 73–93; D.L. Segraves, 'Oneness Theology', in Burgess (ed.), *EPCC*, pp. 342–45.

[16] Menzies and Horton, *Bible Doctrines*, pp. 44, 55–7 (Menzies describes it as a modern form of the heresy of Sabellianism (p. 55)); Macchia, 'Theology, Pentecostal', pp. 1126–128; K.L. Bass, 'Baptism and the Canon: Can/Should We Still Harmonize the Baptismal Formulae in Matthew and Acts' (SPS conference paper, Cleveland, 2007), pp. 32–9; Boyd, *Oneness Pentecostals*, pp. 9, 23.

[17] Reed, 'Oneness Pentecostalism', p. 941.

[18] D. Bernard, *The Oneness of God* (Hazelwood: World Aflame, 1983); idem, *Essentials of Oneness Theology* (Hazelwood: World Aflame, 1984).

[19] Bernard, *The Oneness of God*, p. 66.

understanding of the Spirit does not allow for his being viewed as a distinct person within the Godhead; instead, they believe the Spirit of Jehovah is the Holy Spirit.[20]

Oneness Pentecostals affirm two natures in Jesus, the (human) one identified in his being termed 'Son', in which form he is subordinate to the Father, while his deity retains its integrity; at the same time, they believe that God was not solely present in the body of Jesus for he is omnipresent. At the eschaton, the humanity and sonship of Jesus will be terminated and he will revert to his original mode as God. The issue of the name of Jesus is integral to their identity so much so that adherents have to be rebaptized in the name of Jesus if they have already been baptized in the Trinitarian formula so as to follow the pattern identified in Acts 2.38.

Father

It is the relationality of God that is probably the most fertile area of theological exploration and personal experience that Pentecostals can offer to the theology of God.[21] Traditionally, they have balanced a clear awareness of the awesome nature of the sovereign God with the recognition of the warm relationship that he intends to have with believers, as best defined by his being defined as Father. For them, God is not immutable but interactive, not impassable but permeating their lives, not immoveable but capable of being moved by those he has created. The God they see in the Bible is not capable of being tied down to a creed or neat list of dogmatic truths. They recognize that parts of his being and character are beyond understanding. However, they emphasize the fact that he calls people into a dynamic learning journey with himself that is experiential in its fullest sense, encompassing the mind and the emotions. This means that where unresolved issues remain concerning the nature of God, rather than seek to represent them in carefully prescribed statements, Pentecostals are more prepared to live in the tension and uncertainty of the inexplicable while holding tightly to the central mysterious fact that this fundamentally unknowable God calls them to know him, Pinnock describing Pentecostals as 'boldly relational theists'.[22] Furthermore, Pentecostals believe that God willingly invites believers to partner him in achieving his will, even though he does not need their involvement to achieve his objectives; it may be a risky procedure for him, insofar as he shares his work with weak humanity, but one that involves a real participatory relationship with believers.

[20] Boyd, *Oneness Pentecostals*, pp. 9, 23.
[21] Pinnock, 'Divine Relationality', pp. 3–26.
[22] Pinnock, 'Divine Relationality', p. 14.

Jesus

Introduction

Because of the Pentecostal emphasis on the Spirit, it may be deduced that they have a faulty perception of Jesus. However, they seek to provide a theology that is both theocentric and Christocentric; indeed, it may be argued that Pentecostalism is rather more 'Jesu-centric' than Spirit centred,[23] Padilla identifying it as 'pneumatalogically Christocentric'.[24] Most Pentecostals affirm the full deity, sovereignty and sinless humanity of Jesus, providing a range of verses to substantiate both characteristics.[25] They have a high regard for the humanity of Jesus, sometimes at the expense of his divinity. That is not to suggest that they do not believe he is divine or that he was sinful; although severely tempted, they believe he did not succumb to any temptation (Heb. 2.16–18; 1 Pet. 2.22). However, they take seriously the incarnation and the notion that Jesus 'emptied' (*ekenōsen*) himself (Phil. 2.7), identifying that process as 'divesting himself of the glory and privileges he enjoyed with the Father in past eternity'.[26] Similarly, they believe that he exists in eternity in bodily form and bears the marks of his crucifixion on his hands and in his side. Thus, he is the Mediator par excellence (Heb. 9.12, 26–28), who understands the pressure of sin experienced by all believers (Heb. 4.15) and intercedes on their behalf (Heb. 8.3).

Salvation

As with other evangelicals, Pentecostals believe that a fundamental reason for Jesus becoming incarnate was to die on behalf of all people, who would

---

[23] See Land, *Pentecostal Spirituality*, p. 96; R. Del Colle, 'Theological Dialogue on the "Full Gospel": Trinitarian Contributions from Pope John Paul II and Thomas A. Smail', *Pneuma* 20 (1998), pp. 141–60; M. Habets, 'Veni Cinderella Spiritus!', *JPT* 10.1 (2001), pp. 65–80 (76); J.J. Glass, 'Eschatology: A Clear and Present Danger – A Sure and Certain Hope, in Warrington (ed.), *Pentecostal Perspectives*, pp. 120–46 (136); Chan, *Pentecostal Theology*, p. 68; V-M. Kärkkäinen, '"Encountering Christ in the Full Gospel Way": An Incarnational Pentecostal Spirituality', *JEPTA* 27.2 (2007), pp. 9–23 (10–11); P. Risser, 'Embracing a Balanced "Pentecostal Theology"', *Spirit and Church* 2.2 (2000), p. 188.

[24] E. Padilla, 'Pentecostal Theology', in Burgess (ed.), *EPCC*, p. 356. Colle, a Roman Catholic, similarly speaks of the importance of a pneumatologically informed Christology (R. Del Colle, 'Incarnation and the Holy Spirit', *Spirit and Church* 2.2 (2000), pp. 199–229 (223); idem, 'Spirit-Christology' ('Spirit-Christology: Dogmatic Foundations for Pentecostal-Charismatic Spirituality' *JPT* 3 (1993), pp. 91–112).

[25] D.R. Nichols, 'The Lord Jesus Christ', in Horton (ed.), *Systematic Theology*, pp. 291–324; Divinity – Mt. 2.2, 11; 14.33; 16.16; Jn 1.1; 14.9; 20.28; Eph. 1.22–23; Col. 1.15; Rev. 5.6–13. Humanity – Mk 2.15; Lk. 2.40, 52; Jn 4.6; Heb. 2.9, 14, 17; Menzies and Horton, *Bible Doctrines*, pp. 61–6; Rowe, *One Lord, One Faith*, pp. 59–75.

thus potentially be able to experience a relationship with God and enjoy eternal life.[27] At best, they view the atonement as potential for all but a reality only for those who take advantage of it. The motivation of this free act of God is his holiness (Isa. 6.3; Jn 17.25), mercy and love (Jn 3.16; Eph. 2.4–5; Tit. 3.4–5; 2 Pet. 3.9). The death of Jesus on the cross was the culmination of this mission and thus, Jesus was able to pronounce 'It is finished', whereupon he died, having achieved that which he came to do, the resurrection providing indisputable evidence that he had victoriously overcome death (1 Cor. 15.54–57). Pentecostals affirm the literal, bodily resurrection of Jesus and identify it as an integral marker of the mission of Jesus, affirmed by the writers of the NT as having significant implications for an accurate understanding of Jesus.[28]

It is not surprising that for Pentecostals, the literal, historical resurrection of Jesus is viewed as 'essential to the Christian faith'[29] while Pentecostal preaching has been described as 'the preaching of the Cross and the Resurrection'.[30] Steinmetz sums up much Pentecostal thinking on the resurrection of Jesus by stating, 'the resurrection is that key event on which all else depends . . . No resurrection, no Christianity'.[31]

Pentecostals believe that all people have sinned,[32] sin being defined as breaking God's laws and also as offending or displeasing God. Although sin obstructs the achievement of God's will and breaks his standards, it is viewed much more personally as an individual's resistance to God, a rebuttal of the love of God to the individual, a betrayal of God and an undermining of the purposes to which God has called them. Pentecostals do not believe that the body is inherently evil. However, they do believe that everybody is born contaminated by the sins that Adam and Eve committed when they disobeyed God (Rom. 5.14–21); thus, a belief in original sin would be accepted by most, though the nuances of such a view (realistic, federal, voluntarily adopted depravity views) would be rarely articulated. As a result of these 'original' sins, each person possesses an inclination to sin, as a result of which sins are inevitably committed. Pentecostals subscribe to the need for individual repentance, the receiving of God's grace and forgiveness, by faith, and a determined commitment to an active following of Jesus by lifestyle

---

[26] Menzies and Horton, *Bible Doctrines*, p. 68.
[27] D.B. Pecota, 'The Saving Work of Christ', in Horton (ed.), *Systematic Theology*, pp. 325–73; B.C. Aker, 'Born Again', in Burgess (ed.), *EPCC*, pp. 67–72; Bloch-Hoell, *The Pentecostal Movement*, pp. 122–41.
[28] Mt. 28.1–20; Mk 16.1–8; Lk. 24.1–48; Jn 20.1–29.
[29] G.R. Carlson, 'The Word in the Ministry of Miracle', *Paraclete* 7 (1982), pp. 4–9 (4).
[30] R.L. Brandt, 'Pentecostal Preaching', *Paraclete* 2 (1981), pp. 14–18 (16).
[31] D.C. Steinmetz, 'The Necessity of the Past', *Heritage* (Spring 1995), pp. 22–7 (25).
[32] Ps. 51.5; Rom. 3.23; 5.19; 1 Cor. 15.21–22; Eph. 2.3; Jas 3.9; 1 Jn 3.4; 5.17.

and witness.[33] Whereas unbelievers exist in a state of enmity with God (Col. 1.21) and are objects of his anger (Rom. 5.10), they can know reconciliation because of the death of Jesus (2 Cor. 5.18–19). As a result of this reconciliation, believers are adopted as God's children (Rom. 8.15; Eph. 1.4–5) on the basis of which they enjoy an exalted and unparalleled relationship with God, having been welcomed into a new family, enabling them to benefit from the resources that God, their Father, makes available to them.

The death of Jesus is closely associated with the concept of sacrifice (Isa. 53.7; Heb. 10.1–4, 11–14), Jesus being the perfect fulfilment of the sacrificial system of the OT. He is defined as the one who became the substitute sin bearer for individuals (1 Pet. 1.19; 2.24), despite his never having sinned (Jn 8.46; 1 Cor. 15.3). As a result of his willingness to die, Jesus procured redemption (Mt. 20.28), having paid the penalty for sin, namely death (Heb. 9.27–28), penal substitution being accepted by most Pentecostals.[34] This redemption, at the cost of his life (Mt. 20.28; 1 Cor. 6.20; 15.3), resulted in believers being enabled to enter a relationship with God, to be forgiven of all their sins and experience the removal of the relational gulf between God and themselves. As a result of this transaction, people are justified and enabled to enter a relationship with God as worthy partners, because of that which Jesus has done on their behalf (Rom. 5.9). Arrington describes it as 'the starting place from which the other saving works of God can begin'.[35] Thereafter, the Spirit enables them to benefit from the resources of God (Rom. 8.15–17).

Pentecostals are uncomfortable about dividing sins into venial and mortal sins, as if the former were less significant than the latter in the estimation of God. The unforgivable sin (Mt. 12.31) is generally identified as a wilful, determined rejection of God and is generally descriptive of unbelievers. The only person who cannot be forgiven is one who refuses to ask for forgiveness (1 Jn 1.9). Most Pentecostals believe that after death, there is no further possibility of salvation for those who die unrepentant (Heb. 9.27).

Pentecostals believe that those who have never heard of Jesus may benefit from the death of Jesus and go to heaven after death.[36] Pentecostals have not clearly articulated a belief that identifies what happens to children who die

---

[33] B.R. Marino, 'The Origin, Nature, and Consequences of Sin', in Horton (ed.), *Systematic Theology*, pp. 255–90.

[34] This is the belief that Jesus died on the cross as a substitute for people who have sinned. Furthermore, God imputed the guilt of those sins to him, and he bore their punishment instead of those who had committed them.

[35] F.L. Arrington, 'Justification by Faith in Romans', in T.L. Cross, E.B. Powery (eds), *The Spirit and the Mind. Essays in Informed Pentecostalism* (Lanham: University Press of America, 2000), pp. 105–18 (117); C. Dye, 'Are Pentecostals Pentecostal? A Revisit to the Doctrine of Pentecost', *JEPTA* 19 (1999), pp. 56–80 (64–65); Pecota, 'The Saving Work of Christ', pp. 365–67.

before they are culpable for sin. Rather, they speak of an age of accountability or responsibility before which it is assumed a child is not liable for punishment and that God is to be trusted to do that which is just.[37] Most accept that unbelievers are destined to eternal punishment in Hell; neither annihilationism, universalism nor conditional immortality are accepted by the majority of Pentecostals though there has been a debate among evangelicals on these topics that has fuelled some discussion among Pentecostal scholars.[38]

That which Pentecostals also emphasize is the place of experience in salvation and the ensuing transformation of their lives. A significantly emotional experience (often more than an intellectual one) is anticipated as occurring at the moment of conversion and many testify to that effect. Although this is not unique to Pentecostalism, it does fit in with their emphasis and expectation of religious experience. Furthermore, it adds to the incisive nature of conversion; for Pentecostals, conversion functions as a watershed moment before which the person was an unbeliever and after which s/he became a believer. Fewer Pentecostals speak of a coming to faith that took a period of time; most are able to identify the month and day when they became Christians.

Korean Pentecostal or Full Gospel theology offers a development to the normal soteriology of Pentecostals that includes the concept of 'Blessing', the latter being a distinctive contribution of Yonggi Cho.[39] In it, Cho argues that God desires prosperity in all aspects of the life of a believer, 3 Jn 2 being a key verse.[40] Anderson locates Cho's theology in the context of a developing (and especially suffering) Korea and not in association with the Western form of prosperity theology or quasi-Shamanism, though he does acknowledge

---

[36] T. Richie, 'Azusa-Era Optimism: Bishop J.H. King's Pentecostal Theology of Religions as a Possible Paradigm for Today', *Pneuma* 14.2 (2006), pp. 247–260 (251–260); H.D. Hunter, 'Some Ethical Implications of Pentecostal Eschatology', *JEPTA* 22 (2002), pp. 45–55 (49–50).

[37] Menzies and Horton, *Bible Doctrines*, p. 89.

[38] Hunter, 'Some Ethical Implications', pp. 45–55; J. Moltmann ('The Hope for the Kingdom of God and Signs of Hope in the World: The Relevance of Blumhardt's Theology Today', *Pneuma* 26.1 (2004), pp. 4–16 (15–16) writes, 'Jesus gave himself up in order to look for all the lost and in order to save. He endured the suffering of hell in order to open up hell'. Thus, for him, the Final Judgement is the 'final day of reconciliation . . . salvation of human beings in spite of their sins'.

[39] Cho, *Five-Fold Gospel*.

[40] Cho, *Salvation, Health and Prosperity*, pp. 11–18, 55; D.Y. Cho, *The Story of the Five-fold Gospel for Modern People* (Seoul: Malssuma, 1998); see also H.L. Landrus, 'Hearing 3 John 2 in the Voices of History', *JPT* 11.1 (2002), pp. 70–88; J. Moltmann, 'The Blessing of Hope: The Theology of Hope and the Full Gospel of Life', *JPT* 13.2 (2005), pp. 147–61.

that the Shamanism that permeates Korean thought may have contributed to the success of Cho's teaching on this issue in that it prepared them to consider it.[41] K.S. Lee also offers an apologetic for it, noting, for example, that it does not exclude the place of suffering in the life of the believer though Y.H Lee expresses concerns relating to the materialistic and immediate expectations of believers that have been stimulated by their Shamanist backgrounds.[42] Similarly, Chan is concerned that the expectation of blessings now removes the possibility that they may instead occur in heaven[43] while Lim is concerned about the absence of a 'theology of the cross'.[44]

Predestination

The question of predestination is not one that concerns many Pentecostals, most believing that although God has provided the means of salvation, he has left it to individuals to decide whether or not to take advantage of it. The notion of election is one that many are uncomfortable with, if it means that some are elected to salvation and others are not. At the same time, many verses refer to the concept of election, including God's choice of people (Neh. 9.7), cities (2 Kgs 23.27), the Israelites (Deut. 7.6) and believers (Rom. 8.33; 16.13; Eph. 1.4–5). Thus, Pentecostals often offer the equation that the foreknowledge of God is the flipside of the doctrine of election and combine Rom. 8.29 with Eph. 1.4, the first referring to the foreknowledge of God, the latter relating to the election of believers. Thus, those whom God foreknew were to be elected became believers.[45] Since they are activistic, Pentecostals are less attracted to a notion that may result in passivity with regard to preaching the Gospel. Similarly, their emphasis is on the concept of 'whosoever will, may come' (Jn 3.16) rather than a predetermined choice of God to identify those who will come.

Because of its Wesleyan and Holiness background, there has been a tradition, in Pentecostalism, of Arminian theology.[46] Pentecostals have been

---

[41] A.H. Anderson, 'The Contextual Pentecostal Theology of David Yonggi Cho', in Ma, Menzies and Bae (eds), *David Yonggi Cho*, pp. 133–59; idem, 'The Contribution', pp. 85–105.

[42] K.S. Lee, 'A Response to Jürgen Moltmann's "Blessing of Hope"', *JPT* 13.2 (2005), pp. 163–71; Lee, 'The Holy Spirit Movement', pp. 19–21.

[43] Chan, 'The Pneumatology', pp. 79–99.

[44] D. Lim, 'A Missiological Evaluation of David Yonggi Cho's Church Growth', *AJPS* 7.1 (2004), pp. 125–47 (141); it should be noted that Cho denounces Shamanistic practices (D.Y. Cho, *How Can I Be Healed?* (Seoul: Logos Co., 1999), pp. 98–100) while Park articulates the view that Cho's theology emanates from the American Pentecostal/Charismatic movement and not Shamanism (Park, 'David Yonggi Cho', pp. 107–28).

[45] Pecota, 'The Saving Work of Christ', pp. 355–61.

[46] F.L. Arrington, *Unconditional Eternal Security: Myth or Truth?* (Cleveland: Pathway Press, 2005); Pecota, 'The Saving Work of Christ', pp. 368–72.

described as not only an 'offshoot' of this tradition, but have also been deemed by external as well as internal observers to be 'solidly Arminian'.[47] Central to this view has been the notion that grace is not irresistible, as in classical Calvinism, but can be rejected. Individual responsibility has therefore been highlighted, an impetus which inspired John Wesley's *Plain Account of Christian Perfection* (1766), the subsequent evangelical quest for 'Scriptural Holiness,' and indeed the 'baptism of the Holy Spirit' which, it was initially taught, would enable the attainment of these standards.[48] This is significant in that justification is viewed by many to be valid only if one maintains one's commitment to Christ throughout one's life. An active, consistent and high level of morality is viewed as a practical outworking of such a commitment but also a demonstration of the fact that one has been justified. Macchia thus concludes, 'sanctification is the means by which the Spirit achieves justification' in the believer.[49] Consequently, Pentecostals believe that it is important to retain a close walk with God because of the possibility of losing one's salvation.[50] For some, death is not just the door to heaven but also the final hurdle to be overcome before they can be certain that they have gained salvation, in the context of an ever present danger of falling along the way. Fear and guilt have long been soul mates of Pentecostals and these elements have often been taken advantage of by leaders who have encouraged a maintenance of one's spirituality, witness, giving of time and money, attendance at church meetings on the basis of this being a means to prove or maintain one's pedigree as a child of God. The notion of backsliding or allowing one's spirituality to become weak has traditionally been a dangerous possibility for many Pentecostals, to be feared and guarded against. However, there is an increasing awareness of the concept of the commitment of God to the salvation of believers and his preservation of them in this life.[51]

There are practical dangers with both views. Those who advocate that it is possible to lose their salvation can never be completely assured that they

---

[47] R.E. Olson, 'Calvinism/Arminianism', in R.E. Olson, *The SCM A-Z of Christian Theology* (London: SCM Press, 2005), pp. 296–97; Dayton, *Theological Roots of Pentecostalism*, p. 42.

[48] D. Dayton, 'From Christian Perfection to the "Baptism of the Holy Ghost"', in Synan (ed.), *Aspects of Pentecostal-Charismatic Origins*, pp. 39–54.

[49] F. Macchia, '2000 Presidential Address: Justification and the Spirit: A Pentecostal Reflection on the Doctrine by which the Church Stands or Falls', *Pneuma* 22.1 (2000), p. 13.

[50] Mt. 12.32; Col. 1.21–23; Heb. 2.1–4; 6.1–8; 10.26–38 (though see 10.39). Gajewski and Wawrzeniuk, 'A Historical and Theological Analysis', p. 41; Pecota, 'The Saving Work of Christ', pp. 369–70.

[51] Eph. 1.4–5, 13–14; 2.8–9; 1 Thess. 5.24; Heb. 6.9; 9.14–15; 10.15–22; 2 Pet 1.4; 2.25; Jude 24.

are saved (since they may lose it in the future), their spirituality may be infused with a sense of danger and their motivation to follow Jesus may be motivated more by fear rather than love. Those who believe that their salvation is eternally secure may be passive in their spirituality and witness, assuming that the responsibility for the development of their Christianity belongs to God, not to them. Perceptions of God can also differ in each scenario, the latter viewing God as a Shepherd or Father, the former viewing God more as a Lord or King. Similarly, the notion of salvation as a gift is different for each group. Those who believe that salvation may be lost view it as a gift that may be withdrawn by God on the basis of bad behaviour; for others, it is viewed as a gift given by God, the role of the Spirit being to ensure that believers benefit from its full potential (Eph. 1.14).

Because of various verses that seem to support both views, the logical arguments that may be offered for each and the differing claims as to how each improves one's spirituality, caution needs to be applied in coming to a conclusion. To a large degree, Pentecostals have not made the issue a matter of doctrinal imperative and certainly not a disciplinary issue with regard to leaders who adopt either view. Both God and believers are viewed as having a part to play in the developing spirituality of believers, the exact nature of each component being left to individuals to decide.

Other Religions

Some Pentecostal scholars are beginning to call for greater dialogue with other religions.[52] Anderson notes, 'the relationship between Christian faith and other faiths is . . . seldom discussed by Pentecostals'.[53] Most Pentecostals are exclusivists, believing that the only way to salvation is through a relationship with Jesus; everyone else, they deduce is eternally lost.[54] They identify verses such as Jn 3.3 as supporting their perspective, their strong missionary emphasis being driven by the desire to save people from an eternity

---

[52] B.A. Anderson, 'Missional Orientation and Its Implications for Pentecostal Theological Education', *JEPTA* 26.2 (2000), pp. 134–36 (136); Anderson, 'Towards a Pentecostal Missiology', pp. 36–46.

[53] Anderson, *An Introduction to Pentecostalism*, p. 235; V-M, Kärkkäinen, '"Truth on Fire": Pentecostal Theology of Mission and the Challenges of a New Millennium', *AJPS* 3.1 (2000), pp. 33–60 (54); idem, *Toward a Pneumatological Theology*, pp. 229–39; Yong, 'Not Knowing Where the Wind Blows', pp. 88–9; T. Richie, 'Eschatological Inclusivism: Exploring Early Pentecostal theology of Religions in Charles Fox Parham', *JEPTA* 27.2 (2007), pp. 138–52.

[54] E.S. Williams, *Systematic Theology* (3 vols; Springfield: Gospel Publishing House, 1954), vol. 3, p. 15; Duffield and Van Cleave, *Foundations of Pentecostal Theology*, pp. 268–70; Kärkkäinen, 'Truth on Fire', pp. 54–7; M.D. McLean, 'The Holy Spirit', in Horton (ed.), *Systematic Theology*, pp. 375–95 (392); Larbi, *Pentecostalism*, p. 435.

without God. Thus, the notion of universalism is one from which they would distance themselves. At the same time, they do not spend much time exploring the implications of other verses that may indicate an inclusivist position (Jn 1.29; Heb. 2.9, 1 Jn 4.14).

The normal perspective of most Pentecostals is that adherents to non-Christian religions place themselves outside the grace of God and in effect, destine themselves to hell. However, a minority of Pentecostals are exploring the possibility of the Spirit working in the lives of people who are presently engaged in other religions or no religion.[55] Kärkkäinen engages in discussion with Richie concerning the seeds of such a discussion as reflected in the theology of one of the pioneers of Pentecostalism, Bishop J.H. King, demonstrating that this is not simply a modern issue to have been explored by Pentecostals.[56] Yong, who is a Pentecostal and the Professor of Systematic Theology at the School of Divinity, Regent University, has offered a landmark study in which he posits a 'pneumatological theology of religions' as providing a contribution that may ultimately help because it provides a broader framework of theological enquiry while remaining committed to Trinitarian theology. He broaches the question as to whether the Spirit is at work only in and through the Church.[57] This concentration on the Spirit (without a similar emphasis on the Son) has been critiqued and Yong has recognized the value of this criticism.[58]

He establishes his pneumatological theology, briefly identified as the quest to explore that which the Spirit has been doing, is doing and will do, as a result of which he concludes that the Spirit is busier in more contexts than many have assumed. The creativity of the Spirit (Gen. 1.2), his omnipresence (Ps. 139.7–10; Acts 17.24–28), his role in salvation (Jn 3.3–7) and in the

---

[55] Kärkkäinen, 'Truth on Fire', pp. 56–9; idem, '"How to Speak of the Spirit among Religions": Trinitarian Prolegomena for a Pneumatological Theology of Religions', in M. Welker (ed.), *The Work of the Spirit. Pneumatology and Pentecostalism* (Grand Rapids: Eerdmans, 2006), pp. 47–70; see also C.H. Pinnock, *Flame of Love: A Theology of the Holy Spirit* (Downers Grove: InterVarsity Press, 1996), pp. 200–02; O. Leirvik, 'Charismatic Mission, Miracles and Faith-Based Diplomacy: The Case of Aril Edvardsen', in Stålsett (ed.), *Spirits of Globalization*, pp. 131–44; A. Lord, 'The Pentecostal-Moltmann Dialogue: Implications for Mission', *JPT* 11.2 (2003), pp. 271–87.

[56] V-M. Kärkkäinen, 'A Response to Tony Richie's "Azusa Street Optimism: Bishop J.H. King's Pentecostal Theology of Religion" as a Possible Paradigm for Today', *JPT* 15.2 (2007), pp. 263–68; T. Richie, 'A Reply to Veli-Matti Kärkkäinen's Response', *JPT* (2007), pp. 269–75; idem, 'Azusa-Era Optimism', pp. 247–60.

[57] A. Yong, *Beyond the Impasse: Toward a Pneumatological Theology of Religion* (Grand Rapids: Eerdmans, 2003), pp. 13–33; I.J.M. Haire, 'Animism in Indonesia and Christian Pneumatology', in Jongeneel (ed.), *Pentecost, Mission and Ecumenism*, pp. 177–88.

[58] A. Yong, D.T. Irvin, F.D. Macchia, R. Del Colle, 'Christ and Spirit: Dogma, Discernment, and Dialogical Theology in a Religiously Plural World', *JPT* 12.1 (2003), pp. 15–83.

eschatological restoration of the earth (Rom. 8.18–27) demonstrate his ubiquitous presence.[59]

He provides three axioms that are foundational to his thesis: 'God is universally present and active in the Spirit', 'God's Spirit is the life-breath of the *imago Dei* in every human being' (drawing support from Gen. 2.7 and Jn 1.9), and, more controversially, 'The religions of the world, like everything else that exists, are providentially sustained by the Spirit of God for divine purposes',[60] one of which may be to direct people to the ultimate Saviour via the Spirit. Yong rejects the notion that 'the religions lie beyond the pale of divine presence and activity',[61] partly because he emphasizes the role of the Spirit as the one 'who leads the quest for truth amidst all those who are searching for it (Jn 14.17; 16.13; 1 Jn 2.27)',[62] Jn 3.6 being a verse of considerable importance to him.[63] Aware of objections to particularly the latter two axioms (including his own acknowledgement of the fact that the Bible includes examples where God is actively opposed to other religions), he seeks to respond to them by emphasizing that to concentrate on the possibility of the presence of the Spirit in other religions should not de-emphasize the centrality of Christ to salvation nor should it undermine the important role of evangelism. However, he perceives his task as being to find a way to dialogue with other religions in their quest for 'otherness' rather than to provide a means of evangelizing their members. Although there is a connectedness between dialogue and conversion with reference to Christianity and other faiths, it is possible that the one can occur without the other and that even without the occurrence of the latter, the process be still be recognized as a positive development and not a failure.[64] Richie goes so far as to question whether it is appropriate or even blasphemous to relegate 'all religious experience beyond the borders of the institutional Church to the demonic realm'.[65] He prefers to conclude that although there is no salvation outside

---

[59] Yong, *Beyond the Impasse*, pp. 35–56; R.L. Galligher, 'The Holy Spirit in the World: In Non-Christians, Creation and Other Religions', *AJPS* 9.1 (2006), pp. 17–33.

[60] Yong, *Beyond the Impasse*, pp. 44–6.

[61] Yong, *Beyond the Impasse*, p. 46.

[62] Yong, *Beyond the Impasse*, p. 54.

[63] Yong, 'Not Knowing Where the Wind Blows', p. 100.

[64] Yong, *Beyond the Impasse*, pp. 51–3; Similar observations are offered by the Orthodox theologian S. Bulgakov who writes, 'the pagan world remains open to the waftings of the Spirit of God both in its religion and in its culture' concluding that 'all true religions . . . that contain the experience of Divinity, necessarily have a ray of Divinity, the breath of the Spirit' (*The Comforter* (trans. B. Jakim; Grand Rapids: Eerdmans, 2004), p. 238); Similarly, S. Solivan concludes that 'the Spirit is at work among other people of faith' where he is referring to non-Christian faiths ('Interreligious Dialogue: An Hispanic American Pentecostal Perspective' in S.M. Heim (ed.), *Grounds for Understanding: Ecumenical Responses to Religious Pluralism* (Grand Rapids: Eerdmans, 1998), p. 43).

Christ that does not mean that there is no possibility of salvation outside the Church.[66] Yong is aware that in advocating a pneumatological paradigm, there is the danger that the normativeness of Christ as Mediator of salvation may be undermined. At the same time, he is aware that where the latter is stressed in interfaith dialogue, such a danger breaks down irretrievably and very quickly.

Yong takes the experience of the Spirit as the basis for his attempt to construct a theology of religions[67] and he promotes charismatic and phenomenological discernment as essential criteria in determining the presence of the Spirit. In this regard, one may hear what the Spirit may say internally and also what experience and outward manifestations may offer to the determining of the conclusion, though he notes that a dogmatic method cannot be devised that determines for certain where the Spirit is or is not.

Similarly, Macchia concludes, 'Though I believe Christ to be the only Lord of all creation and salvation, I also regard him as more inclusive and expansive in significance through the witness than many of us wish to admit'.[68] The challenge for Pentecostals, and others, is to enter into dialogue and to discuss beliefs and practices in order to bring to explicit reality that which may be implicit. Lord continues this discussion on the basis that the Spirit has already introduced his mission to this world by his personal involvement in the act of creation. In particular, he also deduces that Pentecostals and others have neglected to consider the general and universal workings of the Spirit. Thus, he writes, 'That is not to deny our particular experience of the Spirit centred around Christ, but rather to say that this cannot exclude other workings of the Spirit in people and creation'.[69]

This need not result in a universalistic perceptive or a weakened Christianity but demands a careful articulation by Pentecostal scholars.[70] Richie concludes,

[65] T. Richie, '"The Unity of the Spirit": Are Pentecostals Inherently Ecumenists and Inclusivists?', *JEPTA* 26.1 (2006), pp. 21–35 (31).

[66] Richie, 'The Unity of the Spirit', p. 33.

[67] A. Yong, *Discerning the Spirit(s): A Pentecostal-Charismatic Contribution to Christian Theology of Religions* (Sheffield; Sheffield Academic Press, 2000), pp. 96–182, 215–19; idem, 'Not Knowing Where the Wind Blows', pp. 92–102; Kärkkäinen, 'How to Speak', p. 68.

[68] F.D. Macchia, *Baptized in the Spirit. A Global Pentecostal Theology* (Grand Rapids: Zondervan, 2006), p. 221.

[69] A.M. Lord, 'Principles for a Charismatic Approach to other Faiths', *AJPS* 6.2 (2003), pp. 235–46 (244–45); J. Moltmann, *The Spirit of Life: A Universal Affirmation* (trans. M. Kohl; Minneapolis: Fortress, 1992), pp. 34–5.

[70] Ma, 'Asian (Classical) Pentecostal Theology', in Anderson and Tang (eds), *Asian and Pentecostal*, pp. 59–92 (81); D.T. Irvin, 'A Review of Amos Yong's *Beyond the Impasse*', *JPT* 12.2 (2004), pp. 277–80; A. Yong, 'Beyond *Beyond the Impasse*? Responding to Dale Irvin', *JPT* 12.2 (2004), pp. 281–85.

'Inclusivism by no means necessitates even a nascent compromise of Christian integrity or of Pentecostal theology and spirituality; rather, it enables Pentecostals to witness with respect to everyone of the limitless love of God in his Son by the power of the Spirit'.[71]

The Holy Spirit

Introduction

The Spirit is of fundamental importance to Pentecostals, Fee describing him as 'the *sina qua non* of all Christian life and experience'.[72] Speaking of some of the older Pentecostal churches, Spittler concludes that 'these groups in fact honor the Holy Spirit instead of a celebrated founder'.[73] However, it is significant to note that while two of the sixteen fundamental truths of the AoG relate to the baptism in the Spirit, there is no separate definition relating to the person of the Spirit (though this is provided in a fuller explanation of the nature of God). Indeed, the person of the Spirit, in contrast to his empowering facility, has received limited comment by Pentecostals, though there are exceptions to this norm.[74]

Most of the beliefs held by Pentecostals concerning the Spirit are gleaned from the NT; there has been little reflection on the writings of others

---

[71] Richie, 'The Unity of the Spirit', p. 34.

[72] G.D. Fee, *Listening to the Spirit in the Text* (Grand Rapids: Eerdmans, 2000), p. 37.

[73] R.P. Spittler, 'Maintaining Distinctives: The Future of Pentecostalism', in Smith (ed.), *Pentecostals from the Inside Out*, pp. 121–34 (122); Gee, *The Pentecostal Movement*, p. 3; du Plessis, 'Golden Jubilee', p. 194.

[74] F. Arrington, *Encountering the Holy Spirit: Paths of Christian Growth and Service* (Cleveland: Pathway Press, 2005); G.D. Fee, *God's Empowering Presence* (Peabody: Hendrickson, 1994); idem, *Paul, the Spirit*; V-M. Kärkkäinen, *Pneumatology: The Holy Spirit in Ecumenical, International and Contextual Perspective* (Grand Rapids: Baker, 2002); idem, *Toward a Pneumatological Theology*; A.D. Palma, *The Holy Spirit: A Pentecostal Perspective* (Springfield: Gospel Publishing House, 2001); C.S. Keener, *The Spirit in the Gospels and Acts* (Peabody: Hendrickson, 1997); R.P. Menzies, *Empowered for Witness: The Spirit in Luke-Acts* (Sheffield: Sheffield Academic Press, 1994); L.T. Holdcroft, *The Holy Spirit: A Pentecostal Interpretation* (Springfield: Gospel Publishing House, 1979); W.W. Menzies, R.P. Menzies (eds), *Spirit and Power. Foundations of Pentecostal Experience* (Grand Rapids: Zondervan, 2000); J.B. Shelton, *Mighty in Word and Deed. The Role of the Holy Spirit in Luke-Acts* (Peabody: Hendrickson, 1991); R. Stronstad, *The Charismatic Theology of St. Luke* (Peabody: Hendrickson, 1984); idem, *The Prophethood of All Believers: A Study in Luke's Charismatic Theology* (Sheffield: Sheffield Academic Press, 1999); K. Warrington, *Discovering the Holy Spirit in the New Testament* (Peabody: Hendrickson, 2005); idem, *The Holy Spirit* (Leicester: IVP, 2008).

throughout the Church age.[75] The fact that the Spirit is relatively infrequently mentioned in the OT[76] and the monotheistic emphasis therein have not helped Pentecostals to be confident in their exploration of the Spirit in these texts. However, Pentecostals have increasingly listened to and dialogued with those outside their tradition who write about the Spirit.[77] Pentecostals have thus been able to contribute their experience and knowledge to the wider dialogue, often resulting in a new spirit of openness towards other believers of very different denominational streams.

[75] Though see S.M. Burgess, *The Holy Spirit. Medieval Roman Catholic and Reformation Traditions* (Peabody: Hendrickson, 1997; idem, *The Holy Spirit. Ancient Christian Traditions* (Peabody: Hendrickson, 1984); idem, *The Holy Spirit. Eastern Christian Traditions* (Peabody: Hendrickson, 1989; idem, *The Spirit and the Church: Antiquity* (Peabody: Hendrickson, 1984).

[76] Though see L.R. McQueen, *Joel and the Spirit: The Cry of a Prophetic Hermeneutic* (Sheffield: Sheffield Academic Press, 1993); W. Ma, *Until the Spirit Comes. The Spirit of God in the Book of Isaiah* (Sheffield: Sheffield Academic Press, 1999).

[77] Y. M-J. Congar, *I Believe in the Holy Spirit* (trans. D. Smith; New York: Seabury, 1983); D.L. Gelpi, *The Divine Mother: A Trinitarian Theology of the Holy Spirit* (Lanham: University Press of America, 1984); J. Moltmann, *The Spirit of Life: A Universal Affirmation* (trans. M. Kohl; Minneapolis: Fortress, 1992); M. Welker, *God the Spirit* (trans. J.F. Hoffmyer; Minneapolis: Fortress, 1994); J. McIntyre, *The Shape of Pneumatology: Studies in the Doctrine of the Holy Spirit* (Edinburgh: T & T Clark, 1997); G.D. Badcock, *Light of Truth, Fire of Love: A Theology of the Holy Spirit* (Grand Rapids: Eerdmans, 1997); D. Bloesch, *The Holy Spirit: Works and Gifts* (Downers Grove: InterVarsity Press, 2000). Issue 4 (1994) of *JPT* provides six responses by mainly Pentecostals to Jürgen Moltmann's works on the Spirit. See also J. Moltmann, 'A Pentecostal Theology of Life', *JPT* 9 (1996), pp. 3–15; Lord, 'The Pentecostal-Moltmann Dialogue', pp. 271–87; F.D. Macchia, 'Discerning the Spirit in Life: A Review of *God the Spirit* by Michael Welker', *JPT* 10 (1997), pp. 3–28; J. Goldingay, 'The Breath of God of Yahweh Scorching, Confounding, Anointing: The Message of Isaiah 40–42', *JPT* 11 (1997), pp. 3–34; M. Welker, 'Spirit Topics: Trinity, Personhood, Mystery and Tongues', *JPT* 10 (1997), pp. 29–34; Pinnock is another with whom Pentecostals have enjoyed a fruitful dialogue – C.H. Pinnock, 'The Work of the Holy Spirit in Hermeneutics', *JPT* 2 (1993), pp. 3–23; C.H. Pinnock, 'A Review of Veli-Matti Kärkkainen's *Pneumatology: The Holy Spirit in Ecumenical, International, and Contextual Perspective*' (Grand Rapids: Baker, 2002); idem, 'A Bridge and Some Points of Growth: A Reply to Cross and Macchia', *JPT* 13 (1998), pp. 49–54; V-M. Kärkkainen, 'Surveying the Land and Charting the Territory of the Spirit': A Biographical Footnote to Clark Pinnock's Review of My *Pneumatology*', *JPT* 12.1 (2003), pp. 9–13; T.L. Cross, 'A Critical Review of Clark Pinnock's *Flame of Love: A Theology of the Holy Spirit*, *JPT* 13 (1998), pp. 3–29; F.D. Macchia, 'Tradition and the *Novum* of the Spirit: A Review of Clark Pinnock's *Flame of Love*', *JPT* 13 (1998), pp. 31–48; idem, 'Toward a Theology of the Third Article in a Post-Barthian Era: A Pentecostal Review of Donald Bloesch's Pneumatology', *JPT* 10.2 (2002), pp. 3–17; E. Schweizer, 'A Very Helpful Challenge: Gordon Fee's *God's Empowering Presence*', *JPT* 8 (1996), pp. 7–21; G.D. Fee, 'God's Empowering Presence: A Response to Eduard Schweizer', *JPT* 8 (1996), pp. 23–30; J.D.G. Dunn and

The following aspects of the Spirit, and, in particular, his experiential and empowering dimensions, are of importance to Pentecostals though most are also held in common with other believers:

- The Holy Spirit is a separate person in the Godhead (Mt. 28.19; Lk. 1.35; 1 Cor. 3.16; 1 Thess. 4.8).[78] As such, the Spirit is involved in a number of significant occasions, including creation (Gen. 1.2; Ps. 104.30; Isa. 32.15–20), regeneration and renewal (Tit. 3.5) and eschatological renewal (Isa. 44.3–5). Although a variety of descriptions are offered for the Spirit (Spirit of God (1 Cor. 2.11), Holy Spirit (Acts 16.6), Spirit of Jesus (Acts 16.7)) only one person is being referred to. For Fee, the Spirit is central to Trinitarian thought in that 'it is through the Spirit's indwelling that we know God and Christ relationally, and through the same Spirit's indwelling that we are being transformed into God's own likeness'.[79]
- The Holy Spirit is, by definition, set apart, the term 'holy' (*hagios*) best being translated as a reference to his uniqueness rather than merely his sinlessness.
- The coming of the Spirit at Pentecost is a vitally significant event. Although the Spirit functioned in the lives of people in the OT era (Ps. 51.11) and

---

M.M.B. Turner are two 'scholarly friends' of Pentecostals who have nevertheless disagreed with their understanding of the role of the Spirit and with whom Pentecostals have dialogued (R.P. Menzies, 'Luke and the Spirit: A Reply to James Dunn', *JPT* 4 (1994), pp. 115–38; J.B. Shelton, 'A Reply to James D.G. Dunn's "Baptism in the Spirit: A Response to Pentecostal Scholarship on Luke-Acts"', *JPT* 4 (1994), pp. 139–43; K.J. Archer, 'Pentecostal Hermeneutics: Retrospect and Prospect', *JPT* 8 (1996), pp. 63–81 (69–74); P. Hocken, 'Baptized in the Spirit – An Eschatological Concept: A Response to Norbert Baumert and His Interlocutors', *JPT* 13.2 (2005), pp. 257–68; V-M. Kärkkäinen, 'Towards a Theology and Ecclesiology of the Spirit: Marquette University's 1998 Symposium, "An Advent of the Spirit: Orientations in Pneumatology"', *JPT* 14 (1999), pp. 65–80; J.C. Thomas, 'Max Turner's *The Holy Spirit and Spiritual Gifts: Then and Now* (Carlisle: Paternoster Press, 1996): An Appreciation and Critique', *JPT* 12 (1998), pp. 3–21; M.M.B. Turner, 'Readings and Paradigms: A Response to John Christopher Thomas', *JPT* 12 (1998), pp. 23–38; idem, *The Holy Spirit and Spiritual Gifts: Then and Now*; idem, *The Power from on High: The Spirit in Israel's Restoration and Witness in Luke-Acts* (Sheffield: Sheffield Academic Press, 1996); idem, '"Empowerment for Mission?" The Pneumatology of Luke-Acts: An Appreciation and Critique of James B. Shelton's *Mighty in Word and Deed*', *Vox Evangelica* 24 (1994), pp. 103–22; idem, 'The Spirit of Christ and "Divine" Christology', in J.B. Green, M. Turner (eds), *Jesus of Nazareth: Lord and Christ* (Grand Rapids: Eerdmans, 1994), pp. 413–36; idem, 'Spirit Endowment in Luke/Acts: Some Linguistic Considerations', *Vox Evangelica* 12 (1979), pp. 45–63; A. Yong, 'On Divine Presence and Divine Agency: Toward a Foundational Pneumatology', *AJPS* 3.2 (2000), pp. 167–88.

78. G. Chilvers, 'The Godhead of the Holy Spirit', *Paraclete*, 4 (1971), pp. 27–30; T.H. Lindberg, 'The Holy Spirit – God at work', *Paraclete* 26.3 (1992), pp. 10–13.
79. Fee, *To What End Exegesis?*, p. 350.

lived with believers before Pentecost (Jn 14.16–17), he did not initiate the Church until the day of Pentecost. Furthermore, the ministry of the Spirit on behalf of and through believers is much more comprehensive after Pentecost than before.[80]

- The Spirit exalts and inspires worship of and belief in Jesus.[81]
- The Spirit is a personal, immediate, dynamic and perfect guide. He speaks and so must be listened to. This demands developing a personal relationship with him, learning to recognize and respond to his guidance.[82] The Spirit is committed to relationship with believers and to ensure that such a relationship is inclusive of the Father and the Son. Together, they are integrally related to believers, both individually and corporately. The Spirit is to be experienced and his presence to be enjoyed, though such closeness has serious consequences including the possibility that believers may hurt him (Eph. 4.30).
- The Spirit is involved in the process of salvation,[83] committed to setting believers apart,[84] affirming them,[85] proactively transforming them ethically and spiritually,[86] inspiring and empowering them.[87] He energizes them, creating faith, motivating sanctification and inspiring prayer.
- The Spirit is a limitless resource for believers with regard to their spirituality. He is the one who makes it possible for people to enter the Kingdom of God (Jn 3.5–6), to know that they are adopted (Rom. 8.15–16), with all the privileges and responsibilities of that fact and to relate to God as Father, experiencing eternal life from the start of that relationship. His presence in their lives is the evidence that believers are authentic children of God (Rom. 8.9).
- The Spirit provides resources for all believers and expects them to be used, and used sensitively for every task he sets, diversely distributing gifts[88] to function for the benefit of all in the development of the Church,

---

[80] Eph. 1.3, 13–14; 2.8, 22; 3.16, 20; 4.4, 30; 5.18; 6.17–18; Fee, *Paul, the Spirit*, pp. 9–23.
[81] Jn 4.23–24; 1 Jn 4.2, 6; 5.6–8; C. Dye, *Living in the Presence. The Holy Spirit's Agenda for You* (Eastbourne: Kingsway, 1996), pp. 114–15.
[82] Jn 14.16–17, 26; 15.26; 16.7; Acts 1.2, 16; 4.25; 8.29; 10.19; 11.12; 13.4; 15.28; 166–67; 20.22–23; 28.25; Rom. 8.14–27; Gal. 5.17–18; Eph. 1.16–17; 3.4–5; Dye, *Living in the Presence*, p. 35; Rowe, *One Lord, One Faith*, p. 36; Fee, *Listening to the Spirit*, pp. 28–9.
[83] 1 Cor. 6.11; 12.3, 13; Heb. 2.4; 6.4; 9.8, 14; 10.29.
[84] Rom. 1.4; 1 Pet. 1.2.
[85] 1 Jn 3.24; 4.13.
[86] 2 Cor. 3.16–18; 6.6–7; 2 Thess. 2.13; Tit. 3.5–6.
[87] Acts 6.3, 5; 8.39; 10.38; 13.2; 20.28; Rom. 14.17; 15.13, 16, 18–19; 1 Cor. 2.4; Eph. 3.16; 2 Tim. 1.6–7.
[88] Rom. 1.11; 12.6–8; 1 Cor. 1.7; 12.4–11, 27–31; 14.1, 12; Fee, *God's Empowering Presence*, pp. 158–271.

inspiring and initiating evangelism,[89] preaching,[90] prophecy[91] and other charismata.[92] He brings liberty, and inspires joy, wisdom, faith, truth and revelation among other gifts.

- The Spirit expects believers to be active in improving their lifestyles (Eph. 5.18–19). If they are controlled by him, they will benefit from his influential presence, his fruit being personally and corporately experienced, and their lifestyles will increasingly become reflective of his character (Gal. 5.22–6.1).
- The Spirit, who establishes the Church as a body (1 Cor. 3.16–17), is committed to unity (Phil. 1.27; 2.1–2) and believers are to maintain unity, recognizing that the aim of the Spirit is to welcome folk from all people-groups and backgrounds and to shed the love of God through each one (2 Cor. 13.14; Eph. 4.3).
- The Spirit is eternal and, being omniscient, is available to guide believers as they gaze at God who beckons them come ever closer to enjoy the benefits of a remarkable salvation with the help of the remarkable Spirit.

Experience

Anderson deduces that Pentecostalism is best defined 'as a movement concerned primarily with the *experience* of the working of the Holy Spirit[93] while Kärkkäinen notes that, 'Rather than reflecting on the doctrine of the Holy Spirit, they have relied on the supernatural dynamics of the Spirit'.[94] Of fundamental importance to Pentecostals is the fact that the Spirit is to be encountered and experienced. Fee underscores the fact that the Spirit is more than a creedal belief and is better recognized as 'God's empowering presence'.[95] Similarly, when Paul sought to remind the believers of the validity of their salvation, he reminded them of the activity of the Spirit in their lives (Gal. 3.2). Similarly, Paul asked the Ephesian disciples whether they had received the Spirit (Acts 19.2), indicating that he expected them to know whether this

---

[89] Acts 1.8; 4.8, 31; 6.10; 7.55; 9.31; 11.24; 13.9, 52; 1 Pet. 1.12.

[90] Lk. 1.15–17; 2.29–32; 4.14–15, 18–19.

[91] Lk. 1.41–45, 67–79; 2.25–32; Acts 2.17–18; 11.28; 19.6; 21.4, 11; 1 Tim. 4.1; Heb. 3.7–8; 10.15; 1 Pet. 1.11; Rev. 1.10; 4.2; 17.3; 21.10.

[92] Examples of charismatic endowments by the Spirit are also located in the OT: strength (Judg. 14.6, 19; 15.14); leadership (Gen. 41.38; Is. 11.1–3); military authority (Judg. 6.34; 11.29–33); skill (Exod. 31.3–4; 35.31); wisdom (Dan. 5.14); prophecy (Num. 11.25, 29; 24.2; 1 Sam. 10.10; 19.19–24; Mic. 3.8); W. Ma, 'The Empowerment of the Spirit of God in Luke-Acts: An Old Testament Perspective', in Ma and Menzies (eds), *The Spirit and Spirituality*', pp. 28–34; G.J. Leeper, 'The Nature of the Pentecostal Gift with Special Reference to Numbers 11 and Acts 2', *AJPS* 6.1 (2003), pp. 23–38.

[93] Anderson, *An Introduction to Pentecostalism*, p. 14.

[94] Kärkkäinen, 'Truth on Fire', p. 37.

[95] Fee, *Listening to the Spirit*, p. 29.

was the case or not. That which is of particular importance to Pentecostals is the role of the Spirit in relating the believer to God. Since the Spirit indwells believers and also is God (Rom. 8.27), he relationally bonds the believer to God (Eph. 2.18), functioning with Jesus as the mediator (1 Tim. 2:4) between the believer and God. As Pinnock aptly writes, the Spirit 'choreographs the dance of God' and enables believers to join in, teaching them as they go.[96]

Thus, he inspires and fills, empowers and encourages, supports and affirms all believers in an immediate, immanent and ongoing context. In coming to believers on the day of Pentecost, he did not leave the Father and Jesus behind, for in his presence, they also are present. Although he is supra-spatial and supra-temporal, he is also intimately present with every believer. He is the gift of Jesus to the Church, but insofar as the Spirit is God, he is also his own gift to the Church. That which is central to Pentecostals is that he is presented by the biblical authors as being dynamic.[97]

The Bible often uses metaphors to express characteristics of the Spirit, including the wind. As the wind functions powerfully, so does the Spirit (Jn 3.8), controlling his own destiny and the lives of the people he directs. He is sovereign, uncontrollable, dynamic but also personal, life-impacting and life-changing. He may be known intellectually and experientially, making a mark on believers, developing them as the wind provides the opportunity for a young tree to become strong, facilitating its growth by creating testing opportunities that result in it clinging to its roots. He is supremely in control of that development and in that regard, he can be trusted in his ongoing relationship with believers, providing them with fresh encounters with himself.

From the earliest days of Pentecostalism, there have been evidence of these Spirit-led experiences as often identified in occurrences of physical phenomena that have resulted in people falling to the ground in a swoon, laughing (recently associated with the 'Toronto Blessing'[98] though predating it by

[96] Pinnock, *Flame of Love*, p. 37.
[97] S. Summers, '"Out of My Mind for God": A Social-Scientific Approach to Pauline Pneumatology', *JPT* 13 (1998), pp. 77–106.
[98] G. Chevreau, *Catch the Fire* (London: HarperCollins, 1994); D. Pawson, *Is the Blessing Biblical?* (London: Hodder and Stoughton, 1995); D. Roberts, *The Toronto Blessing* (Eastbourne: Kingsway, 1994; M. Stibbe, *Times of Refreshing* (London: Marshall Pickering, 1995); M.M. Poloma, 'The "Toronto Blessing" in Postmodern Society: Manifestations, Metaphor and Myth', in Dempster, Klaus and Petersen (eds), *The Globalization of Pentecostalism*, pp. 363–85; idem, 'The Spirit Movement in North America at the Millennium: From Azusa Street to Toronto, Pensacola and Beyond', *JPT* 12 (1998), pp. 83–107; idem, *Main Street Mystics: The Toronto Blessing and Reviving Pentecostalism* (Walnut Creek: Altamira Press, 2003); idem, 'Toronto Blessing', in Burgess and van der Maas (eds), *NIDPCM*, pp. 1149–152; D.N. Hudson, 'Worship: Singing a

decades), crying, and manifesting strange sounds or behaviour (similar to drunkenness).[99] They often occur during times of prayer or worship and generally result in the person concerned having an experience that often leads them closer to God, physically and emotionally drained but also euphoric. Generally, these experiences are explained as physical and emotional responses to supernatural visitations of God. In revival times, their frequency is noted with greater regularity.[100] Psychological factors (mass hysteria, crowd manipulation, heightened and preconceived expectations,) may be associated with such phenomena though this has been infrequently explored.[101]

So common, currently, is the phenomenon of falling when people are being prayed for that it is not uncommon for chairs to be removed behind them and people to be strategically placed to catch them if they fall (almost always backwards). If they fall, they often remain on the floor for a few minutes, during which time they are generally quiet and look as if they are in a deep sleep. Some have testified that they have been physically healed after such experiences, though normally, they are described as times of peace and love in the presence of God. A key to determining the validity and value of such manifestations relates to the benefit that results from these moments of ecstasy.[102] Macchia notes the 'fine line between festivity and frivolity' and advocates discernment to tell the difference[103] while Kydd cautions 'physical manifestations may have significant negative consequences through reinforcing an invalid spirituality'.[104] Schatzmann offers careful counsel concerning

---

New Song in a Strange Land', in Warrington (ed.), *Pentecostal Perspectives,* pp. 177–203 (193); D.N. Hudson, 'Personal reflections of a most unusual year', *EB* 14 (1995), pp. 101–06; D. Hilborn (ed.), *Toronto in Perspective: Papers on the New Testament Wave of the Mid 1990's* (Carlisle: Paternoster, 2001); R.A.N. Kydd, 'A Retrospectus/ Prospectus on Physical Phenomena Centred on the "Toronto Blessing"', *JPT* 12 (1998), pp. 73–81; W.K. Kay ('Sociology of British Pentecostal and Charismatic Movements', in Burgess and van der Maas (eds), *NIDPCM,* pp. 1080–083 (1091)) identifies 60% of Pentecostal ministers from the three main British Pentecostal denominations in 1999 approving of the Toronto blessing.

[99] Walsh, 'To Meet and Satisfy', pp. 132–44.
[100] P.H. Alexander, 'Slain in the Spirit', in Burgess and van der Maas (eds), *NIDPCM,* pp. 1072–074 (1073); Kydd, 'A Retrospectus/Prospectus', p. 77.
[101] See 'Concerning Extraordinary Bodily Phenomena in the Context of Spiritual Occurrences' (The Theological Commission of the Charismatic Renewal in the Catholic Church of Germany) *Pneuma* 18.1 (1996), pp. 5–32 (6–11); M. Cartledge, 'Interpreting Charismatic Experience: Hypnosis, Altered States of Consciousness and the Holy Spirit?', *JPT* 13 (1998), pp. 117–32.
[102] 'Concerning Extraordinary' (The Theological Commission), pp. 13–32; see also T.D. Pratt, 'The Need to Dialogue: A Review of the Debate on the Controversy of Signs, Wonders, Miracles and the Spiritual Warfare Raised in the Literature of the Third Wave Movement', *Pneuma* 13.1 (1991), pp. 7–32.
[103] F.D. Macchia, 'The "Toronto Blessing": No Laughing Matter', *JPT* 8 (1996), pp. 3–6 (6).

the attempt to appropriate biblical texts to support the phenomena concerned, noting inherent dangers in such a process.[105] Rather than assume that such experiences should be normative for everyone, it is more appropriate to recognize the role of the Spirit in providing them for individuals when appropriate and relevant to them.

Increasingly, Pentecostals are appreciating the fact that the Spirit is encountered in a variety of ways, often determined by the personality, temperament or the current situation of the believer concerned. It is important that they do not assume that a particular event should be viewed as normative for all since the dynamic and creative Spirit has the capacity to encounter believers in ways that are most appropriate to them. Some encounter God in the presence of loud worship, others in silence; some in the cacophony of the city, others in the stillness of the countryside; some in the depths of their emotions, others in their intellect; some in prayer, others in the reading of the Bible; some often, others infrequently. It is important to develop a relationship with God, allowing him to be the initiator of such experiences, enjoying them when they occur and still enjoying him in their absence.

The Spirit and Jesus

The terms 'Pneumatological Christology' or 'Spirit Christology' are sometimes used to identify the influential partnership of Jesus and the Spirit. The concept has been explored by a number of scholars, though not resulting in a clear consensus,[106] though Habets comes closest to offering a sympathetic presentation that views 'the Christ event as thoroughly pneumatological in itself'.[107] In general, Pentecostals recognize the role of the Spirit in the life and ministry of Jesus including his birth (Mt. 1.20), death (Heb. 9.14) and resurrection (Rom. 1.4).

Many have commented on the empowering role of the Spirit in supporting Jesus to achieve his Messianic task (Lk. 4.18–19; Acts 10.37–38),[108] assumed

---

[104] Kydd, 'A Retrospectus/Prospectus', p. 80.

[105] S. Schatzmann, 'Towards a Biblical Understanding of Phenomena in Revival', *JEPTA* 16 (1996), pp. 30–9; Poloma, 'The Spirit Movement', pp. 83–107.

[106] H. Hunter comes to this conclusion having surveyed ten authors who have written on the topic ('Spirit-Christology: Dilemma and Promise (1)', *Heythrop Journal* 24/2 (1983), pp. 127–40; R. Del Colle, *Christ and the Spirit: Spirit-Christology in Trinitarian Perspective* (Oxford: Oxford University Press, 1994).

[107] M. Habets, 'Spirit Christology: Seeing in Stereo', *JPT* 11.2 (2003), pp. 199–234 (234); H.D. Hunter, 'The Resurgence of Spirit Christology', *EB* 11.1, 2 (1992), pp. 50–7.

[108] cf. J.D.G. Dunn, *Baptism in the Holy Spirit: A Re-Examination of the New Testament Teaching on the Gift of the Spirit in relation to Pentecostalism Today* (London: SCM, 1970), pp. 28–9; J. Jeremias, *New Testament Theology: The Proclamation of Jesus* (London: SCM, 1972), p. 52; Menzies, *Empowered for Witness*, 152–58; Shelton, *Mighty in Word*, p. 161; B. Aker, 'New Directions in Lucan Theology: Reflections on

to have been initiated at his baptism in the Jordan.[109] Nichols states that at his baptism, 'Jesus moved into a new relationship to the Holy Spirit'.[110] Although he offers no support for this statement, this forms a common assumption of many Pentecostals that results in their belief that Jesus needed the Spirit to enable him to complete his mission. Thus, Dye, senior minister of the largest Classical Pentecostal church in Western Europe, writes, 'Because of his anointing with the Holy Spirit, Jesus was enabled to do that which – as a man – he had previously been unable to do'.[111] Prior to this anointing, he speculates that although Jesus had lived a sinless life, 'with rare exception, nobody noticed any power or authority'.[112]

Dye explains the practical relevance thus:

> As God, Jesus was able to . . . heal the sick . . . but he had chosen not to 'use' his divinity, and he also made it clear that – in his humanity – he was utterly powerless. The miraculous did not occur because Jesus was God, but because he was filled with the Spirit without measure and always moved in perfect harmony with the Father.[113]

The perception, however, that Jesus' miraculous ministry was dependent on the resources provided by the Spirit is only to a very limited degree indicated in the Gospels; indeed, there are very few references to the Spirit in the Gospels and Acts in the context of the miraculous ministry of Jesus (and the Apostles). And although Jesus is often viewed as a model for all believers to emulate with the help of the Spirit, it needs to be borne in mind that the mission of Jesus was different to that of believers. Thus, rather than hope to imitate Jesus in his ministry, believers should seek to fulfil their individual

---

Luke 3.21–22 and some implications', in P. Elbert (ed.), *Faces of Renewal: Studies in Honor of Stanley M. Horton* (Peabody: Hendrickson, 1988), pp. 110–11; M.M.B. Turner, 'The Spirit of Christ and Christology', in H.H. Rowdon (ed.), *Christ the Lord* (Leicester: IVP, 1982), pp. 168–90; idem, 'The Spirit of Prophecy and the Power of Authoritative Preaching in Luke-Acts. A Question of Origins', *NTS* 38 (1992), pp. 72–6; Keener, *The Spirit*, p. 190; D. Petts, 'The Baptism in the Holy Spirit: The Theological Distinctive', in Warrington (ed.), *Pentecostal Perspectives* (Carlisle: Paternoster Press, 1998), pp. 109–13.

[109] R.M. Riggs, *The Spirit Himself* (Springfield: Gospel Publishing House, 1949), pp. 47–61.

[110] Nichols, 'The Lord Jesus Christ', p. 323.

[111] Dye, *Living in the Presence*, p. 32; H. Carter, *The Gifts of the Spirit* (London: Defoe Press, 1946), p. 72; M. Wenk, *Community-Forming Power: The Socio-Ethical Role of the Spirit in Luke-Acts* (Sheffield: Sheffield Academic Press, 2001), p. 199; Turner, 'Empowerment for Mission?', p. 113.

[112] Dye, *Living in the Presence*, p. 55.

[113] C. Dye, *Healing Anointing. Hope for a Hurting World* (London: Hodder and Stoughton, 1997), p. 28.

God-given objectives with the help of the Spirit who partnered Jesus in the achievement of his.

There is no dispute that the Gospels record the ministry of Jesus in much greater detail after the Jordan narrative. However, that which may be questioned is the assertion that Jesus was only able to function supernaturally after this event. If this is so, it begs the question as to how Jesus was functioning sinlessly until this moment and overlooks the references to supernatural abilities in his earlier life (Lk. 2.46–47).

Relatively speaking, there is not a great deal of material in the Gospels that relates to the Spirit, and even less that indicates that Jesus was dependent on the Spirit. This is especially significant in Luke, where the pneumatological emphasis is most pronounced, yet rare in the context of Jesus' miracles. However, the Spirit is prominent when Jesus is absent, as identified in the book of Acts. The concern of the Gospel writers is foremost to present Jesus as unique, the Messiah, who will confer the Spirit,[114] a responsibility afforded to God in the OT.[115] Rather than the Spirit supporting Jesus, Jesus is viewed as being the Lord of the Spirit. The presence of the Spirit at Pentecost is proof that the promise and authority of Jesus to send the Spirit is valid and authentic (Lk. 24.49; Acts 1.4–5).

Although the presence of the Spirit is a useful pointer to the fact that Jesus functioned with divine power, it should not be understood as indicating that Jesus was helpless without the Spirit or that the two are to be viewed as completely distinct. The Synoptics are not attempting to suggest that before the baptism of Jesus, the Spirit was not present in the life of Jesus. It is simply that at the baptism, the fact was being made known, initially to John, and then, through the Gospels, to others. The value of this is to identify the fact that Jesus exists in association with the Spirit. It is not that Jesus was just a man who now becomes a superman. He always was supreme but now, the evidence is presented in the context of his living in the presence of the Spirit who accompanies him. Rather than the Spirit be thought to be supporting Jesus, it is preferable to recognize the significance of Jesus, precisely because the Spirit is with him. Such a feature begs the question 'What kind of man is this to have the Spirit as his constant companion?' The Spirit thus functions as a marker and witness to the special nature of Jesus.

Of particular significance is the role of the Spirit to affirm Jesus. It is unnecessary to assume Jesus needed affirmation as if he was in danger of forgetting his identity or the exalted nature of his person. The affirmation is for the benefit of those who were with Jesus, as well as for the readers of the Gospels. In the OT, the Spirit functioned as a 'marker' especially in terms of identifying people as leaders (Exod. 33.15, 16; Judg. 6.34; 1 Sam. 16.13).

---

[114] Mt. 3.11; Mk 1.8; Lk. 3.16.
[115] Gen. 6.3; Num. 11.29; Isa. 42.1; 63.11; Joel 2.28–32.

The descent of the Spirit upon Jesus affirms him as an appropriate and worthy vessel for the activity of the Spirit. This, of course comes as no surprise to Jesus (despite some suggestions to the opposite by some non-Pentecostal theologians), for he is God incarnate, but it does have value for John and the readers who are to be introduced to Jesus through the Gospels. The message is clear. If the Spirit validates Jesus, he must be authentic. Thus, Fee[116] describes the Spirit as 'God's presence'. The baptism of Jesus provides the occasion for an affirmation of Jesus and a confirmation of his Messianic role by the voice of the Father and the presence of the Spirit (Lk. 3.21–22). The allusions to Ps. 2.7, a royal psalm relating to the Son and heir, and Isa. 42.1, referring to the Servant (Mt. 3.17), are powerful affirmations of Jesus who, at the Jordan, was legitimized by the Spirit.

Thus, Lk. 1.35 describes the Spirit as overshadowing Jesus in the womb, the motif of 'presence' rather than 'power' being of significance. Insofar as this is the first reference of the Spirit to Jesus in his incarnate life, its significance is not to be overlooked.[117] The Spirit was not protecting Jesus but identifying the grandeur of his status by being with him, even as a baby. Even though the threat on Jesus' life was severe, Luke did not identify the Spirit as the bodyguard of Jesus. Rather, Luke intends his readers to be impressed with a baby whose birth is supervised by the Spirit. This theme is developed through the Gospels. So also, the descent of the Spirit, at the baptism of Jesus, was the means of divine affirmation to John of the identity of the Son of God and the Saviour of the world (Lk. 1.32–33; Jn 1.29–34). The significance of the presence of the Spirit was thus to confirm to John the Baptist the identity of the Messiah.

The redactional note by Luke that results in the statement that 'he was led in the Spirit' does not necessarily indicate an infusion of charismatic wisdom, but of charismatic affirmation. Jesus' commitment to his Messianic mission affirms him as the appropriate one in whom the Spirit will reside. The Spirit is not leading Jesus in order for him to function as Messiah; it is because Jesus is the Messiah that the Spirit is leading him (Mt. 4.1). It is not about leading and following, the superior guiding the inferior, the director of the journey steering the uncertain traveller, but about the destiny of the one being inextricably entwined with the destiny of the other. Thus, it is because of the association of the Spirit with Jesus that his going into the wilderness is to be understood as evidence that it is part of the divine agenda. He goes with the Spirit; therefore, to enter the wilderness must be appropriate for the Spirit is going with him. It is because of the remarkable grandeur of Jesus (as described in the gospels) that none other than the Spirit is identified as

---

[116] Fee, *God's Empowering Presence*, p. 8.

[117] Turner (*Power from on High*, p. 161) describes it as 'an interpretational gateway to Luke's pneumatology'.

partnering him. The message to the reader is clear – such a person with whom the Spirit walks should be followed by all.

Similarly, in the temptations of Jesus, it was Jesus' use of Scripture, not his use of the power of the Spirit, which enabled him to overcome the devil. Although some hold the view that it was by the power of the Spirit that Jesus prevailed, such a view is improbable and not supported by the text. Luke (4.12) records Jesus as reminding the devil of his true identity, 'you shall not tempt the Lord your God'. The Devil's temptations here were not directed at a mere prophet, inspired and empowered by the Spirit, but at one who legitimately owned the name of God. It is because of his remarkable worth and identity that none other than the Spirit is his travelling partner.[118]

It is in this light that Lk. 4.18, where Jesus is described as being anointed for his Messianic mission, is to be analysed. Lk. 4.16–30 records the sermon preached by Jesus in Nazareth at the commencement of his ministry, immediately after his temptations.[119] Jesus begins the reading from Isa. 61.1–2 with the words, 'The Spirit of the Lord is upon me'. Only Luke describes Jesus as being anointed (Lk. 4.18; Acts 4.27; 10.38; cf. Heb. 1.9), a term he never applies to believers.[120] The next passage relates to the coming Messianic mission. Jesus thus functions as a prophet, declaring good news, and identifies himself as the one who will fulfil that prophecy (4.24). The role of the Spirit is to affirm Jesus as a prophet before any prophetic ministry is achieved. Power, be it in miracles or proclamation, is not the focus of this pericope; it is the identification and affirmation of the prophet that is most important. The miracles he performs affirm the message of which they are a part, while the Spirit affirms him, the messenger. The purpose of the Spirit is to formalize the role of Jesus, not to facilitate his supernatural ministry, to approve Jesus in the minds of his audience, not to enable him to gain one.[121] To stress the influence of the Spirit on Jesus at the expense of a recognition of the unique status of Jesus is inappropriate in the pedagogical framework of the Gospels.

---

[118] R.P. Menzies, 'The Spirit of Prophecy, Luke-Acts and Pentecostal Theology: A Response to Max Turner', *JPT* 15 (Oct. 1999), pp. 49–74 (61); B. Charette, '"Speaking against the Holy Spirit": The Correlation between Messianic Task and National Fortunes in the Gospel of Matthew', *JPT* 3 (1993), pp. 51–70 (70).

[119] This contrasts with Matthew (13.53–58) and Mark (6.1–6).

[120] Paul uses the term once (2 Cor. 1.25); see also 1 Jn 2.20, 27.

[121] Acts 10.38 may be viewed as undermining this perspective. However, the author is probably identifying, to his Gentile audience, that Jesus operated as the envoy of God in association with the Spirit. It may be true that his desire is to teach that Jesus functioned miraculously as a result of the empowering of the Spirit but, in view of the limited evidence to this elsewhere in Luke-Acts, another interpretation may be advanced, namely that everything Jesus did (doing good and healing people (10.38)),

The Spirit is seen to function in the lives of the early Church believers in just such a fashion. The Spirit affirms Stephen during his martyrdom by providing a vision of his destiny, heaven (Acts 7.55), and affirms the salvation of Saul (Acts 9.17–18). Also, the Gentile household of Cornelius are confirmed by the Spirit to be valid members of the Church (Acts 10.44–48) without mention of prophetic, miraculous or proclamatory activity on their part.

Thus, although the motif of power is present in the experience of Jesus with the Spirit at the Jordan and at Pentecost in the experience of the disciples, it need not be the only, or even the main, motif. Jesus, at the Jordan, is legitimized by the Spirit. Jesus may be empowered by the Spirit; he is certainly endorsed by him (cf. 1 Tim. 3.16). writes, 'The Spirit confirms more than he empowers Jesus'.[122]

The Spirit and Believers

Pentecostals acknowledge the varied roles of the Spirit in the Church. Although they are sometimes accused of concentrating on his power, to the exclusion of all else, there is an increasing awareness on their part that he is more generous than has often been assumed and that he has an agenda for them that is broader and more significant than has often been thought.

The Spirit Empowers Believers

One of the keywords relating to Pentecostals is 'power'[123] and one of the most important verses for them (Acts 1.8) identifies 'power' as that which follows an experience with the Spirit. Conn writes, 'Through the Holy Spirit we have all the spiritual equipment and provision we require'.[124] For many Pentecostals, that power is associated specifically with the baptism in the

---

will do (judge everyone (10.42)), or that happened to him (his resurrection (Acts 10.40)) was authenticated by the Spirit, even including those who witnessed his resurrection being chosen by God (10.41). His life was stamped by the presence of the Spirit and thus authenticated. Similarly, Jn 5.19 may be understood to indicate that Jesus is to be recognized as operating a divine agenda, authorized by God, rather than that he has to receive permission or guidance from God before he can function. He is not so much a servant of God as God who becomes a servant of humanity. His humiliation is not that he is guided by the Spirit how to act and live but that he allows his creation to (apparently) determine to his destiny.

[122] D.L. Bock, (*Luke 1:1–9:50* (Grand Rapids: Baker, 1994), p. 345), writes, 'The Spirit confirms more than he empowers Jesus'.

[123] H. Yung, 'Endued with Power: The Pentecostal-Charismatic Renewal and the Asian Church in the Twenty-First Century', *AJPS* 6.1 (2003), pp. 63–82; G. Canty (*The Practice of Pentecost* (Basingstoke: Marshall Pickering, 1987), pp. 69–75) dedicates a chapter to it; P.J. Gräbe, 'The Pentecostal Discovery of the New Testament Theme of God's Power and Its Relevance to the African Context', *Pneuma* 24.2 (2002), pp. 225–42.

Spirit, though this has often diminished the expectation of the Spirit in the lives of believers prior to and after that occasion.

Shelton stresses Jesus' relationship with the Spirit for carrying out aspects of his Messianic ministry and, following from this, deduces that believers, if they are similarly dependent on the Spirit, may function with the power of Jesus.[125] Similarly, Stronstad concludes, 'The Spirit anointing of Jesus, the Spirit baptism of the disciples, and the Spirit baptism of Cornelius are all functionally equivalent experiences'.[126] Thus, he parallels Jesus with some of the characters in Acts to indicate the belief that believers may have 'the same kind of prophetic ministry he himself had'.[127]

It is true that Luke clearly parallels Jesus with Peter, Paul and Stephen; however, it is not certain that this is in order to draw the conclusion offered by Stronstad, Turner concluding that 'if Luke wished to suggest that all who received the Spirit thereby became robustly charismatic/prophetic figures like Stephen and Philip, he missed glorious opportunities to make such a point'.[128] Turner appositely writes,

> Jesus' experience at Jordan (as) a unique Messianic anointing (was) without a clearly intended parallel in the disciples' experience',[129] concluding, 'the point of the parallels between Jesus' ministry in the Spirit and what takes place in Acts is not that the Church has inherited Jesus' anointing but that the risen Lord himself continues his redemptive activity, as Lord of the Spirit, through the charismata he bestows in his Church.[130]

It is thus more appropriate to view the experience at Pentecost as analogous, rather than identical or parallel, to the Jordan experience of Jesus. Thus, the presence of the Spirit was valuable to Jesus and is invaluable now to believers in enabling them to fulfil their respective and different destinies.

Although the source of power and the essential nature of that power may be identical, the role of Jesus as Messiah was unique and any empowering

---

[124] Conn, *A Balanced Church*, p. 19; T.W. Walker, 'The Baptism in the Holy Spirit', in Brewster (ed.), *Pentecostal Doctrine*, pp. 27–37 (30–3).

[125] Shelton, *Mighty in Word*, pp. 59–61; cf. idem, 'A Reply to James', pp. 139–43.

[126] R. Stronstad, 'They Spoke with Tongues and Prophesied', *Enrichment* 10.1 (2005), pp. 80–6 (85).

[127] Stronstad, *The Prophethood of All Believers*, pp. 16–17.

[128] M.M.B. Turner, 'Does Luke Believe Reception of the "Spirit of Prophecy" makes all "Prophets"? Inviting Dialogue with Roger Stronstad', *JEPTA* 20 (2000), pp. 3–24 (9–10).

[129] M.M.B. Turner, 'Jesus and the Spirit in Lucan perspective', *Tyndale Bulletin* 32 (1981), p. 40.

[130] Turner, 'Jesus and the Spirit', pp. 28–9.

by the Spirit was dedicated to the achievement of his specifically Messianic duties. Although the Spirit also functions in the lives of believers, it is to achieve different purposes that are related to their individual God-given missions and objectives as members of the Church. Thus, Shelton writes, 'the experiences of believers with the Holy Spirit can *not* be equivalent to Jesus' relationship with the Spirit'.[131] Although the power is of a similar quality, the tasks that are to be empowered are different. If a parallel is then to be drawn with the reception of the Spirit by the disciples in Jerusalem, it is to confirm them in the role that Jesus had prepared for them as newly commissioned witnesses to himself (Acts 1.8). Both Jesus and believers have been commissioned by God. The Spirit's presence with both indicates the fact that the commissions have the potential of being fulfilled and most importantly, that those commissioned are authentic messengers.

Pentecostals have recognized that a specific role of the Spirit, as reflected in Luke-Acts, is prophecy/proclamation, especially in evangelism (Acts 1.8).[132] Mark also identifies the Spirit's role as the inspirer of revelation (12.35–37).[133] Thus, Stronstad argues that the phrase 'filled with the Holy Spirit' 'specifically describes prophetic inspiration and vocation'[134] and should be understood as a 'technical term to introduce the office of the prophet . . . or prophetic speech'.[135] In response, Hui explores the exception of Lk. 1.15[136] (in that John the Baptist was filled with the Spirit from birth and not immediately prior to his prophesying) while Turner notes Acts 6.3 as a further exception.[137] Hui argues that the context should be considered when the consequence of the filling with the Spirit is to be determined for the aftermath of the Spirit's involvement in the lives of people differs; it was speech by Elisabeth

---

[131] Shelton, *Mighty in Word*, p. 53.

[132] Y. Cho, 'Spirit and Kingdom in Luke-Acts: Proclamation as the Primary Role of the Spirit in Relation to the Kingdom of God in Luke-Acts', *AJPS* 6.2 (2003), pp. 173–97; Menzies, *Empowered for Witness*, passim; Stronstad, *The Charismatic Theology*, passim.

[133] R. Mansfield, *The Spirit and the Gospel of Mark* (Peabody: Hendrickson, 1987); E.B. Powery, 'The Spirit, the Scripture(s), and the Gospel of Mark: Pneumatology and Hermeneutics in Narrative Perspective', *JPT* 11.2 (2003), pp. 184–98.

[134] R. Stronstad, '"Filled with the Holy Spirit": Terminology in Luke-Acts', in R. Stronstad, M. Van Kleek (eds), *The Holy Spirit in the Scriptures and the Church* (Clayburn: Western Pentecostal Bible College, 1987), pp. 1–13 (4).

[135] Stronstad, 'Filled with the Holy Spirit', pp. 7–9, 12; (John the Baptist (Lk. 1.15); the Jerusalem disciples (Acts 4.31); Paul (Acts 9.17) and the Pisidian disciples (Acts 13.52)); also Shelton, 'Filled with the Holy Spirit', pp. 81–3, 90–2; idem, *Mighty in Word*, pp. 136–44 (Acts 2.4, 14); J.M. Penney, *The Missionary Emphasis of Lukan Pneumatology* (Sheffield: Sheffield Academic Press, 1997), pp. 96–9. He offers evidence from Acts 6.3, 5, 8, 10; 7.55; 11.23–24.

[136] A.W.D. Hui, 'Spirit-Fullness in Luke-Acts: Technical and Prophetic?', *JPT* 17 (Oct. 2000), pp. 24–38.

[137] Turner, "Empowerment for Mission?', pp. 108–10.

(Lk. 1.42), prophecy by Zechariah (Lk. 1.67–79), praise by the disciples at Pentecost (Acts 2.4), wisdom with regard to the seven deacons (Acts 6.3), faith with Stephen and Barnabas (Acts 6.5; 11.24), boldness for Peter (Acts 4.8, 231) and power for Jesus (Lk. 4.14, 18).[138]

Nevertheless, Menzies is right to identify the power derived from the Spirit in Luke-Acts as more related to prophetic witness and proclamation than miracles.[139] Although the latter suggestion has been debated by Pentecostals and others,[140] Menzies does provide a helpful corrective to an inaccurate assumption that the role of the Spirit in the life of Jesus, and in the life of believers, is specifically for empowerment for miracles.[141] With reference to Jesus, 'the anointing of the Spirit *primarily* related to the proclamation of the good news' (Lk. 4.18–19).[142] This emphasis on inspired and empowered proclamation is then carried on into the lives of the disciples (Lk. 24.44–49; Acts 1.8), Philip (Acts 8.4–12, 26–40) and Paul (Acts 20.22–28). Thus, while Paul concentrates on the role of the Spirit being the source of the life of the Kingdom (while also noting his empowering of believers (Rom. 15.19; 1 Cor. 12.4–31; 14.1–33)), Luke offers the perspective that the Spirit enables believers to proclaim the Kingdom powerfully.

The Spirit Establishes a New Community

A fundamental purpose of the book of Acts was to signal that the eschatological aspirations of the Jews were now realized; the Spirit (and the Kingdom) had come. The Spirit who was anticipated in the future (Joel 2.28) is now present, the evidence being the experience of his presence in the lives of believers. Once the Spirit was rarely experienced; now he has franchised all believers to manifest him in their lives personally and for the benefit of others. Little wonder that the Spirit's coming was so exciting to the early

---

[138] Hui, 'Spirit-Fullness in Luke-Acts', p. 30.

[139] R.P. Menzies, *The Development of Early Christian Pneumatology* (Sheffield: Sheffield Academic Press, 1991), pp. 161–77, 258–62; idem, 'The Distinctive Character of Luke's Pneumatology', *Paraclete* 25.4 (1991), pp. 17–30 (18); M. Wenk, 'Reconciliation and Reversal: John's Pneumatic Ministry', *EB* 14 (1995), pp. 5–22 (13); F.L. Arrington, *The Acts of the Apostles* (Peabody: Hendrickson, 1984), pp. xxxvii-xl; Stronstad, *The Charismatic Theology*, pp. 13, 52, 55, 72, 80; Shelton, *Mighty in Word*, pp. 125–27; Turner, 'The Spirit of Prophecy', pp. 69–72.

[140] G. Twelftree, *Jesus the Miracle Worker* (Downers Grove: InterVarsity Press, 1999), pp. 168–70; R.P. Menzies, 'Spirit and Power in Luke-Acts: A Response to Max Turner', *JSNT* 49 (1993), pp. 46–55; idem, 'Luke and the Spirit', pp. 115–38.

[141] Turner prefers to understand the purpose of any empowerment to be in experiencing the full potential of sonship, including miraculous empowerment (Turner, 'Empowerment for Mission?', p. 113.

[142] Cho, 'Spirit and Kingdom', p. 185 (italics in original).

believers whose lives took on a dynamic character that was often accompanied by miraculous phenomena.

In particular, the day of Pentecost provided the basis for a nationally undivided community, demonstrated by the expansion of the Christian community to include Samaritans and even Gentiles; those outside have now been included.[143] Ramachandra, referring to Acts 10.9–23, concludes that the day of Pentecost resulted in 'the stupendous sight, unimaginable in their contemporary world, of a Jewish peasant and a Roman centurion living together under one roof'.[144] The gift of tongues and the sign of fire served to set believers apart and identify them as appropriate recipients of the promise of Joel 2.28–32. The Spirit affirmed those whom others were wishing to exclude. Such racial unity was also present in the early days of Pentecostalism as reflected in the Azusa Street revival. Then, Pentecostals were criticized for their racial inclusivity, the tragedy now being that Pentecostalism is one of the most fragmented of all religious movements.[145] The work of the Spirit to create a community in which he dwells as a corporate grouping as well as individuals (1 Cor. 3.16) needs greater emphasis in the lives of Pentecostals rather than he be solely viewed as the empowerer of individuals.

Where Paul describes the proximity of the Spirit to the believer (Eph. 2.18), his expectation is that the readers will realize that they are constantly in the presence of God and learn to experientially enjoy it. It is the Spirit who makes this possible. Paul uses the term 'access' (prosagōgos) to describe that which the Spirit creates. The term has a varied history of literary usage, though basically, it refers to a prosagogue whose role was to introduce people to rulers. Similarly, the Spirit facilitates the development of relationship with God and the opportunity to serve him as members of a new community dedicated to him. Furthermore, this is a grouping that exists in an eternal context. In Eph. 1.14 (also 2 Cor. 1.21, 22; 5.5), Paul uses arrabōn (guarantee, down-payment) with reference to the Spirit. The Spirit is defined as God's down payment in the believer's life and as such, he acts as a guarantee and a taste of the future. Although it may be assumed that the guarantee refers to that which is to be redeemed by believers after this life, elsewhere in the Bible, redemption is always an act initiated by God. The former view indicates that the Spirit guarantees that believers will possess the inheritance graciously promised by God to them; the latter, more likely interpretation, indicates that the Spirit guarantees to protect believers in order to present

---

[143] T-C.M. Ling, *Pentecostal Theology for the Twenty-First Century* (Aldershot: Ashgate, 2007), pp. 33–70; M. Wenk, 'The Fullness of the Spirit', *Evangel* 21.2 (2003), pp. 40–4 (43).

[144] V. Ramachandra, *The Recovery of Mission. Beyond the Pluralist Paradigm* (Grand Rapids: Eerdmans, 1996), p. 269.

[145] Ling, *Pentecostal Theology*, pp. 45–51.

them to God so that he can redeem them as the inheritance chosen by himself, for himself. The cumulative effect is to provide the readers with a sense of well-being and security; their membership of the Christian community is not restricted to time only but is defined by eternity also.

The Spirit Convicts People of Sin

The role of the Spirit at salvation is one that has, at times, been overlooked by Pentecostals because of their emphasis on his empowering and facilitating ministry in the life of the believer. Studebaker, however, expresses the view that salvation is 'comprehensively pneumatological' and argues against the subordination of the Spirit in salvation. Thus, against the classically Protestant view that assumes the Spirit to be practically involved in sanctification and only to a limited degree in justification (Heb. 9.14), he articulates a different proposal that retains a central role for the Spirit (and Jesus) in achieving salvation and not just identifying the Spirit as the one who applies redemption with Jesus being the procurer of it.[146]

On the basis of Jn 16.8–9, Pentecostals affirm a significant role of the Spirit as being to convict unbelievers of their sin[147] while the Spirit releases the believer from the power of sin and death (Rom. 8.2), as forecast in Ezek. 36.26–28, and enables people to enter the Kingdom of God (Jn 3.7) and to participate in eternal life (Jn 4.14).[148] The Spirit also affirms the believer in a variety of other ways. As in the OT, the Spirit authenticates those he chooses (Num. 11.25; 1 Sam. 19.18–24),[149] enabling believers to know they are adopted as children of God (Rom. 8.9, 14–17; 1 Cor. 12.3; Gal. 4.6).[150]

---

[146] S.M. Studebaker, 'Pentecostal Soteriology and Pneumatology', *JPT* 11.2 (2003), pp. 248–70 (250); W.C. Kaiser Jr ('The Holy Spirit in the Old Testament', in W. Ma, R.P. Menzies (eds), *Pentecostalism in Context. Essays in Honour of William W. Menzies* (Sheffield: Sheffield Academic Press, 1997), pp. 38–47) comes to same conclusion through the OT corpus; contra J.R. Williams, *Renewal Theology* (3 vols; Grand Rapids: Zondervan, 1992), vol. 2, p. 43.

[147] P.S. Brewster, 'The Seven-Fold Work of the Holy Spirit', in P.S. Brewster (ed.), *Pentecostal Doctrine* (Cheltenham: Elim, 1976), pp. 9–24 (12–16); G.R. Carlson, 'The Conviction of the Holy Spirit', *Paraclete* (Fall 1967), pp. 9–13.

[148] J.A. Bertone, 'The Function of the Spirit in the Dialectic between God's Soteriological Plan Enacted but Not yet Culminated: Romans 8.1–27', *JPT* 15 (Oct. 1999), pp. 75–97 (75–85).

[149] First noted of Moses (Num. 11.17) and Joshua (Num. 27.18); as judges (Othniel (Judg. 3.10); Gideon (6.34); Jephthah (11.29); Samson (14.6, 19)); as kings (David (1 Sam. 16.13)); as Messiah (Isa. 11.2; 42.1–2; 59.21); W. Ma, 'Full Circle Mission: A Possibility of Pentecostal Missiology', *AJPS* 8.1. (2005), pp. 5–27 (10–11); idem, '"If It Is a sign": An Old Testament Reflection on the Initial Evidence Discussion', *AJPS* 2.2 (1999), pp. 163–75 (172).

[150] Warrington, *Discovering the Holy Spirit*, pp. 88–91.

The Spirit is the source of cleansing (Rom. 15.16; 1 Cor. 6.11) and righteousness (Rom. 2.29; 8.1–17; 14.17; Gal. 5.5, 16–26) who also provides knowledge of God (1 Cor. 2.6–16; 2 Cor. 3.3–18) and facilitates fellowship with God (Rom. 8.14–17; Gal. 4.6). It is little wonder that Fee describes conversion as 'an experienced realization of God's own presence by his Spirit'.[151] Similarly, Charette surveys the role of the Spirit in Matthew and concludes that the author has been careful in his associating the Spirit with key events in the life of Jesus (his birth, baptism, temptation, his mission of exorcism and his death) to demonstrate that the Spirit is centrally involved in the process of redemption.[152]

The Spirit Transforms Believers

Jesus uses the metaphor of water in association with the Spirit (Jn 3.5; 7.8–39). The Spirit, as water, is indispensable to life (Exod. 17.1–6). Similarly, the Spirit is presented throughout the NT as offering a life changing relationship with God in the context of facilitating positive change and dynamism in the life of the believer (2 Cor. 3.16–18; Eph. 1.3–14). The Spirit will do for parched spirits that which water does for parched throats. He has come to revitalize but also to enliven people in ways that are reminiscent of a bubbling stream that tumbles down a mountainside, symbolizing youthful joy, sparkling release and energetic excitement. As indicated by Paul (Rom. 8.2), the Spirit brings life to the believer.

Water represented wisdom in Jewish literature, especially the wisdom that comes from God.[153] Similarly, the Torah and its teaching were described as water. The Spirit, who preceded the Torah, was described by Jesus as life giving water and he is given as a personal guide and tutor to believers refining and refreshing them (Jn 4.14, 26; 15.26).[154] In this regard, the association between the Spirit and wisdom is reflective of the linkage presented in the OT (Prov. 1.23; Ezek. 36.27).

Pentecostals recognize the role of the Spirit to empower believers in terms of personal development, sanctification and to exhibit fruit,[155] holding similar

---

[151] Fee, *Listening to the Spirit*, p. 38.

[152] B. Charette, '"Never Has Anything Like This Been Seen in Israel": The Spirit as Eschatological Sign in Matthew's Gospel', *JPT* 8 (1996), pp. 31–51 (50–1); idem, *Restoring Presence: The Spirit in Matthew's Gospel* (Sheffield: Sheffield Academic Press, 2000).

[153] Sir. 15.3; 24.25; Exod. Rab. 31.3; Philo, *Somn.* 2.242–243; 1QS 10.12.

[154] Gen. 18.4; 24.32; Ex. 29.4; Lev. 15.13; Num. 8.7.

[155] Gal. 3.3, 5.16–25; 1 Pet. 1.2; see D. Gee, *Concerning Spiritual Gifts* (Springfield: Gospel Publishing House, 1930), pp. 56–63; Menzies, *Spirit and Power*, pp. 201–08; M. Wenk, 'The Holy Spirit as Transforming Power within a Society: Pneumatological Spirituality and Its Political/Social Relevance for Western Europe', *JPT* 11.1 (2002), pp. 130–42; idem, *Community-Forming Power*; idem, 'Community-Forming Power: Reconciliation

views with regard to the fruit of the Spirit as other believers.[156] Although, traditionally, Pentecostals have stressed the gifts of the Spirit, this has not intentionally been to disregard the importance of the fruit of the Spirit. Indeed, without love, spiritual gifts lose much, if not all, of their significance (1 Cor. 13.1–3). Conn writes, 'First among the essential qualities of the church is spiritual fruit'[157] and places the fruit above the gifts of the Spirit in terms of importance. Similarly, Brewster concludes that 'any manifestation of the gifts of the Holy Spirit without the accompanying fruit of the Spirit becomes unacceptable to God and to the Church'.[158] The main aspects of the fruit of the Spirit in the life of the believer is to reflect God and to emulate Jesus for the benefit of others, including unbelievers. Since the Spirit is associated with the believer at salvation (Jn 3.6), evidence of his fruit is anticipated from then, resulting in an ethical transformation of the believer.

It is not assumed that the nine fruits mentioned in Gal. 5.22–24 are a comprehensive listing; others may be added (2 Pet. 1.4–8). However, they have often been individually explored and analysed.[159] Many Pentecostals would presuppose that only believers are able to manifest fruit of the Spirit (Rom. 8.9–11). Therefore, positive attributes in unbelievers are viewed as being natural and not truly spiritual. However, although unbelievers may not

---

and the Spirit in Acts', *JEPTA* 19 (1999), pp. 17–33; W.C. Kaiser Jr, 'The Holy Spirit's Ministry in Personal Spiritual Development: Ephesians 5.15–21', in Ma and Menzies (eds), *The Spirit and Spirituality*, pp. 62–9; D. Tarr, 'The Fruit of the Spirit', *Paraclete* 25.4 (1991), pp. 1–6.

[156] L.W. Hurtado, 'Fruit of the Spirit', in Burgess and van der Maas (eds), *NIDPCM*, pp. 648–52; S.S. Schatzmann, 'The Gifts of the Spirit: Pentecostal Interpretation of Pauline Pneumatology', in K. Warrington (ed.), *Pentecostal Perspectives* (Carlisle: Paternoster Press, 1999), pp. 80–97 (86–8); D. Lim, 'Spiritual Gifts', in Horton (ed.), *Systematic Theology*, pp. 479–84; F.L. Arrington, *Christian Doctrine: A Pentecostal Perspective* (3 vols; Cleveland: Pathway Press, 1992–1994), pp. 97–112.

[157] Conn, *A Balanced Church*, p. 31; H.M. Ervin, *Spirit Baptism. A Biblical Perspective* (Peabody: Hendrickson, 1987), pp. 119–24.

[158] Brewster, 'The Seven-Fold Work', p. 24; Other early Pentecostal leaders who offered a similar perspective included D. Gee, *Concerning Spiritual Gifts*, pp. 70–1; G. Canty, *In My Father's House: Pentecostal Exposition of Major Christian Truths* (Basingstoke: Marshall, Morgan and Scott, 1969), pp. 104–06.

[159] L.W. Hurtado, 'Fruit of the Spirit' in Burgess and van der Maas (eds), *NIDPCM*, pp. 648–52 (650–52); Rowe, *One Lord, One Faith*, pp. 121–30; J.D. Hernando, 'Love', *Paraclete* 25.4 (1991), pp. 7–11; J.C. Katter, 'Joy', *Paraclete* 25.4 (1991), pp. 12–16; M. Williams, 'Peace', *Paraclete* 26.1 (1992), pp. 8–11; P.A. Lee, 'Patience', *Paraclete* 26.1 (1992), pp. 11–13; D.J. Lotter, 'Kindness', *Paraclete* 26.2 (1992), pp. 23–7; R.D. Cotton, 'Goodness', *Paraclete* 26.2 (1992), pp. 27–32; V.R. Ostrom, 'Faithfulness', *Paraclete* 26.3 (1992), pp. 20–3; S.M. Horton, 'Gentleness-Meekness', *Paraclete* 26.3 (1992), pp. 23–7; G.B. McGee, 'Self-Control', *Paraclete* 26.3 (1992), pp. 28–30; Conn, *A Balanced Church*, pp. 39–95; J. Lancaster, 'The Nine-Fold Fruit of the Spirit', in Brewster (ed.), *Pentecostal Doctrine*, pp. 63–77; Tarr, 'The Fruit of the Spirit', pp. 1–6.

knowingly benefit from the work of the Spirit, since they do not acknowledge him, it is not clear that Paul rules out the possibility that they also may exhibit some of his attributes since they have been made in the image of God and Christ enlightens everyone (Jn 1.4, 9; see also Rom. 2.14–15).

Speaking to the Christians living in the region of Galatia (Gal. 5.16–18), Paul states that the Spirit is to be their guide in life and that they should take advantage of his influence (v. 16). It is possible that Paul is presenting two imperatives, 'Walk by the Spirit' and 'Do not gratify the desires of the flesh' (v. 16). However, it is more likely that he is presenting an imperative, followed by a promise, 'Walk by the Spirit' and 'You will not gratify the desires of the flesh'. If believers continuously walk with the Spirit, they will naturally develop a lifestyle that is not dominated by sinful activities because the Spirit will enable them to live the Christian life. Whereas the OT Law (and the NT) point the person in the right direction, the Spirit enables the believer to reach the destination. The Spirit heralds a new era, enabling believers to enter it and empowering them to be improved. Such a process is not dependent on human effort alone though, of course, believers have to exert effort in ethical development (2 Cor. 7.1; 2 Tim. 2.21). But Paul is insistent that they recognize that the Spirit is on their side, changing them into the likeness of Jesus.[160]

Paul precedes the reference to being filled with the Spirit (Eph. 5.18) with a reminder to his readers that they should exercise self discipline with regard to their behaviour (Eph. 5.15), use of time (Eph. 5.16) and in determining the will of God (Eph. 5.17). After he encourages them to be filled with the Spirit (Eph. 5.18), he emphasizes the importance of worship and thanksgiving (Eph. 5.19–20), issues of respectful submission to others (Eph. 5.21–6.9) and the battle against evil (Eph. 6.10–20). The context of being filled with the Spirit is instrumental in determining its meaning. Although some see a link with the fact that the disciples were thought to be drunk on the day of Pentecost, most view the link between drunkenness and being filled with the Spirit (Eph. 5.17–18) as associated with the element of control. Thus, while acknowledging that drunkenness results in a person being controlled by the wine and functioning inappropriately, the continuous (present passive, imperative verb) nature of being filled with the Spirit results in the Spirit controlling the behaviour, words, thoughts and motives of the believer in ways that are positive for all concerned. Paul refers to the importance of living (Gal. 5.25) and walking by the Spirit (Gal. 5.16, 25) in ways that are reminiscent of that which he expects here. Therefore, to use the term 'filled with the Spirit' to describe someone who has experienced the baptism in the Spirit is not

---

[160] See also 2 Cor. 12.9; Col. 1.9–11; G.D. Fee, *Gospel and Spirit: Issues in New Testament Hermeneutics* (Peabody: Hendrickson, 1991), pp. 140–51.

always helpful as Paul uses it here to describe someone who is controlled by the Spirit in the present, rather than to refer to a spiritual experience in the past.

The transforming effect of the Spirit is also promoted by Paul in the context of the weakness of believers, for the Spirit is presented as operating on their behalf, helping and even praying for them (Rom. 8.26).[161] Paul uses a rare verb for 'help' in the Bible and prefaces it with another word (*huper*) that emphasizes the intensity of the help offered. Paul then refers to the fact that the Spirit identifies with believers with groans that are too deep for words (Rom. 8.26).[162] Although the meaning is uncertain, it indicates that the Spirit feels not just for believers but also that which they feel; he empathizes rather than simply sympathizes with them, such is the quality of his involvement in their lives.

Some Pentecostals identify Rom. 8.26 as referring to the act of speaking in tongues in which the Spirit takes a leading role.[163] Thus, Bertone deduces that Paul intends to relate the 'Spirit's empathetic alignment with the believer', the latter benefiting 'from the Spirit-induced glossolalic utterance'.[164] Fee, who also assumes the reference is to tongues, conjectures that the reason that the term 'tongues' is not used here by Paul is because he prefers to use the term *stenagmos* (sigh/groan) which has already been used in v. 22.[165]

However, notwithstanding any possible association between tongues and Rom. 8.26–27, there are issues that make an identification of tongues as being the mode through which the Spirit prays for the believer less likely. First, whereas Paul indicates that the Spirit inspires tongues (1 Cor. 12.8–11), he does not state that the content of the tongue is determined by the Spirit. Secondly, the Spirit takes a much more prominent part in the prayer offered in Rom. 8.26–27 than is evident elsewhere in the NT where tongues are mentioned. Indeed, the believer seems not to be involved in the process, the Spirit apparently not praying with or through the believer but on his/her behalf. Thirdly, if tongues are in view in Romans 8.26, it would exclude believers who are not so gifted in benefiting from the prayer of the

---

[161] C.S. Keener, *Gift Giver. The Holy Spirit in the World Today* (Grand Rapids: Baker, 2001), pp. 66–8; Fee, *Paul, the Spirit*, pp. 140–51.

[162] See also Childbirth (Gen. 3.16), suffering (Ex. 2.24), grief (Jn 14.16), repentance (Mal. 2.13) and in relation to prayer (Ps. 79.11).

[163] Fee, *God's Empowering Presence*, p. 577; J. Bertone, 'The Experience of Glossolalia and the Spirit's Empathy: Romans 8:26 Revisited', *Pneuma* 25.1 (2003), pp. 54–65 (55); A.J.M. Wedderburn, 'Romans 8:26 – Towards a Theology of Glossolalia?', *SJT* 28 (1975), pp. 369–77 (374–75); H.W. Steinberg, 'What Is Praying in the Spirit?', *Paraclete* 25.2 (1991), pp. 1–4.

[164] Bertone, 'The Experience of Glossolalia', p. 58.

[165] G.D. Fee, 'Toward a Pauline Theology of Glossolalia', in Ma and Menzies (eds), *Pentecostalism in Context*, pp. 29–31.

Spirit on their behalf. Fourthly, the term *alalētos* does not easily relate to tongues since it is best translated as 'wordless' communication or an inability to express oneself. However, the gift of tongues is an expression of an articulated mode of communication in which quasi-words are used. Fifthly, if the Spirit prays for the believer only when s/he is speaking in tongues, the level of commitment on the part of the Spirit is severely reduced. Sixthly, Paul, in Rom. 8.26, appears to be more interested in identifying the fact that the Spirit is praying on the behalf of the believer rather than identifying how or when it occurs. Finally, it is most likely that this is a metaphor, a picture that Paul is offering to best explicate a truth that is ultimately inexplicable – the Spirit prays, and for believers.

Seeking to identify whether Paul refers to tongues or not obscures the significance of the passage which is to explore the mystery and marvel that the Spirit is integrally engaged in the lives of believers and is wholly committed to their future. The principle embedded in this truth must not be lost by an intricate examination of how the Spirit, who is God, can pray. The metaphor must be carefully unwrapped. Paul is declaring a truth that is precious and therefore to be appropriated but also a mystery and therefore not necessarily to be completely understood, though there is a welcome encouragement to explore it intellectually and experientially. The picture is of the Spirit, who is God, so intimately relating to believers that, for a moment, it is as if his closeness to them is greater than it is to God, enabling him to pray for them. It is the remarkable commitment of the Spirit to the development of the believer that is paramount, not deciphering how it occurs.

The Spirit Guides Believers

Although the Bible is a fundamentally important source of guidance, it does not exist to provide answers to every question that may be posed. It was fundamentally written for readers who existed in ancient cultures and eras that are inevitably different to those living in later generations. Therefore, to view it as the basis for all decision making for all times, even with reference to the life and practices of believers, is not always appropriate. Principles may be gleaned and applied but care in providing contextually appropriate guidance is always necessary.

When the Bible is not and cannot be an influential guide, the Spirit is. Pentecostals are aware of the fact that as well as looking to the Bible for guidance (Ps. 119.9–11) they are also to be led by the Spirit (Rom. 8.4; 1 Cor. 2.13). Reliance on a relationship with the creative, dynamic and personal Spirit demands trust, honesty, maturity and a determination to listen to the rarely silent Spirit. It is the pathway of Paul who also encourages his readers to 'live by the Spirit' (Gal. 5.25), 'walk by the Spirit (Gal. 5.16, 25), and 'be filled with the Spirit' (Eph. 5.18), as a result of which they will develop godly lifestyles.

John (14.16–17) specifies that a role of the Spirit is to guide believers into all truth and he records Jesus referring to him as the Spirit of truth. Similarly, John 14.25–26 identifies the Spirit as the one who will teach the disciples everything and remind them of all that Jesus had taught them.[166] Furthermore, and radically, Paul teaches that the Law has now been superseded as the ethical guide of the believer (Rom. 10.4; Gal. 3.2–5, 19–29; 4.4–7; 5.1, 5), probably referring to the OT guidelines for behaviour. Klaus concludes that the Law is irrelevant for the believer in the light of the presence of the Spirit in the life of the believer.[167] For Paul, the Spirit provides the most sensational insights and privileges for the believer. He is a better resource than the Torah for a number of reasons. The Spirit offers specific guidance, being able to advise the believer in multiple situations, his advice being more precise and explicit.[168] He is a superior guide and he is associated fundamentally with relationship, not rules. The Spirit brings a person into relationship with God whereas the Law can only provide the standard expected by God and warn of the consequences of disobedience. The Spirit acts as a personal guide and influence whereas the Law is impersonal. The Spirit not only points out sin but also provides strength to overcome it whereas the Law only highlights sin and condemns the sinner (Rom. 7.7–11; Gal. 3.10). Finally, the Spirit acts as an ever-present guide while the Law, inasmuch as it is a collection of books, is less immediate.

In Eph. 1.17, Paul also describes the role of the Spirit as enabling believers to be able to accurately and experientially know certain aspects of truth concerning God, particularly relating to their salvation. Although the Spirit is granted to provide guidance for the believer and power for service, a fundamental aspect of the Spirit is also to enable the believer to explore God, intellectually and experientially. It is an absorption with an examination of God that gives the Christian life dynamism and the Spirit is central in helping believers in the pursuit of that eternal quest.

These factors, of course, offer challenges as well as privileges. It is often easier to consult a list of rules for guidance, as contained in the Bible, than to listen to an intimate friend; the Bible calls for developing a relationship with the Spirit that demands discipline and time, and a readiness to obey that which he commands. The challenge for Pentecostals is that they do not slip into using the Bible as their only guide, forgetting that the Spirit who inspired and preceded it also speaks outside it as well as through it.

---

[166] D. Kim ('The Paraclete: The Spirit of the Church', *AJPS* 5.2 (2002), pp. 255–70 (265)) suggests that this is not simply a reminder of the words taught by Jesus but a greater appreciation or understanding of their import.

[167] B.D. Klaus, 'Fruit of the Spirit', in Burgess (ed.), *EPCC*, p. 209.

[168] S.E. Parker, *Led by the Spirit. Toward a Practical Theology of Pentecostal Discernment and Decision Making* (Sheffield: Sheffield Academic Press, 1996), p. 9.

The Spirit may choose to speak through the language of the Bible but he may as easily speak in other ways (Jn 15.7–12; Acts 15.28).[169] The guidelines in the Bible are recognized as being valuable but so also are other occasions when the dynamic and transforming Spirit may speak to believers. Land argues that the Spirit 'speaks scripturally but also has more to say than Scripture'.[170] That is not to suggest that the Spirit is superior to the Word or the Word to the Spirit. The Spirit and the Word function together, on occasion the former through the latter but also sometimes spontaneously and without specific reference to the written Word.[171] While the Spirit is always available to clarify that which the Bible teaches, he is also able to develop the content and even to provide fresh revelation. The Spirit thus provides a canon outside the canon in a relentless river of revelation that includes the vitally important biblical text. This concept releases believers into being able to affirm the presence of the Spirit in a contemporary setting without having to locate a text which describes the Spirit so functioning as affirmation of that which is being currently experienced.

However, where the Spirit functions outside the written Word, caveats must be carefully instituted in order to check for errors in the listening process.[172] Thus, the Spirit will never correct or contradict the Word and extra-biblical revelation must be assessed in the context of the Christian community which has itself been developed by the Spirit and the Word (1 Cor. 12.3; 14.29; 1 Jn 4.1–3).

The Bible without the Spirit can result in barren exegesis but to emphasize a quest for the Spirit without the balance of the Word can degenerate into effervescent emptiness. The Spirit and the Word functioning in the Christian community is the ideal framework to counteract imbalance and to recognize the intrinsic value of any revelation.[173] An example of the Spirit-community model in identifying the will of God is reflected in Acts 15.22, 28. Thomas and Shelton explore the Jerusalem council and note the role of the community in arriving at the conclusion to welcome Gentiles into the Church.[174] Where there was uncertainty and limited scriptural guidance, the believers looked to the Spirit to facilitate the correct conclusion. Shelton concludes, 'It is not

---

[169] J.W. Wyckoff, 'The Inspiration and Authority of Scripture', in J.K. Bridges (ed.), *The Bible, the Word of God* (Springfield: Gospel Publishing House, 2003), pp. 17–52 (24).

[170] Land, *Pentecostal Spirituality*, p. 100; K. Archer, *A Pentecostal Hermeneutic for the Twenty-First Century. Spirit, Scripture and Community* (London: Continuum, 2004), p. 147.

[171] Land, *Pentecostal Spirituality*, pp. 100, 118; Archer, 'Pentecostal Hermeneutics', p. 80; J. Ruthven, 'A Place for Prophecy', *Paraclete*, 6.2 (1972), pp. 8–14; W.A. Grudem, 'Can All Believers Prophesy?', *Paraclete*, 15.4 (1981), pp. 11–14.

[172] See Kärkkäinen, *Toward a Pneumatological Theology*, p. 14; Cargal, 'Beyond the Fundamentalist-Modernist Controversy', pp. 173–74.

[173] M.D. McLean, 'Toward a Pentecostal Hermeneutic', *Pneuma* 6 (1984), pp. 35–56 (50).

the text of Scripture that is our normative authority but the Holy Spirit-filled church living in the now in connection with the apostolic tradition . . . with the latter being the Holy Spirit speaking through the Church to the Church'.[175]

The Spirit Inspires Charismata in the Church

The Spirit is identified in the OT as enabling, among others, Elijah and Elisha to function charismatically. Gräbe similarly links the concept of power to miraculous activity in the book of Acts (Acts 3.12; 4.7) though it is to be noted that Luke associates the person of Jesus to the miracles not the Spirit. However, the relationship of the Spirit with miraculous activity is clearly and particularly identified by Paul (1 Cor. 12, 14).[176] Pentecostals strongly assert a belief in the existence of *charismata* (more popularly referred to as 'spiritual gifts'), given not on merit but as a result of the grace of God (Judg. 3.10; 6.34; 11.29; 14.19; 2 Kgs 2.9–14). Not only are the gifts of the Spirit bestowed by the Spirit to believers but the Spirit also manifests himself through those gifts. They are not derived remotely from a distance as a result of divine initiation from heaven so much as resulting from his being present in believers.[177]

The term *pneumatikos* emphasizes the fact that the gifts are related to the Spirit (*pneuma*) (Rom. 15.27; 1 Cor. 2.13; 9.11; 12.1; 14.1; Eph. 1.3; 5.19; Col. 3.16), the former term literally meaning, 'spiritual man/one' and hence 'spiritual gift'; Ervin suggests 'spiritual manifestations' as a more accurate designation of that which Paul describes.[178] The manifestation of spiritual gifts does not indicate a superior spirituality on the part of the one who manifests them.[179] Rather, they are designated as being 'spiritual' because the Spirit is the source, not because those so gifted have passed a certain threshold of spirituality.

The other main term used by Paul to describe these phenomena (*charismata*, Rom. 1.11; 11.29; 12.6; 1 Cor. 12.4, 9, 28–31; 1 Pet. 4.10) is generally translated as a '(free) gift' or 'gift of grace'.[180] It is possible that Paul uses the

---

[174] J.C. Thomas, 'Women, Pentecostals and the Bible: An Experiment in Pentecostal Hermeneutics', *JPT* 5 (1994), pp. 44–50; J.B. Shelton, 'Epistemology and Authority in the Acts of the Apostles: An Analysis and Test Case Study of Acts 15:1–29', *Spirit and Church* 2.2 (2000), pp. 231–47.

[175] Shelton, 'Epistemology and Authority', pp. 246–47.

[176] Gräbe, 'The Pentecostal Discovery', *Pneuma* 24.2 (2002), pp. 233–36.

[177] R.A.N. Kydd, *Charismatic Gifts in the Early Church* (Peabody: Hendrickson, 1984).

[178] Ervin, *Spirit Baptism*, pp. 85–96.

[179] S.M. Horton, *What the Bible Says about the Holy Spirit* (Springfield: Gospel Publishing House, 1976), p. 208.

[180] Though see B.C. Aker, '*Charismata*: Gifts, Enablements, or Ministries?', *JPT* 11.1 (2002), pp. 53–69; see also K. Bending, 'Confusing Word and Concept in "Spiritual Gifts": Have we forgotten James Barr's Exhortations?', *JETS* 43.1 (2000), pp. 37–51.

different terms interchangeably (Eph. 4.11 uses neither in referring to the ministries mentioned therein). Ellis believes that while Paul uses *charismata* for all gifts, he refers *pneumatikoi* to 'gifts of inspired utterance or discernment'.[181] Menzies supports this perspective, suggesting that although the terms are apparently used interchangeably (in 1 Cor. 12.1, 4, 31; 14.1), the *pneumatikoi* may be best understood as a sub group of the *charismata*. Thus, Paul would be understood to be using the former term in responding to the questions concerning the 'speech' gifts by the Corinthians (1 Cor. 12.1) and in introducing the gift of prophecy (1 Cor. 14.1, 37), both references relating to a narrow range of speech orientated gifts. In response to Menzies, it may be proposed that Paul uses the term *pneumatikos* when referring to the questions of the Corinthians because this was their preferred term, possibly because of the emphasis on the Spirit (*pneuma*) (1 Cor. 12.1), while Paul prefers to educate them by replacing it with the term *charismata* with its relationship to grace, in his response (1 Cor. 12.4). A difficulty with this position is that if Paul is less comfortable with *pneumatikos*, it is unclear as to why he should use it in 1 Cor. 14.1 to introduce the discussion of tongues, interpretation and prophecy. Other words are also used for spiritual gifts including *dōrea* (Eph. 3.7; 4.7), *domata* (Eph. 4.8), *energēmata* (1 Cor. 12.6, 10) and *diakonioi* (Rom. 12.7; 1 Cor. 5.5).

Cessationism

Pentecostals reject any notion that spiritual gifts and other supernatural phemonena recorded in the NT were restricted to the early Church era.[182] Their early decrease in the Church era is largely believed to be due to the unwillingness of believers to accept their validity and to facilitate their operation.[183] At the same time, occurrences of the manifestation of spiritual

---

[181] E. Ellis, 'Prophecy in the New Testament Church – And Today', in P. Panagopoulos (ed.), *Prophetic Vocation in the New Testament and Today* (Leiden: Brill, 1977), pp. 46–57 (48).

[182] C. Brumback, *What Meaneth This?* (Springfield: Gospel Publishing House, 1947), pp. 59–96; DeArtega, *Quenching the Spirit*, pp. 62–70; W.R. Jones, 'The Nine Gifts of the Holy Spirit' in Brewster (ed.), *Pentecostal Doctrine*, p. 49; J.R. Williams, 'Biblical Truth and Experience. A Reply to *Charismatic Chaos* by John F. MacArthur', *Paraclete* 27.3 (1993), pp. 16–30; J. Deere, *Surprised by the Power of the Spirit* (Grand Rapids: Zondervan, 1993); P. Elbert, 'Pentecostal/Charismatic Themes in Luke-Acts at the Evangelical Theological Society: The Battle of Interpretive Method', *JPT* 12.2 (2004), pp. 181–205; J.M. Penney, 'The Testing of New Testament prophecy', *JPT* 10 (1997), pp. 35–84 (72–82); J. Ruthven, 'The "Foundational Gifts" of Ephesians 2.20', *JPT* 10.2 (2002), pp. 28–43; idem, *On the Cessation of the Charismata* (Sheffield: Sheffield Academic Press, 1993); idem, 'On the Cessation of the Charismata: The Protestant Polemic of Benjamin B. Warfield', *Pneuma* 12.1 (1990), pp. 14–31.

[183] Brumback, *What Meaneth This?*, pp. 84–7; DeArtega, *Quenching the Spirit*, pp. 83–106.

gifts throughout the centuries has been well documented, though their appearances are irregular.[184] Pentecostals dispute that 1 Cor. 13.8–10 undermines the ongoing nature of spiritual gifts. Against those who believe that some of the gifts are temporary (healing, tongues, prophecy) while others are permanent (teaching, administration), Pentecostals react by stating that Paul makes no such distinction. Against the suggestion that 1 Cor. 13.8–10 indicates that prophecy, tongues and knowledge are no longer in existence, being replaced by love, the following responses may be offered:–

- The contrast between these three gifts and love is in the context of the superiority of love over all other manifestations of the Spirit. It is not that the former are insubstantial but that love is supreme, the impermanence of the former being evidence of that fact.
- Impermanence does not indicate that the gifts associated with it are at fault; it relates to the fact that they will not be necessary in the age of completion which is to come.
- The timing of the demise of these gifts (13.10) is believed to be the return of Jesus, not the closing of the canon of Scripture. This deduction is based on the fact that Paul nowhere refers to the NT canon but he does refer to the return of Jesus in ways that demonstrate that such gifts are no longer necessary (1 Cor. 1.7; 13.12). Furthermore, to suggest that the word 'perfect' (13.10) refers to the closure of the NT canon is improbable since that notion would not have been understandable to the readers of the letter since, at the time, there was no indication that there would be a NT.[185]

Principles

Some principles concerning these gifts which are acknowledged by most Pentecostals may be gleaned from 1 Cor. 12.4–11.

- Paul asserts that spiritual gifts should be operated harmoniously in diversity, not uniformly, but as a result of a dynamic relationship with the Spirit, resulting in beneficial relationships with each other (1 Cor. 12.4–31). The fact that these gifts are given by the Spirit should increase the sense of responsibility felt by those who administer them and, in particular, encourage them to do so appropriately, as indicated by the nature of the

---

[184] Brumback, *What Meaneth This?*, pp. 90–5; DeArtega, *Quenching the Spirit*, pp. 62–9, 73–4; A.J. Gordon, *The Ministry of Healing: Miracles of Cure in All Ages* (Harrisburg: Christian Publications, 1961); F.W. Puller, *The Anointing of the Sick: Scripture and Tradition* (London: SPCK, 1904); E. Frost, *Christian Healing* (London: Bradford and Dickens, 1940); Allen, 'Signs and Wonders', pp. 1063–068.

[185] G.D. Fee, *How to Read the Bible for All Its Worth* (Grand Rapids: Zondervan, 1982, rev. edn 1993), p. 64.

Giver of the gifts. Paul associates the gifts with the words 'service' (12.5) and 'working' (12.6). They are described as being given for the benefit of the corporate group (12.7; Eph. 4.12). Thus, they are not to be administered selfishly but selflessly, not for personal gain but for the benefit of others.[186] When the manifestation of a gift ceases to exalt the person of Jesus (1 Cor. 12.3) or to edify or develop other believers (Rom. 1.11; 1 Cor. 12.7), it ceases to be divinely inspired.[187] When there is an absence of a manifestation of love, there is an absence of a manifestation of God through the gift (1 Cor. 13.1–3).

- Each member of the Godhead is involved in the charismata being given to the Church (12.4–6).[188] Paul is not necessarily assuming that the bestowal of the gifts is the responsibility of the Spirit only, as opposed to Jesus or the Father. He does not separate them so functionally. Nevertheless, given the presence of the Spirit in the life of the corporate church and the individual believer, it is logical that he should focus on the Spirit as representatively functioning in the distribution of the gifts.

- Every Christian receives a manifestation of the Spirit to facilitate their service in and on behalf of the local church (12.6, 11; Rom. 12.4–6; Eph. 4.7, 15–16; 2 Tim. 1.7; 1 Pet. 4.10). By definition, all Christians are people of the Spirit and in that respect, they are eligible to function as channels through whom he can minister to others. But with the privilege comes the responsibility of maintaining a close relationship with the Spirit. Although the potential is that all believers may manifest any of the gifts, Paul is clear that not all should be expected to manifest any in particular (1 Cor. 12.29–30). The concentration of Paul in 1 Cor. 12 is not on the gifts referred to or even on their diversity. Rather, it is on the diversity of their distribution. The fact that the Spirit controls the manifestation of

---

[186] R. Tate, 'Christian Childishness and "That Which Is Perfect"', *Paraclete* 24.1 (1990), pp. 11–15; also M. Volf, 'Human Work, Divine Spirit, and New Creation: Toward a Pneumatological Understanding of Work', *Pneuma*, 9.2 (1987), pp. 184–86.

[187] G.D. Fee, *The First Epistle to the Corinthians* (Grand Rapids: Eerdmans, 1987), p. 582; Jones, 'The Nine Gifts', p. 48.

[188] Although it is possible that Paul may have referred to each member of the Godhead in order to identify their differing functions with regard to the provision of the gifts referred to (1 Cor. 12.4–6), it is as likely that he is seeking to emphasize that although these gifts are varied (thus described as 'gifts', 'service' and 'working' (vv. 4–6)), they are all divinely motivated. To attempt to divide them between the members of the Godhead seems unnecessary and counterproductive to Paul's theme in the chapter, namely a diversity of gifts but a unity of purpose. Thus, to conclude, for example, that the Spirit provides the gifts while the Son administers them and the Father provides the power to manifest them is too nuanced a perspective and compartmentalizes the function of the Godhead unnecessarily (though see W.G. Hathaway, *Spiritual Gifts in the Church* (London: Elim Publishing, 1933), p. 11).

the gifts is an important factor in the context of an attempt to identify how one might function as a channel of the gifts (1 Cor. 12.7–11). Pentecostals have always believed that one of the roles of the Spirit in empowering believers is to enable all to function in the Christian community. However, in practice, this has rarely resulted in many, or even a majority, of the believers in a local church manifesting the gifts in the way indicated by Paul. The concept of 'body ministry' is loudly applauded by Pentecostals but the leadership of a local church appears to be the depository of most of the gifts, especially the audible ones.[189] This is often not due to the desire of the leaders to monopolize but often because of the lack of a framework for identifying how individuals may be used by the Spirit and limited provision for opportunities to function thus.

Thus, although it is recognized that the Spirit inspires gifts in all believers, there is value in believers, in the context of the Christian community, helping to identify gifts that have already been granted to others. There are dangers with this in that a rather mechanistic procedure may be devised to help associate gifts with individuals. However, with sensitivity, this can enable believers to recognize that they are manifesting gifts of the Spirit in their lives more than they may have realized, as well as help others to discover giftings that the Spirit has already given that can be developed and exercised. Some Pentecostal churches are developing ways whereby believers are being encouraged to identify their passions, gifts and strengths and then to discover how they might use them for the benefit of others. In this respect, they are seeking to apply to the contemporary church the Pauline recognition that diverse gifts are presented to believers for the benefit of the local church and the wider community.

Pentecostals have generally distrusted the notion that one may transmit one's gifts to another or bestow a gift on another, Rom. 1.11 being interpreted as not relating to the spiritual gifts as discussed above.[190] Neither has it been accepted that 2 Tim. 1.6 should be interpreted as indicating that one may grant to another a gift via the laying on of hands.[191] But this perception does not undermine the value of recognizing or affirming gifts that have been bestowed on others and encouraging their use. It is in this regard that Paul encourages Timothy to develop his gift (2 Tim. 1.6) and

---

[189] For statistical data concerning UK Pentecostal churches see Kay, *Pentecostals in Britain*, pp. 74–81.

[190] Canty, *The Practice of Pentecost*, pp. 100–01; Conn, *A Balanced Church*, pp. 108–09; D. Petts, *Body Builders: Gifts to Make God's People Grow* (Mattersey: Mattersey Hall, 2002), p. 246; the 1949 conference of the US AoG passed a resolution disapproving such a procedure.

[191] J. Tipei, 'The Function of the Laying on of Hands in the New Testament', *JEPTA* 20 (2000), pp. 93–115 (113–14).

Barnabas and Paul were entrusted to fulfil the mission delegated to them by God (Acts 13.3), both occasions incorporating the laying on of hands. Similarly, the purpose behind the presentation of the gifts in Rom. 12.6–8 is to encourage the readers to use those gifts that God has given to them and to do it in ways that are appropriate.

In order to ensure that such a process does not lead to self-centredness and arrogance, it is important to identify needs that are to be met by the manifestation of certain gifts and the latter sought in order to minister to those issues. Aker consequently advocates the use of the concept of 'ministries' rather than 'spiritual gifts' insofar as the element of benefiting others is more readily conveyed in the former term.[192] For some, this may be a permanent capacity to function in a particular way, though it is possible for all to function in any gift, depending on the sovereign plan of the Spirit who delegates the gifts when and to whom he wishes. Although the notion of a gift is that it belongs to the recipient and not the one who has given it, Pentecostals prefer to accept that the charismata are on loan from the Spirit; they are manifestations of the Spirit through believers that are expected to be used in ways that are appropriate to his character and will.[193] Even when an individual frequently manifests a particular gift, it is still preferable to understand this as a manifestation of the Spirit through that person and not that s/he is using the gift of her/his own volition. It is difficult to be completely clear in the formulation of a precise practical framework for the use of the charismata; some (miracles, healings) are manifested more infrequently than others (administration, teaching) which are more permanent. Flexible, rather than rigid, contexts of use need to be embraced.

- The manifestation of the gifts in a public context must be subject to careful assessment.[194] Sanctified common sense, the shared wisdom of the Christian community, a comparison with the teachings located in the Bible and receptivity to the Holy Spirit will help to confirm or reject the manifestation.

- The gifts are intrinsically equal to each other. The appropriate manifestation of any gift is determined by its value as compared to other gifts on any given occasion. Thus, Paul identifies prophecy as having greater value than tongues without interpretation because the former benefits those present while uninterpreted tongues do not (1 Cor. 14.1–6). It is not that prophecy is intrinsically superior to the gift of tongues since both are manifestations of the Spirit but that the former is more valuable to the

---

[192] Aker, 'Charismata', pp. 53–69.
[193] Conn, *A Balanced Church*, pp. 104–107; Canty, *The Practice of Pentecost*, p. 99.
[194] Hathaway, *Spiritual Gifts*, pp. 96–114; Gee, *Concerning Spiritual Gifts*, pp. 71–87.

community since it is understandable and therefore beneficial. Similarly, on occasions, some gifts are more valuable to the Christian community than others; in that restricted sense, they may be identified as having greater value. Paul is not therefore necessarily seeking to demonstrate a hierarchy of gifts. Nevertheless, some Pentecostals unfortunately assume a hierarchy of sorts in which the more sensational and publicly demonstrated gifts are accorded more honour than others that are less spectacular. Paul, on the other hand, identifies the important underlying principle of ensuring that the gifts are administered for the greater good of the community.[195]

- Gifts may be manifested in association with others. Thus, in healing, it is appropriate to expect the gifts of faith and discernment to be also operative; similarly, the exercise of the gift of administration would anticipate the presence of the gift of wisdom.

- The gifts are varied (12.4–6), Paul providing five major lists of gifts (Rom 12.6–8; Eph 4.11; 1 Cor. 12.8–10, 28–29 cf. 13.1–3; 14.6, 26), none of which are intended to be comprehensive but representative (cf. 1 Cor. 7.7 which refers to the gifts of celibacy/singleness or being married). One of the main purposes of these lists is to demonstrate the diversity of gifts available to believers. Hollenweger questions the distinction between 'natural' and 'supernatural' gifts, preferring to identify a spiritual gift on the basis of its value to the Christian community, deducing that 'a charism is a natural gift that is given for the common good'.[196] Others, however, have refused to identify natural talents as spiritual gifts.[197] Thus, Hathaway concludes, 'These gifts are divinely given, not humanly developed'.[198] Schatzmann, however, deduces 'because their own experience is often crisis-related and hence resulting in radical turnabouts, Pentecostals are apt to read radical discontinuity also into God's ways of working out his purposes' resulting in many disavowing the possibility that a spiritual gift may be a natural talent that has been invested with supernatural energy by God.[199] Lim however concludes, 'God touches all our abilities and potential with supernatural power'.[200]

---

[195] Schatzmann, 'The Gifts of the Spirit', p. 91; D. Gee, *Spiritual Gifts in the Work of the Ministry Today* (Springfield: Gospel Publishing House, 1963), p. 5.

[196] W.J. Hollenweger, 'Gifts of the Spirit: Natural and Supernatural', in Burgess and van der Maas (eds), *NIDPCM*, pp. 667–68; Volf, 'Human Work', pp. 184–85.

[197] Hathaway, *Spiritual Gifts*, pp. 11–16; Carter, *The Gifts of the Spirit*, p. 30; Petts, *Body Builders*, p. 228.

[198] Hathaway, *Spiritual Gifts*, p. 13; Gee, *Spiritual Gifts*, p. 10.

[199] Schatzmann, 'The Gifts of the Spirit', pp. 82, 95; also M.L. Rice, '"Pneumatic Experience as Teaching Methodology an Pentecostal Tradition", *AJPS* 5.2 (2002), pp. 289–312 (299).

[200] D. Lim, 'The Incarnational Nature of the Gifts', *Paraclete* 26.3 (1992), pp. 14–19 (15).

It is better, with many Pentecostals, to acknowledge the possibility that the Spirit can empower believers to function in ways that are beyond their normal powers and/or to enable them to utilize the gifts that they have already been granted as part of their personalities as created by God. After salvation, these gifts and sensitivities may be enhanced and supernaturally energized so as to achieve a higher potential of benefit for others. Thus, the abilities of individuals prior to their conversion may be channelled by the Spirit for the benefit of others as well as the possibility of irregular or frequent manifestation of gifts that may not have been present in their lives hitherto.

Some Pentecostals have sought to separate the gifts mentioned in 1 Cor. 12.8–10 from other gifts[201] while others have preferred a more inclusive understanding of the gifts.[202] The danger with the former assessment is that some of the gifts are viewed as being of greater intrinsic value than others.[203] As well as attempting to differentiate between the lists of gifts, others have subdivided the gifts within the lists[204] though this is not a particularly helpful or easy exercise, especially because it is not supported by Paul and such attempts at categorization are tentative at best.[205]

---

[201] Pentecostals often concentrate on the nine gifts mentioned in 1 Cor. 12.4–11. For example, until 1994, the Elim Pentecostal Church Fundamental Beliefs stated, 'We believe that the church should claim and manifest the nine gifts of the Holy Spirit: wisdom, knowledge . . .' Since then the revised statement reads 'We believe in . . . the present operation of the manifold Gifts of the Holy Spirit according to the New Testament'; see also T.N. Turnbull, *What God Hath Wrought* (London: Puritan Press, 1959), p. 107; Gee, *Concerning Spiritual Gifts*, pp. 21–55; A.G. Hadden, 'Gifts of the Spirit in Assemblies of God Writings', *Paraclete* 24.1 (1990), pp. 20–32; C.S. Keener, *Three Crucial Questions about the Holy Spirit* (Grand Rapids: Baker, 1996), pp. 110–25; D. Lim, 'Spiritual Gifts', in Horton (ed.), *Systematic Theology*, pp. 457–72; Jones, 'The Nine Gifts', p. 47; Petts, *Body Builders*, pp. 117–244; H. Horton, *The Gifts of the Spirit* (Nottingham: AoG Publishing House, 1935), p. 68; Arrington, *Christian Doctrine*, pp. 129–61.

[202] Gee, *Spiritual Gifts*, pp. 5–6.

[203] As demonstrated by Horton's (*The Gifts of the Spirit*, p. 35) omission of some of the gifts in 1 Cor. 12.28 (helpers, administrators) while others are referred to (miracles, healers and tongues).

[204] Conn (*A Balanced Church*, p. 112) in agreement with others suggests that the nine gifts mentioned in 1 Cor. 12.8–10 may be grouped as follows:– gifts of revelation (wisdom, knowledge, discernment), gifts of operation (faith, healing, miracles), gifts of inspiration (prophecy, tongues, interpretation); Jones ('The Nine Gifts', p. 50) suggests illumination, action and communication; Hadden ('Gifts of the Spirit', p. 22) suggests 'the power to know supernaturally . . . to act supernaturally . . . to speak supernaturally'.

[205] Petts, *Body Builders*, pp. 115–16; Fee, *Paul, the Spirit*, p. 164.

An examination of the variety[206] within the five main lists of gifts illustrates the difficulty in determining a pattern:

1 Cor. 12.8–10	1 Cor. 12.28	1 Cor. 12.29f	Eph. 4.11	Rom. 12.6–8
Wisdom	Apostles	Apostles	Apostle	Prophecy
Knowledge	Prophets	Prophets	Prophet	Service
Faith	Teachers	Teachers	Evangelist	Teaching
Healing	Miracles	Miracles	Pastor/teacher	Exhortation
Miracles	Healings	Healings		Giving
Prophecy	Helps	Tongues		Mercy
Discernment	Administration	Interpretation		
Tongues	Tongues			
Interpretation				

Although most Pentecostals tend to treat the individual gifts as they are referred to by Paul as distinct gifts with discrete definitions, it is not always clear that this is the most appropriate way of understanding them. Indeed, if Paul is not seeking to be comprehensive in his presentation of the gifts but simply remarking on the plurality and diversity of gifts, they may overlap with one another more than may have been assumed. Thus, to distinguish prophecy, wisdom, revelation and knowledge as if each were a separate manifestation of the Spirit may be an unnecessary exercise since Paul may rather be intending to emphasize the fact that the Spirit is the source of all divinely imparted communication however it may be designated. Notwithstanding the fact that Paul explicitly identifies nearly thirty different gifts of the Spirit, most are self explanatory. However, those identified in 1 Corinthians may benefit from more explication because of their prominence among Pentecostals.

A Collection of Charismata

WORD OF WISDOM

Most Pentecostals view this gift as relating to the inspiration of Spirit-inspired revelation for a particular occasion rather than a natural propensity towards wisdom.[207] Lim suggests it will 'reflect God's plans, purposes, and ways of accomplishing things'.[208] However, a number of suggestions have

---

[206] See also 1 Pet. 4.9–10. Canty (*The Practice of Pentecost*, p. 97) adds Mt. 19.10–11, Mk 16.17–18.

[207] Conn, *A Balanced Church*, pp. 113–15; Canty, *The Practice of Pentecost*, pp. 165–66; Petts, *Body Builders*, pp. 226–27; Horton, *The Gifts of the Spirit*, pp. 58–62.

[208] D. Lim, *Spiritual Gifts: A Fresh Look* (Springfield: Gospel Publishing House, 1991), p. 71; Jones ('The Nine Gifts', p. 51) offers Acts 10.13–15; 27.21–25 as support.

been offered for the content of such wisdom. Canty suggests that the gift is to be used in the context of the spiritual development of the one to whom it is given,[209] while Arrington associates it with the interpretation of the Bible.[210] Gee deduced that the gift may be active in preaching and teaching[211] while Horton anticipates its value in determining the future.[212] This gift is often associated with the gift of knowledge; where the latter relates to familiarity with facts, the gift of wisdom is assumed to relate to the application of those facts in a particular way.[213] The fact that the word 'wisdom' is used elsewhere with reference to the wisdom available from Christ (1 Cor. 1.23–24, 30; Col. 2.3) may indicate that this refers to knowledge concerning the person and mission of Jesus. However, there appears to be little reason to be restrictive in this regard and it is probably safest, in the absence of Pauline guidance, to keep the definition of the anticipated wisdom wider rather than narrower.

WORD OF KNOWLEDGE

Closely related to the word of wisdom, it is generally assumed that the word of knowledge is a supernatural awareness of facts that would be otherwise unknown to the recipient (Acts 5.1–2; 9.10–12).[214] Because the word *gnōsis* (knowledge) is used elsewhere in contexts that relate to the knowledge of God (2 Cor. 2.14; 4.6; Eph. 1.17), it is possible that this gift reflects those occasions when some aspect of God is being revealed. However, there is evidence of supernaturally inspired knowledge being recorded in other settings (Jn 1.48; 4.17–18; Acts 5.1–6; 27.10) and this suggests that a broader base of knowledge may also be appropriate.

DISCERNMENT OF SPIRITS

Although discernment can occur naturally as a result of experience and maturity, Pentecostals believe that Paul is here referring to a charismatic gift of the Spirit. However, Yong suggests,

> If discernment is solely a gift from God, there is not much we can do except pray that we are blessed with the gift when we need it. If, however, discernment requires cultivation as well as the continued and purpose-

---

[209] Canty, *The Practice of Pentecost*, pp. 167–68.

[210] Arrington, *Christian Doctrine*, pp. 132–133.

[211] Gee, *Concerning Spiritual Gifts*, p. 35–9.

[212] Horton, *The Gifts of the Spirit*, pp. 60–1.

[213] Petts, *Body Builders*, pp. 224–25; Rowe, *One Lord, One Faith*, pp. 168–70; M.J. Cartledge, 'Charismatic Prophecy: A Definition and Description', *JPT* 5 (1994), pp. 91–3.

[214] Conn, *A Balanced Church*, p. 116; Menzies and Horton, *Bible Doctrines*, p. 166; F. Martin, 'Knowledge, Word of', in Burgess and van der Maas (eds), *NIDPCM*, pp. 823–25 (825); Gee, *Concerning Spiritual Gifts*, pp. 134–37.

ful exercise of our human faculties, then we need to think about how we should most effectively proceed.[215]

Pentecostalism has experienced its fair share of deceptions that have caused pain to sincere but misguided believers who thought that they were acting under the guidance of the Spirit only to find later that their discernment had been faulty or non-existent, resulting in tragedy.[216] It is generally believed by Pentecostals that this gift describes the supernatural ability to identify the presence of an evil spirit (Acts 8.9–23; 16.16–17),[217] the Spirit[218] or to identify the source of power motivating an act or word.[219]

FAITH

Pentecostals distinguish the gift of faith from the fruit of faithfulness and saving faith. The faith referred to may be identified as the facility to trust God in a particular situation[220] and the gift of faith refers to a God-given assurance to undertake a particular action or offer a specific prayer (often in the absence of a biblical mandate or promise). The gift of faith is identified as a readiness to believe that which God has promised or stated will occur. It is particularly present in contexts when a biblical promise or guideline is unavailable. In those settings, the Spirit may choose to support a believer to follow a particular course of action by providing a 'burst' of supernatural assurance or faith that their proposed action is the correct one. Thus, even though there may be no biblical mandate, the Spirit grants confirmation

---

[215] A. Yong, '"Spiritual Discernment: A Biblical-Theological Reconsideration" in Ma and Menzies (eds), *The Spirit and Spirituality*, pp. 83–107 (99).

[216] J. Salomonsen, 'The Dark Side of Pentecostal Enthusiasm: Abraham's and Sara's Sacrifice in Knutby, Sweden', in Stålsett (ed.), *Spirits of Globalization*, pp. 107–30; for an earlier call to be aware of the dangers of deception, see A. Boddy, 'Prophetic Messages and Their Trustworthiness', *Confidence* (February, 1909), pp. 42–4.

[217] Canty, *The Practice of Pentecost*, pp. 194–97; Petts, *Body Builders*, pp. 210–23; Carter, *The Gifts of the Spirit*, pp. 45–50; E. R. Corsie, 'The Ministry Gifts', in Brewster (ed.), *Pentecostal Doctrine*, pp. 95–111 (106–07); A.L. Hoy, 'The Discernings of the Spirit', *Paraclete* (1984), pp. 11–16; P.L. King, 'Searching for Genuine Gold: Discerning Spirit, Flesh, and Demonic in Pentecostal Experiences' (SPS conference paper, Cleveland, 2007), pp. 174–76.

[218] Yong, *Beyond the Impasse*, pp. 152–54.

[219] J.D. Hernando, 'Discerning of Spirits', *Paraclete* 26.2 (1992), pp. 6–9; F. Martin, 'Discernment of Spirits, Gift of', in Burgess and van der Maas (eds), *NIDPCM*, pp. 582–84; Yong, 'Spiritual Discernment', pp. 93–9.

[220] Acts 3.2–10; 13.6–12; Z.J. Bicket, *We Hold These Truths* (Springfield: Gospel Publishing House, 1978), p. 57; F. Martin, 'Faith, Gift of', in Burgess and van der Maas (eds), *NIDPCM*, pp. 629–30; Carter (*The Gifts of the Spirit*, p. 66) unnecessarily assumes that it is normally associated with dangerous or extreme situations.

prior to the action being undertaken. It is this that protects the believer from functioning precipitously, precociously or presumptuously (Rom. 10.17; Eph. 2.8). The confidence provided by the Spirit to support one's actions or words is to be understood as a gift of faith. It is not to be identified with a belief that God can do that which is needed but that he will do so. That which Paul refers to is a particular acknowledgement by God that the prayer, act or word to be offered is in keeping with his will and therefore he provides encouragement to act accordingly.

Gifts of Healing

The term *charismata* (gifts) prefaces *iamatōn* (healings), in a combination that occurs only in the Pauline literature. The fact that both terms are in the plural has resulted in a range of explanations. It is possible that Paul believed that each healing was to be identified as a gift of healing; thus, the person who is healed receives a gift of healing.[221] It may be that he is demonstrating the comprehensive power of the Spirit to provide restoration for all kinds of illnesses. It is possible that some believers are enabled by the Spirit to facilitate the healing of particular illnesses.[222] Although some have claimed this to be a true reflection of their own healing ministries, it begs the question as to what one should do if the particular restorative capacity is not available to those wishing to minister to someone in need of specific restoration. It is also not reflected in the healing narratives in Acts or in James 5.14–18. It is probable that the term 'gifts of healings' best explains the purpose of the Spirit to provide a variety of healings through a diversity of believers, the gift being given when the Spirit wills it.[223] Although it need not be assumed that such ability resides permanently in a believer, Paul assumes the presence of healers in the Church (1 Cor. 12.28). Such a definition may be applied to those who function in this gift more than other people. Pentecostals are prepared to identify individuals with a more prominent God-given gift of healing (1 Cor. 12.28)[224] though the ministry of healing would be more generally

---

[221] So Canty, *The Practice of Pentecost*, p. 180; H.M. Ervin, *Healing. Sign of the Kingdom* (Peabody: Hendrickson, 2002), p. 29; Kay, *Pentecostals in Britain*, p. 89; Arrington (*Christian Doctrine*, p. 137) suggests 'as there are many illnesses, so are there many gifts of healing'.

[222] K. Warrington, 'Major Aspects of Healing with British Pentecostalism', *JEPTA* 19 (1999), pp. 34–55 (40); Bloch-Hoell, *The Pentecostal Movement*, p. 149.

[223] Conn, *A Balanced Church*, p. 126; Petts, *Body Builders*, pp. 158–59; Fee, *God's Empowering Presence*, pp. 168–69; J.C. Thomas, *The Devil, Disease and Deliverance: Origins of Illness in New Testament Thought* (Sheffield: Sheffield Academic Press, 1998), p. 40; S. Schatzmann, *A Pauline Theology of the Charismata* (Peabody: Hendrickson, 1987), p. 37.

[224] So A.B. Tee ('The Doctrine of Divine Healing', in Brewster (ed.), *Pentecostal Doctrine*, pp. 197–209 (207)), though he notes that this does not mean that they can produce healings whenever they please, since the onus for healing is on God.

understood as being available to all and effected through (m)any believer(s) (1 Cor. 12.7, 14). Gifts of healing are most appropriately manifested in conjunction with the gift of faith (1 Cor. 12.9), and words of wisdom and knowledge or prophecy (1 Cor. 12.8–10).[225]

MIRACLES

This is viewed as a reference to the ability to perform miracles other than healings. Thus, although without NT justification, many Pentecostals particularly associate this with the ability to conduct exorcisms, though other miraculous interventions may also be included.[226]

PROPHECY

The association of the Spirit with prophecy has long been recognized and is still being explored both with regard to the OT,[227] the NT,[228] the ancient world[229] and the early Church.[230] In general, Pentecostals have distinguished prophecy before the day of Pentecost from that which is referred to afterwards.[231] Thus, the death penalty for a false prophet (Deut. 13.1–5, 18, 20)

---

[225] Dye, *Healing Anointing*, pp. 143–44, 179, 181–82.

[226] Conn, *A Balanced Church*, pp. 129–32; F. Martin, 'Miracles, Gift of', in Burgess and van der Maas (eds), *NIDPCM*, pp. 875–76 (876); Canty, *The Practice of Pentecost*, pp. 186–87.

[227] David (2 Sam. 23.2); Saul (1 Sam. 10.9–12); Amasai (1 Chron. 12.18); Azariah (2 Chron. 15.1); Jahaziel (2 Chron. 20.14); Zechariah (Zech. 7.12); Micah (Mic. 3.8); Ezekiel (Ezek. 11.5); for all (Num. 11.29; Joel 2.28–29); Daniel (Dan. 4.8, 9, 18; 5.11, 14); Messiah (Isa. 11.2); Keener, *The Spirit*, pp. 9–48; R.D. Cotton, 'The Pentecostal Significance of Numbers 11', *JPT* 10.1 (2001), pp. 3–10; R.D. Moore, 'The Prophet as Mentor: A Crucial Facet of the Biblical Presentations of Moses, Elijah, and Isaiah', *JPT* 15.2 (2007), pp. 155–72.

[228] C. Stefan 'The Paraclete and Prophecy in the Johannine Community', *Pneuma* 27.2 (2005), 273–96; K. de Smidt, 'Hermeneutical Perspectives on the Spirit in the Book of Revelation', *JPT* 14 (1999), pp. 27–47; R. Stronstad, 'The Prophethood of All Believers: A Study in Luke's Charismatic Theology', in Ma and Menzies (eds), *Pentecostalism in Context*, pp. 60–77; idem, 'Affirming Diversity: God's People as a Community of Prophets', *Pneuma* 17.2 (1995), pp. 145–57. Keener, *The Spirit*, pp. 190–213; Turner, *The Holy Spirit*, pp. 185–220; Stronstad, 'Affirming Diversity', 145–57; Menzies, *Empowered for Witness*, passim; Wenk, *Community-Forming Power*, passim; W.K. Kay, *Prophecy* (Nottingham: Life Stream, 1991).

[229] C.M. Robeck Jr, 'Prophecy, Gift of', in Burgess and van der Maas (eds), *NIDPCM*, pp. 999–1012 (1000–002); this exploration has largely been left to non-Pentecostal scholars such as C. Forbes, *Prophecy and Inspired Speech in Early Christianity and Its Hellenistic Environment* (Peabody: Hendrickson, 1997); W. Grudem, *The Gift of Prophecy in 1 Corinthians* (Washington: University Press of America, 1982).

[230] Robeck, 'Prophecy, Gift of', p. 1007–010; idem, *Prophecy in Carthage: Perpetua, Tertullian, and Cyprian* (Cleveland: Pilgrim Press, 1992).

[231] W.K. Kay, 'Perspectives on Prophecy', *Paraclete* 26.1 (1992), pp. 1–7 (1).

is not applied to NT prophets who speak in error and the prophecies recorded in the NT are mainly intended for believers.[232] The ecstatic prophecies and somewhat bizarre behaviour sometimes associated with some OT prophets (Isa. 20.3–5; Jer. 4.5; 9.1; Ezek. 1.24; 4.1–5.4) is much less prominent in the NT church (Acts 21.10–11; 1 Cor. 14.32) where sensitivity, care and good order are important elements of the manifestations (1 Cor. 14.40).

Pentecostals increasingly view themselves as people through whom prophecies can be offered[233] though they rarely anticipate that this will be of a foretelling nature, though that does sometimes occur, as it did in the NT (Acts 11.28; 21.10–11). Fundamentally, Pentecostals acknowledge that prophecy is a gift given by the Spirit according to his will (1 Cor. 12.11), though Stronstad calls for the recapturing of 'Luke's vision of God's people as the prophethood of all believers'.[234]

In general, most Pentecostals identify prophecies as those occasions when an individual, inspired by God, speaks spontaneously and extemporarily with an emphasis on edification and or exhortation,[235] thus reflecting the NT norm (1 Cor. 14.3–5). Wenk, using speech-act theory and with evidence drawn from the NT, makes a case for prophecy not being viewed exclusively as proclamation but also as a call to dialogue within the community concerning the revelation. As such, prophecy becomes 'a way of initiating dialogue and a process of transformation'.[236]

Prophecy of a personal nature has generally been offered with care or even cautioned against,[237] though many look to prophecy as a means of determining direction or confirmation in decision making and for encouragement.[238] Increasingly, the expectation and practice is for prophecies to be offered by a variety of believers in a congregation rather than a set few, although some individuals and Pentecostal denominations prefer to identify prophets through whom it is expected the Spirit will speak to the community.[239]

---

[232] Stronstad, 'Affirming Diversity', p. 156.

[233] L. Lugo (*Spirit and Power. A 10-Country Survey of Pentecostals* (Washington: Pew Forum on Religion and Public Life, 2006), p. 16) records that 37% of Pentecostals in the countries researched, testified that they had given a prophecy (ranging from 27% (USA) to 55% (South Africa)).

[234] Stronstad, 'Affirming Diversity', p. 157.

[235] Canty, *The Practice of Pentecost*, 202–04; Conn, *A Balanced Church*, p. 134.

[236] M. Wenk, 'The Creative Power of the Prophetic Dialogue', *Pneuma* 26.1 (2004), pp. 118–29.

[237] The 1949 annual conference of the US AoG disapproved of the practice.

[238] Canty, *The Practice of Pentecost*, p. 204; E.L. Hyatt, 'Personal Prophecy. How Much Can We Trust It?', *Pneuma Review* 10.1 (2007), pp. 6–11 (7–8); Riggs, *The Spirit Himself*, p. 161.

[239] The Apostolic Church and similar movements; Conn, *A Balanced Church*, p. 133.

Pentecostals accept that prophecies and other verbal utterances of a charismatic nature are often associated with or preceded by mental pictures, images, words or physical sensations, the person who receives them then describing or explaining them to the congregation. The form of the prophecy is moving away from the use of the language that assumes that the words are directly spoken by God (in the first person singular) to a presentation that recognizes the importance of their being examined as to the quality and relevance of their content, as anticipated in 1 Cor. 14.29–32.

The fallibility of prophecy is generally assumed to be due to its impermanent nature (1 Cor. 13.8). It is generally left to individual believers to decide for themselves the authenticity of the information delivered, the prophecy rather than the prophet being the subject of scrutiny, though the lifestyle or the way in which the prophecy was offered may count towards its legitimacy.[240] It is unclear from 1 Cor. 14.29 whether the prophecy should be scrutinized by other prophets or by the wider congregation though, in practice, the latter is assumed by most Pentecostals.[241] The means whereby the prophecy is to be examined are manifold.[242] A basic premise is that it should not contradict that which is contained in the Bible.[243] Since most prophecies offer little more than representations of truth which are already contained in the Bible, such an exercise is rarely problematic. Where the prophecy is foretelling or unrelated to the Bible, other tests are needed. These relate to the confidence that people have in the one prophesying, common sense, the perception of the community of believers and personal discernment that may be manifested by the Spirit.[244] In accordance with the guidelines of Paul (1 Cor. 14.29), most Pentecostals prefer to allow no more than two or three prophecies in a given meeting though, increasingly, it is assumed that Paul's guidance may have had relevance for the Corinthian context in particular and that contemporary application needs careful contextualisation.

Pentecostals prefer not to identify preaching with prophecy, suggesting that it is offered independently of the Bible and thus to be contrasted with preaching and also reckoned to be inferior to the Bible.[245] They refer to preaching as transmitting the words of God and the Bible as the Word of God. However, many are prepared to accept that, on occasions, a person may preach prophetically, even without their knowledge that they are

---

[240] See Hathaway, *Spiritual Gifts*, pp. 54, 60–70; G. Jeffreys, *Pentecostal Rays* (London: Elim Publishing, 1933), pp. 178–79, 186–89.
[241] Robeck, 'Prophecy, Gift of', p. 1004; Penney, 'The Testing', p. 61.
[242] Penney, 'The Testing', pp. 49–64.
[243] Petts, *Body Builders*, p. 144; Hadden, 'Gifts of the Spirit', p. 30.
[244] C.M. Robeck Jr, 'Written Prophecies: A Question of Authority', *Pneuma* 2.2 (1980), pp. 26–45; Penney, 'The Testing', pp. 49–64.
[245] Petts, *Body Builders*, p. 142; Jones, 'The Nine Gifts', p. 58.

so operating.[246] Indeed, many Pentecostals would aspire to preach in a way that the Spirit is inspiring their words and infusing the message with a supernatural dimension reflective of the Spirit and not merely defined by the speaker, however good s/he may be.

TONGUES AND INTERPRETATION

Glossolalia has been associated with (and understood to be a defining aspect of) Pentecostalism since the earliest days of its existence.[247] The popular term used is 'speaking in tongues' rather than the more technical term of glossolalia (from *glōssa* (tongue) *lalein* (to speak) (1 Cor. 14.2, 6). The descriptions of 'new tongues' (Mk 16.7) and 'tongues of angels' (1 Cor. 13.1) are also believed to refer to glossolalia. Similarly, the notion that one may 'have' a tongue (1 Cor. 14.26 cf. 12.10, 28) is believed to refer to the capacity to speak in tongues. Pentecostals have spent minimal time exploring the actual science or theology of tongues;[248] neither have they significantly interacted with those who have sought to identify possible socio-linguistic,[249]

---

[246] D. Gee advocates this in *The Ministry Gifts of Christ* (Springfield: Gospel Publishing House, 1930), pp. 40–5.

[247] B. Bay, 'Glossolalia in Korean Christianity: An Historical Survey', *ERT* 30.3 (2006), pp. 237–48; see W.E. Mills, 'Glossolalia: A Survey of the Literature', in W.E. Mills (ed.), *Speaking in Tongues: A Guide to Research on Glossolalia* (Grand Rapids: Eerdmans, 1986), pp. 13–31; M.T. Girolimon, 'A Real Crisis of Blessing. Part 1', *Paraclete* 27.1 (1993), pp. 17–26.

[248] For theological studies, see D. Christie-Murray, *Voices from the Gods – Speaking with Tongues* (London: Routledge, 1978); W.E. Mills, *A Theological/Exegetical Approach to Glossolalia* (Lanham: University Press of America, 1985); idem, 'Glossolalia: A Survey of the Literature', in Mills (ed.), *Speaking in Tongues*, pp. 13–31; G. Hovenden, *Speaking in Tongues: The New Testament Evidence in Context* (Sheffield: Sheffield Academic Press, 2002); M.J. Cartledge, 'Tongues of the Spirit: An Empirical-Theological Study of Charismatic Glossolalia' (unpublished doctoral dissertation, University of Wales, 1999); idem (ed.), *Speaking in Tongues: Multi-Disciplinary Perspectives* (Carlisle: Paternoster Press, 2006); H.G. Baker, 'Pentecostal Experience: Towards a Reconstructive Theology of Glossolalia' (unpublished doctoral dissertation, King's College, London University, 1996); for sociological perspectives, see Poloma, *The Assemblies of God*, pp. 33–8, 47–50; W.H. Horton (ed.), *The Glossolalia Phenomenon* (Cleveland: Pathway, 1966); H.N. Maloney, A.A. Lovekin, *Glossolalia: Behavioral Science Perspectives on Speaking in Tongues* (New York: Oxford University Press, 1985), pp. 22–38; F.D. Macchia, 'Sighs Too Deep for Words: Toward a Theology of Glossolalia', *JPT* 1 (1992), pp. 47–73 (50–4); J.M. Ford, 'Toward a Theology of "Speaking in Tongues"', *Theological Studies* 32 (1971), pp. 3–29.

[249] For socio-scientific studies, see W.J. Samarin, *Tongues of Men and Angels* (New York: MacMillan, 1972); F.D. Goodman, *Speaking in Tongues* (London: University of Chicago Press, 1972); J.L. Henderson, 'A Sociolinguistic Analysis of Glossolalia' (unpublished doctoral dissertation, Northwestern University, 1997); W.J. Rarick, 'The Socio-Cultural Context of Glossolalia: A Comparison of Pentecostal and

phenomenological,[250] socio-scientific,[251] psychological[252] or multidisciplinary[253] reasons for the phenomenon. MacDonald robustly concludes 'Biblical glossolalia has no antecedents, no precedents, no parallels – in the Old Testament,

Neo-Pentecostal Religious Behaviour' (unpublished doctoral dissertation, Graduate School of Psychology, Fuller Theological Seminary, 1982); K.A.B. Phipps, 'Glossolalia and Health: The Perceived Effect in Health Promotion' (unpublished doctoral dissertation, University of Indiana, 1993); M.M.B. Turner, 'Early Christian Experience and Theology of "Tongues" – A New Testament Perspective', in Cartledge (ed.), *Speaking in Tongues*, pp. 1–33 (11–20); J.K.A. Smith, 'Tongues as "Resistance Discourse" – A Philosophical Perspective', in Cartledge (ed.), *Speaking in Tongues*, pp. 81–110; D. Hilborn, 'Glossolalia as Communication – A Linguistic-Pragmatic Perspective', in Cartledge (ed.), *Speaking in Tongues*, pp. 111–46; V.S. Poythress, 'Linguistic and Sociological Analyses of Modern Tongues-Speaking: Their Contributions and Limitations', in Mills (ed.), *Speaking in Tongues*, pp. 469–89; M.T. Motley, 'A Linguistic Analysis of Glossolalia: Evidence of Unique Psycholinguistic Meaning', *Communication Quarterly* 30.1 (1981), pp. 18–27.

[250] J. Ruthven, 'Is Glossolalia Languages?', *Paraclete* 2 (1968), pp. 27–30; for phenomenological studies, see C.G. Williams, *Tongues of the Spirit: A Study of Pentecostal Glossolalia and Related Phenomena* (Cardiff: University of Wales Press, 1981).

[251] For behavioural and socio-scientific studies, see Maloney and Lovekin, *Glossolalia: Behavioral Science Perspectives*; M.M. Poloma, 'Glossolalia, Liminality and Empowered Kingdom Building – A Sociological Perspective', in Cartledge (ed.), *Speaking in Tongues*, pp. 147–73 (151–54).

[252] For psychological studies, see J.P. Kildahl, *The Psychology of Speaking in Tongues* (London: Hodder and Stoughton, 1972); A.A. Lovekin, 'Religious Glossolalia: A Longitudinal Study of Personality Changes' (unpublished doctoral dissertation, Graduate School of Psychology, Fuller Theological Seminary, 1975); R.L. Pavelsky, 'The Physiological Correlates of Acts and Process Glossolalia as a Function of Socio-Economic Class, Expectation of Glossolalia and Frequency of Glossolalic Utterance' (unpublished doctoral dissertation, Graduate School of Psychology: Fuller Theological Seminary, 1975); J.L. Smith, 'Glossolalia, Manual', in Burgess and van der Maas (eds), *NIDPCM*, pp. 677–78; L.A. Mumford, 'An Expanded Psychological Understanding of Religious Glossolalia among Women' (unpublished doctoral dissertation, University of Boston, 1996); F.S. Meeks, 'Pastoral Care and Glossolalic Implications of the Contemporary Tongues Movement in American Churches' (unpublished doctoral dissertation, Southwestern Baptist Theological Seminary, 1976); H.E. Gonsalvez, 'The Theology and Psychology of Glossolalia' (unpublished doctoral dissertation, Northwestern University, 1979); J.J. Gowins, 'A Pastoral Psychological Study of Glossolalia' (unpublished doctoral dissertation, Iliff School of Theology and the University of Denver, 1990); W.K. Kay, 'The Mind, Behaviour and Glossolalia – A Psychological Perspective', in Cartledge (ed.), *Speaking in Tongues*, pp. 174–205; idem, 'Personality, Mental Health and Glossolalia', *Pneuma* 17.2 (1995), pp. 253–63; F. Stagg, E.G. Hinson, W.E. Oates, *Glossolalia: Tongues Speaking in Biblical Historical and Psychological Perspective* (New York: Abingdon Press, 1967).

[253] Cartledge, *Speaking in Tongues*; Stagg, Hinson and Oates, *Glossolalia*; Mills, *Speaking in Tongues*.

or paganism, or pathology'.[254] Kay offers an optimistic view in that he concludes that "Psychologists now tend to be studiously neutral in the study of religion. There is an unwillingness to condemn glossolalics for weird or outlandish behaviour and the advent of neurological research helps to confirm the real, as opposed to the hallucinatory, nature of glossolalia'.[255] Pentecostals dismiss suggestions that it is socio-psychologically induced,[256] the result of subconscious awareness of the languages being aroused by the experience of being filled with the Spirit or due to learned behaviour,[257] ecstasy[258] or hysteria[259] or to be identified as gibberish or babbling.[260] Indeed, Ervin concludes that 'there is nothing inherently emotional in glossolalia'.[261] They also reject the claims of some that it is satanically inspired,[262] though they are aware of its presence in pagan religions.[263] Instead, they prefer to believe that although it has certain inexplicable elements, the gift of tongues is best understood if it is viewed functionally. In other words, its role is more important than its internal mechanism. Although research on the phenomenon of tongues has resulted in a number of doctorates, they have rarely been by Pentecostals.[264] Indeed, although the topic has been the subject of significant

---

[254] W.G. MacDonald, 'Biblical Glossolalia. Thesis 3', *Paraclete* 27.2 (1993), pp. 7–14 (7).

[255] Kay, 'The Mind, Behaviour and Glossolalia', p. 262.

[256] R.P. Spittler, 'Glossolalia', in Burgess and van der Maas (eds), *NIDPCM*, pp. 670–76 (674).

[257] For which see W.J. Samarin, 'Glossolalia as Learned Behaviour', *CJT* 15 (1969), pp. 60–4.

[258] Petts, *Body Builders*, p. 118; MacDonald, 'Biblical Glossolalia. Thesis 3', p. 8; for an alternative perspective, see Williams, *Systematic Theology*, vol. 3 p. 55; Turner, 'Early Christian Experience', pp. 31–2.

[259] Brumback, *What Meaneth This?*, pp. 39–46, 104–15.

[260] W.G. MacDonald, 'Biblical Glossolalia. Thesis Four', *Paraclete* 27.3 (1993), pp. 33–43.

[261] Ervin, *Spirit Baptism*, p. 126.

[262] Brumback, *What Meaneth This?*, pp. 119–46.

[263] Spittler, 'Glossolalia', pp. 670–71; Turner, 'Early Christian Experience', pp. 29–31; see also Forbes, *Prophecy and Inspired Speech*, chs 5–6; Maloney and Lovekin, *Glossolalia: Behavioral Science Perspectives*, pp. 28–9; Samarin, *Tongues of Men*, pp. 109–15; Christie-Murray, *Voices from the Gods*, pp. 109–41; L.C. May, 'A Survey of Glossolalia and Related Phenomena in non-Christian Religions', *American Anthropologist* 58 (1956), pp. 75–96.

[264] N.I.J. Engelsen, 'Glossolalia and Other Forms of Inspired Speech according to 1 Corinthians 12–14' (unpublished doctoral dissertation, University of Yale, 1970); M.E. Hart, 'Speaking in Tongues and Prophecy as Understood by Paul at Corinth, with reference to early Christian usage' (unpublished doctoral dissertation, University of Durham, 1975); W.E. Richardson, 'Liturgical Order and Glossolalia in 1 Corinthians 14.26c–33a' (unpublished doctoral dissertation, Seventh Day Adventist Theological Seminary, 1983); C.F. Robertson, 'The Nature of New Testament Glossolalia' (unpublished doctoral dissertation, Dallas Theological Seminary, 1975); N.G. Aubrey, 'The Nature of New Testament Glossolalia' (unpublished doctoral dissertation, Dallas Theological Seminary, 1975).

interest to some non-Pentecostals, until recently, it has received little other than pastoral and historical comment by Pentecostals.[265] This may be due, in part, to the pragmatic recognition that this is a gift to be used rather than discussed. Even its linguistic properties are viewed as having little significance and therefore little time has been spent on attempting to analyse or explore it phenomenologically.[266] MacDonald deduces that it 'bears the character of language'[267] though Turner provides substantial evidence for the opposite view that 'it is fundamentally non-linguistic'.[268] Pentecostals are less interested in determining whether it can function as a language, has linguistic forms or can be accurately translated. It is less important to define glossolalia and more important to experience and realize that which it does for the speaker and hearer.

The gift of tongues is best understood as an extemporaneous or spontaneous manifestation in a form that is a quasi-language. The speaker is in control of her/his speech and the forming of the sounds; the Spirit does not manipulate or coerce the speaker into a particular speech pattern. It is possible that the sounds themselves already existed in the mind and experience of the speaker, being reconstituted in the form of the tongues s/he employs though it also possible that they are previously unimagined phonetic forms. Most Pentecostals have concluded that speaking in tongues is a phenomenon that has divine and human elements in that the Spirit inspires the manifestation but the person articulates the sounds.[269]

It is difficult to be certain as to the percentage of Pentecostals who regularly speak in tongues, Poloma writing, 'In some Classical Pentecostal circles, glossolalia is in danger of becoming a doctrine devoid of experience with an estimated 50% or more of followers reporting that they do not speak in tongues'.[270] Indeed, apparently, more Charismatic believers speak in tongues in the USA than Pentecostals.[271]

---

[265] J.T. Bunn, 'Glossolalia in Historical Perspective", in Mills, *Speaking in Tongues*, pp. 165–203; D.N. Hudson, 'Strange Words and Their Impact on Early Pentecostals – A Historical Perspective', in Cartledge (ed.), *Speaking in Tongues*', pp. 52–80; E.G. Hinson, 'Glossolalia in Historical Perspective', in Mills, *Speaking in Tongues*, pp. 165–203 (181–203).

[266] For some exploration, see Mills, *Speaking in Tongues*, sects 4–5; MacDonald, 'Biblical Glossolalia. Thesis Four', pp. 32–43.

[267] MacDonald, 'Pentecostal Theology', p. 72.

[268] Turner, 'Early Christian Experience', pp. 11–20; Ford, 'Toward a Theology', pp. 3–29; Ervin, *Spirit Baptism*, pp. 135–36.

[269] Gee, *Concerning Spiritual Gifts*, p. 58; D. Petts, *The Dynamic Difference* (Springfield: Gospel Publishing House, 1978), p. 35.

[270] Poloma, 'Glossolalia', p. 151; Chan, *Pentecostal Theology*, p. 8; B. Charette, 'Reflective Speech: Glossolalia and the Image of God', *Pneuma* 28.2 (2006), pp. 189–201 (189).

[271] Lugo (*Spirit and Power*, p. 14) records that 49% of Pentecostals in the USA never speak in tongues as contrasted to 32% of Charismatic Christians. Of the ten countries

The rules of tongues and interpretation

Most Pentecostals assume that the Pauline advice that a manifestation of tongues should occur no more than three times in a given setting (1 Cor. 14.27) is to be taken literally[272] though others assume that the issue of orderliness rather than frequency of use is most important. Increasingly, it has been questioned whether his advice should be viewed as timeless or specifically for the Corinthian church that had abused the gift of tongues.[273] Brumback argues that the one who receives the gift of interpretation should normally be the one who spoke in tongues[274] while affirming that the interpretations should be offered by one person at a time (1 Cor. 14.28). However, although the one speaking in tongues may pray for the ability to interpret those tongues, others may also appropriately do so. The form of the interpretation has also received some enquiry. The general assumption is that an interpretation may be shorter or longer in length than the original glossolalia.[275] The personality of the one interpreting is also assumed to have a bearing on the formulation of the content though the latter should substantially be the same whoever offers the interpretation.[276]

Speaking and singing in tongues corporately without any interpretation is a phenomenon that often occurs in Pentecostal gatherings, generally as an expression of worship or prayer and many Pentecostals testify to its emotional and spiritual benefits.[277] Although 1 Cor. 14.13–20 indicates that such a practice is inappropriate (at least, in Corinth), it nevertheless still occurs, the reference to 'spiritual songs' in Col. 3.16 (1 Cor. 14.15) being used to support the phenomenon. It could be suggested that Paul's advice concerning its circumscribed use was specifically intended for the first century Corinthian church due to the fact that they had so severely abused it.

---

surveyed, an average of 40% of Pentecostals never speak in tongues (ranging from 54% (India) to 18% (South Korea)) while only an average of 37% speak in tongues weekly or more regularly (ranging from 25% (Chile) to 53% (Guatemala); see also Kay, *Pentecostals in Britain*, p. 74–5.

[272] Brumback, *What Meaneth This?*, p. 309; Rowe, *One Lord, One Faith*, p. 183.

[273] Canty, *The Practice of Pentecost*, pp. 199–200; Petts, *Body Builders*, pp. 131–32.

[274] Brumback, *What Meaneth This?*, p. 304; Horton, *What the Bible Says*, p. 232.

[275] Conn, *A Balanced Church*, pp. 141–42; Brumback, *What Meaneth This?*, p. 306; Arrington, *Christian Doctrine*, p. 157.

[276] Brumback, *What Meaneth This?*, p. 307; Petts, *Body Builders*, p. 130.

[277] W. Ma, 'Doing Theology in the Philippines: A Case of Pentecostal Christianity', *AJPS* 8.2 (2005), pp. 215–33 (220); M.J. Cartledge, 'The Practice of Tongues-Speech as a Case Study – A Practical-Theological Perspective', in Cartledge (ed.), *Speaking in Tongues*, pp. 206–34 (210); C.M. Johansson, 'Singing in the Spirit', *Paraclete* 24.2 (1990), pp. 20–3.

Underlying significance and purposes

Although it is sometimes, with the gift of interpretation, placed at the end of the Pauline lists of charismata (1 Cor. 12.10, 30), Pentecostals value speaking in tongues and recognize that it is intrinsically equal to other charismata.[278] Pentecostals generally understand speaking in tongues as having a number of purposes.

- Many believe that it signifies that one has experienced the baptism in the Spirit,[279] though others are less convinced.[280] The evidence for it being a sign of the baptism in the Spirit tends to be drawn from Acts while the references concerning tongues in the Pauline literature are generally viewed as information provided to guide the believer in its use in personal and public worship. In other words, the gift of tongues is viewed by many as having two distinct purposes, the one as a sign of the baptism in the Spirit, the other offering ongoing personal benefit for prayer and praise.
- The use of tongues in a private context is often described as a prayer-language.[281] Thus, it provides an opportunity for a dramatic and intensely personal union of the human with the divine.[282] Charette identifies tongues

---

[278] D.R. Bundrick, 'Equal for Edification: A Response to "Biblical Glossolalia-Thesis 7" and Its Critics', *Paraclete* 29.1 (1995), pp. 1–12 (7–9).

[279] R. Hurst, 'Practical Empowerment for Everyday Living', *Enrichment* 10.1 (2005), pp. 88–91 (91); D. Petts, *The Holy Spirit – An Introduction* (Mattersey: Mattersey Hall, 1998), pp. 70–8; M.W. Dempster ('The Structure of a Christian Ethic Informed by Pentecostal Experience: Surroundings in the Moral Significance of Glossolalia', in Ma and Menzies (eds), *The Spirit and Spirituality*, pp. 108–40 (111)) describes it as 'an indigenous part of Spirit baptism' and not '*only* a sign'.

[280] V-M. Kärkkäinen, *Spiritus Ubi Vult Spirat: Pneumatology in Roman Catholic – Pentecostal Dialogue 1972–1989* (Helsinki: Luther-Agricola-Society, 1998), p. 379; M.M. Poloma ('Pentecostal Prayer as a Complementary Healing Practice within the Assemblies of God' (SPS conference paper, Cleveland, 2007), pp. 275–278 (277)) identified, among US AoG believers, that 77% expressed a belief that they had been baptized in the Spirit while only 66% reported they spoke in tongues. In the same survey, 51% agreed or strongly agreed that tongues are the initial evidence of the baptism in the Spirit while 20% disagreed or strongly disagreed, 18% being uncertain. However, only 32% agreed or strongly agreed that a person who has never spoken in tongues cannot already be baptized in the Spirit.

[281] J. Hayford, *The Beauty of Spiritual Language: My Journey toward the Heart of God* (Dallas: Word, 1992), pp. 95–8; Land, *Pentecostal Spirituality*, p. 111; Hollenweger, *The Pentecostals*, p. 342; Turner, 'Early Christian Experience', pp. 23–6; Keener, *Three Crucial Questions*, p. 75; Bertone, 'The Experience of Glossolalia', pp. 54–65.

[282] S.K.H. Chan, 'The Language Game of Glossolalia, or Making Sense of the "Initial Evidence"',in Ma and Menzies (eds), *Pentecostalism in Context*, pp. 80–95 (86); Smith, 'Tongues as "Resistance Discourse"', p. 110; See further R. Hutch, 'The Personal Ritual of Glossolalia"', in Mills, *Speaking in Tongues*, 1986), pp. 381–95; A. Yong, 'The Truth of Tongues Speech: A Rejoinder to Frank Macchia', *JPT* 13 (1998), pp. 107–15.

as demonstrating 'a unique encounter with God', insofar as believers use a divinely imparted language form through which they speak to God.[283] Paul, in particular, provides evidence for this (1 Cor. 14.2, 4, 28), referring to praying in tongues (1 Cor. 14.15). Steinberg suggests that it may also be related to the personal spiritual development of the individual being used in 'spiritual warfare',[284] as a defence against temptation or negative emotions or to protect one's mind.[285] MacDonald argues that glossolalia provides 'a new level of intimacy . . . with God' because communing in tongues with God provides a context for authentic prayer and Spirit-inspired content.[286] Rybarczyk, exploring tongues through the lens of apophatic theology, concludes that speaking in tongues is a God-created mode of communion with him which, as a result of bypassing the mind, enables the worshipper to experience God in a superior way than cognitive dialogue ever could.[287] Fundamentally, the manifestation of the gift of tongues thus functions as a symbol of the presence of God, his closeness and his mystery, his immanence and his transcendence, in the Christian community.[288]

- Paul declares that the use of tongues has the capacity to edify the speaker (1 Cor. 14.4) though does not clarify the specific nature of that edification. In speaking in tongues, the speakers anticipate that the Spirit will be empowering them and, in that respect, there is the potential for their being edified.[289]

- Glossolalia is also valuable as a sign that the tongues speaker is now part of a charismatic community and therefore is expected to function in charismatic ministry.[290] In particular, whenever glossolalia was experienced, in its historical setting in Acts, it removed barriers of class and race, affirmed non-Jews as valid members of the new Christian community and allowed for the integration of all into the newly constituted community of God (Acts 10.46; 11.15).[291] In this regard, it may be viewed as a reversal of

---

[283] Charette, 'Reflective Speech', p. 197.

[284] H.W. Steinberg, 'Utterance Gifts and the Believer's Responsibility', *Paraclete* 26.2 (1992), pp. 1–6 (3).

[285] Poloma, 'Glossolalia', pp. 161–69; Cartledge, *Charismatic*, p. 88.

[286] W.G. MacDonald, 'Biblical Glossolalia. Thesis 6', *Paraclete* 28.1 (1994), pp 23–6 (25).

[287] E.J. Rybarczyk, 'Reframing Tongues: Apophaticism and Postmodernism', *Pneuma* 27.1 (2005) pp. 83–104 (90–6).

[288] F.D. Macchia, 'Tongues and Prophecy. A Pentecostal Perspective', in Moltmann and Kuschel (eds), *Pentecostal Movements*, pp. 63–9 (64); Samarin, *Tongues of Men*, p. 154.

[289] Fee ('Toward a Pauline Theology ', p. 25) argues that the value of tongues is best understood when it is viewed as a sign of one's weakness, as particularly contrasted with the perception of the Corinthians that it indicated spiritual authority on their part. However, there is little evidence that Paul has this suggestion in mind.

[290] J.E. Powers, 'Missionary Tongues?', *JPT* 17 (Oct. 2000), pp. 39–55 (52–3).

Babel where language became the reason for the disintegration of the society[292] and a remaking of history by the Spirit in the initiation of the Church.[293] Macchia identifies it as the 'first ecumenical language of the church',[294] demonstrating the unity available to believers because of their common experience in Christ as facilitated by the Spirit.[295] It indicates that which is centrally important to Jesus (Jn 13.34–35; 17.21–23) and the Spirit (Eph. 4.2) – the unity of the Church. The Spirit's gift of tongues, available to all believers, is thus a means of reminding individuals of their equal place within the Church, breaking through all racial and economic divisions.[296] Furthermore, since most Pentecostals come from the Majority world, the gift of tongues may be identified as the language of the poor, 'the language of the dispossessed – or the language of the "multitude"'.[297] As a sign, it also highlights truths including the fact that God functions through weakness, that all believers can benefit from God's resources, that God's gifts do not result from human endeavour or natural talent and that he enables believers to communicate with him.

• Although some anticipate their value to unbelievers (1 Cor. 14.20–22),[298] most Pentecostals are wary of this perspective. Paul identifies tongues as

[291] See also Powers, 'Missionary Tongues?', pp. 54–5; M.W. Dempster, 'The Church's Moral Witness: A Study of Glossolalia in Luke's Theology of Acts', *Paraclete* 23.1 (1989), pp. 1–7; F.D. Macchia, 'Babel and the Tongues of Pentecost: Reversal or Fulfilment? – A Theological Perspective', in Cartledge (ed.), *Speaking in Tongues*, pp. 34–51 (35); idem, 'Tongues and Prophecy', p. 64–5.

[292] T.B. Edwards, 'Babel or Pentecost?', *Paraclete* 25.1 (1991), pp. 4–9; R.P. Menzies, 'Coming to Terms with an Evangelical Heritage-Part 2', *Paraclete* 28.4 (1994), pp. 1–10 (9); Land, *Pentecostal Spirituality*, pp. 111, 130.

[293] Dempster, 'The Church's Moral Witness', pp. 1–7.

[294] Macchia, 'Babel and the Tongues of Pentecost', p. 47; idem, 'The Tongues of Pentecost: The Promise and Challenge of Pentecostal/Roman Catholic Dialogue', *Journal of Ecumenical Studies*, 35.1 (1998), pp. 1–18.

[295] Macchia, 'Babel and the Tongues of Pentecost', pp. 36–51; Chan, *Pentecostal Theology*, p. 52.

[296] Dempster, 'The Church's Moral Witness', *Paraclete* 23.1 (1989), pp. 1–7; Chan, *Pentecostal Theology*, p. 103; A. Ayers, 'Can the Behavior of Tongues Utterance still Function as Ecclesial Boundary? The Significance of Art and Sacrament', *Pneuma* 22.2 (2000), pp. 271–301 (274–79); B. Charette, '"Tongues as of fire": Judgment as a Function of Glossolalia in Luke's Thought', *JPT* 13.2 (2005), pp. 173–86; F.D. Macchia, 'Glossolalia', in Burgess (ed.), *EPCC*, pp. 223–25 (224).

[297] Smith, 'Tongues as "Resistance Discourse"', p. 109.

[298] Brumback (*What Meaneth This?*, p. 330) believes that tongues have value in attracting the attention of unbelievers, as reflected in Acts 2.13–14; see R.J. Gladstone, 'Sign Languages in the Assembly: How Are Tongues a Sign to the Unbeliever in 1 Cor 14:20–25', *AJPS* 2.2 (1999), pp. 177–93.

having the potential of confirming unbelievers in their unbelief (1 Cor. 14. 20–22), a negative, not a redemptive, sign. Thus, Paul quotes from Isa. 28.11 where the Jews did not listen to God's prophets when they spoke of judgement, so he sent the same message actualized through the invading armies of foreign nations who spoke different languages. The Jews did not understand the languages of the foreign invaders but the content was of judgement, the same as that previously spoken by their prophets. Speaking in tongues that could not be understood did not lead to repentance but ushered in judgement. Likewise, although some assume that the crowds referred to in Acts 2 became believers having heard the believers speaking in tongues, their salvation is recorded only after Peter preaches his sermon (Acts 2.41).

In early Pentecostalism, the gift of tongues was assumed incorrectly to provide the means whereby missionary activity could take place without the need for the learning of languages, the gift of tongues being assumed to be a divinely inspired ability to communicate in a given language.[299] However, this belief did not last long as the expectation was not fulfilled in the lives of the vast majority, Wacker describing it quickly 'receding into the hazy realm of Pentecostal mythology'.[300] Nevertheless, many testimonies of human languages being spoken in the form of tongues are available that support the notion that the gift of tongues can function as xenolalia (speaking (human) languages).[301]

• The gift of tongues has also been identified as a liberating or empowering act,[302] Hollenweger viewing it as a possible motivation for social transformation.[303] Similarly, Dempster indicates that since glossolalia is one

---

[299] L.G. McClung, 'Explosion, Motivation, and Consolidation: The Historical Anatomy of a Missionary Movement', in McClung, *Azusa Street and Beyond*, pp. 3–20 (12–4); C.M. Robeck Jr, 'An Emerging Magisterium? The Case of the Assemblies of God', in Ma and Menzies (eds), *The Spirit and Spirituality*, pp. 212–52 (219–21); Hudson, 'Strange Words', p. 61.

[300] Wacker, *Heaven Below*, p. 51.

[301] Conn, *A Balanced Church*, p. 138; Canty, *The Practice of Pentecost*, p. 123; Ruthven, 'Is Glossolalia Languages?', pp. 27–30; Powers, 'Missionary Tongues?', pp. 49–50; T.R. Edgar, *Miraculous Gifts* (New Jersey: Loiseaux, 1983), pp. 110–94; J.R. Goff Jr, 'Initial Tongues in the Theology of Charles Fox Parham', in G.B. McGee (ed.), *Initial Evidence: Historical and Biblical Perspectives on the Pentecostal Doctrine of Spirit Baptism* (Peabody: Hendrickson, 1991), pp. 57–71 (64); Hudson, 'Strange Words', pp. 52–80 (59–63); D.W. Faupel, 'Glossolalia as Foreign Language: An Investigation of the Early Twentieth-Century Pentecostal Claim', *WTJ* 31.1 (1996), pp. 95–109; A.H. Anderson, 'Burning Its Way into Every Nation: The Experience of the Spirit in Early Pentecostal Mission' (SPS conference paper, Cleveland, 2007), pp. 1–15 (5–8); Faupel, *The Everlasting Gospel*, p. 23.

[302] Dempster, 'The Structure of a Christian Ethic', p. 116;

[303] W.J. Hollenweger, *Pentecostalism. Origins and Developments Worldwide* (Peabody: Hendrickson, 1997), pp. 201–07.

particular expression of the divine-human encounter, as a result of which the flawed believer engages with the morally sacred divine, it provides 'a spiritual encounter with the God who is, and a moral encounter with the God who values'.[304] As a result of this, a change is expected in the morality of the believer.

Content of tongues and interpretation

The NT, other than Acts 2.6, indicates that an earthly language is not being assumed by the writers when they refer to glossolalia. Acts 2.6, which details an occasion when people heard their languages being spoken by others who did not naturally know them, is generally understood to describe xenolalia whereby the verbal expression is understandable to the hearer without the need for an interpretation. A few have suggested that in Acts 2.6, the glossolalia was accompanied by a miracle of hearing on the part of the observers, resulting in their being able to understand the content of the tongues.[305] Macchia offers the possibility that this was a unique occasion intended to mimic the Sinaitic giving of the Law in the language of the recipients.[306] Spittler views glossolalia and xenolalia as phenomenologically the same[307] though others seek to distinguish between the former language forms.[308]

For many years, the common perception of many Pentecostals has been that tongues and interpretation are equivalent to prophecy in that both result in information being presented to the hearers.[309] Thus, the concept of 'a message in tongues' has been common among Pentecostals, the message being from God to people.[310] Bundrick[311] suggests that Acts 2.11, which states that people heard the believers declaring the wonders of God in

---

[304] Dempster, 'The Structure of a Christian Ethic', p. 115; Macchia, 'Theology, Pentecostal', p. 1133.

[305] Turner, 'Early Christian Experience', p. 4; see J.M. Everts, 'Tongues or Languages? Contextual Consistency in the Translation of Acts 2', *JPT* 4 (1994), pp. 71–80 for an alternative view.

[306] Macchia, 'Glossolalia', p. 224.

[307] Spittler, 'Glossolalia', p. 672.

[308] See the history of the debate in the American AoG in Robeck, 'An Emerging Magisterium?', pp. 217–42; also T.B. Barratt, *In the Days of the Latter Rain* (London: Elim Publishing, 1928), p. 72; Jeffreys, *Pentecostal Rays*, p. 36; Hathaway, *Spiritual Gifts*, p. 113.

[309] So, Conn, *A Balanced Church*, pp. 133–34, 141; Riggs, *The Spirit Himself*, pp. 87, 166; Canty, *The Practice of Pentecost*, p. 115–17; R.P. Spittler, 'Interpretation of Tongues, Gift of', in Burgess and van der Maas (eds), *NIDPCM*, pp. 801–02; Land, *Pentecostal Spirituality*, 172; Bicket, *We Hold These Truths*, p. 58; Horton, *What the Bible Says*, p. 226; Ervin, *Spirit Baptism*, pp. 129–32, 166.

[310] Brumback, *What Meaneth This?*, p. 302–04.

[311] Bundrick, 'Equal for Edification ', p. 6; K.C. Keene, 'A Response to "Biblical Glossolalia-Thesis 7"', *Paraclete* 29.1 (1995), pp. 26–8.

their own languages supports the idea of tongues being directed to people, not God, on other occasions. However, it is not clear from the text that the believers were speaking to people; the author identifies the believers glorifying God in tongues, the contents simply being understood by the hearers. Nevertheless, Aker concludes that when an interpretation is offered, the 'message' in tongues may be received by the hearers as a revelation from God.[312]

This perspective has increasingly been called into question.[313] Part of this shift has been due to the fact that (excluding Acts 2.6) on the occasions when tongues are referred to in the NT, the contents are prayer or praise[314] and are directed to God, not believers.[315] MacDonald concludes, 'Glossolalia is always directed to God, and only to Him'.[316] There is no biblical support for the suggestion that the gift of tongues was intended to be a means whereby God communicated with believers; neither is there any indication that when a tongue is interpreted, it becomes equivalent to prophecy.[317] Those who argue that interpretations of tongues should be viewed as expressions of prayer or praise to God have also suggested that the interpretations that often occur in Pentecostal gatherings more likely result from well intended but mistaken believers who assume they have received them from God, or may be prophetic utterances mistakenly linked with tongues. It is possible that received Pentecostal traditions that have assumed that interpretations of tongues are intended to be prophetic messages have resulted in the promulgation of this practice.[318] Alternatively, it may be argued that the NT does not provide all the information needed to comprehensively identify the purpose of the gift of tongues; thus, the practice of many to associate interpretation with a message to believers may be appropriate even though NT evidence does not support it, Spittler, concluding that attempts to limit the interpretations 'seem needlessly restrictive'.[319]

---

[312] B.C. Aker, 'The Gift of Tongues in 1 Corinthians 14:1–5', *Paraclete* 29.1 (1995), pp. 13–21 (18–9).

[313] B. Caldwell, 'A Pastor's Reaction to William MacDonald's "Biblical Glossolalia"', *Paraclete* 29.1 (1995), pp. 22–5.

[314] Acts 2.11; 10.46; 1 Cor. 14.2, 14–16.

[315] 1 Cor. 14.2, 14–16, 28.

[316] W.G. MacDonald, 'Biblical Glossolalia. Thesis 7', *Paraclete* 28.2 (1994), pp. 1–12 (1); Lim, *Spiritual Gifts*, pp. 140–41, 144; R.L. Brandt, *Charismatics, Are We Missing Something?* (Plainfield: Logos International, 1981), p. 55; Fee, *1 Corinthians*, p. 656; R.K. Levang, 'The Content of an Utterance in Tongues', *Paraclete* 23.1 (1989), pp. 14–20.

[317] Fee, 'Toward a Pauline Theology', p. 33; Schatzmann, 'The Gifts of the Spirit', pp. 92–3.

[318] MacDonald, 'Pentecostal Theology', pp. 72–3.

[319] Spittler, 'Interpretation of Tongues', p. 802; D. Lim, 'Many Gifts, One Spirit', *Paraclete* 26.4 (1992), pp. 3–7 (5).

Perhaps this uncertainty partly explains the decrease of tongues and interpretation in Pentecostal churches today, in addition to a prolonged diet of repetitious, simple and simplistic interpretations over the years. Poloma, in a survey of US AoG believers, identified 70% who have never spoken in tongues in expectation of an interpretation and 83% who have never offered an interpretation, concluding that 'this once common practice appears to be disappearing from many AG congregations'.[320] Guidance needs to be offered to acquaint Pentecostals with the value and relevance of this gift to their ongoing development as believers for it is a gift from God intended to 'become the "occasion" for a new theophany and a new level of intimacy with God'.[321]

The Baptism in the Spirit

Introduction

A main distinctive of Pentecostalism is the baptism in the Spirit.[322] Although it is acknowledged that the term 'baptism in the Spirit' is not located in the NT, the concept is mentioned in each of the Gospels (Mt. 3.11; Mk 1.8; Lk. 3.16; Jn 1.33) as well as Acts (1.5; 11.16) and the Pauline literature (1 Cor. 12.13), and the experience resonates throughout Pentecostalism and is the basis for a significant amount of literature written by Pentecostals. Harrell writes, 'It was this craving for the baptism of the Holy Spirit that set Pentecostals apart from other evangelicals'.[323] However, the baptism in the Spirit has been interpreted in different ways by believers in and outside of Pentecostalism resulting in a reframing of the doctrine by some Pentecostals.[324] Thus, while many Pentecostals affirm the propositional nature of the

---

[320] Poloma, 'Pentecostal Prayer', p. 277.

[321] Chan, *Pentecostal Theology*, p. 78.

[322] Bond, 'What Is Distinctive', in Clark and Lederle (eds), *What Is Distinctive*, pp. 133–42 (134); S.K.H. Chan, 'Evidential Glossolalia and the Doctrine of Subsequence', *AJPS* 2.2 (1999) pp. 195–211; Anderson, *Zion and Pentecost*, p. 244; Dunn, *Baptism in the Holy Spirit*, pp. 23–44; Alvarez, 'The South', p. 141; H.I. Lederle, *Treasures Old and New: Interpretations of 'Spirit-Baptism' in the Charismatic Renewal Movement* (Peabody: Hendrickson, 1988), p. xi; Dye, 'Are Pentecostals Pentecostal?', *JEPTA* 19 (1999), p. 60; Oneness Pentecostals have a different understanding of the baptism in the Spirit which associates it more closely with repentance, faith and water baptism in the name of Jesus.

[323] D.E. Harrell, 'Foreword', in Smith (ed.), *Pentecostals from the Inside Out*, pp. 9–16 (10).

[324] T.A.C. Bush, 'The Development of the Perception of the Baptism in the Holy Spirit within the Pentecostal Movement in Great Britain', *EB* 11. 1–2 (1992), pp. 24–41; Dayton, *Theological Roots of Pentecostalism*, pp. 87–113; R. Lovelace, 'Baptism in the Holy Spirit and the Evangelical Tradition', in Elbert (ed.), *Faces of Renewal*, pp. 209–36; Lederle, *Treasures Old and New*; N.C. Dionson, 'The Doctrine of the

baptism in the Spirit and defend it biblically,[325] others accept the validity of the experience but question the biblically based justification often offered for it by Pentecostals.[326] The discussion is not helped by the fact that the experience is referred to by a variety of terms including 'being filled with the Spirit' which can lead to confusion especially where the NT uses the same phrase to describe different experiences.[327] It is probable that the attempts to identify the most accurate definition of the baptism in the Spirit are not perceived as being relevant to most Pentecostals. They have benefited from the experience and are more impressed by that than a comprehensive explanation and articulation of its nature. Indeed, it is possible that too much scholarly attention has been focused on a biblical articulation of the doctrine instead of an exploration of the experience itself. The former has resulted in a significant variety of views while the omission of the latter has contributed to the decrease in popularity of the experience for many Pentecostals.

Further complicating the issue is the variety of uses of the term 'baptism in the Spirit' employed by believers. Historically, the term 'baptism in the Spirit' was used by Methodist-Wesleyan and Holiness believers in the nineteenth century to describe an event that was associated with an experience of sanctification, believed to occur after conversion.[328] Later, believers, associated

---

Baptism in the Holy Spirit: From a Pentecostal Pastor's Uneasy Chair', *AJPS* 2.2 (1999), pp. 233–42; Schatzmann, 'The Gifts of the Spirit', pp. 83–5; J.S. Clifton, 'The Spirit and Doctrinal Development: A Functional Analysis of the Traditional Pentecostal Doctrine of the Baptism in the Holy Spirit', *Pneuma* 29.1 (2007), pp. 5–23; D.L. Gelpi, 'Pentecostal Theology: A Roman Catholic Viewpoint', in Spittler (ed.), *Perspectives on the New Pentecostalism*, pp. 86–103; C.H. Pinnock, 'The New Pentecostalism: Reflections of an Evangelical Observer', in Spittler (ed.), *Perspectives on the New Pentecostalism*, pp. 182–92; J.M. Ford, 'The New Pentecostalism: Personal Reflections of a Participating Roman Catholic Scholar', in Spittler (ed.), *Perspectives on the New Pentecostalism*, pp. 208–29; N. Baumert, '"Charism" and "Spirit-Baptism": Presentation of an Analysis', *JPT* 12.2 (2004), pp. 147–79; J.W. Wyckoff, 'The Baptism in the Holy Spirit', in Horton (ed.), *Systematic Theology*, pp. 423–55; K.D. Yun, *Baptism in the Holy Spirit: An Ecumenical Theology of Spirit Baptism* (Lanham: University of America Press, 2003); R. Wessels, 'The Spirit Baptism, Nineteenth Century Roots', *Pneuma* 14.2 (1992), pp. 127–57; W.J. Hollenweger, 'Rethinking Spirit Baptism: The Natural and the Supernatural', in Anderson and Hollenweger (eds), *Pentecostals after a Century*, pp. 164–72.

[325] Menzies, *Spirit and Power*, pp. 109–44, 189–208.

[326] Fee, *Gospel and Spirit*; Schatzmann, 'The Gifts of the Spirit', pp. 83–5; Macchia, *Baptized in the Spirit*, pp. 61–8.

[327] R.C. Cunningham, 'The Importance of the Spirit's Fullness', *Paraclete* (Fall 1967), pp. 14–17; C.L. Holman, 'What Does It Mean Today to be Spirit-Filled? Ephesians and Ecumenism (or Ecumenical Pneumatology)', *SC* 4.2 (2002), pp. 151–60; J.B. Shelton, '"Filled with the Holy Spirit" and "Full of the Holy Spirit": Lucan Redactional Phrases', in Elbert (ed.), *Faces of Renewal*, pp. 81–107.

with the Keswick conferences (that took place in England from 1875 to the present), coupled the concept of the baptism in the Spirit with the belief that the recipients would be empowered to adopt a Christian lifestyle more completely as well as an expectation that it was to be the precursor of a restoration of miracles. By the beginning of the twentieth century, the term was used much more regularly to refer to a post-conversion experience that was associated, by some, with speaking in tongues and, by many, with power to witness for Christ. Over time, the belief in a crisis experience of sanctification (as contrasted to a lifestyle of increasing commitment to God and an absorption of his character into one's own through personal discipline and the work of the Spirit) was reduced, although it is present in some Pentecostal denominations today.

The challenge for Pentecostals is to adequately conceptualize the baptism in the Spirit in such a way that the validity and authenticity of the experience can be supported as well as enjoyed. Chan's accurate perception is that it is often presented inadequately to second generation Pentecostals resulting in many of them not actualizing it personally.[329] It may be of interest to note, in this context, that Harvey Cox does not include a discussion of the baptism in the Spirit as a separate experience in *Fire from Heaven*. Furthermore, Macchia deduces that 'Spirit baptism is no longer regarded as the most distinctive Pentecostal doctrine or as having central significance to Pentecostal theology without qualification or even rejection among leading Pentecostal theologians or historians'.[330] Although he overstates his case, the very fact that he, a Pentecostal, could articulate such a view indicates that there has been a significant shift in Pentecostal emphasis.

There is, at present, a desire to retain the experience but a readiness to articulate it in terminology other than that historically used and to defend it from a different perspective other than a strictly biblical one based in the book of Acts. Macchia has offered a number of reasons why this is an appropriate task.[331] Similarly, Fee, while uncomfortable with the beliefs of subsequence and initial evidence, nevertheless affirms the dynamic empowering presence of the Spirit as well as the experience of the baptism of the Spirit as biblically based concepts.[332]

---

[328] See R.H. Gause, *Church of God Polity* (Cleveland: Pathway Press, 1958), p. 159; Hughes, *Church of God Distinctives*, pp. 30–5; J. Campbell, *The Pentecostal Holiness Church: 1898–1948: Its Background and History* (Franklin Springs: Pentecostal Holiness Church, 1951), p. 195.

[329] Chan, *Pentecostal Theology*, pp. 10–13.

[330] Macchia, *Baptized in the Spirit*, p. 23.

[331] Macchia, *Baptized in the Spirit*, pp. 27–8.

[332] Fee, *Gospel and Spirit*, p. 111.

Another cause of confusion relates to the variety of guidelines that have been offered to enable people to experience the baptism in the Spirit. Pentecostals have articulated a number of conditions that need to be fulfilled prior to the baptism in the Spirit though these have not always been carefully identified.[333] What is at times incongruous is that some of these are more stringent than those needed to receive salvation. Pentecostals generally teach that ultimately it is God's prerogative as to when he bestows the baptism in the Spirit though they also assume that since the only prerequisite is conversion, the experience is open to all believers.[334]

Fundamentally, repentance leading to salvation (Acts 8.12, 17), a desire to be baptized in the Spirit (Lk. 11.13; Acts 1.14; 4.31; 8.15)[335] and a readiness to worship[336] are identified as important precursors to the baptism in the Spirit. Another important qualification for the baptism in the Spirit was often deemed to be a holy life or a life of obedience.[337] Riggs suggests that this is part of 'God's elimination test to determine whom He considers worthy to receive this priceless gift'.[338] However, others have resisted the notion that holiness was a precursor of the baptism in the Spirit;[339] the fact that the NT does not clearly support this position undermines its value.[340]

Other more detailed conditions have been identified while, at the same time, reasons have been offered for people not receiving their baptism.[341]

---

[333] C.W. Conn, *Pillars of Pentecost* (Cleveland: Pathway Press, 1956), p. 96.

[334] Wyckoff, 'The Baptism in the Holy Spirit', p. 453.

[335] J.R. Flower, 'Holiness, the Spirit's Infilling, and Speaking with Tongues', *Paraclete* 2 (1968), pp 7–9 (8); Riggs, *The Spirit Himself*, p. 105–06, 112; Menzies and Horton, *Bible Doctrines*, p. 130; M. Pearlman, *Knowing the Doctrines of the Bible* (Springfield: Gospel Publishing House, 1937), p. 318; Williams, *Systematic Theology*, vol. 3, pp. 59–61; however, there is no clear indication in Acts 1.14 or 4.31 that the believers were praying for the Spirit to come.

[336] Brumback, *What Meaneth This?*, pp. 259–60; Menzies and Horton, *Bible Doctrines*, p. 130; A.D. Palma ('Spirit Baptism: Before and After', *Enrichment* 10.1 (2005), pp. 92–6 (94)) suggests 'praising God in one's language often facilitates the transition to praising Him in tongues', reflecting a common view by Pentecostals.

[337] Conn, *Pillars of Pentecost*, p. 96; Robeck, 'An Emerging Magisterium?', p. 219; J.R. Williams, 'Baptism in the Holy Spirit', in Burgess and van der Maas (eds), *NIDPCM*, pp. 354–63 (362); idem, *Renewal Theology*, vol. 2, p. 301; B. Pugh, '"There Is Power in the Blood": The Role of the Blood of Jesus in the Spirituality of Early British Pentecostalism', *JEPTA* 25 (2005), pp. 54–66 (63–4); Land, *Pentecostal Spirituality*, p. 129; Arrington, *Christian Doctrine*, p. 86.

[338] Riggs, *The Spirit Himself*, p. 104.

[339] J. Lancaster, *The Spirit-Filled Church* (London: Grenehurst Press, 1987), p. 28.

[340] Robeck, 'An Emerging Magisterium?', p. 221.

[341] Conn (*Pillars of Pentecost*, pp. 96–104) offers repentance, baptism in water, desire, obedience and holiness; Pearlman (*Knowing the Doctrines*, pp. 316–19) lists prayer by oneself and others, obedience, cleansing; see also Bruner, *A Theology of the Holy Spirit*, pp. 92–117.

However, the arbitrariness of the reasons offered why some have not received the baptism in the Spirit and the diversity of means engaged to achieve it have resulted, for many, in an undermining of the expectation or even validity of the experience itself. In the light of such differing opinions, it is no surprise that many Pentecostals welcomed the arrival of renewal movements (including the Third Wave) which elevated and sought to experience the Spirit but did not concentrate on a post-conversion crisis experience for this to occur.

On the basis that the baptism in the Spirit is a gift from God, it is taught that it is not possible to earn it; rather one may receive it. Traditionally, times were (and to a lesser extent still are) set apart for people to 'seek' for the baptism in the Spirit, often known as 'tarrying meetings' (based on the AV translation of Lk. 24.49). On these occasions, people would be 'helped' to receive the baptism and many did. However, there is a good deal of popular evidence that sincere but mechanistic procedures were used to facilitate people speaking in tongues. Some of the latter elements not only fuelled the opposition to Pentecostals but also did a great deal of damage to those who were desirous of this experience but found themselves in situations where they received inept guidance that sometimes left them emotionally exhausted, confused, disappointed and spiritually deflated. The numbers of those who left disappointed or who were prepared to receive a pale reflection of the experience of the believers in Acts rather than leave empty handed will never be known. This incongruity of the promised baptism in the Spirit being viewed as a gift of God that, ironically for many, proved so difficult to receive was further compounded by statements that the experience was readily available to all.[342] Such tarrying meetings are much less frequent now.

The often unwitting tendency to create a second-class mentality for those who have not received the baptism in the Spirit has caused division and further eroded its significance for many. However, while some have been disenchanted by their experience in that the anticipated blessings proved limited or non-existent, for a significant number, the experience has resulted in a re-envisioning of their Christian pilgrimage.

Subsequence

The subsequent nature of the baptism in the Spirit to conversion, an undoubted Pentecostal distinctive,[343] has created a great deal of discussion

---

[342] D. Gee, *God's Great Gift: Seven Talks Together about the Holy Spirit* (Springfield: Gospel Publishing House, n.d.), p. 57; Poloma, *The Assemblies of God*, pp. 41–5.

[343] Article 7 of the AoG tenets of Faith identifies the baptism in the Spirit as 'distinct from and subsequent to the experience of the new birth (Acts 8.12–17; 10.44–46; 15.7–9)'; also Menzies, *Spirit and Power*, pp. 109–19; Petts, 'The Baptism in the Holy Spirit', p. 99; H.M. Ervin, *These Are Not Drunken as Ye Suppose* (Plainfield: Logos, 1968), p. 57; Pearlman, *Knowing the Doctrines*, pp. 311–12; Gee, *Wind and Flame*, p. 7; Horton, *What the Bible Says*, pp. 159–61; Arrington, *Christian Doctrine*, pp. 60–2.

in recent years, not without diversity of opinion.[344] Much of the debate between Pentecostals and those expressing opposing views revolves around whether the gift of the Spirit as recorded in Acts was subsequent to salvation or not. Both sides have been guilty of attempting to make the facts fit their case and/or to allow the writings of Paul and John concerning the Spirit to influence their understanding of Luke.

Fundamentally, the perception of most Pentecostals is that after conversion, a further experience is available for believers, identified as the baptism in the Spirit.[345] Rather than this being described as 'baptism *of* the Spirit', most Pentecostals now refer to it as 'baptism *in* the Spirit' in order to retain the belief that it is Christ who actualizes this latter experience. Thus, the baptism *of* the Spirit refers to the occasion when the Spirit baptizes the believer into the Church, at salvation, while the baptism *in* the Spirit is a distinct experience, initiated by Jesus, who baptizes the believer into the Spirit. However, Pentecostals also use a variety of terms (outpouring (Acts 2.17–18); receive (Acts 2.38); fill (Acts 2.4, 9.17); baptize (Mt. 3.11; Acts 11.16)) to describe the baptism in the Spirit.[346] The adoption of these terms is sometimes unhelpful as they are used to refer to different aspects of the work of the Spirit by the NT authors depending on the context. Thus, being 'filled with the Spirit' has a different meaning in Acts 2.4 compared to Ephesians 5.18. This terminological issue has often been at the heart of difficulties in the acceptance, or otherwise, of Pentecostal pneumatology by non-Pentecostals.[347]

Generally speaking, Pentecostals deduce that all become recipients of the Spirit at salvation (1 Cor. 12.13) while this is to be followed by a further and distinct infusion of the Spirit, known as the baptism in the Spirit. Thus, three days after Paul encountered Christ (Acts 9.4–6), his filling by the Spirit occurred (Acts 9.9, 17). Similarly, after the Samaritans believed (Acts 8.12), they received the Spirit (Acts 8.17), while also the Spirit came on the Ephesians after they had believed (Acts 19.5–6). Most Pentecostals conclude that all Christians should and could function charismatically, and the baptism in the Spirit, variously defined, is identified as a catalytic and integral element in that process.

---

[344] See Fee, *Gospel and Spirit*, chs 6–7 ('Baptism in the Holy Spirit: The Issue of Separability and Subsequence', *Pneuma* 7.2 (1985), pp. 87–100.); Chan, 'Evidential Glossolalia', pp. 195–211; idem, *Pentecostal Theology*, p. 85–95; Anderson, *An Introduction to Pentecostalism*, pp. 192–95; Williams, 'Baptism in the Holy Spirit', pp. 354–55; Macchia, 'Theology, Pentecostal', pp. 1129–131.

[345] Canty, *The Practice of Pentecost*, 76–85; Petts, 'The Baptism in the Holy Spirit', in Warrington, *Pentecostal Perspectives*, pp. 98–119.

[346] Petts, 'The Baptism in the Holy Spirit', p. 102; Riggs, *The Spirit Himself*, p. 63.

[347] R. Howard, 'David du Plessis: Pentecost's "Ambassador-at-Large"', in Ma and Menzies, *The Spirit and Spirituality*, pp. 271–97 (279).

Although they assume that the baptism in the Spirit could take place immediately after or simultaneous with salvation,[348] it is mostly assumed that these are rare events[349] and while accepting the possibility that there may be no chronological separation, Pentecostals affirm a theological difference.[350] It is at this point that many Pentecostals have often struggled to articulate their beliefs carefully.[351] This has sometimes resulted in a careless and insubstantial presentation of the role of the Spirit in the life of the believer prior to the baptism in the Spirit. It has also resulted in some feeling that a two tier Christianity has been established.[352] When they have resorted to metaphors to explain the progression in the role of the Spirit from salvation to the baptism in the Spirit, they have often encumbered themselves with exegetical and practical difficulties. Thus, Riggs deduces, without offering clarification, that it is as the Spirit of Christ that the believer experiences the Spirit at salvation while at the baptism in the Spirit, he comes as 'the Third Person of the Trinity'.[353] In an attempt to maintain a significant place for the baptism in the Spirit, Horton writes,

> it is the cross that saves and renders one a member of the family, but it is the enduement, anointing, infilling, baptism of the Holy Spirit that equips with gifts and renders one a miraculous member of the miracle-working body of Christ.[354]

However, this inappropriately assumes that gifts may not be granted to believers nor miracles manifested prior to the baptism in the Spirit. Bruner, who is not a Pentecostal, cautions against the danger of placing a 'higher valuation on the further or subsequent experience for which the first experience

---

[348] Y. C. Lim, 'Acts 10: A Gentile Model for Pentecostal Experience', *AJPS* 1 (1998), pp. 70–1.

[349] Pearlman, *Knowing the Doctrines*, pp. 316–17.

[350] A.D. Palma, 'The Promise of the Spirit', *Paraclete* 28.1 (1994), pp. 12–16 (13). There was a popular belief among many early Pentecostals that the Spirit did not indwell the believer at conversion but only at a later occasion when the baptism in the Spirit was experienced but this has been rejected on the basis of Jn 14.17; Rom. 8.9, 11; 1 Cor. 12.13; Eph. 2.1, 5.

[351] M. Robinson ('The Charismatic Anglican – Historical and Contemporary: A Comparison of Alexander Boddy and Michael C. Harper' (unpublished master's dissertation, University of Birmingham, 1976)) described Boddy as undertaking 'fairly primitive attempts at theological interpretation' on behalf of Pentecostalism (and he was one of the most articulate and theologically literate figures of his day).

[352] J.R. Williams, 'Pentecostal Theology: A Neo-Pentecostal Viewpoint', in Spittler (ed.), *Perspectives on the New Pentecostalism*, pp. 76–85 (82).

[353] Riggs, *The Spirit Himself*, p. 80.

[354] Horton, *The Gifts of the Spirit*, p. 45.

serves as a threshold'.[355] The reason why this issue is most contentious is that if the baptism in the Spirit is merged with salvation, it ceases to be a valid description of the subsequent experience as accepted by Pentecostals. Chan concludes, 'A position that grounds Spirit-baptism experientially in conversion will eventually lose its distinctive qualities'.[356] Therefore, they have sought to separate salvation from the baptism in the Spirit and emphasize both as valid experiences.[357]

Confusion sets in for many when attempts are made to explain the place of the Spirit in salvation and the baptism in the Spirit. In general, Pentecostals have explained the latter as the manifestation of the Spirit which has been accompanied by a significant lack of appreciation of his purposes on other occasions. In particular, the emphasis on the secondary experience of the baptism of the Spirit has had the tendency to weaken the role and significance of the Spirit in the believer at and subsequent to salvation. Many Pentecostals have engaged with this notion and argued that while there may be an enhanced role or experience of the Spirit on the occasion of the baptism in the Spirit, nevertheless, his presence and potential from conversion should be increasingly explored and recognized as having significant importance in the development of the believer.

An alternative framework may need to be identified that recognizes the fundamentally important role of the Spirit at salvation and also the valuable encounter with the Spirit to be experienced at the baptism in the Spirit – while also anticipating more experiences in the future (and prior to it) when his grace, power and influence may be manifested. For too long, the baptism in the Spirit has been a battlefield when the focus has been on defending a doctrinal perspective instead of promulgating the benefits of the Spirit and the multiple encounters he plans with believers. This may mean that Pentecostal terminology is to be reconsidered. Thus, Sepúlveda describes the initial encounter of people with God in a Pentecostal setting as truly Pentecostal in that 'God the Father and his only Son Jesus Christ have become present in real and active form through the Holy Spirit . . . *new birth = birth (Baptism) in the Spirit*'.[358] This however, does not necessitate the removal from one's theology or spirituality of experiences with the Spirit when believers are baptized afresh into his destiny and the destiny he has determined for them. Some Pentecostals have already begun to move in this direction, seeking to maintain an emphasis on the role of the Spirtit at

---

[355] Bruner, *A Theology of the Holy Spirit*, p. 72.

[356] Chan, 'Evidential Glossolalia', p. 209.

[357] G. Duffield, *Pentecostal Preaching* (New York: Vantage Press, 1957), pp. 76–7.

[358] J. Sepúlveda, 'Born Again: Baptism and the Spirit. A Pentecostal Perspective', in Moltmann and Kuschel (eds), *Pentecostal Movements*, p. 106.

conversion and thereafter also. Thus, Clifton states that the baptism in the Spirit occurs 'with or at a moment distinct from Christian initiation', but is also 'the ongoing orientation of the believer to the leading of the Spirit', thus including a continuous as well as a crisis component.[359] Similarly, Lim advocates the view that rather than being a single event, Spirit baptism may be a possible series of crisis experiences encountered throughout the normal Christian life.[360] Anderson helpfully suggests that the baptism in the Spirit is best understood if it is integrated theologically, if not chronologically, with the experience of conversion insofar as the former fulfils the potential of the latter.[361] Needless to say there have been extensive and lively dialogues between Pentecostals and others exploring this issue.[362]

Petts, advocating subsequence, bases his case on the fact that the disciples

had already confessed Jesus as the Christ (Mt. 16.16), been pronounced clean (Jn. 15.3), been told that their names were written in heaven (Lk. 10.20), and had forsaken all to follow him (Mt. 19.27). Thus, their reception of the Spirit at Pentecost is seen as subsequent to their conversion.[363]

However, Fee suggests that although there are references in the book of Acts that indicate that the baptism in the Spirit occurred subsequent to conversion (and also possibly Jn 15.26–27), others do not (Acts 10.43–44). For it to have normative value, it must be shown that this is related to the intent of the author, in particular, that he intended the readers to believe that the experience was to be repeated in the lives of future believers.[364] This results in Fee stressing the validity of the Pentecostal experience but questioning the theology and in particular, the suggestion that the timing of the experience

---

[359] Clifton, 'The Spirit and Doctrinal Development', p. 21.

[360] D.S. Lim, "An Evangelical Critique of "Initial Evidence" doctrine', *AJPS* 1/2 (1998), pp. 219–29.

[361] G.L. Anderson, 'Baptism in the Holy Spirit, Initial Evidence, and a New Model', *Paraclete* 27.4 (1993), pp. 1–11.

[362] J.D.G. Dunn, 'Baptism in the Holy Spirit . . . yet once more', *JEPTA* 18 (1998), pp. 3–25; idem, 'Baptism in the Spirit: A Response to Pentecostal Scholarship on Luke-Acts', *JPT* 3 (1993), pp. 3–27; idem, 'Spirit-Baptism and Pentecostalism', *SJT* 23.4 (Nov. 1970), pp. 397–401; P. Hocken, 'The Meaning and Purpose of "Baptism in the Spirit"', *Pneuma* 7.2 (1985), pp. 125–34; M. Duggan, 'The Cross and the Holy Spirit', *Pneuma* 7.2 (1985), pp. 135–46; R. Lovelace, 'Baptism in the Holy Spirit and the Evangelical Tradition', *Pneuma* 7.2 (1985), pp. 101–24; W.P. Atkinson, 'Pentecostal Responses to Dunn's "Baptism in the Holy Spirit": Luke-Acts', *JPT* 6 (1995), pp. 87–131 (129).

[363] Petts, 'The Baptism in the Holy Spirit', p. 99.

[364] Fee, *Gospel and Spirit*, pp. 92–110.

is always post-conversion. Thus, Fee questions the validity of historical precedent being used to set a norm with regard to the baptism in the Spirit.[365] While accepting that such precedents may be identified as repeatable patterns, he disputes that they be viewed necessarily as normative. Allied to this is a plea to recognize that Luke has written a historical narrative which although it contains much theology, its genre and overall purpose needs to be borne in mind in seeking to identify normative patterns of belief and praxis. Thus, while Luke may be identified as establishing the development of the Church and the Spirit's involvement in that process, it may be less clear that he intended to establish a procedure of Spirit impartation and reception.[366]

In response, however, other Pentecostals have argued that it is the intention of Luke-Acts to demonstrate the charismatic role of the Spirit and that therefore the narratives concerning the baptism in the Spirit become much more relevant as they are not examples of occasional elements of early Church life but central to the purpose of the author and to be treated as such.[367] Thus, Pentecostals (and others) argue that the gift of the Spirit in Luke is charismatic rather than associated with salvation.[368] Thus, the intent of Luke is not to link the Spirit with salvation (as does Paul) but with another experience; thus, Luke does infer that a charismatic manifestation of the Spirit is to be experienced by believers separate from and subsequent to conversion.[369]

Petts broadly agrees with Fee, noting that to encourage believers to visit Jerusalem in order to be baptized in the Spirit (Acts 1.4–5) would be absurd, because, like the presence of the wind (Acts 2.2), that only occurred once. However, he draws attention to the fact that this 'does not mean that frequently repeated historical incidents may not be understood to be normative'.[370] Responding to the discussion between Fee and Stronstad on this topic,[371] Holman suggests that sometimes historical precedent may determine normative practice in some circumstances; the difficulty for him

---

[365] G.D. Fee, 'Hermeneutics and Historical Precedent – a Major Problem for Pentecostal Hermeneutics', in Spittler (ed.), *Perspectives on the New Pentecostalism*, pp. 118–32 (128–29); idem, *How to Read*, ch. 6; idem, 'Response to Roger Stronstad's "The Biblical Precedent for Historical Precedent"', *Paraclete* 27.3 (1993), pp. 11–14.

[366] Fee, *Gospel and Spirit*, pp. 90–1.

[367] Menzies, *Empowered for Witness*, p. 239; R. Stronstad, 'The Biblical Precedent for Historical Precedent', *Paraclete* 27.3 (1993), pp. 1–10.

[368] Menzies, 'Coming to Terms', p. 23.

[369] Menzies, 'Coming to Terms', p. 24.

[370] Petts, 'The Baptism in the Holy Spirit', p. 106.

[371] Fee, 'Hermeneutics and Historical Precedent, pp. 118–32; R. Stronstad, 'Pentecostal Hermeneutics: A Review of Gordon D. Fee's *Gospel and Spirit: Issues in Pentecostal Hermeneutics*', *Pneuma* 15.2 (1993), pp. 215–22.

is determining when it does and when it does not.[372] Fee concludes some-what similarly by stating that it is never valid as the only criteria for determining that which may be identified as normative practice.[373] Fee has been the object of much criticism by some Pentecostals, Stronstad in partic-ular disagreeing with his stance and offering biblical precedents for historical precedent;[374] others have appreciated his candour and the case he presents.

There may be value in dispensing with the term 'subsequent' and replacing it with 'separate' to concentrate on its identity as that which is more impor-tant than its timing. It is the distinctive nature of the baptism in the Spirit rather than its subsequence that is of particular value.[375] Indeed, Lederle, after an exhaustive exploration of various definitions of the baptism in the Spirit concludes that a more appropriate explanation of the baptism in the Spirit should concentrate on its value as 'the legitimate rediscovery of the charismatic or experiential dimension of the normal integrated Christian life' excluding the need for a subsequent event but anticipating a deeply experiential and 'ongoing openness to the full range of charisms as a present-day reality which the Holy Spirit freely distributes'.[376] However, the concept of subsequence has value to the extent that it develops the concept of pro-gression in the life of the believer.

This is a tension with which Pentecostals have lived for decades and they have sometimes articulated the issue insensitively. In their fervour to enhance the significance of the baptism in the Spirit, Pentecostals have often uninten-tionally implied that his role is of greater import in the latter than the act of salvation or his ongoing influential presence in the life of the believer. A greater awareness of the Pauline contribution to the ministry of the Spirit is valuable in helping to present the comprehensive ministry of the Spirit.[377] However, Pentecostalism has succeeded in rediscovering the role of the Spirit whereas in the past, to a large degree, he was too frequently assumed to per-form a supplementary and inferior role when compared to Jesus and the Father.

---

[372] C.L. Holman, 'A Response to Roger Stronstad's "The Biblical Precedent for Historical Precedent"', *Paraclete* 27.4 (1993), pp. 11–14.

[373] Fee, *Gospel and Spirit*, pp. 94–5.

[374] Stronstad, 'The Biblical Precedent', pp. 1–10; for an historical overview of the debate, see B.T. Noel, 'Gordon Fee and the Challenge to Pentecostal Hermeneutics: Thirty Years Later', *Pneuma* 26.1 (2004), pp. 60–80.

[375] See also Chan, 'The Language Game', pp. 90–2; Robeck, 'An Emerging Magisterium?', pp. 241–42; Fee, 'Hermeneutics and Historical Precedent', pp. 130–131.

[376] H.I. Lederle, 'An Ecumenical Investigation into the Proprium or Distinctive Elements of Pentecostal Theology' in Clark, *What Is Distinctive?*, **pp. 158–171**.

[377] Fee, *God's Empowering Presence*, passim; Warrington, *Discovering the Holy Spirit*, passim.

The NT Evidence

Pentecostals have sought to defend the baptism in the Spirit by addressing the biblical text.

John 20.19–23

This verse reflects the action of Jesus of breathing on the disciples and stating, 'Receive the Holy Spirit' (20.22), and following his commission of them (20.21). Thereafter, Jesus grants them the authority to forgive and withhold forgiveness. Opinions are divided as to the meaning of Jesus' action. Many assume that this verse supports the belief in a two-fold impartation of the Spirit to the believer, the first here (relating to their salvation), the second on the day of Pentecost.[378] Thus, Menzies argues that 20.22 refers to 'the disciples' reception of the life-giving Spirit . . . the Spirit of new creation'.[379] He makes a strong case, noting that *enephusēsen* (he breathed) is also used in Gen. 2.7, of the breathing by God into Adam, and, in Ezek. 37.9, 14, of the breathing of the Spirit of God into the dry bones, but rarely elsewhere.[380] Thus, it may be viewed as a description of the conversion of the disciples as evidenced by their receiving the Spirit in a way that is reminiscent of the way that God breathed life into people in the OT and as the fulfilment of John 7.37–39 and 16.7.[381] Menzies maintains that, based on John's account, 'the Spirit of new creation (Jn 20.22) and the Pentecostal gift are received in two, theologically distinct experiences'.[382] In contrast to those who argue that 20.22 and the day of Pentecost are theologically unified, it may be asserted that if this is so, it is difficult to identify why there is a time lapse between these events.

However, as Thomas notes, the fact that the next pericope identifies the disciples as still hiding (20.26) may suggest that a life transforming infusion of the Spirit has not yet occurred.[383] Thus, Thomas concludes that 20.22

---

[378] See Article 8 of the AoG Fundamental Beliefs; Ervin, *Spirit Baptism*, pp. 15–21; H.O. Bryant, 'Filled with the Spirit', in Burgess (ed.), *EPCC*, p. 205; L.T. Holdcroft, 'The Breath of the Risen Christ', *Paraclete* 1 (1975), pp. 27–32; B. Aker, 'Breathed, A Study on the Biblical Distinction between Regeneration and Spirit Baptism', *Paraclete* 2 (1983), pp. 13–16.

[379] R.P. Menzies, 'John's Place in the Development of Early Christian Pneumatology', in Ma and Menzies (eds), *The Spirit and Spirituality*, pp. 41–52 (49).

[380] Menzies, 'John's Place in the Development', p. 49.

[381] See the similar use of the word 'receive' in both texts and the association of the giving of the Spirit with the glorification of Jesus at his ascension.

[382] Menzies, 'John's Place in the Development', p. 52.

[383] J.C. Thomas, 'The Spirit in the Fourth Gospel: Narrative Explorations', in Cross and Powery (eds), *The Spirit and the Mind*, pp. 87–104 (103).

refers to a 'symbolic, parabolic and/or proleptic action that points beyond itself to a reception of the Spirit that is not described in the narrative'.[384]

Alternatively, the information that follows in v. 23 may provide an explanation in that there, Jesus transfers his authority concerning the granting and withholding of forgiveness to the disciples.[385] The reason that the disciples are able to undertake any mission, even though Jesus is to leave them, is that they are granted the ability to function in the power of the Spirit. This action of Jesus thus may describe a charismatic or partial empowering of the disciples for evangelism until the day of Pentecost. It is true that they had evangelized before the death of Jesus and been given the privilege of offering salvation to people earlier (Mt. 16.19; Lk. 9.2, 6), but now Jesus is to leave them. Then they were the delegates of Jesus functioning in his authority. Now, they obey his commission, not in his presence but, in the presence of the Spirit. The arrival of the Spirit on the day of Pentecost will however be for a different purpose – to indwell them permanently and to institute the Church.

Acts 1.8

Pentecostals have reacted strongly to the suggestion that the book of Acts is an inappropriate basis for doctrine, given its stress on historically based narrative.[386] They have countered this perspective in a number of ways including the recognition that intrinsically, it is unproven and also, on the basis of 2 Tim. 3.16, it is false. Increasingly, it has been demonstrated that Luke was not merely an historian but a theologian who crafted his theology in a narratival framework. Petts, recognizing that Acts provides information about how believers should live, concludes, 'if doctrine relates to faith and practice, there is no self-evident reason why we cannot glean doctrine from Acts'.[387] This is important because traditionally, Pentecostals have relied on Luke-Acts to support their view of the baptism in the Spirit.[388]

---

[384] Thomas, 'The Spirit in the Fourth Gospel', p. 104; J. Lancaster ('The Life-Style of the Spirit', *Paraclete*, 2 (1979), pp. 4–7 (4)) understands it to be a symbolic impartation of the Spirit who was actually received at Pentecost.

[385] R.K. Levang, 'The Holy Spirit and the Keys of the Kingdom', *Paraclete* 1 (1969), pp. 21–3.

[386] This was a position popularly advocated by the evangelical leader J.R.W. Stott (*The Baptism and Fullness of the Holy Spirit* (Leicester: IVP, 1975), pp. 15–17), though subsequently revised (*The Message of Acts* (Leicester: IVP, 1990), pp. 11–12).

[387] Petts, 'The Baptism in the Holy Spirit', p. 104.

[388] H.M. Ervin, *Conversion-Initiation and the Baptism in the Holy Spirit: An Engaging Critique of James D.G. Dunn's Baptism in the Holy Spirit* (Peabody: Hendrickson, 1984), pp. 1–14, 79–160.

Acts 1.8 refers to the day of Pentecost and is associated with the endowment of power as promised in Lk. 24.49, Acts 1.4–5. However, although Pentecostals have understood the power of the Spirit as relating to spreading the Gospel, it is possible, that they have inappropriately reduced the focus to power for evangelism when the Spirit has a wider agenda in empowering the believers in ways that may include evangelism but also in other respects, as reflected throughout the book of Acts.

Acts 2.1–39

This passage describes the events that occurred on the day of Pentecost. Pentecostals affirm that before the day of Pentecost, the disciples were believers who were following Jesus, owning him as the Son of God and provide verses to substantiate this view (Lk. 10.20; Jn 15.3–5; 17.14).[389] They believe that the event that occurred on the day of Pentecost was a fulfilment of John 7.37–38 in which Jesus prophesied that the Spirit would come after he had been glorified. It is in this respect that the Pentecostal paradigm is best presented in Acts (2.38; 4.31). Prior to this event, the disciples received the Spirit, to a degree (20.22), but on the day of Pentecost, they experienced a different dimension of his involvement in their lives.[390] This perspective has support in that Luke himself makes this association in Acts 2.17–21.

Acts 8.14–17

In these verses, Luke records the event following the sensational news that Samaritans have 'received the word of God'. After this demonstration of faith on their part and following a prayer of Peter and John, the Samaritans 'receive the Holy Spirit'. There is no mention of the Samaritans receiving the gift of tongues when they receive the Spirit. It is surprising that Luke omits this, especially if he is intending to indicate that it always accompanies the reception of the Spirit by believers in Acts. However, many Pentecostals argue that it is probable that they did, on the basis of the fact that elsewhere in Acts, when the Spirit was received for the first time, the recipients did speak in tongues,[391] while others suggest that it may have been speaking in tongues that encouraged Simon the Magician to want the experience

---

[389] Shelton, *Mighty in Word*, pp. 126–30; Wyckoff, 'The Baptism in the Holy Spirit', p. 429; Ervin, *Spirit Baptism*, pp. 68–9.

[390] Menzies, 'Coming to Terms', p. 26; Stronstad, *The Charismatic Theology*, p. 69; M.D. Caldwell, 'Interpreting Spirit-Baptism in Acts 2:37–39 as a Paradigm' (unpublished doctoral dissertation, Southwestern Baptist Theological Seminary, 2007); Shelton, *Mighty in Word*, p. 130; R.G. de la Cruz, 'Luke's Application of Joel 2:28–32 in Peter's sermon in Acts 2', *CPCR* 4.

[391] Petts, 'The Baptism in the Holy Spirit', p. 102; Brumback, *What Meaneth This?*, pp. 206–14.

also (8.18).[392] The fact that the Samaritans had 'received the word of God' (8.14) and 'been baptised in the name of the Lord Jesus' (8.12, 16) in response to Philip preaching about Christ (8.5) and the good news of the Kingdom of God (8.12) indicates that the reception of the Spirit was subsequent to conversion.[393] On this basis, many Pentecostals believe that although they received the Spirit at conversion, it is the baptism in the Spirit that is being referred to by Luke which had not been received.[394] What Luke does not appear to be advocating is that the reception of the Spirit indicates that salvation has now been affirmed for that had already been guaranteed on the basis of their having 'received the word of God' (8.17).

Pentecostals reject the view that the Samaritan experience was exceptional, defective[395] or that they were not Christians[396] before they received the Spirit and therefore not normative. Stronstad views the separation of conversion from the receiving the Spirit as being 'typical of the outpourings of the Spirit in Acts'.[397] However, others view it as abnormal or anomalous in that although it is normal to receive the Spirit when one becomes a believer, this provides an incident where it is possible to have been a believer without having received the Spirit.[398] The fact that Paul never indicates the possibility that someone may be a believer without having received the Spirit does at least point to the possibility of decidedly different emphases by both Luke and Paul for Luke is prepared to accept the possibility of salvation even where the Spirit is apparently not yet present in the lives of the believers (Acts 8.16).

It is not clear that the issue of subsequence is the main reason for the inclusion of this event by Luke and it is as likely that his motivation may have been to record the 'dynamic quality of the gift of the Spirit' and, in particular, the Spirit's readiness to include in his community those who had been outsiders for centuries.[399] Atkinson offers some helpful reminders when he notes that 'five accounts of Spirit-reception do not constitute a statistically

---

[392] Walker, 'The Baptism in the Holy Spirit', p. 35.
[393] Petts, 'The Baptism in the Holy Spirit', p. 99; Ervin, *Spirit Baptism*, p. 73; contra M.M.B. Turner, 'Interpreting the Samaritans of Acts 8: The Waterloo of Pentecostal Soteriology and Pneumatology', *Pneuma* 23.2 (2001), pp. 265–86.
[394] Petts, 'The Baptism in the Holy Spirit', pp. 109–11; Ervin, *Spirit Baptism*, pp. 71–4.
[395] Petts, 'The Baptism in the Holy Spirit', pp. 110–11; Menzies, 'The Distinctive Character', pp. 23–5; Ervin, *Conversion-Initiation*, pp. 25–40.
[396] See Dunn, *Baptism in the Holy Spirit*, pp. 63–8; he admits that this is not his strongest point (J.D.G. Dunn, '"They believed Philip preaching" (Acts 8:12): A Reply', *Irish Biblical Studies* 1 (1979), pp. 175–83).
[397] Stronstad, *The Charismatic Theology*, p. 65.
[398] Petts, 'The Baptism in the Holy Spirit', pp. 65, 74.
[399] Fee, 'Hermeneutics and Historical Precedent', p. 130; Fee, *Gospel and Spirit*, pp. 96–9.

significant sample' to draw dogmatic conclusions as to the timing of the reception of the Spirit by individuals.[400] As Hunter concludes, 'The "pattern" in Acts is the absence of uniformity in sequence'.[401]

The involvement of the Apostles, on this occasion, was not to approve the acceptance of the Samaritans into the Church so much as to indicate that they, as Jews and leaders of the Christian community, were part of the procedure, thus establishing a framework of fellowship and harmony for the present and future. The incorporation of the Samaritans into the Church was a momentous occasion. Given the animosity between Jews and Samaritans and their exclusion from Jewish worship for centuries, it was most unusual that they should participate in that which was, at the time, a Jewish Church. However, no one could now doubt their inclusion because of their reception by the Spirit, and as witnessed by the Apostles. In this regard, the agenda established in 1.8 is being fulfilled in part for Samaritans have benefited from the witness of the early believers. Although the presence of Jewish apostles was not needed when the Ethiopian came to faith and was baptized (8.26–38), Luke appears to heighten the importance of this occasion by noting that the word of God had been received by Samaria, not simply by Samaritans.

It is wise to be cautious in establishing a reason for this event and even to express uncertainty as to why it happened. That there was a delay is evident and that it suggested a deficiency, soon rectified by the arrival of the Apostles, is clear. To advance beyond this is to move into speculation which, at times, is a worthy task, but one that does not easily result in consensus. Furthermore, to go beyond that which Luke clearly states may miss the point of the narrative. That which may be gleaned about the Spirit from this occasion is that he is integral to the incorporation of people into the Church; without him, something is wrong and needs to be resolved. Given the stress by Luke on the sovereign role of the Spirit in Acts, there is no suggestion that the Spirit is at fault. Rather, in his sovereignty, he allows the delay for purposes of his own choosing. What must not be overlooked also is the importance of the fact that the Samaritans had been welcomed into the Church and the reception of the Spirit by them was the final and public evidence of that fact.

Acts 10.44–46

Remarkably, Gentiles also receive the Spirit and are enabled to speak in tongues, as were the Jews earlier in Jerusalem (Acts 2.4). This is another

---

[400] Atkinson, 'Pentecostal Responses: Luke-Acts', pp. 128–29.

[401] H.D. Hunter, *Spirit-Baptism. A Pentecostal Alternative* (Lanham: University Press of America, 1983), p. 90.

momentous occasion, described by Chuen as 'the second Pentecost'.[402] As such, it is no surprise to note that tongues are present as the sign of such a remarkable addition to the Church.

It appears that Cornelius had been accepted by God prior to his having received the Spirit (Acts 10.2, 32–35; 30–33) though some dispute this, viewing him as merely religious.[403] Acts 11.14, however, indicates that Peter's coming is to lead to the salvation of Cornelius and his household. It appears therefore that his being a God-fearer (10.2) meant that there was still the potential for a deeper development of his relationship with God, such that Peter could anticipate his being 'saved' (11.14) and forgiven.[404] The reception of the Spirit is evidence that the latter had occurred.[405] Peter informs his hearers that the Spirit came to Cornelius in a way that reflected the occasion when Peter and his colleagues also received the Spirit when they also believed (11.17). Peter's faith was demonstrated in that he obeyed Jesus and waited for the Spirit in Jerusalem, as instructed (Acts 1.4). Cornelius' faith was demonstrated in that he also obeyed God and sent for Peter as instructed by God (Acts 10.5). The faith referred to does not refer to an expression of faith needed to expedite the Spirit. Rather, it designated the lifestyle of commitment to God that was the basis for the Spirit entering into the life of a believer in order to continue the work already initiated.

It is of interest to note that other conversions of Gentiles are not recorded as being accompanied by a reception or filling of the Spirit (Lydia, 16.15; Philippian jailor, 16.30–33; Thessalonians, 17.1–9; Beroeans, 17.10–12; Athenians, 17.34; Corinthians, 18.8–9). In the cases of Lydia, the Philippian jailor and the Corinthians, Luke records that, having believed, they were baptized though he does not clarify whether this was in water or in the Spirit. Given that nowhere else does he refer to people being baptized in the Spirit, it may be more likely that he is referring to water baptism. The absence of a reference to an experience of the Spirit by these people should not be taken to mean that this did not occur, since elsewhere Paul assumes that the Spirit engages with believers experientially. However, rather than assume that which he does not record, it is more appropriate to focus on the events he does record and identify the reasons for their being recorded.

The significance, here, of the Gentiles, including Cornelius, being filled with the Spirit has been a cause for discussion. It is possible that the Spirit affirmed their salvation or that he came to empower them for their witness

---

[402] L.Y. Chuen, 'Acts 10: A Gentile Model for Pentecostal Experience', *AJPS* 1.1 (1998), pp. 62–72(67).

[403] D.V. Hurst, T.J. Jones, *The Church Begins. A Study Manual on the First Twelve Chapters of the Acts* (Springfield: Gospel Publishing House, 1959), p. 111.

[404] Petts, 'The Baptism in the Holy Spirit', pp. 70, 80.

[405] Menzies, *The Development of Early Christian*, pp. 266–67.

as believers though there is no indication in the text that Cornelius' family engaged in evangelistic activity immediately after their experience. Many Pentecostals suggest that they received a secondary experience of the Spirit, believing that the Spirit filled them at the commencement of the sermon (11.15) to affirm their salvation, and filled them again during the sermon (10.44) as a subsequent experience. While not doubting the role of the Spirit in filling believers on more than one occasion, there seems little exegetical support for this explanation. If Luke had intended to present a two-fold expression of the Spirit, one wonders why he did not make it clear.

An alternative solution, and one in keeping with the experience of the Samaritans, is to recognize the role of the Spirit here as the one who sanctions the entrance of people groups into the Church. Thus, the importance of the event is due to Gentiles being welcomed into the Church by the Spirit, an event causing amazement (10.45) and initial criticism (11.2) on the part of some believers. Despite the prophecy of 1.8, the possibility that the Church should incorporate more than Jews was a surprise to many. Given the debate recorded in Acts 15 as to whether Gentile believers should be circumcised or not, it is clear that such nationality issues were very important to many in the early Church. Thus, in 15.28, Paul refers to the giving of the Spirit to the Gentiles as evidence that there was no distinction between them and Jewish believers. Therefore, the Spirit is presented by Luke as taking the initiative in baptizing the Gentiles into the Church and demonstrating his presence in them by granting them the capacity to speak in tongues. Since the Spirit had affirmed their initiation, it was incumbent on the believers to add their affirmation by baptizing them in water.

Acts 19.1–7

The Ephesian disciples (*mathētai* – 19.1)[406] were believers (19.2) who had not yet received the Spirit until Paul met them. These verses describe that encounter. Although some have suggested that their status as believers was in question or that they needed confirmation that they were believers or, furthermore, that their baptism by John was inauthentic, Pentecostals conclude that the author clearly identifies them as being true believers who have not yet received the Spirit.[407] Atkinson notes, 'Luke presents a believer (or apparent believer) without the Spirit as an anomaly, an anomaly which calls for an immediate corrective response from the Church (Acts 8.15; 19.2–6)'.[408] Having already been baptized in water (19.3), and rebaptized in

---

[406] Commonly used to describe Christians (16.1; 18.23, 27; 19.9; 20.1, 30; 21.4, 16).

[407] Riggs, *The Spirit Himself*, pp. 53, 61; Menzies, *The Development of Early Christian*, pp. 268–77; Ervin, *Spirit Baptism*, pp. 79–80.

[408] Atkinson, 'Pentecostal Responses: Luke-Acts', pp. 87–131 (129).

the name of Jesus (19.5), the Spirit then 'came on them' and they spoke in tongues and prophesied (19.6). This provides a paradigm for the Pentecostal perspective of a post-conversion filling of the Spirit. However, it is clear that there was something deficient about their initial situation, even though they were authentic believers, and this is supported by the fact that Paul rebaptized them (19.3), suggesting that he was dissatisfied with their previous baptism. Shelton concludes, 'Luke's redactional interests must be respected, and we must not read too much into the text concerning the converted state of the recipients of the Holy Spirit since Luke himself does not clarify the point'.[409]

Although Luke chooses not to explain the precise nature of any deficiency in their spirituality thus far, he does indicate that without the Spirit, they would have missed the substantial benefits that come with his presence in their lives.

1 Corinthians 12.13

Some have interpreted this verse as indicative of a subsequent experience of the Spirit after salvation.[410] Petts argues for a translation of 'we have all been baptised in one Spirit for (for the purpose or benefit of) one body' arguing that not only is this an accurate translation, but it also fits the context (of the use of charismatic gifts, not conversion) better than the normal translation offered.[411] However, he builds a weak case for translating *eis* as 'for' instead of 'in'[412] and Atkinson questions his translation, offering other Pauline texts (Rom. 6.3; 1 Cor. 1.13, 15; 10.2; Gal. 3.27) where the meaning of *baptidzō eis* is used with the clear translation of 'into'.[413] Other Pentecostals more appropriately believe that this reference relates to the occasion when the believer is baptized into the Church by the Spirit at salvation, identifying the reading of 'by one Spirit' as indicating the agency of the Spirit to incorporate believers into the Church.[414]

---

[406] Commonly used to describe Christians (16.1; 18.23, 27; 19.9; 20.1, 30; 21.4, 16).
[407] Riggs, *The Spirit Himself*, pp. 53, 61; Menzies, *The Development of Early Christian*, pp. 268–77; Ervin, *Spirit Baptism*, pp. 79–80.
[408] Atkinson, 'Pentecostal Responses: Luke-Acts', pp. 87–131 (129).
[409] Shelton, *Mighty in Word*, p. 136.
[410] Petts, 'The Baptism in the Holy Spirit', p. 80; Ervin, *Conversion-Initiation*, pp. 100–02; see a critique of both by W.P. Atkinson, 'Pentecostal Responses to Dunn's Baptism in the Holy Spirit: Pauline literature', *JPT* 7 (1995), pp. 49–72 (57–58).
[411] Petts, *Body Builders*, pp. 109–111.
[412] Petts, 'The Baptism in the Holy Spirit', p. 113.
[413] Atkinson, 'Pentecostal Responses: Pauline literature', pp. 58–9.
[414] Menzies and Horton, *Bible Doctrines*, p. 129; Williams, 'Baptism in the Holy Spirit', p. 355; W.P. Atkinson, 'Worth a Second Look: Pentecostal Hermeneutics', *Evangel* 21.2 (2003), pp. 49–54 (51).

Galatians 4.6

Paul here identifies the reception of the Spirit as occurring at conversion, as referenced in 3.14, as a result of which the Spirit affirms that believers are children and heirs of God. Ervin argues, however, for subsequence and rejects the idea that *pneuma huiothesias* (Spirit of the Son) refers to the Spirit but to 'the animating, or vital principle that characterises sonship'.[415] Romans 8.15–16 undermine this perspective, Paul clearly identifying the Spirit as the one who affirms sonship.

Ephesians 1.13 (2 Cor. 1.22; Eph. 4.30)

Some Pentecostals have assumed that Paul is distinguishing in time between the act of salvation and the sealing of the Spirit that is referred to in this verse.[416] However, there is little evidence that would indicate that belief in Jesus is separated in time from the sealing of the Spirit. The reference to sealing is a description of that which takes place at salvation, not to a subsequent experience, be it water baptism or a secondary Spirit-experience. Some point to the aorist tense of the word, 'believe' ('having believed in him, you were sealed'), suggesting that it implies a prior conversion experience followed by an experience of sealing. However, the aorist tense is not always used to describe a past event but, as here, to refer to a distinct event. Thus, Paul is pointing to the distinct event of sealing. The events are separate, but not in time. Because of faith in Christ, the believer is sealed with the Spirit. To assume that Paul is referring to a separate experience is to read into the text that which Paul is not expressing. On the contrary, he is anxious to help the readers discover the enormous resources invested in them by the Spirit when they expressed faith in Christ. To anticipate that Paul is discussing a future event is to deny the immediacy of the promised Spirit to the believer; indeed, without the Spirit, the believer has no guarantee of any future inheritance (1.14).

The concept of 'sealing with the Spirit' provides Paul with an opportunity to explore the radical nature of the salvation that the believers have received and the remarkable Spirit who has chosen to be their partner throughout their lives. The practice of sealing letters, objects (Rev. 5.1–2) and even people (Rev. 7.4) was common in the ancient world. The seal represented a number of features, each of which may have stimulated Paul to use the concept to explicate the comprehensive nature of the Spirit's involvement in the life of a believer.

Fundamentally, the seal signified ownership; that which was sealed (cattle, slaves, objects) was owned by someone. Secondly, the seal signified security.

---

[415] Ervin, *Conversion-Initiation*, p. 88.
[416] Dye, *Living in the Presence*, p. 69.

The Spirit is described as owning and providing security for believers. Not only does someone own the believer but also he happens to be the one who owns all authority. To seek to harm a believer would thus be equivalent to attempting to harm the Spirit. The seal of the Spirit is God's way of sending out a warning to any potential aggressors (Rev. 7.1–8). The seal also signified a finished transaction (Est. 8.8; Jer. 32.10). The Spirit is God's way of reminding believers that the act of salvation has been completed. The Spirit, by his presence, is a constant reminder that the transfer has already taken place from one kingdom into another (Rom. 8.15–17). Finally, the seal signifies that the object sealed is valuable. Paul indicates that the Spirit acts as an eternal flame, whose presence is evidence that God has valued the believer as someone in whom he chooses to dwell. The reminder that the Spirit would guarantee them throughout their lives and beyond, despite the uncertainties of life, would have helped their confidence increase, reminded them of the remarkable nature of their salvation while also grounding them in the security guaranteed by the Spirit.

Ephesians 5.18

Although some have understood this verse as describing the post-conversion baptism in the Spirit, this is less the case by modern Pentecostals. Instead, they identify it as an imperative to benefit from the controlling influence of the Spirit in the lives of believers on a daily basis and distinct from the baptism in the Spirit. In this respect, it is the iterative sense of the verb 'be filled' that is often advocated though some prefer to identify it with a meaning that indicates not repeated fillings but a continued experience of the Spirit in the light of an earlier filling of the Spirit.[417]

Titus 3.5–7

Holman suggests that these verses may be supportive of the Pentecostal view of the baptism of the Spirit, partly because of the language used (reminiscent of Joel 2.28–29), the fact that Jesus is the one who bestows the Spirit, and the suggestion that v. 6 is parenthetical in vv. 5–7, 'and thus somewhat disassociated from a necessary connection with the 'salvation' of v. 5'.[418] At the very least, the experiential nature of the involvement of the Spirit in a believer's life is clear by the metaphors used. However, although it is conceivable that the washing of regeneration may be different to the renewal of the Spirit, it is unlikely as the references to the washing, renewal of the Spirit, being justified and becoming an heir of eternal life are more appropriately

---

[417] So Ervin, *Spirit Baptism*, pp. 57–9.
[418] C.L. Holman, 'Titus 3.5–6: A Window on Worldwide Pentecost', *JPT* 8 (1996), pp. 53–63 (61).

to be identified synonymously.[419] Thus, it is more likely that the writer is referring to the role of the Spirit in salvation.

Consequences/Purposes

Basic to Pentecostalism is a fervency to experience the baptism in the Spirit. This has largely been due to the assumption that one will be more effective as a Christian as a result,[420] a perspective that has begun to be reassessed and even criticized by some Pentecostals.[421] Indeed, although Pentecostals have traditionally tended to maintain a narrow focus on the aftermath of the baptism in the Spirit, it may be more appropriate, especially with regard to the variety of consequences of the Spirit's involvement in the lives of believers in Luke-Acts, to anticipate a range of subsequent experiences. These may include power for evangelism, a desire to follow Jesus more intently, to fulfil one's God-given ministry more effectively, to seek God's presence more intentionally, to experience the Spirit more fully or to function as a believer more strategically. That which is fundamental to each of the above is that it is expected that the Spirit will impact the believer powerfully and in a particular way as directed by the Spirit.[422]

The demonstration of that power has been largely related to three main areas, evangelism, personal transformation and charismata.[423] Indeed, the Spirit and power are interchangeable terms in Luke (1.35; 3.22; 4.1, 14; 5.17), Acts (1.8) and the Pauline literature (1 Cor. 2.4; Gal. 3.5; 1 Thess. 1.5). Thus, Chesnut describes the baptism in the Spirit as categorized by an 'explosive power'.[424]

---

[419] Dunn, *Baptism in the Holy Spirit*, pp. 166–67.

[420] Lim, 'Many Gifts, One Spirit', p. 3; R. Stronstad, 'The Holy Spirit in Luke-Acts', *Paraclete* 23.2 (1989), pp. 18–26 (26); Wyckoff, 'The Baptism in the Holy Spirit', pp. 448–51.

[421] Anderson, 'Baptism in the Holy Spirit', p. 1.

[422] Canty (*The Practice of Pentecost*, p. 92) deduces that this experience will 'not make us more effective than others but only more effective than we ourselves would otherwise be'.

[423] See Article 7 of the Fundamental Truths of the AoG which states that with the baptism in the Spirit comes 'the enduement of power for life and service'; D.J. Ayling, 'A Baptism of Power', in Brewster, *Pentecostal Doctrine*, pp. 227–38; A.A. Biddle, 'The Holy Spirit prompting Evangelism', in Brewster, *Pentecostal Doctrine*, pp. 307–17; A. Chia, 'Biblical Theology of Power Manifestation: A Singaporean Quest', *AJPS* 2.1 (1999), pp. 19–33.

[424] Chesnut, *Born Again in Brazil*, p. 92; A common misconception of many Pentecostals is that prior to the day of Pentecost, the disciples were frightened but that fear was replaced with authority on that day. However, Luke (24.52–53) records the disciples, after the resurrection of Jesus, being filled with joy and regularly visiting the temple in Jerusalem.

Evangelism

Many Pentecostals anticipate being granted power for evangelism, taking Acts 1.8 (also 4.8–12, 31; 9.17–20) as the basis for such an expectation.[425] Although the disciples of Jesus were empowered by Jesus in his earthly life (Mt. 10.1), Pentecostals believe that the authority granted then was only for his lifetime, Gause identifying the period between the ascension of Jesus and the day of Pentecost as a 'relatively inactive' period.[426] However, a fresh infusion of supernatural power was to be needed as the evangelism of the early Church was to be undertaken by a small group of ordinary people who were to take on the pagan world. Their frailty would, however, be transformed by the power of the Spirit as a result of which the Spirit's agenda (Acts 1.8) would be achieved. Macchia also sees benefit in advocating 'a kind of "second conversion", an awakening to one's vocation in the world and giftings to serve as a witness to Christ'.[427] Keener explores the purpose of Luke in that he associates tongues with the baptism in the Spirit, concluding that since the latter was intended to empower believers in their (cross-cultural) mission, 'what better sign to evidence this particular empowerment of the Spirit than inspiration to speak in languages of other cultures'.[428] He argues that there is a logical connection between speaking in tongues and universal mission, concluding that to receive the former without engaging in the latter is to neglect the underlying purpose of tongues.[429] Whether he is right or not, the association between power to evangelize and the baptism in the Spirit is clear in the theology of Pentecostals. What needs to be demonstrated, however, is whether this expectation is realized in the lives of those who have experienced the baptism in the Spirit. It is not clear that the anticipated power and increased evangelistic fervour has always (or even frequently) been received by many Pentecostals. It is possible that a deficiency of power thus exists in the lives of many. Alternatively, it may be that the power to

---

[425] Hughes, *What Is Pentecost?*, pp. 19, 21; Keener, *Gift Giver*, 51–68; Stronstad, 'The Prophethood of All Believers', p. 75; Arrington, *Christian Doctrine*, pp. 71–2, 82–4; Williams, *Systematic Theology*, vol. 3, p. 53; also Menzies and Horton, *Bible Doctrines*, pp. 123–25; Rowe, *One Lord, One Faith*, pp. 134–38; L.G. McClung Jr, '"Try to Get People Saved". Revisiting the Paradigm of an Urgent Pentecostal Missiology', in Dempster, Klaus and Petersen (eds), *The Globalization of Pentecostalism*, pp. 30–51 (36–7).

[426] Gause, 'Issues in Pentecostalism', p. 109.

[427] F.D. Macchia, 'The Kingdom and the Power: Spirit Baptism in Pentecostal Ecumenical Perspective', in Welker, *The Work of the Spirit*, pp. 109–25 (118–19).

[428] C.S. Keener, 'Why Does Luke Use Tongues as a Sign of the Spirit's Empowerment?', *JPT* 15.2 (2007), pp. 177–84 (177).

[429] Keener, 'Why Does Luke Use Tongues', pp. 177–84.

evangelize was specifically granted to the early believers because of the particular circumstances facing them as they presented the good news of the resurrection of Jesus to those who had crucified him and those who treated them as fools because they chose to believe in a Messiah who died as a convicted criminal. The power for evangelism anticipated in Acts 1.8 was clearly appropriate for them as they confronted an alien culture antagonistic to their message as it will also be for many contemporary believers. However, other aspects of the power of the Spirit may be more relevant for those who have been granted different commissions and who function in alternative contexts. Perhaps the emphasis should be placed on the empowering nature of the Spirit's impact rather than restrict it only and always to evangelism; the template of Acts 1.8 may be thus be but one of many that the Spirit can use when infusing a believer with his authority and power.

Personal Transformation

Others have taught that the power granted relates to developing a more consecrated Christian lifestyle[430] (associated with 'a more active love for Christ',[431] a greater sense of his presence[432] and an increased desire to read and study the Bible[433]) or even to result in a crisis experience of sanctification.[434]

Charismata

It has often been assumed by Pentecostals that as a result of the baptism of the Spirit, spiritual gifts (especially tongues) will be made available to believers; it functions thus as the gateway to the gifts.[435] In particular, the nine gifts

---

[430] See Article 8 of the AoG Fundamental Beliefs; Land, *Pentecostal Spirituality*, pp. 91–3; MacDonald, 'Pentecostal Theology', p. 66; Palma, 'Spirit Baptism', p. 96; Macchia, 'The Kingdom and the Power', pp. 119–20; Hurst, 'Practical Empowerment', p. 89–90; Larbi, *Pentecostalism*, p. 423; Chan, *Pentecostal Theology*, pp. 64–6; G.T. Montague, *The Holy Spirit: Growth of a Biblical Tradition* (Peabody: Hendrickson, 1976), p. 309; D.N. Bowdle, 'Informed Pentecostalism: An Alternative Paradigm', in Cross and Powery (eds), *The Spirit and the Mind*, pp. 9–19 (16–17).

[431] Robeck, 'An Emerging Magisterium?', p. 239; Walker, 'The Baptism in the Holy Spirit', p. 36; W.G. MacDonald, 'Biblical Glossolalia. Theses One and Two', *Paraclete* 27.1 (1993), pp. 1–7 (4–7).

[432] MacDonald, 'Pentecostal Theology', p. 66; Arrington, *Christian Doctrine*, pp. 78–81; Gause, 'Issues in Pentecostalism', p. 115.

[433] See Robeck, 'An Emerging Magisterium?', p. 239; Arrington, *Christian Doctrine*, p. 79; Stronstad, 'The Prophethood of all Believers', pp. 60–77 (75); MacDonald, 'Pentecostal Theology', p. 66; H.M. Ervin, 'Hermeneutics: A Pentecostal Option', *Pneuma* 3.2 (1981), pp. 11–25 (22); Conn, *A Balanced Church*, p. 45.

[434] See D.W. Dayton, 'Rejoinder to Laurence Wood', *Pneuma* 27.2 (2005), pp. 367–75; Macchia, 'Theology, Pentecostal', p. 1131.

[435] See Article 7 of the Fundamental Truths of the AoG which states that with the baptism in the Spirit comes 'the bestowment of the gifts and their uses in the work of the

referred to in 1 Cor. 12.8–10 have often been associated with the baptism in the Spirit[436] though this emphasis has been challenged by both early and later Pentecostals.[437] A difficulty with this view relates to the manifestation of spiritual gifts in the lives of believers who have not apparently experienced the baptism in the Spirit, as it is promoted by Pentecostals. Petts, while still defending the view that the baptism in the Spirit is the gateway to the gifts, suggests that God can work outside the norm and enable any believer to manifest spiritual gifts if they so desire.[438] Menzies, however, promotes the view that the baptism in the Spirit is the precondition for prophecy because of the Lukan association with it (Lk. 2.38–39).[439] Stronstad, in the main, has also argued that prophecy is a significant consequence of the baptism in the Spirit and he draws on evidence from Jewish literature. However, Atkinson and Turner have critiqued this emphasis, calling into question the assumption that prophecy is central to Luke's presentation of the aftermath of the baptism in the Spirit and suggesting that Luke anticipates a wider role of the Spirit in the lives of believers who have received the Spirit though that may include prophecy.[440]

It is difficult to defend the 'gateway' model exegetically or experientially. Since the Spirit indwells every believer (1 Cor. 12.13) and in the light of the fact that the Spirit gives every believer gifts (1 Cor. 12.6–7, 11), it is unclear why his gifts should only be granted after the baptism in the Spirit.[441]

The Place of Tongues

It is not apparently of great significance to Luke to make a clear case for tongues being the initial evidence.[442] If he did intend to do so, it is to be assumed that he would have presented the evidence more consistently and in every reference to the baptism in the Spirit; but he does not (Acts 8.17; 9.17–18). Similarly, even where he does provide an association of the two,

ministry'; see also Pearlman, *Knowing the Doctrines*, p. 313; W. Cantelon, *The Baptism of the Holy Spirit* (Springfield: Acme Printing, 1951), p. 15; Williams, *Systematic Theology*, vol. 3, pp. 63–75; Gee, *Spiritual Gifts*, p. 18; Petts, *Body Builders*, pp. 110–13; Menzies and Horton, *Bible Doctrines*, pp. 126–27; Arrington, *Christian Doctrine*, pp. 79–80.

[436] Pearlman, *Knowing the Doctrines*, pp. 321–27; Brumback, *What Meaneth This?*, p. 153.
[437] Gee, *Spiritual Gifts*, p. 5; Lederle, *Treasures Old and New*, p. 218.
[438] Petts, *Body Builders*, p. 112.
[439] Menzies, *The Development of Early Christian*, pp. 124, 185–98, 244–45, 248, 258; Shelton, *Mighty in Word*, pp. 130, 171; Stronstad, *The Charismatic Theology*, p. 69; Cruz, 'Luke's Application of Joel', p. 4; Chan, *Pentecostal Theology*, p. 43.
[440] Atkinson, 'Pentecostal Responses: Luke-Acts', pp. 121–24; Turner, 'Does Luke Believe', pp. 15–17.
[441] Schatzmann, 'The Gifts of the Spirit', pp. 84–5; Canty, *The Practice of Pentecost*, p. 96.
[442] Menzies, 'Coming to Terms', p. 2.

it is not clear that it is to declare that the gift of tongues is normative in connection with the baptism in the Spirit.[443] Partly due to the difficulty of demonstrating the case for the integral presence of tongues with the baptism in the Spirit as located in the NT, some have attempted to argue for a theological relationship between the two.[444] Chan explores the role of tongues as providing a personal encounter with God and, in that regard, it may be best viewed as '*the* sign of Spirit-baptism'.[445] The gift of tongues may thus be identified as the best response to the baptism in the Spirit. To those who suggest that tongues may be a valid but not the only response, he responds by comparing it with sadness and tears; as the one indicates the other, so also tongues is best associated with the baptism in the Spirit. However, in his own analogy, there is flexibility since tears may not always signify sadness. For some, sadness may best be expressed by deep silence, not speech (tongues); similarly, others have experienced intimate encounters with God differently and the sign of that encounter to them has been silence, not tongues. It is not clear that he has indicated that tongues are the normative sign though he has provided extra support for it being one of the better candidates for the role.

This of course, does not mean that the gift of tongues is an invalid sign of the baptism in the Spirit. Indeed, Menzies provides a conclusion with which most Pentecostals would agree, writing, '"tongues as initial evidence", although not explicitly found in the New Testament, is an appropriate inference' drawn from the text, especially when it is appreciated that for Luke, inspired speech (in particular, tongues and prophecy) is integral to people receiving the Spirit in Acts.[446]

Many Pentecostals associate the gift of speaking in tongues with the baptism of the Spirit, viewing it as the initial evidence,[447] particularly among

---

[443] L.W. Hurtado, 'Normal but Not the Norm: Initial Evidence and the New Testament', in McGee (ed.), *Initial Evidence*, pp. 189–201; Chan, 'Evidential Glossolalia', pp. 196–97; contra D. Lim, 'A Reflection on the "Initial Evidence" Discussion from a Pentecostal Pastor's Perspective', *AJPS* 2.2 (1999), pp. 223–232 (226); Fee, *Gospel and Spirit*, p. 98.

[444] F.D. Macchia, 'Groans too Deep for Words: Towards a Theology of Tongues as Initial Evidence', *AJPS* 1.2 (1998), pp. 149–73 (156); Chan, 'Evidential Glossolalia', p. 198.

[445] Chan, 'The Language Game', p. 86.

[446] Menzies, 'Coming to Terms Part 2', p. 7; C.A. Taylor ('Deaf and the Initial Physical Evidence', *Paraclete* 29.3 (1995), pp. 37–45) refers to accounts of deaf people speaking in tongues when baptized in the Spirit and also using sign language as a manifestation of tongues speech (see also P.E. Graham, 'Do the Deaf Speak in Tongues?', *Paraclete* 24.2 (1990), pp. 21–7.

[447] Paragraph 8 of the AoG Fundamental Truths reads 'The baptism . . . in the Holy Ghost is witnessed by the initial physical sign of speaking with other tongues . . .'; Article 5 of the constitution of the Pentecostal Fellowship of North America; W.G. MacDonald ('Biblical Glossolalia. Thesis 5', *Paraclete* 27.4 (1993), pp. 15–22 (15)) identifies it as 'the one constant biblical indicator'; A.R. Hartwick, 'Speaking in Tongues: The Initial Physical Evidence of the Baptism in the Holy Spirit', *Paraclete* 29.3 (1995) pp. 9–15;

Pentecostals in the USA,[448] McGee identifying it as the 'chief doctrinal distinctive of Classical Pentecostalism'.[449] However, other Pentecostals do not view tongues as the initial evidence of the baptism in the Spirit[450] including some major Pentecostal denominations.[451] Pluess notes that many European Pentecostals have often preferred to distance speaking in tongues from the

Wyckoff, 'The Baptism in the Holy Spirit', pp. 437–42; Ervin, *Spirit Baptism*, pp. 80–4; Arrington, *Christian Doctrine*, pp. 62–5; Hughes, *Church of God Distinctives*, pp. 32–3; Brumback, *What Meaneth This?*, pp. 229–60; Menzies, *Spirit and Power*, pp. 121–31; Menzies, *Empowered for Witness*, pp. 246–55; idem, 'Evidential Tongues: An Essay on Theological Method', *AJPS* 1.2 (1998), pp. 111–23; V. Synan, 'The Role of Tongues as Initial Evidence', in Wilson, *Spirit and Renewal*, pp. 67–83; W. Caldwell, *Pentecostal Baptism* (Kisumu; Evangel Publishing House, 1963), pp. 28–30; Macchia, 'Groans too Deep for Words', pp. 153–72; Canty, *The Practice of Pentecost*, pp. 84, 104–05; M.S. Clark, 'Initial Evidence: A Southern African Perspective', *AJPS*, 1.2 (1998), pp. 209–17; Lim, 'A Reflection', pp. 223–32; Spittler, 'Maintaining Distinctives', pp. 132, 136; G.B. McGee, 'Initial Evidence', in Burgess and van der Maas (eds), *NIDPCM*, pp. 784–91; W.K. Kay, 'The "Initial Evidence": Implications of an Empirical Perspective in a British Context', *JEPTA* 20 (2000), pp. 25–31; idem, 'Assemblies of God: Distinctive Continuity and Distinctive Change', in Warrington, *Pentecostal Perspectives*, pp. 40–63 (55–6); Chan, *Pentecostal Theology*, pp. 40–72.

[448] Anderson, *An Introduction to Pentecostalism*, pp. 10–12, 53; Robeck, 'An Emerging Magisterium?', pp. 249–52; Macchia ('Discerning the Spirit in Life', p. 23) notes dissenting voices in Europe and Third World Pentecostalism.

[449] McGee, 'Initial Evidence', p. 784.

[450] George Jeffreys, T.B. Barratt and Jonathan Paul were three major early European Pentecostal leaders who did not believe that tongues was the sign of the baptism in the Spirit; so also does the Chilean Pentecostal Church (Sepúlveda, 'Indigenous Pentecostalism', p. 133) and many current Charismatics; see Hudson, 'Strange Words', pp. 57–80 for a historical overview of the debate among early European Pentecostals; see also Turner, 'Early Christian Experience', pp. 8–11; G.B. McGee, 'Early Pentecostal Hermeneutics: Tongues as Evidence in the Book of Acts', in McGee (ed.), *Initial Evidence*, pp. 96–118; R.G. de la Cruz, 'Salvation in Christ and Baptism in the Spirit', *AJPS*, 1.2 (1998), pp. 126–46; M.T. Girolimon, 'A Real Crisis of Blessing. Part II', *Paraclete* 27.2 (1993), pp. 1–6; G. Menzies, 'Tongues as "The Initial Physical Sign" of Spirit Baptism in the Thought of D. W. Kerr', *Pneuma* 20.2 (1998), pp. 175–89.

[451] The 1923 Fundamentals of the British Elim Pentecostal Church stated that the baptism in the Spirit was 'accompanied by speaking in other tongues . . .', though this was excluded in a revision in 1934 which read that the baptism in the Spirit was accompanied by 'signs following', a position affirmed in the 1993 revision. Kay identified, in a survey of Elim ministers, that 49% disagreed with the statement, 'Speaking with tongues is necessary as initial evidence of the baptism in the Holy Spirit' while 42% agreed; 18% disagreed with the statement, 'Baptism in the Spirit can occur without speaking in tongues' while 73% agreed; 91% agreed that 'The baptism in the Holy Spirit is evidenced by "signs following"' (Kay, 'The "Initial Evidence"', pp. 30–1); also the Church of God in Christ, Pentecostal Assemblies of the World and many Argentinian Pentecostals (including the Brazil for Christ Evangelical Pentecostal Church with 1.2 million affiliates in 4,500 congregations in 2000).

baptism in the Spirit.[452] He offers the suggestion that the difference in emphasis between North American and European Pentecostals was that while the former 'were occupied with *legitimization* of glossolalia, the Europeans sought for a *validation* of tongues'.[453] Different circumstances resulted in different emphases and conclusions with regard to the place of speaking in tongues in relationship to the baptism in the Spirit.[454]

Others offer a different perspective[455] or suggest that speaking in tongues is valid, or even normative, evidence of the baptism in the Spirit but that it does not always occur.[456] Many Pentecostals encourage speaking in tongues but some disconnect it from the baptism in the Spirit.

The perception of tongues as a sign of the baptism in the Spirit has been a divisive issue among Pentecostals, especially where those who do not speak in tongues often feel marginalized.[457] Their relationship with God has sometimes been harmed since despite all their efforts, their expectation has remained unfulfilled. Of great concern is the fact that speaking in tongues has waned in the lives of many Pentecostals, of particular concern to those who view it as the initial evidence of the baptism in the Spirit. The danger is that as well as concentrating on the experience of tongues rather than providing a coherent biblical explanation for it, the latter has too often been confusing, and this may have resulted in its decrease. Thus, although Christenson writes, 'It was not the doctrine, but the event of speaking in tongues, which midwifed the birth of modern-day Pentecostalism',[458] the child that was born has not always benefited from the new language that was enjoyed by its parents. This has often resulted in lipservice being paid to the official dogma by many Pentecostals while private (and even public) experience does not reflect it.

---

[452] J-D. Pluess, 'Initial Evidence or Evident Initials? A European Point of View on a Pentecostal Distinctive', *AJPS* 2.2 (1999), pp. 213–22 (214–17).

[453] Pluess, 'Initial Evidence or Evident Initials?', p. 218.

[454] H.I. Lederle, 'Initial Evidence and the Charismatic Movement: An Ecumenical Appraisal', in McGee (ed.), *Initial Evidence*, pp. 131–41.

[455] W. Ma, '"If It Is a Sign": An Old Testament Reflection on the Initial Evidence Discussion', *AJPS* 2.2 (1999), pp. 163–75.

[456] Canty, *The Practice of Pentecost*, 119–21; Keener, *Three Crucial Questions*, 69–76; T.M. Ling, 'A Response to Frank Macchia', *AJPS* 1.2 (1998), pp. 180–85; R.H. Hughes, 'The New Pentecostalism: Perspective of a Classical Pentecostal Administrator', in Spittler (ed.), *Perspectives on the New Pentecostalism*, pp. 166–80 (171–72); Petts, *The Dynamic Difference*, p. 23; W.G. Hathaway, *A Sound From Heaven* (London: Victory Press, 1947), pp. 61–2; Chan, 'The Language Game', pp. 80–95.

[457] Robeck, 'An Emerging Magisterium?', pp. 221–42; Cerillo and Wacker, 'Bibliography and Historiography', p. 394; McGee, 'Initial Evidence', pp. 784–90; Macchia, *Baptized in the Spirit*, p. 36.

[458] Christenson, 'Pentecostalism's Forgotten Forerunner', p. 42.

There has been recent discussion over whether tongues should be viewed as the evidence or a sign of the baptism in the Spirit. Menzies suggests the value of the latter[459] while Dye indicates that as a sign, tongues need not be evidenced in the lives of all those who have been baptized in the Spirit especially if it is viewed as a 'community sign'.[460] Macchia[461] affirms the value of this perspective, noting that it avoids 'the negative result of formalising . . . or proving' of the baptism in the Spirit.

The universality of tongues as a gift for all believers is a belief that most Pentecostals would affirm.[462] Paul writes that he would be pleased if all believers spoke in tongues (1 Cor. 14.5, 28) though he accepts that not all do (1 Cor. 12.30). Those who identify speaking in tongues as the initial evidence of the baptism in the Spirit argue that this verse relates to the ability to speak in tongues publicly in association with the gift of interpretation. On this basis, all who are baptized in the Spirit would be assumed to receive the gift of tongues for personal use while only some would be enabled to use it in a public context.[463] Thus, although the phenomena may be the same, their purposes differ.[464] This may be an appropriate interpretation though it is not clear from the text that this is what Paul had in mind. It may be fairer exegesis to deduce that Paul is speaking about the value of speaking in tongues per se for he does not, here or elsewhere, associate it with the baptism in the Spirit.

Some Ways Forward

- While affirming the place of the baptism in the Spirit as a valid experience for many that results in a new development in spirituality and service, 'the challenge is how to explain more fully theologically such a dramatic experience of charismatic renewal'.[465] The context of such a challenge is

---

[459] W.W. Menzies, 'Reflections on Suffering: A Pentecostal perspective', in Ma and Menzies (eds), *The Spirit*', p. 5.

[460] Dye, 'Are Pentecostals Pentecostal?', p. 67; Ma, 'If It Is a Sign', p. 164.

[461] Macchia, 'Groans too Deep for Words', p. 153.

[462] P. Kaminer makes a case for this to include Jesus ('Did Jesus Speak in Tongues?', *Paraclete*, 26.2 (1992), pp. 10–13) though this rejected by S.M. Horton ('Did Jesus Speak in Tongues?', *Paraclete* 26.2 (1992), pp. 14–16).

[463] Gee, *Concerning Spiritual Gifts*, 79; Menzies, *Spirit and Power*, 133–44; Chan, 'The Language Game, pp. 80–95; Menzies and Horton, *Bible Doctrines*, p. 140; R.P. Menzies, 'Paul and the Universality of Tongues: A Response to Max Turner', *AJPS* 2.2 (1999), pp. 283–95 (287).

[464] Article 8 of the Fundamental Beliefs of the AoG states, 'the initial physical sign of speaking with other tongues . . . is the same in essence as the gift of tongues . . . but different in purpose'.

[465] Macchia, 'Theology, Pentecostal', p. 1130.

that there has been a decrease in the numbers of Pentecostals who claim to have experienced the baptism in the Spirit, especially in the West, and this is coupled by concerns that the experience is only encouraged to a limited extent by Pentecostal leaders. Thus, Harrup identifies that although the number of converts has increased in AoG churches in the USA, the numbers of those who experienced the baptism in the Spirit have plateaued for the past 25 years; currently, for every five converts, there is one Spirit-baptism.[466] The danger facing contemporary Pentecostalism is that the experience of the Spirit as encountered by those in the early Church is largely irrelevant to many Pentecostals, compounded by the fact that the experiences of the early Pentecostal generations have also largely been forgotten. Few people are modelling the dynamic transformation following the baptism in the Spirit; for too many, the models died decades ago.

- Macchia speaks of, 'the Spirit's empowerment of believers as bringing the Spirit's initiation of conversion to Jesus to greater "fullness" in the lives of believers'.[467] Thus, rather than see the baptism in the Spirit as completely separate from conversion, it may be more appropriate to understand it as the continuity of the liberating, transforming and empowering salvation initiated at conversion by Jesus. This framework allows for the recognition of the fundamentally important experience of salvation while retaining a pneumatic experience at and also distinctive to conversion. In this regard, Maachia retains the term 'baptism in the Spirit' to describe Luke's empowering motif and Paul's soteriological and initiatory emphases with regard to the work of the Spirit, arguing that both regeneration[468] and empowerment[469] are appropriate experiences associated with it.[470] This will be rejected by some Pentecostals because they will see it as a watering down of the secondary work of the Spirit and a compromise too far with the evangelical premise that the term is best used with reference to salvation.[471] However, there is little reason not to recognize the value of combining both emphases in the term and thus reflect more accurately the distinctive and complementary messages of Paul and Luke. The significance of this position is that it values both salvation and the baptism in the Spirit, recognizing the distinctive importance of each while encouraging the experiential realities of both events as being dynamically present

---

[466] S. Harrup, 'Practicing Pentecost', *Enrichment* 10.1 (2005) pp. 40–7; Anderson, 'Baptism in the Holy Spirit', p. 14.

[467] F.D. Macchia, 'The Struggle for Global Witness: Shifting Paradigms in Pentecostal Theology', in Dempster, Klaus and Petersen (eds), *The Globalization of Pentecostalism*, pp. 8–29 (16).

[468] Macchia, *Baptized in the Spirit*, pp. 134–40, 201.

[469] Macchia, *Baptized in the Spirit*, pp. 160–68, 195.

[470] Macchia, *Baptized in the Spirit*, pp. 62–77, esp. 70, 74, 77.

[471] Menzies, 'Coming to Terms', pp. 21–2.

in the lives of the recipients. The alternative has often resulted in Pentecostals overlooking the soteriological role of the Spirit while evangelicals
miss the empowering nature of the Spirit. It may be helpful to recognize
that the phrase 'baptism in the Spirit' is a metaphor for an experience
rather than a title to describe an experience and that it is more fluid than
static, more related to the eschaton as a sign of that which is to come
rather than to the present, more rooted in variety than uniformity, more
diverse than its association with tongues would indicate, more a language
with many accents than a single voice, more central and less peripheral,
more relevant to normative Christian spirituality than Pentecostals and
evangelicals might assume.

- There is an ongoing need to challenge Pentecostals that whether or not
they have been baptized in the Spirit, they are to develop their walk with
God and their ability to listen to the Spirit, both being integral elements
of their spiritual journeys. When some Pentecostals conclude that the
baptism in the Spirit is the goal of their spirituality, they need to be warned
of the folly of this perspective and its inherent danger as it indicates that
they have misunderstood the reason behind the Spirit's involvement in
their lives. In the same way that some evangelicals have assumed that
conversion is all that is needed on their part, so also Pentecostals need to
be aware that they do not take lightly the significance of the baptism in
the Spirit. As salvation is not merely the passport to heaven, so also the
baptism in the Spirit should not be viewed as the membership card into a
Pentecostal club but as another opportunity to interface with the divine,
with repeated infillings of the Spirit in the future and an increasing control of the Spirit being actively enacted in their lives. He has not been
given as a badge of normality or a mark of having attained a particular
level, or the highest level, of spiritual honour. Rather, he has been given to
affirm the believer in a number of respects and to be the resource for the
activities of the believer thereafter. His presence is a privilege and a
responsibility, an honour and a challenge, to be treasured but not to be
stored, to be enjoyed not to be memorialized, an entrée to the future not
merely a testimony to the past.
- There is value in remembering that the emphases of Luke and Paul concerning the Spirit are different to one another. Thus, Menzies concludes,
'The pneumatologies of Luke and Paul are different but compatible; and
the differences should not be blurred, for both perspectives offer us valuable insight into the dynamic work of the Holy Spirit'.[472] Paul examines
the role of the Spirit in salvation and the Christian life[473] while Luke iden-

---

[472] Menzies, 'The Distinctive Character', p. 25.
[473] Stronstad, *The Charismatic Theology*, pp. 1–12; R.P. Menzies, 'Spirit–Baptism and
Spiritual Gifts', in Ma and Menzies (eds), *Pentecostalism in Context*, pp. 48–59 (54–6);

tifies the role of the Spirit in mission (empowering and proclamation).[474] To read Luke through the eyes of Paul is as unacceptable as reading Paul through the eyes of Luke.[475] Atkinson deduces that 'no good evidence has been offered from Paul's letters or Luke's record that Paul taught two Spirit-receptions. The only one he describes is that which is inextricably bound up with justification and the onset of new covenant life'.[476] Thus, he stresses the fact that the Spirit has been given by God (1 Cor.2.12; 2 Cor. 1.21–22; Gal. 3.5; 4.6; Eph. 1.17; 1 Thess. 4.8), Jesus being designated as the one who gives ministry gifts (Eph. 4.8), and that every Christian has the Spirit (Rom. 8.9). Luke, however, describes the Spirit's role as fundamentally to create a proclamation-community, in which the believer acts prophetically as the mouthpiece of God, Shelton concluding that the 'role of the Spirit in conversion is not his major interest'.[477] Paul, while recognizing the prophetic impact of the Spirit, presents a broader range of emphases than Luke who presents the Spirit as the guiding dynamic in the kerygmatic function of the Church, both to believer and unbeliever.

The different (and similar) terms used by Paul and Luke for the manifestation of the Spirit in the life of the believer may thus be understood in the context of their emphases and not assumed necessarily to be referring to the same experience as described by each other. Thus, Luke's references to being filled with the Spirit resulting in the disciples' speaking in tongues (Acts 2.4) or speaking boldly (Acts 4.31) have different purposes to Paul who uses the phrase to refer to spirituality in a corporate setting of worship and service (Eph. 5.18). Similarly, while Luke refers to the concept of receiving the Spirit, resulting in prophecy (Acts 19.6), Paul refers to it in relationship to salvation (Gal. 3.2, 14). Menzies concludes, 'Spirit-baptism in the Lukan sense (the gift of the Spirit or the Pentecostal gift) then must be distinguished from the gift of the Spirit which Paul associates with conversion'.[478]

Paul's presentation of the work and person of the Spirit is more comprehensive than that of Luke, identifying a continuum of new experiences of the believer with the Spirit (Eph. 1.17). To assume that each says the

---

[474] Atkinson, 'Pentecostal Responses: Luke-Acts', pp. 96–8; Stronstad, *The Charismatic Theology*, pp. 10–11; Petts, 'The Baptism in the Holy Spirit', pp. 83–5; Menzies, 'The Distinctive Character', pp. 26–7.

[475] M.W. Mittelstadt, *The Spirit and Suffering in Luke-Acts. Implications for a Pentecostal Pneumatology* (London: T & T Clark, 2004), p. 27; Menzies, 'The Distinctive Character', pp 21–2; Macchia, 'Discerning the Spirit in Life, pp. 3–28 (25–6).

[476] Atkinson, 'Pentecostal Responses: Pauline literature', p. 67

[477] Shelton, *Mighty in Word*, p. 135.

[478] Menzies, 'Spirit-Baptism and Spiritual Gifts', p. 55.

same as the other and thus may be blended is not just inaccurate but also underestimates the individual purposes of the authors. It is more appropriate to recognize that although both often have the person and ministry of the Spirit as a focus, each charts a path that explores sometimes very different characteristics of the Spirit. Menzies concludes, 'This indicates that the Lukan gift of the Spirit should not – indeed, cannot – be equated with the Pauline gift of the Spirit'.[479]

This does not necessarily mean that Paul does not believe in a secondary experience of the Spirit after salvation. On the contrary, he indicates that ongoing experiences of the Spirit are to be anticipated, as a result of which individuals may function or develop in new ways (2 Tim. 1.6; Gal. 5.16; Eph. 5.18). Similarly, fresh infusions of power are also expected by Paul in his ministry (Rom. 15.19; Eph. 3.20; Col. 4.3–4). Thus, Stronstad writes, 'There is no tension between the fact of the indwelling of the Holy Spirit in the life of every believer and an additional experience of receiving the prophetic or charismatic gift of the Spirit'.[480]

Although Acts may be recognized as having value at determining and teaching theology, it is to be remembered that caution is needed when theology is being deduced from narrative because it is possible to learn different (even widely divergent) lessons from the same narrative.[481] Therefore, it may be more appropriate to first explore Paul who offers more clearly theological perspectives and then, into his more theological framework, incorporate the phenomenologically grounded pneumatology of Luke. In other words, although Luke and Paul complement one another, because of Paul's comprehensive presentation of the Spirit (in both soteriology and charismatic activity, in the individual believer and the Church), it is wise that he be recognized as offering a normative theology alongside which Luke's nuanced (though valid) perspective of the Spirit is to be set.

- There has been such an emphasis on receiving *from* the Spirit that he has not always been the focus of attention. Thus, there has been a tendency to seek the baptism in the Spirit in order to speak in tongues rather than to be influenced by the Spirit in one's life and behaviour. Instead of being valued as the most important element, he has been often been viewed simply as the source of those aspects most desired by believers. Associated with this has been a limited recognition of his person and character, and a greater acknowledgement of his power and resources. To many, he has become a powerful source of energy rather than a personal guide, a

---

[479] Menzies, 'Spirit-Baptism and Spiritual Gifts', p. 55.
[480] Stronstad, *The Charismatic Theology*, p. 68; Ervin, *Conversion-Initiation*, p. 115.
[481] Chan, 'The Language Game', p. 82–4.

miraculous force rather than a mentoring friend.[482] He has been largely viewed functionally as the one who can facilitate the believer to be a useful disciple of Jesus. The intermittent reminder to Pentecostals (often by Pentecostals) has been that they do not so concentrate on the gifts of the Spirit that they forget the Giver of the gifts, the Spirit.

- The importance of the Spirit, other than that reflected in the baptism in the Spirit and the gifts bestowed by the Spirit, has been little explored by Pentecostals. However, a growing awareness of the diverse ministry of the Spirit to and on behalf of believers has occurred, particularly as a result of increased appreciation of the writings of Paul concerning the Spirit. The more Paul's contribution concerning the Spirit has been explored, the more the Spirit has been understood as having a varied and encompassing role in the development of the lives of believers. Consequently, the association of the Spirit with conversion, his commitment to spiritual development, his affirmation of the believer's position in Christ and his guiding and transforming influence are enabling Pentecostals to relate to the Spirit of power as well as the power of the Spirit.[483] Such a quest enables believers to experience the Spirit on multiple occasions through their Christian lives, resulting in a multilayered bestowal of the Spirit depending on their given need or his sovereign manifestation.

Although Pentecostal theologians stress that the baptism in the Spirit, as understood by Pentecostals, does not indicate that believers are devoid of the Spirit until they experience it, this message has not always been disseminated throughout the movement. Traditionally, Pentecostals have separated the Spirit from the act of salvation to such an extent that it has been difficult to deduce his role in salvation; indeed, the implicit understanding for many has been that his influence in the life of the believer is limited or even non-existent until the occurrence of the baptism in the Spirit. This has led many of those who did not receive the baptism in the Spirit to be disappointed and even marginalized as those who were somehow lacking in the best that God had to offer, whose Christianity was second class, despite the quality of their spirituality or even the effectiveness of their witness. In this regard, an inappropriate presentation of the baptism in the Spirit can result in it appearing to be dangerously elitist.[484] While not denigrating the baptism in the Spirit, or any other

---

[482] McLean, 'The Holy Spirit', pp. 375–95; Cross, 'A Proposal to Break', pp. 71–2.

[483] Fee, *Gospel and Spirit*, 74–161; Warrington, *Discovering the Holy Spirit*, passim; Wenk, 'The Fullness of the Spirit', pp. 40–4; Warrington, *The Holy Spirit*, passim.

[484] Thus, W.D. Collins ('An Assemblies of God Perspective on Demonology. Part 2', *Paraclete* 28.1 (1994), pp. 18–22 (22)) writes, 'When a believer is baptized in the Holy Spirit, he is anointed . . . so he can move against the works of the devil as Christ did' as if this only relates to those who have been baptized in the Spirit.

Spirit-inspired experience, it is crucial to enable believers to experientially and intellectually realize the Spirit-inspired event of conversion and his involvement in their lives thereafter. Furthermore, to suggest that all believers are indwelt by the Spirit but that only those who have received the baptism in the Spirit are empowered by him undermines the richness of the resources of the Spirit made available to all believers at salvation.

- In concentrating on power, Pentecostals are in danger of viewing their Christian experience as best defined by concepts of strength, victory and charismatically enabled progress (*theologia gloriae*) while forgetting that the latter also occur in times of weakness (Rom. 8.17–8, 23, 35–7; 2 Cor. 4.7–11; 6.4–10; 12.7–10), eclipse and even apparent defeat (*theologia crucis*). Experiences of the Spirit should result in triumph but not triumphalism, freedom and release but not licence, love not selfishness, the presence of God though not necessarily the absence of pain and suffering. Ling warns, 'The overemphasis on the Spirit and power within contemporary Pentecostalism is an index of the inadequacy of its "traditioning" practice'.[485]

- Pentecostals need to be careful that they do not (unintentionally) create a framework outside of which it may be assumed that the Spirit does (or should) not function. Thus, in their desire to embrace a schema comprising conversion followed by a baptism in the Spirit (with its varied potential consequences of tongues, power, prophecy or sanctification), they may have made it theoretically inappropriate for the creative and free Spirit to minister as he wishes and to impress his particular agenda on those he inspires. It is in this regard that Pentecostals may learn to widen their expectation of the work of the Spirit by considering how the Spirit has led others into new dimensions of spirituality (whose denominational or spiritual traditions may not be Pentecostal). In this regard, other believers may have much to teach (and learn from) Pentecostals, especially where it refers to the expectation of a plurality of renewals of the Spirit.[486] Some Pentecostals (unwittingly) assume that the Spirit did little until the Pentecostal revivals at the start of the twentieth century. The tendency to elitism is a constant threat to any who espouse a particular spiritual experience and Pentecostals are not immune to this.[487]

- Pentecostals have tended to see the baptism in the Spirit as a personal experience benefiting the individual rather than a baptism of the individual

---

[485] Ling, *Pentecostal Theology*, p. 101.
[486] K. Stendahl, 'The New Pentecostalism: Reflections of an Ecumenical Observer', in Spittler (ed.), *Perspectives on the New Pentecostalism*, pp. 194–207; Ford, 'The New Pentecostalism', 208–29; T-M. Cheung, 'Understanding of Spirit-Baptism', *JPT* 8 (1996), pp. 121–24.
[487] Macchia, *Baptized in the Spirit*, pp. 27, 32, 210–13.

into a re-envisioned awareness of his/her place in the body of believers. Macchia prefers to understand the idea that the believer is the temple of the Spirit 'for the sake of the world' as 'the sign of grace to an all-too graceless world'.[488] Similarly, Chan states, the 'primary focus of Spirit-baptism is to actualize our communal life or our fellowship in Christ'.[489]

- Pentecostals need to emphasize the role of the Spirit to experientially impact the lives of believers. Thus, Macchia writes, 'A theology deeply committed to the life of the Spirit cannot neglect aspects of experience in Christ that lie outside the limits of rational discourse'.[490] Theology can be uninspiring or reductionistic if it is exclusively word-based and an experiential theology of the Spirit is essential in the life of the believer and the Church. That which is central to being a Pentecostal is the desire to encounter the Spirit. However, Pentecostals are in danger of existing in a spiritual desert – devoid of the Spirit, except for the rare occasions when the Spirit breaks through into their lives or they break into his. For many, there exists an assumption that this is normal. For too long, they have believed the myth that the Spirit only rarely encounters believers. Pentecostal praxis also indicates that such encounters are often narrowly focused and infrequent. Many Pentecostals are also only aware of a very small capacity of the Spirit's agenda for believers. Too often they think of him as Cinderella who comes to the Ball late, leaves early and deposits something small – precious, but small – in their lives. Thereafter, like Cinderella, he must be searched for – in the hope that he may give more in the future – but too often that is only for the princely few. A challenge to Pentecostal leaders is to ensure that they enable believers to view the Spirit as desiring to be their personal mentor, encourage them to recognize that he is committed to proactively transforming them, providing limitless resources for them with regard to their salvation and their spirituality, including gifts for all to be used sensitively for the benefit of others and in partnership with him.

---

[488] Macchia, *Baptized in the Spirit*, p. 204.

[489] C. Chan, 'Mother Church: Toward a Pentecostal Ecclesiology', *Pneuma* 22.2 (2000), pp. 177–208 (180–81).

[490] Macchia, *Baptized in the Spirit*, p. 52.

4

THE CHURCH

Introduction

In reality, Pentecostals do not own a distinctively Pentecostal theology of the church. Kärkkäinen observes that one reason for the limited stress on developing an ecclesiological theology may have been due to the belief in the imminent return of Jesus as well as the need to evangelize that was uppermost in their thoughts.[1] Furthermore, he deduces, 'Pentecostals . . . were "doers" rather than "thinkers" and instead of writing theological treatises they went on living and experimenting with the New Testament type of enthusiastic church life'.[2] Similarly, Chan advocates the importance of the interactive nature of the Pentecostal Church which is dedicated to healing and dynamically traditioning the truth, living in the keen recognition that it is an eschatological community whose existence and development is based on the work of the Spirit who, by his presence, is a constant reminder that this world is not its home.[3]

Perhaps indicative of this lack of emphasis, the entries relating to the Theology of the Church in the *Dictionary of Pentecostal and Charismatic Movements*[4] and the later *New International Dictionary of Pentecostal and Charismatic Movements*[5] are both written by Peter Hocken, a Charismatic

---

[1] V-M, Kärkkäinen, 'Church as Charismatic Fellowship: Ecclesiological Reflections from the Pentecostal-Roman Catholic Dialogue', *JPT* 18 (2001), pp. 100–121 (108).

[2] Kärkkäinen, *Toward a Pneumatological Theology*, p. 110; H. Zegwaart, 'The Place of the Church in the Economy of Salvation. Roman Catholic and Pentecostal Perspectives: Room for Rapprochement', *JEPTA* 21 (2001) pp. 26–40 (33–8); M.L. Dusing, 'The New Testament Church', in Horton (ed.), *Systematic Theology*, pp. 525–66 (525).

[3] Chan, 'Mother Church', pp. 184–208; V-M. Kärkkäinen, 'Theology and Ecclesiology of the Spirit', *JPT* 14 (April, 1999), pp. 65–80.

[4] P. Hocken, 'Church', in S. Burgess, G. McGee, P. Alexander (eds), *DPCM* (Grand Rapids, Regency Reference Library, 1988), pp. 211–18.

[5] P. Hocken, 'Church, Theology of', in Burgess and van der Maas (eds), *NIDPCM*, pp. 544–51.

Roman Catholic. Pentecostals are much more interested in soteriology than ecclesiology.[6] Nevertheless, increasingly, they are prepared (at least in the scholarly world) to explore ecclesiological issues and to dialogue with and listen to others outside of their tradition.[7] While they have not provided a systematized ecclesiology, they have left valuable room for improvisation, adaptation and pragmatism. Clark writes, 'The rise of world Pentecost has relativized the whole concept of structures for thinking Pentecostals by bringing home the fact that the best structure is the one that works in its local context'.[8] The provision of a pragmatic, rather than an imposed, solution also ensures that any office does not replace charisma. Institutionalization that incorporates the concept of office without the spiritual charismatic authority necessary to empower the believer to function in that role is an obstruction to the mission of the Church.

The Local Church

Cross offers key ecclesiological characteristics that best define a Pentecostal church. As such it will experience the immediate presence of God, be capable of reflecting the nature of God in areas such as unity and mission, is transformed by God and engaged in the transformation of others as set by the agenda of God for the world.[9] Similarly, Macchia identifies key marks of the Church as being called to be united, holy, catholic (in the sense of being diverse) and apostolic (in the sense that it has been sent by God to fulfil his commission.[10]

---

[6] In this respect, Pentecostals offer a more accentuated tendency of that which also afflicts many evangelicals (B. Hindmarsh, 'Is Evangelical Ecclesiology an Oxymoron? A Historical Perspective' in J. Stackhouse (ed.), *Evangelical Ecclesiology: Reality or Illusion?* (Grand Rapids: Baker, 2003), pp. 15–37.

[7] V-M, Kärkkäinen, *An Introduction to Ecclesiology: Ecumenical, Historical and Global Perspectives* (Downer's Grove: InterVarsity Press, 2002); idem, '"The Nature and Purpose of the Church" Theological and Ecumenical Reflection from Pentecostal/Free Church Perspectives', *Ecumenical Trends* 33 (2004), pp. 97–103; R. Del Colle, 'Communion and the Trinity: The Free Church Ecclesiology of Miroslav Wolf – A Catholic Response', *Pneuma* 22.2 (2000), pp. 303–27; F.D. Macchia, 'The Nature and Purpose of the Church: A Pentecostal Response', *Ecumenical Trends* 34 (2005), pp. 97–102; S.K.H. Chan ('Spirit, Church and Liturgy: The Making of a Pentecostal Ecclesiology' (EPCRA conference paper, Uppsala University, 2007), pp. 1–17) explores the relevance of the Orthodox tradition to a development of Pentecostal ecclesiology in order to make explicit some of the implicit elements of Pentecostal spirituality, especially with reference to church leadership and the Lord's Supper.

[8] Clark and Lederle (eds), *What Is Distinctive*, p. 41.

[9] T. Cross, 'A Response to Clark Pinnock's "Church in the Power of the Holy Spirit"', *JPT* 14.2 (2006), pp. 175–82 (177–80).

[10] F. Macchia, 'Church, Theology of the', in Burgess (ed.), *EPCC*, pp. 104–06.

Pentecostals recognize all believers to be members of the universal Church but also encourage individuals to become members of local churches.[11] The local church is of significant importance to Pentecostals and although many local churches are part of large denominations, they are granted significant autonomy, including the freedom to appoint their own leaders, develop ministries, initiate mission activities and often invest in projects and buildings. Furthermore, the local church provides opportunities to facilitate individuals to develop their own abilities and gifts. Hocken notes that although Pentecostals may have infrequently explored the theology of the church in written form, 'the most distinctive Pentecostal contribution to ecclesiology' has been made with regard to their understanding of the local church.[12] In association with many other evangelicals, Pentecostals emphasize the relational importance of the Church, 'fellowship' being a key concept.[13] Thus, they expect to engage in participatory worship and corporate edification where every believer is viewed as charismatic and therefore can function as a channel for the Spirit (Rom. 12.6; 1 Cor. 12.7; Phil. 4.15; 1 Pet. 4.10).

People are welcomed as members of local churches on the basis of a personal claim to salvation and a willingness to function within the group as a committed Christian. Many also emphasize the importance of water baptism and regular church attendance as criteria for membership. Few demand that the prospective members should be baptized in the Spirit or speak in tongues, though some demand that members tithe.[14] In reality, the rules for membership are often very limited, perhaps indicating the fundamental belief that membership of a local church is less important than membership of the global Church. Membership is not essential to one's involvement in a local church though generally, it would be encouraged if official roles in the fellowship were to be undertaken. Membership is also generally needed if one wishes to participate in church polity. On occasions where a member has engaged in immoral activity or lifestyle, the membership is often removed and the person concerned even excluded from meeting with other church members for a predetermined time as an exercise in discipline.[15]

Pentecostals affirm similar beliefs to other evangelicals concerning the identity and responsibilities of members of local churches. Rather than develop a strictly laity-clergy divide, they tend to facilitate the involvement of multiple church members in the ministry of the local church, the priesthood

---

[11] Lugo (*Spirit and Power*, p. 18) records that 80% of Pentecostals in the countries researched stated that they attended religious services at least once a week (ranging from 65% (USA) to 92% (Philippines)).

[12] Hocken, 'Church, Theology of', pp. 546–47.

[13] Kärkkäinen, *Toward a Pneumatological Theology*, p. 116.

[14] Rowe, *One Lord, One Faith*, p. 368.

[15] D.J. Wilson, 'Church Membership', in Burgess and van der Maas (eds), *NIDPCM*, pp. 529–30.

of all believers being taken for granted by Pentecostals.[16] Theoretically, Pentecostal churches anticipate the possibility that all may participate in most settings within the structure of the church. Given that the Spirit initiates gifts (1 Cor 12.4–7, 11) and that it is his desire that all believers should so function (Rom. 12.4–9), there is often less of a clear line between the laity and leadership. However, for a number of reasons, the involvement of the majority of attendees in the ministry of the local church is often minimal. These reasons include the rise of numerically large urban churches that anticipate a multidisciplined and full-time leadership, the increasing numbers of leadership roles being undertaken by skilled exponents, the desire of attendees to have less involvement in the mission of the church than may have been the case in previous generations and societal changes that have affected the social dynamic of local churches. The ideal of 'body ministry' where all are anticipated as having the opportunity to function practically in the local church is often less of a phenomenon than would be expected among Pentecostals who are generally open to the creative work of the Spirit in individuals.

The resources to be tapped in order to achieve ministry in the local church are located in the believer's relationship with Jesus (Jn 15.1–8) and the empowering role of the Spirit (Jn 14.12–17), a fundamental tenet being that the Church is a community of the Spirit.[17] Theirs is a charismatic community at heart, in which the community functions through the charismata of the Spirit; theirs is a Spirit ecclesiology. His is a transforming role for he is the Creator Spiritus and the Pentecostal Church must ensure that it follows his agenda. What is of central importance to leaders in Pentecostal settings is that they be led by the Spirit rather than rely on their office for their authority. Of importance also is that that they be charismatic (dependent on the Spirit) rather than they merely have charismatic personalities.[18] Thus, Hocken describes the Pentecostal pastor who leads worship as one who 'ideally discerns what is happening more than he determines what will happen'.[19]

Among other terms, Pentecostals view themselves as part of the body of Christ (1 Cor. 12.27; Eph. 1.22–23). The value of the term is that it indicates

---

[16] MacDonald, 'Pentecostal Theology', p. 67; B. Sun, 'The Holy Spirit: The Missing Key in the Implementation of the Doctrine of the Priesthood of Believers', in Ma and Menzies (eds), *Pentecostalism in Context*, pp. 173–94.

[17] R. Hunston, 'The Church-the Body of Christ', in Brewster, *Pentecostal Doctrine*, pp. 139–48 (147); Macchia, 'Church, Theology of the', pp. 104–07 (104); Arrington, *Christian Doctrine*, pp. 165–85; C.D. Kham, 'Theology and Building Healthy Churches' (SPS conference paper, Cleveland, 2007), pp. 379–86.

[18] Clark and Lederle (eds), *What Is Distinctive*, p. 76.

[19] P. Hocken, S. Tugwell, G. Every, J.O. Mills, *New Heaven? New Earth? An Encounter with Pentecostalism* (Springfield: Templegate, 1977), p. 33.

the possibility of growth and maturity (Eph. 4.15–16; Col. 2.19), can be used to represent local and global expressions of the Church (1 Cor. 3.1–4; Eph. 1.22–23), is associated with the concepts of mutual support (Rom. 12.6–8), diversity (1 Cor. 12.14, 20) and unity (1 Cor. 12.12–31) and may be associated with the characteristics of direction and leadership (1 Cor. 12.27–28). They also refer to believers as the temple in whom the Spirit dwells (1 Cor. 3.16–17; Eph. 2.21–22) and the bride of Christ (2 Cor. 11.2; Rev. 21.2). The term often used to define God's people in the Bible is *laos* (people; Exod. 19.5; Acts 15.14; Tit. 2.14; 1 Pet. 2.9–10), defined as such by the fact that a covenant undergirds their relationship with God (2 Cor. 3.6; Heb. 8.7–12). As such, Pentecostals recognize that they are different to unbelievers and are to act as such for they are saints (*hagioi*), the main term used by Paul to describe believers. Rather than this be assumed to be equated with being sinless, it is more appropriate to recognize its fundamental meaning of people who have been set apart (Exod. 19.5–6; Heb. 6.10; Rev. 8.4); after all, they are described as royal priests (1 Pet. 2.9–10) and ought to live accordingly. They have also been chosen (Eph. 1.4, 11; 1 Thess. 1.4; 2 Thess. 2.13) as the Israel of God (Gal. 6.16),[20] this term referring to the Church, which comprises Jew and Gentile, a celebration of continuity and discontinuity (Rom. 2.28–29; Phil. 3.3).

One of the dangers of the increasing size of Pentecostal churches is that encounters with God experienced by attendees will be less personal and more congregational based. Rather than individuals expecting to meet with God personally, as well as corporately, there is a subtle move to the latter in which encounters with God are shared experiences with others. The emphasis on an individual encounter with God is in danger of being replaced by a communal one, in which one may even be a passive element.

Increasingly, Pentecostal churches are slipping into a clergy-laity divide, where the former are ordained and resourced and the latter function voluntarily and unpaid. Those who are in full time positions tend to function with greater authority and receive the greater support from the members of a congregation. Generally, potential leaders receive training and are affirmed by the leadership of the denominations. Although Fee argues that the NT model is of an identifiable leadership who were simply part of the congregation, this model is rarely reflected in any other than the smallest of Pentecostal churches.[21] Poloma notes that Pentecostalism has become different to its earlier expression where charisma determined function and 'continues to give way to a priestly clergy with lines drawn between the leaders and the led'.[22]

---

[20] See further Fee, *Gospel and Spirit*, pp. 122–33.
[21] Fee, *Listening to the Spirit*, pp. 123–24.

A challenge associated with the rise of urban churches, that are filled with Pentecostals who have professional qualifications and positions, is that leaders will need to develop their own leadership strategies and teaching programmes to make sure they meet the needs and expectations of such people. The less educated Pentecostals of the past needed and were offered a different diet to that expected and needed by modern Pentecostal urbanites. As a result, Cerillo calls for the establishment of a Pentecostal urban studies centre to explore ways of understanding the geographical, social, ethnic, racial, gender, spiritual and economic complexities of the city, integrating social action with the presentation of the message of salvation while providing a means for preparing leaders to function successfully therein.[23]

In contrast to early Pentecostalism when attempts were made to be inclusive,[24] Pentecostalism is rife with division.[25] Although there are signs of increasing fellowship and dialogue (especially among Pentecostal scholars), there is room for more.[26] Robeck regrets the fact that although 'Pentecostals are multi-cultural, we haven't yet learned how to act like it without hurting one another'.[27] A worrying trend has been the proliferation of independent churches, often Pentecostal by way of style and spirituality, but often led by people with little theological training. Although churches can grow in the absence of the latter, the danger of error being developed is clear.

Leadership Models

Kärkkäinen[28] notes that 'Pentecostals have written surprisingly little on ecclesiology' though that is less surprising when one recognizes the very nature of Pentecostalism which has tended to be pragmatic, resulting in a diversity of ecclesiologies.[29] However, this should not be understood to mean

---

[22] Poloma, *The Assemblies of God*, p. 121.

[23] A. Cerillo Jr, 'Pentecostals and the City', in Dempster, Klaus and Petersen (eds), *Called and Empowered*, pp. 98–119 (111–14).

[24] D.T. Irvin, ' "Drawing All Together in One Bond of Love": The Ecumenical Vision of William J. Seymour and the Azusa Street Revival', *JPT* 6 (1995), pp. 25–53.

[25] E. Javier, 'The Pentecostal Legacy: A Personal Memoir', *AJPS* 8.2 (2005), pp. 289–310 (300–04); this, of course, is not unique to Pentecostalism (see A. Walker, 'Sectarian Reactions: Pluralism and the Privatization of Religion', in H. Wilmer (ed.), *20/20 Visions: The Futures of Christianity in Britain* (London: SPCK, 1992)).

[26] S. Land, 'A Passion for the Kingdom: Revisioning Pentecostal Spirituality', *JPT* 1 (1992), pp. 19–46 (38–46).

[27] Robeck, 'Taking Stock of Pentecostalism', p. 45.

[28] Kärkkäinen, 'Church as Charismatic Fellowship', p. 102.

[29] S. Clifton, 'Pentecostal Ecclesiology: A Methodological Proposal for a Diverse Movement', *JPT* 15.2 (2007), pp. 213–32.

that Pentecostals have nebulous or ill thought through models of church leadership. On the contrary, they have expended much time and effort in defining their perspectives on developing church leadership as it was meant to be.[30] As a result, global Pentecostalism has a rich variety of ecclesiologies and forms of leadership, many of which claim to reflect a NT church model though many actually represent cultural tendencies or the personalities of the founders.

There is a general recognition among Pentecostals that the NT does not offer one model of ministry or leadership; instead, several may be identified or supported from the text.[31] While some Pentecostal denominations function along Congregational or Presbyterian lines, where the concept of *koinonia* is more easily reflected, others are Episcopal, while the Apostolic churches have a clearer apostolic framework.[32] Some Pentecostal denominations are decentralized while many have a centralized modus operandi; some have headquarters while others emphasize the autonomy and independence of the local church albeit in a fellowship with other like-minded assemblies.[33] Some groups have attempted to be theocracies, some have descended to autocracies, while most are somewhat in between often mixing a Congregational model in the local church and a Presbyterian model in regional or national contexts.[34] Some have offices that include apostles, prophets and teachers, others officially recognize nobody by these terms while others substitute other identifying titles.

The reason for the choice of governmental form is often related to the historical context during which the particular movement was formed. Some reacted to the contemporary structures of other denominations while others adopted elements with which they were in agreement. Those that were established by missionaries often imposed the ecclesiology of the sending denomination while others have developed their own structures that are best fitted to their mission strategy and socio-economic contexts.[35]

The terms 'pastor', 'elder' and 'overseer' are sometimes used interchangeably in Pentecostal churches, as they are in the NT, their main responsibility

---

[30] D.A. Coulter, 'The Development of Ecclesiology in the Church of God (Cleveland, TN): A Forgotten Contribution?', *Pneuma* 29.1 (2007), pp. 59–85.

[31] Kärkkäinen, *Spiritus Ubi Vult Spirat*, p. 336–37; Fee, *Listening to the Spirit*, pp. 132–62.

[32] Rowe, *One Lord, One Faith*, pp. 242–77; H.D. Hunter, 'We Are the Church: New Congregationalism. A Pentecostal Perspective', *Concilium* 3 (1996), pp. 17–44.

[33] Especially Scandinavia, see N-O, Nilsson, 'The Development of the Church-Concept: 1913–1948', *CPCR* 11 (Feb. 2002); Kärkkäinen, 'The Pentecostal Movement', pp. 110–12.

[34] Poloma, *The Assemblies of God*, pp. 122–27.

[35] See Hollenweger, *The Pentecostals*, p. 426; S.D. Glazier (ed.), *Perspectives on Pentecostalism: Case studies from the Caribbean and Latin America* (Washington: University Press of America, 1980).

being to care for believers (Acts 20.28; Eph. 4.11; Tit. 1.5–7). In general, a plurality of leaders is preferred where possible, in agreement with NT practice (Tit. 1.5). Their role is to provide spiritual leadership of a local congregation (1 Tim. 5.17). Deacons are located in many Pentecostal churches, their role often associated with the administration and practical development of the life of the local church and maintenance of the church buildings.

The appointment of leaders and the selection procedure of ministries in local churches vary widely, though generally it is determined by the church leadership on the basis of criteria that include recognition of relevant gifting, membership, experience and their acceptance by the wider group. Pentecostals have traditionally preferred to allow their ecclesiologies to develop on the basis of recognized gifts as they are reflected in people rather than appoint people to an office in the hope that charismatic authority will be later added.

Ministry Gifts

Pentecostals often distinguish between all the other gifts mentioned in the NT and those identified in Ephesians 4.11–12, the latter often described as 'Christ's gifts'.[36] Petts notes that the list refers, not to gifts but, to people who are themselves given to the church,[37] 'anointed persons with specialized callings'.[38]

Apostle

Pentecostals have a preference for restoring that which they perceive to be apostolic Christianity.[39] Thus, many early Pentecostals expected to see a re-emergence of the role of the apostle and some Pentecostal denominations have included the word 'Apostolic' in their names (The Apostolic Church; Apostolic Faith Mission). There is a measure of disagreement over this role among Pentecostals, not helped by the limited descriptions offered in the NT for the identification of the apostle and by the fact that some of those not designated as apostles functioned with significant (and sometimes similar) authority to the Twelve (the 70 – Lk. 10.1–2; Stephen – Acts 6.3–7.60;

---

[36] D. Gee (*The Ministry-Gifts of Christ* (London: AoG Publishing House, 1930), p. 28) identifies the gifts mentioned in Eph. 4.11 as those given to the church by Jesus for its 'spiritual growth and activity' and are to be differentiated from the other gifts granted by the Spirit; Corsie, 'The Ministry Gifts', p. 95; Ervin, *Spirit Baptism*, p. 114; Conn, *A Balanced Church*, pp. 34–8.

[37] Petts, *Body Builders*, p. 17; Menzies and Horton, *Bible Doctrines*, p. 176.

[38] G.R. Carlson, 'Christ's Gifts to His Church', *Paraclete* 25.3 (1991), p. 2.

[39] V-M, Kärkkäinen, 'Pentecostalism and the Claim for Apostolicity: An Essay in Ecumenical Ecclesiology', *Ecumenical Review of Theology* 25 (2001), pp. 323–36.

Philip – Acts 6.3–5, 8.5–13). The authority of the apostle is referred to in 2 Pet. 3.2 though it is unclear as to whom the writer is referring. Ervin simply states that their function is generally recognized though does not clarify its identity.[40]

The uncertainty is further complicated by the fact that the Twelve received their apostolic commission from Jesus while he was on earth (Mk. 3.13–15), had to be witnesses to his resurrection (Acts 1.22; 1 Cor. 9.1; 15.7) and functioned supernaturally, such activity demonstrating a claim to apostleship (2 Cor. 12.12). Paul defended his inclusion as an apostle of similar status to the Twelve in 1 Cor. 15.7–9. Since that procedure can no longer occur, it is not clear whether any other apostles can be legitimately appointed. The role of the Twelve and Paul seems to have been of a foundational nature (1 Cor. 9.2; Eph. 2.20) in a way that is reminiscent of the work of a church planter.[41] However, although an apostle may be defined as one who starts a church, there is limited NT evidence to prove this. Not only is there a lack of evidence as to the ministries of the apostles chosen by Jesus that could substantiate this presupposition, but even when apostles, like Paul, did establish churches, he did not use that feature as evidence of his apostleship. It is more likely that apostles may be designated as such by reason of their foundational and influential role, as identified in Eph. 2.20. However, even here, the evidence is limited, this verse possibly solely referring to the primary nature of the role of the apostles in the early Church.

The eschatological references to the status and function of the apostles, howsoever they are to be interpreted, also make it difficult to equate them with modern leaders (Mt. 19.28; Rev. 21.14). The NT identifies other believers as apostles, including Barnabas and James (Acts 14.14; Rom. 16.7(?); Gal. 1.18–19; 1 Thess. 2.6) who were appointed by fellow believers or local churches. As such, the latter may represent apostles who could be identified in the modern Church, apostles in a secondary sense, sent to fulfil a particular responsibility (Rom. 16.7; 2 Cor. 8.23).

Many Western Pentecostals appear to prefer to identify people as apostles after they have died and some have suggested that the office of apostle is rarely to be expected.[42] If this is so, as Canty notes, it is odd that Pentecostals who are non-cessationist make an exception here.[43] Even though the Charismatic Renewal raised the issue again, and identified a number of apostles as well as offering reasons why they should be acknowledged as such,[44]

---

[40] Ervin, *Spirit Baptism*, p. 114.
[41] D. Cartledge, *The Apostolic Revolution: The Restoration of Apostles and Prophets in the Assemblies of God in Australia* (Chester Hill: Paraclete Institute, 2000), p. 264.
[42] Conn, *A Balanced Church*, pp. 153–54.
[43] Canty, *The Practice of Pentecost*, p. 125.
[44] P.C. Wagner, *Apostles and Prophets: The Foundation of the Church* (Ventura: Regal, 2000).

Pentecostals, by and large, have preferred to remain cautious in this respect and major Pentecostal denominations have chosen not to incorporate apostles as part of their leadership nomenclature. This has been, to a degree, due the fact that some so-called apostles have been divisive, their ministries inappropriate and their teachings false.[45] Other Pentecostal denominations are more relaxed about using the title 'apostle' for people who have significant roles and responsibilities indicative of such a designation.[46]

Though they may not always be identified as apostles, many Pentecostal leaders function analogously to the early apostles in their leadership of churches and denominations. In the best examples of this model, they remain accountable to the churches they lead and whom they ultimately serve.

Prophet

Apostles and prophets are on a few occasions associated with one another in the NT (Eph. 2.20; 3.5) and these references are often understood to identify prophet/esses who had a role in the wider Church.[47] However, although some have popularly assumed that the NT prophet/ess was itinerant, there is little evidence to support this. Most Pentecostals distinguish between the roles of apostle and prophet.[48] They are prepared to accept that a member of a local church may be identified as a prophet/ess though many are reticent to grant a person a trans-local role, partly due to uncertainty caused in the event of a prophet/ess losing his/her sense of accountability and because of some notable failures in the lives of those who had been so designated.[49]

The difficulty is further compounded by there being limited definitions concerning the role of the prophet in the NT that would encourage one to be easily identified. Although Silas and Judas are described as prophets, there is limited information concerning their role other than that they exhorted and strengthened the believers by their words (Acts 15.32). Agabus, who foretold a famine (Acts 11.27–29) and the arrest of Paul (Acts 21.10–11),

---

[45] Hathaway, 'The Role', pp. 40–9; Gee (*The Pentecostal Movement*, pp. 117–18) concludes, '"It is a sorry fact that grave errors and extravagances quickly marred both the use of the prophetic gift and the office of the self-styled "apostle" leader'.

[46] Church of Pentecost, Ghana; H.B. Llewellyn, 'A Study of the History and Thought of the Apostolic Church in Wales in the Context of Pentecostalism' (unpublished master's dissertation, University of Cardiff, 1997), pp. 86–8; N.I. Ndiokwere, *Prophecy and Revolution: The Role of Prophets in the Independent African Churches and in Biblical Tradition* (London: SPCK, 1981).

[47] Petts, *Body Builders*, pp. 53–5.

[48] contra W. Grudem, *The Gift of Prophecy in the New Testament and Today* (Eastbourne: Kingsway, 1988), pp. 45–63.

[49] T. Grass, 'The Taming of the Prophets: Bringing Prophecy under Control in the Catholic Apostolic Church', *JEPTA* 16 (1996), pp. 58–70.

is also described as a prophet while Philip's four daughters are defined as prophetesses (Acts 21.8–9) though nothing is reported of their prophetic activities.[50] Although this would indicate the possibility of modern prophetesses, Ervin argues against this on the basis of Paul's injunction that a woman should not teach (1 Tim. 2.12), that there is only one other example of women prophesying (Lk. 2. 36) and that their experience was more akin to a member of the church giving a word of prophecy rather than functioning in a larger capacity as a prophetess.[51] However, his evidence is insufficient to support such a sweeping conclusion, especially given the awareness by Paul that women are expected to prophesy (1 Cor. 11.5) and the absence of a wider prophetic mandate for men only. Another challenge in identifying prophets, as opposed to those who prophesy irregularly, is that all believers are capable of ministering thus (Acts 2.17–18; 19.6; 1 Cor. 14.31).

The role of the prophet (as compared with the gift of prophecy) is to provide foundational ministry in a church or churches (Eph. 2.20)[52] though, as has been indicated, few are identified as such in the NT. It is also unclear that this is intended to refer to all prophets and more likely refers to those who were central in the development of the Church by the preaching of the gospel.[53] They are differentiated from church planters and preachers though the ideal of a preacher is that s/he should function prophetically.[54] The quasi-cessationist position of some Pentecostals, with regard to the identification of prophets, sits uneasily with their views concerning other manifestations of the Spirit. Nevertheless, some Pentecostal churches are prepared to acknowledge believers as prophets and to facilitate their role in helping the church or denomination to move forward.

Moore is one of the few Pentecostal scholars who has sought to explore the role of the OT prophet and then gleaned principles of relevance to the prophetic vocation today,[55] noting the role of the prophet as a messenger (Isa. 6.8–9), who revealed, on behalf of the Lord (Hos. 1.2), the words heard, the vision seen or the experience felt.[56] The OT prophet often functioned as

---

[50] Acts 13.1–2 provides a list of those who were described as teachers and prophets; D.M. Gill, 'The Disappearance of the Female Prophet: Twilight of Christian Prophecy' in Ma and Menzies (eds), *The Spirit*, pp. 178–93.

[51] Ervin, *Spirit Baptism*, pp. 117–18.

[52] Petts, *Body Builders*, p. 55; Conn (*A Balanced Church*, pp. 154–56) goes beyond the information in Acts by suggesting that this 'was emotional, even ecstatic, exhortation . . . essentially spontaneous, unpolished, emotional, exhortative, and corrective').

[53] Penney, 'The Testing', pp. 66–7.

[54] Conn (*A Balanced Church*, p. 156) writes, 'The emotional preaching of a prophet may lack the form, the order, and the logic of a teacher or a pastor . . .'

[55] Carlson, 'Christ's Gifts to His Church', pp. 1–9 (4).

[56] R.D. Moore, 'The Prophetic Calling: An Old Testament Profile and Its Relevance for Today', *JEPTA* 24 (2004), pp. 16–29 (17–20).

a poet whose prophecies were couched in ways that aided the memory or graphically encapsulated the message (Ezek. 33.30–32). Moore also identifies the ecstatic element of the prophet that sometimes placed them outside normal conventions of behaviour, the zeal of the prophet being reflective of the zeal of the Lord who chose to speak through the prophet.[57] Finally, the radical theophanic encounters experienced by the OT prophets separated them from all others. Some of these characteristics may be applied in order to identify modern prophet/esses.

Evangelist

Being identified in Acts 21.8, Eph. 4.11 and 2 Tim. 4.5, this ministry was of importance to the development of the early Church and has been central to the development of Pentecostalism. Indeed, Conn develops evangelism as 'a prominent and distinguishing feature of the Pentecostal Revival'.[58] Perhaps because it better fits the ethos of Pentecostalism, there has been little difficulty in acknowledging those with evangelistic tendencies. It appears from the limited evidence of Acts, that the work of the evangelist was intended to be itinerant (Acts 8.40), though on the basis of Eph. 2.12, it may be anticipated that another role of the evangelist was to train others to do likewise. Similarly, most Pentecostal evangelists have functioned on an itinerant basis, though they have generally been associated with a local church or denomination. Although all believers are to be evangelistic, the role of an evangelist, as one who is dedicated to this occupation, has long been recognized, as has the association of the evangelist with miracles of healing. The supernatural emphasis and the commitment to the conversion of many in large missions has resulted in a long history of Pentecostal evangelists who have often become much better known than Bible teachers or pastors.[59]

Pastor/Teacher

Traditionally, these roles have been separated from one another. Furthermore, while many Pentecostals believe that a pastor should have the ability to teach, they advocate that one may be a teacher and not necessarily a pastor, thus allowing for the possibility of itinerant teachers, where the latter have been 'given a special ability to explain and interpret the truth of God's revelation (Matt. 28.19–20)'.[60] However, a strong case may be made for

---

[57] Moore, 'The Prophetic Calling', pp. 24–7.
[58] Conn, A Balanced Church, p. 159.
[59] See D. Cartwright, The Great Evangelists: The Remarkable Lives of George and Stephen Jeffreys (Basingstoke: Marshall Pickering, 1986); L.G. McClung Jr, 'Evangelists', in Burgess and van der Maas (eds), NIDPCM, pp. 620–23 (621–22).
[60] Menzies and Horton, Bible Doctrines, p. 178; also Petts, Body Builders, pp. 91–2.

combining them and such a view has been accepted by many Pentecostals.[61] Thus, the pastor is anticipated as functioning in a pastoral, shepherding way (1 Pet. 5.2) as well as one who teaches (1 Tim. 3.2; 5.17; Tit. 1.9). Both aspects enable the persons concerned to offer spiritual leadership and counselling. Some Pentecostals view the terms *poimen* (pastor, shepherd),[62] *presbuteros* (elder)[63] and *episcopēs* (overseer)[64] as being used synonymously.[65] In accordance with the pattern in the NT,[66] many Pentecostal churches are led by a team of full-time or part-time leaders, often entitled pastors or ministers, with varying responsibilities.

The Role of Women in Leadership

Introduction

The place of women in Pentecostalism has changed over the years and they are currently very underrepresented in the leadership of most Pentecostal churches and denominations.[67] There is, however, much evidence of women

---

[61] Conn, *A Balanced Church*, p. 162; Carlson, 'Christ's Gifts to His Church', p. 8, Dye, *Living in the Presence*, p. 76.

[62] Eph. 4.11.

[63] Acts 20.28.

[64] 1 Tim. 3.1.

[65] Petts, *Body Builders*, p. 71, providing 1 Pet. 5.2 and Tit. 1.5–7 as evidence; also Menzies and Horton, *Bible Doctrines*, p. 179.

[66] Acts 14.23; 15.22; 20.17; Jas 5.14.

[67] Anderson, *An Introduction to Pentecostalism*, p. 127. Writing in 1946, Brumback (*What Meaneth This?*, p. 315) could state of Pentecostalism, 'On the whole, women are not given undue prominence in the movement; they represent a very small percentage of the ministry; and they are virtually silent with respect to doctrinal and governmental questions. We have endeavoured conscientiously to abide by the Word in this matter'; L. Scanzoni, S. Setta, 'Women in Evangelical, Holiness and Pentecostal Traditions', in R. Ruether, R. Keller (eds), *Women in Religion in America Vol. 3, 1900–1968* (Cambridge: Harper and Row, 1981), pp. 223–35; E. Alexander, 'Gender and Leadership in the Theology and Practice of Three Pentecostal Women Pioneers' (unpublished doctoral dissertation, Catholic University of America, Washington, 2002); D.M. Gill, 'The Biblical Liberated Woman', *Paraclete* 29.2 (1995), pp. 1–9 (6–8).

[68] W.K. Kay, 'A Woman's Place Is on Her Knees: The Pastor's View of the Role of Women in the Assemblies of God', *JEPTA* 18 (1998), pp. 64–75 (67–8); Bundy, 'Historical and Theological Analysis', pp. 86–9; Irvin, 'Drawing All Together', pp. 30–1; J. C. Ma, 'Asian Women and Pentecostal Ministry', in Anderson and Tang (eds), *Asian and Pentecostal*, pp. 129–46; J.E. Powers, '"Your Daughters Shall Prophesy": Pentecostal Hermeneutics and the Empowerment of Women', in Dempster, Klaus and Petersen (eds), *The Globalization of Pentecostalism*, pp. 313–37 (313–23); C.J. Sanders, 'History of Women in the Pentecostal Movement', *CPCR* 2; W.E. Warner, 'At the Grass-Roots: Kathryn Kuhlman's Pentecostal-Charismatic Influence on the Mainstream Churches', *Pneuma* 17.1 (1995), pp. 51–65; A. Butler, *Women in the Church of God in Christ*

playing an active role in evangelism, church planting, teaching and preaching as well as writing in early Pentecostalism.[68] Indeed, the Azusa Street Revival reveals that women played prominent roles in it and its aftermath.[69] A number of women set up Pentecostal churches and even Pentecostal denominations.[70] In particular, the International Church of the Foursquare Gospel (ICFG), established by Aimee Semple McPherson in Los Angeles but with centres throughout the world, ordains women. Anderson notes that over 30% of the pastors of the Brazilian Foursquare Gospel Church, established by evangelists from the ICFG, are women.[71]

Early Pentecostalism provided the means for women to be much more active in the Church, as was then possible in some Holiness traditions of the time. This was well expressed by Maria Woodworth-Etter, an early Pentecostal preacher, who wrote in 1916, 'It is high time for women to let their lights shine, to bring out their talents that have been hidden away rusting, and use them for the glory of God'.[72] A strong emphasis on the imminent return of Jesus partly facilitated an early readiness to accommodate women in leadership.[73] In 1914, a third of AoG ministers were women as were two-thirds of its missionaries.[74] However, the seeds of division were developing even then in that, despite this, women were not allowed to be elders

(University of North Carolina Press: Chapel Hill, 2007); K.D. Welch, 'Oklahoma Women Preachers, Pioneers and Pentecostals' (unpublished doctoral dissertation, The University of Arizona, 2007).

[69] D.G. Roebuck, 'Go and Tell My Brothers: The Waning of Women's Voices in American Pentecostalism' (SPS conference paper, 1990), pp. 1–10 (2); R.M. Griffith, D.G. Roebuck, 'Women, Role of', in Burgess, *NIDPCM*, pp. 1203–204; Javier, 'The Pentecostal Legacy', pp. 304–05; E. Alexander, *The Women of Azusa Street* (Cleveland: Pilgrim Press, 2006); idem, 'Women', in Burgess (ed.), *EPCC*, pp. 460–61.

[70] Anderson, *An Introduction to Pentecostalism*, p. 274; C. Hoehler-Fatton, *Women of Fire and Spirit: History, Faith and Gender in Roho Religion in Western Kenya* (Oxford: Oxford University Press, 1996); R. Barnes III, 'F.F. Bosworth and the Role of Women in His Life and Ministry', *JEPTA* 27.1 (2007), pp. 25–38; D. Chapman, 'The Rise and Demise of Women's Ministry in the Origins and Early Years of Pentecostalism in Britain', *JPT* 12.2 (2004), pp. 217–46; E.L. Blumhofer, 'Reflections on the Source of Aimee Semple McPherson's Voice', *Pneuma* 17.1 (1995), pp. 21–4; D.G. Roebuck, 'Perfect Liberty to Preach the Gospel: Women Ministers in the Church of God', *Pneuma* 17.1 (1995), pp. 25–32.

[71] Anderson, *An Introduction to Pentecostalism*, p. 72; D.M. Epstein, *Sister Aimee: The Life of Amy Semple McPherson* (New York: Harcourt, Brace and Jovanovich, 1993).

[72] M. Woodworth-Etter, *Signs and Wonders* (New Kensington: Whitaker House, 1916), p. 202.

[73] Macchia, 'The Struggle for Global Witness', p. 23.

[74] B. Cavaness, 'God Calling: Women in Pentecostal Missions', in L.G. McClung Jr (ed.), *Azusa Street and Beyond: 100 Years*, pp. 53–66; Anderson, *An Introduction to Pentecostalism*, p. 274.

(though they could be missionaries and evangelists) or vote in the General Council. Despite the fact that many women undertook very important positions in the war effort, this did not translate into their being encouraged to take on similarly important roles in the Church.[75] Similarly, Anderson notes that although ordination of women was instituted in 1935, it was so restrictive that few women sought it.[76] Despite these obstacles, 'by 1936, two thirds of the members and half of the preachers and missionaries of US Pentecostal churches were women'.[77]

However, the emphasis on the role of the woman as homemaker and protector of the family, dominated Pentecostal denominations after the chaotic times of World War II.[78] Roebuck and Mundy show that, at least in the Church of God, male leaders increasingly circumscribed the roles of women partly to protect that which they viewed as the demise of family values and traditions, resulting in a reduction of women ministers from 1950 to 1990 from 18.2% to 7.7%.[79] Increasingly though, even from its earliest days, the role of women in leadership has often been restricted in many Pentecostal churches.[80] This has been exacerbated in cultures where a patriarchal culture is maintained.

Tensions

Most Pentecostal denominations accept that women have a specific right to prophesy and pray publicly, as reflected in 1 Cor. 11.5.[81] Thereafter, there is a reluctance to depart from the standard evangelical view, as expressed by Poythress that with regard to church leadership, 'Paul insists that women not take on that role but submit to the leadership of men'.[82] The increasing

---

[75] C.H. Barfoot, G.T. Sheppard, 'Priestly versus Prophetic Religion: The Changing Roles of Women Clergy in Classical Pentecostal Churches', *RRR* 22.1 (1980), pp. 2–17.

[76] Anderson, *An Introduction to Pentecostalism*, p. 274.

[77] Anderson, *An Introduction to Pentecostalism*, p. 274.

[78] Griffith and Roebeck, 'Women, Role of', pp. 198–203.

[79] D.G. Roebuck, K.C. Mundy, 'Women, Culture, and Post-World War Two Pentecostalism', in Cross and Powery (eds), *The Spirit and the Mind*, pp. 191–204 (192–93, 197); see a more in-depth treatment of the topic in the Church of God by C.R. Dirksen, 'Let Your Women Keep Silence', in D.N. Bowdle (ed.), *The Promise and the Power: Essays on the Motivations, Developments, and Practices of the Church of God* (Cleveland: Pathway Press, 1980), pp. 165–96.

[80] Alexander, 'Women', p. 462.

[81] D.M. Gill, 'The Contemporary State of Women in Ministry in the Assemblies of God', *Pneuma* 17.1 (1995), pp. 33–6.

[82] V.S. Poythress, 'The Church as Family: Why Male Leadership in the Family Requires Male Leadership in the Church', in J. Piper, W. Grudem (eds), *Recovering Biblical Manhood and Womanhood* (Wheaton: Crossway, 1991), pp. 237–50 (238); see also G.W. Knight III, 'Husbands and Wives as Analogues of Christ and the Church: Ephesians 5:21–23 and Colossians 3:18–19', in Piper and Grudem, *Recovering Biblical Manhood*, pp. 161–75.

numbers of male ministers have, to a degree, reduced the pressure to appoint church leaders and thus the incentive for women to function in such positions has receded. Increasingly, women have taken upon themselves other roles, including prayer and intercession.[83] In a survey of the views of AoG pastors in the United Kingdom, it was discovered that 60% of them thought that the greatest contribution of women to the life of the local church was through prayer while 29% identified it as practical involvement.[84] Other countries express similarly limited views concerning the role of women in church leadership.[85]

The situation in the early twenty-first century is that women are increasingly accepted in roles of leadership by Pentecostal denominations although they are not so easily welcomed by congregations, despite the increasing presence of women in the global marketplace, education and politics. Whereas denominational leaders and Pentecostal scholars and theologians are increasingly less comfortable with forbidding women from functioning in the church in leadership, individual churches are more resistant though this appears to be changing slowly.[86] It is possible that this is due to the power of tradition and current praxis, though it may also be due to the fact that a hiatus exists; women are infrequently represented in positions of leadership in Pentecostal churches and denominations and the impetus to change is restricted as there are very few role models in existence. As in secular society, where men dominate the boardrooms, the same is the case in national and regional offices of many Pentecostal Churches also.

However, Korea, in particular, has been used to the idea of women leaders in the Pentecostal Church.[87] Nilsson also provides a case study of the Swedish Pentecostal movement, demonstrating that there has been a substantial shift towards facilitating the possibility for women to function more in the Swedish Pentecostal Church. This has largely resulted from a willingness to move from a literalistic interpretation of the biblical text to a desire to contextualize it. It has also been aided by the involvement of the laity in the debate and, practically, because of the absurdity of women missionaries being restricted from functioning in leadership capacities on returning to Sweden when in their mission activities, they had engaged in broad leadership roles.[88]

---

[83] Griffith and Roebuck, 'Women, Role of', pp. 1206–207.

[84] Kay, 'A Woman's Place', pp. 69–73.

[85] Gajewski and Wawrzeniuk, 'A Historical and Theological Analysis', p. 44.

[86] Lugo (*Spirit and Power*, p. 40) records that 70% of Pentecostals in the countries researched agreed that women should be allowed to be church leaders, ranging from India (39%) to South Korea (90%); clearly, cultural contexts play a significant part in the issue.

[87] Y-H. Lee, 'The Life and Ministry of David Yonggi Cho and the Yoido Full Gospel Church', in Ma, Menzies and Bae (eds), *David Yonggi Cho*, p. 7.

[88] N-O. Nilsson, 'The Debate on Women's Ministry: Summary and Analysis', *CPCR 5* (Feb. 1999).

Reasons that have been (and still are) offered for a restricted involvement of women in the Church include the suggestion that the NT provides little evidence that women were appointed to any office or had significant leadership roles in the early Church.[89] Therefore, to encourage this development would be to set a precedent that the NT does not recognize. Consequently, early Pentecostalism provides few examples of women being ordained to positions consisting of ministerial authority; they could be missionaries or evangelists but not pastors or elders.[90] Griffith identifies controversies in the American Pentecostal denominations over this issue, particularly in the early twentieth century.[91]

Another tension arose due to the uncertainty as to whether women could have authority over men in the context of local or international churches when Paul encouraged them to be submissive to their husbands (Eph. 5.22). If women were to fulfil this Pauline exhortation, it was felt by many that they were to be excluded from any position of authority over men. Thus, women were not allowed to vote in the general councils of the AoG in the USA until 1920 and ordination was only granted in 1935, though this was not a popular move, evidenced by the fact that no one was appointed to a national office.[92] However, women in missionary settings, in mainly non-Western countries, were often afforded significant positions of authority and over men, though this was rarely commented on by their colleagues in their home countries.

Closer relationships with evangelical believers have further restricted Pentecostal women from functioning in leadership as a result of Pentecostals adopting the restrictions placed on women by evangelical and Fundamentalist scholarship.[93] Similarly, Poloma notes the restrictions that have been placed on women from social pressures and biblical exegesis that has arisen from the 'marriage with non-Pentecostal conservative Protestantism (which) is moving the Assemblies of God away from its historical ambivalence toward

---

[89] J.E. Powers, 'Recovering a Woman's Head with Prophetic Authority: A Pentecostal Interpretation of 1 Corinthians 11:3–16', *JPT* 10.1 (2001), pp. 11–37 (13).
[90] B. Cavaness, 'God Calling: Women in Assemblies of God Missions', *Pneuma* 16.1 (1994), pp. 49–62.
[91] Griffith and Roebuck, 'Women, Role of', pp. 1204–206.
[92] E.L. Blumhofer, C.R. Armstrong, 'Assemblies of God', in Burgess and van der Maas (eds), *NICPCM*, p. 335.
[93] M.D. Palmer, 'Ethics in the Classical Pentecostal Tradition' in Burgess and van der Maas (eds), *NIDPCM*, p. 608; P. Althouse (*Spirit of the Last Days: Pentecostal Eschatology in Conversation with Jurgen Moltmann* (London: T&T Clark, 2003), pp. 61, 160–61) comments generally that Pentecostalism had come under the thrall of Fundamentalism by the middle of the twentieth century. He regards this development as being responsible for the quelling of both the 'charismatic dimension' and the 'early Pentecostal vision'.

women in ministry and toward silencing its prophesying daughters'.[94] Powers argues that the Charismatic Renewal brought further pressure against women in ministry because although the Spirit renewed mainstream churches, it did so in the context of church structures that had traditionally been dominated by men. In general, they were so to remain.[95] Barfoot and Sheppard claim that Pentecostals moved from an emphasis on calling, where women were able to follow the call they believed they had received from God and thus function charismatically, to a position where regimentation and structure dominated the processes of leadership, resulting in a decrease in women in leadership.[96] This development of hierarchical structures was encouraged by the demise in the belief in the imminent return of Jesus, resulting in a perception that to survive and increase, organizations needed to be developed. Although this did not by necessity preclude the involvement of women, it provided a contributory element since those who worked in such organizations were paid whereas women had previously often functioned voluntarily.

Everts also identifies social reasons for the limited opportunities for women to function in church leadership including the view that women are viewed as being more emotional and less rational than men. She also identifies maternalism and sexuality as powerful and restrictive forces.[97]

The Influence of the Bible

Increasingly, it has been recognized that a major difficulty in seeking to be guided by the Bible with reference to this issue is that it does not provide clear guidelines, as demonstrated by the many books that have been written claiming to reflect the teaching of the Bible whose conclusions are often at variance with others who have claimed similar reliance on the biblical text. Some Pentecostals argue that the discussion needs to bear in mind the wider presentation of that which the Bible says of women. For example, Paul indicates that there is no distinction in the Church on the basis of gender (Gal. 4.28). Thus, Fee argues that where Paul elsewhere refers to the issue of male/female relationships (1 Cor. 7.1–40; 11.2–16), he is dealing with abuse of this fundamental notion of mutuality rather than refusing to allow women the same roles as men.[98] Paul is arguing for complementarity, but not the removal of a differentiation between the sexes. He concludes, 'Ministry is thus the result of God's gifting and has nothing to do with being male or female, any more than it has to do with being Jew or Gentile, or slave or free'.[99]

---

[94] Poloma, *The Assemblies of God*, pp. 103–21 (119).
[95] Powers, 'Recovering a woman's head', pp. 14–17.
[96] Barfoot and Sheppard 'Priestly versus Prophetic Religion', pp. 2–17.
[97] J.M. Everts, 'Brokenness as the Center of a Woman's Ministry', *Pneuma* 17.2 (1995), pp. 237–43.
[98] Fee, *Listening to the Spirit*, pp. 61–76.
[99] Fee, *Listening to the Spirit*, p. 76.

It is to be remembered that the texts that refer to this issue are occasional letters to first-century settings where cultural norms needed to be observed to ensure that the effectiveness and witness of the Church were not compromised. Bearing this in mind will guard against the assumption that all the advice of the writers, including Paul, is timeless. Although that may be the case in many situations, it is possible that some of the propositions written were meant to relate to the original setting primarily and possibly exclusively.[100] Thus, passages including 1 Tim. 2.9–15 may be interpreted appropriately when they are recognized as containing specific guidance to specific believers living in a particular era and context, the latter being a situation where false teaching was being promulgated.[101] Although there are dangers in holding to such a potentially fluid hermeneutic, it does allow for the possibility that what the Spirit may seem to be affirming in other contexts and eras, which is not reflected in the biblical material, may still nevertheless be appropriate since the Spirit is dynamic and not static. Furthermore, other verses indicate that men were not always the leaders in the Church (Acts 16.3–5, 13–15, 40; Rom. 16.1–2, 7; Col. 4.15; Phil. 4.2–3).

Recognizing the ambiguity over the meaning of *kephalē* in 1 Cor. 11.3,[102] Powers deduces that rather than argue over which meaning is most accurate ('head' or 'source'), it is more appropriate to recognize the ambiguity and allow the context to determine the most appropriate translation and not simply conduct a literary examination of the word.[103] She provides a case for the ongoing functioning of women in the church through an exegesis of 1 Cor. 11.3–16.[104] As a result, she concludes that the passage reminds the readers that 'one should not break convention if that would distract from the glory of God in worship' and that 'not all distinctions between the sexes are obliterated'.[105] A careful balance is to be promulgated – to encourage women to function as part of the eschatological community but, as with men, to do so appropriately and with a clear support and authority in place. That which Paul is not doing (in 1 Cor. 11.3–16) is advocating a subordination of women to men but suggesting that they wear a veil as an appropriate form of attire to the culture of the day, not because of the importance of accommodating oneself to one's culture, but because it serves to act as a sign of their authority, in an appropriate way in first-century Corinth.[106] At the

[100] Powers, 'Recovering a Woman's Head', p. 20.
[101] Fee, *Listening to the Spirit*, p. 75.
[102] For a discussion of the options see, W. Grudem, 'The Meaning of Kephale: A Response to Recent Studies', in Piper and Grudem, *Recovering Biblical Manhood*, pp. 424–76.
[103] Powers, 'Recovering a Woman's Head', pp. 22–4.
[104] Powers, 'Recovering a Woman's Head', pp. 11–37.
[105] Powers, 'Your Daughters Shall Prophesy', p. 330.
[106] C.S. Keener, *Paul, Women, and Wives: Marriage and Women's Ministry in the Letters of Paul* (Peabody: Hendrickson, 1992), pp. 19–69.

very least, women are not subjugated by Paul nor does the veil signify their inferior place. Rather, it demonstrated that they are functioning authoritatively in their own right. Most importantly, although Paul makes a clear case for identifying male leadership, even basing such a gender distinctive on Creation, it is not clear that his exposition is to be related to the Church universal and throughout all the ages. It is after all included in a letter to a first-century church.

The role of women as reflected in 1 Cor. 14.33–35 has also been the basis of much discussion, especially the recommendation that they remain silent in church gatherings. Brumback assumes that Paul is reprimanding those women in the Corinthian church who 'were attempting to claim full equality with men', a situation that needed to be corrected.[107] Associating this issue with 1 Tim. 2.11–12, he understands this to be a general rather than an absolute rule.[108]

Munyon asserts that the prohibition of women to speak (14.34–35) referred to a practice instituted by the Corinthians that Paul rejected (in v. 36); as in 1 Cor. 1.12, 6.12, 10.23, these verses may be identified as the Corinthians' beliefs that Paul is quoting.[109] In support of this view, he notes that for Paul to refer to the Law (v. 34) is unusual, and asserts that elsewhere Paul had allowed the possibility of public worship by women (1 Cor. 11.2–16) and leadership (Rom. 16.12). Thus, he concludes that it is possible that a Jewish influence has restricted the role of women in the church in Corinth. Others believe that rather than this being an injunction against women teachers, it is more likely referring to women interrupting the speaker with inappropriate questions, Paul suggesting that their learning would improve if their (more educated) husbands taught them in the privacy of their homes. There are many other possible interpretations that attempt to explicate these verses but it is not clear which (if any) are correct. It is of greater value to the debate to recognize that there is little evidence that Paul intended his injunction to be applied for all time. Indeed, Keener identifies this as a local problem that demanded a local solution,[110] albeit a practice followed in 'all the churches' of the day.

The reference to submission in Eph. 5.18–33 is often viewed as being very influential to the discussion. However, Paul is probably referring to the topic of submission in a desire to affirm the norm in Graeco-Roman society and he qualifies it by instructing men to love their wives as Christ loves the Church

---

[107] Brumback, *What Meaneth This?*, p. 313.

[108] Brumback, *What Meaneth This?*, p. 314; he identifies exceptions (Judg. 4.4; 2 Chron. 34.22–28; Acts 18.26.

[109] T. Munyon, '1 Corinthians 14:34–35: The Jewish Influence View. Part 1', *Paraclete* 29.2 (1995), pp. 15–24.

[110] Keener, *Paul, Women, and Wives*, pp. 70–100.

(5.2, 25), thereby encouraging mutual submission. This guidance ensures that, if followed, believers could not be accused of subverting the status quo while at the same time, Paul encourages men to have higher standards of care and affection for women than the current society advocated.

1 Timothy 2.8–15 is a key passage that has received considerable attention in recent years. The historical Pentecostal context for the interpretation of these verses has been literalistic, resulting in their being applied in such a way as to discourage women from teaching or to function in leadership in church. Increasingly, it has been indicated that an alternative and more preferable application needs to be taken into consideration on the basis that the passage was written 'to correct a very ad-hoc problem in Ephesus' and was never intended to be a timeless injunction.[111] Thus, although the NT references to women in leadership appear to prohibit or reduce such opportunities, one's hermeneutical method is an important factor. If the Bible is accepted as offering timeless guidelines in all respects, those guidelines are to be adopted and applied in all circumstances. However, if the contents are to be contextualized in different settings and eras, different procedures will need to be implemented to ensure that the principles established by the biblical authors are appropriately applied. Thus, one may be true to the s/Spirit of the text.

The Role of the Spirit in the Community

It is possible that a consideration of the role of the Spirit may be a helpful guide to determining the validity of women functioning in leadership. The empowering of believers by the Spirit in ways determined by him (1 Cor. 12.4–7, 11), irrespective of gender, indicates that restrictive measures that would exclude some from ministry or leadership may be inappropriate. Thus with Macchia, it is appropriate to ask, 'Why Pentecostals have in general not followed this contextual hermeneutic with regard to the obvious anointing of women in a limitless variety of roles today is impossible in my view to explain in a way that justifies it'.[112] He notes that the evidence that proved to Jewish Christians that Gentiles could be affirmed as equal partners was similarly 'based on the obvious fact that the Spirit anointed and gifted them as well as the Jews'.[113]

Bundy translates the conclusion of an early European Pentecostal leader, T.B. Barratt, who wrote in a book dedicated to the issue of the role of women in church leadership, 'When the Spirit calls her and the church understands

---

[111] Fee, Gospel and Spirit, p. 64; Keener, Paul, Women, and Wives, pp. 101–32.
[112] Macchia, Baptized in the Spirit, p. 220; Powers, 'Your Daughters Shall Prophesy', p. 324; E.D. Rios, '"The Ladies Are Warriors": Latina Pentecostalism and Faith-Based Activism in New York City', in McClung (ed.), Azusa Street and Beyond: 100 Years, pp. 217–32.
[113] Macchia, Baptized in the Spirit, p. 220.

the call, then the inspired woman may assume any role as her place in the Christian church'.[114] Similarly, Thomas advocates allowing the community of believers, who share the Spirit, to listen to the testimonies of others (especially those who have been endowed with gifts, past and present) and reflect the leading of the Spirit as they perceive it in their setting.[115] He offers the astute comment that, in response to those who may say they have not seen leadership gifts in women and therefore cannot countenance the possibility, 'Most of those in Jerusalem had not seen Gentile converts with their own eyes, but in the end were willing to accept the testimony of others who had'.[116] Given the impasse that exists on this topic because of the various and even opposing views that may be gleaned from the Bible, this approach provides a radical and Spirit-directed framework for enquiry; such a procedure may be open to abuse and misunderstanding but it is part of the quest to which Pentecostals have been called – to walk and be led by the Spirit.

The Role of Historical Precedent

Benvenuti argues that Pentecostalism should look to its history for guidance as to appropriate practice for providing current opportunities for women in ministry and leadership as it did in its early years, as exemplified by Aimee Semple McPherson.[117] Not only did women function in significant ways but also they did so with the blessing of male colleagues who recognized that they were authentically gifted by God, as confirmed through the success of their ministries, and were living testimonies of the fulfilment of Joel 2.28.

Training and Education

Introduction

For most of their existence, Pentecostal Theological Colleges have been the venues for short-term preparation for ministry, not places for exploration and contemplation. Studies were not expected to last for longer than 2 years and were often much shorter, the teachers often being successful or experienced ministers or evangelists. Neither has all the teaching been of a high academic calibre nor was it intended to provide an opportunity for discourse

---

[114] Bundy, 'Historical and Theological Analysis', pp. 88–9 (trans. T.B. Barratt, *Kvinnens stilling I Menigheten* (Oslo: Korset Seier Forlag, 1933), p. 33).

[115] Thomas, 'Women Pentecostals and the Bible', pp. 52–4.

[116] Thomas, 'Women Pentecostals and the Bible', p. 53.

[117] S.R. Benvenuti, 'Pentecostal Women in Ministry: Where Do We Go from Here?', *CPCR* 1; S.R. Nenvenuti, 'Anointed, Gifted and Called: Pentecostal Women in Ministry', *Pneuma* 17.2 (1995), pp. 230–34; G.D. Townsend, 'The Material Dream of Aimee Semple McPherson: A Lesson in Pentecostal Spirituality', *Pneuma* 14.2 (1992), pp. 171–83.

or analysis. McClung writes of study conducted in Pentecostal institutions as, 'more experiential than cognitive, more activist than reflective, more actualized than analyzed'.[118] The major purpose for the establishment of such Colleges was to prepare people for evangelism and leading churches rather than for objective enquiry or the development of Pentecostal scholarship.[119] Also, in the early days of Pentecostalism, there was a strong belief in the imminent return of Jesus and therefore to engage in extended periods of study was felt to be inappropriate.[120] Similarly, in the quest for evangelism, education has generally suffered; while church growth has emphasized the status of the pastor/preacher, the teacher has been marginalized. Such a context causes Palmer to call for a return to the fundamental raison d'être of the believer – to commune with the Creator, as a result of which the creation of a Christian world view becomes paramount;[121] such a challenging and responsible objective is potentially best served in a Theological College setting. In an interesting empirical investigation, Kay demonstrates that, as recently as 1999, 36% of UK Pentecostal ministers had not received any formal theological training while only 10% had gained a degree in theology.[122]

In recent years, there has been considerable discussion by Pentecostals concerning the role and development of Theological Colleges and Christian education.[123] In some areas of the world, there has been a resurgence in

---

[118] L.G. McClung, 'Salvation Shock Troops', in Smith *Pentecostals from the Inside Out* , pp. 81–90 (86).

[119] Macchia, 'The Struggle for Global Witness ', p. 9.

[120] L.F. Wilson, 'Bible Institutes, Colleges, Universities', in Burgess and van der Maas (eds), *NIDPCM*, pp. 372–80 (373).

[121] M. Palmer, 'Orienting Our Lives: The Importance of a Liberal Education for Pentecostals in the Twenty First Century', *Pneuma* 23.2 (2001), pp. 197–216 (204–06).

[122] Kay, 'Sociology of British Pentecostal', pp. 1080–083 (1081).

[123] K. Warrington, 'Would Jesus Have Sent His Disciples to Bible College?', *JEPTA* 23 (2003), pp. 30–44; D. Tarr, 'Transcendence, Immanence, and the Emerging Pentecostal Academy', in Ma and Menzies (eds), *Pentecostalism in Context*, pp. 195–222; C.M. Robeck Jr, 'Seminaries and Graduate Schools', in Burgess and van der Maas (eds), *NIDPCM*, pp. 1045–050; R.W. Ferris (ed.), *Renewal in Theological Education: Strategies for Change* (Billy Graham Center: Wheaton College, 1990); E. Lee, 'What the Academy Needs from the Church', *AJPS* 3.2 (July 2000), pp. 311–18; J.S. Hittenberger, 'Toward a Pentecostal Philosophy of Education', *Pneuma* 23.2 (Fall 2001), pp. 217–44; P.J. Dovre (ed.), *The Future of Religious Colleges* (Grand Rapids: Eerdmans, 2002); Johns, *Pentecostal Formation*, pp. 111–40; J. Ruthven, 'Are Pentecostal Seminaries a Good Idea?', *Pneuma* 26.2 (2004), pp. 339–45; W.K. Kay, 'Pentecostal Education', *JBV* 25.2 (2004), pp. 229–39; J. Sepúlveda, 'The Challenge for Theological Education from a Pentecostal Standpoint', *Ministerial Formation* 87 (1999), pp. 29–34; P. Alexander, 'Conceiving Christian Ministry training' (EPTA conference paper, Iso Kirja, Sweden, 2006); Kärkkäinen, 'Pentecostal Theological Education'; J. Hittenberger, 'The Future of Pentecostal Higher Education' in Patterson and Ryberczyk, *The Future of Religious Colleges*, pp. 83–103.

the growth of both Pentecostal Theological Colleges and scholarship.[124] However, in other regions, this has not been reflected, Sepulveda, for example, describing Chilean Pentecostals as still exhibiting a 'strong anti-theological, anti-academic prejudice'.[125] Similarly, Hedlund cautions against this tendency among some Indian Pentecostals[126] as does Ayuk of Nigerian Pentecostals.[127] This propensity is often most espoused where Pentecostal leaders are less educated as well as where the perception of ministerial success is viewed as being solely or significantly due to the Spirit.[128] In general, Pentecostals have preferred to live in contexts dominated by exclamation marks rather than question marks.

However, there have been significant developments in Pentecostal education:

- The concept of teaching in Pentecostalism is being increasingly recognized as crucially important to its wellbeing. Although theological reflection in the early decades of Pentecostalism was often defensive, reactionary, intermittent and narrow in scope, the more recent decades have seen a marked increase in scholarship and exploration by Pentecostals of issues relating to their theology, spirituality and history. Bowdle encourages this development, noting that 'Jesus is Lord of learning'.[129]
- Pentecostals are redeeming the concept of scholarship, enabling and encouraging those who have been so gifted to engage in it for the benefit of the Church, the development and training of leaders[130] and the exploration

---

[124] Wilson, 'Bible Institutes, Colleges, Universities', pp. 375–79; G. Espinosa, 'Bible Institutes, Spanish-Speaking', in Burgess and van der Maas (eds), *NIDPCM*, pp. 380–81; H.D. Hunter, 'International Pentecostal-Charismatic Scholarly Associations', in Burgess and van der Maas (eds), *NIDPCM*, pp. 794–97; Hedlund, 'Critique of Pentecostal Mission', pp. 83–4; B. Sun, 'Assemblies of God Theological Education in Asia Pacific: A Reflection', *AJPS* 3.2 (2000), pp. 227–51 (232–41); D. Daniels, 'Live so Can Use Me Anytime, Lord, Anywhere (sic): Theological Education in the Church of God in Christ, 1970–1997', *AJPS* 3.2 (2000), pp. 295–310; J.S. Hittenberger, 'Globalization, "Marketization", and the Mission of Pentecostal Higher Education in Africa', *Pneuma* 26.2 (2004), pp. 182–215.

[125] Sepùlveda, 'The Challenge for Theological Education', p. 29; Wilson, 'Bible Institutes, Colleges, Universities', p. 374.

[126] Hedlund, 'Critique of Pentecostal Mission', p. 89.

[127] A.A. Ayuk, 'Portrait of a Nigerian Pentecostal Missionary', *AJPS* 8.1 (2005), pp. 117–41 (133–36).

[128] T. Pagaialii, 'The Pentecostal Movement of Samoa: Reaching the Uttermost', *AJPS* 7.1 (2004) pp. 265–79 (273–75).

[129] Bowdle, 'Informed Pentecostalism, pp. 12, 13–15; Bundy notes that in early Pentecostalism in Norway, there was much evidence of theological dialogue, even of controversial issues (Bundy, 'Historical and Theological Analysis', p. 82.

[130] Pandrea, 'A Historical and Theological Analysis', pp. 128–29.

of doctrinal truths.[131]The importance of reflection and studious thinking has neither been more necessary nor more available in Pentecostalism. There was a time when the term 'Pentecostal scholar' was viewed as an oxymoron. It is now much more acceptable to acknowledge that one's intellect is God given and that it can be used for the glory of God in the context of teaching and research.[132] Allied with the Spirit, a powerful combination is anticipated.

- Colleges are increasingly recognizing that they are not meant to be places where sacred Pentecostal dogmas are safeguarded at the expense of encouraging students to think about their beliefs. Learning needs to be more than simply receiving and reproducing information but also about the exploration of truth (not simply of key concepts of one's cultural or religious heritage). If a learning process exists solely to transmit and reinforce a cultural and theological heritage, it cannot empower the learner to think creatively, reflect independently and articulate transparently; it cannot ask the awkward questions for fear of what answers may be raised. The concept of problem solving does not easily fit into such a mould and yet learning by solving problems is a developing educational initiative, providing the possibility of moving beyond the traditional perspectives, received traditions and previously determined answers to those that can be determined in the context of mature thinking and critical objectivity. Education is thus not only restricted to cognitive thinking but also embraces the development of sensitive understanding of issues and the possibility of shaping views and practices in a context that encourages careful thought as well as listening to and learning from others.

Pentecostals are exploring their own histories objectively. This sometimes results in painful discoveries but it demonstrates an integrity and readiness to be less polarized and polemical in maintaining one's distinctive Pentecostal views without the loss of objective discussion and analysis. Increasingly, study is dialogical and contextual – far removed from the programmed memorization of biblical texts to undergird doctrines felt to be important to the Pentecostal constituency concerned. Instead of seeking to indoctrinate students with preformed ideas or truths, Colleges have become centres where learning is facilitated and enquiry is encouraged

---

[131] W. Ma, 'Biblical Studies in the Pentecostal Tradition: Yesterday, Today, and Tomorrow', in Dempster, Klaus and Petersen (eds), *The Globalization of Pentecostalism*, pp. 52–69 (57–64); Bowdle, 'Informed Pentecostalism', pp. 9–10; Brenkus, 'A Historical and Theological Analysis', pp. 49–65 (63); D. Jacobsen, 'Knowing the Doctrine of Pentecostals: The Scholastic Theology of the Assemblies of God, 1930–1955', in Blumhofer, Spittler and Wacker (eds), *Pentecostal Currents*, pp. 90–107.

[132] W.J. Hollenweger, 'Pentecostalism and Academic Theology: From Confrontation to Cooperation', *EB* 11. 1–2 (1992), pp. 42–9; R.M. Nañez, *Full Gospel, Fractured Minds? A Call to Use God's Gift of the Intellect* (Grand Rapids: Eerdmans, 2005).

in a Spirit-inspired context where commitment to integrity, transparency and authenticity is prized. This is most important where Pentecostals are increasingly being confronted with an ever changing culture and society. At the same time, whereas Pentecostal theology was previously taught using textbooks written by evangelical authors, which in some areas (the role of women in ministry, supernatural phenomena, the inerrancy of the Bible) tended to gradually move Pentecostal students away from their traditional values, students are now guided in their exploration of their own Pentecostal distinctives while benefiting from literature offered by Pentecostal scholars.[133]

- College faculties are becoming more interested in offering education that meets the needs of people, including church leaders,[134]rather than follow a programme of study that was relevant to previous eras and offered solutions for questions that were asked by different audiences.[135] They are also becoming more aware of the need to determine syllabi (including those that will be validated by external educational authorities) that reflect the needs of their students' future vocations rather than an inflexible framework of learning that lacks the opportunity to practically discover and experience God in an applied context.[136] As such, since the 1950s and increasingly, the 1980s, College curricula have increasingly been determined by Pentecostal faculties, even when the qualification receives university or governmental accreditation. Nevertheless, there are still challenges to tertiary education for Pentecostals that need to be addressed.

Some Ways Forward

The Church and the Academy

Although this has been greatly reduced in some countries, a continuing anti-intellectual stance by some Pentecostals still exists, Larbi acknowledging that African 'Pentecostals would like to hide behind closed doors and pray instead of presenting the gospel at the open market of ideas'.[137] Kennedy makes the valid point that 'Pentecostals have historically focused their

---

[133] J.C. Thomas, 'Pentecostal Explorations of the New Testament: Teaching New Testament Introduction in a Pentecostal Seminary', *JPT* 11.1 (2002), pp. 120–29.

[134] M.R. Hathaway, 'Trends in Ministerial Training' (EPTA conference paper, Brussels, 1980), pp. 16–27.

[135] H. Jurgensen, 'Theological Trends and Our Pentecostal Commitments' (EPTA conference paper, Brussels, 1980), pp. 28–49.

[136] Macchia, 'The Struggle for Global Witness', p. 9; G.M. Flattery, 'Accreditation of Pentecostal Colleges in Europe' (EPTA conference paper, Brussels, 1980); D. Petts, 'Classroom Methods and Theological Education' (EPTA conference paper, Brussels, 1980), pp. 50–5.

[137] Larbi, *Pentecostalism*, p. 447.

attention on missionary projects rather than on establishing research institutions'[138]though the rise in the latter and the increasing quality of the education being offered there has seen significant advance in recent decades. At the same time, Pentecostals have stood against an excessive intellectualizing of their faith which would render it inaccessible to believers.

A symbiotic partnership needs to be strengthened between Colleges and the Church constituencies who send students there in order to maximize the learning process for all concerned, recognizing the different emphases and expectations of each. The fear of being marginalized from the training of future leaders should cause all involved in Theological College education to reconsider that which they are offering and its relevance. The Church functions as a hermeneutical context for the learning and practice of the student. It can provide the College with the knowledge as to whether the latter is providing that which the Church needs; the Academy must never forget that it is the servant of the Church (not its replacement) and that as such, it must prove its value by helping it fulfil its potential.[139] Syllabi need to be envisaged that reflect the needs of society and the Church as well as students, rather than reflecting a model of the past that is assumed to be normative but is rarely tested. Both groups need to talk to each other with ears open wide. Thus, rather than the College being the only setting for learning, it is to be recognized that the better setting for prospective church leaders is the church community where mission can be developed in the appropriate context. A partnership between the local church and a residential College for intensive, dedicated sessions may be a suitable framework for ministry training/discipleship. Pentecostal denominations are already aware of this issue and are seeking to develop new models of training for pastors outside the College framework. Interestingly, this has resulted in a proliferation of church-based colleges, established for a variety of reasons including a reluctance to send their best people to College and a commitment to hands-on experience. A further significant reason is a commitment to leadership development through discipleship and impartation of vision from a successful leader. However, there are dangers of a multiplicity of small Colleges being established, sometimes church-based. Although these often have value and make education more widely available, they can also cater to the narrow beliefs of a given group and restrict wider engagement with and learning from other believers. Nevertheless, rather than allow a division to develop, Colleges ought to consider ways of supporting the learning and training processes that are taking place in churches. There remain important and valuable reasons for the existence of Colleges and Seminaries. They have

---

[138] J.R. Kennedy, 'Anti-Intellectualism', in Burgess, *EPCC*, pp. 35–9.
[139] R. Dresselhaus, 'What Can the Academy Do for the Church?', *AJPS* 3.2 (2000), pp. 319–23.

unique value in 'promoting deep knowledge, careful research, and critical evaluation of thought' and do not, by default, restrict charismatic expression.[140]

The Learning Journey

Develop Cross-Cultural Participation

There is a need for trained personnel and Pentecostal literature, especially in Majority world settings, as highlighted by Larbi.[141] Western Colleges, in particular, can function as conduits and resources for providing educational development and training for leadership in settings where the infrastructure has not yet been established and finances are limited. They can also provide guidance with regard to the increasing need for accreditation by Colleges and, in particular, to ensure that a balance is maintained in the academic, applied and Pentecostal-nuanced components of the courses offered.[142] At the same time, Colleges in non-Western countries can provide invaluable cross-cultural experiences especially in areas where the Church is expanding rapidly.

Form a Context of Spiritual Formation

From earliest times, some Pentecostals and others have spoken in disparaging terms of Theological Colleges, describing seminaries as 'cemeteries' and lampooning the titles of degrees earned or questioning their relevance or necessity.[143] Although these comments have been exaggerations, nevertheless, some Colleges have lost their expectation of the supernatural, their spirituality has been less clearly Pentecostal and they have been less vocational or, at least, that has been the perceptions of outside observers.[144] This has been in part not only due to the personalities and giftings of those who have functioned in educational contexts but also due to the fact that spirituality is a personal discipline and that students often commence their studies with an inadequate spiritual formation. However, where it has resulted in the students imbibing those features while in College, it has had a detrimental affect on the Church and the College. Instead, campuses should be the context for more proactive spiritual formation.[145]

---

[140] J.L. Castleberry, 'Pentecostal Seminaries Are Essential to the Future Health of the Church', *Pneuma* 26.2 (2004), pp. 346–54 (351).

[141] Larbi, *Pentecostalism*, pp. 446–48.

[142] Ayuk, 'The Pentecostal Transformation', pp. 198–99.

[143] Walsh ('To Meet and Satisfy', pp. 206–07) quotes T.K. Leonard ('The Gospel School Department', *Word and Witness* (August 1914), p. 3) who dismisses theological training because 'time is too precious, Jesus is coming too soon and education has proven too futile'.

[144] Tarr, 'Transcendence', pp. 206–07, 211–12.

[145] M. Wenk, 'Do We Need a Distinct European Pentecostal/Charismatic Approach to Theological Education', *JEPTA* 23 (2003), pp. 61–2 (58–71).

There is a danger that theology can be taught in the absence of a spiritual framework. However, as Hudson notes, education and training for ministry cannot be in the context of 'a disembodied spirituality'.[146] In this respect, it may be appropriate to revisit the topic of 'the call of God', once the normal reason for people applying to Colleges, in order to encourage the value of recognizing the role of God's guidance in the determining of one's destiny. The learning experience must help to develop personal spirituality and transform character, to impart vision as well as learning.[147] This must start with the teachers themselves, McKinney encouraging 'faculty to model a desire for continual spiritual renewal'.[148] It is often the lasting impact of the life of a teacher that affects students more than the information they have gained from the lectures. Also, the occasions where encounters with God are more likely, including corporate worship, need to be prioritized in the curriculum as do issues relating to service and mission.[149]

Provide a Place for the Spirit

In the pedagogical process, there needs to be an involvement of the Spirit and recognition that the learning journey is a holy one in which the Spirit is present as the supreme Teacher.[150] Anderson calls for a 'renewed focus on the role of the Holy Spirit in terms of learning and spiritual formation'.[151] However, Hudson warns, 'The ultimate irony is that the Spirit, that blows wherever he wills, has been codified, systematised and analysed'[152] whereas he also needs to be experienced. This need not be identified only in worship settings but by an awareness that he is speaking through the learning journey, the learners, the teachers, the questions, the probing analysis and the silence. This calls for a particular type of learning environment. Teachers need to be Spirit-led learners and model Spirit-controlled lives, recognizing the Spirit's presence in the lives of their students, facilitating the students' exploration of the Spirit and giving him the opportunity to be a participatory guide and dialogue partner in the learning process. In the quest for rational

---

[146] D.N. Hudson, 'It's Not What We Do: It's the Way We Do It. Uncomfortable Thoughts for a Lecturer in a Residential Bible College at the Turn of the Century', *JEPTA* 23 (2003), pp. 45–57.

[147] E.L. McKinney, 'Some Spiritual Aspects of Pentecostal Education: A Personal Journey', *AJPS* 3.2 (2000), pp. 253–79; M. Alvarez, 'Distinctives of Pentecostal Education', *AJPS* 3.2 (2000), pp. 282–93.

[148] McKinney, 'Some Spiritual Aspects', p. 262.

[149] Hittenberger, 'Toward a Pentecostal Philosophy', p. 223.

[150] C.B. Johns, 'The Meaning of Pentecost for Theological Education', *Ministerial Formation* 87 (1999), pp. 42–7.

[151] Anderson, 'Missional Orientation and Its Implications, p. 145; Hittenberger, 'Toward a Pentecostal Philosophy', pp. 217–44.

[152] Hudson, 'It's Not What We Do', p. 49.

theological models, it is essential that the mystery of God be embraced in the quest for divine discoveries and that room be allowed for a dynamic interaction with him. Paul modelled this by walking with the Spirit, encouraging his readers to listen to the Spirit and expecting him to impact them experientially; Pentecostal teachers need to emulate him.

Identify the Pre-College Journey of the Student

Teaching in Colleges is best offered when it is appropriately contextualized in the life settings of the students.[153] It is important to offer a learning environment for students that takes into consideration their previous experiences, spiritual journeys and cultural distinctives.[154] To offer a form of theological education which follows the pattern of a Western educational ethos with a high stress on the cerebral may not be the most appropriate for the student. Theology is not stagnant; it develops in a context. Therefore, for example, exorcism could be explored differently with students from Africa to those from the UK because their worldviews, experience and praxis differ markedly. The road to be undertaken in the educational process needs to reflect the road already travelled by the student while enabling their level of consciousness to be raised to encompass vistas relevant to them though as yet not appreciated by them. Such education calls for a more individualistic, intensive and dynamic approach that may not be replicated in a predetermined format which includes set reading and set notes and that assumes a static pedagogy within carefully defined limits. The best teacher responds to the prior experience of the learner or stimulates his/her curiosity, then goes to the subject, develops, contextualizes and applies it.

Identify the Requirements of the Student

College tutors need to identify the academic, theological, spiritual, socioeconomic needs and aspirations of the individual student. Educators need to be listeners as well as communicators, learners as well as teachers,[155] askers of questions not just providers of answers, indulging in dialogue with fellow learners; not functioning only in a teacher-pupil, expert-novice relationship but also in a Learner-learner relationship (where the lecturer is the Learner).

---

[153] A.H. Anderson, 'The "Fury and Wonder": Pentecostal-Charismatic Spirituality in Theological Education', *Pneuma* 23.2 (2001), pp. 287–302; L. Wanak, 'Theological Education and the Role of Teachers in the 21st century: A Look at the Asia Pacific Region', *JAM* 2.1 (2000), pp. 3–24 (11).

[154] Warrington, 'Would Jesus Have Sent', pp. 39–41.

[155] See A.G. Harkness, 'De-Schooling the Theological Seminary: An Appropriate Paradigm for Effective Ministerial Formation', *TTR* 4.3 (2001), pp. 141–54 (150–51).

The role of the teacher is not to be an expert who gathers together ever-increasing knowledge, some of which may be imparted to the listener; rather, they are to be facilitators. This needs a paradigm change away from learning how to teach, to learning more about learning in order to teach. This dynamic process driven by the students' needs, not the content of the predetermined course, is difficult to be accommodated in a static framework of education with pre-set objectives. Training for ministry and discipleship is different to academic theological education, though both have value; that which is to be determined is the model best suited for the individual student. The theological issues in the lives and contexts of some students will be different to others. To try to meet each of their aspirations would be a challenge, but one that must be attended to carefully to facilitate a relevant and empowering learning journey. It means that one must offer different learning tracks, core and elective modules relevant to each student, as far as possible, in an interdisciplinary format; new delivery systems need to be created for the diverse requirements of the learning communities in the Church. In the process, the student is incorporated as a partner in the learning journey in which the teacher is a guide and fellow traveller though not exclusively an authoritative determiner of the destination or the road to be travelled or the views or detours on the way. Without the institution of a contextual theological education, there is the danger that syllabi will address issues that are absent from the lives of those who are taught from them.[156]

The content of one's communication should be offered in the context of praxis and practising; less knowledge and more know-how; less information and more application; less intensive data presentation and more inspiration and transformation; less hand-outs and more hands-on-experience; less cerebral and more personal development; less intellectual and more intuitive learning; not just the impartation of information but also the directing of self activity. In this regard, Jesus is the best paradigm of excellent pedagogy.

The Ordinances

Many Pentecostals would refrain from using the term 'ritual' as a descriptor for their central practices (because of the fear that it might be associated with merely a ceremony) or 'sacrament' (because it may indicate to some that the procedure may contain self-inducing power). Instead, the term 'ordinances'[157] has often been used, though on the basis of little semantic or

---

[156] Anderson, 'The "Fury and Wonder"', pp. 287–302.
[157] R. Bicknell, 'The Ordinances: The Marginalised Aspects of Pentecostalism', in Warrington (ed.), *Pentecostal Perspectives*, pp. 204–22 (205); J. Lancaster, 'The Ordinances', in Brewster (ed.), *Pentecostal Doctrine*, pp. 79–92 (79); Dyer, 'An Examination of Theology', pp. 66–81, 85–96.

biblical support; others choose to identify the events as neither 'sacrament' nor 'ordinance'. Pentecostals believe that without faith on the part of the recipient, participation in these ceremonies has little, if any, benefit. They do not restrict the administration of the ordinances to the clergy, though traditionally this has been the practice, though not because of a biblical paradigm.

Many of the central practices of Pentecostal/Charismatic spirituality are shared with other streams of Christianity, including water baptism and the Lord's Supper. However, other practices observed by Pentecostals, and also identified as ordinances by some, include anointing the sick with oil, laying on of hands[158] and foot washing.[159] The practice of anointing, in a wider setting, is used by especially African Pentecostals in a number of respects with some unfortunate as well as positive ramifications.[160]

Water Baptism

Most Pentecostals (along with many other evangelicals) undergo water baptism because of their desire to emulate the baptism of Jesus (Mt. 3.16), to obey the command of Jesus (Mt. 28.19) and to be aligned to the practice of the earliest believers as recorded in the book of Acts (9.18; 10.47; 16.33; 18.8). The background for such a practice may be traced to Jewish beliefs that the ceremonial application of water represented cleansing from defilement and sin, parallels with OT events (1 Cor. 10.1–5; 1 Pet. 3.20–21), and its symbolism with reference to new life (1 Cor. 10.2). Pentecostals do not accept that the water is charged with any supernatural properties nor do they teach that it confers salvation or that babtism is essential for salvation, though it is recognized as being very important,[161] regarded as normative practice and therefore expected of all believers as a sign of obedience to the

---

[158] J.R. Williams, 'Laying on of Hands', in Burgess and van der Maas (eds), *NIDPCM*, pp. 834–36.

[159] Based on the narrative in John 13.1–17, in which Jesus washed the feet of his disciples and commanded that they do likewise, some Pentecostals have adopted a similar practice. Because John records this as taking place after the Last Supper, it is sometimes undertaken in association with this event. The purpose is to remind everyone present that service is at the heart of the Christian community and that equality and unity are paramount in the family of God. At the same time, it offers an opportunity to convey the principles of servanthood and fellowship; F.D. Macchia, 'Is Footwashing the Neglected Sacrament? A Theological Response to John Christopher Thomas', *Pneuma* 19.2 (1997), pp. 239–49; J.C. Thomas, *Footwashing in John 13 and the Johannine Community* (Sheffield: Sheffield Academic Press, 1991.

[160] J.K. Asamoah-Gyadu, '"Unction to Function"': Reinventing the *Oil of Influence* in African Pentecostalism', *JPT* 13.2 (2005), pp. 231–56.

[161] Gajewski and Wawrzeniuk, 'A Historical and Theological Analysis', p. 43; many Polish Pentecostals have made it a precondition for church membership, to be followed, for the first time, with participation in the Lord's Supper.

command of Jesus.[162] Increasingly, it occurs after a (short) period of teaching concerning essential elements of the Christian life although Rowe, for one, argues that the biblical pattern is that it should occur immediately after one's conversion (Acts 16.33).[163] Prior to the baptism of an individual, the Trinitarian formula, recorded in Mt. 28.19, is pronounced, though this is amended among Oneness Pentecostals by the substitution of the name of Jesus Christ (Acts 2.38; 10.48) or 'the Lord Jesus' (Acts 8.16; 19.5).[164]

Because, occasionally, those being baptized have experienced physical healing or the baptism in the Spirit, Dyer suggests the act of water baptism may be understood as a 'sacramental encounter such that the moment of baptism becomes a moment of encounter with the Divine'.[165] Most Pentecostals practice baptism by full immersion, on the basis of verses such as Mk 1.10, Rom. 6.1–4 that indicate immersion, rather than sprinkling.[166] The act of baptism is viewed by many as reflecting a distinct break from one's previous life and an opportunity to publicly declare one's commitment to Christ, in which the pictorial 'dying and rising' metaphors refer to the renunciation of one's previous life which was not under the authority of Jesus (Rom. 6.4). In particular, the act of baptism is intended to signify repentance, the forgiveness of sins, salvation and the integration of the believer and Christ (Gal. 3.27), though there is no suggestion that such a relationship is initiated during baptism, the latter being the public affirmation of a previous integration into the family of God at salvation (1 Cor. 12.13; Eph. 4.5).[167] Furthermore, water baptism is viewed as providing 'an experience of God's acceptance and calling'.[168] In the act of baptism, 'God confirms . . . His acceptance and approval' of the believer.[169]

Bicknell notes, 'By concentrating its efforts upon personal faith over against corporate identity . . . the Pentecostal understanding of the ordinances may

---

[162] Oneness Pentecostals view baptism in the name of Jesus as effecting salvation.

[163] Rowe, *One Lord, One Faith*, p. 196.

[164] For further exploration of this belief and practice, see Anderson, *An Introduction to Pentecostalism*, pp. 47–51 (some hold to the belief that salvation is constituted when a person has been thus baptized, been baptized in the Holy Spirit and spoke in tongues); Reed, 'Oneness Pentecostalism', pp. 89–91.

[165] Dyer, 'An Examination of Theology', p. 223.

[166] Lancaster, 'The Ordinances', p. 85; Rowe, *One Lord, One Faith*, pp. 196–97.

[167] Bicknell, 'The Ordinances', pp. 205–06; Lancaster, 'The Ordinances', p. 83; some Oneness Pentecostals teach that water baptism is a prerequisite to salvation (offering Acts 2.38; 22.16 as evidence), arguing that it should be administered in the name of Jesus, rather than the Father, Son and the Holy Spirit.

[168] F.D. Macchia, 'Astonished by Faithfulness to God: A Reflection on Karl Barth's Understanding of Spirit Baptism', in Ma and Menzies (eds), *Spirit and Spirituality*, 2004), pp. 164–76 (173).

[169] Lancaster, 'The Ordinances', p. 85.

have been robbed of corporate significance'.[170] Whereas Pentecostals (and others) have focused on the individual nature of the faith of the one being baptized, the value of his/her incorporation into the body of believers is worthy of greater emphasis. Finally, baptism is sometimes viewed as the Christian parallel to the Jewish Passover (Lk. 22.7–8; 1 Cor. 5.7), in which the death of Jesus replaces the death of the Passover lamb in providing not freedom from slavery, but from sin and its consequences. Pentecostals do not believe that water baptism is the occasion for the reception of the Spirit by the one being baptized. They gain support for this from the fact that on only one occasion did the Spirit come upon people in the context of water baptism (Acts 19.5–6).

It is administered mainly to adults and less so to children, the baptism of infants being rejected by most Pentecostals because the act would be devoid of personal faith on the part of the recipient.[171] However, the Methodist Pentecostal Church of Chile does practice infant baptism[172] and Tan explores the value of baptizing the infants of believing parents. He argues that the NT does not explicitly condemn it and therefore argues that unless 'there are unimpeachable theological grounds for excluding them', such children should be considered as acceptable baptismal candidates. He views this as a possibility because he considers the stress on individual confession of one's faith before baptism as more appropriate to a Western worldview where individualism is more important than it is in an Asian setting, where a greater emphasis is placed on the social construct of the family. Furthermore, he deduces that many of the aspirations associated with the dedication of children to the Lord need be no different to those associated with infant baptism, in which case, there is even less reason to deny them and their parents this hopeful sign of their becoming members of the Christian community.[173] Although few Pentecostals will accept this view, at the very least, it demonstrates a flexible Pentecostalism that is prepared to explore alternative views and to recognize the value of culture in one's hermeneutic.

The Lord's Supper

Hollenweger concludes that 'the service of the Lord's Supper is the central point of Pentecostal worship',[174] though interestingly, *The New International Dictionary of Pentecostal and Charismatic Movements* only dedicates three

---

[170] Bicknell, 'The Ordinances', p. 218.

[171] Lancaster, 'The Ordinances', pp. 83–4; Macchia, *Baptized in the Spirit*, p. 250.

[172] Sepúlveda, 'Indigenous Pentecostalism', p. 119.

[173] S.G.H. Tan, 'Reassessing Believer's Baptism in Pentecostal Theology and Practice', *AJPS* 6.2 (2003) pp. 219–34 (232–33).

[174] Hollenweger, *The Pentecostals*, p. 385.

paragraphs to it. This is more in line with Bond's conclusion that 'the attitude to the elements of bread and wine betrays a doctrinal shallowness' among Pentecostals.[175] Pentecostal beliefs and practice concerning the Lord's Supper may be traced to the Reformation theology and practice of Zwingli and Calvin via Congregationalism and Brethren traditions.[176] Fundamentally, Pentecostals adhere to that which they perceive to be a Zwinglian rather than a Lutheran form of the Eucharist. In reality, Zwingli anticipated more than retrospection and remembrance but also and because of the former acts, a realization of the presence of the Lord. However, for most Pentecostals, it is fundamentally a celebration of a past event though in recognition that it is destined to redundancy in heaven (1 Cor. 11.26).

The commendation of this event by Jesus to his followers (Lk. 22.14–20), his desire to share it with them (Lk. 22.15), his invitation that they share it with him (Lk. 22.8), his command, 'Do this in remembrance of me' (Lk. 22.19) and its reiteration by Paul (1 Cor. 12.23–26) form significant reasons for the practice. Indeed, it is viewed as an important event in the calendar of the local church and is generally held every Sunday, on the basis of Acts 20.7.[177]

More generally known as the Lord's Supper (1 Cor. 11.20), Communion (1 Cor. 10.16), the Lord's Table (1 Cor. 10.21) or the Breaking of Bread (Acts 2.42), it is observed with simplicity of form, frequently under the supervision of the leader(s) of the church, aided by others who distribute the emblems at the appropriate time, prior to which they are often covered by a white linen cloth in full view of the congregation. Although no written liturgy is used, there is often a demonstrable pattern. The actual partaking traditionally follows a time of reflection, thanksgiving and open worship, focusing on the death of Jesus, and the reading of one of the NT passages describing the event. It is a bittersweet experience for many as they consider the cost to Jesus and the consequences for them. Most Pentecostals view the occasion as one of remembrance of the death of Jesus and less of his resurrection, the broken bread representing the body of Jesus on the cross, the cup representing his blood, the association with the forgiveness of sins being paramount (Mt. 26.28, Heb. 9.22). Associated with this act of remembrance is the opportunity to express gratitude for salvation and worship to Jesus, the Lord's Supper being a 'ratification of the New Covenant'.[178] The foundational

---

[175] Bond, 'What Is Distinctive' p. 140.
[176] R. Bicknell, 'In Memory of Christ's Sacrifice: Roots and Shoots of Elim's Eucharistic Expression', *JEPTA* 17 (1997), pp. 59–89 (59–65); Dyer, 'An Examination of Theology', pp. 31–65.
[177] Rowe (*One Lord, One Faith*, p. 201) writes, 'The Breaking of Bread service is the barometer of spirituality' (201).
[178] Lancaster, 'The Ordinances', p. 87; Dyer, 'An Examination of theology ', pp. 133–35; 203–10.

element of 'proclaim(ing) the Lord's death' (1 Cor. 11.26) underscores its importance to Pentecostals who have traditionally been strongly motivated to evangelize the world.[179] It is also viewed as a sign of the eschatological life to come, to be celebrated 'until he comes' (Lk. 22.16; 1 Cor. 12.26).[180] Unlike much of Pentecostal worship, this is often a quiet and even sober occasion, the concentration being on the cost to Jesus in terms of his passion. It is a personal and private event, albeit in the context of a congregational act, with the emphasis on reflection. Increasingly, congregational worship has become a more significant feature, and introspection has been joined by corporate praise and the singing of worship songs.[181] A more relaxed and less formal style is partly due to the fact that the act of Communion is not now restricted to a Sunday service.

Although some have suggested that 'the partaking of the bread and wine is understood simply as a memorial' of the death of Jesus,[182] others have reacted against it being identified as merely memorial. Instead, they prefer to identify it as an opportunity to remember the past in order to be transformed in the present and prepared for the future. Furthermore, as well as acknowledging that one's spiritual life may be revitalized,[183] some have suggested that healing of sickness may also be anticipated.[184] To a lesser degree, there has been an expectation, on the part of some, that the presence of Jesus during this time should be of a more intense nature, attention being drawn to the concept of participation in the blood and body of Christ (1 Cor. 10.16–17), as well as the experience of the two disciples in Emmaus whose eyes were opened when Jesus broke bread with them (Lk. 24.30–31).[185] Thus, as well as celebrating their salvation and refreshing their memories with all that they have as a result of the death of Jesus, many also expect to encounter him in a significant way,[186] Dyer suggesting that in, at least, British Pentecostalism, there is 'a subliminal sacramentalism'.[187] However, this view needs to

---

[179] Bicknell, 'The Ordinances', p. 217; Lancaster, 'The Ordinances', p. 87.

[180] Menzies and Horton, *Bible Doctrines*, pp. 116–17; Lancaster, 'The Ordinances', p. 89; Dyer, 'An Examination of Theology', pp. 146–48.

[181] Dyer, 'An Examination of Theology', pp. 136–40.

[182] B. Wilson, *Sects and Society* (London: Heinemann, 1961) p. 19; see Dyer, 'An Examination of Theology', pp. 125–33, 195–99; Rowe, *One Lord, One Faith*, p. 200.

[183] C. Dye, 'What Happens When We Take Communion?', *Direction* 67 (Dec. 1994), p. 8.

[184] Kärkkäinen, *Toward a Pneumatological Theology*, pp. 142–44; Dyer, 'An Examination of theology', pp. 144–46, 226–29.

[185] H.D. Hunter, 'Ordinances, Pentecostal', in Burgess and van der Maas (eds), *NIDPCM* (2002) pp. 947–49 (948); W.P.F. Burton, *What Mean Ye by These Stones* (London: Victory Press, 1947), p. 40; Kärkkäinen, 'Encountering Christ', p. 19.

[186] W.D. Arteaga, *Forgotten Power: The Significance of the Lord's Supper in Revival* (Grand Rapids: Zondervan Publishing House, 2002).

[187] Dyer, 'An Examination of Theology', p. 149–53, 200–03, 226–29.

be contextualized in the recognition that the presence of Christ can be experienced at any time.

The recommendation by Paul that participants examine themselves to ensure that they participate worthily and, in particular, that they do not dishonour 'the body' of the Lord (1 Cor. 12.29) has been a cause of confusion. Many have assumed this to be a recommendation that unbelievers should not participate because they may not fully appreciate the significance of the death of Jesus on the cross. However, Paul is reminding the readers that if they participate without honouring the body of believers who share in the act with them, their participation in the Lord's Supper is inappropriate and even counterproductive, especially since the death of Jesus brought unity among diverse peoples (1 Cor. 11:17–22; 31–34). The issue at stake is not personal failings but a recognition of the importance of corporate fellowship.[188] Williams notes that the issue 'is not our worthiness but our coming in a worthy manner'.[189] The warning of potential judgment, sickness and death (1 Cor. 12.29–30) is taken seriously by Pentecostals, resulting in a call to confess any sins (generally privately) prior to partaking of the emblems. Some advocate excluding errant or unrepentant believers from the event on the basis of 1 Cor. 5.2, 11, though this runs the risk of making Communion a test of personal sanctification, a feature not present in its institution by Jesus.

Only believers are encouraged to partake, including those who may not be members of the local congregation; indeed, many Pentecostal churches actively discourage the participation by those who are not believers, such a recommendation being often audibly stated prior to the congregational participation. Whereas children were often not allowed to partake, even when they had professed salvation, for fear of participating naïvely, there has been a considerable weakening of this position. It is possible that this is due to the lessening of the sobriety and sanctity of the occasion and the elevation of the place of children in many congregational settings.

Most Pentecostals use broken bread (sometimes unleavened), crackers or a loaf to represent the body of Jesus and the community of believers (1 Cor. 10.17),[190] presented on plates by servers from which the congregation partake while seated. As a substitute for the wine of the NT, most Pentecostals offer grape juice. Very few use fermented wine, often due to historical practice, a stance of total abstinence or an assumption that Jesus only drank unfermented juice.[191] The juice is generally administered in small goblets,

---

[188] Kärkkäinen, *Toward a Pneumatological Theology*, p. 142.
[189] Williams, *Renewal Theology*, p. 258; Dyer, 'An Examination of Theology', pp. 140–44.
[190] Dyer, 'An Examination of Theology', pp. 210–12.
[191] See Dyer, 'An Examination of Theology', pp. 114–16; Bicknell, 'In memory of Christ's Sacrifice', pp. 67–8.

contained in communion trays that are passed around the congregation, though some use a common cup. It is the normal practice for the communicants to eat the bread and drink the juice, in that order. They are not viewed as being special in themselves, retaining the same constituent elements before, during, and after the event. There has been limited experimentation with the form of the Lord's Supper; sometimes, congregants are invited to celebrate it in family or small groups or invited to the front of the church to receive from those administering it.

There has always been a rebuttal of any suggestion that salvific grace is available in the Communion event[192] or that the body and/or blood of Jesus are present in the elements, texts including Jn 6.52–57 and 1 Cor. 11.24 being interpreted symbolically.[193] Rather than acknowledge the real presence of Jesus in the emblems, they celebrate his realized presence[194] through the Spirit and thus reject a sacramental understanding of the event.[195] Any benefit gained is due to the person of Christ not the elements themselves. The concept of an altar is not present in Pentecostal language, the term *table* being preferred, as a sign of fellowship both with the Lord and each other. Similarly, they often speak of the bread and juice as emblems or symbols to distance themselves from any association with transubstantiation or consubstantiation.[196]

Traditionally, Pentecostals have not engaged in critical or evaluative discussion concerning Communion.[197] Bicknell draws attention to the fact that for many Pentecostals, the emphasis on the Communion event being an act of obedience in which they remember Christ's death has resulted for many in a loss of the element of mystery. Instead, it has been replaced by a minimalistic understanding and practice, often now encapsulated in only a brief section within a corporate gathering of believers.[198] Allen is similarly concerned that a trend has occurred within Western Pentecostalism that has resulted in the occasion being marginalized and swamped by singing, into which the partaking of the symbols is inserted rather than it being the central aspect of the event.[199]

---

[192] Though see Dyer, 'An Examination of Theology', pp. 156–57.

[193] Canty, *In My Father's House*, p. 54.

[194] Dyer, 'An Examination of Theology', pp. 153–55; H. Burton-Haynes, 'The Breaking of Bread', *Four Essentials of a Virile Pentecostal Church* (Cheltenham: Grenehurst Press, n.d.), p. 13; W.S. Biddy, 'Re-Envisioning the Pentecostal Understanding of the Eucharist: An Ecumenical Proposal', *Pneuma* 28.2 (2006), pp. 228–51 (230–49).

[195] Bicknell, 'The Ordinances', p. 209; though see dialogue between Pentecostals and Catholics (Kärkkäinen, *Toward a Pneumatological Theology*, pp. 135–46).

[196] Bicknell, 'In Memory of Christ's Sacrifice', pp. 68–9.

[197] Though see Dyer, 'An Examination of Theology', passim.

[198] Bicknell, 'The Ordinances', p. 219.

[199] D. Allen, *Neglected Feast: Rescuing the Breaking of Bread* (Nottingham: New Life, 2007), pp. 53–7, 61, 67–70, 82–5.

The role of the Spirit in communion, as explored by the Eastern Orthodox tradition of the Church is worthy of greater appreciation by Pentecostals.[200] As with water baptism, the individualism, often present, removes the Communion act from the corporate setting as reflected in the NT, resulting in its communal significance being largely marginalized. For many Pentecostals, the event has become so personalized that its value for reminding the participants that they are part of a body, one loaf (1 Cor. 10.16–17; 11.29) with consequent privileges and responsibilities is overlooked or at least routinized.[201] The danger of the event becoming a formality because of its regular celebration is also to be borne in mind. A fresh appreciation of its significance as well as creativity in its celebration will help ensure that its vitalizing impact may not be lost.

Ecumenism

Introduction

Although Pentecostals have over the years increasingly sought and responded to dialogue with other Protestant denominations,[202] discussions with the Roman Catholic Church and ecumenical debate have been much more tenuous.[203] This has been in part due to the rejection of Pentecostals by many mainline churches, especially in the earliest years. They themselves have often disregarded formal relationships with those who hold significantly different beliefs to them. Some denominations have accused Pentecostals of

---

[200] Kärkkäinen, *Toward a Pneumatological Theology*, pp. 139–46; Macchia, *Baptized in the Spirit*, pp. 252–56.

[201] Lancaster, 'The Ordinances', pp. 88–9; Dyer, 'An Examination of Theology', pp. 242–43.

[202] 'Word and Spirit, Church and World: The Final Report of the International Dialogue between Representatives of the World Alliance of Reformed Churches and Some Pentecostal Churches and Leaders 1996–2000', *AJPS* 4.1 (2001), pp. 41–72; see responses by Pentecostals Walter Hollenweger, Sang Hwan Lee, Jane Everts Powers, Paul van der Laan, Henry H. Knight III, Douglas Jacobsen among others – *Pneuma* 23.1 (2001), pp. 44–97. C.M. Robeck Jr ('The Assemblies of God and Ecumenical Cooperation: 1920–1965' in Ma and Menzies (ed.), *Pentecostalism in Context*, pp. 107–50 (110–25)) notes that a measure of relationship was developed between the AoG and the Foreign Missions Conference of North America (founded in 1893, this provided a basis for dialogue and action with regard to missions by a large variety of denominations) prior to the establishment of the WCC in 1948.

[203] Robeck, 'The Assemblies of God', pp. 107–50; Kärkkäinen, *Toward a Pneumatological Theology*, pp. 39–51; idem, '"Anonymous Ecumenists"? Pentecostals and the Struggle for Christian Identity', *JES* 37.1 (2000), pp. 13–27; H.D. Hunter, 'Two Movements of the Holy Spirit in the 20th Century? A Closer Look at Global Pentecostalism and Ecumenism,' *One in Christ* 38.1 (2003), pp. 31–9.

proselytism and, although there may be valid reasons for people transferring their allegiance to Pentecostal churches, it has resulted in hurt and suspicion on the part of non-Pentecostal denominations and their leaders and has hindered dialogue.[204]

Furthermore, the tendency of Pentecostals to have serious organizational disagreements[205] and to split from one another has not helped in a quest for unity with those who are not Pentecostal. Even when some Pentecostals and other denominations began to dialogue with one another, to worship together and be prepared to learn from each other, many Pentecostals still maintained an isolationist position. The call to 'come out from among them and be separate' (2 Cor. 6.17) was often applied as readily to other Christians from differing traditions to one's own as it was to secular society.

Thus, cross-church activities have often been difficult to develop; indeed, on many occasions, they were not even considered. Joint expressions of opposition against or support for wider ethical or behavioural issues affecting the broader community have been rare. The perceived preservation of the integrity and purity of the Pentecostal community was viewed as more important than any joint attempt to develop the Kingdom of God with people who may have held different beliefs to one's own.

There has been a greater flexibility and a readiness to engage in dialogue with other Christian traditions in recent years and a willingness to recognize that this is a worthy and necessary role for Pentecostals, with benefits for cooperation on socio-ethical issues, to foster good relationships and break down barriers harmful to evangelism.[206] This has also been partly fed by the desire to fulfil the prayer of Jesus in Jn 17 and the Pauline recognition of the

---

[204] Kärkkäinen, *Toward a Pneumatological Theology*, pp. 193–205; idem, 'Proselytism and Church Relations: Theological Issues Facing Older and Younger Churches', *ER* 52.3 (2000), pp. 379–90; idem, *Ad Ultimum Terrae: Evangelization, Proselytism and Common Witness in the Roman Catholic Dialogue (1990–1997)* (Frankfurt: Peter Lang, 1999); C.M. Robeck Jr, 'Mission and the Issue of Proselytism', *IBMR* 20.1 (1996), pp. 2–8; idem, 'Do We Agree as to When Evangelism Becomes Proselytism?', *Ecumenical Trends* 29.10 (November 2000), 7/151–14/158.

[205] Robeck, 'The Assemblies of God', p. 128; D.L. Cole, 'Pentecostal Koinonia: An Emerging Ecumenical Ecclesiology among Pentecostals' (unpublished doctoral dissertation, Fuller Theological Seminary, Los Angeles, 1998), pp. 243–57.

[206] Moltmann and Kuschel (eds), *Pentecostal Movements*; C.M Robeck Jr, 'Pentecostals and Ecumenism in a Pluralistic World', in Dempster, Klaus and Petersen (eds), *Called and Empowered*, pp. 338–62; J. Gros, 'Toward a Dialogue of Conversion: The Pentecostal, Evangelical and Conciliar Movements', *Pneuma* 17.2 (1995), pp. 189–202; C.M. Robeck Jr has collected an invaluable and substantial index of articles and books, written between 1982 and 2006, relating to dialogue between Pentecostals and the wider Church titled, 'Resourcing Ecumenical Formation among Pentecostals. A Select Bibliography: Ecumenical (and Inter-Religious) Promise'.

role of the Spirit to fuse all believers into one Church (Eph. 2.11–18; 4.3).[207] Indeed, one of the reasons for dialogue occurring between Pentecostals and the WCC was the joint recognition of the role of the Spirit to bring unity and to establish spiritual communion.[208] Similarly, the Pentecostal-Catholic dialogue commenced in 1970 on the basis of an agreement that the essence of Pentecostalism was best identified as 'the personal and direct awareness and experiencing of the Holy Spirit by which the risen and glorified Christ is revealed and the believer is empowered to witness and worship'.[209]

The establishment of Pentecostal academic societies[210] and other Pentecostal fellowships[211] has also helped build bridges.[212] Robeck offers regular clarion calls concerning the issue that reflect sound spirituality and a desire to concentrate on the essentials, overcome fear of the other, slow down the trend to further disunity while recognizing that 'the nature of dialogue is a process of discovery',[213] a potentially positive and life-enhancing quest. Similarly, Rybarczyk offers lessons that may be learned by Pentecostals by exploring spiritualities different to their own; indeed, he also notes that there are often commonalities in experience and aspiration in apparently diverse traditions.[214]

---

[207] W.G. Rusch, 'The Theology of the Holy Spirit and the Pentecostal Churches in the Ecumenical Movement', *Pneuma* 9.1 (1987), pp. 17–30; Macchia, *Baptized in the Spirit*, pp. 210–13; Robeck, 'Pentecostals and Ecumenism', pp. 341–44.

[208] Moltmann (*The Spirit of Life*, p. 4) speaks of the importance of different believers, recognizing '"the fellowship of the Spirit" as something that transcends . . . denominational boundaries'; Habets, 'Veni Cinderella Spiritus!', pp. 66–80; V-M. Kärkkäinen, 'Pneumatology as a New Ecumenical "Model"', *Ecumenical Trends* 27.9 (1998), pp. 10–16; idem, 'The Ecumenical Potential of Pneumatology', *Gregorianum* 80.1 (1999), pp. 121–45; O. Ortega, 'Ecumenism of the Spirit', in B. F. Gutierrez, D.A. Smith (eds), *In the Power of the Spirit: The Pentecostal Challenge to Historic Churches in Latin America* (Louisville: Presbyterian Church, Worldwide Ministries Division, 1996), pp. 171–83.

[209] K. McDonnell, 'Five Defining Issues: The International Classical Pentecostal/Roman Catholic Dialogue', *Pneuma* 17.2 (1995), pp. 163–88 (178).

[210] Society of Pentecostal Studies, European Pentecostal Theological Association, European Pentecostal Charismatic research Association, Pentecostal Charismatic Research Fellowship.

[211] Pentecostal World Conference, Pentecostal/Charismatic Churches of North America, Pentecostal European Fellowship.

[212] J. Gros, 'Confessing the Apostolic Faith from the Perspective of the Pentecostal Churches', *Pneuma* 9 (1987), pp. 5–16.

[213] C.M. Robeck Jr, 'Pentecostals and Christian Unity: Facing the Challenge', *Pneuma* 26.2 (2004), pp. 307–38 (334).

[214] E.J. Rybarczyk, 'Spiritualities Old and New: Similarities between Eastern Orthodoxy and Classical Pentecostalism', *Pneuma* 24.1 (2002), pp. 7–25.

World Council of Churches

McClung[215] identifies early Pentecostals as experiencing the challenge of accommodating believers from many different church backgrounds who related together under the common experience of the baptism in the Spirit, McGee[216] identifying a similar spirit of cooperation among early Pentecostal missionaries. Bundy traces the early history of Pentecostal ecumenical development concluding, 'Ecumenism has been an essential and foundational quest of Pentecostalism'.[217] Robeck identifies cooperation between the WCC and some representatives of the AoG in the USA in the years after its establishment though it was rarely made public.[218] However, within a decade of it being established, criticism of the WCC was voiced because of its apparent formality, liberal tendencies and its call for unity, viewed as a sign of an end-time apostate and antichristian federation.[219] During the 1950s and 1960s, the debate concerning the WCC continued with most Pentecostals exhibiting a suspicious if not openly hostile attitude towards it. However, there were some leading Pentecostals who provided an alternative stance and argued that such dialogue and interaction did not necessarily indicate compromise.[220] Anderson[221] identifies a number of Pentecostals who espoused ecumenical ideals,[222] the most renowned being David du Plessis[223] (such people have often been misunderstood and maligned as a result). Nevertheless, in 1965 and 1969, the General Council of the AoG expressed its disapproval of the WCC, stipulating that it was at variance with biblical priorities and spiritual unity, associated it with Babylon of Rev. 17 and 18 and thus disapproved of ministers being involved.[224] Most Western Pentecostals have railed against the WCC as a liberal, or worse, an antichristian organization.[225]

---

[215] McClung, 'Try to Get People Saved', p. 40.

[216] G.B. McGee, 'Missions, Overseas (N. American Pentecostal)', in Burgess and van der Maas (eds), *NIDPCM*, pp. 885–901 (888).

[217] D.D. Bundy, 'The Ecumenical Quest of Pentecostalism', *CPCR* 5 (1999); Robeck, 'Pentecostal Origins from Global Perspective', pp. 166–80.

[218] Robeck, 'The Assemblies of God', pp. 125–32; idem, 'Pentecostals and the Apostolic Faith', pp. 64–6; idem (ed.), *Confessing the Apostolic Faith: Pentecostal Churches and the Ecumenical Movement* (Pasadena: The Society for Pentecostal Studies, 1987); Richie, 'The Unity of the Spirit', pp. 24–5.

[219] Robeck, 'The Assemblies of God', pp. 127, 129; K. Kendrick, *The Promise Fulfilled: A History of the Modern Pentecostal Movement* (Springfield: Gospel Publishing House, 1961), pp. 203–04; D.M. Coulter, 'Pentecostal Visions of the End: Eschatology, Ecclesiology and the Fascination of the *Left Behind* Series', *JPT* 14.1 (2005), pp. 81–98 (93–4).

[220] D. Gee, 'Contact Is not Compromise', *Pentecost*, 53 (Sep.–Nov., 1960).

[221] Anderson, *An Introduction to Pentecostalism*, pp. 67–8, 73, 249.

[222] T.B. Barratt, Alexander Boddy, Aimee Semple McPherson, Donald Gee, Walter Hollenweger, C.M. Robeck.

There are a number of basic reasons that cause Pentecostals to be wary of developing relationships with the WCC. The first relates to the concept of an ecumenical movement itself. Pentecostals believe that they, as believers, are part of the invisible Church that comprises all believers. Therefore, they are suspicious of a movement that seeks to demonstrate unity, a unity they believe already to be demonstrable by the individual members owning a relationship with Jesus.

Robeck also identifies the formalism that many Pentecostals associated with the liberal churches of the WCC.[226] Pentecostals viewed their doctrinal statements as being suspect and their (often liturgical) worship lacked the warmth and authenticity of a true expression of spirituality. Interestingly, Robeck deduces that the exuberance of Pentecostal worship was often viewed by members of the WCC as dangerous and likely to lead to disorder.[227] Thus, misunderstanding reigned on both sides of the ecumenical fence.

Partly as a result of the unwillingness by members of each constituency to explore the strengths of each other and only to concentrate on the perceived weaknesses, other valid issues were also sidelined by Pentecostals. Thus, for Pentecostals, because the WCC was seen to be a movement that concentrated on the social gospel, Pentecostal denominations denounced the latter. Similarly, because of the educated calibre of many of the leaders in the churches associated with the WCC, a fear grew among Pentecostals that to adopt an educated portfolio (especially in theology) was to run the risk of compromising one's faith or sliding towards the adoption of a liberal theology.

A more obvious problem relates to the different doctrines espoused by Pentecostals and those held (or perceived to be held) by members of the WCC.[228] Over recent decades, more Pentecostals have dialogued with the WCC,[229] though it has taken non-Western Pentecostals, in the main, to be at

---

[223] Howard, 'David du Plessis', pp. 271–97; M. Robinson, 'David du Plessis – A Promise Fulfilled', in Jongeneel (ed.), *Pentecost, Mission and Ecumenism*, pp. 143–55; D. du Plessis, *The Spirit Bade Me Go. The Astounding Move of God in the Denominational Churches* (Plainfield: Logos, 1970).

[224] Robeck, 'The Assemblies of God', p. 147.

[225] S. Durasoff, *Bright Wind of the Spirit: Pentecostalism Today* (London: Hodder and Stoughton, 1972), pp. 87, 99; Menzies, *Anointed to Serve*, pp. 220–21.

[226] Robeck, 'Pentecostals and the Apostolic Faith', pp. 69–70.

[227] Robeck, 'Pentecostals and the Apostolic Faith', p. 70.

[228] C.M. Robeck Jr, 'World Council of Churches' in Burgess and van der Maas (eds), *NIDPCM*, pp. 1213–217 (1214).

[229] G.W. Gilpin, 'The Place of the Pentecostal Movements Today' in Brewster (ed.), *Pentecostal Doctrine*, pp. 113–26 (118); M. Conway, 'Helping the Ecumenical Movement to Move On: Hollenweger and the Rediscovery of the Value of Diversity', in Jongeneel (ed.),

the forefront of engaging in discussions with the WCC and they have begun to make substantial changes to its membership and emphases.[230] Some Pentecostal denominations are members of the WCC including the Iglesia Pentecostal de Chile (the first to do so, joining in 1946),[231] the Misión Iglesia Pentecostal (1961), the Church of God in Argentina, the Igreja Evangélica Pentecostal (1969) and the Unión Evangélica Pentecostal Venezolana, Iglesia de Dios (Argentina, 1980), the Missâo Evangélica Pentecostalies Libres de Angola (1985) and the Iglesia de Misiones Pentecostalies Libres de Chile (1991). Many other Pentecostal denominations are members of national councils of churches.[232] Anderson concludes, 'It appears as if Majority World Pentecostals have far fewer "hang-ups" when it comes to ecumenism than their western counterparts have'.[233] The consultations on faith and healing

Pentecost, Mission and Ecumenism, pp. 273–87; G. Wainwright, 'The One Hope of Your Calling? The Ecumenical and Pentecostal Movements after a Century', *Pneuma* 25.1 (2003), pp. 7–28; J. Gros, 'A Pilgrimage in the Spirit: Pentecostal Testimony in the Faith and Order Movement', *Pneuma* 25.1 (2003), pp. 29–53; R. Pfister, 'Pentecostalism and Ecumenism: A Critical Examination of Seeming Antipodes in Light of Recent developments within French Pentecostalism', *SC* 2.3 (2001), pp. 209–26; C.M. Robeck Jr, 'Pentecostalism and Ecumenical Dialogue: A Potential Agenda', *Ecumenical Trends* 16.11 (1987), pp. 185–88; idem, 'Pentecostal/Charismatic Churches and Ecumenism: An Interview with Cecil M. Robeck, Jr', *The Pneuma Review* 6.1 (2003), 22–35; idem, 'The Challenge Pentecostalism Poses to the Quest for Ecclesial Unity', in P. Walter, K. Krämer and G. Augustin (eds), *Die Kirche en ökumenischer Perspektive* [a festschrift for Cardinal Walter Kasper on his 70th Birthday] (Freiburg: Herder, 2003), pp. 306–20; idem, 'Pentecostals and Christian Unity: Facing the Challenge', *Pneuma* 26.2 (2004), pp. 307–38; idem, 'The Holy Spirit and the Unity of the Church: The Challenge of Pentecostal, Charismatic, and Independent Movements', in D. Donnelly, A. Denaux and J. Famerée (eds), *The Holy Spirit, the Church and Christian Unity: Proceedings of the Consultation Held at the Monastery of Bose, Italy (14–20 October 2002)* (Leuven: Leuven University Press, 2005) pp. 353–81; idem, 'The Pentecostal Movement Should Open Her Eyes to the Ecumenical Movement', *CGJ* 4 (April 2003), pp. 32–8; idem, 'Pentecostals and Ecumenism', pp. 338–62; J.L. Sandidge, 'The Pentecostal Movement and Ecumenism: An Update', *Ecumenical Trends* 18 (1989), pp. 102–06; idem, 'An Update on the Ecumenical Activities of Pentecostals', in Jongeneel (ed.), *Experiences of the Spirit: Conferences on Pentecostal and Charismatic Research in Europe at Utrecht University 1989* (Frankfurt: Peter Lang, 1991), pp. 239–46.

[230] Gros, 'Toward a Dialogue of Conversion, pp. 189–202.
[231] A.E. Fernandez, 'The Significance of the Chilean Pentecostals' Admission to the World Council of Churches', *IRM* 51 (1962), pp. 480–82.
[232] C.M Robeck Jr, 'Do "Good Fences Make Good Neighbors"? Evangelization, Proselytism, and Common Witness', *AJPS* 2.1 (January 1999), pp. 87–103 (94–8).
[233] Anderson, *An Introduction to Pentecostalism*, p. 253; E.A. Wilson, 'Latin American Pentecostals: Their Potential for Ecumenical Dialogue', *Pneuma* 9.1 (1987), pp. 85–90; C.E. Alvarez, 'Latin American Pentecostals: Ecumenical and Evangelical', *Pneuma* 9.1 (1987), pp. 91–95.

initiated by the WCC have seen a majority number of Pentecostals and Charismatics involved.[234] Three consultations (held in Lima (1994); San Jose, Costa Rica (1996) and Switzerland (1997)) have been initiated by the WCC relating to issues that are important to Pentecostals; on each occasion, there were 25–30 Pentecostal attendees. More recently, a WCC/Pentecostal Joint Consultative Group was commissioned in 1998 in Zimbabwe that included 29 Pentecostals.[235] Staples identifies the adoption of major pneumatological concepts by the WCC with which Pentecostals are in complete agreement, including the roles, gifts and mission of the Spirit in the Church and lives of individual believers.[236] Indeed, Hollenweger believes he can identify 'a growing ecumenical commitment of many Pentecostals', a trend that he views as healthy.[237]

Roman Catholicism

Fear, ignorance and prejudice have resulted in deep divisions between Pentecostals and the Roman Catholic Church, Rev. 18.4 ('Come out of her, my people, so that you do not take part in her sins . . .') being used by some Pentecostal leaders as a call to those who would seek to engage with it. Since the early1970s, there has been some significant movement with regard to dialogue between some Pentecostals and leaders of the Roman Catholic Church, resulting in five specific discussions that occurred over a period of years (1972–1976, 1977–1982, 1985–1989, 1990–1997, 1998–2004).[238] This has

---

[234] C.M. Robeck Jr, 'A Pentecostal Looks at the World Council of Churches', *ER* 47.1 (1995), pp. 60–9.

[235] See D.L Cole, 'Ecumenism and the Ecumenical Movement', in Burgess (ed.), *EPCC*, pp. 153–58.

[236] P. Staples. 'Ecumenical Theology and Pentecostalism', in Jongeneel (ed.), *Pentecost, Mission and Ecumenism*, pp. 262–71 (264–69).

[237] W.J. Hollenweger, 'Biblically Justified Abuse: A Review of Stephen Parson's *Ungodly Fear: Fundamentalist Christianity and the Abuse of Power*', *JPT* 10.2 (2002), pp. 129–35 (134–35).

[238] K. McDonnell, 'Classical Pentecostal/Roman Catholic Dialogue: Hopes and Possibilities', in Spittler (ed.), *Perspectives on the New Pentecostalism*, pp. 246–68; idem, *Catholic Pentecostalism: Problems in Education* (Pecos, NM: Dove Publications, 1970); idem, 'Five Defining Issues.', pp. 163–88; C.M. Robeck Jr, J.L. Sandidge, 'Dialogue, Catholic and Pentecostal', in Burgess (ed.) *DIPCM*, pp. 576–82; E. O'Connor, *The Pentecostal Movement in the Catholic Church* (Notre Dame: Ave Maria Press, 1971); K. and D. Ranaghan, *Catholic Pentecostals* (New York: Paulist Press, 1969); Habets, 'Veni Cinderella Spiritus!', pp. 65–80; C.M. Robeck Jr, 'Specks and Logs, Catholics and Pentecostals', *Pneuma* 12.2 (1990), pp. 77–83; idem, 'John Paul II: A Personal Account of His Impact and Legacy', *JPT* 27.1 (2005), pp. 3–34; Gros, 'Toward a Dialogue of Conversion', pp. 189–201; J.L. Sandidge (ed.), *The Roman Catholic-Pentecostal Dialogue (1977–1982): A Study in Developing Ecumenism* (Frankfurt: Peter Lang, 1987); P.D. Lee, *Pneumatological Ecclesiology in the Roman*

sometimes been facilitated by Pentecostal scholars and, in particular, the Society for Pentecostal Studies, as a result of which consultations between Pentecostals and Catholics have been held in 1996, 1997 and 1998.[239] Similarly, Pentecostal journals have often been the vehicles for delivering the findings of such dialogues and for Pentecostal and Catholic scholars to write on issues of shared interest.[240] Macchia, a Pentecostal theologian, writes of the Catholic Church, 'There is a lifeline historically that leads us to view ourselves in relation to her and in appreciation for her, despite legitimate complaints that we might be able to recall against her (and she against us!)'.[241] Robeck offers a helpful insight into the relationship between Pentecostals and Catholics noting concerns on both sides; in their own way, each has been and still is concerned, if not worried, about the other.[242] However, on the basis of Eph. 4.1–6, he argues that working towards unity with other members of the Church is to follow the agenda set by the Spirit.[243]

Dialogue has concentrated on various issues including the Bible, both Pentecostals and Catholics identifying it as having priority in spirituality and theology, as being, without error and inspired by the Spirit, its interpretation needing the help of the Spirit and the Christian community.[244] The Charismatic Renewal in the Catholic Church (commencing around 1967) has made dialogue easier between some Pentecostals and Catholics, and especially since the Second Vatican Council.[245] Hollenweger believes that Pentecostals and Roman Catholics have a great deal in common, including their interest in renewal, the Spirit and ecclesiology, though his assessment

---

Catholic-Pentecostal Dialogue: A Catholic Reading of the Third Quinquennium (1985–1989) (Rome: Pontifical University, 1994); T.R. Crowe, *Pentecostal Unity: Recurring Frustration and Enduring Hopes* (Chicago: Loyola University Press, 1993); D.L. Cole, 'Dialogues, Catholic and Pentecostal', in Burgess (ed.), *EPCC*, pp. 129–34; idem, 'Current Pentecostal/Ecumenical Tensions', *Ecumenical Trends* 24.5 (May, 1995), 1/65–2/66, 9/73–16/80.

[239] See further Robeck, 'Do "Good Fences Make Good Neighbors"?', pp. 99–100.

[240] The full report of the Fourth Phase of the International Dialogue (1990–1997) between the Catholic Church and some Pentecostal Leaders was included in the *AJPS* 2.1 (1999), pp. 105–51; so also the third set of discussions between similar groups was published in *JPT* 12.2 (1990); A.D. Canales, 'A Rebirth of Being "Born Again": Theological, Sacramental and Pastoral Reflections form a Roman Catholic Perspective', *JPT* 11.1 (2002), pp. 98–119; J.L. Sandidge, 'Roman Catholic/Pentecostal Dialogue: A Contribution to Christian Unity', *Pneuma* 7.1 (1985), pp. 41–60.

[241] Macchia, *Baptized in the Spirit*, p. 227.

[242] C.M. Robeck Jr, 'Roman Catholic-Pentecostal Dialogue: Some Pentecostal Assumptions', *JEPTA* 21 (2002), pp. 3–25 (3–9); K. McDonnell, 'Improbable Conversations: The International Classical Pentecostal/Roman Catholic Dialogue', *Pneuma* 17.2 (1995), pp. 163–74; idem, 'Five Defining Issues', pp. 163–88.

[243] Robeck, 'Roman Catholic-Pentecostal Dialogue', pp. 9–25.

[244] Kärkkäinen, *Toward a Pneumatological Theology*, pp. 25–38.

that they share a similar ecclesiology is largely based on an inadequate and rather inflated perception of the authority of the Pentecostal pastor.[246] However, the issue of ecclesiology has proved to be a useful matrix within which dialogue has taken place.[247] Indeed, Zegwaart explores the possibility for further dialogue between Pentecostals and Catholics on the central issues of ecclesiology, soteriology and the sacraments[248] while Kärkkäinen identifies pneumatology[249] and ecclesiology[250] as having valuable potential for extended fruitful dialogue.

There have been positive moves by some leaders in both communities resulting in a readiness to learn from each other.[251] Thus, in 1976, McDonnell encouraged fellow Catholics to learn from the Pentecostal 'willingness to let the Spirit come to visibility in the full spectrum of His gifts',[252] their readiness to acknowledge a 'personal moment in faith and a personal relationship with Jesus',[253] while encouraging Pentecostals to be less suspicious of international structures that seek to reflect the message of the Gospel.[254] He also offered an apology on behalf of Catholics towards Pentecostals for a range of issues including intolerance, discrimination and exclusivism.[255] This was, in turn, accepted by the president of the Society for Pentecostal Studies who also requested forgiveness for negative attitudes and statements towards the Catholic Church.[256] At the same time, that there are major differences is clear and these may not be simply overlooked by either side.

[245] J.M. Ford, *Which Way for Catholic Pentecostals?* (New York: Harper and Row, 1976); O'Connor, *The Pentecostal Movement*; T.P. Thigpen, 'Catholic Charismatic Renewal', in Burgess and van der Maas (eds), *NIDCPM*, pp. 460–67; Kärkkäinen, *Toward a Pneumatological Theology*, pp. 47–50; P. Hocken, 'Charismatic Renewal in the Roman Catholic Church: Reception and Challenge', in Jongeneel (ed.), *Pentecost, Mission and Ecumenism*, pp. 301–09; D.L. Gelpi, 'The Theological Challenge of Charismatic Spirituality', *Pneuma* 14.2 (1992), pp. 185–97.

[246] W.J. Hollenweger, 'Common Witness between Catholics and Pentecostals', *Pneuma* 18.2 (1996), pp. 185–216 (194–99).

[247] Cole, 'Pentecostal Koinonia', pp. 103–89.

[248] Zegwaart, 'The Place of the Church', *JEPTA* 21 (2001), pp. 26–40; Kärkkäinen, 'Church as Charismatic Fellowship', pp. 100–21.

[249] Kärkkäinen, *Toward a Pneumatological Theology*, pp. 65–79.

[250] Kärkkäinen, *Toward a Pneumatological Theology*, pp. 109–22.

[251] J.M. Ceresoli, 'Critical Mass: "We Had Church" in a Holy Catholic Way', *JPT* 17 (Oct. 2000), pp. 7–11.

[252] McDonnell, 'Classical Pentecostal/Roman Catholic Dialogue', p. 252.

[253] K. McDonnell, 'The Pros and Cons of Dialogue with Catholics', *JPT* 16 (2000), pp. 90–101 (91).

[254] McDonnell, 'Classical Pentecostal/Roman Catholic Dialogue', p. 250–52.

[255] K. McDonnell, 'A Confession of Sins', *JPT* 17 (2000), pp. 20–21.

[256] F.D. Macchia, 'A Response and Corresponding Request for Forgiveness', *JPT* 17, pp. 22–3 (2000).

McDonnell, a Catholic, writes, 'Primary biblical truthes unite us. Important theological convictions divide us. What can we do together?' and suggests prayer together, sharing of pulpits as well as speaking together on issues on which agreement may be established. He also calls for clearer information to be offered in theological institutes with regard to each other's traditions.[257] He also offers a candid overview of the mistakes made by Catholics against Pentecostals, notes measures taken by the Catholic Church to support Pentecostal churches and individuals, and offers his gratitude to Pentecostalism for that which he has learned that has profited his spiritual growth.[258]

Some Ways Forward

Robeck offers a number of perspectives that, if developed, could advance the dialogue between Pentecostals and the wider Church.[259] He suggests that areas of agreement should be identified, strengths affirmed and weaknesses acknowledged. Patience and forgiveness is needed on the part of all as well as a greater realization of the universal nature of the Church. Finally, he advocates the strategic 'breaking down of barriers at all levels of the church, but particularly among those in church leadership'.[260] Pluess, drawing a parallel with the fairy story of the ugly frog who turns into a handsome prince when she receives him as her companion, concludes that this piece of fiction may provide a model for the emergence of a readiness to engage in dialogue and companionship with those who may initially appear uncomfortably different to oneself but who may become a companion of a type that would not have been previously anticipated.[261]

Sandidge also identifies ways whereby the development of bridges could be created between both groups by national dialogues, the sharing and exploration of differing doctrinal distinctives in seminaries, a readiness to learn from one another, repentance on both sides for words, deeds, unfounded criticisms and assumptions, and engaging in corporate prayer.[262]

Macchia argues that the identification of a movement as 'Pentecostal . . . begs for an ecumenical vision of the kingdom of God yet to come', identifying the early Church as a movement 'struggling through encounters with the

---

[257] K. McDonnell, 'Can Classical Pentecostals and Roman Catholics Engage in Common Witness', *JPT* 7 (1995), pp. 97–106 (103–05).

[258] McDonnell, 'The Pros and Cons', pp. 90–101.

[259] Robeck, 'Pentecostals and the Apostolic Faith', pp. 74–5; Kärkkäinen, *Toward a Pneumatological Theology*, pp. 50–1.

[260] Robeck, 'Pentecostals and the Apostolic Faith', p. 75.

[261] J-D. Pluess, 'The Frog-King or the Coming of Age of Pentecostalism', *CPCR* (2001).

[262] J.L. Sandidge, 'Consultation Summary: A Pentecostal Perspective', *Pneuma* 9.1 (1987), pp. 96–8.

Spirit of God to realize more and more of the ecumenical witness to which God has called them'.[263]

Part of the difficulty in developing dialogue between Pentecostals and either Catholics or ecumenical believers is that any developing rapprochement will be limited among Pentecostals simply because few are aware of the discussions being held between the various groups. Developments in dialogue and closer examples of fellowship are rarely recorded in popular Pentecostal magazines. Similarly, there have been very few attempts to provide reports to Pentecostals by their denominational leaders of these often unofficial discussions. Indeed, some of the barriers to dialogue on the part of Pentecostals are created by other Pentecostals.[264] Suspicions and assumptions are still common among the members of each constituent body and the issue of proselytism still plagues the dialogue.

However, given the emphasis of Pentecostals on the Bible and the Spirit, there is much that can be gained by the WCC and the Catholic Church developing relationships with Pentecostals.[265] The day of Pentecost acted as a model of unity in the context of diversity. Pentecostals need to be aware of the possibility that their questioning whether God may be working in other parts of the Church may be as inappropriate as the Jewish Christians in the early Church who were concerned about the possibility that God could be working among the Gentiles. Macchia writes, 'We have no right to criticise the ecumenical conversation taking place in a variety of contexts unless we are involved in the blood and sweat of labouring alongside it'.[266]

---

[263] Macchia, 'The Struggle for Global Witness', p. 25.
[264] Robeck, 'Do "Good Fences Make Good Neighbors"?', p. 101.
[265] C. Randall, 'The Importance of the Pentecostal and Holiness Churches in the Ecumenical Movement', *Pneuma* 9.1 (1987), pp. 50–60.
[266] Macchia, *Baptized in the Spirit*, p. 221.

5

THE BIBLE

Introduction

Pentecostals are in agreement with the traditional evangelical position regarding the establishment of the biblical canon. Similarly, they accept the trustworthiness of the Scriptures, as affirmed by the significant numbers of manuscripts that support them, and conclude that the canon is closed.[1] Many still have a fondness for the Authorised Version though more modern translations are increasingly used.[2]

Creeds are less important to Pentecostals as doctrinal formulations; they prefer to track their theology through the pages of Scripture, allowing for the Spirit and their Church traditions to guide them on their journey. They have often felt that many creeds have locked out some of their beliefs which they maintain are located in the Bible.[3] Wyckoff notes that the AoG established a creed only after much discussion for they wanted to maintain the ideal that 'the Bible is our all-sufficient rule for faith and practice'.[4] All other religious books, however good, are relegated to a lower place, to such an extent that some early Pentecostals were dismissive of them.[5] Part of this

---

[1] Menzies and Horton, *Bible Doctrines*, pp. 30–9; J.R. Higgins, 'God's Inspired Word', in Horton (ed.), *Systematic Theology*, pp. 61–115 (107–09).

[2] Rowe, *One Lord, One Faith*, p. 223. Rowe writes in the 1950s, 'The Authorised Version . . . is not likely to be ousted from its place of supreme regard . . .'; W.K. Kay ('Pentecostals and the Bible', *JEPTA* 24 (2004), pp. 71–83 (81)) notes in his survey of UK Pentecostal leaders that some rate the AV as the best version (Apostolic 46%, AoG 19.5%, Church of God 34%, Elim 10.5%) while others think the NIV is the best version (Apostolic 24%, AoG 29.4%, Church of God 10%, Elim 29.5%).

[3] Horton, *What the Bible Says*, pp. 14–15.

[4] Wyckoff, 'The Inspiration and Authority', pp. 30–1.

[5] See Nichol, *Pentecostalism*, pp. 77–8; S.H. Frodsham (*Smith Wigglesworth: Apostle of Faith* (Springfield: Gospel Publishing House, 1951), p. 109) notes the proud boast of Wigglesworth that the only book that he had ever read was the Bible.

trend has been due to a high appreciation of the significance of the Bible as God's Word.[6] It is thus no surprise that most early Pentecostal Colleges were known as Bible Colleges, where the Bible was the main textbook and libraries often numbered no more than a few hundred books. Much has changed in the past few decades.

Inspiration

To a very large degree, Pentecostals are in agreement with many other evangelicals concerning the inspiration and authority of the Bible.[7] Because of its divine source, Pentecostals have always revered its contents.[8] Hollenweger, in his introduction to *Pentecostalism. Origins and Developments Worldwide*, writes, 'To my friends and teachers in the Pentecostal Movement who taught me to love the Bible'.[9] Allied to this is a passion which characterizes their exploration of the Bible.[10] Pentecostals view the Bible as being the most important source of information concerning God, especially important because it is inspired by God (Acts 28.25; 1 Cor. 2.13; 2 Tim. 3.16; 2 Pet. 1.21).[11] Such inspiration carries with it an authority that is above tradition and that which reason might dictate. Indeed, Pentecostals affirm that the Bible is authoritative with regard to issues concerning salvation and faith,[12] conveying propositional truth and guidance for life.[13] However, Massey[14] notes, 'Despite this firm stance . . . Pentecostal churches and scholars have had to accept elements of change and development in their approach to Scripture'. This has not resulted in a demeaning of the truth of Scripture;

---

[6] Wilson, 'Bible Institutes, Colleges, Universities', in Burgess and van der Maas (eds), *NIDPCM*, pp. 372–73.

[7] R.D. Massey, 'The Word of God: "Thus Saith the Lord"', in Warrington (ed.), *Pentecostal Perspectives*, pp. 64–79 (64–5).

[8] T.F. Zimmerman, 'The Reason for the Rise of the Pentecostal Movement', in McClung (ed.), *Azusa Street and Beyond*, pp. 57–61 (58–9).

[9] Hollenweger, *Pentecostalism*; he also adds '. . . and to my teachers and friends in the Presbyterian Church who taught me to understand it'.

[10] R.D. Moore, '"And also Much Cattle?!": Prophetic Passions and the End of Jonah', *JPT* 11 (1997), pp. 36–9.

[11] Kay, 'Pentecostals and the Bible', pp. 71–83; Massey, 'The Word of God', p. 64; Larbi, *Pentecostalism*, p. 423; Menzies and Horton, *Bible Doctrines*, p. 21; Anderson, 'Pentecostals Believe', pp. 54–8; G.W. Gilpin, 'The Inspiration of the Bible', in Brewster (ed.), *Pentecostal Doctrine*, pp. 127–36 (128); Higgins, 'God's Inspired Word', pp. 109–13.

[12] Wyckoff, 'The Inspiration and Authority', pp. 19, 21; Anderson, 'Pentecostals Believe', p. 57.

[13] Menzies and Horton, *Bible Doctrines*, p. 22; McLean, 'Toward a Pentecostal Hermeneutic', p. 36; Gilpin, 'The Inspiration of the Bible', pp. 128–36.

[14] Massey, 'The Word of God', p. 68.

yet, it does reflect a growing awareness of its mystery, complexity of inter-pretation and need for contextualization.

Most Pentecostals would accept that God transmitted his words through the personalities and experiences of the writers who were involved, resulting in an interdependent partnership with God, without this, in any sense, detracting from their divine source and authority.[15] Nevertheless, the precise role of the writers of the Bible is often unclear. Though they are reticent to assume that the writers functioned as human word processors through whom the words of God tumbled out onto the page, they acknowledge the difficulty of determining how best to understand the association between the divine and the human in the writing process. Becker concludes,

> the Bible is the Word of God and the word of man, breathed by the Spirit and approved by Him in the shape that we have it today. The Bible is not the pure word of God, neither is it the pure word of man, but it became something new: it became an incarnated word.[16]

There is an increasing awareness that the authors wrote in their own words and style, reflecting their native cultures and eras as well as their personali-ties and educative backgrounds. There is also a growing readiness to read the text in the recognition that it is an ancient document that was written to people whose lives and situations were very different to present readers and to whom the writers of the Bible were offering specific and applied wisdom.

Infallibility and Inerrancy

Questions concerning inerrancy or infallibility and their differences to one another have rarely troubled most Pentecostals.[17] Indeed, Kay concludes that one of the reasons for earlier Pentecostals drawing up a position paper on inerrancy was largely due to the desire to facilitate collaboration and fellowship with the National Association of Evangelicals and not to strengthen existing Pentecostal understanding of the Bible as 'the inspired Word of God'.[18]

---

[15] Menzies and Horton, *Bible Doctrines*, p. 22; J.C. Thomas, *Ministry and Theology: Studies for the Church and Its Leaders* (Cleveland: Pathway Press, 1996), pp. 7–18.

[16] M. Becker, 'A Tenet under Examination: Reflections on the Pentecostal Hermeneutical Approach', *JEPTA* 24 (2004), pp. 30–48 (43).

[17] Ellington ('Pentecostalism and the Authority', p. 19) suggests the adoption of inerrancy may have been due to a desire to be more closely aligned with, and accepted by, Evan-gelicals rather than it being prompted by a desire from Pentecostals to adopt inerrancy because of its internal coherence.

The majority of Pentecostals would be prepared to subscribe to the Chicago Statement on Biblical Inerrancy drawn up in 1978[19] and the Lausanne Covenant (1974).[20] However, many would be unaware that the declaration refers to the text as originally given being inerrant and that those original texts are no longer extant. The tradition of textual criticism and the copious number of variants of the biblical text, which most Pentecostals (as well as other believers) are blissfully unaware of, make it difficult to determine which of the copies are the authentic links in the chain back to the first text. Nevertheless, because of the inspired nature of the Bible, most Pentecostals simply assume that the received text (in whatever version they use) must be true, that the autographs were inerrant and that the original record has been accurately transmitted from the copies of the originals. Thus, Higgins confidently announces that although 'the *act* of inspiration happened only once (in the autographs), the *quality* of inspiration was retained in the apographs'.[21]

The possibility of (even unintentional) imperfections being inserted by the writers would receive a cautious reaction from Pentecostals. Issues dependent on cultural and time considerations, and apparent contradictions have been addressed only in recent decades, most Pentecostals preferring to live with any potential ambiguities rather than call into question the integrity of Scripture. Rather than acknowledge (less so, to accept) any inaccuracies in the text, there has been a determination to harmonize or spiritualize them, or wait for the 'truth' to be revealed, as a result of which it is assumed that the authenticity of the text will be affirmed. They would prefer to believe that errors are impossible rather than countenance the possibility that the Bible contains them; the danger for many is that if it were proven that errors were contained in the Bible, it would cease to be the word of God, Higgins concluding, 'Scripture does not err because God does not lie'.[22] There has thus been a general unwillingness to accept that such a sacred text, inspired

---

[18] W.K. Kay, 'Do Doctrinal Boundaries Protect Our Identity or Prevent Fellowship?', *EB* 12 (1993), pp. 38–48 (41); in particular, see the process documented by C.M. Robeck Jr, 'National Association of Evangelicals', in Burgess, *NIDPCM*, pp. 922–25.

[19] *Paraclete* (Fall 1979, 1–5) incorporated the full transcript of the Chicago Statement on Biblical Inerrancy; see J.I. Packer, *God Has Spoken* (London: Hodder and Stoughton, 1979) for an exposition of it.

[20] Article 2 reads 'We affirm the Divine inspiration, truthfulness and authority of both OT and NT Scriptures in their entirety as the only written word of God, without error in all that it affirms and the only infallible rule of faith and practice'; Higgins, 'God's Inspired Word', pp. 61–115; C.R. Clarke, 'A Review of *Toward a Pneumatological Theology: Pentecostal and Ecumenical Perspectives on Ecclesiology, Soteriology, and Theology of Mission* by Veli-Matti Kärkkäinen', *JPT* 14.1 (2005), pp. 123–37 (127); Massey, 'The Word of God', p. 68.

[21] Higgins, 'God's Inspired Word', p. 107 (italics in original).

[22] Higgins, 'God's Inspired Word', p. 103.

by God, could have been tainted as a result of the process of transmission. A sense of awe for the text is preferred to an over eager assumption to believe that it can always be comprehended, especially where there are apparent contradictions; after all, it is God's book. It is too complex a book for a mere human; to assume a complete understanding of it presumes too much.

As a result of wider theological training and a maturing process within Pentecostalism, issues of infallibility and inerrancy have received greater attention.[23] In a survey of UK Pentecostal leaders, reported in 2004, while nearly all (99.5%) the ministers accepted that the Bible is infallible, nearly 40% disagreed with inerrancy, accepting that there were errors in the Bible.[24] This trend towards a greater association with a belief in infallibility rather than inerrancy is reflected elsewhere by Pentecostals.[25] In this respect, infallibility and inerrancy are clearly not viewed synonymously by many Pentecostals. Although both terms describe the notion of truthfulness and accuracy, in association with the Bible, 'infallibility' is used to refer to its reliability in matters of faith and practice, but not necessarily when related to all issues of history, science, grammar or style. Inerrancy is the term used to define the belief that the contents of the original texts are completely true and without error. A basic perspective of Pentecostals is that the 'Bible is a reliable revelation of God, and that it states the exact truthes the Holy Spirit intends to convey',[26] Massey concluding, 'The decisive truth-revealing role of the Holy Spirit has to be affirmed, if not fully understood in its operation'.[27]

Hermeneutics

Pentecostals have traditionally held to the position of the Reformers concerning the clarity of the meaning of Scripture for all believers and tended to

---

[23] A.D. Millard, 'The Pentecostal Movement and Inerrancy', *Paraclete* 20.2 (1986), pp. 4–7; Menzies and Horton, *Bible Doctrines*, p. 26.

[24] Kay ('Pentecostals and the Bible', pp. 77, 81) identifies some interesting characteristics associated with those who hold such views on the issue that indicate a conservative disposition. Thus, more inerrantists evaluated speaking in tongues higher than those who advocated an infallible position and were more likely to be opposed to allowing equality of opportunities to women in ministry. Similarly, they were more rigorous with regard to church activities including tithing and attendance, more conservative in lifestyle issues and more likely to support abstention from alcohol or gambling. Similarly, with regard to doctrines, they tend to be supportive of healing in the atonement, creationism and a belief that there is a clear biblical eschatological perspective.

[25] Gajewski and Wawrzeniuk, 'A Historical and Theological Analysis', p. 38.

[26] F.L. Arrington, 'The Use of the Bible by Pentecostals', *Pneuma* 16.1 (1994), pp. 101–07 (101).

[27] Massey, 'The Word of God', p. 67.

treat the Bible in a literalistic manner.[28] Thus, most Pentecostals are creation-ist, believing in the literal interpretation of Gen. 1–2 and thus the creation of Adam and Eve, and a young earth.[29]

Whereas systematic theology has often traditionally been the basis for a believer's exploration of God, Pentecostals have preferred to allow a popu-lar form of biblical theology to guide them in their quest. This has often occurred either because of a lack of awareness or appreciation of systematic theological works, because they did not reflect the emphases or spirituality of Pentecostals, or simply because they were often encyclopedic, perceived as inaccessible and unlikely to stimulate enthusiasm for an exploration of God or the development of personal spirituality. Although the terms are capable of a wide range of meanings, systematic theology tends to concen-trate on the topical ordering of biblical truths as logically and as synchronically as possible whereas biblical theology tends to be descriptive, inductive and as diachronic as possible. Whereas the former is once-removed from the text, in that it seeks to rearticulate it, the latter prefers to understand the text as being a message in its own right. Biblical theology holds more attraction to Pentecostals than systematic theology. Fundamentally, there has been a profound desire to be guided by the teachings of the Bible, rather than the formulations of commentators on the Bible. As Archer has demonstrated, early Pentecostals explored the Bible not in order to construct a systematic theology but 'a praxis-driven "Jesus-centrism" Christianity . . . pietistic and practical'.[30]

---

[28] Lugo (*Spirit and Power*, pp. 6, 23) records that 76% of Pentecostals in the countries researched held a literal view of the Bible; Anderson, 'Pentecostals Believe', p. 57; Clark, 'Pentecostalism's Anabaptist Roots', pp. 205–07; Bond, 'What Is Distinctive', p. 134; G. Wacker, 'The Functions of Faith in Primitive Pentecostalism', *Harvard Theological Review* 77. 3–4 (1984), pp. 353–75 (365); Ma, 'Biblical Studies', pp. 54–5.

[29] See Kay 'Pentecostals and the Bible', p. 81; in his survey, UK Pentecostal leaders responded to this issue with an interesting measure of disagreement. The figures of those who thought that God made the world in six 24 hour days was Apostolic 67.4%, AoG 70.3%, Church of God 65.3%, Elim 55.6%; W.A. Wedenoja, 'Anthropology', in Burgess (ed.), *EPCC*, pp. 34–5. Some Pentecostals hold to theistic evolution in which God is believed to supervise the evolutionary development of humanity and the Gen-esis record is interpreted allegorically. Others have begun to look to creative design theories to dovetail the Bible with scientific discoveries though with mixed success. Munyon reviews the evidence for the gap theory, the young age theory and the age day theory and (wisely) offers no conclusion as to which is the most likely to be closest to the truth (T. Munyon, 'The Creation of the Universe and Humankind', in Horton (ed.), *Systematic Theology*, pp. 215–53 (223–35)). However, he rejects theistic evolution associating it with 'secular evolution . . . with the proviso that God was superintending the process' (p. 223).

[30] Archer, 'Early Pentecostal Biblical Interpretation', p. 43.

This emphasis on the Bible as the guide for Pentecostals has probably been the reason for the fact that the few systematic theology books written by Pentecostals have been largely biblical theological explorations.[31] Rather than refer to the views of others, they have assumed that all they need is contained in the Bible. One of the earliest and most widely read Pentecostal books exploring Christian doctrines contained references to only about 50 authors, with limited bibliographical information concerning them. It is clear that these references were little more than asides, the concentration being on that which the Bible revealed about the doctrines under investigation, resulting in the author's assumption that his work will be accepted as 'authoritative'.[32] Similarly, nearly 20 years later, Horton wrote a book exploring theology on the basis of 'what the Bible actually teaches' with deliberately 'few references to books other than the Bible'.[33]

Nevertheless, for much of its earlier existence, Pentecostal students studied the Bible through the writings of systematic theologians and a staple item on the timetable of many Pentecostal Colleges was that of systematic theology.[34] This resulted, for many, in the inappropriate assumption that the Bible was only to be viewed as a formulation of doctrines, to be systematically presented as a result of a trawling through its books to identify common themes. This approach often resulted in a loss of a sense of the dynamic; the Bible was increasingly sought to be 'understood' and doctrines itemized in an ever growing list. Instead of it being a life-giving letter from God to believers, it became a repository of doctrines that were sometimes impenetrable and generally impersonal; a book of rules and dogmas that lacked the relational dynamic with God that the Spirit had intended.

This assumption that the Bible is a clear guide on all theological matters concerning belief and praxis has not always been helpful. For example, the desire of many to prove that tongues is the initial evidence of the baptism in the Spirit, to establish the subsequent nature of the baptism in the Spirit, the role of women in leadership or particular eschatological schemas on the basis of the biblical text has resulted in their being critiqued for claiming more than the text affirms. It has also sometimes resulted in naïve interpretations of the Bible, elitism and an assumption that humanly authored books

---

[31] Though see Pearlman, *Knowing the Doctrines*; Williams, *Systematic Theology*; J. Stone, *An Introduction to Basic Theology* (Cleveland: White Wing Publishers, 1971); Pruitt, *Fundamentals of the Faith*; Hughes, *Church of God Distinctives*; Arrington, *Christian Doctrine*; Duffield and Van Cleave, *Foundations of Pentecostal Theology*; see also D.D. Bundy, 'The Genre of Systematic Theology in Pentecostalism', *Pneuma* 15 (1993), pp. 89–107.

[32] Pearlman, *Knowing the Doctrines*, pp. 7–9.

[33] S.M. Horton, *Into All Truth: A Survey of the Course and Content of Divine Revelation* (Springfield: Gospel Publishing House, 1955), pp. 14–15.

[34] Bundy, 'The Genre of Systematic Theology', pp. 89–107.

exploring the biblical texts are inferior to one's own analysis. Sometimes, the more academic a book, the more likely it has been shunned. There was in much of Pentecostalism, at least until the latter third of the twentieth century, a strong anti-intellectual feeling, Hathaway noting that 'University degrees were considered a hindrance to Pentecostal ministry', acknowledging that 'the movement has struggled for most of its life with the mind-Spirit tension'.[35]

However, Pentecostals have moved on. The fact that the issue of hermeneutics is a major section of the seminal work by Hollenweger[36] and the subject of increasing numbers of articles in Pentecostal journals[37] identifies how this topic has been elevated in importance[38] while *The Pentecostal*

---

[35] M.R. Hathaway, 'The Elim Pentecostal Church: Origins, Development and Distinctives', in Warrington (ed.), *Pentecostal Perspectives*, pp. 1–39 (33); Bicknell, 'The Ordinances', p. 213; Nañez, *Full Gospel, Fractured Minds?*; Kärkkäinen, *Toward a Pneumatological Theology*, p. 7; Wilson, 'Bible Institutes, Colleges, Universities', pp. 372–73.

[36] Hollenweger, *Pentecostalism*, pp. 307–25; cf. F.L. Arrington, 'Hermeneutics', in S.M. Burgess, G.B. McGee, P.H. Alexander (eds), *DPCM* (Peabody: Hendrickson, 1988), pp. 376–89.

[37] Ervin, 'Hermeneutics: A Pentecostal Option', pp. 11–25; R.K. Johnston, 'Pentecostalism and Theological Hermeneutics: Evangelical Options', *Pneuma* (Spring 1984), pp. 51–64; G.T. Sheppard, 'Biblical Interpretation after Gadamer', *Pneuma*, 16.1 (1994), pp. 121–41; idem, 'Pentecostals and the Hermeneutics', pp. 5–34; R. Stronstad, 'Trends in Pentecostal Hermeneutics', *Paraclete* 22.3 (1988), pp. 1–12; idem, 'Pentecostal Experience and Hermeneutics', *Paraclete*, 26.1 (1992), pp. 14–30; R. Israel, D.E. Albrecht, R.G. McNally, 'Pentecostals and Hermeneutics: Texts, Rituals and Community', *Pneuma*, 15.2 (1993), pp. 137–62; Cargal, 'Beyond the Fundamentalist-Modernist Controversy', pp. 163–88; A.C. Autry, 'Dimensions of Hermeneutics in Pentecostal Focus', *JPT* 3 (1993), pp. 29–50; J. Byrd, 'Paul Ricoeur's Hermeneutical Theory and Pentecostal Proclamation', *Pneuma* 15.2 (1993), pp. 203–14; M.S. Clark, 'Pentecostal Hermeneutics: The Challenge of Relating to (Post)–Modern Literary Theory', *AJPS* 1 (2002), pp. 67–92; J.C. Thomas, K. Alexander, 'And the Signs Are Following. Mark 16:9–20', *JPT* 11.2 (2003), pp. 147–70; J. Abrahams, 'Feminist Hermeneutics and Pentecostal Spirituality: The Creation Narrative of Genesis as a Paradigm', *AJPS*, 6.1 (2003), pp. 3–21; C.S. Keener, 'Rightly Understanding God's Word. Context', *PR* 6.2 (2003), pp. 50–8; idem, 'Rightly Understanding God's Word. Learning Context', *PR* 6.4 (2003), 30–53; idem, 'Rightly Understanding God's Word. Whole Book Context. Part 1', *PR* 7.1 (2004), pp. 26–49; idem, 'Rightly Understanding God's Word. Whole Book Context. Part 2', *PR* 7.2 (2004), pp. 16–45; idem, 'Rightly Understanding God's Word. More Principles of Context', *PR* 7.3 (2004) pp, 44–55; idem, 'Rightly Understanding God's Word. Bible Background', *PR* 8.1 (2005), pp. 42–61; Noel, 'Gordon Fee and the Challenge', pp. 60–80; G.D. Fee, 'Why Pentecostals Read Their Bibles Poorly – and Some Suggested Cures', *JEPTA* 24 (2004), pp. 4–15.

[38] M. Turnage, 'The Early Church and the Axis of History and Pentecostalism: Facing the 21st Century: Some Reflections', *JEPTA* 23 (2003), pp. 4–29; Warrington, 'Would Jesus Have Sent', pp. 30–44; Hudson, 'It's Not What We Do', pp. 45–57; Wenk, 'Do We

Commentary[39] seeks to provide a mouthpiece for distinctly Pentecostal exposition. In 1985, Menzies noted that hermeneutics was now the 'bedrock issue' that was at the heart of much of Pentecostal theology[40] though not many years earlier, Fee had noted that many defined the interpretative methodologies of Pentecostals as 'bad hermeneutics'.[41] Hermeneutics and a readiness to explore the biblical text analytically are currently issues of increasing interest to many Pentecostals and a number of values are important to Pentecostals in interpreting the Bible.

The Value of Personal Application

Pentecostals believe that the main purpose of the Bible is to help them develop their experience of and relationship with God, to be more available to the ministry of the Spirit and to be drawn closer to Jesus. These are more important to Pentecostals than the value of the Bible as a resource for the identification and elaboration of various doctrines. Although they would state that they hold to an orthodox theology and accept the fundamental place of the Bible in the identification of such a theology, few would see the establishment of that as its primary purpose. Thus, Clark concludes, 'the Bible is associated with activity and experience rather than viewed as a textbook of doctrine'.[42] It is recognized as a collection of stories intended to lead a person to God and to be transformed as a result rather than a database of dogma to be discussed. It is less to be studied as an academic exercise and more to be seen as the altar of sacrifice to which they bring their lives for renewal. It is identified as a friendly partner, reflecting their joys and sorrows, their achievements and challenges, their present and future lives and, functioning as a guide to better relationships with God and others. A consequence of this has been that the task of studying and understanding the Bible has been identified as being both the responsibility and privilege of

Need', pp. 58–71; Ma, 'Biblical Studies', pp. 57–64; G.T. Sheppard, 'Pentecostals, Globalization and Postmodern Hermeneutics: Implications for the Politics of Scriptural Interpretation', in Dempster, Klaus and Petersen (eds), *The Globalization of Pentecostalism*, pp. 289–312; Powers, 'Your Daughters Shall Prophesy', pp. 313–37, 57–64; M.P. Brooks, 'Bible Colleges and the Expansion of the Pentecostal Movement', *Paraclete*, 23.2 (1989), pp. 9–17; Arrington, 'Hermeneutics', pp. 376–89.

[39] Pilgrim Press: Cleveland, OH, 2004.

[40] N.M. Menzies, 'The Methodology of Pentecostal Theology: An Essay on Hermeneutics', in Elbert (ed.), *Essays on Apostolic*, pp. 1–14 (5).

[41] Fee, 'Hermeneutics and Historical Precedent', p. 119.

[42] Clark and Lederle (eds), *What Is Distinctive*, p. 101; Anderson, *An Introduction to Pentecostalism*, p. 225; Archer, 'Early Pentecostal Biblical Interpretation', pp. 32–70; J. Hattingh, 'The Proprium of Pentecostal Theology', in Clark and Lederle (eds), *What Is Distinctive*, pp. 153–57 (155); Macchia, 'Theology, Pentecostal', p. 1122; Ellington, 'Pentecostalism and the Authority', p. 29.

all believers. The Bible is viewed primarily as a place of encounter, an encounter with the divine author.[43] Ellington notes that Pentecostals expect 'to encounter in the Scripture the very words of God speaking directly to their needs and guiding them'.[44]

They feel that the Bible is theirs and that they have the authority to access it for themselves. Hocken describes one of his clearest impressions of Pentecostalism as being 'a directness of relationship to God with corresponding expectations of divine revelation'.[45] To miss out on such revelations is viewed as not merely regretful but harmful to one's progress as a believer. Anderson[46] writes, 'Their purpose in reading the Bible is to find there something that can be experienced as relevant to their felt needs' and Wagner accounts for the growth of Pentecostalism as, in part, due to the 'extensive Bible-teaching ministry which is focused on the *felt needs* of church members'.[47]

In many ways, Pentecostals have tended to see their relationship with God functioning as a theocracy in which God makes the rules, punishing the disobedient and rewarding the obedient, in ways that are reminiscent of his responses to the Jews, as reflected in the OT. They live their lives through those described in it, their own lives being viewed as part of the Biblical drama.[48] Thus, they sometimes view their own journeys as paralleled with those of the Israelites from Egypt to the Promised Land or of the early Church from Jerusalem to the uttermost parts of the earth.[49] The Bible portrays God as being centrally involved in the lives of his people and these biblical characters are linked to the readers, offering templates for understanding how God works today.

The Bible is anticipated as being for the purpose of touching the readers emotionally, not simply to teach them intellectually; to result in an experience, not merely better exegesis; to facilitate an exposure of God not only an exposition of truth. Their worldview is one that incorporates a dynamic God who impacts his people – then and now. Cargal speaks of the 'immediacy of the text';[50] they do not just want to know what the text meant then

---

[43] Synan, 'Pentecostalism', p. 39; Kärkkäinen, *Toward a Pneumatological Theology*, pp. 4–5; Johns, 'Pentecostalism and the Postmodern Worldview', p. 90.

[44] Ellington, 'Pentecostalism and the Authority', p. 22.

[45] P. **Hocken**, 'A Charismatic View on the Distinctiveness of Pentecostalism', in W. Ma, R.P. Menzies (eds), *Pentecostalism in Context. Essays in Honour of William W. Menzies* (Sheffield: Sheffield Academic Press, 1997), pp. 96–106 (98).

[46] Anderson, *An Introduction to Pentecostalism*, p. 225; Archer, 'Early Pentecostal Biblical Interpretation', pp. 32–70; idem, 'Pentecostal Hermeneutics', pp. 63–81.

[47] C.P. Wagner, 'America's Pentecostals: See How They Grow', *Christianity Today* 31 (Oct. 16, 1987), p. 28 (italics mine).

[48] Archer, 'Pentecostal Hermeneutics', p. 67.

[49] Land, *Pentecostal Spirituality*, pp. 74–5.

[50] Cargal, 'Beyond the Fundamentalist-Modernist Controversy', p. 164.

but what it means now. Macchia[51] writes, 'There is for Pentecostals a certain "present-tenseness" to the events and words of the Bible, so that what happened then, happens now.'

The phrase 'This is That' was used to identify present experiences with those described or promised in the Bible[52] and often resulted in a determination to find information in the text that may be readily applied to one's own spiritual journey. Wacker[53] identifies the Pentecostal 'conviction that the Bible offered a compendium of answers for all significant questions. It needed only to be read, believed and obeyed'.

There are changes taking place among Pentecostals in the way that they read the Bible, but the latter description is a fair assessment of where the emphasis has been laid in the past, and, to a degree, the present also, in that truth is valued when it is not just conceptualized but also personally applied.[54] This provides a personal vitality and excitement to the text, though it has also, on occasions, resulted in naïve, superficial and inappropriate interpretations because of the non-critical stance that often undergirds it. This has often meant, for example, that some Pentecostals have too readily adopted promises that were originally given to other followers of God and treated them as if they were automatically relevant for themselves with no consideration of the context of their original application. Thus, OT promises to Israel are often indiscriminately applied to the Church.[55] As such, Exod. 15.26, a verse relating to the Jews, linking not only sickness with disobedience but also health with obedience, has often been applied to contemporary believers as well, with unhelpful consequences in that it suggests that healing is to be expected if one is obedient. Similarly, some early Pentecostals were reticent to benefit from medical practice on the basis of verses such as 2 Chron. 16.12.[56]

For many Pentecostals, there is no historical gap to be bridged between themselves and the text. Although this is changing dramatically, there is still a strong belief that the Bible is to be taken at face value; it has been assumed that there is little reason to separate that which it said to a previous generation from that which it says now; the message is assumed to be the same. God's warnings of punishment to the Israelites are taken seriously by Pentecostals while the songs and poetry of the OT echo the fluid dynamism of

---

[51] Macchia, 'Theology, Pentecostal', *NIDPCM*, p. 1122.
[52] G.R. Carlson used the phrase to give Biblical support for the Pentecostal baptism of the Spirit (*Paraclete* 8.2 (1974), pp. 22–5) as did A.W. Pettet (*Paraclete* 18.4 (1984), pp. 5–7).
[53] Wacker, *Heaven Below*, p. 71.
[54] Bond, 'What Is Distinctive', p. 135.
[55] Larbi, *Pentecostalism*, p. 423.
[56] Exod. 15.26; Deut. 32.39; Ps. 103.3.

Pentecostal worship and spirituality. Similarly, the history of the early Church as reflected in the book of Acts is often visited to help them refine their experience and lifestyles in order to emulate the earliest Christians.[57] The determination to appropriate the message for the modern reader has often obscured the fact that the original message was addressed to a first-century audience. It is important that Pentecostals realize that an initial appreciation of the ancient context would enable them to understand that which the writer intended to convey to his original readers. Thereafter, the message may be contextually re-applied for later generations. Ebojo explores this concept more, seeking to draw lessons for contemporary application of the text for Pentecostals from the ways the earliest scribes sought to contextualize the written traditions for their own communities. He describes them as 'not detached transmitters of the text working in a context-less vacuum. The truth is, they were also participant-readers, with particular interests and agenda that were largely shaped and dictated by their sociocultural contexts'.[58] Thus, he argues that the differences in some parallel texts (Mk 9.29//s; 16.1–20) may be due to the perspectives of the scribes who copied and adapted the originals to benefit their particular constituencies and thus provided a relevant contextuality of application. He concludes, 'The reality was that early Christians reflected on the "Word" and made it relevant in *their* own "world" even if it meant "rewriting" Scripture'.[59] That a Pentecostal could articulate such a flexible view of inspiration indicates that, at least, some Pentecostals are prepared to re-examine issues relating to the interpretation and contextualization of the ancient text.

The Value of Narrative

Pentecostals esteem the biblical narrative highly and believe that it does not just provide examples of that which God has done in the past but also has 'normative theological value'.[60] Stories in which people have encountered God are generally preferred to didactic sections that explore the theology of that encounter. Thus, traditionally, they have related more easily to the Gospels and Acts than the epistles; they have enjoyed pausing with the historical books before Psalms more than the prophetic books that follow. The emphasis on narrative resonates with their own storytelling pilgrimages

---

[57] Wacker, *Heaven Below,* pp. 71–2.
[58] E.B. Ebojo, 'The "Other-Worldly" in the Hands of "This-Worldly" Scribes', in T.D. Gener, A.A.O. Gorospe (eds), *Principalities and Powers. Reflections in the Asian Context* (Manila: OMF, 2007), pp. 202–23 (208).
[59] Ebojo, 'The "Other-Worldly"', p. 222.
[60] J.E. Powers, 'A "Thorn in the Flesh": The Appropriation of Textual Meaning', *JPT* 18 (2001), pp. 85–99 (89).

and is reflected in the preponderance of anecdotes and narrative in their preaching.[61]

Pentecostalism is also comfortable with emotion and the capacity to express various emotions in a corporate context. The latter are often best expressed in the biblical narratives – in the stories of the wanderings of the Israelites, the travails and joys of the Psalmists, the sufferings of the prophets who stood for God and righteousness and the emphasis on a holy God who responded to his people with hot rage and tender compassion. All resonate with the experiences of Pentecostals in their relationship with God and the world in which they live.

The Value of Personal Experience

That which is consistently integral to Pentecostal interpretations of the text is their experience with God.[62] Consequently, it is no surprise to read Fee's assessment that, 'In general, the Pentecostals' experience has preceded their hermeneutics'.[63] Where Pentecostals have encountered God in a given setting, that often subsequently determines how they respond to a particular issue as referred to in the Bible.[64] Thus, they are prepared to draw their conclusions with reference to empirical as well as textual evidence; personal experience has, at times, preceded their hermeneutics.[65] Thus, even though the Christian tradition may not often record the baptism in the Spirit or the regular occurrence of charismatic gifts, the fact that they have been experienced by Pentecostals is more important as an affirmation of their understanding of the biblical phenomena than the historical silence on the topic.[66] Thus, Stronstad concludes, 'the Pentecostal experience is a valid hermeneutical presupposition'.[67] Similarly, Hattingh states, 'For the Pentecostal theologian, subjective experience is important not because it becomes the grounds of faith, but because it is in this area that truth is realised'.[68] Furthermore, he writes, 'An objectivity which accepts a historical reality by means of reason alone is deprived of that which the Bible proclaims'.[69]

---

[61] Hocken, 'A Charismatic View', p. 98.

[62] Kärkkäinen, *Toward a Pneumatological Theology*, p. 28; L. Hurtado, 'Why Pentecostals Need the Bible', *Paraclete* 6.1 (1972), pp. 20–1.

[63] Fee, 'Hermeneutics and Historical Precedent', p. 122; G.L. Anderson, 'Pentecostal Hermeneutics Part II', pp. 18–19.

[64] Arrington, 'Hermeneutics', p. 383; Ervin, 'Hermeneutics: A Pentecostal Option', pp. 11–25.

[65] G.L. Anderson, 'Pentecost, Scholarship, and Learning in a Postmodern World', *Pneuma* 27.1 (2005), pp. 115–23 (121); Atkinson, 'Worth a Second Look', pp. 50–1.

[66] K.J. Archer, 'Pentecostal Story: The Hermeneutic Filter for the Making of Meaning', *Pneuma* 26.1 (2004), pp. 36–59 (54–9).

[67] Stronstad, 'The Biblical Precedent', p. 1.

[68] Hattingh, 'The Proprium of Pentecostal Theology', p. 155.

Pentecostals also believe that the supernatural events which are recorded in the pages of the Bible may also occur today.[70] This belief in the possibility of supernatural activity provides a pre-understanding of the Bible, 'an experiential presupposition'.[71] It inevitably affects their hermeneutics as they interpret the text with an expectation that God may similarly move in their lives now just as he did then. It is this personal encounter that is often a stronger basis for the belief that the Bible is authoritative than a doctrinal or doctrinaire framework.[72] Similarly, those Pentecostals who accept the role of women as teachers in the Church are influenced not only by exegesis of relevant passages but also (and even more so) by the fact that they have benefited from such teaching.

As Kärkkäinen writes, 'Experience came first; theology followed'[73] while Jacobsen concludes, 'Pentecostal experience has been circumscribed by theology and Pentecostal theology has been grounded in experience.'[74] Often times, experience bridges the text and its application and can inform one's interpretation of the text.[75] Thomas explores the Jerusalem council (Acts 15) and notes the value placed on experience (the experiences of Peter, Paul and Barnabas with regard to Gentile converts and the impact of the Spirit on them).[76] Only after this is offered does James refer to scripture (15.16–18), and that somewhat ambiguously (Amos 9.11–12) but dynamically, in arriving at the conclusion to welcome Gentiles into the Church.

However, Pentecostals are aware that experience, however valid, is not sufficient to determine truth or praxis. The need to construct a methodology that recognizes its value but protects from its inherent dangers has been articulated by Pentecostals as being an important quest.[77] Thus, Arrington cautions against relying only on personal experience and argues that any theological formulation should begin with scripture.[78] Stephenson, however, advocates that Pentecostals should 'intentionally draw upon aspects of their spirituality to inform their doctrine and vice versa' in a reciprocal and

---

[69] Hattingh, 'The Proprium of Pentecostal Theology', p. 155.

[70] Elbert, 'Pentecostal/Charismatic Themes', pp. 181–215; Byrd, 'Paul Ricoeur's Hermeneutical Theory', p. 205; Arrington, ' The Use of the Bible', p. 105.

[71] Stronstad, 'Pentecostal Experience and Hermeneutics', p. 17.

[72] Ellington, 'Pentecostalism and the Authority', pp. 16–18.

[73] Kärkkäinen, *Toward a Pneumatological Theology*, p. 6.

[74] Jacobsen, *Thinking in the Spirit*, p. 2; G.T. Sheppard, 'Word and Spirit: Scripture in Pentecostal Tradition. Part 1', *Agora* 1 (1978), pp. 4–22 (14–19).

[75] Yong, 'Not Knowing Where the Wind Blows', p. 93; Arrington, 'The Use of the Bible', pp. 105–07.

[76] Thomas, 'Women Pentecostals and the Bible', pp. 44–50.

[77] Parker, *Led by the Spirit*, pp. 39–61; Gause, 'Issues in Pentecostalism', p. 114.

[78] Arrington, *Christian Doctrine*, vol. 1. pp. 79–80.

continuing dialogue to ensure that experience and scripture have the opportunity to refine and correctly determine truth.[79]

Thus, even though it needs to be validated by outside criteria, as well as the Bible, Pentecostals recognize that one's experience may be included as a vital component in the hermeneutical process.[80] Stronstad concludes, 'a Pentecostal hermeneutic will have a variety of cognitive and experiential elements' and he defends the significance of both.[81]

The Value of the Mind

There has been a strong commitment to the discipline of preparing well crafted sermons.[82] A greater emphasis on the priority of teaching that is accompanied by careful attention to the message of the Bible as part of the preparation for the sermon has increasingly resulted in preaching being more the product of studious, exegetically sound research with the consequence that sermons are often more thoughtfully crafted than once they were.[83] As always, there is the perceived danger that the application of such resources to preaching may result in a sophistication that lacks the cutting edge of the Spirit. That which is feared is the absence of that all important, vibrant spontaneity of the Spirit and thus preaching is often accompanied by private and public prayer.[84] At all times, the sermon must be judged, not only on its presentation and style but also on its effectiveness and aftermath. The model of Jesus, the Galilean teacher is valued above that of the Jerusalem scribe for contemporary Pentecostal preaching.

Indeed, historically, there has been a fear of the intellect by Pentecostals with regard to the interpretation of Scripture. For much of its history, Pentecostals engaged in a pre-critical engagement with the text (and many still do).[85] The willingness to interact with the text while benefiting from some of the twentieth-century methods of biblical interpretation has only in recent years been accepted by Pentecostals.[86]

---

[79] C.A. Stephenson, 'Epistemology in Pentecostal Systematic Theology: Myers Pearlman, E.S. Williams, and French L. Arrington' (SPS conference paper, Cleveland, 2007), pp. 307–14 (313–14).

[80] R.L. Gabriel, 'A Response to Wonsuk Ma's "Toward an Asian Pentecostal Theology"', *AJPS* 2.1 (1999), pp. 77–85 (79); Anderson, 'Pentecostal Hermeneutics Part II', pp. 13–22 (19); Parker, *Led by the Spirit*, pp. 11, 20–38.

[81] Stronstad, 'Pentecostal Experience and Hermeneutics', pp. 14–30.

[82] J. Gordy, 'Toward a Theology of Pentecostal Preaching', p. 87.

[83] Byrd, 'Paul Ricoeur's Hermeneutical Theory', pp. 203–14.

[84] R.D. Cotton, 'Walking in the Spirit in Spontaneity', *Paraclete* 25.1 (1991), pp. 1–3.

[85] Cargal, 'Beyond the Fundamentalist-Modernist Controversy', p. 179.

[86] Landrus, 'Hearing 3 John 2', pp. 70–88; M.E. Roberts, 'A Hermeneutic of Charity: Response to Heather Landrus', *JPT* 11.1 (2002), pp. 89–97; E.B. Powery, 'Ulrich Luz's *Matthew in History*: A Contribution to Pentecostal Hermeneutics', *JPT* 14 (1999), pp. 3–17; U. Luz, 'A Response to Emerson B. Powery', *JPT* 14 (1999), pp. 19–26.

This has partially resulted from the historical roots of Pentecostalism, which mainly attracted adherents from the working, and therefore less well educated, classes. This was compounded by the fact that early Pentecostals were opposed by other denominations, which were often populated by more professional, and better educated, people. It has also resulted from the belief that the Spirit is the sole interpreter of Scripture; any competitor to his role has been viewed with suspicion. Consequently, there has developed a reticence to credit the mind with significant value as far as interpretation of Scripture is concerned for fear that it might militate against the work of the Spirit who has been given to lead believers into truth.

This reticence to value the intellect has also been prompted by the fact that those who were engaged in critical biblical analysis for much of the twentieth century were reflecting liberal and rationalist perspectives relating to the inspiration of the Scriptures and the person of Christ, while exhibiting antagonism to the idea of a miracle working God and a charismatic Church, inspired and empowered by the Spirit. Because of the provenance of such individuals, it was largely assumed that the fruit of their labour was to be ignored, if not condemned.[87] Thus, they were rarely engaged with and the notion of significant biblical analysis was to lie dormant for most of the Pentecostal era. Because of this, Pentecostals lacked training in the use of literary analytical tools and they retreated into the artificial security of assuming that they had the truth and that, because they apparently relied so much on the Spirit as their guide, no further discussion or investigation of the text was needed.

However, it is precisely a careful use of the intellect in conjunction with a commitment to appropriate guidelines for interpretation of the text that have increasingly been recognized by most Pentecostals as holding significant value for its development as a movement and protection from error.[88] This is demonstrated by the advance in graduate and postgraduate education for Pentecostals worldwide[89] and a recent flurry of academic journals and academic societies[90] dedicated to issues of interest to Pentecostals.

---

[87] R.R. Hammer, 'From Atheism to a High View of Scripture', *Paraclete* 16.1 (1982), pp. 16–18; Hathaway, 'The Elim Pentecostal Church', p. 33.

[88] Bundrick, 'Ye Need Not That Any Man Teach You', *Paraclete* 15.4 (1981), pp. 15–17; S.D. Gear, 'The Holy Spirit and the Mind', *Paraclete* 18.4 (1984), pp. 25–30; W.P. Atkinson, *Now Read This* (Eastbourne: Kingsway, 1996), pp. 79–94.

[89] Ma, 'Biblical Studies', 57–64; Brooks, 'Bible Colleges and the Expansion', pp. 9–17; Tarr, 'Transcendence', pp. 195–222.

[90] *Asian Journal of Pentecostal Theology, Australian Journal of Pentecostal Theology, Journal of the European Pentecostal Theological Association, Journal of Pentecostal Theology, Pneuma, Pneuma Review, Spirit and Church* plus online journals; societies including – The Society for Pentecostal Studies, European Pentecostal Theological

Two extremes are to be avoided. The one locks the Bible into an academic environment to which only the scholar may be admitted; the other is that which opens the floodgates of inappropriate interpretations of the text, initiated by a reliance on private interpretation. Pentecostals are increasingly aware that the Bible is a collection of books through which the divine author has invited the reader to experience a creative journey of discovery. A readiness to listen to the text and others who comment on it indicates that a maturing process is taking place in Pentecostalism. A new sense of self-confidence is developing that enables Pentecostals to explore the text more objectively, thoughtfully and with integrity in order to be enlightened by truth.

As to whether there is a Pentecostal hermeneutic is a question that has been explored by many in recent years.[91] A definitive answer has not yet been determined, with some expressing concern that some expressions of Pentecostal hermeneutics are little more than elitist forms of interpretation, albeit based on the assumption that the Spirit is motivating the interpretation. Ervin argues that there is no specifically Pentecostal hermeneutic, suggesting that Pentecostals have benefited from evangelical hermeneutics but have also uniquely emphasized the role of the Spirit in the interpretative process.[92]

Association, European Pentecostal Charismatic Research Association; see W.J. Hollenweger, 'The Challenge of Reconciliation', JEPTA 19 (1999), pp. 5–16 (8–12); D.D. Bundy, 'Historical Perspectives on the Development of the European Pentecostal Theological Association', *Pneuma* 2.2 (Fall 1980), pp. 15–25.

[91] G.L. Anderson, 'Pentecostal Hermeneutics Part 1', *Paraclete* 28.1 (1994), pp. 1–11; Parker, *Led by the Spirit*, pp. 24–7; L.W. Oliverio Jr, 'The Classical Pentecostal Hermeneutic and Its Successors' (SPS conference paper, Cleveland, 2007), pp. 261–66; V-M. Kärkkäinen, 'Pentecostal Hermeneutics in the Making: On the Way from Fundamentalism to Postmodernism', *JEPTA* 18 (1998), pp. 76–115; McLean, 'Toward a Pentecostal Hermeneutic', pp. 35–56; B.C. Aker, 'Some Reflections on Pentecostal Hermeneutics', *Paraclete* 19.2 (1985), pp. 18–20; Arrington, 'The Use of the Bible', pp. 101–07; H.K. Harrington, R. Patten, 'Pentecostal Hermeneutics and Postmodern Literary Theory', *Pneuma* 16.1 (1994), pp. 109–14; R.P. Menzies, 'Jumping off the Postmodern Bandwagon', *Pneuma*, 16.1 (1994), pp. 115–20; Powery, 'Ulrich Luz's *Matthew in History*', pp. 3–17; Y.S. Eim, 'Pentecostal Hermeneutics. The Critical Task of Pentecostalism for the 21st century', *SC* 2.1 (2000), pp. 1–5; W.J. Hollenweger, 'The Contribution of Critical Exegesis to Pentecostal Hermeneutics', *SC* 2.1 (2000), pp. 7–18; Y.J. Ahn, 'Various Debates in Contemporary Pentecostal Hermeneutics', *SC* 2.1 (2000), pp. 19–52; F.D. Macchia, 'The Spirit in the Text. Recent Trends in Pentecostal Hermeneutics', *SC* 2.1 (2000), pp. 53–65; Clark, 'Pentecostal Hermeneutics', pp. 67–92; P.W. Lewis, 'Towards a Pentecostal Epistemology: The Role of Experience in Pentecostal Hermeneutics', *SC* 2.1 (2000), pp. 95–125; Becker, 'A Tenet under Examination', pp. 30–48.

[92] Ervin, 'Hermeneutics: A Pentecostal Option', pp. 25–35.

Key elements that Pentecostals recommend in their reading and interpreting of the text are as follows:

- A recognition that the Bible is an authentic resource for one's relationship with God and lifestyle development.
- An acknowledgement that the transmission of the Bible through the centuries has not diluted its authority for Christians in all eras or undermined its divine inspiration.
- An approval of the view that contextualization of some of the Biblical information is valid because of the difference in contexts, cultures and eras.[93]
- A readiness to accept that faith and reason are integral elements of a coherent hermeneutic.
- An acceptance of the fact that exegetical and hermeneutical aids may be valuable for a better appreciation of the meaning of the text especially in that they help to determine the original meaning of the text.[94] It should be noted that the following comments are more realized in the Pentecostal Academy, though are increasingly reflective also of the Pentecostal pulpit.[95] Issues relating to the purposes of the biblical authors in writing, methodology and historical context have been increasingly recognized as important characteristics in the interpretation of Scripture.[96] The fact that a best selling book guiding people in their reading and understanding of the Bible has been written by a Pentecostal scholar is significant.[97] Thus, Pentecostals are prepared to explore the value of literary criticism (including reader-response or reader-centred criticism, literary genres,[98] feminist hermeneutics,[99] redaction criticism,[100] narrative criticism[101] and a cautious

---

[93] Sheppard, 'Pentecostals, Globalization', pp. 289–312.
[94] Ellington, 'Pentecostalism and the Authority', p. 20; Anderson, 'Pentecostal Hermeneutics Part 1', p. 6 and 'Pentecostal Hermeneutics Part II', *Paraclete* 28.2 (1994), pp. 13–14; Powery, 'Ulrich Luz's *Matthew in History*', pp. 3–17; Luz, 'A Response to Emerson B. Powery', pp. 19–26; G.L. Anderson, 'Why Interpreters Disagree', *Paraclete* 24.1 (1990), pp. 1–10; Fee, *To What End Exegesis?*
[95] Cargal, 'Beyond the Fundamentalist-Modernist Controversy', p. 170; Kärkkäinen, 'Pentecostal Hermeneutics in the Making', pp. 81–2.
[96] C.S. Keener, 'Rightly Understanding God's Word: The Reader's "Social Location"', *PR* 9.2 (2006) pp. 44–56; Kärkkäinen, *Spiritus Ubi Vult Spirat*, 1998, pp. 138–41.
[97] Fee, *How to Read*.
[98] C.S. Keener, 'Rightly Understanding God's Word: Context of Genre Continued', *PR* 8.4 (2005), pp. 40–61; idem, 'Rightly Understanding God's Word: Context of Genre: Revelation', *PR* 9.1 (2006), pp. 40–61; Anderson, 'Pentecostal Hermeneutics Part II', pp. 16–18; Fee, 'Hermeneutics and Historical Precedent', pp. 124–26; idem, *Gospel and Spirit*, pp. 89–92.
[99] Abraham, 'Feminist Hermeneutics and Pentecostal Spirituality', pp. 3–21.

recognition of the value of tradition-historical-grammatical methodologies[102]) and engage in exegetical evaluation of the text.[103] The issue of authorial intent has been championed in particular by Fee, as a result of which he seeks to differentiate timeless truths from ones that relate to particular historical circumstances. The former may be identified as those that were central to the intention of the author and have more didactic value than secondary concerns.[104] A balance is to be maintained in that though it is increasingly recognized that the Bible, like many other books, is to be studied, using appropriate interpretative methodologies, the fact is that it is not like any other book.

The Value of the Christian Community

Interpretations of the text are best determined in the context of a community of believers (including Christian traditions other than Pentecostal ones), past and present, which offer an environment for a safe enquiry of the text.[105] It provides the opportunity for balance and accountability while protecting its members from subjective tendencies.[106] Without the involvement and consensus of the wider community, one's interpretation of the text can become stridently dogmatic, divisive and thus ultimately and fundamentally flawed. In particular, the Pentecostal community brings its own unique comment on the text, based on its social and religious contexts and belief in the dynamic nature of the Spirit and the experiential aspect of their faith, such

---

[100] D.A. Johns ('Some New Directions in Hermeneutics of Classical Pentecostalism's Doctrine of Initial Evidence', in McGee (ed.), *Initial Evidence*, pp. 145–67 (157)) identifies redaction criticism as 'one of the areas that is similar to what Pentecostals have been doing all along'. Redaction criticism is a popular tool by some Pentecostals including Shelton, *Mighty in Word;* Warrington, *Discovering the Holy Spirit;* idem, *Jesus the Healer. Paradigm or Phenomenon* (Carlisle: Paternoster Press, 2000); W.W. Menzies, 'Synoptic Theology: An Essay on Pentecostal Hermeneutics', *Paraclete* 13.1 (1979), pp. 14–21.

[101] S.A. Ellington, 'History, Story and Testimony: Locating Truth in a Pentecostal Hermeneutic', *Pneuma* 23.2 (2001), pp. 245–63.

[102] Cargal, 'Beyond the Fundamentalist-Modernist Controversy', p. 163; Arrington, 'The Use of the Bible', pp. 102–03.

[103] G.D. Fee, *New Testament Exegesis. A Handbook for Students and Pastors* (Philadelphia: Westminster Press, 1983).

[104] Fee, *Gospel and Spirit*, pp. 39–44, 85–93, 103–04.

[105] Archer, *A Pentecostal Hermeneutic;* also Coulter, 'What Meaneth this?', pp. 62–3; McClung, 'Explosion, Motivation, and Consolidation', pp. 6–7; Pinnock, 'The Work of the Holy Spirit', pp. 16–17; Ellington, 'Pentecostalism and the Authority', p. 29; Israel, Albrecht and McNally, 'Pentecostals and Hermeneutics: Texts, Rituals and Community', *Pneuma* 15.2 (1993), pp. 154–61; Chan, *Pentecostal Theology*, p. 44.

[106] Chan, *Pentecostal Theology*, p. 45.

a context being as important to the hermeneutical process as any exegetical or theological method.[107]

The Value of the Spirit

Pentecostals believe that the Spirit has been given, among other reasons, to function as a teacher of believers, his role being to lead them into truth.[108] The potential dynamic that is resident in the text when illuminated by the Spirit and the possibility of multidimensional interpretations have ensured that Pentecostals have not found themselves isolated in the deserts of higher criticism. This Spirit-led journey results in the text being enlivened by his inspiration,[109] McKay describing the impact of the Spirit as being so dramatic as to warrant the phrase, 'taking the veil away'.[110]

Ervin[111] writes of the importance of recognizing the value of linguistic, literary and historical analysis to an understanding of the Bible, a process that is best attained by 'human rationality . . . quickened by the Spirit'. Rather than explore the text only through the grid of human hermeneutics, however valid, discovering the meaning of the text as a result of benefiting from its original inspirer, the Spirit, is inevitably superior. In this regard, the Spirit is centrally valued in the creation, transmission, reception and application of the text. This pneumatic hermeneutic is a valuable means of restoring to the text the integral characteristic of the Spirit who is the most important element of the transmission process from God to the believer.[112] Thus, Land records, 'Scripture is normative but not the text alone. It is text as

---

[107] Archer, 'Pentecostal Story', p. 37; Chan, *Pentecostal Theology*, p. 45.

[108] Fee, 'Hermeneutics and Historical Precedent', p. 122; Hollenweger, *Pentecostalism*, pp. 307–21; J. McKay, 'When the Veil Is Taken Away. The Impact of Prophetic Experience in Biblical Interpretation', *JPT* 5 (1994), pp. 17–40.

[109] K. Warrington, 'Bible or Spirit, Cold Text or Warm Friend: Who's Best for You?', (EPTA conference paper, Regents Theological College, Nantwich, 2004).

[110] F.B. Rice ('The Holy Spirit and the Intellect', *Paraclete* 10.3 (1976), pp. 3–7) explores the possibility of the Spirit working with the intellect of those who seek to interpret the text; McKay, 'When the Veil Is Taken Away', p. 21; Land, *Pentecostal Spirituality*, pp. 100, 106; Anderson, 'Pentecostal Hermeneutics Part 1', p. 2 and 'Pentecostal Hermeneutics Part II', pp. 14–16; Kärkkäinen, *Spiritus Ubi Vult Spirat*, p. 138; Sheppard, 'Word and Spirit. Part 1', pp. 4–5, 17–22 and 'Word and Spirit: Scripture in Pentecostal Tradition. Part 2', *Agora* 2 (1978), pp. 14–19; R. Stronstad, *Spirit, Scripture and Theology: A Pentecostal Perspective* (Baguio City: Asia Pacific Theological Seminary Press, 1995).

[111] Ervin, 'Hermeneutics: A Pentecostal Option', 18; Anderson, 'Pentecostal Hermeneutics. Part 1', pp. 1–2 and 'Pentecostal Hermeneutics. Part II', pp. 13–22.

[112] So also J.M. Bonino, 'Changing Paradigms: A Response', in Dempster, Klaus and Petersen (eds), *Called and Empowered*, pp. 117–19; Ellington, 'Pentecostalism and the Authority', pp. 16–20; Ervin, 'Hermeneutics: A Pentecostal Option', p. 23.

inspired and illuminated by the Spirit which is authoritative and transforma-tive'.[113] Powery concludes, on the basis of an examination of Mk 12.35–37, 'one cannot know or understand the meaning [or narrative function] of the scriptural text without the proper engagement with or endowment by the Spirit'.[114] The Bible is not simply a collection of (Spirit-inspired) words, but a living letter from the Spirit who is as much alive now as when he penned those words through human authors. He is still desirous to lead readers into, not just truth, but a true relationship with himself, not just factual ortho-doxy but also friendship that is authentic. To lose the charismatic, prophetic dimension is to potentially absent the Spirit from that which he desires to do most – encounter the reader himself.[115] As Coulter notes, this 'dynamic view of revelation establishes a distinct marker' over against other evangeli-cal traditions.[116]

Smith cautions that being exclusively 'a community of the Book' can result in an undermining of the expectation of the dynamic Spirit speaking.[117] An implication of his perspective is that there can be an assumption that the Spirit has already spoken – in the Bible. Although this is true, the timeless Spirit also continuously provides guidance for behaviour and praxis and this pneumatic hermeneutic needs to be borne in mind in one's hermeneuti-cal deliberations.[118] Although the Bible is central to the formulation of orthodox beliefs, that truth may not be reduced to propositional statements as located in the Bible only. The dynamic Spirit speaks today through the ancient word but often in fresh, new and innovative ways – sometimes with revelations that are additional to those received by the original readers. It is a Spirit-filled book, neither static nor stagnant but dynamic, and to be engaged with in a process of exploration and discovery.

However, to benefit from the creative and authoritative potential of the Spirit demands a readiness and ability to listen to him. The encouragement of the gift of discernment to enable believers to identify when and how the Spirit is speaking is also important. What may be one person's illumination by the Spirit or ability to see 'multiple dimensions of meaning'[119] can be a 'subjectivizing hermeneutic'[120] or eisegesis to another. Of more immediate importance is the offering of guidance to believers to be aware that the Spirit

---

[113] S.J. Land, 'Response to Professor Harvey Cox', *JPT* 5 (1994), pp. 13–16 (13).

[114] Powery, 'The Spirit, the Scripture(s)', p. 186.

[115] Cross, 'A Proposal to Break', pp. 60–70; J.K.A. Smith, 'The Closing of the Book: Pente-costals, Evangelicals and the Sacred Writings', *JPT* 11 (1997), pp. 49–71; McKay, 'When the Veil Is Taken Away', pp. 17–40.

[116] Coulter, 'What Meaneth This?', p. 54.

[117] Smith, 'The Closing of the Book', pp. 49–71.

[118] McLean, 'Toward a Pentecostal Hermeneutic', pp. 35–56.

[119] Cargal, 'Beyond the Fundamentalist-Modernist Controversy', p. 175.

[120] Dayton, *Theological Roots of Pentecostalism*, p. 50.

is not as silent as many may assume but that he desires to enlighten and encounter them as they listen to him speaking to them through the text. It is possible that the Spirit might surprise the reader,[121] even to the point of offering different messages of hope, guidance, revelation and tuition depending on the cultural or spiritual context in which the believer is located. The Spirit is more creative and flexible than many assume.

Pentecostalism, which came into being proclaiming that it was reintroducing the liberating person of the Spirit, has in recent years developed a greater appreciation of the implications of this in relation to the Bible. To a large degree, Pentecostal theology starts with the Spirit. Although the Bible records, 'In the beginning was the Word' (Gen. 1.1), the Spirit preceded the beginning. He may not be restricted by the text that he inspired; he is also free to speak when and what he wishes. Believers in the Christian community, past and present, need to take advantage of all the guidelines available to them for ensuring that in listening for the Spirit, they hear the authentic word of their divine mentor. It is in this regard that rather than seeking to locate a Pentecostal hermeneutic, it is preferable to speak of the best kind of hermeneutic as being one that is fundamentally inspired by the Spirit.

Preaching

Not a great deal of literature has been written exploring Pentecostal preaching though there are some notable exceptions.[122] The dynamics of preaching have largely been developed from guidance provided by evangelical authors, as well as from personal contexts of ministry or past experiences within the Pentecostal tradition. Pentecostals have traditionally learnt about their faith more through the medium of hearing the spoken word rather than reading the written word. Thus, preaching has been crucially important to the spiritual development of Pentecostals.[123] Using the Nazareth sermon pericope in

---

[121] K. Tanner, 'Workings of the Spirit: Simplicity or Complexity?', in Welker (ed.), *The Work of the Spirit*, pp. 100–04.

[122] R.H. Hughes, *Pentecostal Preaching* (Cleveland: Pathway Press, 1981); idem, 'The Uniqueness of Pentecostal Preaching', in McClung (ed.), *Azusa Street and Beyond: 100 Years*, pp. 117–128; idem, 'The Uniqueness of Pentecostal Preaching', pp. 91–6; Brandt, 'Pentecostal Preaching', pp. 14–18; J. Byrd, 'Formulation of a Classical Pentecostal Homiletic in Dialogue with Contemporary Protestant Homiletics' (unpublished doctoral dissertation, Southern Baptist Theological Seminary, 1990), esp. pp. 255–64; A. Raganooth, 'Pentecostal Preaching in North America' (unpublished doctoral dissertation, University of South Africa, 1999); idem, *Preach the Word: A Pentecostal Approach* (Winnipeg: Agape Teaching Ministry, 2004); Gordy, 'Toward a Theology of Pentecostal Preaching', pp. 81–97.

[123] J. Camery-Hoggart, 'The Word of God from Living Voices: Orality and Literacy in the Pentecostal Tradition', *Pneuma* 27.2 (2005), pp. 225–55 (226); idem, *Speaking of God: Reading and Preaching the Word of God* (Peabody: Hendrickson, 1995).

Mk 1. 21–28 as an example, Davies describes Pentecostal preaching as 'a dialogic, listener-focussed process, where the individual listener needs to play an active role in the production of the meaning'.[124]

Sermons are viewed not simply as opportunities to impart truth but to communicate life. The text is viewed as being alive even though ancient, and capable of enlivening its readers and hearers. Pentecostals are not alone in using narrative in their preaching but it is also certainly an important aspect of their communication. It is no surprise that not only is the Bible central to their preaching but also the narrative sections that are most popular.[125] As a result, they use stories and personal testimony to illustrate and apply the truths they seek to express.[126] Pentecostal preachers are often emotional and extemporaneous communicators, engaging in storytelling to make a point, retelling the biblical narratives in their own words, often packaged in lengthy sermons. Hocken defines Pentecostal preaching as comprising 'a use of Scripture and a style of preaching and ministry that was more anecdotal and narrative than schematic and doctrinal'.[127] Cox argues that Pentecostals are 'experiential and not text oriented' and view the Bible as 'a symbol of authority, not a text to be exegeted'. He concludes, 'Sermons are not lectures sprinkled with a few anecdotes, but stories, often dramatically re-enacted, with an occasional doctrinal observation interjected'.[128] To a degree, he is correct although there has been transition and development.

Pentecostal preaching anticipates achieving something beneficial for the hearers, Myung identifying the central message of freedom.[129] Pentecostals preach in order to facilitate development in personal spirituality.[130] Thus, not only does the Bible inform their preaching, but the latter is also intended to result in the hearers responding to the sermon as if it was the word of God to them in their individual settings.[131] They anticipate a decision for lifestyle change on the part of the listeners and call for a response either in a corporate setting at the conclusion to the sermon or more immediately while the sermon is being preached. At its best, Pentecostal preaching appeals to the affections and also anticipates the possibility of an encounter with God;

---

[124] A. Davies, 'A New Teaching without Authority: Preaching the Bible in Postmodernity', *JEPTA* 27.2 (2007), pp. 161–71 (170).

[125] R.H. Hughes, 'The Uniqueness of Pentecostal Preaching', pp. 91–6.

[126] T.H. Lindberg, 'The Power of Simplicity in Spirit-Filled Preaching', *Paraclete* 24.4 (1990), pp. 10–15.

[127] Hocken, 'A Charismatic View', p. 98.

[128] H. Cox, 'Spirits of Globalization: Pentecostalism and Experiential Spiritualities in a Global Era', in Stålsett (ed.), *Spirits of Globalization*, pp. 11–22 (19).

[129] Myung and Hong, *Charis and Charisma*, pp. 78–9.

[130] H.R. Yim, 'Preaching God's Word in Demonstration of the Spirit and Power', in Elbert (ed.), *Essays on Apostolic*, p. 81.

this might relate to conviction of sin, a sense of awe and worship, a readiness to praise God or a determination to develop as a Christian.[132]

Clark thus describes Pentecostal preaching as 'kerygmatic, par excellence' in that, although it may contain exposition, it is a dynamic event that anticipates a change in the hearers, be it conviction, challenge, encouragement or guidance.[133] It is intended to be effective and effectual, meaningful and motivational. The sense of immediacy also undergirds much of Pentecostal preaching in which the preacher attempts to identify that which the text means for now and for the particular group of people to whom the sermon is being preached. There is an expectation that the preacher and hearer will 're-experience the text', learning old lessons as presented in the text for the benefit of the original readers but also be open to the possibility of hearing from God in a new way.[134] The best sermon is the one that may be defined as prophetic, Massey deducing that 'true Pentecostal preaching is inspirational or prophetic';[135] that is to say, it includes a particular word or becomes a personal word from God to the listeners. Even though the preacher may not be cognizant of it, the individual hearer may receive it as a specific communication from God.[136] Perhaps because of this, the term 'message' is often used by Pentecostals for the sermon, thus identifying it as a message (from God) rather than a mere formulation of statements. In this regard, the presence of the Spirit in the act of preaching is paramount.

Gordy deduces that the involvement of the Spirit in the preparation and delivery of the sermon provides a distinctive of Pentecostal preaching[137] (though many non-Pentecostals would make the same affirmation). Thus, instead of preaching merely being cerebral, it should also have the capacity of being revelational and transformational, both of which are aspects of

---

[131] D.L. Tucker, 'Biblical Preaching: Theology, Relevance, Empowerment', *Paraclete* 25.3 (1991), pp. 23–9.

[132] R.O. Baker, 'Pentecostal Bible Reading: Toward a Model of Reading for the Formation of Christian Affections', *JPT* 7 (1995), pp. 34–48; Byrd, 'Paul Ricoeur's Hermeneutical Theory, p. 205.

[133] Clark and Lederle (eds), *What Is Distinctive*, pp. 77–9.

[134] A. Raganooth, 'Pentecostal Preaching' (SPS conference paper, Cleveland, 2007) p. 295; Albrecht, *Rites in the Spirit*, pp. 162–63.

[135] Massey, 'The Word of God', p. 70.

[136] McKay, 'When the Veil Is Taken Away', pp. 28–9; Albrecht, *Rites in the Spirit*, p. 164.

[137] Gordy, 'Toward a Theology of Pentecostal Preaching', p. 89; idem, 'Toward a Theology', pp. 81–97; Hughes, 'The Uniqueness of Pentecostal preaching', p. 91; Myung and Hong, *Charis and Charisma*, pp 83–5; C.T. Crabtree, 'What a Name to Live Up to', *Enrichment* 10.1 (2005), p. 55–9 (57); Baker, 'Pentecostal Bible Reading', *JPT* 7 (1995), p. 47; E.C. Elser, 'Charismatic Preaching', *Paraclete* 10.4 (1976), pp. 14–17; J.K. Moon, 'The Holy Spirit in Preaching', *Paraclete* 11.4 (1977), pp. 23–6; H.W. Steinberg, 'Anointed Preaching', *Paraclete*, 24.4 (1990) 6–9.

the Spirit.[138] Indeed, Pentecostals often use the term 'anointed' of the preaching they seek to engage in; it refers to the desire to benefit from the impartation of the Spirit as they speak.[139] It is reminiscent of the use of oil in the OT to indicate that a person had been set apart to fulfil a commission (Exod. 40.13–15; 1 Kgs 19.16). In particular, it is referred to by Luke (4.18) as the mode in which Jesus preached his first recorded sermon in Nazareth.

Some Ways Forward

- The present (and especially Western) culture offers many attractions and distractions that impede the reading and study of the Bible. Lugo records that only 42% read the Bible daily (ranging from South Korea (27%) to Brazil and Kenya (51%).[140] Increasingly, people are conditioned to only being able to occupy their minds with short attention based exercises and this also provides a powerful hindrance to both reading the Bible. Reading the Bible publicly is less common than it was in Pentecostal churches. Not only does this decentralize it from church practice but it also encourages the belief that reading the Bible is an exercise that should be undertaken in private, if at all. Therefore, Pentecostal leaders need to ensure that a central place is provided for the reading of the Bible in corporate gatherings. Similarly, a regular reliance on the Bible in preaching will elevate its importance in the perceptions of the listeners.
- In an age where questions are expected to be answered quickly, the complexities of the Bible, its stories and doctrines, make for an uncomfortable source of truth for many modern readers. This is accentuated when believers struggle to read an ancient text that, despite modern translations, clearly speaks to a different culture, a different age and is presented in a literary style that is foreign to the modern mind. More importantly is the assumption on the part of many that the Bible can function as a comprehensive resource on all issues and that it can provide the answers to all the questions asked of it. However, it was never intended to be an exhaustive database of endless wisdom but was largely provided as a record of how God related to his people in previous generations. The purpose of the Bible is not only to be a source that contemporary believers may examine for guidance relating to their lives, but also a stimulus for them to develop a personal relationship with the author himself, leading to their being able to travel in companionship with, not the Bible only, but also the immediate, personal, and comprehensive source of wisdom and enabling,

---

[138] Johns and Johns, 'Yielding to the Spirit', pp. 114–16.
[139] Steinberg, 'Anointed Preaching', pp. 6–9.
[140] Lugo, *Spirit and Power*, p. 19.

the Spirit. As well as inspiring the ancient text itself, he seeks to inspire believers with unique whispers, special words spoken through the mouths of others and specific messages reflected in the Biblical text – some of which may be just for them.

Therefore, it is important that Pentecostals cultivate the art of listening for and to the Spirit as they read the text. Asking questions of the authors as one reads is a means whereby one can interact with the ultimate author. Pentecostals need to be aware of the possibility that the Spirit may speak additionally to the message that he supervised thousands of years ago. Sermons thus can become opportunities to share that which one has discovered as a result of the adventure of listening to and learning from the Spirit. It is important also to remember that preaching/teaching is a trialogue involving the speaker, the audience and the Spirit. Each has something to offer to the communicative process.

- The danger of assuming that all the promises of the Bible may be applied to one's personal life without contextualization can lead to inappropriate or unhelpful consequences. The danger of subjectivism is always close to a community that espouses the role of individual interpretation and reliance on the Spirit to guide one's understanding of the text. To engage in the latter as an isolated individual without an appreciation of historical traditioning and the importance of the local Christian community in providing an interpretative framework can lead to elitist and divisive outcomes for all concerned. If Pentecostals communicate truth in a context of reflection and learning from a wider believing community, including their own, they will be protected from offering it in an unnecessarily rigid or dogmatic framework.

6

SPIRITUALITY AND ETHICS

Personal Spirituality

Introduction

Traditionally, Pentecostals have assumed the importance of discipleship in an ongoing process of sanctification in the lives of believers (Rom. 8.18),[1] Bowers writing, 'Discipleship or Christian formation is a critical facet of the missional work of Pentecostals'.[2] As a result of salvation, they view themselves as having been set apart to God (1 Cor. 1.30; Heb. 10.10) whereupon their role is to practically live as followers of Jesus, in as close a replication of his lifestyle as they can (1 Thess. 4.7) by a process of self discipline (Col. 3.5) and reliance on divine help (1 Cor. 10.13), taking advantage of the possibility of forgiveness when they fail (1 Jn 1.9).

The concepts of holiness and sanctification are popular maxims of Pentecostalism.[3] Two uses of the noun 'sanctification' are employed by Pentecostals. The first refers to the act of believers being sanctified (set apart) at salvation, righteousness being imputed to them by God; this act results in them being declared by God as being his people with the consequent privileges and responsibilities of that position. The second characteristic of the word 'sanctification' relates to a life of ongoing discipleship, demonstrated by commitment to a transformed lifestyle.[4]

---

[1] Menzies and Horton, *Bible Doctrines*, pp. 147–54; Rowe, *One Lord, One Faith*, pp. 94–120; J. Bowers, 'A Wesleyan-Pentecostal Approach to Christian Formation', *JPT* 6 (1995), pp. 55–86.

[2] Bowers, 'A Wesleyan-Pentecostal Approach', p. 55.

[3] D. Powell, 'The Doctrine of Holiness', in Brewster (ed.), *Pentecostal Doctrine*, pp. 357–70.

[4] D. Leggett, 'The Assemblies of God Statement on Sanctification', *Paraclete* 25.2 (1991), pp. 19–27; Land, *Pentecostal Spirituality*, p. 76.

Some expressions of Pentecostalism, especially within the Wesleyan/ Holiness constituencies, believe that an act of sanctification may be experienced as a second work of the Spirit after salvation, sometimes confusingly also known as the baptism in the Spirit[5] that results in the possibility that a believer may live without intentionally committing sin.

This emphasis was largely undermined among Pentecostals, initially as a result of the teaching of William H. Durham, who, in 1910, espoused the belief that the process of sanctification was ongoing and that salvation resulted in believers being set apart to God (1 Cor. 1.2–3, 30; 6.9–11; 1 Pet. 1.1–2).[6] The General Council of the AoG adopted a statement concerning sanctification that was more clearly in line with this notion of progressive sanctification.[7] This is the more popular view among Pentecostals today.[8] Whether Pentecostals accept progressive sanctification or a crisis experience, there has always been a desire to maintain a radical sense of holiness.

Motivations for Holiness

The Bible

A Pentecostal model of ethics or morality has not been formally developed, most preferring to rely on that which may be gleaned from the Bible for personal and corporate moral conduct. Traditionally, the OT has played an important part in this process. Thus, the Ten Commandments, part of God's covenant with Israel (Deut. 4.13), would be viewed by most Pentecostals as part of their covenant with God also, and therefore to function as a platform for one's morality. Thus, because of the commandment 'Thou shalt not kill', for many years, most Pentecostals were pacifists.

---

[5] R.T. Hughes, 'Christian Primitivism as Perfectionism: From Anabaptists to Pentecostals', in S.M. Burgess (ed.), *Reaching Beyond: Chapters in the History of Perfectionism* (Peabody: Hendrickson, 1986), pp. 213–55; Land, *Pentecostal Spirituality*, pp. 88–93, 128; Dayton, *Theological Roots of Pentecostalism*, pp. 63–100; contra A.F. Missen, 'Doctrine and Modern Society', in Brewster (ed.), *Pentecostal Doctrine* (Cheltenham: Elim, 1976), pp. 373–79 (378).

[6] D.W. Faupel, 'William H. Durham and the Finished Work of Calvary', in Jongeneel (ed.), *Pentecost, Mission and Ecumenism*, pp. 85–95; Faupel, *The Everlasting Gospel*, pp. 231–70; R.W. Bishop, 'Walking in the Spirit in Sanctification', *Paraclete* 24.3 (1990), pp. 2–30 (26).

[7] Part of it reads 'Sanctification is an act of separation from that which is evil . . . By the power of the Holy Ghost, we are able to obey the command: "Be ye holy, for I am Holy" (1 Peter 1.15, 16)'.

[8] Kärkkäinen, *Spiritus Ubi Vult Spirat*, p. 182; T.P. Jenney, 'The Holy Spirit and Sanctification', in Horton (ed.), *Systematic Theology*, pp. 397–421 (414–20); Hollenweger, *The Pentecostals*, pp. 23–5.

Similarly, tithing is practiced by most Pentecostals,[9] despite this being largely based on Malachi 3.10 (Deut. 12.6; Prov. 3.9), referring to Jews and not specifically Christians. NT verses are also employed to indicate the importance of giving to the Christian community (Mk 12.42–44; 1 Cor. 16.1–2; 2 Cor. 9.7) and many Pentecostals are encouraged (and historical practice has supported this) to present their offerings weekly or monthly to the local church which they attend (based on Lev. 27.30).

Encouragements to godly life as related in the OT are also often reflected in Pentecostal contexts. Thus, 2 Chron. 7.14 ('If my people, who are called by my name, will humble themselves and pray and seek my face and turn from their wicked ways, then I will hear from Heaven and will forgive their sin') has become, for many, the basis for confidence that one's sins will be forgiven if the guidelines are followed; more importantly, revival is assumed to follow. The fear of punishment from God or the withholding of his blessings, including healing, has resulted in many choosing to maintain their curtailed lifestyles (Lev. 26.15–16; Jer. 11.11, 14).

The guidelines offered in the NT have also regularly been adopted in determining appropriate Christian behaviour. Increasingly, they have been contextualized in ways that retain the underlying principles but fit the modern and cultural contexts of believers though often times, they can be applied directly to a modern Christian setting.

However, there are a number of challenges facing modern Pentecostal leaders. First, there is a decrease in the personal reading of the Bible by many believers that has resulted in an increasing unawareness of the guidelines contained therein. Secondly, modern society is becoming increasingly diverse and complex, and answers to the plethora of confusing questions and complicated issues concerning morality are not always clearly identifiable from the Bible. This has resulted in a more fluid context for determining norms for one's behaviour. Some of the accepted views of the past have been rejected as being unnecessarily dogmatic, in need of contextualization[10] or simply not reflective of the guidance actually contained in the Bible.

The Pentecostal Community

A major guide in the determining of one's lifestyle remains the received practices and teachings of one's denomination or church. Although it would not

---

[9] Hollenweger, *The Pentecostals*, pp. 399–412; Anderson (*An Introduction to Pentecostalism*, p. 70) identifies the Brazilian Pentecostal Congregação Christã (Christian Congregation), numbering around 1.5 million, as one denomination that does not insist on tithing.

[10] G.H. Stassen ('Recovering the Way of Jesus in the Sermon on the Mount', *JEPTA* 22 (2002), pp. 103–26) calls for a new appreciation of the Sermon on the Mount as a guide for the transformation of attitudes and actions but not as a presentation of idealistic or legalistic propositions.

be true to state that standards were deliberately set and maintained in order to strengthen these groups as a sociological tool of enforcement to maintain cohesion, it did mean that not conforming to the praxis of the majority of believers meant that one was in danger of being excluded from the group and having therefore to function in a very different context. The place of the community as the setting for the development of Christian formation has always been important for Pentecostals; it has been a significant context for discipleship, affirmation and transformation and Boone calls for Pentecostals to continue as 'an intentional tradition-bearing community'.[11]

For much of the history of Pentecostalism, the outworking of this Christian formation has been by retreating from the morality of the secular environment. An appropriate pattern of life was, to a large degree, identified by what one chose not to do as much, if not more, than by what one chose to do. Those activities associated with 'the world' included smoking, alcohol,[12] cinema[13] (though to a much lesser degree television), dancing, gambling (even playing cards were often viewed as unacceptable), inappropriate sexual activity and bad language.[14] This list could be broadened in some countries and eras to include issues as diverse as chewing gum, cosmetics, mixed bathing and involvement in politics.

Associated with this stance of abstinence was a reticence to develop friendships with unbelievers for fear of being influenced inappropriately. The gap between the church and the 'world' was rigidly maintained. Associated with, and sometimes caused by such an emphasis on this brand of holiness, is legalism, a phenomenon that still haunts many Pentecostals who, in their attempt to achieve and maintain standards of holiness, sometimes

---

[11] R.J. Boone, 'Community and Worship: The Key Components of Pentecostal Christian Formation', *JPT* 8 (1996), pp. 129–42 (131).

[12] Although this is changing (especially in Europe and areas influenced by European culture, many Pentecostals adopt a stance of abstinence from alcohol; Lugo (*Spirit and Power*, p. 8) records that 71% of Pentecostals in the countries researched concluded that drinking alcohol was inappropriate though there were wide divergences (USA = 48%, South Korea = 54%; South Africa = 56% and Kenya = 88%, Nigeria = 84%, Philippines = 82%); see Conn, *A Balanced Church*, p. 90; Pandrea, 'A Historical and Theological Analysis', p. 127; Kay ('Sociology of British Pentecostal', p. 1091) identifies 51% of all Pentecostal ministers in 1999 advocating that Christians should not drink alcohol (though the average for UK AoG and Elim ministers was 39%).

[13] Kay ('Sociology of British Pentecostal', p. 1091) identifies 33% of all Pentecostal ministers in 1999 advocating that Christians should not go to the cinema, though the average of AoG and Elim ministers was 15%.

[14] Palmer, 'Ethics in the Classical', p. 608; Anderson, *An Introduction to Pentecostalism*, p. 108; Wacker, *Heaven Below*, pp. 184–91; J.N. Horn, 'Power and Empowerment in the Political Context of South Africa', *JEPTA* 25 (2005), p. 7 . . . South Africa; Lugo (*Spirit and Power*, p. 36) records that 77% of Pentecostals in the countries researched stated that premarital sex was never justified.

inappropriately imposed on them by others, have struggled to rid themselves of unnecessary guilt that has been caused by an inability to achieve the standard expected by others, by themselves and (so they often assumed) also by God.[15] Spittler notes that 'legislated holiness has long characterised the Pentecostals'[16] though this tendency has reduced in recent years as a result of an emphasis on the grace of God and the benefits of security, love and acceptance that come with being a child of God.

Personal Application

Pentecostal spirituality is very practical, including how one relates to God and others, including one's family,[17] especially if unbelievers, the hope being that they may come to faith. The role of the Spirit in facilitating such practical holiness in the life of the believer is very important (Gal. 5.16, 22–23; 1 Pet. 1.2) though Pentecostals are generally unaware of the significant information relating to this feature in the NT and thus often unacquainted with the potential of the Spirit to develop this characteristic in the individual and corporate life of believers.

Pentecostals recognize the role of the Spirit to purify believers, especially as located in the Pauline literature (1 Cor. 6.11; 2 Cor. 5.17; Gal. 5.22), though Keener sees this theme also developed in Jn 7.37–39[18] and Wenk and Turner indicate its presence in Luke.[19] Adewuya explores the relationship between the Spirit and ethics in Rom. 8.1–17, concluding that the Spirit is to be identified as the moral stimulus and power for daily living.[20]

Pentecostals are uncomfortable with the notion of spiritually standing still. They prefer to be challenged to consider their relationship with the Lord and to improve it than to be simply affirmed in it. Earlier Pentecostals were brought up with the maxims, 'You're saved to serve', 'Redeem the time', 'Being a Christian is not a bed of roses', 'Fight to win'. Thus, commands of God in the Bible and the challenge to change are issues with which

---

[15] J.M. Harris III, 'Eysenck's guilt construct in male and female Anglican Clergy in the United Kingdom and male and female Assemblies of God ministers in the United States', *JEPTA* 27.1 (2007), pp. 39–54.

[16] Spittler, 'Maintaining Distinctives', p. 131.

[17] V.T. Nolivos, 'A Pentecostal Paradigm for the Latin American Family: An Instrument of Transformation', *AJPS* 5.2 (2002), pp. 223–34; J.K. Vining, *Nurturing Pentecostal Families: A Covenant to Nurture Our Families* (Cleveland: Pathway Press, 1996); J. Sims, 'Exploring Pentecostal Ethics: Reclaiming Our Heritage', in Cross and Powery (eds), *The Spirit and the Mind*, p. 227; Jenney, 'The Holy Spirit and Sanctification', pp. 397–421.

[18] Keener, *The Spirit*, pp. 157–60.

[19] Wenk, *Community-Forming Power*, passim; Turner, *The Holy Spirit*, p. 49.

[20] J.A, Adewuya, 'The Holy Spirit and Sanctification in Romans 8.1–17', *JPT* 18 2001), pp. 71–84; Sims, 'Exploring Pentecostal Ethics', p. 227.

they easily identify. When Jesus commissions Peter to feed his sheep (Jn 20.15–19), they readily expect to also participate in obeying Peter's assignment. When Jesus authorizes the disciples to offer the forgiveness of sins to people, they automatically assume this is to be undertaken by them also (Jn 20.22–23). When they read of the reception of the Spirit granted by Jesus to the disciples (Jn 20.22), they gladly place themselves among the waiting disciples to also receive the Spirit. They, like Peter, are desirous of moving beyond failure and imperfect obedience to new levels of discipleship. As he moved from denial to become a leading apostle, so also they desire to progress, not 'backslide', itself a term common to the psyche of many Pentecostals.

Some Ways Forward

There is an increasing recognition of the importance of offering and experiencing a faith that is culturally relevant.[21] Although, this may be viewed by some as compromising the old ways or relinquishing one's standards, it is more based on the recognition that some of the practices of earlier Pentecostals were as much due to a reaction to the prevailing culture as they were gleaned from the Bible. Thus, increasingly, many seek to explore their faith in recognition of their culture while maintaining a readiness to hold to Biblical standards and principles and functioning authentically with regard to their spirituality. This is often motivated by a desire to ensure that the message of Jesus and the lifestyles of his followers are not misunderstood by unbelievers as culturally irrelevant.[22]

The issue of holiness is in need of careful consideration by Pentecostals. The danger is that it may be viewed as an aspect of spirituality that was appropriate to earlier Pentecostalism but now, in an enlightened age, other emphases are to be concentrated on. There are a number of reasons why there has been a decrease in standards of holiness or teaching concerning it. There has been an increased unwillingness for Pentecostal leaders to teach on holiness for fear that they may be accused of hypocrisy since they are not sinless either. Oo suggests that the greater attention given to charismata than to right conduct may be a contributory factor.[23] The assumption that morality is less important has resulted in well documented accounts of leaders losing their ministries and their freedom, resulting in further calls to rediscover

---

[21] D. Livermore, 'Emerge or Submerge', *PR* 10.1 (2007), pp. 31–55.

[22] M. Mittelberg, B. Hybels, *Building a Contagious Church: Context, Growth, Leadership, and Worship* (Downers Grove: InterVarsity Press, 2000).

[23] S.T.S. Oo, 'In Search of Holiness: A Response to Yee Tham Wan's "Bridging the Gap between Pentecostal Holiness and Morality"', *AJPS* 5.2 (2002), pp. 313–20 (314–15).

the morality associated with early Pentecostalism.[24] Similarly, there is too often a belief that morality may be distanced from spirituality; this is sometimes further assumed where people who have been living immorally are still functioning supernaturally and their ministries still benefiting others. There is a challenge to Pentecostal leaders to be able to instil in the lives of particularly younger believers the spiritual and moral attitudes of a previous generation where they are biblically based.

Speaking of North American Pentecostalism, Wacker cautions that 'its uncritical identification with the values of Middle America represents a major loss of prophetic vision' while acknowledging that 'there are numerous exceptions'.[25] Similar concerns may be voiced of the Church as a whole, Volf reminding his readers that, 'without disruption, there can be no Christian faith' since 'the gospel disrupts the equilibrium of our cultural identity'.[26]

To a very large degree, Western Pentecostals and those influenced by the West have now adopted different views to many of their predecessors and a much more liberal stance is held though this is less clearly reflected among many Pentecostal clergy.[27] This change has largely been due to the removal of the economic hardships experienced by early Pentecostals when the hope of heaven was stronger in the context of the deprivation felt by many. Developing economic prosperity, influences from others more culturally aware or affluent Christians, and the infiltration of social and moral nuances have taken their toll. This is increasingly affecting Pentecostals in countries where economies are getting stronger and wealth is becoming more widespread. Where standards of holiness were central to Pentecostal spirituality, greater choice in life has not always resulted in the retention of these standards. The pervasive nature of modern culture with its easy access to the internet which provides a consequent exposure to unhealthy visual and verbal materials, the increasingly liberal nature of the media, the huge increase in the popularity of television and associated technology, the ease of travel and rapid exchange of views with believers who may have different moral perspectives, the slipping standards of some church leaders and a reticence to adopt the lifestyles of older believers unthinkingly, have all affected the lifestyles of many Pentecostals, often retrogressively. In many non-Western cultures, there are stricter rules of behaviour and dress and, sometimes, higher standards of morality are maintained.[28]

---

[24] Y.T. Wan, 'Bridging the Gap between Pentecostal Holiness and Morality', *AJPS* 4.2 (2001), pp. 153–80.

[25] Wacker, 'Wild Theories', 28.

[26] M. Volf, 'When Gospel and Culture intersect: Notes on the Nature of Christian Difference', in Ma and Menzies (eds), *Pentecostalism in Context*, pp. 223–36 (234).

[27] W.K. Kay, 'Job Satisfaction of British Pentecostal Ministers', *AJPS* 3.1 (2000), pp. 83–97 (97).

[28] Chesnut, *Born Again in Brazil*, pp. 108–25.

The emphasis on the grace and fatherhood of God, as contrasted to the earlier emphasis of the holiness of God, has resulted, for some, in the unfortunate consequences of a greater tendency to sin and to offer less resistance to temptation insofar as the message of forgiveness, rather than judgement, is stressed.[29] Similarly, the weakening of Arminian trends and the increasing adoption of a quasi-Calvinistic theology, particularly where it relates to the security of believers, may have exacerbated the situation. Although the latter may allow the believer to live in freedom of guilt and fear to a greater extent, it can also result in a readiness to take advantage of that new liberty and translate it into licence.

Pentecostals are less radical and less restorationist than they were. They have moved from the days when spirituality was too heavily viewed by the activities that one did or did not do to a spirituality that is less identified by rules or guidelines with positive and negative consequences. Whereas, for example, earlier Pentecostals would carry Bibles (through the streets) to church (albeit a small spiritual discipline that carried with it some suggestion of being a witness of one's faith to onlookers), now there is little reason to do so since many preachers do not make exposition of the text central to their preaching and if they do, the text is often, at least in affluent societies, presented on a screen at the front of the church. Dowdle, more generally, similarly warns of the danger of 'substituting style for substance' and measuring effectiveness 'in terms of numbers, finances, buildings, and programs'.[30]

There are also fewer taboos now than there once were. Many activities are now accepted as normal or tolerated as less than ideal but not restrictive to the development of one's spirituality. Although, in some cases, this has been a welcome development, there is now a reluctance to identify some practices as unhealthy or unacceptable partly due to the increased freedom of people living in a democratic society: the accentuated emphasis on the individual; the fear of legalism and heavy shepherding; concerns over cultural differences; the recognition that many now become Christians and still carry the memories and behaviours of their past that may not easily be removed; and differences in standards as to that which is right and wrong. Younger, mobile, independent, educated and affluent Pentecostals are less influenced by a desire to maintain the cohesion of social Christian groups by their behaviour unless it is demonstrably clear that to act and believe thus has a supported rationale. Whereas the local church was the place for social gatherings, relationship development and entertainment, much of that is now also possible through modern technology and in ways that are sometimes more sophisticated, personal and convenient. Conversely, there is a much greater potential to be entertained in an individualistic setting via the internet or television; this

---

[29] Oo, 'In Search of Holiness', pp. 315–16.
[30] Bowdle, 'Informed Pentecostalism', p. 17.

also militates against community based activities and experiences. Finally, there is ignorance with regard to the role of the Spirit and instead of recognizing his mission to sanctify believers and provide experientially based encounters with God, which have the potential of radically transforming their lives, many operate on a merely emotional and superficial level.

Prayer

Pentecostals treasure the personal nature of their spirituality and central to it is prayer,[31] Land identifying it as 'the primary theological activity of Pentecostals . . . the most significant activity of the Pentecostal congregation'.[32] Throughout its history, Pentecostals have encouraged each other to develop a disciplined and regular personal prayer life that has been associated with programmes intended to create frameworks in which prayer can become a lifestyle component.[33] They emphasize the importance of the development of a relationship with God that is both warm and intense. Pentecostals base their beliefs relating to prayer on the Bible, though temperament and church tradition also play a part in forming the motivation for and practice of prayer.[34] Wagner identifies the fact that for Pentecostals, 'prayer is a significant, explicit, and up front component of the churches' philosophy of ministry' and a major reason for the growth of Pentecostalism.[35] It is often believed to be a major reason for revival[36] and, especially expressed in African and Asian Pentecostalism but also in some Western Pentecostal churches, viewed as a power encounter with supernatural forces.[37]

Prayer Is Primarily an Encounter with God

Prayer is not just an opportunity for a monologue to God. It is intended to be dialogical. Fundamentally, it is intended to be a God-conscious moment

---

[31] Yonggi Cho ('Prayer Can Change the Course of Your Life', *Pentecostal Evangel* (October 18, 1998), p. 11) describes it as 'the first priority' for Koreans; Poloma, 'Pentecostal Prayer' p. 275; R.L. Brandt, Z. Bicket, *The Spirit Helps Us Pray: A Biblical Theology of Prayer* (Springfield: Gospel Publishing House, 1994), passim.

[32] Land, *Pentecostal Spirituality*, p. 166.

[33] Brandt and Bicket, *The Spirit Helps Us Pray*, pp. 387–99; Lugo (*Spirit and Power*, p. 19) records that 75% of Pentecostals in the countries researched stated that they prayed daily (ranging from South Korea (34%) to the Philippines (93%)).

[34] J.C. Ma, 'Korean Pentecostal Spirituality: A Case Study Of Jashil Choi', in Ma and Menzies (eds), *The Spirit and Spirituality*, pp. 298–313.

[35] Wagner, 'America's Pentecostals', p. 28.

[36] Brandt and Bicket, *The Spirit Helps Us Pray*, pp. 369–85.

[37] Ma, 'Korean Pentecostal Spirituality', pp. 307–08; Myung and Hong, *Charis and Charism*, pp. 69–72; Brandt and Bicket, *The Spirit Helps Us Pray*, pp. 277–78.

when the transcendent God opens a window into the world of the believer and announces his presence – maybe in a cataclysmic setting but more often in a whisper, so quiet that it may be missed. But in that encounter, a prayer is born. Prayer is offered to the Father, Son and Spirit though most often the Father is viewed as the recipient of a believer's prayers. The recognition that the Spirit has an important function in prayer is increasingly being recognized by Pentecostals (Rom. 8.26; Jude 20).

Prayer Is Intended to Be Corporate As Well As Individual

Prayer is a regular element in the context of the gathered body of believers. It has been traditional to hold a 'prayer meeting' during the week when prayer is the main function of the gathering. During the past years, the latter has occurred less, partly due to the growth in cell or home groups, though in some parts of the non-Western Pentecostal world, corporate prayer meetings have been retained and even grown in importance with sizeable periods of time being given to corporate prayer. Similarly, while the numbers of Western Pentecostals have reduced in prayer meetings, there has been considerable growth in Africa, South America and parts of Asia, where thousands have gathered to pray for periods in excess of 2 or 3 hours at a time.

Prayer camps are popular gatherings in parts of Africa, particularly Ghana, the ones regulated by or associated with mainstream Pentecostal denominations being more structured and safeguarded against excesses. In South Korea, in particular, the emphasis on prayer has resulted in prayer mountains being designated as places for extended communal and individual prayer. The prayer mountain phenomenon commenced in the early 1940s and became so successful (currently over 500 prayer mountains have been established in South Korea) that it is appropriate to refer to it as the Prayer Mountain Movement.[38] The significance of the location is, to a degree, based on the fact that prayer was sometimes enjoyed by Jesus in mountainous areas, though the obvious peace and absence of distraction in these places is also a reason for their choice.

In the USA, prayer towers have been erected in which prayer is offered, the best known being sited at the Oral Roberts University, Tulsa. Although individuals come to pray in these buildings, their function is different to the prayer camps and prayer mountains in that people often staff the prayer towers and intercede for people who send their requests to them.

---

[38] Y.S. Eim, 'South Korea', in Burgess, *NIDPCM*, pp. 240–43; Anderson, *An Introduction to Pentecostalism*, p. 137; Lee, 'The Life and Ministry', pp. 3–23 (6); Menzies, W.W., 'David Yonggi Cho's Theology of the Fullness of the Spirit: A Pentecostal Perspective', in Ma, Menzies and Bae (eds), *David Yonggi Cho*, pp. 27–42 (34–6).

Prayer Is Meant to Be Heard by Others

In the main, Pentecostals have not viewed silence as a significant element of individual or corporate prayer. Consequently, the characteristics of meditation and contemplation with regard to prayer are considerably less common than in other forms of Christian spirituality. Pentecostals are more inclined to be actively involved in articulating their requests. Praying aloud is a means of sharing one's request with others, their spoken affirmation of it as it is being uttered providing communal and personal significance. Not only is extemporary prayer common in Pentecostal gatherings, but so also is the corporate nature of such prayer in unison, either in tongues or in the first language of the individuals concerned.[39] The latter form of prayer is particularly common in cultures that value the solidarity of the group, but even in the more individualistic and democratic West this form of communal prayer is becoming more popular, especially among younger people who are often less inhibited than older people groups.

Prayer offered in public or private is rarely written or preformulated. Because of the emphasis on the personal nature of prayer, the more informal prayer is much more common with all the strengths and weaknesses that may be associated with it. Thus, it tends to be more familiar, personal and warm with the danger that it may lack thoughtful sobriety and careful expression and be repetitious and bland. Pentecostals tend to view God as their personal Father, Jesus as their personal Saviour and the Spirit as their personal guide, thus resulting in a form of prayer that is more conversational and less liturgical.

Prayer Is Expected to Be Answered

Pentecostals assume that God listens when they pray and are consequently expectant of his intervention into their lives and in response to their prayers.[40] The Bible contains much that encourages this perspective, identifying the fact that God is prepared to hear and answer the prayers of his people (2 Kgs 20.6; Pss. 38.15; 50.15; Mt. 16.24; 1 Jn 5.15). Thus, Moore uses Job 42.7 to identify aspects of prayer that relate to the Pentecostal practice of 'praying through' to a belief that God has heard or will respond as one has requested.[41]

For some, open theology[42] is a natural context for many Pentecostals, Thompson concluding that the God of open theism 'looks far more like the

---

[39] Synan, 'Pentecostalism', pp. 38–9; Land, *Pentecostal Spirituality*, p. 166.

[40] Hocken, 'A Charismatic View', p. 98; Boone, 'Community and Worship', p. 140.

[41] R.D. Moore, 'Raw Prayer and Refined Theology: "You have not spoken straight to me, as my servant Job has"', in Cross and Powery, *The Spirit and the Mind*, pp. 35–48 (46–8).

God Pentecostals know and worship' for they believe that they can effect changes as a result of prayer.[43] However, prayer is not an opportunity to encourage God to change his mind or the future but of engaging with God and bringing the future into a reality in the present.

Pinnock offered a challenge to Pentecostals to explore open theism[44] and some have responded, positively and negatively.[45] However, traditionally, Pentecostals, along with evangelicals, have articulated the belief that God is unrestricted in matters of knowledge of the future. Furthermore, since it is anticipated that he exists outside time (since he created it), he must constantly live in a kind of eternal present, knowing everything there is to know, even of the future (since the future is part of his present) (Prov. 16.9; Isa. 42.9; Rom. 11.33–34).

Pentecostals often use verses from the Bible as part of their prayer and praise. The ancient stories and promises are regularly referred to as part of the tapestry of their prayer. Such narratives provide examples of how to pray and what to pray for as well as encouragement and reasons to pray. The experiences of OT believers and the promises spoken by the earthly Jesus are drafted into modern prayers by many who would seek to ascribe those experiences and promises to themselves. However, this belief does not assume that all prayer requests will always be granted by God. There are other issues to be considered including the appropriate nature of the prayer (1 Jn 5.16), its relationship to the will of God (1 Jn 5.14) and the possibility that the divine response may result in the prayer not being answered in the way hoped for.

The parables of the friend at midnight (Lk. 11.5–8) and the importunate widow (Lk. 18.1–8) are often employed by Pentecostals as test cases for the value of persistency in order to receive that for which one prays. Kim argues

---

[42] This relates to a theological position that attempts to explain the concept of God's foreknowledge, concluding that God does not exercise complete control of the future (or chooses not to), leaving it 'open' for people to exercise their free will. This leads to the belief that God does not exhaustively know the future.

[43] M.K. Thompson, 'Does God Have a Future? A Pentecostal Response to Christopher Hall's and John Sanders' Recent Book', *Pneuma* 26.1 (2004), pp. 130–37; J. Sanders, *The God Who Risks: A Theology of Providence* (Downers Grove: InterVarsity Press, 1998).

[44] Pinnock, 'Divine Relationality', pp. 3–26.

[45] S.A. Ellington, 'Who Shall Lead Them Out? An Exploration of God's Openness in Exodus 32.7–14', *JPT* 14.1 (2005), pp. 41–60; K.J. Archer, 'How Much Does God Control? Open View Response to the Arminian View', *The Pneuma Review* 7.1 (2004), pp. 60–4; idem, 'Open Theism: "Prayer Changes Things"', *The Pneuma Review* 5.2 (2002), pp. 32–53; G. Boyd, *God of the Possible: A Biblical Introduction to the Open View of God* (Grand Rapids: Baker, 2000); T.L. Cross, 'The Rich Feast of Theology: Can Pentecostals Bring the Main Course or Only the Relish?', *JPT* 16 (2000), pp. 27–47 (30–31).

that both provide sound exegetical foundations for the importance of persistency in prayer.[46] Unfortunately, some Pentecostals assume that the parables justify crossing the line between persistence and insistence. A careful balance needs to be struck which encourages believers to recognize that God is not irritated with persistent prayers (1 Kgs 18.42; Mt. 7.7–8; 26.36–44; Acts 12.5) but also to learn to listen to his response to those prayers. His answer may be 'no'; to continue to ask for that prayer to be answered differently thereafter would thus be inappropriate.

Prayer and Fasting

Pentecostals accept the spiritual discipline of fasting and engage in it with regard to prayer especially when praying about something important. Korean Pentecostals, in particular, identify prayer and fasting as two of the key components in the development of one's spirituality and the mission of the Church, regularly engaging in both.[47]

Although the Bible presents the value of fasting in association with prayer (1 Kgs 21.27–29; Est. 4.16; Joel 2.12; Acts 13.2–4; 14.23), especially associated with the Day of Atonement (Lev. 16.29, 31), many Pentecostals are not clear as to its significance, some assuming that it provides an improved chance of one's prayer being answered, on the basis that it demonstrates to God the serious intent of the one offering the prayer.[48] It is not hard to see the illogicality of this argument when one recognizes the fact that God knows everything about believers before they pray and Brandt advises against such a motivation.[49] Many Pentecostals affirm that fasting can result in a more powerful prayer being offered or that it more readily overcomes malevolent spiritual obstacles. Although Dan. 10.13 is sometimes used as evidence that malignant spiritual forces can obstruct angelic responses to prayer, there is no biblical evidence that suggests that prayers can be hindered from being heard by God and very little basis for believing that his response may be delayed by demonic forces.

More importantly, it is to be recognized that fasting may provide an opportunity for reflection to better determine how one should pray about a given situation. It also provides more time to pray though it is also increasingly recognized that fasting is best undertaken when the Spirit has motivated it;[50] otherwise, there is a danger that it will be viewed as a way of encouraging

---

[46] D. Kim, 'Lukan Pentecostal Theology of Prayer: Is Persistent Prayer Not Biblical?', *AJPS* 7.1. (2004), pp. 205–17.

[47] Ma, 'Korean Pentecostal Spirituality', p. 299.

[48] C.W. Conn, 'Fasting', in Burgess and van der Maas (eds), *NIDPCM*, pp. 634–35.

[49] Brandt and Bicket, *The Spirit Helps Us Pray*, p. 230.

[50] Ma, 'Korean Pentecostal Spirituality', p. 302.

or, worse, manipulating God to answer prayer in the way that has been requested.

Worship

Although worship was written about infrequently in the past, that is now changing, especially as worship in Pentecostal churches is also changing.[51] Although Pentecostals recognize that worship is a term best used to refer to the adoration of God which should be contextualized in the lifestyle of the believer, it is generally used to refer to those occasions when believers engage in an act of private or corporate praise of God. The latter is now rather more structured, varied and continuously developing as new musical forms and genres are adopted, including occasions where worship is listened to or even watched as well as participated in.[52] Increasingly, the concept of worship is equated with singing and less with service and sacrifice.[53]

Encounter

Two pertinent words when referring to Pentecostal spirituality are 'expectancy' and 'encounter'.[54] Pentecostals expect to encounter God. It undergirds much of their worship and theology and may even be identified as another way of defining worship. Wacker concludes that 'experience has undeniably functioned as a cornerstone of Holy Ghost (Spirit) worship from the beginning' of Pentecostalism[55] while Cox describes Pentecostalism as 'the experiential branch of Christianity'.[56] Thus, Pentecostals expect to experience an intimate relationship with God in which he is felt and they are moved emotionally. The question of Paul to the Galatians (3.4) concerning that which they experienced when they came to faith resonates with Pentecostal spirituality; theirs is a *felt* faith. Du Plessis, a significant Pentecostal statesman, identifies the elements of 'a good Pentecostal meeting' as 'There is atmosphere.

---

[51] D. Eastman, 'Worship Realities for a New Millennium', in McClung (ed.), *Azusa Street and Beyond: 100 Years*, pp. 271–80.

[52] D. Zschech, *Extravagant Worship* (Minneapolis: Bethany House, 2002).

[53] D. Morgan, 'Contemporary Australian Pentecostal Worship in Trouble: An Analysis of Hillsong Worship' (SPS conference paper, Cleveland, 2007), pp. 245–51 (248).

[54] B. Houston, *Worship: A God Encounter* (Castle Hill: Maximised Leadership, 2004); Albrecht, *Rites in the Spirit*, pp. 226, 238–39.

[55] G. Wacker, 'Early Pentecostals and the Study of Popular Religious Movements" in Welker (ed.) *The Work of the Spirit*, pp. 126–46 (131); Kärkkäinen, *Spiritus Ubi Vult Spirat*, p. 47.

[56] Cox, 'Some Personal Reflections', p. 30; McDonnell ('The Experiential and the Social', p. 46) describes its theology as 'a theology of experience'.

Everyone knows something is happening'.[57] Although this could now describe many Christian gatherings, nevertheless, this is the historical context in which Pentecostalism grew and, to a degree, still exists with similar expectations.

Pentecostals believe that their worship is based on the practice of the early Church and they have attempted to adopt principles of worship that they have identified in the NT, especially where these relate to opportunities for all to participate, in ways that are meaningful, edifying and honouring of the group (1 Cor. 14.26).[58] The Spirit is identified as the one who facilitates worship, the aim of Pentecostals being to worship God in Spirit and in truth (Jn 4.24) where they interpret the former to relate to the Spirit who leads them in their worship of God. They also acknowledge the Spirit as being the one who made it possible for them to be in a position where they are able to access God (Eph. 2.18) and to function as corporate (Eph. 2.22) and individual dwelling places of God (1 Cor. 6.18–19). Fee describes the Spirit 'as the experienced, empowering return of God's own personal presence in and among us'[59] while Hocken describes 'a directness of relationship to God with corresponding expectations of divine revelation' as being one of his clearest impressions of Pentecostalism.[60] Similarly, Bruner writes of the expectation of Pentecostals of 'divine invasion'.[61] Pentecostalism provides for the possibility of an experience with the divine.

Although it can be overstated, believers do not come to a church so much as to a meeting – with each other and with God and their expectation is that God will come and meet with them.[62] However, although experience is important in Pentecostal spirituality and worship, it is important to acknowledge that it is not experience per se but that which is associated with God, often related to the Spirit but central to which is the person of Jesus.[63] Clark confirms that for Pentecostals, 'experience is normal, but it is Christ who is the dominant theme'.[64] The desire of Paul to know Christ (Phil. 3.10) is

---

[57] Du Plessis, *A Man Called Mr. Pentecost*, p. 183.

[58] G.D. Erickson, *Pentecostal Worship* (Hazelwood: Word Aflame, 1989).

[59] Fee, *God's Empowering Presence*, p. xv.

[60] Hocken, 'A Charismatic View', pp. 96–106 (98).

[61] Bruner, *A Theology of the Holy Spirit*, p. 137.

[62] Hocken ('A Charismatic View', p. 98) identifies the 'genuinely participatory pattern of worship' as one of the clearest identifying marks of Pentecostalism.

[63] Clark and Lederle (eds), *What Is Distinctive*, pp. 37, 43–7; D.E. Albrecht, 'An Anatomy of Worship: A Pentecostal Analysis', in Ma and Menzies, *The Spirit and Spirituality*, pp. 70–82 (74); H. Cox, *Fire from Heaven: The Rise of Pentecostal Spirituality and the Reshaping of Religion in the Twenty-First Century* (London: Cassell, 1996), pp. 71, 299–300; Petersen, *Not by Might nor by Power*, pp. 94–6.

[64] Clark and Lederle (eds), *What Is Distinctive*, p. 45.

automatically assumed by most Pentecostals to include an emotional, relational development with Christ as well as an intellectual knowledge of Christ.

The central feature of Pentecostal meetings is worship and this tends to be expressive and free, in the sense that there is not a liturgical framework, although there is often a structure.[65] Pentecostal worship can be identified by the content and way in which it is conducted, with generally a great deal of communal activity, including corporate singing and praying. Black Pentecostals have always enjoyed a greater degree of liberty and expressiveness in their songs and singing styles, partly related to their culture but also due to their readiness and desire to allow experience to be the filter through which their worship is offered.[66]

There is a danger that corporate worship may become the occasion when Pentecostals expect to experience God to the exclusion of other opportunities for such encounters and that more will be expected of it in terms of spiritual dynamism than it can deliver, leading to disillusion or attempts to increase its emotional and spiritual charge. At the same time, Pentecostals need to ensure that worship is not passive observation by the many in the context of a few enthusiastic worshippers.[67] Pentecostals have rarely exploited the benefits of silence and meditation as means of responding to God in a corporate gathering; to do so will provide another means of engaging with God.

Response

Albrecht, speaking of Pentecostals, concludes, 'In a real sense all worship is "responsive"'.[68] Theirs is a spirituality characterized by a readiness to respond to God. Anderson concludes that 'experiences with God provide a basis for their faith',[69] as a result of which, transformation is anticipated.[70] Pentecostals identify worship as a response to that which God has done for them, either as a result of salvation or in provision of other benefits. They have a strong sense of gratitude that they articulate in a variety of ways and that motivates them to action both in their verbal thanksgiving, social concern and evangelism.[71]

---

[65] T. Walsh, '"A Sane People Free from Fads, Fancies and Extravagances": Rhetoric and Reality of Collective Worship during the First Decade of the Pentecostal Movement in Britain', *JEPTA* 24 (2004), pp. 101–19.

[66] J. Edwards, *Let's Praise Him Again* (Eastbourne: Kingsway, 1992), pp. 68–70, 90–3.

[67] Chan, *Pentecostal Theology*, pp. 7, 11, 17–24.

[68] Albrecht, 'An Anatomy of Worship', p. 71.

[69] Anderson, 'Pentecostals Believe', p. 55.

[70] D.E. Albrecht, 'Pentecostal Spirituality: Looking through the Lens of Ritual', *Pneuma* 14.2 (1992), pp. 107–25.

[71] Land, *Pentecostal Spirituality*, pp. 141, 147–50.

Albrecht describes Pentecostal worship as an occasion when 'God is the audience and the congregation performs the drama of praise'.[72] This drama is often accompanied by physical movements (clapping, hands raised, dancing), ejaculatory expressions of praise in the forms of words or phrases which may be pronounced aloud, and/or emotional responses of joy and laughter or tears and sorrow.[73] The praise to God is often accompanied with prayer for and ministry to others present and on behalf of those who may be absent. The concept of touch and the laying on of hands or holding hands are common expressions of unity of mind and purpose on these occasions.

An integral part of Pentecostal worship is the concept of testimony in which believers relate how God has affected them, often in ways deemed to be supernatural.[74] This phenomenon rests on the premise that God seeks to transform believers individually and to relate practically to their everyday lives. Such testimonies have the potential of imparting lessons to the hearers[75] and they are also powerful evangelistic tools, revealing how God has transformed them.[76] Whereas the sermon will often relate how God worked in the lives of people in the Bible, the personal testimony allows for the possibility of being reminded that this feature occurs in the present also. It also has the added benefit of transferring something personal to the wider group in a shared narrative. In general, these testimonies have described positive experiences; the opportunity to relate difficulties and challenges has been less welcome in public settings. There is the danger that testimonies can become the vehicle for relating only good things that happen and not for sharing those occasions when defeat and not victory beckons, when the silence of God rather than clear awareness of his presence is being experienced, when fear of the future is the reality but the testimony is assumed to be the inappropriate vehicle for such self offering. However, one suspects

---

[72] Albrecht, 'An Anatomy of Worship', p. 72.

[73] F. Bixley, 'Dancing in the Spirit', in Burgess and van der Maas (eds), *NIDPCM*, pp. 570–71.

[74] Bruner, *A Theology of the Holy Spirit*, pp. 135–36; Kärkkäinen, *Toward a Pneumatological Theology*, p. 5; Chan, *Pentecostal Theology*, pp. 23–24; R.D. McCall, 'Storytelling and Testimony: Reclaiming a Pentecostal Distinctive' (unpublished doctoral dissertation, Columbia Theological Seminary, 1998); M.S. Park, 'Korean Pentecostal Spirituality as Manifested in the Testimonies of Believers of the Yoido Full Gospel Church', in Ma, Menzies and Bae, *David Yonggi Cho*, pp. 43–67 (43–6); Archer, 'Pentecostal Story', p. 66; S.A. Ellington, 'The Costly Loss of Testimony', *JPT* 16 (2000), pp. 48–59; Matviuk, 'Latin American Pentecostal Growth', pp. 217–18; Land, *Pentecostal Spirituality*, pp. 78–9.

[75] Land, *Pentecostal Spirituality*, p. 80; Johns and Johns, 'Yielding to the Spirit', pp. 109–34 (126).

[76] Asamoah-Gyadu, 'An African Pentecostal on Mission', pp. 311–12; Cox, *Fire from Heaven*, p. xvii.

that such honest reflections of life would be appreciated by many who infrequently see God working in their lives in dramatic ways. Ellington calls for the place of lament in Pentecostal testimonies to be introduced, partially as a response to the sometimes bland and stereotypical testimony that reflects little development on the part of the believer and assumes no personal pain on the journey.[77]

Spontaneity

Albrecht identifies this as another distinctive aspect of Pentecostal worship. It is based on the belief that the Spirit is the controller of the worship event and that since he is sovereign, he may develop an unpredictable route in worship that allows for spontaneity on the part of the worshipper. Even when Pentecostal services are scripted, songs to be sung have been chosen, the worship teams have practised and the sermon topic has been identified and prepared in readiness to be delivered, there is a readiness to discard these plans for that which the Spirit may wish to introduce that has not been anticipated. In it all, he is ideally viewed as the worship director.

The feature of spontaneity has sometimes resulted in Pentecostal worship being informal (and on rare occasions, disorderly). Nevertheless, Pentecostals would rather run the risk of making mistakes in worship in their exuberance than restrict the Spirit from doing that which he wants on account of a desire for propriety. Although they aim for balance, they recognize that when a sovereign God interacts with flawed humanity, the result may not be that which the believers anticipated. Although modern worship is less formal than it was in many Pentecostal churches, especially in the latter quarter of the twentieth century, this is not to suggest that there is no order. Often, there is a predictability about the order of the service although it might appear to be flexible and spontaneous. Nevertheless, there is a greater degree of freedom and opportunity for expressions of corporate and extended praise in most modern Pentecostal churches than would have been the case in the past.

Music and Song

Yong writes of 'the centrality of music in Pentecostal praxis',[78] loosely based on the prominence of song in worship in the OT (1 Chron. 16.37–42) and

---

[77] Ellington, 'The Costly Loss of Testimony', p. 53; J-D. Pluess, *Therapeutic and Prophetic Narratives in Worship* (Frankfurt: Peter Lang, 1988), pp. 186–87.

[78] A. Yong, 'Academic Glossolalia? Pentecostal Scholarship, Multi-Disciplinarity, and the Science-Religion Conversation', *JPT* (14.1 (2005), pp. 61–80 (73); G. Hinson, *Fire in My Bones: Transcendence and the Holy Spirit in African American Gospel* (Philadelphia: University of Pennsylvania, 2000).

NT (1 Cor. 14.26; Eph. 5.19; Col. 3.16[79]) and on the history of the Church. From the early years of Pentecostalism, there has been a rich tradition of song, with strong influence from Black music.[80] American and Scandinavian Pentecostals, in particular have, developed a wide range of song types and musical accompaniment, in the form of choirs and instrumentation, both of which are used in corporate gatherings. Congregational singing is the backbone of Pentecostal worship, often in celebratory form, generally forming the first half and conclusion of services. Pentecostals tend not to adopt a liturgical pattern of worship though they do have their rituals of style and sound that change over the years, and often in response to contemporary music styles.

Whereas their music was historically dominated by traditional hymns, the last 30 years have seen an increase in the singing of many new choruses and hymns.[81] Increasingly, these are sung over extended periods in which the congregation often remains standing as opposed to a format in which hymns were intermingled with other elements of the service, such as the reading of the Bible or prayer. Music in Pentecostal worship is often very personal in terms of endearment and communication between the singer and God and songs are increasingly viewed as 'vehicles for people to communicate directly with God'.[82] The songs have increasingly taken the form of more directional expressions to God than doctrinal reflections on his character. They function as modern day psalms expressing a wide range of emotions, requests and statements of praise to God.[83] The doctrinally based hymns of past decades have been largely replaced by simpler songs that are easier to memorize and contain more emotionally charged lyrics of affection for God, readiness to serve him and prayer for his increasing involvement in the lives of the singers.

Hudson challenges Pentecostals to recognize that sometimes, 'newer choruses have been accepted on the basis of the emotions that are raised, and so the words of the songs are sacrificed to the music that accompanies them'. He expresses even greater concern over some of the 'unquestioning acceptance of the language used and concepts expressed'.[84] Another concern is related to the fact that earlier hymns expressed a wide range of doctrinal truths and personal experiences (of joy and sadness, hope and confusion, a close

---

[79] See further Fee, *Listening to the Spirit*, pp. 100–04.
[80] R.A. Mills, 'Musical Prayers: Reflections on the African Roots of Pentecostal Music', *JPT* 12 (1998), pp. 109–26.
[81] D.L. Alford, 'Music, Pentecostal and Charismatic', in Burgess and van der Maas (eds), *NIDPCM*, pp. 911–20 (914–19); Hudson, 'Worship', pp. 183–84; A.E. Dyer, 'Some Theological Trends Reflected in the Songs used by the British Charismatic Churches of 1970s – early 2000s', *JEPTA* 26.1 (2006), pp. 36–48.
[82] Hudson, 'Worship', p. 194.
[83] Bond, 'What Is Distinctive', p. 141.
[84] Hudson, 'Worship', p. 195.

awareness of God and a sense of abandonment by God, triumph and fear, health and sickness); many modern songs, however, are triumphant and even triumphalistic with all the attendant dangers of such emphases, particularly of dualism where the believer is depicted or envisaged as always living in victory while concepts relating to alternative emotions can be viewed as illegitimate, unhelpful and unnecessary. An imbalance in worship can also lead to an inadequate view of spiritual encounter with the devil in which songs sung, ever more fervently, can be assumed to be achieving spiritual victories in themselves. As Hudson concludes, 'To presume that, because we are singing about spiritual warfare, we are actually engaged in it is fallacious'.[85] Worship for many has become less intellectual and more experiential, less theological and more practical, less doctrinal and more relational, less declaratory and more intimate, less reflective of the full breadth of human experience and more consistent with a narrow band of experiences that are generally devoid of some of the less palatable characteristics of life, including suffering, and can have escapist elements.

Increasingly, where possible, hymn books are not used, the words of the songs being revealed on screens, thus enabling greater freedom of physical responses in the worship. Similarly, musical accompaniment is increasingly important as is the role of the worship leader, often one of the musicians whose responsibility is to supervise a choir, musicians, and the praise and worship of a service. Thus, whereas the leader, generally the minister, of the church used to be the focus of attention for most of the service, s/he is now mainly called upon to preach, the rest of the service being delegated to others. Pentecostals need to ensure that the increasing role of the worship leader does not become a substitute for the leading of the Spirit, nor allow it to result in an unhealthy homogeneity of worship and the disenfranchisement of some of the worshipping community who may not relate to the particular style in which the worship experience is packaged. The worship group needs to marry the preparation for playing with an observation of the Spirit as the true conductor of the worship.

Post-modernism's openness to varieties of religious experience is a challenge to Pentecostalism to ensure that the experiences it advocates are authentic and not simply reflections of the aspirations of post-modern culture.[86] One attribute of music, especially in the context of a group where a heightened expectation is present, is that emotional and psychological states are developed that may function as substitutes for worship and even without

---

[85] Hudson, 'Worship', p. 197.
[86] R. Jaichandran, B.D. Madhav, 'Pentecostal Spirituality in a Postmodern World', *AJPS* 6.1 (2003), pp. 39–61; D. MacInnes, 'Problems of Praise', in E. England, *Living in the Light of the Pentecost* (East Sussex: Highland, 1990), pp. 241–49; C.M. Johansson, 'Music in the Pentecostal Movement', in Patterson and Rybarczyk (eds.), pp. 49–69.

the celebrant realizing the presence of a surrogate form of worship. Chan suggests that by contextualizing worship in the celebration of the Lord's Supper, the celebrant is protected from simply being captivated by the music and practising a reductionistic worship.[87]

Integrity of worship needs authenticity and honesty mingled with faith in God and trust in his ability and willingness to accommodate all one's emotions, for those times when believers can joyfully give all to God and those times when with heads bowed they can only lift their hands to receive his mercy and forgiveness, for those times when they can confidently march forward and those times when bewildered, they can only stand still and hope not to slip back.

Public Responsibility: Socio-political-economic Concerns

The Past

In general, Pentecostals have been criticized for having a limited political and social justice agenda,[88] one Pentecostal educator memorably describing Pentecostalism as a 'glossolalic ostrich'.[89] La Poorta largely agrees, noting that some moral issues such as homosexuality, alcohol abuse, pornography and abortion have received greater attention and condemnation than others, particularly social injustice.[90] There are sometimes understandable reasons for this. Thus, Donev notes that in countries where Communism controlled the political agenda (to the disadvantage of believers), faith and politics are still not compatible with one another in the minds of many; thus, it is not surprising that many believers are reticent to support engagement

---

[87] Chan, *Pentecostal Theology*, pp. 37–8.

[88] J.C. Hoffnagel, 'Pentecostalism: A Revolutionary or Conservative Movement?', in Glazier, *Perspectives on Pentecostalism*, pp. 111–24; S. Chan, 'Asian Pentecostalism, Social Concerns and the Ethics of Conformism', *Transformation*, 11.1 (1994), pp. 29–32; V-M. Karkkainen, 'Spirituality as a Resource for Social Justice: Reflections from the Catholic Pentecostal Dialogue, *AJPS* 6.1 (2003), pp. 83–96; G.B. McGee, 'Pentecostal Missiology: Moving Beyond Triumphalism to Face the Issues', *Pneuma* 16.2 (1994), pp. 275–82; Petersen, *Not By Might nor by Power*, p. 231; D.J. Bosch, 'Church Growth Missiology', *Missionalia* 16.1 (1988) pp. 3–24 (23); Anderson, 'Towards a Pentecostal Missiology', p. 37; W.J. Hollenweger, 'An Irresponsible Silence', *AJPS* 7.1 (2004), pp. 219–24.

[89] D. Allen, 'The Glossolalic Ostrich: Isolationism and Other-Worldliness in the British Assemblies of God', *EB* 13 (1994), pp. 50–62.

[90] J. La Poorta, 'Church and Society: A Pentecostal Perspective from the Southern Hemisphere' (EPCRA conference paper, University of Uppsala, 2007), pp. 1–9 (9).

in politics.[91] Kuzmic is one of a very few number of Pentecostals who has sought to explore affinities and dissimilarities between Marxism and Christianity in order to better respond to Marxist policies and practices.[92]

At times, instead of engaging practically to make a difference, Pentecostals have resorted to prayer as a substitute for or adjunct to such engagement.[93] Larbi concludes that African Pentecostal 'contributions on national issues like unemployment, poverty alleviation, corruption, political intolerance, ethnic and racial conflicts, breakdown of law and order . . . have been minimal',[94] their contribution in these areas largely being restricted to prayer.[95] Pentecostals have tended to emphasize individual salvation of an eschatological nature with concomitant personal moral development rather than wider and community related social and political concerns.[96] Indeed, there has been a suspicion among many Pentecostals that 'an emphasis on social concerns corresponds with a de-emphasis on spiritual fervor', sometimes leading to criticism of active social evangelism.[97] It is in this regard that many have preferred to invest in personal evangelism rather than other forms of indirect evangelism, leaving the moral and political debate to others.[98] Indeed, some early Pentecostals advocated that even voting in elections was unacceptable.[99] Similarly, Möller notes that many in Southern Africa were actively discouraged from involvement in politics.[100] Watt notes that early AoG leaders believed that political and economic liberation would be

---

[91] D.K. Donev, 'Bulgarian American Congregations: Cultural, Economic and Leadership Dimensions' (SPS conference paper, Cleveland, 2007), pp. 87–102 (99); Teraudkalns, 'Pentecostalism in the Baltics', p. 107; F. Macchia's editorial ('Democrat or Republican: Theological Reflections on Party Loyalty', *Pneuma* 26.2 (2004), pp. 177–81) is a recent exception to this norm.

[92] P. Kuzmic, 'Pentecostal Ministry in a Marxist Context', *EB* 9.1 (1990), pp. 4–32.

[93] J.L. Suico, 'Pentecostalism and Social Change', *AJPS* 8.2 (2005), pp. 195–213 (200); Larbi (*Pentecostalism*, p. 431–33) records that the Church of Pentecost requires prayers for political leaders at every major church service.

[94] Larbi, *Pentecostalism*, p. 447.

[95] Ayuk, 'The Pentecostal Transformation', pp. 197–98.

[96] R. Pfister, 'Some Reflections on Social Ministry in European Pentecostal Churches: Three Case Studies', *EB*, 10.1 (1991), pp. 19–24 (19); G. Wacker, 'Early Pentecostals and the Almost Chosen People', *Pneuma* 19.2 (1997), pp. 141–66.

[97] J.T. Snell, 'The Gift of Mercy. Its role in Formulating a Pentecostal Theology of Social Ministry', *Paraclete* 24.2 (1990), pp. 24–32 (24); Pfister, 'Some Reflections on Social Ministry', pp. 20–1.

[98] Clark and Lederle (eds), *What Is Distinctive*, 85; Macchia, *Baptized in the Spirit*, p. 277.

[99] Wacker, 'Early Pentecostals and the Almost', pp. 149–51.

[100] F.P. Möller, *Church and Politics: A Pentecostal View on the South African Situation* (Braamfontein: Gospel Publishers, 1998), p. 3.

achieved through the gospel, rather than socio-political pronouncements[101] though there is evidence of social concern being the motivation of action among some early American Pentecostals.[102]

The emphasis on evangelization, as equated with the preaching of the Gospel, has further undermined any reason to engage in political debate or exploration of issues relating to social concern. The fact that those who did explore these topics were often associated with the liberal wing of the Church ensured that most Pentecostals assumed that they themselves must be following the correct agenda. Since the 'social gospel' was the raison d'être of 'liberal' Christians, it was concluded by many Pentecostals that it must therefore be rejected.[103] Service to unbelievers is still predominantly viewed in terms of evangelism or activities that are directly related to the possibility of evangelism.[104] The spread of the Gospel has been largely identified with a message that concentrates on forgiveness, resulting from the death of Jesus, that leads to a relationship with God and eternity in heaven. This has tended to obscure the possibility that a parallel message of hope may also be presented that could include social programmes for improving the living conditions of those outside (and inside) the Christian community.

Thus, Villafañe regrets that Pentecostals have not offered 'their services and prophetic voices against sinful social structures and on behalf of social justice'[105] while Palmer identifies only limited official responses by Pentecostal denominations to ethical issues including abortion, participation in war, race relations and gender issues.[106] Indeed, a position of neutrality has sometimes been articulated as the most appropriate response to political matters in the belief that this 'will enhance the effectiveness of its evangelistic witness'.[107]

---

[101] Watt, *From Africa's Soil*, p. 178; see also A.A. Dubb, *Community of the Saved: An African Revivalist Church in the East Cape* (Johannesburg: Witwatersrand University Press, 1976), pp. 119–20.

[102] C.M. Robeck Jr, 'The Social Concern of Early American Pentecostalism', in Jongeneel (ed.), *Pentecost, Mission and Ecumenism*, pp. 97–106; D.D. Bundy, 'Social Ethics in the Church of the Poor: The Cases of T.B. Barratt and Lewi Pethrus', *JEPTA* 22 (2002), pp. 30–44.

[103] S.L. Georgianna, 'The American Assemblies of God: Spiritual Emphasis and Social Activism', in Elbert, *Faces of Renewal*, pp. 265–77 (268–69).

[104] McClung 'Try To Get People Saved', pp. 30–51.

[105] E. Villafañe, *The Liberating Spirit: Toward an Hispanic American Pentecostal Social Ethic* (Grand Rapids: Eerdmans, 1993), p. 202; V-M, Kärkkäinen, 'Missiology: Pentecostal and Charismatic', in Burgess and van der Maas (eds), *NIDPCM*, pp. 877–85 (880–81).

[106] Palmer, 'Ethics in the Classical', pp. 605–09 (607–08); Klaus, 'The Holy Spirit', p. 342; E. Wilson, 'Latin American Pentecostalism: Challenging the Stereotypes of Pentecostal Passivity', *Transformation* 11.1 (1994), pp. 19–24; R. Shaull, W. Cesar, *Pentecostalism and the Future of the Christian Churches: Promises, Limitations, Challenges* (Grand Rapids: Eerdmans, 2000), pp. 146, 211–12.

What is often the case is that Pentecostals have been less involved in writing about such issues, preferring to concentrate on their traditional strength of *oral* denunciation of injustice and proclamation of ethical morality, albeit from the pulpit and to believers rather than secular society.

Butler identifies the dilemma felt by many Pentecostals, especially in earlier years, of living 'within a world that they were both called to influence and sworn to "come out of"'.[108] In general, the latter stance was adopted, especially because of the belief in the imminent return of Jesus.[109] Why attempt to change a society that was doomed and, moreover, was doomed to end soon?[110] If Jesus was soon to return, it was viewed as questionable why one should criticize the practices and the pleasures associated with a world that was soon to be non-existent.[111] It was viewed by many as an exercise in futility, by others as a movement away from that which was central to their mission of preaching the gospel. Rather than make better citizens, many felt their role was to create more citizens for heaven. This world was not their home; they were simply passing through and their perspective was increasingly viewed as being eternal, as a result of which they were at times accused of enjoying 'pie in the sky' instead of engaging in social action. Thus, traditionally, Pentecostals have viewed the present through the lens of an imminent return of Jesus, resulting in a tendency towards passivity with regard to social change. Indeed, the emphasis has been on saving the world and its people spiritually rather than physically, socio-economically, politically or ecologically. Although there has been valuable involvement by Pentecostals in the latter, Macchia deduces, 'they lack the concern to transform the existing structures of society' and challenges Pentecostals 'to revise their eschatology' and thus retain their social relevance while discarding their 'escapist tendencies'.[112]

The Present

It is true that the result of the salvation of individuals is that new believers often become upwardly mobile as a result of a change of lifestyle, including

---

[107] Larbi, *Pentecostalism*, p. 430.

[108] A. Butler, 'Pentecostal Traditions We Should Pass on: The Good, the Bad and the Ugly', *Pneuma* 27.2 (2005), pp. 343–53 (346).

[109] J.N. Horn, 'Prophetic Chiliasm: A Clarion Call for the Bride of Christ or a Call to Enlist in Hell's Armies? Re-Evaluating the Political Significance of Prophetic Chiliasm in Pentecostal Thinking' (EPCRA conference paper, Uppsala University, 2007), pp. 1–22 (18).

[110] V-M, Kärkkäinen, 'Are Pentecostals Oblivious to Social Justice? Theological and Ecumenical Perspectives', *Missionalia* 29.3 (2001), pp. 387–404.

[111] Georgianna, 'The American Assemblies of God, p. 268.

[112] Macchia, 'Theology, Pentecostal', p. 1139.

the adoption of a work ethic that may not have been previously present. Thus, Wedenoja, speaking in a Jamaican context, describes Pentecostalism as a 'subtle revolution ... and not obviously political ... because it effects changes in self and the relations between self and others, which ... generates an ideological force promoting corresponding changes in society, economy and polity'.[113] Similarly, Klaus affirms that 'Grass-roots-level programs of personal renewal have had far-reaching implications for social transformation'.[114] Thus, the change in the lives of those who become Christians is often so remarkable that it positively effects change in their contexts also. Gros thus deduces that although 'Pentecostals do not have a social policy, they are a social policy.[115]

However, Pentecostals are now more often engaging with those who are in positions of national and international authority and who have the power to make major changes.[116] Increasingly, in the past few decades, Pentecostals have reflected political concerns,[117] especially in non-Western Pentecostal churches.[118] Shaull[119] and Mariz[120] note this in Brazil, Waldrop[121] of Guatemalan Pentecostals while Sepulveda comments on developments in Latin America.[122] The Universal Church of the Kingdom of God, one of the

---

[113] W. Wedenoja, 'Modernisation and the Pentecostal Movement in Jamaica', in Glazier *Perspectives on Pentecostalism*, pp. 27–48 (42–3); A.G. Miller, 'Pentecostalism as a Social Movement: Beyond the Theory of Deprivation', *JPT* 6 (1996), pp. 97–114.

[114] Klaus, 'The Holy Spirit', p. 342.

[115] Gros, 'Confessing the Apostolic Faith', pp. 5–16 (12).

[116] D. Petersen, 'Toward a Latin American Pentecostal Political Praxis', *Transformation* 14.1 (1997), pp. 30–3; F.G. Wessels, 'Charismatic Christian Congregations and Social Justice – A South African Perspective', *Missionalia* 25.3 (1997), pp. 360–74.

[117] Lugo (*Spirit and Power*, p. 7) records that 79% of the Pentecostals in the countries reviewed express support for religious involvement in politics and public life, the percentages being higher in South America and Africa; McDonnell, 'The Experiential and the Social', p. 53; I. Lundgren, 'Lewi Pethrus and the Swedish Pentecostal movement', in Elbert, *Essays on Apostolic*, pp. 158–72; Clark and Lederle (eds), *What Is Distinctive*, pp. 90–6; Anderson, *An Introduction to Pentecostalism*, pp. 264–67; M.L. Hodges, 'A Pentecostal's View of Mission Strategy', in McClung, *Azusa Street and Beyond*, pp. 83–9 (87–8); R.S. Beckford, *Dread and Pentecostal: Political Theology for the Black Church in Britain* (London: SPCK, 2000); idem, 'Black Pentecostals and Black Politics', in Anderson and Hollenweger (eds), *Pentecostals after a Century*, pp. 48–59.

[118] P. Freston, 'Researching the Heartland of Pentecostalism: Latin Americans at Home and Abroad' (EPCRA conference paper, University of Uppsala, 2007), pp. 1–14 (6).

[119] Shaull and Cesar, *Pentecostalism and the Future*, p. 197.

[120] C. Mariz, *Coping with Poverty* (Philadelphia: Temple University Press, 1994), p. 110.

[121] R.E. Waldrop, 'The Social Consciousness and Involvement of the Full Gospel Church of God in Guatemala', *CPCR* 2 (July 1997).

[122] Sepulveda, 'Reflections on the Pentecostal Contribution', pp. 105–07; Petersen, 'Toward a Latin American', pp. 30–3.

fastest denominations in Brazil with over a million members, participates in national politics and has a political party.[123] Anderson identifies other Pentecostals who are involved in politics in South America and Africa.[124] It is also true that some ethnic minority groups have become much more socially aware, partly as a result of their own experiences as minority groups.[125] At the same time, they have also been practically involved in ventures that provide help to people in need, especially in marginalized and mission-based sectors as well as among indigenous groups where poverty is common.[126]

Similarly, especially in settings where the challenges of poverty are greatest, there is an increasing recognition that a stance that encourages the believer to simply wait for heaven when all wrongs will be righted is less helpful. Instead, there has been a desire to respond holistically to the debilitating impact that poverty, disease and lack of education has on people.[127]

At the same time, individual Pentecostals and churches have championed socio-ethical causes[128] and explored ethical issues[129] as well as commented on socio-ethical aspects of society.[130] Indeed, there is significant growth in these areas among Pentecostal churches.[131] Thus, for example, the Redeemed

---

[123] Anderson, *An Introduction to Pentecostalism*, p. 73; P. Freston, 'The Transitionalisation of Brazilian Pentecostalism: The Universal Church of the Kingdom of God', in Corton and Marshall-Fratani (eds), *Between Babel and Pentecost*, pp. 196–235; see also E.A. Wilson, 'Brazil', in Burgess (ed.), *EPCC*, pp. 74–5.

[124] Anderson, *An Introduction to Pentecostalism*, p. 262; Kim, 'Filipino Pentecostalism', pp. 252–54; Chesnut, *Born Again in Brazil*, pp. 145–66.

[125] J.L. Hall, '"Hispanic Pentecostalism" in Burgess and van der Maas (eds), *NIDPCM*, pp. 715– 23 (722).

[126] D.E. Miller, T. Yamamori, *Global Pentecostalism: The New Face of Christian Social Engagement* (Berkeley: University of California Press, 2007); Bonino, *Faces of Latin*, pp. 66–7; A. Ruuth, 'Problems of Transition', in J-A. Alvarsson, *The Missionary Process* (Uppsala: Studia Missionalia Svecana XCIX, 2005), pp. 129–46 (142–44); A.H. Anderson, 'Global Pentecostalism in the New Millennium', in Anderson and Hollenweger (eds), *Pentecostals after a Century*, pp. 209–23 (212–14); Brenkus, 'A Historical and Theological Analysis', pp. 64–5.

[127] Larbi, *Pentecostalism*, p. 428.

[128] Pfister, 'Some Reflections on Social Ministry', pp. 21–4; Pandrea, 'A Historical and Theological Analysis', p. 133; C.M. Robeck Jr, 'Pentecostals and Social Ethics', *Pneuma* 9.2 (1987), pp. 103–07.

[129] See W.J. Hollenweger, 'Social Justice and the Pentecostal/Charismatic Movement', in Burgess, *NIDPCM*, pp. 1076–079; Griffith and Roebuck, 'Women, Role of', pp. 1203–209; D.J. Wilson, 'Pacificism', in Burgess, *NIDPCM*, pp. 953–55.

[130] B. Charette, 'Messiah without Anointing: A Missing Element in Cinematic Portrayals of Jesus', *Pneuma* 27.2 (2005), pp. 355–65.

[131] M.W. Dempster, 'Pentecostal Social Concern and the Biblical Mandate of Social Justice', *Pneuma* 9.2 (1987), pp. 129–53; idem, 'Christian Social Concern in Pentecostal Perspective' (SPS conference paper, 1991); Chan, 'Asian Pentecostalism', pp. 29–32; D.L. Rodríguez, '"A Critical Review of Douglas Petersen's *Not by Might nor by*

Christian Church of God and other Pentecostal churches in Nigeria provide social services (health, education, HIV aids support, rehabilitation centres, politics) in the context of the failure of the State to provide them.[132] Petersen provides a comprehensive survey of Pentecostal involvement in social concern in Latin America.[133] Miller and Yamamori offer a similar profile of African, European and Asian pentecostals.[134]

Minjung theology, in particular, as articulated by Korean Pentecostals, highlights the importance of addressing poverty, freedom of rights and discrimination. Bae views it as the basis for the distinctive Korean Pentecostal theology which seeks to provide 'a wholeness-centred theology seeking for holistic salvation', often affirmed by reference to 3 Jn 1.2.[135] As a result, they have developed a strong socio-political ministry.[136]

The assumption that believers should be disengaged from their society (its culture and its problems) is therefore increasingly being modified, a pietistic view being abandoned and replaced by a more robust determination on the part of some (particularly non-Western Pentecostals) to effect change by other means than only prayer.[137] Instead, it is being recognized that the NT focuses on ethical issues as well as the personal growth of Christians, the former reflecting the heart of God as much as the latter.[138] In general, Pentecostal denominational leaders have, until recently, offered limited comment on ethical issues and initiated even less dialogue with secular groups concerning even some of the more important ethical concerns, such as abortion, euthanasia or birth, gender and marital issues, including cohabitation and divorce, though with some exceptions.[139] Ma comes to the same conclusion

---

Power: A Pentecostal Theology of Social Concern in Latin America', *JPT* 17 (Oct. 2000), pp. 131–38 (136, 138); C.B. Johns, 'Meeting God in the Margins: Ministry among Modernity's Refugees', in M. Zyniewicz (ed.), *The Papers of the Henry Luce III Fellows in Theology* (Atlanta: Scholars Press, 1999), pp. 7–31.

[132] Adeboye, '"Arrowhead" of Nigerian Pentecostalism', pp. 43–55.

[133] Petersen, *Not by Might nor by Power*, pp. 112–85.

[134] D.E. Miller, T. Yamamori, *Global Pentecostalism. The New Face of Christian Social Engagement*, (Berkeley: University of California, 2007), pp. 39–224.

[135] H.S. Bae, 'Full Gospel Theology as a Distinctive Theological Practice for Korean Pentecostal Theology', *Spirit and Church* 2.2 (2000), pp. 169–81.

[136] H. Yung, 'The Missiological Challenge of David Yonggi Cho's Theology', in Ma, Menzies and Bae, *David Yonggi Cho*, pp. 69–93 (82–7); Y-g, Hong, 'Social Leadership and Church Growth', in Ma, Menzies and Bae, *David Yonggi Cho*, pp. 221–51.

[137] Anderson, *An Introduction to Pentecostalism*, pp. 261–28; Ma, 'Asian (Classical) Pentecostal Theology', pp. 76–8.

[138] Suico, 'Pentecostalism and Social Change', p. 205.

[139] Lugo (*Spirit and Power*, pp. 8, 57) records that of Pentecostals in the countries researched concluded that divorce was never justified (though there were wide divergences – USA = 15%, Brazil = 37% but Nigeria = 81%, Philippines = 84%); A. Yong, *Theology and Down Syndrome* (Waco: Baylor University Press, 2007); K. Warrington,

with regard to Pentecostals in Asia also, writing that they have often remained silent and thus neglected their 'prophetic mission . . . to the world'.[140] Hollenweger concludes that although 'Pentecostals can understand the issue of global social justice . . ., they usually come late, when the battle is already over', citing apartheid as an example.[141]

Despite the accuracy of these comments, some moral issues, including the advocacy of marital faithfulness and rejection of homosexuality as an appropriate lifestyle have been taught and promoted by Pentecostals. Similarly, their position concerning abortion would be to oppose it on the basis of the belief that the life of the unborn child is sacred and therefore to be protected.[142] A position paper, adopted by the AoG in 2002 and titled *A Sanctity of Human Life including Abortion and Euthanasia*, states that abortion 'is a morally unacceptable alternative for birth control, population control, sex election, and elimination of the physically and mentally handicapped'.[143]

Palmer identifies two Pentecostal denominations that have commented officially on euthanasia and assisted suicide, namely, the Pentecostal Assemblies of Canada (2001) and the AoG (2002).[144] Each condemns both practices though room is provided that enables people to decide whether the quality of life experienced by an individual is enhanced by the medical treatment offered. Thus, although details and practical application are limited, it is clear that those who drew up the documents were aware of the complexities associated with the issues. The AoG has also provided a formal discussion paper with regard to genetic issues and the implications for birth and therapeutic treatment. It offers a cautious presentation of guidelines that include the acknowledgement that the Bible offers little help in these debates. At the same time, it raises concerns with regard to reproductive cloning, which it views as immoral, and stem cell research which seeks to learn from cultivated stem cells taken from aborted foetuses, which it also views as evil.

Racial issues have recently become the focus of some dialogue. Although the early days of Pentecostalism in the West embraced the notion of a racially

D.N. Hudson, 'Cohabitation and the Church', *EB* 13 (1994), pp. 63–73; K. Warrington, 'Cohabitation and the Church', *Churchman* 111.2 (1997), pp. 127–42; Georgianna, 'The American Assemblies of God', pp. 265–77.

[140] J. Ma, 'Pentecostal Challenges in East and South-East Asia', in Dempster, Klaus and Petersen (eds), *The Globalisation of Pentecostalism*, pp. 197–99.

[141] Hollenweger, 'Social Justice', p. 1077.

[142] Lugo (*Spirit and Power*, p. 380) notes that 85% of Pentecostals in the countries researched concluded that a homosexual lifestyle was never justified, ranging from 64% (USA) to 97% (Philippines).

[143] See also Gajewski and Wawrzeniuk, 'A Historical and Theological Analysis', p. 44.

[144] M.D. Palmer, 'Ethics (Social, Sexual)', in Burgess, *EPCC*, pp. 172–78 (175).

inclusive Church,[145] this ideal did not last and before too long, churches were being established on racial grounds.[146] As Ma has written, 'What the Holy Spirit miraculously put together was miserably divided by humans',[147] and for decades, racism has been a painful and segregating issue in especially US and South African Pentecostalism. This sad part of Pentecostal history has been explored and documented by a number of writers,[148] particularly relating to the USA,[149] India[150] and South Africa.[151]

[145] D. Daniels, 'Charles Harrison Mason: The Interracial Impulse of Early Pentecostalism', in Goff and Wacker (eds), *Portraits of a Generation*, pp. 255–70; Irvin, 'Drawing All Together', pp. 25–30; H.P. Thompson Jr, '"On Account of Conditions that Seem Unalterable": A Proposal about Race Relations in the Church of God (Cleveland, TN) 1909–1929', *Pneuma* 25.2 (2003), pp. 240–64 (241–46).

[146] Logan, 'Black Pentecostalism', p. 61; H. Kenyon, 'An Analysis of Ethical Issues in the History of the Assemblies of God' (unpublished doctoral dissertation, Baylor University, 1988), pp. 40–176; Synan, *The Century of the Holy Spirit*, p. 167; E. Alexander, 'Race Relations', in Burgess, *EPCC*, pp. 401–04.

[147] Ma, 'Doing Theology in the Philippines', p. 230.

[148] MacRobert, *The Black Roots*; A.H. Anderson, 'Dangerous Memories for South African Pentecostals' in Anderson and Hollenweger (eds), *Pentecostals after a Century*, pp. 89–107; L.D. Callahan, 'Redeemed or Destroyed: Re-Evaluating the Social Dimensions of Bodily Destiny in the Thought of Charles Parham", *Pneuma* 28.2 (2006), pp. 203–27 (209–14).

[149] Alexander, 'Race Relations', pp. 402–03; D. Michel, *Telling the Story: Black Pentecostals in the Church of God* (Cleveland: Pathway Press, 2000); L.E. Olena, 'From Paralysis to Action: Robert Harrison and the Assemblies of God-Experiencing Racism in the Pentecostal Fold' (SPS conference paper, Cleveland, 2007), pp. 253–60; D. Daniels, '"Everybody Bids You Welcome": A Multicultural Approach to North American Pentecostalism', in Dempster, Klaus and Petersen (eds), *The Globalization of Pentecostalism*, pp. 222–52; Thompson, 'On Account of Conditions', pp. 240–64; R.J. Newman, 'Race and the Assemblies of God Church: The Journey from Azusa Street to the "Miracle of Memphis"' (unpublished doctoral dissertation, University of Memphis, 2005).

[150] S. Nadar, G.S.D. Leonard, 'Indentured Theology: White Souls/Black Skins? Decolonizing Pentecostals within the Indian Diaspora', in Stålsett, *Spirits of Globalization*, pp. 65–89.

[151] Anderson, 'Dangerous Memories', pp. 90–106; idem, 'Pentecostals and Apartheid in South Africa during Ninety Years 1908–1998' *CPCR* 9; Horn, 'Power and Empowerment', pp. 7–24 (15–24); idem, 'South African Pentecostals and Apartheid: A Short Case Study of the Apostolic Faith Mission', in Jongeneel (ed.), *Pentecost, Mission and Ecumenism*, pp. 157–67; idem, 'Crossing Racial Borders in Southern Africa: A Lesson from History', *CPCR* 3; J. Lapoorta, 'The Necessity for a Relevant Pentecostal Witness in South Africa', *EB* 10.1 (1991), pp. 25–33; idem, *Unity or Division? The Unity Struggles of the Black Churches within the Apostolic Mission of South Africa* (Kuils River: Japie LaPoorta, 1996); idem, 'Unity or Division: A Case Study of the Apostolic Faith Mission of South Africa', in Dempster, Klaus and Petersen (eds), *The Globalization of Pentecostalism*, pp. 151–69; 'Declaration of Solidarity with the Relevant Pentecostal Witness in South Africa', *EB* 10.1 (1991), pp. 34–5.

One of the reasons for the early expressions of racism was British Israelism, a belief that assumed that the lost ten tribes of Israel were located in the Anglo Saxon world, often centralized in England and the USA.[152] Such a belief prioritized white over non-white races as well as supported imperialist pursuits on the part of Western countries. Premillenial dispensationalism also played a part in the maintenance of apartheid in South Africa because it was assumed that Jesus was soon to return and therefore there was no time for political engagement. Other priorities were also presented (such as the communist threat, linked to a dispensational interpretation of Ezek. 38–39) that were viewed as taking precedence over any consideration of whether racial prejudice was worthy of critique.[153]

In recent years, there has been a move to engage in meaningful dialogue and relationship with Pentecostals of different racial backgrounds.[154] In 1994, the Pentecostal Fellowship of North America, an all white grouping, was disbanded in order to be replaced by the racially mixed Pentecostal/Charismatic Churches of North America, led by six white and six African Americans, in an event popularly known as 'the Memphis Miracle'.[155] Its first manifesto

---

[152] H. Davies (*Christian Deviations: Essays in Defence of the Christian Faith* (London: SCM, 1957), p. 20) outlines the central tenets of this belief, describing it as a 'racialist distortion of the faith'.

[153] Horn, 'Prophetic Chiliasm', pp. 16–22.

[154] Anderson, *An Introduction to Pentecostalism*, pp. 270–73; Blumhofer and Armstrong, 'Assemblies of God', pp. 333–40; Kärkkäinen, *Toward a Pneumatological Theology*, pp. 182–83; Martin, *The Life and Ministry*, pp. 196–248; D.R. Rosenior, 'Toward Racial Reconciliation: Collective Memory, Myth and Nostalgia in American Pentecostalism' (SPS conference paper, Cleveland, 2007), pp. 299–306; F.D. Macchia, 'From Azusa to Memphis: Where Do We Go from Here? Roundtable Discussions on the Memphis Colloquy', *Pneuma* 18.1 (1996), pp. 113–16; I.C. Clemmons, 'What Price Reconciliation: Reflections on the "Memphis Dialogue"', *Pneuma* 18.1 (1996), pp. 116–22; L. Lovett, 'Looking Backward to Go Forward', *Pneuma* 18.1 (1996), pp. 122–25; M. Gaxiola-Gaxiola, 'Reverberations from Memphis', *Pneuma* 18.1 (1996), pp. 125–28; S. Solivan, 'A Hispanic/Latino Pentecostal Response', *Pneuma* 18.1 (1996), pp. 128–32; B.M. Amos, 'Race, Gender and Justice', *Pneuma* 18.1 (1996), pp. 132–35; C.M. Robeck Jr, 'Racial Reconciliation at Memphis: Some Personal Reflections', *Pneuma* 18.1 (1996), pp. 135–40.

[155] R.A. Berg, 'Memphis Miracle', in Burgess, *EPCC*, pp. 304–06; F.D. Macchia, 'From Azusa to Memphis: Evaluation of the Racial Reconciliation Dialogue among Pentecostals', *Pneuma*, 17.2 (1995), pp. 203–18; H.D. Hunter, 'A Journey toward Racial Reconciliation: Race Mixing in the CGP', *Refleks* 3.1 (2004), pp. 19–42; A.H. Anderson, 'The Dubious Legacy of Charles Parham: Racism and Cultural Insensitivities among Pentecostals', *Pneuma* 27.1 (2005), pp. 51–64; Robeck, 'The Social Concern', pp. 97–106; idem, 'Taking Stock of Pentecostalism', pp. 45–51; Synan, *The Holiness-Pentecostal Tradition*, pp. 165–84; Horn, 'South African Pentecostals', pp. 157–67.

was dedicated to the issue of racial reconciliation.[156] The context for such a declaration is that for the previous 70 years, American Pentecostals were racially divided.[157] The Church of God of Prophecy has, for much of its history, functioned as a racially integrated church, though even here, 'the egalitarian vision espoused . . . has never been fully put into practice and is always at risk'.[158] Volf, in particular, has emphasized the term 'embrace' on a number of occasions to best encapsulate the attitude that Pentecostals and others should model with regard to issues of race and social inequality.[159]

Pacifism is another area where debate has occurred. Early Pentecostals were by and large pacifist,[160] basing their decision on the belief that it is a sin to shed blood, a command of Jesus to love one's enemies and also that believers were to prepare for the soon return of Jesus rather than engage in military activity.[161] Most of their energy was spent in evangelism; to kill potential converts was incongruous. It was also believed that pacificism was the normative position in the early Church and therefore to hold to such a position was in accordance with a desire to restore the apostolic faith.[162]

However, there was a shift in opinion by World War II when many people enlisted.[163] Butler suggests this was due to the slow encroachment of modernity on Pentecostals as a result of which they increasingly began to adopt the

---

[156] See Conference held in Memphis (Oct. 18, 1994) titled 'Pentecostal Partners: A Reconciliation Strategy for 21st Century Ministry'.

[157] Palmer, 'Ethics (Social, Sexual)', pp. 174–75.

[158] Hunter, 'A Journey toward Racial Reconciliation', pp. 19–42.

[159] M. Volf, 'Exclusion and Embrace: Theological Reflections in the Wake of "Ethnic Cleansing"', *JES* 29.2 (1992), pp. 230–48; idem, 'A Vision of Embrace: Theological Perspectives on Cultural Identity and Conflict, *Ecumenical Review* 48.2 (1995), pp. 195–205; idem, *Exclusion and Embrace: A Theological Exploration of Identity, Otherness and Reconciliation* (Nashville: Abingdon, 1996).

[160] See P.N. Alexander, 'An Analysis of the Emergence and Decline of Pacificism in the History of the Assemblies of God' (unpublished doctoral dissertation, Baylor University, 2000), for a thorough exploration of this issue in the AoG; idem, 'Pacifism and Peace', in Burgess, *EPCC*, pp. 351–55; M.W. Dempster, 'Reassessing the Moral Rhetoric of Early American Pacificism', *Crux* 26 (1990), pp. 23–36; idem, '"Crossing Borders": Arguments Used by early American Pentecostals in Support of the Global Character of Pacificism', *EB* 10.1 (1991), pp. 63–80; idem, 'Pacifism in Pentecostalism: The Case of the Assemblies of God', in T.F. Schlabach, R.T. Hughes (eds), *Proclaim Peace: Christian Pacifism from Unexpected Quarters* (Champaign: University of Illinois Press, 1997), pp. 31–57; P.N. Anderson, 'Spirit Empowered Peacemaking: Toward a Pentecostal Peace Fellowship', *JEPTA* 22 (2002), pp. 78–102; T. Kornweibel Jr, 'Race and Conscientious Objection in World War 1: The Story of the Church of God in Christ', in Schlabach and Hughes (eds), *Proclaim Peace*, pp. 57–81 (61); J. Shuman, 'Pentecost and the End of Patriotism: A Call for the Restoration of Pacificism among Pentecostal Christians', *JPT* 9 (1996), pp. 70–96; Horn, 'Prophetic Chiliasm', pp. 7–16.

[161] Kornweibel, 'Race and Conscientious Objection', pp. 57–81; Wilson, 'Pacificism', p. 953; Kay, *Inside Story*, p. 106.

[162] Dempster, 'Crossing Borders', pp. 64–7.

views of the majority of people in society and of fellow believers with regard to the acceptability of war.[164] Alexander also identifies the limited development of a biblical hermeneutic supporting pacifism,[165] though some literature was available.[166] However, some notable British Pentecostals maintained a pacifist stance; some of these were exempted from military service (Donald Gee, John Carter) while some were imprisoned (Howard Carter). While denominations, including the AoG, have left it to individual members to decide whether one should be a combatant or not, others, including the United Pentecostal Church, have remained pacifist. The issue has been raised in recent years, largely as a result of the initiation in 2001 of the *Pentecostal Peace Fellowship* by Paul N. Alexander.[167]

Other important issues, such as ecology, have largely been ignored by most Pentecostals though there are exceptions and some have written about ecological concerns and health issues caused by pollution, travel and industrial excess and called for prayer for God's creation as well as action to prevent a worsening crisis.[168] Hollenweger, a respected scholar of Pentecostalism, when asked in an interview to identify the three main challenges affecting Pentecostals, offered ecological destruction and the imbalance in world trade as his two primary concerns, and, only thirdly, the interaction between Pentecostal theology and its spirituality.[169] There has been little awareness of the possibility that the Spirit may desire to empower believers to transform

---

[163] Wilson, 'Pacificism', pp. 953–54; Palmer, 'Ethics (Social, Sexual)', p. 173; Alexander, 'Pacifism and Peace', p. 354; Horn, 'Power and Empowerment', p. 12; Shuman, 'Pentecost and the End of Patriotism', pp. 88–90; Horn, 'Prophetic Chiliasm', pp. 7–16.

[164] Butler, 'Pentecostal Traditions', p. 347; Robeck, 'Pentecostals and the Apostolic Faith', p. 70.

[165] Alexander, 'Pacifism and Peace', p. 354.

[166] F. Bartleman, *Christian Citizenship* (Los Angeles: Self publication, 1922); J. Beaman, *Pentecostal Pacifism: The Origin, Development, and Rejection of Pacific Beliefs among the Pentecostals* (Hillsboro: Center for Mennonite Brethren Studies, 1989); Dempster, 'Reassessing the Moral Rhetoric', pp. 23–36.

[167] P.N. Alexander, 'Spirit Empowered Peacemaking: Toward a Pentecostal Peace Fellowship', *JEPTA* 22 (2002), pp. 78–102 (100–02).

[168] Wenk, 'The Holy Spirit', pp. 131–32; J-A, Alvarsson, 'An Anthropological Contribution to the Future of Swedish Pentecostalism' (EPCRA conference paper, University of Uppsala, 2007) pp. 1–13 (8–9); A.K. Gabriel, 'Pneumatological Perspectives for a Theology of Nature: The Holy Spirit in Relation to Ecology and Technology', *JPT* 15.2 (2007), pp. 195–212; Robeck, 'Future Trajectories', p. 19; A. Dermawan, 'The Spirit in Creation and Environmental Stewardship: A Preliminary Pentecostal Response toward Ecological Theology, *AJPS* 6.2 (2003), pp. 199–217 (203–07); H.D. Hunter, 'Pentecostal Healing for God's Sick Creation', *Spirit and Church* 2.2 (2000), pp. 145–167; M. Volf, 'On Loving with Hope: Eschatology and Social Responsibility', *Transformation* 7.3 (1990), pp. 28–31; D.W. Dayton, 'Pentecostal/Charismatic Renewal and Social Change: A Western Perspective', *Transformation* 5.4 (1988), pp. 7–13.

[169] Hollenweger, 'Pentecostalism, Past, Present and Future', pp. 45–6.

the world in which they live, its structures, systems and environment. The hope of Paul (Rom. 8.19–21) that creation will be released from its bondage has tended to be interpreted as an eschatological expectation rather than an issue that believers could help to bring to reality prior to the eschaton. Cho, starting from the recognition that the Spirit was fundamentally involved in the creation of the world, asserts that he should not be removed from such concerns now[170] while Snell uses Mk 16.15–20 as the basis for a similar call for Pentecostals to fulfil their obligations towards creation.[171]

The complementary issues of wealth and poverty have, to a limited degree, been addressed by Pentecostals.[172] The issue of wealth was not central to early Pentecostals partly because most of them were not wealthy, coming from the less privileged groups of society. To a degree, they still do. However, there has been a development with regard to an expectation on the part of some to be prosperous as a manifestation of God's blessing to his people. Cho, pastor of one of the world's largest congregations has offered a framework that he titles 'the three-fold blessings of salvation' that comprises spiritual salvation as well as health and prosperity.[173] That which is often known as the Prosperity Gospel, associated with the largely US Word of Faith movement, is rejected by many Pentecostal leaders[174] though it still influences many Pentecostal believers, especially in parts of the developing world where poverty is common. This aberrant dogma assumes that God promises wealth, health and happiness for all believers in this life; it is theirs to claim and verses such as Phil. 4.19 are used to support such a notion. While it emphasizes the goodness of God and teaches that a belief in Christianity does not mean that one must eschew material benefits, it does not have any room for suffering nor a theology of suffering, presents pastoral difficulties for those who remain in need and ultimately provides a distorted picture of God who appears to arbitrarily bless some but not others.[175]

---

[170] Dermawan, 'The Spirit in Creation', pp. 208–16.

[171] J.T. Snell, 'Beyond the Individual and into the World: A Call to Participation in the Larger Purposes of the Spirit on the Basis of Pentecostal Theology', *Pneuma* 14.1 (1992), pp. 43–57 (48–51).

[172] D.G. Roebuck, 'Pentecostalism at the End of the Twentieth Century: From Poverty, Promise and Passion to Prosperity, Power and Place', in C.E. Norman, D.S. Armentrout (eds), *Religion in the Contemporary South, Changes, Continuities, and Contexts* (Knoxville: The University of Tennessee Press, 2005), pp. 53–73.

[173] Cho, *Salvation, Health and Prosperity*; idem, *The Fourth Dimension* (Seoul: Seoul Logos, 1979).

[174] G.D. Fee, *The Disease of the Health and Wealth Gospels* (Costa Mesa: The Word For Today, 1979); J.N. Horn, *From Rags to Riches: An Analysis of the Faith Movement and Its Relationship to the Classical Pentecostal Movement* (Pretoria: University of South Africa, 1989); A. Perriman (ed.), *Faith, Health and Prosperity: A Report on 'Word of Faith' and 'Positive Confession' Theologies* (Carlisle: ACUTE Paternoster Press, 2003); Robeck, 'Future Trajectories', pp. 28–31.

Fee, in an attempt to redress the balance, calls for a radical faith 'that does not require poverty, but it does require righteousness . . . to use our wealth . . . to alleviate the hurt and pain of the oppressed'.[176] Kung calls for Pentecostals, who have traditionally attracted the poor, not to lose sight of such people, especially in the light of the increasing globalization of the world that has benefits but also spawns massive disruption and leaves many people marginalized and vulnerable to exploitation.[177]

The NT does not set a pattern of mission or social transformation that must be replicated in every setting or age, neither does it show the leaders of the Church encouraging the believers to change their society. Although the basic behavioural characteristics portrayed in the life of Jesus are to be properly emulated, the contemporary context also needs to be considered. The mission of the Church in one society, age or setting may be very different to that in another. Seeking to find a NT paradigm for social transformation is not particularly helpful as that was not the main focus of the early Church leaders. They were looking to establish an alternative society not to change society. This is not to suggest that they anticipated or hoped for a monastic community that was cut off from its social environment, neither is this to set an agenda for a pietistic approach to life. On the contrary, Jesus speaks of believers functioning as salt and light within their society (Mt. 5.13–16) and presents the normative Christian life in the Beatitudes as containing characteristics important for making an impact on society including the aspects of being merciful and peacemakers (Mt. 5.7, 9).

The guidelines offered in Mt. 25.35–46 which refer to actions of mercy to people in need of sustenance, housing, care or visitation are presented by Jesus as evidence of being his follower. Clearly, he anticipated that such actions were appropriate and even expected by his followers but they function not as examples of how a believer should transform society but as dividing markers separating his followers from his opposers. In other words, they are not presented as elements specifically geared to change society so much as they demonstrate evidence of changed lives. In agreement with Hays, 'The question that Luke-Acts puts to the church – then and now– is not "Are you reforming society?" but rather "Is the power of the resurrection at work among you"'.[178] If it is, society will be reformed. However, what neither Jesus nor Paul did was to initiate measures to bring about societal transformation other than through the witness of the believing community.

---

[175] L. Nwankwo, '"You Have Received the Spirit of Power . . ." (2 Tim. 1:7). Reviewing the Prosperity Message in the Light of a Theology of Empowerment', *JEPTA* 22 (2002), pp. 56–77.

[176] Fee, *Listening to the Spirit*, p. 55.

[177] L-Y. Kung, 'Globalization, Ecumenism and Pentecostalism: A Search for Human Solidarity in Hong Kong', *AJPS* 6.1 (2003), 97–122.

[178] R. Hays, *The Moral Vision of the New Testament* (Edinburgh: T & T Clark, 1998), p. 135.

However, the limited information in the NT that would suggest that the early Christians sought to change their societies needs careful evaluation.[179] Wenk explores the issue of Christian responsibility on the basis of the qualitatively unique interactive relationships within the Trinity. Given that humanity has been created to reflect God, he argues that such emphases should also be reflected in the lives of believers with regard to others in and outside their communities.[180] Thereafter, he identifies OT (Exod. 22.20–26; Prov. 14.31; 21.13) and NT (Jas. 1.27) texts that indicate the importance of this attitude.[181] Petersen offers a hermeneutical approach which is based on the Church listening to the 'screaming questions' of the poor and marginalized who are not interested in 'traditionally articulated scientific/theological ideas' but 'want to know how God could abandon them so totally in the physical realm'.[182] Using as his grid the fact that socio-economic inequalities abound and that they are unacceptable, he articulates a response which is to be guided by an awareness of that which the Bible states concerning human suffering.[183] To do this is to seek to ensure the principles of the Kingdom are being worked out in practice. Wenk calls for the Pentecostal Church to be the kind that 'hears the cry of the needy, that sees the pain of the people, that is willing to understand the feeling of a person in despair' for 'such a church will reflect the love of God and be his agent in this world'.[184]

It is true that neither Paul nor other leaders in the early Church initiated discussions that might have led to changes in society. Political debate was not entered into (other than to encourage the believers to submit to the government of the day and maintain the status quo (Rom. 13.1–7; 1 Pet. 2.13–17) and social concerns were not developed by believers for their secular communities. Paul was concerned to develop Christians in society not to Christianize society. His role was dedicated to the development of the Church in society, not the development of society, though it may be assumed that he anticipated that transformation of society may have resulted from the former. Thus, the legitimacy of slavery was not addressed (though elements of its practice were, albeit in the Christian community (1 Pet. 2.18–21). Instead of encouraging slaves to demand their freedom or slave owners to release their slaves, he guided them in their lifestyles (Eph. 6.5–9; Col. 4.1).

---

[179] K. Warrington, 'Social Transformation in the Missions of Jesus and Paul: Priority or Bonus?', in D. Hillborn (ed.), *Movement for Change. Evangelical Perspectives on Social Transformation* (Carlisle: Paternoster Press, 2004), pp. 38–55.

[180] M. Wenk, 'Christian Social Responsibility', *EB* 10.1 (1991), pp. 7–18.

[181] Wenk, 'Christian Social Responsibility', pp. 8–10.

[182] D. Petersen, 'The Kingdom of God and the Hermeneutical Circle: Pentecostal Praxis in the Third World', in Dempster, Klaus and Petersen (eds), *Called and Empowered*, pp. 44–58 (47).

[183] Petersen, 'The Kingdom of God', pp. 47–9.

[184] Wenk, 'Christian Social Responsibility', p. 14.

His letter to Philemon on behalf of Onesimus, his slave, exploring the possibility of his being freed (1.16), is a rare example of Paul seeking to change an example of a practice associated with his culture. Even where he allows for the freedom of women to be developed, in contrast to much of Judaism and Gentile practice, he does not advocate this beyond the confines of the Christian community, though it is again to be assumed that his views could have been adopted if felt to be attractive to the secular society.[185] In that regard, Christianity may be understood to be setting an agenda that was not only right for itself but also of benefit to a wider audience, though the latter application is not clearly presented as being the responsibility of the Church.

This is not to suggest that the early believers did not positively affect their communities. Indeed, there is evidence that they did. Nevertheless, the limited information and examples of social changes in the first 50 years of the Church are curious features of a community that in its later history caused radical change in societal rules. A number of reasons may be offered for the slow development in this direction:

- The evidence of the NT is limited and not intended to be comprehensive. It is possible that the Church was not in existence long enough for such an agenda to be established and an infrastructure for its development to be created. The early believers had enough to do with the internal development of their communities to be concerned with the development of strategies for the broader improvement of its society. Therefore, it is less surprising, in the context of many instructions offered by the writers of the NT, that there is little to guide the believers in effecting changes to the practices of their secular communities.
- The lack of evidence of an agenda to change society may indicate the limited importance of this feature to the early Church. Instead of changing their society, they sought instead to change the hearts of their unbelieving neighbours, perhaps with the secondary aim of changing the wider society, though the latter is not specified. Consequently, 'the focus of Pentecostals has been on individual change, often to the exclusion of social change'.[186] It is possible that the early believers did not recognize it as their responsibility to transform the world in which they lived and it may also be assumed, in the absence of advice to the contrary, that the apostles felt the same. The Spirit who was the one who set the agenda of the early Church in mission, in particular, does not appear to have urged it towards societal change. If the Spirit was not leading them in this direction, they may have thought that there was little reason for them to initiate an alternative programme.

[185] R. Banks, *Paul's Idea of Community* (Peabody: Hendrickson, 1994), pp. 155–58.
[186] Kärkkäinen, *Toward a Pneumatological Theology*, p. 184.

- It is possible that to have attempted to change society may have been premature and thus counter-productive in an era where opposition was viewed with grave suspicion and even fear by the authorities, often resulting in harsh and forceful reactions. For the Church to have a broader schema may have resulted in their evangelism being quickly truncated.
- It is possible that the thought of changing their society never occurred to the earliest believers. The NT believers did not live in a democracy and thus did not have the freedom to voice their opinions and change the direction of the secular world in which they lived. It is not necessarily that they lacked the desire to bring about change but simply that they recognized that it was impractical to attempt it. Those that did were best represented in Israel by Zealots who sought to bring about change by violent means, partly because it was perceived that there was no other way; such a process was not appropriate for followers of the Peacemaker.

  Many today are able to influence change for the better in their societies but for the vast majority of people in the ancient world, such freedom was not only a dream but also an inconceivable option. At the same time, the level of corruption and inequality in the fractured society of the Roman Empire should not be overlooked. The lack of framework for social change, the small numbers of believers, the absence of a tradition of change and experience in effecting social transformation and the sheer enormity of the task all made such an enterprise one that would need to be explicitly expressed by Jesus to his disciples or the Spirit to the Church for it to have been initiated.

- It is possible that, as with early Pentecostals, the first-century believers anticipated the world ceasing to exist in the near future (Mt. 24.29–35). Certainly, Paul anticipates a serious upheaval in society that motivated his writing to the Corinthians concerning entering into marriage (1 Cor. 7.25–31). There would have been limited reason for believers to seek to change the rules of the society in which they lived. Why disburse energy changing the world if it was about to end? Instead, their focus was on developing an alternative community that would have the opportunity to be expressed fully when the current social pattern was finally removed.

Some Ways Forward

Petersen reminds Pentecostals that the motivation to social action should result from 'a transformation of life, empowered by the Spirit to demonstrate love toward all mankind'.[187] Furthermore, he advocates that Pentecostals should engage in social action but not in their exclusive enclaves only and

---

[187] Petersen, *Not by Might nor by Power*, p. 230.

also become more involved in politics.[188] The more that Pentecostals realize that although the Kingdom of God will be finally consummated at the return of Jesus, it may be increasingly anticipated as invading the present, the more this issue will move higher up the agenda of important issues to be developed. However, the more Pentecostals imbibe the mores of Western secularism and materialism and become individualistic, fragmented and subjective, the less engaged they will be with the society in which they live.

In view of this sense of dissonance, Dempster argues for the increase of social concern by Pentecostals precisely because of the return of Jesus.[189] Similarly, Kusmic cautions against a postponement of societal change until the eschaton and instead exhorts Pentecostals to live out the significance of the Sermon on the Mount in the present.[190] Moltmann asks Pentecostals to demonstrate the charismata 'in the everyday world' since 'they are to witness to the liberating lordship of Christ in this world's conflicts',[191] while Cox advocates more sermons on Acts 5 ('They had all things in common') as well as Acts 2.[192]

The fact that Pentecostals have a high theology of the Spirit should manifest itself in social concern and action for one's community, given the role of the Spirit in this regard, as also reflected in the writings of Luke (4.16–30).[193] Pentecostals, more than others, because of their emphasis on the Spirit, should be following in the steps of the Spirit with reference to social concerns.[194] As Hays states, 'Where the Spirit is at work, *liberation is underway*'.[195] Increasingly, a greater awareness of the role of the Spirit as reflected in the NT has the potential of setting frameworks for ethical thinking and decision making, especially where the Bible does not address current ethical dilemmas.[196]

---

[188] Petersen, *Not by Might nor by Power*, pp. 231–33.

[189] M.W. Dempster, 'Christian Social Concern in Pentecostal Perspective: Reformulating Pentecostal Eschatology', *JPT* 2 (1993), pp. 51–64.

[190] P. Kuzmic, 'Eschatology and Ethics: Evangelical Views and Attitudes', in V. Samuel, C. Sugden (eds), *Mission as Transformation* (Oxford: Regnum Books, 1999), pp. 134–65.

[191] Moltmann, *The Spirit of Life*, p. 186.

[192] H.G. Cox, '"Pentecostalism and Global Market Culture": A Response to Issues Facing Pentecostalism in a Postmodern World', in Dempster, Klaus and Petersen (eds), *The Globalization of Pentecostalism*, pp. 386–95 (395).

[193] Wenk ('The Holy Spirit', pp. 135–37) identifies this feature in a number of Lucan passages; Menzies, *Spirit and Power*, pp. 201–08; Kaiser, 'The Holy Spirit's Ministry', pp. 62–9.

[194] M.W. Dempster, 'Evangelism, Social Concern, and the Kingdom of God', in Dempster, Klaus and Petersen (eds), *Called and Empowered*, pp. 22–43; E. Villafañe, 'The Politics of the Spirit: Reflections on a Theology of Social Transformation for the Twenty-First Century', *Pneuma* 18.2 (1996), pp. 161–70.

[195] Hays, *The Moral Vision*, p. 135 (italics in original).

[196] Fee, *Paul, the Spirit*, pp. 98–111.

The manifesto for believers is to walk with the Spirit and listen to his guidance as he seeks to manifest the life of Christ among them, purifying and empowering them to achieve it. Yoder writes, 'God is working in the world and it is the task of the church to know how he is working'.[197] At the same time, social initiatives are to be expected as outworkings of love as believers share 'the good news of God's love, incarnated in the witness of a community, for the sake of the world'.[198]

Dirksen explores the possibility that there may be a specific Pentecostal approach to community support when the latter is undertaken in response to the guidance of the Spirit who has been sought for this express purpose.[199] Villafañe identifies the baptism in the Spirit as a particularly important catalyst in this regard[200] and Dempster similarly advocates speaking in tongues (and the baptism in the Spirit) as a basic stimulation and motivation to social action.[201] Petersen has taken up this challenge and, on the basis that power is a keyword for Pentecostals, argues that they must engage in a wider agenda of social concern to take advantage of the presence of the Spirit in their lives. He writes,

> Spirit baptism empowers one not only to participate in evangelism and supernatural events but also to enjoy the empowerment of the Spirit in the expression of ethical concerns. Therefore, it is only when contemporary Pentecostals, empowered by the Spirit, recognize and practise a confirmed commitment to *both* evangelism and to social concern that integrity of mission is accomplished.[202]

Similarly, Wells argues that Pentecostals are best placed to emulate the resistance to ungodly and unacceptable social practices engaged in by the OT prophets and Jesus because of their attachment to the charisms of the Spirit,

---

[197] J.H. Yoder, *The Politics of Jesus* (Grand Rapids: Eerdmans, 1972), p. 155.

[198] D.J. Bosch, *Transforming Mission: Paradigm Shifts in Theology of Mission* (Maryknoll: Orbis, 1991), p. 519.

[199] M.O. Dirksen, 'Community Development: Is There a Pentecostal Approach?', (SPS conference paper, Cleveland, 2007), pp. 80–6.

[200] E. Villafañe, 'The Contours of a Pentecostal Social Ethic: A North American Hispanic Perspective', *Transformation* 11.1 (1994), pp. 6–9 (9).

[201] Dempster, 'The Church's Moral Witness', pp. 1–7; F. Macchia, 'Tongues as a Sign: Towards a Sacramental Understanding of the Pentecostal Experience', *Pneuma* 15.1 (1993), pp. 61–76 (63).

[202] Petersen, *Not by Might nor by Power*, p. 226 (italics in original); see also Villafañe, *The Liberating Spirit*; L.S.V. de Petrella ('The tension between evangelism and social action in the Pentecostal movement', *IRM* 75 (1986), pp. 34–8) identifies Pentecostal movements as not being 'pietistic or spiritualistic' but as 'instruments of God's intervention' in the world.

especially prophecy which he enlarges to include speaking out against injustice.[203] Indeed, basing his conclusion on an examination of the work of the Spirit in the OT, Kung argues that 'the promised Spirit is the Spirit of justice and peace . . . any form or tendency of privatization . . . of God's promise of the Spirit is misleading and distorted'.[204]

The community in which the Spirit resides is to be the guide for such dialogue and action by believers. The ethics and lifestyles of believers are not to be individualistic; they are to be formulated in a community that is being renewed by the Spirit. Not only does he offer guidance but he also empowers believers to put his guidance into operation (Gal. 5.16). There is an implicit danger in assuming that the Spirit alone transforms society, albeit through the Church, and that this transformation is anticipated as always being at the level of the supernatural. Such thinking has spawned the health and wealth theology that proclaims that issues including poverty, deprivation, unemployment, health, old age, physical incapacity, depression, psychological or mental conditions can all be resolved by following a belief structure, apparently located in the Bible, in which God resolves these situations, believers simply needing to acquiesce to this. What is the need for social action when the Bible has all the answers and the Spirit is available to apply them to all one's problems? The mantra that 'Jesus is the same, yesterday, today and forever' can sometimes be a poor substitute for individual action to effect change; it needs to be stated in association with the call of the same Jesus to pastoral care by his followers (Mt. 25.35–39; Heb. 13.2; Jas. 1.27).

Now, the widening gap between rich and poor, the fragmented nature of society, the unfairness in global structures and the breakdown in many aspects of society, caused by selfishness, corruption, disease, natural disasters and war, all point to the pressing need for Pentecostals to engage in improving the living conditions of the masses. The Spirit of grace and compassion who groans for creation has already provided a stimulus to strategically and intentionally save the world, both physically and spiritually. Pentecostals must learn to catch up with all aspects of the Spirit's agenda.

---

[203] H. Wells, 'Resistance to Domination as a Charism of the Holy Spirit', in Stålsett, *Spirits of Globalization*, pp. 170–82; Kärkkäinen, 'Spirituality as a Resource', pp. 90–4.
[204] L.Y. Kung, 'Outpouring of the Spirit: A Reflection on Pentecostals' Identity', *AJPS* 4.1 (2001), pp. 3–19 (13).

7

MISSION

Introduction

Mission is central to Pentecostalism, Wilson concluding, 'The missionary task for many came close to being their movement's organizational reason-for being'.[1] Although they share similar motivations to their evangelical colleagues, they have traditionally been more robust and enthusiastic in their evangelistic ambition, Dyer describing a 'mission contagion' resulting from itinerating missionaries resulting in others volunteering to function as missionaries.[2] Klaus defines Pentecostals as being passionate about mission, viewing it as an urgent task[3] and van der Laan refers to the readiness of

[1] Wilson, *Strategy of the Spirit*, p. 15; Anderson, 'Towards a Pentecostal Missiology', pp. 36–7; Javier, 'The Pentecostal Legacy', pp. 297–300; B.D. Klaus, 'The Mission of the Church', in Horton (ed.), *Systematic Theology*, pp. 567–95; Lim, 'A Missiological Evaluation', pp. 125–47; G.B. McGee, *This Gospel Shall Be Preached: History of the Assemblies of God Foreign Missions to 1959* (Springfield: Gospel Publishing House, 1986); idem, *This Gospel Shall be Preached: History of the Assemblies of God Foreign Missions since 1959* (Springfield: Gospel Publishing House, 1989); Clark and Lederle (eds), *What Is Distinctive*, pp. 58–60; Ma, 'The Empowerment of the Spirit', p. 29; Goff, *Fields White unto Harvest*, p. 165; A. Langerak, 'The Witness and Influence of Pentecostal Christians in Latin America', *IRM* 87 (April 1998), pp. 175–87.

[2] A.E. Dyer, 'Missionary Candidates to the British Assemblies of God Overseas Mission 1945–1954', *JEPTA* 24 (2004), pp. 84–100 (88); V. Synan, 'Missionaries of the One Way Ticket, in McClung (ed.), *Azusa Street and Beyond: 100 Years*, pp. 41–52.

[3] Klaus, 'The Holy Spirit', p. 335; Kärkkäinen, 'Missiology: Pentecostal and Charismatic', p. 877; Zimmerman, 'The Reason for the Rise', pp. 60–1; L.G. McClung, 'Spontaneous Strategy of the Spirit: Pentecostal Missionary Practices', in McClung (ed.), *Azusa Street and Beyond*, pp. 71–84 (74–6); idem, 'Early Pentecostal Missionaries: They Went Everywhere Preaching the Gospel', in McClung (ed.), *Azusa Street and Beyond: 100 Years*, pp. 35–40; Anderson, 'Burning Its Way into Every Nation', pp. 8–9; R.E. Hedlund, 'Why Pentecostal Churches Are Growing Faster in Italy', *EMQ* 8 (1972), pp. 129–36.

many Pentecostals to be engaged in mission activities.[4] It is seen as the responsibility of the local church and they recognize their part in supporting those who have undertaken a missiological role in other countries.[5] This passion is and has been worked out in the readiness of Pentecostals to financially support those who engage in mission.[6] McClung concludes that 'Pentecostalism by its very nature is intrinsically missiological'[7] while McGee deduces that 'Pentecostalism cannot be properly understood apart from its missionary vision'.[8]

In this regard, it is what Pentecostals do more than that which they believe that best illustrates their core being. This is expressed by the Declaration adopted by the AoG Council on Evangelism in St Louis in 1968 and the Covenant on World Evangelization adopted by the Church of God Congress held in Cleveland in 1983 in which the emphasis was not on doctrines related to evangelism but on the significance of the Spirit and the Bible to the development of evangelism.[9] They treat mission as the means of the enlargement of the Church. For much of its history, global Pentecostalism has conducted missions that often lasted a week or two when a church or locality became the target for a consistent and emphatic drive to ensure that as many people as possible had the opportunity to hear the Gospel, often associated with a readiness to pray for the sick.

In a remarkable assessment of Pentecostal missions, McClung concludes, 'the Pentecostal Movement has encouraged the Church Growth Movement and has been admired by its researchers. Some might dare to say that if it were not for Pentecostal growth around the world, the Church Growth Movement might not have had much growth to study'.[10] Although only just over 100 years since its commencement, the evidence of the remarkable growth of Pentecostalism is clear.[11] Although for much of its history, the

---

[4] P.N. van der Laan, 'Dynamics in Pentecostal mission: A Dutch perspective', *International Review of Mission* 75 (1986), pp. 75–81.

[5] R.O. Innvaer, *Sennepsfroet: En bok om misjon* (Oslo: Rex Forlag, 1993), pp. 23–71.

[6] McClung, 'Spontaneous Strategy of the Spirit, pp. 71–84 (80).

[7] McClung, 'Try to Get People Saved', p. 32; also D.J. Hesselgrave, *Today's Choices for Tomorrow's Mission: An Evangelical Perspective on Trends and Issues in Missions* (Grand Rapids: Zondervan, 1988), p. 118.

[8] G.B. McGee, 'Early Pentecostal Missionaries: They Went Everywhere Preaching the Gospel', in McClung (ed.), *Azusa Street and Beyond*, pp. 33–6 (33).

[9] See in McClung, *Azusa Street and Beyond*, pp. 167–72; S. Myung, 'The Spiritual Dimension of Church Growth as Applied in Yoido Full Gospel Church' (unpublished doctoral dissertation, Fuller Theological Seminary, 1999).

[10] G. McClung, 'From BRIDGES (McGavran 1955) to WAVES (Wagner 1983): Pentecostals and the Church Growth Movement', *Pneuma* 7.1 (1985), pp. 5–18 (12); idem, 'Try to Get People Saved', pp. 42–8; Yung, 'Endued with Power', pp. 63–82.

[11] S.H. Frodsham, *With Signs Following. The Story of the Pentecostal Revival in the Twentieth Century* (Springfield: Gospel Publishing House, 1928), p. 50; McClung,

movement of missionaries has been from the West, now non-Western Pentecostals are evangelizing their own nation's diaspora, especially in the West.[12] This 'mission in reverse' is resulting in Western nationals (and others) coming to faith as a result of the evangelism of those who represent countries that were themselves the object of missionary activity in the past.[13] Furthermore, non-Western Pentecostals are becoming much more aggressive in their mission activity. Increasingly, material is available concerning Pentecostal mission in many settings and countries.[14] Pentecostals have been particularly successful in this area for a number of reasons.

Missional Factors

The Commissions of Jesus

First, Pentecostals take seriously the commissions of Jesus to his disciples where he commanded them to evangelize the world (Mt. 28.19–20) and

'Explosion, Motivation, and Consolidation', p. 10–11; J.T. Dermawan, 'A Study of the Nias Revival in Indonesia', *AJPS* 6.2 (2003), pp. 247–263; G. McClung, 'The Church of God in Germany: Missiological Options for a Maturing Pentecostal Church', *EB* 10.1 (1991), pp. 53–62; V-M. Kärkkäinen, 'One Hundred Years of Pentecostal Missions: A Report on the European Pentecostal/Charismatic Association's 1999 Meeting', *Mission Studies* 16.1–2 (2000), pp. 207–16; G.B. McGee, 'The Azusa Street Revival and Twentieth Century Missions', *IBMR* 12.2 (1988), pp. 58–61.

[12] Asamoah-Gyadu, 'An African Pentecostal on Mission', pp. 297–321; Ayuk, 'Portrait of a Nigerian Pentecostal Missionary', pp. 122–41; M. Wilkinson, 'The Globalization of Pentecostalism: The Role of Asian Immigrant Pentecostals in Canada', *AJPS* 3.2 (2000), pp. 219–26; O. Kalu, 'Preserving a Worldview: Pentecostalism in the African Maps of the Universe', *Pneuma* 24.2 (2002), pp. 110–37 (123–130).

[13] C. van der Laan, 'Pentecostal Migrant Churches in the Netherlands', *JEPTA* 25 (2005), pp. 67–81; Asamoah-Gyadu, 'An African Pentecostal on Mission', p. 298; L.D. Pate, 'Pentecostal Missions from the Two-Thirds World', in Dempster, Klaus and Petersen (eds), *Called and Empowered*, pp. 242–58; R. Ezemadu, 'The Role of the Majority Church in Missions', in McClung (ed.), *Azusa Street and Beyond: 100 Years*, pp. 243–50.

[14] Sayman, 'Some Reflections on the Development', pp. 40–56; C.K. Khia, *The Cross among Pagodas: A History of the Assemblies of God in Myanmar* (Baguio City: Asia Pacific Theological Seminary, 2003); Kim, *History and Theology of Korean Pentecostalism*; McGee, 'Missions, Overseas', pp. 885–901; M.S. Clark, 'Two Contrasting Models of Missions in South Africa: The Apostolic Faith Mission and the Assemblies of God', *AJPS* 8.1 (2005), pp. 143–61; G.L. Pettersen, *Pinse over grensene* (Oslo: Filadelfiaforlaget, 1989); Kärkkäinen, 'From the Ends of the Earth', pp. 116–31; J. Reinke, *Deutsche Pfingstmissionen: Geschichte, Theologie, Praxis* (Bonn: Verlag für Kultur und Wissenschaft, 1997); D. Woods, 'Failure and Success in the Ministry of T.J. McIntosh, the First Pentecostal Missionary to China', *CPCR* 12 (Jan. 2003); P. Smith, *Global Warming: The Fire of Pentecost in World Evangelism* (Antrim: Elim Pentecostal Irish Churches, 2007); A.H. Anderson, *Spreading Fires: The Missionary Nature of Early Pentecostalism* (London: SCM, 2007).

assume it also applies to them.[15] Evangelism is a matter of obedience and they believe that they will be called to account for indolence on their part. There is always the fear that people may have come to faith if they had been faithful in speaking to them; the thought that unbelievers will blame them on the Day of Judgement is one that has haunted countless Pentecostals in years gone by.

Closely associated with this feature is the recognition that for Pentecostals, their mission is Christòcentric, the Spirit enabling them to continue that which Jesus commenced.[16] Their emphasis on heaven, hell and the belief in the eternal punishment awaiting unbelievers has been of major importance in stimulating Pentecostals to evangelism, the concept of the Pentecostal being a 'watchman' (Isa. 21.11; Ezek. 3.17; 33.7), entrusted with the destiny of humanity, being a sobering reminder of the responsibility to share the Gospel with others.

Because of the strong assumption that the mandate of mission was to be accompanied by the power that was available to Jesus in his mission, there has been an expectation of success.[17] To function incarnationally is recognized as a valuable model for mission, the example of Jesus being followed in this respect. Kay concludes, 'Out of this identification, flows true communication and authentic modelling of the radical alternative offered by Jesus'.[18]

The Role of the Spirit

Their belief that the Spirit is an empowering resource has been instrumental in encouraging them to engage in mission.[19] In particular, the experience of

---

[15] L. Wigglesworth, 'The Great Commission', in Brewster (ed.), *Pentecostal Doctrine*, pp. 393–99; W. Ma, 'Selected Areas for Pentecostal Mission Studies: Current Status and Future Agenda' (EPCRA conference paper, University of Uppsala, 2007), pp. 1–14 (3).

[16] Klaus, 'The Holy Spirit', p. 335; Anderson, 'Towards a Pentecostal Missiology', p. 33; C.P. Wagner, 'A Church Growth Perspective on Pentecostal Missions', in Dempster, Klaus and Petersen (eds), *Called and Empowered*, pp. 265–98 (268–70).

[17] C.H. Kraft, 'A Third Wave Perspective on Pentecostal Missions', in Dempster, Klaus and Petersen (eds), *Called and Empowered* (Peabody: Hendrickson, 1991), pp. 299–312 (304); Petersen, 'The Kingdom of God', in Dempster, Klaus and Petersen (eds), *Called and Empowered*, p. 56; G.B. McGee, 'Pentecostals and Their Various Strategies for Global Mission: A Historical Assessment' in Dempster, Klaus and Petersen (eds), *Called and Empowered*, pp. 203–24 (214–16); Cerillo, 'Pentecostals and the City', p. 101.

[18] P.K. Kay, 'Personal Reflections on Incarnation as the Model for Mission', *JEPTA* 26.2 (2006), pp. 127–33 (128).

[19] G.B. McGee, '"Power from on High": A Historical Perspective on the Radical Strategy in Missions', in Ma and Menzies (eds), *Pentecostalism in Context*, pp. 317–36 (324–34); idem, 'The Radical Strategy in Modern Missions: The Linkage of Paranormal Phenomena with Evangelism', in C.D. McDonnell (ed.), *The Holy Spirit and Mission Dynamics*

the baptism of the Spirit has played an important part in developing a mission consciousness among Pentecostals, Land concluding that 'All who had "gotten their Pentecost" were witnesses, tellers of good news',[20] making them 'dynamic missionary people'.[21] Indeed, the emphasis on the Spirit has been identified as being 'central to Pentecostal missiology'[22] in which the Spirit is viewed as the leader of Church growth.[23] The role of the Spirit as a missional force in the book of Acts has significantly contributed to this emphasis (Acts 1.8; 10.19–20; 11.12; 13.2; 16.6–10).[24]

This expectation has been fuelled by the belief that the promise of supernatural power as reflected in Acts 1.8 is a fundamental consequence of the presence of the Spirit in their lives.[25] Associated with the baptism in the Spirit is the phenomenon of speaking in tongues which, in some early Pentecostal settings, was assumed to be the gift of the Spirit to believers in order to enable them to evangelize in foreign languages.[26]

(Pasadena: William Carey Library, 1997), pp. 69–95; B. Klaus, 'The Holy Spirit', p. 334–35; L.G. McClung, 'Evangelism', in Burgess and van der Maas (eds), *NIDPCM*, pp. 617–20 (618); McClung, 'Try to Get People Saved', p. 36; Hodges, 'A Pentecostal's View', pp. 83–84; Anderson, 'Global Pentecostalism', pp. 19–31; D.A. McGavran, 'What Makes Pentecostal Churches Grow?', in McClung (ed.), *Azusa Street and Beyond*, pp. 121–23 (122); J.P. Hogan, 'The Holy Spirit and the Great Commission', in McClung (ed.), *Azusa Street and Beyond: 100 Years*, pp. 97–106.

[20] Land, *Pentecostal Spirituality*, p. 19.

[21] J.A.B. Jongeneel, 'Ecumenical, Evangelical and Pentecostal/Charismatic Views on Mission as a Movement of the Holy Spirit', in Jongeneel (ed.), *Pentecost, Mission and Ecumenism*, p. 234; D. Bays, 'The Protestant Missionary Establishment and the Pentecostal Movement', in Blumhofer, Spittler and Wacker (eds), *Pentecostal Currents*, pp. 50–67; Ma, 'Full Circle Mission', p. 17; McClung, 'Truth on Fire', p. 49; J.R. Flowers, 'Editorial', *The Pentecost* (August, 1908), p. 4.

[22] Lord, 'The Voluntary Principle', p. 86; E. Pousson, 'A "Great Century" of Pentecostal/Charismatic Renewal and Mission', *Pneuma* 16 (1994), pp. 81–100 (94); L.G. McClung, 'Pentecostal/Charismatic Perspectives on a Missiology for the Twenty-First Century', *Pneuma* 16 (Spring 1994), pp. 11–21 (12).

[23] Myung and Hong, *Charis and Charisma*, pp. 51–62; Jongeneel, 'Ecumenical, Evangelical and Pentecostal/Charismatic Views, pp. 231–46.

[24] M. Wenk, 'Light: A Pentecostal Reading of a Biblical Metaphor', *JEPTA* 26.2 (2006), pp. 168–83 (169); Penney, *The Missionary Emphasis*, pp. 122–25; McClung, 'Try to Get People Saved', pp. 38–9; T. Munyon, 'Two Criteria for Revival in Acts 1–8', *Paraclete* 25.1 (1991), pp. 10–3; T.H. Lindberg, 'The Holy Spirit and Missions', *Paraclete* 24.1 (1990), pp. 16–9; M.P. Brooks, 'The Spirit and Mission in Acts', *Paraclete* 25.1 (1991), pp. 14–23.

[25] Ma, 'The Empowerment of the Spirit', p. 28; McClung, 'Truth on Fire', p. 50; idem, 'Salvation Shock Troops', 35; W.J. de Kock, 'Pentecostal Power for a Pentecostal Task: Empowerment through Engagement in South African Context', *JPT* 16 (2000), pp. 103–05.

[26] *The Apostolic Faith* (Sep. 1906, p. 1; Nov. 1906, p. 2); McGee, 'The Azusa Street Revival', p. 59: McGee, 'Power from on High', pp. 325–27; McClung, 'Salvation Shock

As a result of this emphasis on the resources of the Spirit, many (early) Pentecostal missionaries saw little need for theological or cultural education before embarking on their mission activities, often to the cost of their ministry.[27] Neither did it matter if no missionary board accepted them; they went anyway on the basis of the belief that the Spirit had mandated them,[28] often through a prophecy or inner certainty that this was to be their destiny.[29] Anderson identifies this motivation as even more important to many than the sense of their fulfilling the Great Commission;[30] they were obeying the Spirit who was individually directing them. Many women became missionaries in the process and thus functioned in ways that were closed to them in their home countries.[31]

Pomerville suggests that the limited expectation of many non-Pentecostal missionaries to see the Spirit working in their mission activities actually necessitated the emergence of a Pentecostal mission force that gave due attention to the Spirit, anticipating that he would accompany and empower them.[32] Filson notes that in years past, evangelical missionaries often condemned animistic practices but failed to offer an alternative way of dealing with their problems and fill the vacuum left after animistic practices had been abandoned.[33] Pentecostals, because of their awareness of the presence of the dynamic and empowering Spirit within them, exhibit a confidence

---

Troops', p. 82; R. Harris, *Spoken by the Spirit* (Springfield: Gospel Publishing House, 1973); A.H. Anderson, 'Christian Missionaries and "Heathen Natives": The Cultural Ethics of Early Pentecostal Missionaries', *JEPTA* 22 (2002), pp. 4–29 (12–19); McGee, G.B., 'Shortcut to Language Preparation? Radical Evangelicals, Missions, and the Gift of Tongues', *IBMR* 25.3 (2001), pp. 118–25.

[27] A.H. Anderson, 'Signs and Blunders: Pentecostal Mission Issues at "Home and Abroad" in the Twentieth Century', *JAM* 2.2 (2000), pp. 193–210; McGee, 'Early Pentecostal Missionaries', p. 34.

[28] Anderson, 'Burning Its Way into Every Nation', p. 3; as early as 1909, the Pentecostal Missionary Union was established in Sunderland, England with Alexander Boddy as the first Chairman and Cecil Polhill as President (see Gee, *The Pentecostal Movement*, p. 47; P.K. Kay, 'The Pentecostal Missionary Union and the Fourfold Gospel with Baptism in the Holy Spirit and Speaking in Tongues: A New Power for Missions?', *JEPTA* 19 (1999), pp. 89–104); the AoG formalized a Missionary Board in 1919, the Church of God did the same in 1926 and the Pentecostal Holiness Church elected a Board in 1911. See further developments in McClung, 'Explosion, Motivation, and Consolidation', pp. 18–20.

[29] McClung, 'Explosion, Motivation, and Consolidation', pp. 11–17.

[30] Anderson, *An Introduction to Pentecostalism*, p. 207.

[31] McGee, 'Missions, Overseas', p. 889; McClung, 'Spontaneous Strategy of the Spirit', pp. 76–7; J.C. Ma, 'Elva Vanderbout: A Woman Pioneer of Pentecostal Mission among Igorots', *JAM* 3.1 (2000), pp. 121–40; R.M. Riss, 'Women, Role of', *DPCM*, pp. 893–99.

[32] Pomerville, *The Third Force in Mission*, pp. 63–78.

[33] W.R. Filson, 'A Pentecostal Response to Cordilleran Religions', *AJPS* 2.1 (1999), pp. 35–45 (37).

sometimes lacking in non-Pentecostals, which can be effective in overcoming any sense of inadequacy and powerlessness. They are constantly reminded by their Pentecostal identity that they function not on their own but as a result of and in the power of the Spirit.

Signs and wonders are thus anticipated by Pentecostals involved in mission, enabling them to powerfully engage in the task of presenting the supremacy of Christ and of authenticating the gospel,[34] Anderson describes healing and exorcism as 'probably the most important part of their evangelism' and 'church recruitment',[35] resulting in significant numbers of people coming to faith as they witness the reality of God in their midst.[36] McClung describes it as an 'evangelistic door-opener',[37] especially where medical aid is limited. Lartey identifies this particularly in the African context where healing and the imposition of sicknesses and curses have also been present in much tribal religion.[38] Thus, prayer is of significant importance to Pentecostals in their mission activity,[39] Cho identifying it as a major reason for the church growth in Korea.[40]

---

[34] Saayman, 'Some Reflections on the Development', p. 46; Larbi, *Pentecostalism*, p. 429; Ma, 'Pentecostal Challenges', p. 199; C.P. Wagner, 'Characteristics of Pentecostal Church Growth', in McClung (ed.), *Azusa Street and Beyond*, pp. 125–32 (128–29); McGee, 'Power from on High', pp. 317–24; R.P. Menzies, 'A Pentecostal Perspective on "Signs and Wonders"', *Pneuma* 17.2 (1995), pp. 265–78; D. Gee, 'Spiritual Gifts and World Evangelization', in McClung (ed.), *Azusa Street and Beyond: 100 Years*, pp. 107–16.

[35] Anderson, 'Global Pentecostalism', p. 216; Wagner, 'A Church Growth Perspective', pp. 271–72; D.J. Chiquete, 'Healing, Salvation and Mission: The Ministry of Healing in Latin American Pentecostalism', *IRM* 93 .370/371 (2004), pp. 474–85; McGee, 'The Radical Strategy in Modern Missions', pp. 69–95; R.E. Hedlund (*Evangelization and Church Growth: Issues from the Asian Context* (Madras: Church Growth Research Centre, MacGavran Institute, 1992), pp. 217–18) notes a 11.8% growth in conversions where prayer for the sick is included in evangelism.

[36] McGee, 'Power from on High', pp. 317–36; O. Onyinah, 'Matthew Speaks to Ghanaian Healing Situations', *JPT* 10.1 (2001), pp. 120–43 (124); Myung and Hong, *Charis and Charisma*, pp. 57–61; Ayuk, 'The Pentecostal Transformation', p. 192; Anderson, 'Burning Its Way into Every Nation', p. 9; J.C. Ma, *Mission Possible. Biblical Strategies for Reaching the Lost* (Milton Keynes: Paternoster, 2005), p. 62.

[37] McClung, 'Spontaneous Strategy of the Spirit', p. 74; Suico, 'Pentecostalism and Social Change', p. 196; Wenk, 'Light: A Pentecostal Reading', p. 170.

[38] E.Y. Lartey, 'Healing: Tradition and Pentecostalism in Africa', *IRM* 75 (1986), pp. 75–81 (47–50); Glazier, *Perspectives on Pentecostalism*, pp. 67–8, 125–42; Anderson, *Zion and Pentecost*, pp. 120–26.

[39] Wagner, 'A Church Growth Perspective', pp. 272–73.

[40] P.(D).Y. Cho, 'The Secret Behind the World's Biggest Church', in McClung (ed.), *Azusa Street and Beyond*, pp. 99–101; Myung and Hong, *Charis and Charisma*, pp. 63–74; D. Allen, 'Revival – A Classic Pentecostal View', *JEPTA* 27.2 (2007), pp. 118–27; M.J. McClymond (ed.), *Embodying the Spirit: New Perspectives on North American Revivalism* (Baltimore: Johns Hopkins University Press, 2004).

Hughes describes Pentecostal evangelism as 'supernatural evangelism'.[41] Similarly, Larbi identifies that which often results in people coming to faith is when they are offered a salvation that is personal and immediate, concluding that 'what really attracted them to join the Church was the concrete and material help that Jesus provides in the here and now'.[42]

Worldviews

The worldview of Pentecostals was (and still is) similar to those to whom the Gospel was/is presented.[43] Indeed, Cox concludes that Pentecostal theology provides 'both a *bridge* from the spiritual world of the old religion and a *dam* against its powers'.[44] Maxwell explores the relationship between Pentecostalism and traditional culture in Zimbabwe, noting that it is replete with a sense of continuity and cross-fertilization.[45] Dermawan identifies the place of experience in the non-Western worldview, drawing attention to the fact that experience is also a foundational aspect of Pentecostal spirituality and this in turn facilitates the attractiveness of the gospel as presented by Pentecostals to those who value it.[46] The emphasis on the Spirit and supernatural phenomena has also meant that Pentecostals have been better aware of the emphasis on the spirit world in the many societies in which they have ministered. Because Pentecostals are aware of the phenomena of supernatural healing, revelation, blessings, curses and the spirit world, they are better placed to engage with people who have similar worldviews concerning these features. Onyinah notes that early non-Pentecostal missionaries to Africa taught that beliefs in spirit forces were superstitious while at the same time, identified the devil and demons as being the forces behind such phenomena. This had the effect of strengthening the beliefs of the people in the potency

---

[41] Hughes, *Church of God Distinctives*, p. 63; Frodsham, *With Signs Following*, pp. 91–2; Ayuk, 'Portrait of a Nigerian Pentecostal Missionary', pp. 121, 127, 129–130; Dermawan, 'A Study of Nias Revival', p. 256; C.H. Kraft, 'Allegiance, Truth and Power Encounters in Christian Witness', in Jongeneel (ed.), *Pentecost, Mission and Ecumenism*, pp. 215–30 (215–17); S. Malek, 'Islam Encountering Gospel Power', in Dempster, Klaus and Petersen (eds), *Called and Empowered*, pp. 180–97.

[42] E.K. Larbi, 'The Nature of Continuity and Discontinuity of Ghanaian Pentecostal Concept of Salvation in African Cosmology', *AJPS* 5.1 (2002), pp. 87–106 (88–100).

[43] Ma, 'Full Circle Mission', p. 20; J.C. Ma, *When the Spirit Meets the Spirits* (Frankfurt: Peter Lang, 2000), pp. 213–32; McGee, 'Power from on High', p. 334.

[44] Cox, 'Spirits of Globalization', p. 17 (italics in original).

[45] D. Maxwell, *African Gifts of the Spirit: Pentecostalism and the Rise of a Zimbabwean Transnational Religious Movement* (Oxford: James Currey, 2006), pp. 46–52.

[46] Dermawan, 'A Study of Nias Revival', p. 262; J.C. Ma, 'Animism', Burgess (ed.), *EPCC*, pp. 26–7 (27); A. Santiago-Vendrell, 'Popular Religion as a Unifying Factor in the Latino/a Religious Community: A Pentecostal Proposal in US Latino Ecumenical Theology', *JPT* 12.1 (Oct. 2003), pp. 129–141.

of these evil forces but did not offer an alternative that would offer provision for healing, exorcism and protection from such spirit forces.[47] Although these commonalities present significant challenges (because of inherent differences), they do provide a fertile ground for interaction, dialogue and understanding between Pentecostals and those to whom they present the Gospel.

Similarly, the ones to whom they have preached the Gospel have more easily understood the message they brought because of its association with and understanding of supernatural phenomena.[48] The concept of a 'power encounter' is familiar to Pentecostals and pagans alike and the basis for some common ground between them and those who live in animistic societies or whose history has a marked tradition of spirit forces.[49]

Kim suggests that the presence of Shamanistic views in Korea helped prepare the way for Pentecostal teaching concerning the spirit world.[50] Deliverance from such malevolent spirit forces not only easily fits the worldview of many in the Majority world but also the readiness of Pentecostals to engage in the ministry to remove demonic forces from the lives of people has resulted in their being welcomed by many.[51] However, Nwankwo identifies problems in this respect noting, for example, that 'The Prosperity Message also resonates with the wholistic worldview that survives in Africa', the danger

---

[47] O. Onyinah, 'Contemporary "Witchdemonology" in Africa', *IRM* 93.370/371 (July–Oct. 2004), pp. 330–45 (333).

[48] Amenyo, 'The Charismatic Renewal Movement', pp. 180–83; J.C. Ma, 'A Comparison of Two Worldviews: Kankana-Ey and Pentecostal', in Ma and Menzies (eds), *Pentecostalism in Context*, pp. 265–90; idem, 'Pentecostal Challenges', pp. 183–202 (200–01); Anderson, *An Introduction to Pentecostalism*, pp. 63, 197–205; Yong, 'Not Knowing Where the Wind Blows', pp. 85–6, 99–100; H.W. Turner, *African Independent Churches* (Oxford: Oxford University Press, 1967) vol. 2, p. 368; C. de Wet, 'The Challenge of Signs and Wonders in World Missions for the Twentieth Century', in L.G. McClung Jr (ed.), *Azusa Street and Beyond: Pentecostal Missions and Church Growth in the Twentieth Century* (South Plainfield: Bridge, 1986), pp. 161–65; Chia, 'Biblical Theology of Power Manifestation', pp. 29–31; Sepùlveda, 'Indigenous Pentecostalism', in Anderson and Hollenweger (eds), *Pentecostals after a Century*, p. 111.

[49] Chia, 'Biblical Theology of Power Manifestation', p. 20–1; Ma, 'Full Circle Mission', p. 20; R.M. Gen, 'The Phenomenon of Miracles and Divine Infliction in Luke-Acts: Their Theological Significance', *Pneuma* 11.1 (1989), pp. 3–19.

[50] S.G. Kim, 'Pentecostalism, Shamanism and Capitalism within Contemporary Korean Society', in Stålsett (ed.), *Spirits of Globalization*, pp. 23–38; Yoo, 'Pentecostalism in Korea', pp. 171–74; Myung, 'The Spiritual Dimension of Church Growth', p. 235; Lee, 'Pentecostal Type Distinctives', p. 298; Jeong, 'The Formation and Development', pp. 26–30.

[51] P. Gifford, 'The Complex Provenance of Some Elements of African Pentecostal Theology', in Corton and Marshall-Fratani (eds), *Between Babel and Pentecost*, pp. 62–79 (65–74).

being that it will be accepted uncritically because it reflects the African world-view of blessings becoming available if the spirits are appeased or pleased, theirs being a cult of dependency on the spirits.[52] Similarly, Yung cautions against simply accepting that a non-Western worldview (which allows for the possibility of supernatural and spiritual activity) is correct because it more closely fits with the Pentecostal view of supernatural manifestations and calls for the development of a Christian worldview as a protection against slipping into syncretism.[53]

However, although syncretism is a danger,[54] the more positive potential is that such common ground may provide the opportunity for 'truth-encounters'[55] with the message of the Gospel and demonstrations of the power of the Spirit that can result in salvation. A theology without the presence of the dynamic Spirit can become rationalistic and not expectant of the miraculous; it can also be blind to the supernatural, be it good or evil. Pentecostals who combine a theological framework with an appreciation of the role of the Spirit can provide a more appropriate context for discerning and analysing extant supernatural phenomena while also anticipating divinely inspired manifestations of the Spirit.[56] Furthermore, Anderson argues that 'the fact that so many manifestations of the Spirit . . . have parallels in pre-Christian religion should not unduly alarm us' for 'the Holy Spirit has sanctified for his use religious expressions that were found in traditional Africa', offering drumming, clapping, dancing and repetitive singing.[57] Even where there have been differences in doctrine and practice, the emphasis on the Spirit and the role he plays in the life of the believer and the Church has formed a flexible but embracing framework in which the various strands of Pentecostalism may find room to operate effectively.

Experience

The place of experience has been instrumental in Pentecostals presenting their message successfully.[58] They have assumed that authentic spirituality

[52] Nwankwo, 'You Have Received', p. 68.
[53] Yung, 'Pentecostalism and the Asian Church', p. 53.
[54] M.S. Clark, 'The Challenge of Contextualization and Syncretism to Pentecostal Theology and Missions in Africa', *JAM* 3.1 (2001), pp. 79–99; J.C. Ma, 'Santuala: A Case of Pentecostal Syncretism'', *AJPS* 3.1 (2000), pp. 61–82; Hedlund, 'Critique of Pentecostal Mission', p. 88.
[55] Ma, 'A Comparison of Two Worldviews', p. 290.
[56] Yong, *Discerning the Spirit(s)*, pp. 134, 162, 319; S. Aigbe, 'Pentecostal Mission and Tribal People Groups', in Dempster, Klaus and Petersen (eds), *Called and Empowered*, pp. 165–79 (173).
[57] A.H. Anderson, 'Stretching the Definitions? Pneumatology and "Syncretism" in African Pentecostalism', *JPT* 10.1 (2001), pp. 98–119 (116–17).
[58] Pomerville, *The Third Force in Mission*, p. 104; Lord, 'The Voluntary Principle', p. 91.

has an experiential dimension and this has been championed in their evangelism and worship which is often dynamic and exuberant.[59] Lord believes that 'experience, enlightened and empowered by the Spirit, is still at the heart of Pentecostal missiology'.[60] The spontaneity of Pentecostal worship with its emphasis on oral and narrative expressions of praise and dynamic preaching has resulted in Pentecostalism more easily being accommodated into a range of different settings than a more liturgically based spirituality might allow.[61] The Pentecostal emphasis on freedom initiated by the Spirit which encourages all participants to engage with God personally has further enhanced the attractiveness of Pentecostal spirituality.[62] The emphasis on experience also makes Pentecostals most attractive in the post-modern climate which also stresses the importance of individual choice and expression in experiencing one's spirituality. This also poses a great danger in that experience as the determinator of authentic spirituality can lead to vacuous faith. Cox, however, views many of the poor of the world who 'experience the globalizing landscape' as experiencing bewildering chaos. For them, 'Pentecostal worship with its ear-splitting noise and tumultuous prayer is something of a homeopathic cure. It invites people to plunge into the chaos in order to overcome it, by the power of the Holy Spirit'.[63] It offers the possibility of an experience with God that will touch the emotions of people and respond to their aspirations while also promising an eternal dimension that will rescue them from all that imprisons and oppresses them in the present. The place of personal testimony and the presentation of the Gospel in popular language including narrative and story, rather than doctrine and creed, appealing to the emotions rather than the mind are also important features.[64] It is in this regard that Pentecostals may be offering something primal with regard to spirituality in its ecstatic form, a dimension that is dynamically present in Pentecostal worship.

Holistic Support

As a result of the holistic message that has frequently included redemptive aspects of salvation other than forgiveness of sins (including women's issues, disaster relief, provision of education, healthcare and the arresting of poverty), they have found willing listeners especially among the poor and

---

[59] Ayuk, 'The Pentecostal Transformation', p. 191.

[60] A.M. Lord, 'The Holy Spirit and Contextualization', *AJPS* 4.2 (2001), pp. 201–13 (205).

[61] Anderson, 'Towards a Pentecostal Missiology', p. 43; Ayuk, 'Portrait of a Nigerian Pentecostal Missionary', p. 131–32.

[62] McClung, 'Spontaneous Strategy of the Spirit', p. 73.

[63] Cox, 'Spirits of Globalization', p. 17.

[64] Sepulveda, 'Reflections on the Pentecostal Contribution', p. 93.

the marginalized.[65] In particular, the Pentecostal message seeks to bring hope and a spiritual and dynamic perspective to people who live in contexts of powerlessness, deprivation and uprootedness often caused by societal crises.[66] Particularly among the Majority world, Pentecostalism is a popular religion because it appeals to the felt needs of the many.[67] Rather than concentrate on the dissection of doctrinal minutiae, it disseminates a message of hope, particularly of relevance to the poor and oppressed.[68] The receptivity of Pentecostalism in many (especially poor) countries is largely due to the community that is formed by Pentecostals whose familial and caring priorities have provided much needed therapy on a number of levels as has its readiness to incorporate the newest member and offer them a place and a role in the ministry of the church.[69]

Flexibility

A readiness to be pragmatic and flexible, rather than abide by a doctrinaire formula of received practice that was formulated in and for a different setting, has also served many Pentecostal missionaries well,[70] Saayman reflecting on the fact that often mission policies were, in the past, helpfully decided in the mission context rather than by the mission board in the country from which the missionary came.[71] A positive consequence of this perspective is that Pentecostals are prepared to rethink their mission strategies where appropriate.[72] Thus, since Pentecostalism (and the world) is increasingly being urbanized, the readiness of Pentecostals to evangelize their urban

---

[65] Pomerville, 'The Pentecostals and Growth', p. 153; Ayuk, 'Portrait of a Nigerian Pentecostal Missionary', p. 126; Suico, 'Pentecostalism and Social Change', p. 198; Yung, 'The Missiological Challenge', in Ma, Menzies and Bae, *David Yonggi Cho*, p. 70; I.M. Satyavrata, 'Contextual Perspectives on Pentecostalism as a Global Culture: A South Asian View', in Dempster, Klaus and Petersen (eds), *The Globalization of Pentecostalism*, pp. 203–21 (209–10); M. Wilkinson, 'Faith-Based Social Services: Some Observations for Assessing Pentecostal Social Action', *Transformation* 24.2 (2007), pp. 71–9; Ma, 'Selected Areas for Pentecostal Mission Studies', p. 10.

[66] Ma, 'Asian (Classical) Pentecostal Theology', pp. 64–8; Sepulveda, 'Reflections on the Pentecostal Contribution', p. 98; Wagner, 'A Church Growth Perspective', pp. 273–74; C.E. Self, 'Conscientization, Conversion and Convergence: Reflections on Base Communities and Emerging Pentecostalism in Latin America', *Pneuma* 14.1 (1992), pp. 59–72 (69–70).

[67] F.E. Manning, 'Pentecostalism: Christianity and Reputation', in Glazier (ed.), *Perspectives on Pentecostalism*, pp. 177–87 (181–82).

[68] Westmeier, *Protestant Pentecostalism in Latin America*, pp. 127–31.

[69] Aigbe, 'Pentecostal Mission and Tribal People Groups', p. 173; Chesnut, *Born Again in Brazil*, pp. 104–07.

[70] Hodges, 'A Pentecostal's View', p. 86.

[71] Saayman, 'Some Reflections on the Development', p. 42.

neighbours is resulting in consequent societal transformation of some areas of the inner cities (including the development of drug rehabilitation centres and other vital socially significant ministries) and the establishment of mega churches.[73] This readiness to evangelize in flexible frameworks has been present from the earliest days when Pentecostals would rent shops, halls and other town centre buildings to function as places where the Gospel could be preached and to erect tents for evangelistic missions. It is also evident in the numbers of radio and television channels that have been established, often in association with city-wide missions.[74] McGee provides examples of the variety in mission activity that included sharing the Gospel and initiating projects that sought to provide for the physical, educational and financial needs of the people, building and administering schools, orphanages and medical centres.[75]

The Second Coming of Jesus

Pentecostals have traditionally been associated with and motivated by the belief that Jesus' return is imminent.[76] Such a conviction ensures that their mission mandate is one that all are to be engaged in.[77] This has resulted in an ever urgent race to preach the Gospel to as many people as possible before Jesus returns, when the opportunity to come to faith will be terminated (Mt. 24.14, 'This gospel of the kingdom shall be preached in all the world for a witness . . . then shall the end come').[78] Indeed, Boddy, an early

---

[72] McGee, 'Pentecostals and Their Various Strategies', in Dempster, Klaus and Petersen (eds), *Called and Empowered*, pp. 203–24; Aigbe, 'Pentecostal Mission and Tribal People Groups', in Dempster, Klaus and Petersen (eds), *Called and Empowered*, pp. 165–79.

[73] McClung, 'Spontaneous Strategy of the Spirit', p. 78; Cerillo, 'Pentecostals and the City', in Dempster, Klaus and Petersen (eds), *Called and Empowered*, pp. 98–119; L.G. McClung, 'Another 100 Years? Which Way for Pentecostal Missions?', in McClung (ed.), *Azusa Street and Beyond*, pp. 137–48 (145–46).

[74] McClung, 'Evangelism', pp. 619–20; W.E. Warner, 'Radio', in Burgess and van der Maas (eds), *NIDPCM*, pp. 1015–016; D.J. Hedges, 'Television', in Burgess and van der Maas (eds), *NIDPCM*, pp. 1118–120.

[75] G.B. McGee, 'Saving Souls or Saving Lives? The Tension between Ministries of Word and Deed in Assemblies of God Missiology', *Paraclete* 28.4 (1994), pp. 11–23 (13–20); Anderson, 'Burning Its Way into Every Nation', p. 12; Menzies, R.P., 'Complete Evangelism: A Review Article', *JPT* 13 (1998), pp. 133–42.

[76] Faupel, *The Everlasting Gospel*, pp. 21–7.

[77] C. Nienkirchen, 'Conflicting Vision of the Past: The Prophetic Use of History in the Early American Pentecostal-Charismatic Movements', in K. Poewe (ed.), *Charismatic Christianity as a Global Culture* (Columbia: University of South Carolina Press, 1994), pp. 119–133 (121); Dyer, 'Missionary Candidates', pp. 85–6, 89; Anderson, 'Burning Its Way into Every Nation', pp. 3–4; L.G. McClung, 'Missiology', in Burgess, McGee and Alexander (eds), *DPCM*, pp. 607–08; Saayman, 'Some Reflections on the Development', p. 43; Wagner, 'A Church Growth Perspective', pp. 276–77.

Pentecostal, concluded that, given the rapid increase in the translation of parts of the Bible into many languages, 'We cannot see that there is anything now between us and the Coming of the End'.[79] Although the sense of eschatological fervency may have reduced, there is nevertheless, on the part of some, the belief that mission is a significant means of ushering in the eschatological age. Lord argues that eschatology can still motivate mission if key characteristics of the future kingdom are anticipated as being potential in the world today.[80] However, Ma is more concerned,[81] writing, 'The complete absence of the eschatological message in almost a generation is critically worrisome'. The original impetus to evangelism motivated by eschatology needs to be rediscovered. Similarly, eschatological views need to be focused on as a stimulus to mission rather than in order to dogmatically establish one's eschatological timetable.[82]

Transfer of Ownership

Although early Pentecostals succumbed to the same paternalistic tendencies of other Western based missionaries,[83] many Pentecostal missions have recognized the value of transferring ownership of new churches to indigenous Christians, enabling them to determine their future and to contextualize

[78] Klaus, 'The Holy Spirit', pp. 330, 335; Anderson, *An Introduction to Pentecostalism*, pp. 217–20; Petersen, *Not by Might nor by Power*, p. 9–12; G.B. McGee, 'Pentecostal and Charismatic Missions', in J.M. Phillips, R.T. Coote (eds), *Toward the Twenty-First Century in Christian Mission: Essays in Honor of Gerald H. Anderson* (Grand Rapids: Eerdmans, 1993), pp. 41–56; Faupel, *The Everlasting Gospel*, pp. 36–47; McClung, 'Try to Get People Saved', p. 36, 38–40; Frodsham, *With Signs Following*, p. 275–76.

[79] A. Boddy, 'Seven Signs of His Coming', *Confidence* (Dec. 1910), p. 287.

[80] A.M. Lord, 'Mission Eschatology: A Framework for Mission in the Spirit', *JPT* 11 (1997), pp. 111–23 (114, 116–22).

[81] Ma, 'Selected Areas for Pentecostal Mission Studies', p. 5; idem, 'Pentecostal Eschatology: What Happened When the Wave Hit the West End of the Ocean', in H. Hunter, C.M. Robeck Jr (eds), *The Azusa Street Revival and Its Legacy* (Cleveland: Pathway Press, 2006), pp. 227–42.

[82] G. Menzies, G.L. Anderson, 'D.W. Kerr and Eschatological Diversity in the Assemblies of God', *Paraclete* 27.1 (1993), pp. 8–16.

[83] Anderson, 'Christian Missionaries', pp. 4–29; idem, 'The Dubious Legacy of Charles Parham', pp. 58–61; McGee, 'Pentecostals and Their Various Strategies', pp. 210–11; A.L. La Ruffa, 'Pentecostalism in Puerto Rican Society', in Glazier, *Perspectives on Pentecostalism*, pp. 49–65 (60); M.O. Williams, *Partnership in Missions* (Springfield: Division of Foreign Missions, 1979), p. 140; Westmeier, *Protestant Pentecostalism in Latin America*, pp. 69–71; W.J. Hollenweger ('Evangelism: A Non-Colonial Model', *JPT* 7 (1995), pp. 108–15) criticizes colonial attitudes in which Western values and Christian perceptions are presented to the global community with the assumption that they reflect the authentic expression of Christianity.

their faith and praxis interdependently in ways that are most appropriate to their setting.[84] Anderson speaks of the 'remarkable ability of the Pentecostal gospel to spread in different cultural contexts',[85] Hedlund noting that rather than presenting 'the gospel in foreign dress . . . Pentecostals responded with local cultural distinctives'.[86] They have attempted to offer solutions where the social realities may be different in one setting as compared to another.[87] This ability to 'translate the Protestant message into the forms of expression of the local popular culture' is a major reason for the growth of Pentecostalism.[88]

Melvin Hodges was influential in this regard, arguing that a national church should not be dependent on foreign resources.[89] Similarly, Klaus singles out the influence of Roland Allen on early Pentecostal mission strategy, especially with regard to the Pauline model of church planting as described in the book of Acts, McGee writing that 'Pentecostals were among Allen's best students'.[90] Yoo attributes the readiness of early Pentecostal missionaries

---

[84] Kärkkäinen, 'Missiology: Pentecostal and Charismatic', p. 877; McClung, 'Spontaneous Strategy of the Spirit', pp. 77–8; Hodges, 'A Pentecostal's View', p. 84; Lord, 'The Voluntary Principle', p. 93; Anderson, 'Towards a Pentecostal Missiology', p. 37; Suico, 'Pentecostalism and Social Change', p. 197; M. Harper, 'The Holy Spirit Acts in the Church, Its Structures, Its Sacramentality, Its Worship and Sacraments', *One in Christ* 12 (1976), pp. 319–28 (323); B.D. Klaus, L.O. Triplett, 'National Leadership in Pentecostal Missions', in Dempster, Klaus and Petersen (eds), *Called and Empowered*, pp. 225–41; O. Onyinah, 'Pentecostalism and the African Diaspora: An Examination of the Missions Activities of the Church of Pentecost', *Pneuma* 26.2 (2004), pp. 216–41 (230–32); J.L. Amstutz, 'Foursquare Missions: Doing More with Less', *Pneuma* 16.1 (1994), pp. 63–80 (75–8); G.B. McGee, 'Pentecostal Phenomena and Revivals in India: Implications for Indigenous Church Leadership', *IBMR* 20 (July 1996), pp. 112–17.

[85] Anderson, 'Burning Its Way into Every Nation', pp. 11–12.

[86] Hedlund, 'Critique of Pentecostal Mission', p. 69.

[87] L. Svensson, *Den växande förmsamlingen* (Örebrö: Evangeliipress, 1987).

[88] Sepúlveda, 'Indigenous Pentecostalism', p. 128; Cox, *Fire from Heaven*, p. 259; A.H. Anderson, 'The Gospel and Culture in Pentecostal Missions in the Third World', *Missionalia* 27.2 (1999), pp. 220–30.

[89] M. Hodges, *The Indigenous Church* (Springfield: Gospel Publishing House, 1953), p. 13; idem, *A Theology of the Church and Its Mission: A Pentecostal Perspective* (Springfield: Gospel Publishing House, 1977); idem, *The Indigenous Church and the Missionary* (Springfield: Gospel Publishing House, 1978); Hedlund, 'Critique of Pentecostal Mission', pp. 80–2; G.B. McGee, 'The Legacy of Melvin Hodges', *IBMR* 22.1 (Jan. 1998), pp. 2–24 (21); writing in 1999, W.J. Hollenweger ('Crucial Issues for Pentecostals', in Anderson and Hollenweger (eds), *Pentecostals after a Century*, pp. 176–91 (176)) described his work as 'the most significant on mission the Pentecostal movement has yet produced'.

[90] McGee, 'The Legacy of Melvin Hodges', p. 21; idem, 'Missions, Overseas', pp. 896–97; C.H. Long and A. Rowthorn, 'The Legacy of Roland Allen', *IBMR* 13.2 (1989), pp. 65–70

to encourage 'self-propagation, self-government and self-support' as major factors in the adoption of Christianity by Koreans.[91] Similarly, Matviuk concludes that Latin American Pentecostalism has grown largely because of its readiness to develop in association with natural and culturally appropriate forms of leadership and a collectivist mindset, resulting in a 'leadership that is fully contextual and deeply native'.[92] While accepting the benefits of this emphasis, Carter observes the value of the development of a coactive relationship between national churches and missionaries in which interdependence has a part to play in the development towards independence.[93]

Some Ways Forward

- Increasing secularization, economic disharmony and de-Christianization in the West provide a challenging context for mission[94] and these need to be uppermost in Pentecostal mission strategy. Thus, Bonino explores the danger of an overconcentration on missions 'abroad' to the detriment of needs at 'home'.[95]
- The danger of becoming middle class, respectable and adopting a nominal form of spirituality is a constant threat.[96] Allied to this is the 'potential neglect of the masses'[97] and the poor.[98] There is a danger that Pentecostals

(65–6); Klaus, 'The Holy Spirit', p. 336; Kärkkäinen, 'Missiology: Pentecostal and Charismatic', p. 878; Lord, 'The Voluntary Principle', p. 93. In particular, R. Allen, *Missionary Methods: St. Paul's or Ours* (London: Robert Scott, 1912), *Missionary Principles* (London: Robert Scott, 1913) and *Pentecost and the World: The Revelation of the Holy Spirit in Acts of the Apostles* (London: Oxford University Press, 1917); Saayman, 'Some Reflections on the Development', p. 43.

[91] Yoo, 'Pentecostalism in Korea', p. 171.

[92] S. Matviuk, 'Pentecostal Leadership Development and Church Growth in Latin America', *AJPS* 5.1 (2002), pp. 155–72 (165).

[93] J.F. Carter, 'The Indigenous Principle Revisited towards a Coactive Model of Missionary Activity', *AJPS* 1.1 (1998), pp. 73–82; Indeed, Makuyan Pentecostalism may be one example where indigenous practices would benefit from input from the wider Pentecostal family; see Nagasaw, 'Makuya Pentecostalism', pp. 203–18.

[94] Kärkkäinen, 'Truth on Fire', pp. 34–6.

[95] J.M. Bonino, 'Pentecostal Missions Is More Than What It Claims', *Pneuma* 16.2 (1994), pp. 283–88.

[96] Wagner, 'Characteristics of Pentecostal Church Growth', pp. 130–31; McClung, 'Another 100 Years?', pp. 141–42; idem, 'New Cultures. New Challenges. New Churches', in Smith (ed.) *Pentecostals from the Inside Out*, pp. 105–19 (113–15); Kraft, 'A Third Wave Perspective', pp. 306–07.

[97] Wagner, 'Another 100 Years?', p. 141.

[98] Chia, 'Biblical Theology of Power Manifestation', p. 28.

are increasingly being less evangelistic[99] and more complacent[100] and Johnson calls for an increased impetus in reaching the non-evangelized world.[101] The testimony of believers who are suffering for their faith is a constant challenge to others to check that their evangelistic fervour is not diminishing. Although evangelistic methods are increasingly widespread, many Pentecostals still rely on the services of a visiting evangelist to increase the numbers of Christians in their local churches.[102] Kuzmic, speaking of life in a Marxist setting, encourages Pentecostals not to withdraw into a ghetto-style faith driven setting or exit a difficult situation but rather to be 'marked by a theology of the cross'. He concludes, 'Withdrawal is preoccupied with survival; Spirit-filled Pentecostals are concerned with revival'.[103]

- Anderson identifies 'parochialism and rivalry' as making ecumenical cooperation problematic.[104] Furthermore, Pentecostals have often mixed evangelism with proselytism to the detriment of interchurch relations.[105] The value of dialoguing with other Christian traditions has been advocated by some to ensure that competitive practices and insensitivities can be diminished, and understanding and cooperation be increased.[106] However, traditionally, this has not been a priority for Pentecostals. Pentecostals were present at the Second Congress of the Lausanne Movement in 1989 but they were not significantly represented and not without opposition from some Pentecostals and non-Pentecostals. The relationship with the Mission arm of the WCC has been distant though there have been developing relationships since the 1990s especially in the consultations

---

[99] Wagner, 'Another 100 Years?', p. 141; Lugo (*Spirit and Power*, p. 21) records that 61% of Pentecostals in the countries researched stated that they share their faith with unbelievers at least once a week (ranging from 37% (India) to 72% (Guatemala)).

[100] McClung, 'Another 100 Years?', pp. 140–41; Gajewski and Wawrzeniuk, 'A Historical and Theological Analysis', pp. 45–6.

[101] T.M. Johnson, 'Global Plans in the Pentecostal/Charismatic Tradition and the Challenge of the Unevangelized World, World A', in Jongeneel (ed.), *Pentecost, Mission and Ecumenism*, pp. 197–206.

[102] P. Lewis, 'Evangelism', in Burgess (ed.), *EPCC*, pp. 183–86.

[103] P. Kuzmic, 'Pentecostals Respond to Marxism', in Dempster, Klaus and Petersen (eds), *Called and Empowered*, pp. 143–64 (151, 155).

[104] Anderson, *An Introduction to Pentecostalism*, p. 234; idem, 'Signs and Blunders', pp. 193–210; Hedlund, 'Critique of Pentecostal Mission', p. 86; V-M. Kärkkäinen, 'The Working of the Spirit of God in Creation and in the People of God: The Pneumatology of Wolfhart Pannenberg', *Pneuma* 26.1 (2004), pp. 17–35.

[105] Ma, 'Selected Areas for Pentecostal Mission Studies', pp. 11–12.

[106] J. Gros, 'An Ecumenical Perspective on Pentecostal Missions', in Dempster, Klaus and Petersen (eds), *Called and Empowered*, pp. 285–98; A.H. Anderson, 'Diversity in the Definition of "Pentecostalism/Charismatic" and Its Ecumenical Implications', *Mission Studies* 19.2 (2002), pp. 40–55.

on healing and exorcism when Pentecostal scholars had leading roles. Those Pentecostals who have engaged in such dialogue often do so without the support or active backing of their denominational leaders. It has often been left to Pentecostal scholars to explore these potential links rather than other leaders in Pentecostal communities. Allied to this is the increasing rise of institutionalization in Pentecostalism that can result in a marked decline of flexibility and spontaneity.[107] In their place can come consolidation, bureaucratization and structuralism and a preference to determine one's agenda without consulting or dialoguing with others.

- Triumphalism and elitism are dangers;[108] a theology of power where success is always assumed needs to be balanced by a theology of weakness, best reflected in the cross.[109] The excesses of the prosperity gospel, the phenomenon of the megastar leader and overly triumphalistic spirituality are issues to be guarded against.[110] Cox identifies Pentecostal worship as belonging to the age of the supermarket and the encouragement of immediate gratification, concluding with a warning, 'Pentecostalism is almost tailormade for the market-consumer culture'.[111] Such a signal, where appropriate, must be heeded.
- The limited social involvement of some Pentecostals has been an unhelpful aspect of Pentecostal mission.[112] Increasingly, there have been exceptions to this stance[113] and it has been a commendable feature of Scandinavian and Finnish Pentecostalism for many years.[114]
- Syncretism is a danger especially where the Pentecostal worldview, that includes a belief in spiritual forces as well as an expectation of supernatural

---

[107] McClung, 'Another 100 Years?', p. 143.
[108] McGee, 'Pentecostal Missiology', pp. 275–82.
[109] Satyavrata, 'Contextual Perspectives on Pentecostalism', pp. 212–13.
[110] Hedlund, 'Critique of Pentecostal Mission', pp. 87–8; Kraft, 'A Third Wave Perspective', p. 307; V-M. Kärkkäinen, 'Theology of the Cross: A Stumbling Block to Pentecostal/Charismatic Spirituality?', in Ma and Menzies, *The Spirit and Spirituality*, pp. 150–63.
[111] Cox, 'Spirits of Globalization', p. 20.
[112] Satyavrata, 'Contextual Perspectives on Pentecostalism', pp. 214–16.
[113] G.B. McGee, 'The Lord's Pentecostal Missionary Movement'. The Restorationist Impulse of a Modern Mission Movement', *AJPS* 8.1 (2005), pp. 49–65 (57–8); B. Graham (ed.), *Letters from Lillian* (Springfield: Assemblies of God Publishing House, 1983); Petersen, *Not By Might nor by Power*, pp. 186–233.
[114] D. Halberg, 'Swedish Missionary Outreach', *World Pentecost* 1 (1973), pp. 22–3; A. Hämäläinen, *Leadership: The Spirit and the Structure. Missiological Perspectives for Designing Church and Mission Bodies* (unpublished doctoral dissertation, Gordon-Conwell Theological Seminary, 2005), pp. 311–12; D.D. Bundy, 'Swedish Pentecostal Mission Theory and Practice to 1930: Foundational Values in Conflict' (SPS/EPCRA conference paper, 1995).

occurrences, overlaps with that of the people who are adopting it. The potential is that a group may be 'more Pentecostal but less Christian'.[115]

- Anderson argues that the pragmatic nature of Pentecostal mission, especially in the past has resulted in an absence of a clear theology of mission.[116] However, increasingly, Pentecostals have engaged in dialogue concerning mission strategies and have successfully developed programmes and methodologies that include the major components of the Spirit and the Bible.[117] Similarly, Cho argues for the adoption of organized programmes of training and discipling of believers in order that churches might mature and grow.[118] Similarly, Hedlund notes a tendency among some to not engage in careful reflection regarding exorcism, too often assuming that a disorder is demonic without any apparent awareness of the possibility that there may be another explanation, including the possibility of a psychological cause for the behaviour manifested.[119]

- There is a danger that in the desire to train leaders, training centres may become formal instead of dynamic and the training and the teachers be more concerned with orthodoxy rather than openness to the Spirit. College faculties need to guard against concentrating on enabling their students to gain good degrees instead of also developing their spirituality, developing academic prowess to the exclusion of spiritual power, being elitist rather than evangelistic, professional and not also Pentecostal. Conversely, there is a danger of not following supernatural revivals and conversions with careful theological training of leaders and discipling of the converts.[120] Similarly, there is a need to ensure that 'power encounters' must be associated with 'truth encounters' in which the initial reception to the greater power of Jesus is developed into a committed allegiance to Jesus and an ongoing relationship categorized by spiritual, ethical and societal transformation.[121]

---

[115] Ma, 'Doing Theology in the Philippines', p. 231; Kraft, 'A Third Wave Perspective', p. 306; Lartey, 'Healing: Tradition and Pentecostalism', pp. 75–81.

[116] Anderson, 'Missional Orientation and Its Implications', p. 136.

[117] McClung, 'Spontaneous Strategy of the Spirit', pp. 71–6; idem, 'Another 100 Years?', pp. 137–48; Pomerville, 'The Pentecostals and Growth', p. 151; Hodges, 'A Pentecostal's View', pp. 83–9.

[118] Cho, 'The Secret Behind', pp. 99–104 (103–04); also Hollenweger, 'Crucial Issues for Pentecostals', p. 176.

[119] Hedlund, 'Critique of Pentecostal Mission', p. 91; Kraft, 'A Third Wave Perspective', p. 308.

[120] Dermawan, 'A Study of Nias Revival', p. 262.

[121] Kraft, 'Allegiance, Truth and Power Encounters', pp. 218–30.

8

HEALING, EXORCISM AND SUFFERING

Introduction

Pentecostals believe in the possibility of divine healing as a legitimate expression of the ministry of the Church, entrusted to it by Jesus and mediated through the power of the Holy Spirit.[1] Dayton[2] contends in his survey of the rise of the Healing Movements that, 'Pentecostalism . . . understood itself to be restoring a lost concern of the Early Church' while Poloma[3] describes it as one of the major reasons for the growth of Pentecostalism. The AoG, in an official positional paper, describes it as 'an integral part of the Gospel'

---

[1] cf. Lugo (*Spirit and Power*, pp. 5, 15) records that 74% of Pentecostals in the countries researched testified that they have witnessed or experienced divine healing, lowest in South Korea (56%) and the USA (62%); A.H. Anderson, 'Pentecostals, Healing and Ecumenism', *IRM* 93.370/371 (July–Oct. 2004), pp. 486–96; idem, *African Reformation: African Initiated Christianity in the 20th Century* (Trenton, NJ: Africa World Press, 2001), pp. 290–304; D.E. Harrell Jr, *All Things Are Possible: The Healing and Charismatic Revivals in Modern America* (Bloomington: Indiana University Press, 1975; T. Cross, 'The Doctrine of Healing', Y.C. Han, W. Griffith (eds), *Transforming Power: Dimensions of the Gospel* (Cleveland: Pathway Press, 2001), pp. 179–231; D.W. Dayton, 'The Rise of the Evangelical Healing Movement in Nineteenth Century America', *Pneuma* 4.1 (1982), pp. 1–18; Clearly and Stewart-Gambino, *Power, Politics and Pentecostals*, pp. 8, 14, 16, 206–07; F. Martin, 'Gifts of Healing', in Burgess, McGee (eds), *DPCM*, pp. 350–53; P.G. Chappell, 'Healing Movements', in Burgess, McGee (eds), *DPCM*, pp. 353–74; Blumhofer, *The Assemblies of God*, pp. 26–36; Poloma, *The Assemblies of God*, pp. 53–63; J.R. Goff, 'Questions of Health and Wealth', in Smith (ed.), *Pentecostals from the Inside Out*, pp. 60–70; F.H. Kamsteeg, 'Pentecostal Healing and Power: A Peruvian Case', in A. Droogers, G. Huizer and H. Siebers (eds), *Popular Power in Latin American Religions* (Saarbrücken: Verlag Breitenbach Publishers, 1991), pp. 196–218; Kay, *Pentecostals in Britain*, pp. 82–106; C. Währisch-Oblau, 'God Can Make Us Healthy Through and Through: On Prayers for the Sick and

and 'the privilege of all believers',[4] while Marty views it as the 'second Pentecostal distinctive'.[5] That is not to say that Pentecostalism initiated this healing emphasis.[6] Divine healing was a significant feature of early Holiness groups, especially in the USA,[7] and to a lesser degree in the UK,[8] in the latter years of the nineteenth century[9] and many of the current beliefs and practices of Pentecostals may be traced back to these groups.

Healing Experiences in Christian Churches in China and African Immigrant Congregations', *IRM* 90.356/357 (2001), pp. 87–99; M. Bergunder, 'Miracle Healing and Exorcism: The South Indian Pentecostal Movement in the Context of Popular Hinduism', *IRM* 90.356/357 (2001), pp. 103–12; M.J. Cartledge, *Practical Theology. Charismatic and Empirical Perspectives* (Carlisle: Paternoster Press, 2003), pp. 199–214; D.N. Hudson, 'Early British Pentecostals and Their Relationship to Health, Healing and Medicine', *AJPS* 6.2 (2003), pp. 283–301; A. Mohr, 'An Historical Perspective on Faith Healing Evangelism and the Establishment of Zionism and Aladura in Africa' (SPS conference paper, Cleveland, 2007), pp. 213–20; K. Warrington, 'The Teaching and Praxis of supernatural healing of British Pentecostals, of John Wimber and Kenneth Hagin in the Light of an Analysis of the Healing Ministry of Jesus as Recorded in the Gospels' (unpublished doctoral dissertation, Kings College, University of London, 1999), pp. 21–52.

2   Dayton, *Theological Roots of Pentecostalism*, p. 115.

3   M.M. Poloma, 'An Empirical Study of Perceptions of Healing among Assemblies of God members', *Pneuma* 7.1 (1985), pp. 61–77 (61); see also Kim, *History and Theology of Korean Pentecostalism*, pp. 112–14, 146–47.

4   AoG, 'Our Position on Divine Healing', *Paraclete* 9.2 (1975), pp. 7–13 (7, 10); cf. J.R. Williams, *Renewal Theology. Salvation, the Holy Spirit, and Christian Living* (Grand Rapids: Zondervan, 1990), p. 256; C.B. Johns, 'Healing and Deliverance: A Pentecostal Perspective', in Moltmann and Kuschel, *Pentecostal Movements*, (London: SCM, 1996), pp. 45–51 (45).

5   M. Marty, 'Pentecostalism in American Piety and Practice', in Synan (ed.), *Aspects of Pentecostal-Charismatic Origins*, pp. 193–233 (218). In this, he adapts the words of Bruner (*A Theology of the Holy Spirit*) who described healing as 'almost a second Pentecostal distinctive'.

6   R.A.N. Kydd, 'Jesus, Saints and Relics: Approaching the Early Church through Healing', *JPT* 2 (1993), pp. 91–104.

7   V. Synan, 'A Healer in the House? A Historical Perspective on Healing in the Pentecostal/ Charismatic Tradition', *AJPS* 3.2 (2000), pp. 189–201; N. Hardesty, *Faith Cure. Divine Healing in the Holiness and Pentecostal Movements* (Peabody: Hendrickson, 2003), pp. 27–55, 119–28; Dayton, *Theological Roots of Pentecostalism*, pp. 115–41.

8   Hudson, 'Early British Pentecostals', pp. 284–94.

9   See Charles Cullis, A.B. Simpson, A.J. Gordon, J.A. Dowie, W.E. Boardman, Carrie Judd Montgomery and Maria Woodworth-Etter, the latter two joining the Pentecostal movement. D. Dayton notes that interest in divine healing may be identified in the last decades of the nineteenth century, thus pre-dating the rise of Pentecostalism ('"Christian Perfection" to the "Baptism of the Holy Ghost"', in Synan (ed.), *Aspects of Pentecostal-Charismatic Origins*, pp. 39–54 (51)). Divine healing was also debated and practiced in the Wesleyan-Holiness movement in the second half of the nineteenth century (M.E. Dieter, 'Wesleyan-Holiness Aspects of Pentecostal Origins', in Synan (ed.),

So central is it to Pentecostalism that when Pentecostals were condemned by the world Christian Fundamentals Association in Chicago in 1928, they were described as 'tongues-talkers and faith healers'.[10] This emphasis on divine healing is noticeable in Pentecostalism[11] throughout the world, support resting on OT[12] and NT texts,[13] reinforced by occurrences of healings throughout its history.[14]

However, the occurrence of healings and the belief in the ongoing nature of such phenomena is no guarantee for the internal coherence or consistency of Pentecostal teaching or practice concerning such an issue.[15] Beliefs that

Aspects of Pentecostal-Charismatic Origins, pp. 55–80 (68–9); Wacker, 'Travail of a Broken Family', pp. 30–3; W.L. De Arteaga, 'Agnes Sanford: Apostle of Healing, and First Theologian of the Charismatic Renewal. Part 1', *PR* 9.2 (2006), pp. 6–17; W.L. De Arteaga, 'Agnes Sanford: Apostle of Healing, and First Theologian of the Charismatic Renewal. Part 2', *PR* 9.3 (2006), pp. 4–17; D. Vreeland, 'John Alexander Dowie', *PR* (9.1 (2006), pp. 30–9.

[10] For a similar emphasis in Korean Pentecostalism, see Kim, *History and Theology of Korean Pentecostalism*, p. 259.

[11] See the Fundamental Beliefs of the Classical Pentecostal denominations including the AoG; the Elim Pentecostal Church, the Apostolic Church, the Church of God of Prophecy and the New Testament Church of God; A. Tee, *Healing and Health* (London: Evangel Press, n.d.), pp. 6–12; M. Taylor, 'A Historical Perspective on the Doctrine of Divine Healing', *EB* 14 (1995), pp. 54–84; K. Warrington, 'Healing and Exorcism. The Path to Wholeness', in Warrington (ed.), *Pentecostal Perspectives*, pp. 147–76; idem, 'Major Aspects of Healing', pp. 34–55; W.K. Kay, A.E. Dyer, *Pentecostal and Charismatic Studies* (London: SCM, 2004), pp. 47–82.

[12] Exod. 15.26; Pss. 103.2–3; 105.37; Isa. 53.4–5; Mal. 3.6; cf. F.H. Squire, *The Healing Power of Christ* (Southend: Full Gospel Publishing House, 1935), pp. 13–19; G. Wright, *Our Quest for Healing* (Cheltenham: Grenehurst, 1981), pp. 49–51.

[13] Mt. 4.23; 8.16–17; 10.8; Mk 16.15ff; Lk. 9.1–2; Jn 14.12; Acts 10.38; Heb. 13.8; Jas 5.14–15; 1 Pet. 2.24; cf. A. Linford, *Pentecostal Pictures* (London: Peniel Press, 1976), pp. 121–29.

[14] E.C.W. Boulton, *George Jeffreys. A Ministry of the Miraculous* (Clapham: Elim, 1928), pp. 180–98; G. Jeffreys, *Healing Rays* (Clapham: Elim, 1932), pp. 176–209; C.J.E. Kingston, *Fulness of Power* (Clapham: Victory, 1939), pp. 51–7; W.F.P. Burton, *Signs Following* (Luton: Assemblies of God, 1949), pp. 1–8, 16–24; W.T.H. Richards, *Pentecost Is Dynamite* (London: Lakeland, 1972), p. 65; A.F. Missen, *The Sound of a Going* (Nottingham: Assemblies of God, 1973), pp. 5, 22; Christenson, 'Pentecostalism's Forgotten Forerunner', pp. 15–37; C.C. Whittaker, *Seven Pentecostal Pioneers* (Basingstoke: Marshalls, 1983), pp. 35, 59–76; Wacker, *Heaven Below*, pp. 65–8; D. Harrell Jr, 'Healers and Televangelists after World War 2', in Synan (ed.), *The Century of the Holy Spirit*, pp. 325–47; F.W. Jordan, 'At Arm's Length: The First Presbyterian Church, Pittsburgh, and Kathryn Kuhlman', in Blumhofer, Spittler and Wacker (eds), *Pentecostal Currents*, pp. 188–208.

[15] Wacker, 'Travail of a Broken Family', p. 32; J. Wright, 'Profiles of Divine Healing: Third Wave Theology Compared with Classical Pentecostal Theology', *AJPS* 5.2 (2002), pp. 271–87 (286); R.A.N. Kydd, *Healing through the Centuries: Models for Understanding* (Peabody: Hendrickson, 1998).

sometimes differ from one another coexist within Pentecostalism and act as reminders that Pentecostalism is neither a single nor static phenomenon.[16]

Discussions within Pentecostalism concerning healing have been based on the healing ministry of Jesus, the charismatic gifts of healings referred to by Paul and the guidelines in Jas 5.13–18.[17] These, as well as the healing references in the book of Acts, have formed the basis for the belief that supernatural healing may still occur today. There has been, in recent years, an increasing readiness to develop a theology of healing by some Pentecostals that is analytical and critical of excesses and errors. Similarly, there has been a developing recognition that healing may be requested for forms of weakness other than illness, as implied by the guidelines in James 5 which provide a path to wholeness and healing in their fullest sense; a potential harmony of the physical, emotional, mental and spiritual aspects of a person. James is recognized as offering hope to those in his community who are physically ill but also support for those who are lacking wholeness as a result of other forms of weakness.[18] God cares for all aspects of the life of the believer, his aim being to provide restoration and wholeness. Nevertheless, healing is viewed as a divine attribute and therefore it is expected that God will manifest this aspect of his character since it is part of his nature.[19] The biblical schema may be summarized thus:

- The OT presents God as the healer of people and this helps define him as God.
- The Gospels present Jesus as the healer of people. As such, he is identified as the Son of God, Messiah and Saviour who has come to initiate the Kingdom of God.
- The book of Acts provides examples of the ongoing healing ministry in the early Church, mainly through Peter and Paul. Furthermore, it presents Jesus as still healing, the Apostles and others healing in ways that are reminiscent of Jesus in his mission activity. The ascended Christ is not absent; he is still present in the Church.[20]
- The letters of Paul impart limited information about the charismatic and spontaneous nature of the gifts of the Spirit as they relate to healing.[21]

---

[16] K. Warrington, 'The Path to Wholeness. Beliefs and Practices Relating to Healing in Pentecostalism', *Evangel*, 21.2 (2003), pp. 45–8.

[17] K. Warrington, 'An Exegesis of James 5.13–18' (unpublished master's dissertation, London Bible College, 1991).

[18] K. Warrington, 'James 5:14–18: Healing, Then and Now', *IRM* 95.370–371 (July/Oct. 2004), pp. 346–67 (346–51).

[19] V.L. Purdy, 'Divine Healing', in Horton (ed.), *Systematic Theology*, pp. 489–523 (497–99); Tee, 'The Doctrine of Divine Healing', p. 200.

[20] K. Warrington, 'Acts and the Healing Narratives: Why?', *JPT* 14.2 (April 2006), pp. 189–218.

[21] K. Warrington, *Healing and Suffering: Biblical and Pastoral Reflections*, (Carlisle: Paternoster Press, 2005), pp. 128–148.

Paul reflects the interim period between the initiation and consummation of the Kingdom. Although healings still occur, suffering is also present and not all illness is removed. Nevertheless, on occasions, God still heals via the gifts of healings (1 Cor. 12.9). When he chooses not to bring restoration, the promise of 2 Cor. 12.9 ('My grace is sufficient for you, for my power is made perfect in weakness') is a strong support for all believers.

- The letter of James provides guidelines for healing praxis to be undertaken by members of the local church on behalf of one another. James reflects the same premise that healings still occur and he provides guidelines for preparing for this possibility while giving advice concerning the role of the believers to corporately minister to those suffering from varied forms of weakness, including physical sickness. This advice, set in Jewish terms, needs to be recontextualized for the contemporary Church so that it also can minister in the ways anticipated by James for his Christian constituency.[22]

Healing and Jesus

A major reason for the records of the healing ministry of Jesus is to teach the readers about him. The Gospel writers are clear in their intention of presenting Jesus as a healer who has no peer; his authority is superior to anyone else of his time or who had lived before him. However, to conclude that this is all they have to say about Jesus as a result of his healings is to make a fundamental mistake. The physical restorations, although important to those healed, also revealed truth about the healer. The healing narratives were intended to result in the question being asked, 'Who is this man?', closely followed by the more spectacular question, 'Is he God?' As well as relieving suffering, the healing ministry of Jesus is thus to be recognized as demonstrating his Messiahship but, much more importantly, his deity, as well as providing opportunities for unbelievers to come to faith in him.

There are aspects of Jesus' ministry, including his sensitivity and grace that should be incorporated into a person's own ministry and lifestyle, especially when related to scenarios of suffering and sickness. However, there are motifs integral to his healing ministry that distinguish it from their own experiences of healing. His healing powers are signposts to him and not simply to a more successful healing ministry.[23] Indeed, a marked contrast is to be noted between the healing ministry of Jesus and that of his followers:

- Jesus healed *all* who came to him for healing.
- Jesus never prayed before healing people. The reference to his praying prior to the resurrection of Lazarus was for the purpose of informing

---

[22] Warrington, *Healing and Suffering*, pp. 149–179.

[23] Warrington, *Jesus the Healer*, pp. 1–29, 141–63; idem, 'The Role of Jesus in the Healing Praxis and Teaching of British Pentecostalism: A Re-Examination', *Pneuma* 25.1 (2003), pp. 66–92.

those present that his was a divine commission (Jn 11.41–2), not to gain guidance, approval or authority.

- Jesus never unambiguously related sickness to the personal sin of the sufferer (contrast Lk. 1.20; Acts 5.1–11; 13.8–12; Jas 5.15–16).
- Jesus never indicated that sickness had pedagogical value to the sufferer (contrast Acts 5.11; 13.12; 2 Cor 12.7–10; Gal 4.13).
- Jesus' healings had a pedagogical function.[24] Thus, they demonstrated that he had the authority to initiate the Kingdom, he fulfilled OT prophecy, he had authority to forgive sins, he had supremacy over the Law, the Sabbath and the temple, he had come to incorporate the marginalized, and to provide miracles to encourage people to put their trust in him.
- Jesus did not establish a set methodology.
- The guidelines of Jas 5.13–18 are markedly different from the ministry of Jesus.
- Jesus is to be distinguished from other healers in the Church, because his mission is unique and, thus, inevitably different from that of his followers.

Healing and the Death of Jesus

The issue of whether Jesus has guaranteed healing to all believers is often associated with the phrase 'healing in the atonement'. It is a foundational belief of many Pentecostals[25] though it predated Pentecostalism.[26] However, there have been shifts in thinking over the years.[27]

---

[24] Jesus is presented as having authority to heal sicknesses (Mt. 8.14–16; 16ff//s; 13.51–58//s; 14.34–36//s; 15.29–31; 19.2; 21.14; Mk 7.31ff; Lk. 1.20ff; 13.32), cast out demons (Mt. 8.28–34//s; 9.32–34; 15.21–28//s; 17.14–21//s; Mk 1.23–28//s; 1.39; 9.38–41//s) and to raise people from the dead (Mt. 9.18–19; 23–26//s). His healings demonstrate that he has authority concerning issues related to the Jewish Law, including the Sabbath (Lk. 8.2–3; 13.10ff; 14.1–6; Jn 5.1–14; 9.1–41), purity laws (Mt. 8.2–4//s; 9.20–22//s; Luke 7.11ff.) and the temple (Mt. 21.14); the reinstatement of the outcast (Mt. 15.21–28//s; Lk. 13.10–17; 17.11–19); the initiation of the Kingdom (Mt. 4.23–24; 9.35; 10.1, 8//s, 11.4ff//s; 12.22–29//s; Mk 7.31–37; Lk. 7.19–23; 9.1f; 10.8, 17–20); they fulfil prophecy concerning the Messiah (Mt. 12.15–21; Lk. 4.19–21); they demonstrate the authority of Jesus to forgive sins (Mt. 9.1–8); they provide opportunities to develop a more accurate perception of the identity of Jesus (Mt. 12.9–14//s; 12.15–21; 20.29–34//s; 21.14; Lk. 13.10–17; 14.1–6; 17.11–19; Jn 4.46–54; 5.2–47; 9.1–41; 11.2–44); teach about faith (Mt. 8.5–13//s; 9.18f, 23–26//s; 13.51//s; 14.34–36//s; 15.21–28//s; 17.14–21//s) and obedience (Mt. 7.21–23; 12.43–45//s).

[25] Kay (*Pentecostals in Britain*, p. 101) provides the following response figures of ministers who agree with the statement, 'Physical healing is provided by Christ's atonement'

Two different interpretations of this view are generally offered. The one states that because of the death of Jesus, healing is available to believers today as easily as the forgiveness of sins can be received.[28] Thus, Oral Roberts, one of Pentecostalism's most notable healing evangelists writes, 'Healing is in the Atonement. Therefore, it includes all . . . just as He will forgive all our sins, He will heal all our diseases'.[29] This sometimes leads to guilt or confusion if the healing is not forthcoming, the onus for healing falling firmly on the supplicant, with God often unintentionally being depersonalized in the procedure.[30]

The alternative definition is that because of the death of Jesus, healing is available to believers though it may not always (or even often) be actualized until after death; healing is thus defined as being a result of the Atonement though the consequences may not occur in this life.[31]

Menzies[32] offers a nuanced perspective, arguing that because of the death of Jesus, as well as being spiritually transformed, believers also experience a parallel, physical transformation. Realizing that this 'does not mean that our

---

AoG: 88.9%; Elim: 80.9%; Apostolic Church: 87.5%; Church of God: 98%. The Fundamental Beliefs of the AoG (article 12), the Pentecostal Holiness Church (article 14) and the Church of God (Cleveland) (Article 11) affirm that healing is provided for in the Atonement; Hardesty, *Faith Cure*, p. 87 (see pp. 62, 69, 89, 92–4).

[26] A.B. Simpson, *The Gospel of Healing* (Camp Hill: Christian Publications, 1885), p. 34; cf. R. J. Cunningham, 'The Faith Cure in America, 1872–1982', *Church History* 43 (1974), p. 506; R.K. Carter affirmed the doctrine in *The Atonement for Sin and Sickness: Or a Full Salvation for Soul and Body* (Boston: Willard Tract Repository (1884), p. 12) though he retracted it some years later (*'Faith Healing' Reviewed after Twenty Years* (Boston: Christian Witness Co., 1897), p. 167); see also Dayton, *Theological Roots of Pentecostalism*, pp. 127–32.

[27] Synan, 'A Healer in the House?', pp. 189–201; Wright, *Our Quest for Healing*, pp. 62–3; D. Gee, *Trophimus, I Left Sick. Our Problem of Divine Healing* (Clapham: Elim, 1952), p. 25; D. Petts, 'Healing and the Atonement' (Conference paper, Elim/AoG Theological Conference, Swanwick, 1995), pp. 141–56.

[28] C. Urquhart, *The Truth That Sets You Free* (London: Hodder and Stoughton, 1993), p. 149; contra C. Farah, *From the Pinnacle of the Temple* (Plainfield: Logos, 1979), pp. 71–8.

[29] O. Roberts, *If You Need Healing, Do These Things* (New York: County Life Press, 1952), pp. 42, 60.

[30] W.K. Kay, 'Approaches to Healing in British Pentecostalism', *JPT* 14 (1999), pp. 113–25 (116–17).

[31] cf. Jeffreys, *Healing Rays*, p. 37; Wright, *Our Quest for Healing*, pp. 62–3; Gee, *Trophimus, I Left Sick*, p. 25; D. Petts, *Healing and the Atonement* (unpublished doctoral dissertation, Nottingham University, 1993), pp. 31–70 for a survey of the development within Pentecostalism concerning the relationship between healing and the Atonement of Christ.

[32] R.P. Menzies, 'Healing in the Atonement', in Menzies and Menzies, *Spirit and Power*, pp. 159–70 (164).

bodies will be gradually strengthened and energized until we obtain immortality', he nevertheless still holds to the view that as a result of the atonement, believers 'are moving toward our ultimate destiny in Christ, which includes physical wholeness'.[33] However, the parallel between physical and spiritual transformation is not as close or as clear as he asserts for, as he admits, 'our body will grow frail and weak and ultimately die'.[34] However, by contrast, because of the atonement, a spiritual transformation is effected immediately (2 Cor. 3.18). Although a physical transformation is effected at death for all, those promulgating a belief in healing in the atonement generally anticipate a physical transformation much earlier. Although the latter is a possibility, to argue that it will occur as certainly as the Spirit will spiritually dynamize the believer is yet to be clearly biblically supported.[35]

However, some Pentecostals have resisted this linkage between divine healing and the death of Jesus, noting that healings occurred in the OT, and thus prior to Calvary, and also in the life of Jesus (before he died).[36] Rather than look to the death of Jesus as the catalyst for divine healing, it may be more appropriate to recognize that healings have occurred and will continually occur as a result of the sovereign activity of the Spirit, through the ministry of the Church, based on his individual plan for people.

Matthew 8.14–17 is the key passage used to defend the belief of 'healing in the atonement' (though other texts have been advanced also[37]). In it, Matthew records that the exorcisms and healings achieved by Jesus fulfilled Isa. 53.4–5. This OT passage and, in particular, the statement, 'by his stripes we are healed' is regularly interpreted as the basis for the belief that Isaiah prophesied that Messiah would provide physical healing, even though the Isaianic passage indicates a spiritual, not physical context.[38] Matthew provides

---

[33] Menzies, 'Healing in the Atonement', p. 164.

[34] Menzies, 'Healing in the Atonement', p. 164.

[35] Also R. Dickinson, *God Does Heal Today* (Carlisle: Paternoster Press, 1995), pp. 48–57; M.L. Brown, *Israel's Divine Healer* (Carlisle: Paternoster, 1995), pp. 72–8; M. Harper, *The Healings of Jesus* (London: Hodder and Stoughton, 1986), p. 109; Fee, *The Disease of the Health*, p. 19; K.M. Bailey, *Divine Healing. The Children's Bread* (Camp Hill: Christian, 1977), pp. 43–58; M. Scott, *Healing Then and Now* (Milton Keynes: Word, 1993), p. 38.

[36] L.F.W. Woodford, *Divine Healing and the Atonement: A Restatement* (Croydon: Victoria Institute, 1956), p. 53; C.L. Parker, *Covet Earnestly* (London: AoG, 1961), p. 9; see also J.R. Williams (*Renewal Theology. God, the World and Redemption* (Grand Rapids: Zondervan, 1988), p. 365) who writes, 'It is unscriptural to say that Christ took away our diseases in His death or that physical healing as such is to be found in the Atonement'.

[37] C.J. Thomas, 'Healing in the Atonement: A Johannine Perspective', *JPT* 14.1 (2005), pp. 23–39 (26–34).

[38] Menzies and Horton, *Bible Doctrines*, pp. 197–98.

a translation of the original Hebrew of Isa. 53.4 instead of following the Septuagint and makes physical illnesses the subject. He thus clearly links the prophecy with the healing ministry of Jesus. However, he does not record that Jesus provided for the removal of people's sicknesses as a result of his death on the cross. In fact, the death of Jesus is not in view. Rather, Matthew demonstrates that Jesus fulfilled this prophecy in his healing activity, as illustrated by the previous healing of Peter's mother-in-law and of the crowds who came to Jesus for healing that evening. The case for associating the Matthean passage with the death of Jesus is largely based on the fact that the Isaiah text is part of a prophecy largely fulfilled in the death of Messiah.[39] However, given that none of the Gospel writers associate Jesus' healing ministry with his death, it is questionable whether such an association should be assumed on their part. The fulfilment of Mt. 8.17 is presented by Matthew as being during the life of Jesus, not after his death.[40]

1 Peter 2.24 is the other text sometimes referred to in order to support the idea of healing in the atonement. The context of this verse, however, is of impending persecution and suffering (2.12) while the prevailing theme of the letter is that suffering will happen to believers but that it has benefit in that it stimulates Christian growth (1.6–8; 2.18–22; 3.14–17; 4.12–19; 5.9–10). The suffering in view is punishment or physical abuse as a result

---

[39] Thomas, *The Devil, Disease and Deliverance*, pp. 173–74; cf. Twelftree (*Jesus the Miracle Worker*, p. 112) speculates that Matthew assumes the reference is 'an anticipation of the passion . . . That Matthew considers such activity to be a part of Jesus' atoning work seems to be the best reading . . . Matthew considers Jesus' exorcism and healing ministry to be tied to his (future) vicarious death'; similarly, although Menzies ('Healing in the Atonement', pp. 166–67) acknowledges that Matthew's own interpretation of this application of the prophecy to Jesus is that it is fulfilled in his healing ministry, nevertheless, he moves beyond this to speculate that it is 'more than simply a description of Jesus' earthly ministry in terms of healing; rather, he assumes that it is Matthew's summary of the significance of Jesus' messianic mission, which culminates on the cross', concluding that it was 'fulfilled in Jesus' atoning work on the cross'.

[40] See Williams, *Renewal Theology. God*, pp. 364–65; Fee, *The Disease of the Health*, p. 15. Further exegesis of Isa. 53.4 is inappropriate; sufficient to note that Matthew's divergence from the LXX (which relates the work of the Messiah to bearing sins) and his individualistic use of specific verbs (*astheneia* and *nosos*) indicate that he has adapted the passage for his own hermeneutical purposes; his reversion to a more literal rendering of the MT is valuable for Matthew who sees the prophecy being fulfilled in the healing ministry of Jesus. Although Isaiah may have presented the work of Messiah in soteriological terms, Matthew has used them to portray the healing mission of Jesus. To suggest that Matthew carries through the soteriological emphasis of Isaiah into his description of the healing of Jesus is not clear from a reading of Mt. 8.16–17; J. Niehaus, 'O.T. Foundations: Signs and Wonders in Prophetic Ministry and the Substitutionary Atonement of Isaiah 53', in G. Grieg, K. Springer (eds), *The Kingdom and the Power* (Ventura: Regal, 1995), pp. 41–53 (49); Petts, 'Healing and the Atonement', pp. 28–9.

of being a Christian, not physical illness. In 2.22–25, Peter presents Christ as the supreme example of one who suffered unjustly but who bore it honourably.

The 'healing' referred to in 1 Pet. 2.24 relates to the forgiveness of sins, as stated in the previous verse and not to physical healing. The fact that the phrase, 'you have been healed' is in the aorist tense indicates that their salvation is being referred to as it defines a completed action in the past. It is instructive to note that there is no reference to physical healing in this epistle. Although it is possible that the author is encouraging the readers to anticipate physical healing to their wounds that have been the consequence of suffering for their faith, it is much more likely that he is encouraging those who are suffering unjustly to follow the example of Christ who similarly suffered in fulfilling his mission. Petts[41] concludes, 'When correctly exegeted, it cannot reasonably be understood to teach the doctrine that healing is in the Atonement'.

That which is not in dispute is that divine healings occur today. Neither is it disputed that because of the death of Jesus, the plan of salvation (that includes both physical and spiritual restoration and redemption) is guaranteed either in this life or the next. However, that which is contested by some is that Matthew and Peter were seeking to link divine healing with the death of Jesus in a way that might lead to people assuming that it is as easily available as the forgiveness of sins. The limited number of healings in the history of Pentecostalism undermines the quality of the apparent premise that the death of Jesus has introduced the possibility of unqualified healings for all believers. The presence of sickness and death is an obvious reminder that these issues have not yet been resolved in this life although their demise is assured because of the comprehensive nature of the victory of Jesus.[42]

Healing and the Will of God

Throughout the history of Pentecostalism, there have been those who have stated that it is always God's will to heal,[43] Carter,[44] pointing to the fact that

---

[41] Petts ('Healing and the Atonement' (unpublished doctoral dissertation), pp. 154, 192) notes, 'Peter takes Isaiah 53:5 and applies it, in the context of Christ's redemptive work on the Cross, to healing from the wounds of sin, but no thought of physical healing is in mind . . . The "healing" referred to clearly means a spiritual wholeness which results from Christ's bearing our sins on the Cross.'

[42] Kärkkäinen, *Toward a Pneumatological Theology*, pp. 142–44.

[43] Squire, *The Healing Power of Christ*, pp. 28–9; C.J. Montgomery, *The Prayer of Faith* (London: Victory, 1930), pp. 4–5, 27, 40–1, 66, 72; Horton, *The Gifts of the Spirit*, p. 110; R.E. Darragh, *In Defence of His Word* (London: Elim Publishing Company, 1932), p. 104; A.L. Hoy, 'Gifts of Healings', *Paraclete* 12.1 (1978), pp. 10–14.

'Jesus healed *all* who came to him' as evidence. From this assertion, it has been deduced that the desire of Jesus remains constant through all eras and his response to those who come for healing is the same as when he was on earth. Thus, at times, the ministry of healing takes place in a verbal context of claiming or commanding healing, in assumed agreement with the procedure of Jesus. Many Pentecostals, however, prefer to believe that it is God's preference to heal or that it is his normative will so to do, though even here, there is the suspicion that this is a wish that does not bear a great deal of theological weight being placed on it and too often healing appears to be a lottery with a few who get healed but a majority who do not, their lot in life being to wait for their turn patiently.

The Word of Faith movement,[45] in particular, has championed the belief that healing is not only available for all believers now but that it should also be claimed as a promise of God. It has been criticized because much of the teaching has been assessed as not being reflective of the biblical message, the presentation of propositions being on the basis of proof texts. Furthermore, many have rejected their assumption that God works to a formula that will inevitably result in action on his part. They have also been criticized because of their lack of critical comment when healings do not occur even though the formula has been adhered to, their overreliance on God to achieve the results (thus, the popular quoting of Zech. 4.6), their inability to accommodate suffering as a positive component of Christianity, their assumption that lack of health and poverty are spiritual problems that can be remedied by spiritual antidotes (prayer, removal of curses, faith) and their over emphasis on the issue of physical restoration.[46] However, it has influenced many in the

---

[44] J. Carter, *Questions and Answers on Vital Subjects* (Nottingham: AoG Publishing House, n.d.), pp. 9–10 (italics in original).

[45] According to www.rhema.org/khm.htm, the Hagins have distributed 53 million books, with 58,000 tapes being distributed every month.

[46] Goff, 'Questions of Health and Wealth', pp. 65–80; D.R. McConnell, *A Different Gospel. A Historical and Biblical Analysis of the Modern Health Movement* (Peabody: Hendrickson, 1988); B. Barron, *The Health and Wealth Gospel* (Downers Grove: InterVarsity Press, 1987); Perriman, *Faith, Health and Prosperity*; C. Farah, 'A Critical Analysis: The 'Roots and Fruits' of Faith-Formula Theology', *Pneuma* 3.1 (1981), pp. 3–21; D. Hollinger, 'Enjoying God Forever: An Historical/Sociological Profile of the Health and Wealth Gospel', *Tyndale Journal* 9.2 (1988), pp. 131–49; Farah, *From the Pinnacle*; K. Warrington, 'Healing and Kenneth Hagin', *AJPS* 3.1 (2000), pp. 119–38; idem, 'The Use of the Name (of Jesus) in Healing and Exorcism with Partial Reference to the Teachings of Kenneth Hagin, *JEPTA* 17 (1997), pp. 16–36; G.M. Burge, 'Problems in the Healing Ministries within the Charismatic Context' (SPS conference paper, Cleveland, 1983); D.H. Simmons, 'Hagin-Heretic or Herald of God? A Theological and Historical Analysis of Kenneth E. Hagin's claim to be a prophet' (unpublished master's dissertation, Oral Roberts University, 1985); K.S. Kantzer, 'The Cut-Rate Grace of a Health and Wealth Gospel', *Christianity Today*, 29.9 (4 June 1985), pp. 14–15;

global Pentecostal community, both in the rich West and the poverty stricken areas of the Majority world. Thus, some Western Pentecostals thank God for their prosperity while some Majority world Pentecostals cling to the dream of prosperity (understood in terms of wealth and health) fed to them by mainly Western teaching supporting these fantasies.[47]

It has also been a popular belief that a major reason for Jesus healing was due to his compassion. Associated with this assumption is the popular maxim, 'Yesterday, today, forever, Jesus is the same' (Heb. 13.8), resulting in the conclusion that any who are sick are as eligible to receive healing as those who lived in the era of Jesus, on the basis of his compassion. However, the implications of this assumption for people who are not healed are insubstantially explored.[48] More importantly is the paucity of Gospel references identifying compassion as a reason for Jesus healing people, a factor which is rarely acknowledged.

The belief in divine healing has caused tensions in Pentecostal belief and practice, and the distinction between God's will and desire is often blurred. Thus although Dye writes, 'The Bible is packed with promises of healing',[49] he acknowledges, 'The cross does not guarantee us automatic physical healing in this life – even if we are fully obedient and full of faith',[50] concluding that he has learned to accept 'the twin realities of God's willingness to heal and the abiding presence of pain'.[51]

The belief that God appears to have provided a way out of suffering and at the same time, a recognition that, for many, the escape route has not been located is ever present in Pentecostal thought. Consequently, for some Christians who suffer physically or mentally, their presence within some Pentecostal environments sits awkwardly in the context of a perceived belief that healing is available for all; this discomfort is not unique to Pentecostalism.

J.A. Matta, *The Born Again Jesus of the Word Faith Teaching* (Fullerton: Spirit of Truth Ministry, 1987); D.J. Moo, 'Divine Healing in the Health and Wealth Gospel', *Tyndale Journal* 9.2 (1988), pp. 191–205; H.T. Neuman, 'Cultic Origins of Word-Faith Theology within the Charismatic Movement', *Pneuma* 12.1 (1990), pp. 32–55; H.H. Knight III, 'God's Faithfulness and God's Freedom: A Comparison of Contemporary Theologies of Healing', *JPT* 2 (1993), pp. 65–89; T. Smail, A. Walker, N. Wright, '"Revelation Knowledge" and Knowledge of Revelation: The Faith Movement and the Question of Heresy', *JPT* 5 (1996), pp. 57–77; Nwankwo, 'You Have Received', pp. 56–77; A.H. Anderson, 'The Prosperity Message in the Eschatology in the Teaching of Some New Charismatic Churches', *Missionalia* 15.2 (1987), pp. 72–83.

[47] Lugo (*Spirit and Power*, p. 29) records that 80% of Pentecostals in the countries researched accepted that God granted health on the basis of faith, the percentage being the highest in countries from the global South.

[48] Menzies and Horton, *Bible Doctrines*, p. 205.

[49] Dye, *Healing Anointing*, p. 84.

[50] Dye, *Healing Anointing*, p. 99.

[51] Dye, *Healing Anointing*, p. 19.

Similarly, death is a difficult issue for many Pentecostals in that rather than allow a believer to view it as the door to heaven and its coming as the opportunity to prepare for eternity, they tend to pray against its occurrence until it is too late for such preparation to ensue for such an eventuality.[52] Death has been infrequently viewed positively as an entrance into the eternal presence of God. It has often been understood to be a victory for the devil who has robbed the believer of his/her right to life, rather than be recognized as the gateway to the eternity that God has prepared for all believers. Speaking of death and referring to 2 Kgs 13.14, which records the fact that Elisha died of a sickness, Gee[53] notes that since 'the context gives not the slightest indication that he (Elisha) had failed spiritually . . . it is fanatical to rule out all place for possible sickness, and ultimately . . . a sickness unto death'.

These unresolved tensions may be located among Pentecostals throughout their history and are a testimony to their willingness to cling to beliefs that are viewed as being accurate biblical perceptions, rather than accept that which reality dictates. This is a fundamental Pentecostal stance; reality is not viewed as being the sole legitimate arbiter; their beliefs are determined by their interpretation of Scripture. That which is needed is a more carefully scrutinized theology of healing.

A variety of reasons have been offered for the absence of healing when prayer has been offered, mainly being personal sin or insufficient faith. Petts offers the possibility that healing may not occur because it has not been realized that the cause of the sickness is demonic.[54] At other times, absence of healing has been perceived as being due to the inadequacy of those offering prayer. Thus, Canty[55] explains, 'It is the will of God that all shall be well, but not necessarily His will that I can bestow a healing upon everybody in every meeting. Only Christ would operate at that level'. Dye also notes, 'Jesus' divinity, sinlessness, perfect obedience and unlimited anointing must surely mean that we cannot always expect to be as effective in ministry as him'.[56] However, the implication that believers can be obstacles to the healing of others has no biblical basis.

---

[52] J. Katter, 'Divine Healing. Principles and Practical Suggestions', *Paraclete* 27.2 (1993), pp. 24–9 (24).

[53] Gee, *Trophimus, I Left Sick*, p. 16; Tee, *Healing and Health*, pp. 12–13; Wright (*Our Quest for Healing*, p. 15) refers to Paul's awareness of the fact that his body was perishing (Rom. 8.19, 21; 2 Cor. 4.16) and OT heroes who were also sick (Asa (1 Kgs 15.14, 23). He comments that Moses' good health was an exception (Deut. 34.1, 7) in the context of others who were less fortunate (Gen. 27.1; 48.10; Josh. 13.1; 1 Sam. 3.2). Isa. 1.6 and Ezek. 30.21 refer to the skill of binding of wounds/broken bones. Herbs were also used (2 Kgs 20.7; Isa. 38.21).

[54] Petts, *Body Builders*, p. 166.

[55] Canty, *The Practice of Pentecost*, pp. 180–81.

[56] Dye, *Healing Anointing*, p. 84.

Throughout the Pentecostal era and before,[57] there have been others who have reacted to the simplistic suggestion that because Jesus healed all who came to him for healing, the same is unconditionally available today for all believers. Similarly, as a result of the fact that people are not always healed despite prayer being offered, some Pentecostals are prepared to offer practical, sensitive reflection that is intended to be of benefit to those who remain sick and the wider Christian community. This includes asking God for guidance as to how to pray, counselling the suffering person to realize the presence of God despite their continued sickness, helping to remove any sense of guilt from them, reminding them of their ability to authentically reflect God in their circumstances and that God is more concerned about their eternal destiny than their physical well-being.[58]

The issue of the conditional nature of divine healing is one of the areas that has experienced a noticeable change within Pentecostalism. Some have suggested that although God has the power to heal, he does not always choose to heal and in the case of the latter, it is due to his sovereign will[59] and in order to promote benefit for the sufferer.[60] Gee[61] notes, 'We have erred by refusing any place in our doctrine or at least a very insufficient place for the sovereign will of God'. Similarly, he[62] remarks, 'To ask for Divine healing without any accompanying "nevertheless, not my will but Thine be done" seems to pose an attitude out of keeping with every other right attitude we take in prayer'. The official Statements of Faith of the Classical Pentecostal denominations offer the hope and potential of divine healing but refrain from expressing it as a guarantee. Chamberlain thus writes, 'We believe in healing. We also believe God is sovereign'.[63] Pentecostals have also begun to recognize the value of suffering as a form of divine discipline and chastisement. Thus, Parker[64] states, 'God uses sickness . . . for His glory to keep His people humble and obedient'. However, it is also increasingly appreciated that suffering can form a significantly important platform for glorifying God and reflecting his character in a context of

---

[57] Hardesty, *Faith Cure*, pp. 97–8.

[58] Dye, *Healing Anointing*, pp. 206–08.

[59] P.G. Parker (*Divine Healing* (Clapham: Victory Press, n.d.), p. 24) records, 'When our Lord first of all commenced to give out His gifts of healing, all who came to Him received . . . But the time came for the plan to be modified . . . From general giving the plan became discriminate giving'; cf. Gee, *The Pentecostal Movement*, p. 164; P.S. Brewster, *The Spreading Flame of Pentecost* (London: Elim Publishing House, 1970), p. 45; Hollenweger, *The Pentecostals*, p. 357.

[60] Petts, *Body Builders*, p. 167.

[61] Gee, *Trophimus, I Left Sick*, p. 37; Tee, 'The Doctrine of Divine Healing', p. 198.

[62] Gee, *Trophimus, I Left Sick*, pp. 27–8.

[63] R.G. Chamberlain, Editorial, *Pentecostal Evangel*, 3 (1984).

[64] Parker, *Divine Healing*, p. 44.

weakness. Indeed, it may be argued that a most authentic faith is demonstrated when a believer trusts God while simultaneously facing a challenging set of circumstances. Menzies thus advises that we should 'pray until the Lord whispers to our consciousness that other factors are at work beyond understanding, and that we should quit praying for deliverance at that point', recognizing 'this is the point when the Holy Spirit can tenderly enable believers to accept the suffering and its consequences'.[65]

An assessment of current Pentecostalism would suggest an increasing alliance with the latter views.[66] Thus, sickness is viewed as a potential ally to believers and a useful instrument in the hands of God for their benefit. The recognition that benefit may be derived by the believer as a result of illness or disability is a significant shift away from a belief that Jesus has apparently delegated to believers the authority to excise all sickness from the lives of believers.

Thomas provides a helpful survey of the potential pedagogical reasons for the existence of infirmity and death in the life of the believer.[67] Evidence for the latter is also available from the NT (1 Cor. 11.30; Gal. 4.13). Pentecostals are increasingly prepared to view healing in an eschatological context, this perception providing a framework for healing that identifies believers with creation that also groans and awaits its final redemption (Rom. 8.22–23). Consequently, they are encouraged to trust God, recognizing that although they may not be healed in this life, after death, they will experience wholeness. Throughout Pentecostal history, there has been a willingness by some to express ignorance concerning the reasons why some Christians remain ill after prayer for restoration.[68] Increasingly, Pentecostals recognize that they exist in an era that does not experience all that God has available for his people.[69]

Healing and Medicine

Pentecostals tend not to contrast medical and divine healing and the former is not viewed suspiciously or negatively,[70] though in earlier times, it was

---

[65] Menzies, 'Reflections on Suffering', p. 147.
[66] Hollenweger (The Pentecostals, p. 358); G. Allen, R. Wallis, 'Pentecostalists as a Medical Minority', in R. Wallis, P. Morely (eds), Marginal Medicine (London: Peter Owen, 1976), pp. 110–37.
[67] Thomas, The Devil, Disease and Deliverance, pp. 297–300.
[68] Tee, Healing and Health, pp. 9–10; Gee, Trophimus, I Left Sick, pp. 29–30.
[69] S.D. Eutsler, 'Why Are Not All Christians Healed?', Paraclete 27.2 (1993), pp. 15–23 (18).
[70] Calley, God's People, p. 94; AoG, Who We Are and What We Believe (Springfield: Gospel Publishing House, 1982), p. 23; the NTCG Supplement to the Declaration of Faith, article 11, reads, 'It is recognized that all healing is provided by the goodness of God,

assumed to be an inappropriate or even unacceptable form of healing,[71] with some drawing a clear contrast between medical and divine healing.[72] Gee,[73] while recognizing the 'magnificent consistency' of those who held to this view, nevertheless questioned their judgment.

However, it has generally been acknowledged that divine healing and medicine should not be confused, neither should it be assumed that divine healing is 'a substitute for obedience to the rules of physical and mental health'[74] or 'a means of avoiding the effects of old age'.[75] On the contrary, it has been recognized that medicine and natural curative properties of the body are examples of the work of a creative God.[76] Increasingly, the importance of nutrition, exercise and hygiene are appreciated as also important to one's health.[77] In much of the world where medical facilities are limited, the

whether that healing is administered by counsel, medical skills or the application of medicine itself'; cf. R. Baldwin, *Healing and Wholeness* (Milton Keynes: Word, 1988), pp. 168–69; Hollenweger, *The Pentecostals*, p. 367; D. Gee (*Study Hour*, 9 (1950), pp. 2–6, 33–7) argues in favour of psychiatry in the treatment of those depressed and/or mentally ill, commenting favourably on the works of Freud and Jung; Petts ('Healing and the Atonement' (unpublished doctoral dissertation) pp. 263–68) employs Mk 2.17, Lk. 10.29–37 and Rev. 3.18 as evidence for the value of medicine; similarly he argues that Mk 5.25–26 may not be viewed as a condemnation of medicine.

71. Synan, *The Holiness-Pentecostal Tradition*, p. 192; Horton, *The Gifts of the Spirit*, pp. 99, 101.

72. Hardesty, *Faith Cure*, pp. 135–37; W.P.F. Burton (*Missionary Pioneering in Congo Forests* (Preston: R. Seed & Sons, 1922), p. 15) in response to the possibility of his protecting himself via the use of quinine, as did other missionaries, responds, 'I would rather die than disgrace His cause'. Nevertheless, for the sake of the gospel being preached to the unevangelized and out of consideration for his partner, he implies that he would be willing to take it; others in the Congo Mission refused and at least nine died as a result; J.N. Parr (*Divine Healing* (Stockport: AoG Publishing House, 1930), pp. 38–40) questions the necessity and even validity of medicine; H. Carter ('The Supernatural Aspect of All the Gifts', *Study Hour* (13 Sep. 1941), p. 2) argues, 'When we accept the services of the doctor we are standing on no higher level than unconverted people'; it is of interest to note that in his photograph in the book *The Gifts of the Spirit* he is wearing glasses; G. Cove (*God's Covenant of Divine Healing* (Nelson: Coulton's, n.d., p. 30) states, 'Divine healing is the exclusive method of healing the Christian . . . Doctors dislike it when they are treating a case for the patient to secretly call in another doctor for consultation. The Heavenly Father dislikes it as well'; Wacker, *Heaven Below*, pp. 191–92; Synan, *The Old Time Power*, pp. 166–67; Hardesty, *Faith Cure*, pp. 52, 72–3, 77–8.

73. Gee, *Trophimus, I Left Sick*, p. 28.

74. Gee, *Trophimus, I Left Sick*, p. 16; cf. Jeffreys (*Healing Rays*, p. 44) quotes Ps. 107.17–18; Gal. 6.7; Wright (*Our Quest for Healing*, pp. 38, 41) cites 'pollution, folly . . . smoking . . . hectic living, self indulgence . . . denial of . . . exercise . . . recreation . . . overwork as in the case of Epaphroditus'.

75. AoG, 'Our Position on Divine Healing', p. 10.

76. Dye, *Healing Anointing*, pp. 96–8.

desire for supernatural healing is more prominent though this does not mean that proportionately more people are healed there, though the reported numbers of supernatural healings may be greater than in countries where medicine is more available.

Within Pentecostalism, the developing role of the gift of teaching and the increasing recognition of its importance to the stability and edification of the Church has helped to inform and instruct believers from a more biblically circumscribed perspective. Also, in recent years, dialogue with medical practitioners, though as yet inadequately developed within Pentecostalism, has occurred, resulting in some practices being established that consist of doctors, psychologists, counsellors and people who pray for the patients and staff alike.

Healing and Evangelism

In the NT, healing miracles encouraged unbelievers to place their faith in Jesus.[78] Healing is a dynamic demonstration of the supremacy of Jesus and a sign that a new kingdom has been established. The relationship between healing and evangelism has always been prominent in Pentecostalism.[79] Gee[80] notes that healings 'have their true sphere in evangelism rather than among the saints'.[81] Similarly, Williams describes healing as 'not just supplemental, it is instrumental. It can become the avenue for the proclamation of salvation in Jesus Christ'.[82] Therefore, evangelistic missions which prominently advertised the possibility of divine healing have been common in Pentecostal history. This practice however has decreased among Western Pentecostals in recent decades, partly due to the fact that the high expectancy of healings in past evangelistic contexts was rarely fulfilled.[83] Allen confirms that this

---

[77] Dye, *Healing Anointing*, pp. 151–57, 163–68.

[78] Mt. 9.1–8//s; 9.32–34; 12.9–14//s; 12.15–21; 12.22–29//s; 12.43–45//s; 20.29–34//s; 21.14; Lk. 13.10–17; 14.1–6; 17.11–19; Jn 4.46–54; 5.2–47; 9.1–41; 11.2–44.

[79] cf. Hathaway, *Spiritual Gifts*, p. 45; D.A. Womack, *Breaking the Stain-Glass Barrier* (New York: Harper and Row, 1973), pp. 57–8; Brewster, *The Spreading Flame . . .*, p. 46.

[80] Gee (*Trophimus, I Left Sick*, pp. 9–10) notes of Paul, 'neither for himself, nor for those who were members of his missionary band, did he practice Divine healing'.

[81] Gee, *Concerning Spiritual Gifts*, p. 38.

[82] Williams, *Renewal Theology. Salvation*, p. 254.

[83] D. Gee ('Healed – But Not Saved', *Voice of Healing* (Jan. 1954), p. 11) advises evangelists to emphasize the priority of salvation of the soul over that of the body because of those who were healed but refused to become Christians; from 1959, a sharp and marked reduction in testimonies of healings are recorded in the *Voice of Healing*, their place being taken by articles relating to end time prophecy and reports of missionary endeavours.

deterioration in healings had been recognized earlier in the UK, there being considerably less in the 1940s than in the late 1920s and 1930s.[84] The role of the healing evangelist has largely now been replaced by a local church-based-practice of prayer in the context of corporate prayer for those suffering. The 'power-evangelism' model of John Wimber[85] has latterly revived the association of evangelism and divine healing.

However, most healings in Pentecostal contexts are now anticipated for the benefit of believers, rather than unbelievers. Any similarity to the ministry of Jesus, in which healings were partly intended as stepping-stones to salvific faith is, to a large degree for many Pentecostals, much less frequent. An exception may be noted particularly in non-Western countries where divine healing is regularly associated with evangelism.

Healing and Believers

The belief that Jesus delegated his healing authority to all believers permeates Pentecostalism, though it also predates it.[86] Indeed, he is viewed as a paradigm, his achievements potentially being replicated by believers,[87] Jeffreys[88] stating, 'The commission to go and preach and to expect the signs, including healing, to follow, has never been withdrawn: Mk. 16.15–18'. However, the absence of a replication of the success rate of Jesus has resulted in questions being asked over the years of the basic premise; too often, expectations have infrequently been fulfilled. Walker[89] writes, 'Miracles have been testified to in abundance, but rarely verified'. Some who have reflected on such dissimilarity attribute it to the fact that Jesus had a greater anointing of the Spirit and so was able to achieve more miracles or increasingly that the sovereignty of God needs to be recognized as being a significant component in healing.[90]

---

[84] Allen, 'Signs and Wonders', p. 198.

[85] J. Wimber, *Power Healing* (New York: Harper and Row, 1987); idem, *Power Evangelism. Signs and Wonders Today* (London: Hodder and Stoughton, 1985); K. Warrington, 'A Window on Wimber and Healing', *Churchman* 113.1 (1999), pp. 59–69; Knight, 'God's Faithfulness and God's Freedom', pp. 84–6.

[86] Hardesty (*Faith Cure*, pp. 90–1) notes that Holiness groups previously also taught that the commissions of Jesus to the 12 (Mt. 10.1) and the 70 (Lk. 10.9) were transferred to all believers on the basis of Jn 17.18 and the promise of Jn 14.12.

[87] Dye, *Healing Anointing*, pp. 48, 60.

[88] E.C.W. Boulton, *George Jeffreys. A Ministry of the Miraculous* (Clapham: Elim, n.d.), pp. 36–40.

[89] T. Smail, A. Walker, N. Wright, *Charismatic Renewal* (London: SPCK, 1995), p. 125.

[90] Dye, *Healing Anointing*, pp. 90–5.

It is true that Jesus anticipated a continuing healing ministry in the Church after his resurrection as recorded in the book of Acts and prophesied in the Gospels.[91] The description of the ministry of Jesus to the sick in Mt. 9.35 is identical to the commission to the disciples in *their* ministry to the sick, as recorded in 10.1, the implication being that what their Master has done, they are to do likewise. The Synoptists record Jesus' commissioning the disciples to engage in a ministry of healing in the context of preaching the Kingdom (Mt. 10.6–7; Mk 6.12; Lk. 9.2) and many Pentecostals take seriously the suggestion that they should also take up the mandate given to the disciples by Jesus. However, the commission concerning healing in Mt. 10.8//s is located in the context of a number of instructions for evangelism that have relevance only for the Twelve, though principles may be gleaned and applied to other contexts and eras. If it does relate to today, there is a marked imbalance and infrequency concerning the occurrence of resurrections. Similarly, it is noted that some of the injunctions of Jesus are ignored by believers today including his commission that they should take very limited possessions and only go to 'the lost sheep of the house of Israel'. Nevertheless, many Pentecostals assume that Jesus delegated his healing ministry to all believers. It may be more accurate to recognize that all believers may potentially provide divine healing as a result of the Spirit manifesting his healing power through them rather than that they should emulate Jesus in his healing ministry.

To extrapolate from the records of the healings of Jesus the view that since he healed all who approached him with physical ailments so can all his followers provide healing on every occasion, overlooks the importance of his healings as part of his Messiahship, a status unique to him. Attention is drawn to Lk. 7.22 which provides a response to the question of John the Baptist concerning the identity of Jesus. The healings of Jesus mentioned in the response are demonstrable evidences of his Messianic status. This, coupled with the presentation of his ministry in Lk. 4.18–20, indicate the uniquely phenomenological nature of his person and mission. Since Jesus' role as Messiah was unique, his healing ministry is, by definition, unrepeatable to the same degree by any other individual. That is not to say that healings do not occur today or that one may not learn from Jesus' praxis concerning one's own healing ministry.

Indeed, in Jn 14.12–14, Jesus promises that the works he performed (understood by Pentecostals as a reference to his miracles) will be achieved to a greater degree by those who believe in him.[92] To suggest that believers

---

[91] Mt. 10.1, 8//Mk 6.7, 13 (3.15)//Lk. 9.1, 2, 6; 10.9; Mt. 28.19–20; Mk 16.17–20.

[92] The perspective that 'works' in v. 10 could refer to the preaching of the Gospel is not reflected in the text itself. The plural 'works' is an inappropriate way to express the preaching of the Gospel and it more clearly relates to the miracles of Jesus, as also

will be able to achieve greater works in terms of the dramatic impact caused by even more sensational scenarios than the healings or resurrections of Jesus is an unlikely interpretation of the text. Neither is Jesus promising that greater power will be available to believers than was available to himself. The significance of the promise is that such authoritative power will be granted to believers so that even when Jesus has ascended, the purposes of God will still be made manifest through them because they will be living in the age of the Spirit.[93] The reference to the Spirit (14.15–18) indicates that he is the distinguishing feature in this promise.

Thus the greatness of the works is best understood in terms of the new context in which they are achieved. It is not that a superior quality of miracles is to be expected but that they are to be achieved in the new era of the Spirit and in the absence of the physical presence of Jesus. This greater ministry is now available through the Church and no longer limited to the disciples; it is for the world and not just Israel. The contrast is not between Jesus and his disciples but between Jesus and his disciples who will function with the empowering Spirit in a global context when Jesus ascends to heaven. Thus, the statement in v. 17 that the Spirit 'will remain in you *all*', refers to the Church which is the community of the Spirit in which he will dwell (Rom. 8.15–16; 1 Cor. 3.16–17; 6.18–19) and through whom he will minister (Acts 1.8; 2.17–18; 1 Cor. 2.4). In that sense, Jesus' ministry of initiating the Kingdom has been complemented by the ministry of the Spirit through believers.

Faith

The issue of faith is important for Pentecostals with regard to healing though this does not include a belief that someone should become a Christian before they may be healed.[94] Whether faith is to be exerted by the sufferer, the one who is praying or by both of them has been a vexed issue for many. The fear that a lack of faith has obstructed God in his desire to heal has resulted in many experiencing guilt due to an unnecessary perception that one may have been a block to one's own healing or that of another.[95] More to the point, in many Pentecostal writings, the identity of the faith needed is

---

noted in v. 11 (cf. 9.4). Furthermore, the use of the same term in v. 12, first referring to the same works mentioned in v. 11 as being achieved by Jesus and secondly as potential realities in the experience of the disciples, suggests a continuation of meaning. The following verses then present a promise of Jesus in response to prayer but the context is not of evangelization but the achievement of those works.

[93] cf. Turner, *The Holy Spirit*, p. 338.

[94] Many early Holiness and Pentecostal writers stressed the importance of someone coming to personal faith in Christ before healing could be expected or even requested (Hardesty, *Faith Cure*, p. 130).

not clarified.[96] Roberts encouraged those who were sick to 'Turn your faith loose – now' though it is difficult to determine what is meant and more difficult to ascertain that which the listeners should do.[97] To some, it appears little different to positive thinking though most view it as equivalent to an expression of trust that God is listening and is desirous of responding to the prayer offered. Some have been influenced by a view that is often associated with the Word of Faith movement that anticipates that without an expression of 'faith', the answer to the prayer will not be forthcoming. The 'faith' referred to is described as a belief that God will answer the prayer as it has been requested, some thus choosing to 'claim' the answer to the prayer. However, although there are promises in the Bible relating to some issues that believers are encouraged to pray for, believing that God will respond on the basis of his promise (Jas. 1.5–8), to assume that this is automatically true for requests that are not related to a promise are presumptuous and not supported by Scripture.

Nevertheless, the phenomenon of claiming one's healing has been popularized as a form of prayer, further encouragement being offered that the prayer offered should not include the phrase, 'if it be your will', but 'according to your will'. Similarly, some have taught that prayer should result in believing that the answer to the prayer has already been received, even though the subject of the prayer may still remain.

These perspectives are not supported by many Pentecostals but where they are held, they can cause immense pastoral difficulties for those involved, especially when the prayer is not answered positively. Biblical support for God subjecting people to such treatment to prove their faith concerning an apparent promise is lacking. One's integrity is maintained by acknowledging one's problems, not pretending that they do not exist and it is unhelpful to live as if one's problems are not real. What must at all times be maintained is the recognition that to know God's will and seek to pray within it is at the heart of prayer.

Some view positively the possibility of increasing the faith that one has, as a result of which restoration will occur. Those who have not been healed are often deemed not to have had enough faith and those who are healed are assumed to have passed the faith threshold, whether they are believers or not. The statements 'just have faith' or 'only believe' are however, almost meaningless, because faith requires an object; faith in itself has no power.

---

[95] Canty (*In My Father's House*, p. 90) states concerning healing, 'We may be sure of his will, but has he the power? . . . its release depends on us . . . He only has as much power as we let him use'.

[96] See Warrington, 'Major Aspects of Healing', pp. 34–5.

[97] Roberts, *If You Need Healing*, p. 24; Menzies and Horton, *Bible Doctrines*, pp. 200–02.

The power of faith lies in its object and faith is only as valid as the validity of its object. One does not simply have faith; one has faith in something or someone and in this case, God and his supernatural revelation. Faith does not take up where facts leave off. Faith is not believing something one is not sure of. It is not a leap in the dark but a leap into the light – the light of the revealed word of God, either contained in the Bible or revealed by the Spirit. It is not to be equated with determination or presumption neither is it to be associated with effort, Canty concluding, 'Trying to believe is like trying to be seven foot tall'.[98]

For many Pentecostals, the faith that is expected by God is equated with belief in a promise; a promise that healing is the guaranteed right of the believer. Thus, they assume that before God will heal them, they have to believe that he is going to do so. Tee[99] states that it is 'VITAL' that the person who is ill must have 'an unwavering assurance, deep in their spirit, that it really is the will of God for them to be healed' stating that one can 'emphatically claim that it is the will of God for us to receive healing'. Furthermore, the absence of such 'belief' has been identified as being sin. Finally, it has been suggested by some that one should thank God for one's healing before it has taken place as evidence of one's 'faith' that the healing will occur. Such expressions of faith are not substantiated by the Gospel data and there is a paucity of reflective assessment of these claims by the adherents of such views against the background of a limited number of healings.[100] If healing has been guaranteed by God for believers, such advice may be appropriate. However, in the absence of such a promise, such an attitude is more readily associated with presumption; it is, in effect, an anthropocentrically initiated faith and, as such, is little better than positive thinking.

There is no indication that Jesus expected that people should have an assurance that they would be healed when they came to him. Neither were they encouraged to claim their healing from him. People came simply because they were aware that he had healed before and assumed that he could do so again. The faith that looks to Jesus for help is that which he commends. It is the faith that affirms 'he can' not necessarily that 'he will'.

The suggestion that an insufficient amount of faith could restrict Jesus is wrong on two counts. First, the teaching of Jesus concerning faith is related to its existence, not its quantity. The person who came to Jesus for help had

---

[98] Canty, *The Practice of Pentecost*, p. 172.

[99] Tee, *Healing and Health*, p. 19 (capitals in original); Wacker (*Heaven Below*, pp. 26–8, 189) and Farah (*From the Pinnacle*, pp. 53–4, 121–22) identify consequences of this stance in US Pentecostalism; Gee (*Trophimus, I Left Sick*, pp. 27–8) warns against 'claiming' one's healing which he describes as 'very difficult and disheartening'. Likewise, he criticizes those who 'treat with merciless suspicion as harbouring doubt and unbelief' Christians who ask questions concerning healing being the will of God.

[100] See also Williams, *Renewal Theology. Salvation*, p. 371.

already expressed faith. Secondly, the belief that a person's faith can be developed to achieve a greater level of success is a distortion of the NT teaching concerning faith. It undermines the majesty and love of Jesus, making him a servant of a 'faith' by which he may be coerced or enabled to function. The encouragement by some today that Christians should develop greater faith in order that healing might occur causes heartache for those who remain unhealed. It also reflects a fundamental misunderstanding of the concept of faith as recorded in the Gospels.[101]

On only one occasion is it recorded that Jesus' ministry of healing was partially impeded by a lack of faith on the part of those present (Mt. 13.54–58; Mk 6.1–6; Lk. 4.16–30). However, the unbelief on the part of the people is to be understood as an absence of faith, an unwillingness to believe, rather than an insufficient faith that needed development. It is not to be identified as limited faith in him but as rejection of him. It is not they had too little faith to be healed; they had no faith. On the contrary, they were scandalized by his apparent presumption to speak as he did in their synagogue, resulting in their attempt to kill him.

However, whereas Matthew records that Jesus 'did not do many mighty works there', Mark records that 'he could do no mighty work there' except to heal a few sick folk. Some have understood the latter to imply that Jesus needed an expression of faith on the part of those present to activate his healing power. However, this passage is to be understood as providing a reason for his decision not to perform miracles because they had rejected his person, message and mission. If Jesus had healed people in Nazareth, that would have placed them in a state of greater condemnation; it would have accentuated their guilt, not just for rejecting Jesus but for doing so in the context of his providing miracles on their behalf (Mt. 11.21).

However, that Jesus healed all who came to him for healing then does not necessarily mean that all believers will be healed now. This is not necessarily due to sin on their part or a lack of faith but because the same Jesus who healed people to demonstrate who he was chooses now to demonstrate who he is to believers, sometimes by healing them instantaneously or progressively but sometimes by enabling the suffering context of their lives to be the means whereby he is glorified and to provide them with a platform to demonstrate their trust in him, to be witnessed by both people and supernatural beings.

Prayer

Pentecostals have always affirmed the importance of prayer in the context of a request for healing.[102] Increasingly, however, prayer has been recognized

---

[101] Warrington, *Jesus the Healer*, pp. 15–28; idem, *Healing and Suffering*, pp. 27–38.
[102] Kay, 'Assemblies of God', p. 60.

as an opportunity not only for requesting healing but also for listening to divine advice and guidance as to how one should pray in contexts of sickness as well as other settings.[103] In the context of Jas 5.15, the relationship between the sufferer and God must be developed to bring about interaction and absorption of the former into the will of the latter. The characteristic, which brings faith into existence, is the will of God. The prayer of faith can only thus be offered if the will of God is in keeping with the prayer. It is only in this context that James can offer a guarantee of restoration.

The process of praying for those who are suffering should be undertaken in the expectation that God will provide wisdom concerning how to pray. While one ear should be attuned to the person receiving prayer, the other should be available to receive the wisdom and guidance offered by God. James clearly expects 'the prayer of faith' (5.15) to succeed. It is possible that Jas 5.15 finds its closest parallel in 1.6 inasmuch as the shared context is a prayer of request. The faith that is anticipated in 1.6 is trust in God's promise that he will provide wisdom, on the basis of which one is encouraged to pray and expect a positive response. It is in this respect that faith, as recorded in 5.15, is most appropriately interpreted as trust that God will do as he has promised.

The prayer of faith is thus best identified as knowledge of God's will for a particular situation. The faith referred to is thus equivalent to a divine assurance or revelation to pray in a particular way. Resulting from such divinely imparted knowledge, an individual may confidently expect that the outcome, as revealed, will occur. If God has not provided a revelation or promise, no matter how much 'faith' may be 'manufactured', the desired result cannot be guaranteed. On those occasions when there is no biblical guarantee that prayer will be answered in a particular way, it is more appropriate to pray according to the knowledge and wisdom available at the time. On occasions, God will answer prayer in the way that has been requested because it is allied to his will. On some of those occasions, God will also provide a gift of faith that will enable one to pray in the assurance that the prayer will be answered in the way that it has been offered.

Consequently, when prayer is offered, an attempt should be made to ascertain the will of God in order to pray most appropriately (1.6). For James, the elders (5.14)[104] and/or the righteous person (5.16), because of their experience, wisdom and righteous lifestyles, were identified as those best able to pray appropriately. Such a prayer is to be offered by one who has taken time to tap God's resource of wisdom and appropriate it to a particular situation. Only this prayer can provide the comprehensive guarantee of restoration

---

[103] Dye, *Healing Anointing*, p. 191; Thomas, *The Devil, Disease and Deliverance*, p. 305; Warrington, *Healing and Suffering*, pp. 151–165.

[104] Acts 11.30; 14.23; 15.2, 4, 6, 22–23; 16.4; 20.17; 21.18; 1 Tim. 5.17, 19; Tit. 1.5; 1 Pet. 5.1.

promised by James. In the absence of a certainty that restoration will occur, prayer should still be offered. Whatever occurs, one can be certain that in bringing the person to the Lord, a positive impact is to be expected. Indeed, Onyinah suggests that the healing ministry of Jesus is to encourage people to pray for healing but also 'to trust him to bring good out of every situation whether he cures or not'.[105]

The corporate activity of elders is central to the pattern advocated by James; they act together, rather than individually. The significance of their being summoned may be due to their age or wisdom or both and also linked to the fact they represent the Christian community,[106] their desire being to remind sufferers of their important place within the community, despite any temporary absence[107] and, most importantly, to pray for them.

The significance of the role of the elder is further appreciated when the righteousness of the person offering prayer is explored (5.16). It is possible that James is using the term 'righteous' to describe a Christian, thus indicating that all believers may so pray effectively; this is how the term is sometimes used by Paul (Rom. 5.19). However, given the Jewish background of James, it is more likely that he is using the term to describe those believers whose lives are particularly godly. In Jewish society, righteous people were identified by their moral lifestyles in relationship to God and their community.[108] The righteous person, identified by James, is able to offer effective prayers because s/he will pray in the context of enjoying a close relationship with God. Such a person will seek God's will for the occasion. Thus, the prayer offered by such a person is powerful, not because it is related to the meritorious nature of the one praying but because the one praying is willing and able to discern how best to pray.

Sin and Forgiveness

It is a well established belief among Pentecostals that sickness may be the result of divine judgement or chastisement because of personal sin.[109] Sickness has been regularly traced back to Satan and the Fall and various texts have been provided to substantiate this view.[110] It has been assumed that sickness

---

[105] O. Onyinah, 'God's Grace, Healing and Suffering', *IRM* 95 Nos. 376/377 (2006), pp. 117–27 (126).

[106] Exod. 3.16; 4.29; 12.2–3; Josh. 8.33; 23.2.

[107] In Jewish culture, illness often had an anti-social aspect (Lev. 13–4; Job 19.13–22; Ps. 69.2; Isa. 38.10–18). The presence of the eldership no doubt helped offset this characteristic.

[108] Gen. 18.23, 26, 28; Deut. 4.8; Job 15.14; Pss. 10.3; 36.16, 30–31; Prov. 15.28; Mal. 3.18.

[109] Exod. 9.14; Num. 14.37; 1 Sam. 25.36–9; 1 Kgs 13.4–6; Pss. 31.4–5; 37.3.

[110] Job 2.7; Lk. 11.20–25, 13.11–17; Acts 10.38; Jas 5.16.

may also be caused by demonic influence. Most Pentecostals reject the equation that illness is always linked to individual sin[111] though personal sin has been cautiously recognized as a reason for a healing not occurring, as reflected in the NT (Acts 5.1–11; 1 Cor. 11.29–30; Jas 5.16).[112]

Gee,[113] commenting on Trophimus who was sick, acknowledges that there is nothing to suggest that he was spiritually or morally in error, as a result of which he advises, 'If no apparent reasons for failure to receive supernatural healing are made clear to the conscience . . . we . . . leave the case in the hands of our Heavenly Father . . . without condemnation of ourselves or others'. Similarly, Canty[114] writes, 'It is wrong to suggest that some unknown state of soul can prevent healing and that it needs careful searching to discover it . . . sin is usually obvious'.

The Name of Jesus

One of the clearest emphases in Pentecostal prayer for healing is the incorporation of the name of Jesus (Jas 5.15), though the reason for this is not always clearly presented. Dye, however, accurately writes that the use of the name of Jesus is only appropriately incorporated if one's prayer 'lines up perfectly with the will of God'.[115]

The clearest derivation of this practice is the apostolic use of the name of Jesus in prayer as recorded in the book of Acts.[116] Promises by Jesus to his disciples concerning the efficacy of his name[117] also form a fertile environment for a belief in the importance of the regular articulation of the name. However, it is the context in which the name is used that determines whether contemporary believers are actually following the guidelines of Jesus.[118] The phrase 'in the name of the Lord' in Jas 5.14, is the only occasion where it is used in the context of a prayer for restoration. Its most proximate occurrence is 5.10 where it appears to mean that the prophets spoke with the authority of the Lord or more generally, on behalf of the Lord. The words they spoke were not their own but were initiated by God and thus in keeping with his will.

---

[111] Jeffreys, *Healing Rays*, pp. 150–51; Parr, *Divine Healing*, p. 9; Dye, *Healing Anointing*, p. 189.

[112] Jeffreys, *Healing Rays*, p. 165; Simpson, *The Gospel of Healing*, p. 89; Hardesty, *Faith Cure*, pp. 130–32.

[113] Gee, *Trophimus, I Left Sick*, pp. 12–13.

[114] Canty, *The Practice of Pentecost*, p. 179.

[115] C. Dye, *Prayer That Gets Answers* (London: Dovewell, 1998), p. 12; L.W. Hurtado, 'Healing and Related Factors', *Paraclete* 4.2 (1970), pp. 20–4.

[116] Acts 3.6, 16; 4.10; 9.34.

[117] Jn 14.13–14; 15.16; 16.24.

[118] cf. K. Warrington, 'The Use of the Name (of Jesus) in Healing and Exorcism' (SPS/EPCRA conference paper, Mattersey, 1998).

The 'name' of the Lord and the 'power' of the Lord often appear to be used synonymously in the Bible,[119] and the incorporation of the name of the Lord undergirds an expectation to see his power in operation.[120] However, to use the name of Jesus with an expectation of an automatic release of power is inappropriate.[121] Although the name may serve to remind a person of the power of the name bearer, the will of the owner of that power is to be recognized as being of paramount importance. The legitimate and authoritative use of the name necessitates relationship with the name bearer. The name of the Lord is only appropriately used when the prayer incorporating it is sanctioned by God, for then it will effect a change.[122]

Tee notes,

> There is nothing clockwork or mechanical about prayer . . . no one can ask for this or that . . . and think that, by adding at the end of the sentence 'in the name of Jesus', whatever they request or demand is going to take place forthwith . . . The owner of the name must authorise it.[123]

The most important aspect related to the name of Jesus is thus not its presence in a healing prayer but its symbolic value as an indicator of the importance of a recognition of the will of God by the one offering the prayer.

Anointing with Oil

Anointing with oil has retained its place in the context of prayer for the sick in Pentecostal practice (Jas 5.16)[124] though is not viewed as being essential for a healing to occur. Pentecostals reject any sacramental notions that suggest that the oil has residential curative powers or that it may be blessed in order to be used for the purpose of anointing the sick. Pentecostals have traditionally used oil, sparingly applied to the forehead. Although generally used with reference to healing the sick, some African Pentecostals use it in settings where curses are removed, reversals in life situations are requested or the impartation of power for those who are to undertake specific responsibilities in the church.[125]

---

[119] 2 Kgs 2.24; Ps. 117.10–12, 26; Mt. 7.22; Lk. 10.17; Acts 3.6, 16; 4.7, 10; 16.18.

[120] Mt. 21.9; Mk 9.38; Lk. 9.49, 13.35; Acts 3.6, 4.7, 10; Phil. 2.9–10; Col. 3.17; Heb. 1.4.

[121] cf. Warrington, 'The Use of the Name', pp. 16–36.

[122] Exod. 5.22–23; Deut. 18.18–19; 2 Chron. 26.5; Jn 14.13–14; 15.7, 16; 16.24, 26; Jas 1.25; 1 Jn 3.22; 5.14–15.

[123] Tee, 'The Doctrine of Divine Healing', p. 203; cf. AoG, 'Our Position on Divine Healing', p. 12.

[124] Darragh, *In Defence of His Word*, pp. 1620; Anderson (*An Introduction to Pentecostalism*, pp. 108, 228) notes that some African Pentecostals also include water or other objects in healing settings.

[125] Asamoah-Gyadu, 'Unction to Function', pp. 243–48, 252–56.

Inasmuch as James' addressees are Jewish Christians, and because he does not explain the practice, it may be assumed that, at least in part, it derived from their Jewish culture. Oil had ceremonial, cosmetic and dietary functions in Judaism[126] as well as medicinal properties.[127] However, it is unlikely that James is advocating a medical therapy. Although the medical properties of oil were well known at that time, they were only ever expected to alleviate suffering in a limited range of illnesses. Another major obstacle to the view that James anticipated a medical use of oil is that it presupposes that 5.14–16 reflects a scenario of sickness. Although this may be one of the forms of suffering anticipated by James, it is inappropriate to assume that it is the only one and an exploration of the passage concerned substantiates the probability of a wider arena of weakness and suffering.[128] It is necessary therefore to consider other possible uses of oil in Jewish society that may provide a more appropriate frame of reference for its use in Jas 5.

Oil was regarded by the Jews as symbolizing a number of characteristics that would encourage the one who was being anointed.[129] As such, it indicated the presence of the Spirit[130] and was also used to signify an infusion of the strength[131] or wisdom[132] of God. Anointing was also associated with restoration, occurring when a person had been healed of leprosy, such an act demonstrating her/his purification,[133] based on which s/he was welcomed back into society. On other occasions, oil was used to demonstrate that a new situation had come into being (including the completion of a marriage or business contract and the legitimate emancipation of a slave). It was associated with the bestowal of honour and affirmation[134] and since it was regarded as being precious, the one who was anointed was also deemed to be precious.[135] If the anointing procedure transmitted only some of these implications, it is clear why James included it in his advice. The anointing with oil is thus probably intended to be symbolic and commemorative of

---

[126] Ceremonial use: Exod. 40.13; Cosmetic use: 2 Sam. 12.20; Dan. 10.2; Amos 6.16; Dietary use: Exod. 29.2; 1 Kgs 7.12; 2 Kgs 18.32.

[127] 2 Chron. 28.15; Isa. 1.6; Jer. 8.22; to anoint a sore: b. *Shab.* 53b; b. *Yoma* 77b; to heal toothache: b. *Gittin* 69a; to heal skin diseases: Mid. *Gen.* 85.1; various healings: Josephus, *Wars* 1. 657; *Ant.* 17. 172; Philo, *De Somn.* 2. 58.

[128] K. Warrington, 'The Identification of Weakness in James 5' (SPS conference paper, Springfield, 1992).

[129] Exod. 28.41; 30.30; Lev. 8.12; Judg. 9.15; 1 Sam. 10.1; 2 Sam. 12.7; 1 Kgs 19.16; K. Warrington, 'Anointing with Oil', *EB*, 2 (1993), pp. 5–22.

[130] 1 Sam. 10.1, 6; 16.13; Isa. 61.1; Acts 10.38; 2 Cor. 1.21–22.

[131] Ps. 88.21–25.

[132] Isa. 11.1–4; 1 Jn 2.20, 27.

[133] Lev. 14.12, 16.

[134] Mt. 26.7; Lk. 7.46; Jn 11.2; 12.3.

[135] Mid. *Ex.* 48.1; Lev. 3.6; 26.9; Num. 6.1; 18.9.

certain features that would result in the sufferer feeling secure, knowing that s/he was in the presence of friends who cared and a God who restored and supported.

Laying on of Hands

This is a significant feature of Pentecostal healing praxis,[136] following the practice of Jesus. The hands are generally gently placed on the head rather than the area of the sickness. It has been regarded as an act of compassion more than a formal rite, as well as a symbolic act linking the power of God with the hand(s) of the one(s) doing the action. When used by Jesus, however, the fact that he touched a sick person demonstrated his authority in that he did not anticipate any ceremonial contamination as a result of his action, his authority over the Law being demonstrated by the subsequent healing.

Exorcism

Pentecostals accept the personal and malevolent existence of the devil whose major role is to undermine the mission of Jesus as it is expressed through the Church and to combat the work of the Spirit which is to lead people into truth.[137] They also believe that Jesus has gained victory over the devil, a victory that will be consummated at the eschaton though it is to be experienced in the present, both personally and globally by resisting him through prayer, obedience, self discipline and other strategies of spiritual warfare.[138] The origin of demons is not identified in the Bible and Pentecostals have been reticent to speculate about this topic though a common belief is that they are synonymous with fallen angels (Mt. 25.41; 2 Pet. 2.4; Jude 6; Rev. 12.7–9).

Pentecostals also believe in the possibility of spiritual warfare by which they mean combating demonic forces by means of spiritual power, often prayer, Eph. 6.11–12 being the main verses supporting such a belief. Some have expressed concern about the danger of accepting an inappropriate dualism in which God and the devil are apparently engaged in a struggle in which the final outcome is certain but the prior strife and intensity of battle

---

[136] Kay (*Pentecostals in Britain*, p. 101), as a result of considering results from a major census he conducted concerning Pentecostal beliefs, including healing, identified the laying on of hands in healing scenarios as one of the few items that attracts 100% agreement from Pentecostal ministers across the denominational spectrum.

[137] F.D. Macchia, 'Repudiating the Enemy: Satan and Demons', in Horton (ed.), *Systematic Theology*, pp. 194–212.

[138] C.H. Kraft, 'Spiritual Warfare: A Neocharismatic Perspective', in Burgess and van der Maas (eds), *NIDPCM*, pp. 1091–096.

is high. The framework for such a view is complex but it includes the following elements. Although the war will be won by God, there is an assumption that many skirmishes will also be won by the devil. The battle rages hot and fierce with the believer often in a vulnerable position, such battles also being reflected in the heavenly realm where demons and angels continue the conflict.[139] However, the biblical schema does not reflect a situation in which the Kingdom of God is presented thus in juxtaposition with the kingdom of Satan. The devil is much less significant to God than many believers think. Rather than a cosmic dualism, Jesus is always presented in the NT as superior to Satan and the one to whom the demons give obeisance. Similarly, Jesus is presented as the conqueror of the evil age and the redeemer of people from it (Gal. 1.4; Eph. 2.2; Col. 1.13). That is not to suggest that there are no evil powers or that they are not influential and potentially harmful to the believer (2 Cor. 4.4; Eph. 6.12). However, believers are empowered to defend themselves against such forces (Eph. 6.13).

It is in the NT that demons are more clearly described, possibly because the Jews had an inadequate demonology, largely mythical and one in which their spiritual danger and malevolence were largely ignored; instead, they were viewed often by the populace as being mischievous – but rarely a spiritual threat. They are ruled by (the) Satan (Rev. 12.9–10) and antagonistic to God (1 Cor. 8.4–6; 10.20). The description of demons in the Gospels indicates a readiness to harm those they inhabit, either with an illness (Mk 9.17) or by impelling the victim to self harm (Mk 5.5). They are described as dirty or unclean (Mk 5.2) and evil (Lk. 11.26). Since the devil is characterized as being involved in temptation (Gen. 3.14; 2 Cor. 11.3), many assume that demons have a similar role.[140] Collins proposes that they are engaged in oppressing believers and causing obsessive negative behaviour.[141] Although most Pentecostals understand the depersonalized nature of evil, they have a strong perception of a personal devil and demons.

Pentecostals accept that sickness/suffering may be caused by demons though this is not assumed to be the cause of every illness.[142] Thomas[143] has explored the role of the devil in sickness and notes that this is primarily reflected in Matthew and Luke-Acts while other NT writers, including James and John do not suggest that the devil or demons are influential in sickness

---

[139] See R.A. Guelich, 'Spiritual Warfare: Jesus, Paul and Peretti', *Pneuma* 13.1 (1991), pp. 33–64.

[140] W.D. Collins, 'An Assemblies of God Perspective on Demonology. Part 1', *Paraclete* 27.4 (1993), pp. 23–30 (27).

[141] Collins, 'An Assemblies of God. Part 1', pp. 28–30.

[142] G. Canty, 'Demons and Casting Out Demons', in Brewster (ed.), *Pentecostal Doctrines*, pp. 241–57 (250); see Mt. 4.23; 8.16; Mk 1.32; Lk. 7.21; 13.32.

[143] Thomas, *The Devil, Disease and Deliverance*, p. 301.

and Paul and Mark offer only limited support for such an association. Instead, he concludes, 'Far from being viewed simply as a source of healing, God, in the view of most of the New Testament writers . . ., can be depicted as the origin of infirmity and death'.[144]

The NT does not provide guidance in identifying if a sickness has been caused by a demonic presence. Therefore, such a possibility needs to be considered carefully. Pentecostals in non-Western cultures encounter overt demonic activity more often and the connection between the demonic and illness is much closer in some cultural contexts than in others. It may not be possible to provide a comprehensively satisfactory explanation for this difference though world views, personal history and the socio-cultural and religious contexts of the sufferers may have a part to play in any discussion. The explicit activity of demons in many non-Western societies may coincide with the prevalent views relating to ancestral spirits that can negatively impact people. The identification of demonic activity will benefit from an awareness of the cultural setting while scientific psychological and biblical perspectives are also to be carefully considered. The question remains as to whether Western Pentecostals have been able as accurately to identify the demonic influences in their more secular and post-modern settings.

In general, the impact of Satan upon people has been assumed to be the result of demonic activity and has popularly been subsumed under two categories, possession and oppression[145] though little critical analysis has been undertaken with regard to these classifications. McClung concludes that among Pentecostals, 'exorcism has been practiced but not formally theologized' noting that 'No clarified doctrinal statement on demonology and exorcism exists among major Pentecostal bodies',[146] even though it has been practiced from the commencement of its history. Indeed, Poloma provides evidence from AoG ministers that indicate many differences and even uncertainty concerning demonic issues, noting that 37% of them have never engaged in a deliverance setting.[147] A number of reasons account for this, one of which is a reaction to the tendency to unthinkingly ascribe demonic activity to many problems that affect people; thus many are prone to consider

---

[144] Thomas, *The Devil, Disease and Deliverance*, p. 300; contra Canty ('Demons and Casting Out Demons', p. 249) who states that 'Satan is primarily responsible for the sick'.

[145] L.G. McClung Jr ('Exorcism', in Burgess (ed.), *NIDPCM*, pp. 624–28 (626)) suggests 'oppression, obsession and possession'.

[146] McClung, 'Exorcism', p. 624.

[147] Poloma, *The Assemblies of God*, pp. 199–202; Lugo (*Spirit and Power*, p. 15) records that 58% of Pentecostals in the countries researched testified that they had experienced or witnessed an exorcism (ranging from 30% (South Korea) and 34% (USA) to 80% (Brazil) and 86% (Kenya); J. Theron, 'A Critical Overview of the Church's Ministry of Deliverance from Evil Spirits', *Pneuma* 18.1 (1996), pp. 79–92.

other solutions instead of exorcism. Another reason appears to be largely due to the limited expressions of demonic activity in the West in ways that are reminiscent of the Gospel narrative. However, although there may be less evidence of individuals being affected by demons in ways reflected in the NT that does not mean that they have ceased their malevolence.

Although Pentecostals hold diverse views concerning the demonic and exorcism (increasingly, identified as 'deliverance'),[148] they have sought to maintain a sanguine stance with regard to these issues and to be guided by the biblical narrative for their beliefs and praxis. Fundamentally, they believe that casting out demons is part of the Gospel commission,[149] the authority contained therein being available to believers. There has been a reticence to accept that which is not clearly reflected in the NT, whether it refers to expressions of the demonic or exorcistic practices. This is largely due to an assumption by many that only that which is recorded in the NT should be affirmed as a basis for belief and praxis. This matrix may need to be reconsidered as the NT was not provided as a comprehensive statement of all spiritual activity.

Popular Pentecostal beliefs concerning demonological issues have been generated, by and large, through preaching and the testimonies of people who have engaged in deliverance ministries or been delivered from demonic influences. For many Pentecostals, the popular view of demons owes as much to medieval art and popular fiction[150] as it does to the NT. Similarly, visual experiences and verbal information associated with exorcisms or demonized activity have often been the catalyst for beliefs concerning demons rather than the largely veiled description of the NT.[151]

The lack of Biblical support for much that has been written often makes the practice of exorcism subjective and even suspect, leaving a trail of speculation and, at worst, confusion for the readers.[152] Thus, attempts have been made to

---

[148] Marty, 'Pentecostalism in American Piety', p. 216.

[149] Mt. 10.8; Mk 16.15–20; Lk. 9.1–2; 10.1, 17; Acts 10.38.

[150] F. Peretti, *This Present Darkness* (Minstrel: Eastbourne, 1989).

[151] Canty ('Demons and Casting Out Demons', p. 254) states, 'There is nothing in Scripture about coughing or spitting out demons . . . nor are we given any encouragement to hold conversations with demons . . . they should be told to leave.' Though offering no evidence, he suggests, 'Demons themselves enjoy having attention paid to them and tend to turn up where they are talked about a great deal. There is simply no sense, nor any Scripture, for long battles with a demonised person, battles lasting for many years.'

[152] Wacker, *Heaven Below*, pp. 91–2; J. Richards ('The Church's Healing Ministry and the Charismatic Renewal', in D. Martin, P. Mullen (eds), *Strange Gifts* (Oxford: Blackwell, 1984), pp. 151–58 (151)) describes, 'an over-awareness of spiritual warfare, leading to an inflated demonology' which exists in some Pentecostals; see also A. Walker, 'The Devil You Think You Know: Demonology and the Charismatic Movement', in Smail, Walker and Wright, *Charismatic Renewal*, pp. 86–105.

discern the names, activities and inhabited regions of demons by some,[153] Canty[154] describing it as 'a curiosity of the "lore" of current demonology'.

It is not surprising that Hollenweger described demonic activity as 'an unsolved problem in Pentecostal belief and practice'.[155] One aspect of the problem relates to the causes of demonic activity (known as 'demonic door-ways' by some African Pentecostals[156]) in an individual. Many varied reasons have been offered for the presence of demons including hereditary links, occult activity, ancestral spirits, curses, lust, emotional trauma, drugs, idola-try, negative thoughts and physical weakness.[157] Onyinah identifies dangers in simplistically assuming that all believers need deliverance after salvation, a practice that is common among some African Pentecostals. Even though some people appear to have been helped and released from bondage to ancestral spirits as a result of this, he notes that many stay fearful of the spir-its that oppressed them in the past and become dependent on such exorcistic practices and centres of deliverance for protection for the future.[158]

Pentecostals have, in general, refused to accept the possibility of a Chris-tian being 'possessed' by a demon,[159] Kay[160] concluding that in the 1970s, when neo-Pentecostals, in general, confirmed that a Christian could be pos-sessed, 'the classic Pentecostals, after some debate, said a firm no'. For many Pentecostals, the lack of evidence for such phenomena in the NT is sufficient to indicate that it cannot and does not happen today. However, although the Bible may be silent on believers being seriously affected by demons, the real-ity is often very different and in such cases, dogmatic statements may be less appropriate even where the Bible is drawn in as support. Where reality is different to one's theology, it is sometimes the latter that needs revision, or, at least, the way in which it is presented. The Bible is not meant to be a record of all demonic activity and sometimes, the experiences of those from different cultures may be of significant help in exploring such issues.

---

[153] See McClung, 'Exorcism', p. 626.

[154] Canty, *The Practice of Pentecost*, p. 193.

[155] Hollenweger, *The Pentecostals*, p. 379.

[156] J.K. Asamoah-Gyadu, 'Mission to "Set the Captives Free": Healing, Deliverance and Generational Curses in Ghanaian Pentecostalism', *IRM* 93. 370/371 (July–Oct. 2004), pp. 389–406 (396).

[157] Asamoah-Gyadu, 'Mission to "Set the Captives Free"', p. 397.

[158] Onyinah, 'Matthew to "Set the Captives Free"', pp. 128–30.

[159] See K. Warrington, 'Reflections on the History and Development of Demonological Beliefs and Praxis among British Pentecostals', *AJPS* 7.1. (2004), pp. 281–304; Duffield and Van Cleave, *Foundations of Pentecostal Theology*, p. 494; the official position of the AoG (printed in *The Pentecostal Testimony*, June 1975, pp. 16–18) rejects the view that a Christian may be demon possessed; Collins, 'An Assemblies of God', p. 20.

[160] Kay, *Inside Story*, p. 337.

The experiences, practices and views of many African and Asian Pentecostals have brought a breadth of opinion to the discussion in the last few years.[161] More research needs to be completed with reference to demonic activity and exorcism including the issue of terminology (possession, oppression).

Partly as a result of the great variation in belief concerning demonic issues within British Pentecostalism, in 1975, a Committee was appointed by the Executive Council of the Elim Pentecostal Church to consider these topics and a number of papers were presented and discussed. One of the major results of the documentation provided was to present a cautious response to some of the more unguarded current beliefs and practices. Thus, Walker[162] noted the danger of blaming demons for sinful tendencies instead of emphasizing the importance of a believer being 'a persistent, developing, on-going disciple'. Despite the variety of opinions, a number of constants remain:

- The devil and demons are antagonistic foes of the Church.
- They have been eternally overcome by Jesus.
- They still affect individuals malevolently.
- They can be resisted and overcome by and through Jesus.

Similarly, although forms of exorcism vary, a number of features would be recognized as being important to many Pentecostals involved in exorcistic ministry:

- Preparation including prayer and the gift of discernment.
- The use of the name of Jesus.[163]
- The incorporation of a command that the demon leave its victim.
- A recognition of the authority of Jesus that is invested in the believer.

Other more marginal elements, that have little Biblical precedent, vary depending on the religious, social and cultural context of the people concerned and

---

[161] W. Ma, '"In Jesus' Name!" Power Encounter from an Asian Pentecostal Perspective', in Gener and Gorospe (eds), *Principalities and Powers*, pp. 21–40.

[162] T.W. Walker, 'Demon Possession', *Elim Committee on Demon Possession Report* (1975), pp. 1–2.

[163] Mk 16.17; Acts 16.18. Asamoah-Gyadu, 'Mission to "Set the Captives Free"', p. 395; Canty, 'Demons and Casting Out Demons', pp. 253–54 states, 'The vital element is not the formula but the presence of Jesus in the life of the person casting the demons out . . . The pronunciation of the name . . . was partly a testimony to those who observed what was happening . . . The fact is that demons left people when the name of Jesus was not uttered . . . The casting out of demons does not require a barrage of words with the voluminous repetition of the word "Jesus" or "Christ"'.

have received limited comment by Pentecostals. Such aspects include the use of specific terminology (such as 'binding and loosing'[164]), the laying on of hands on those needing deliverance, physical manifestations of the sufferer, anointing, physical gestures to symbolize the removal of demons, conversation with and identification of demons, and post-exorcistic care of the person concerned.

Onyinah, reflecting African exorcistic phenomena, identifies a number of means whereby people are delivered from demonic forces including the place of dreams in the procedure. He quotes case studies in which revelation has been gained concerning proposed malevolent activities of witches towards believers, the revelation providing a warning to gain protection from that activity.[165] He also describes an absence of deliverance on the part of many Pentecostal believers despite their having engaged in fasting and prayer because underlying emotional and social issues needed prior resolution.[166] Asamoah-Gyadu also notes that some Pentecostals value counselling and a 'lengthy system of diagnosis . . . to help trace the ancestry of victims' though he questions this link with the past, offering Lk. 13.1–5 and Jn 9.3 as evidence that it is more appropriate to repudiate the notion that people always inherit the sins of past members of their family than to assume the opposite.[167] Rather than concentrate on the past, he encourages Pentecostals to bring their needs to God who can transform their lives irrespective of any past issues.[168]

Although exorcisms are included in the Synoptics, it is significant to note that John's Gospel does not record any.[169] The author chose to use a selection of signs to enforce his teaching and it appears that exorcisms did not achieve his purposes.[170] The paucity of exorcisms in the Acts of the Apostles

---

[164] The concepts of 'binding and loosing' are popular in Pentecostalism and are loosely based on their reference by Jesus in Mt. 16.19; 18.18. However, their usage there has no relationship to exorcism. Rather, it was Rabbinic terminology describing the authority to provide or restrict permission to a Jew in a given setting (to teach, to be released from a vow). However, other uses of the term 'binding' (Mk 3.27) and 'loosing/releasing' (Mk 7.34–35; Lk. 13.16) are associated with the expulsion of the devil or demons. Rather than exclusively relate these terms to exorcism or to the granting or withholding of authority in church settings, it may be preferable to recognize the underlying notions relate to the granting of authority to believers by Jesus.

[165] Onyinah, 'Contemporary "Witchdemonology" in Africa', pp. 338–40.

[166] Onyinah, 'Contemporary "Witchdemonology" in Africa', pp. 340–42.

[167] Asamoah-Gyadu, 'Mission to "Set the Captives Free"', p. 401; see B. Meyer, 'Make a Complete Break with the Past: Memory and Post-Colonial Modernity in Ghanaian Pentecostalist Discourse', *JRA* 27.3 (1998), pp. 316–49 (321).

[168] Asamoah-Gyadu, 'Mission to "Set the Captives Free"', pp. 402–06.

[169] Though see E.K. Broadhead, 'Echoes of an Exorcism in the Fourth Gospel?', *ZNTW* 86.1–2 (1995), pp. 111–19.

[170] For further, see Twelftree, *Jesus the Miracle Worker*, pp. 222–24. He suggests that to have presented Jesus as an exorcist may have associated Jesus with contemporary

(16.16–23) and the absence of exorcisms in the rest of the NT are also of interest. It may be that exorcisms were more prominent in the ministry of Jesus, given the dynamic nature of his person and his radical message concerning the Kingdom he was initiating, which resulted in a violent backlash from his demonic foes.

Outside the Synoptics, the guidance offered by other NT writers relating to the demonic is that the most appropriate ways of responding to such forces are through being filled with the Spirit, receiving the Word (Mk 4.15–20) and resisting temptation (1 Pet. 5.8). In Rom. 16.20, Paul encourages his readers to adopt Christian behaviour, as a result of which God will 'crush Satan under your feet'. Similarly, self control (1 Cor. 7.5; Eph. 4.26–27), forgiveness (2 Cor. 2.11) and the ministry of love within the Christian community (Eph. 4.1–6.9) are all viewed as antidotes to Satan's measures against believers. Indeed, Paul deduces that all principalities are subservient to Christ (Col. 2.10), were originally created for him (Col. 1.16) and were disarmed at the Cross (Col. 2.15 cf. Rom. 8.38–39). Thus, Paul asserts that his readers are to recognize that they are supported by the powerful Spirit in their battle with evil. Rather than explore secondary questions related to demons, he identifies the resources of believers to undermine the role of evil in their lives and contexts. Indeed, he implies that the influence of an evil force on believers is largely determined by believers themselves for they have the authority to resist it (Jas 4.7).

Thus, although the biblical text provides information relating to the combat between the believer and demonic forces, it offers little by way of guidance for the implementation of a normative exorcistic procedure, let alone answer many of the questions that have been asked in recent years concerning issues relating to the demonic. It is instructive to note the paucity of such comment by the writers in the NT outside the ministry of Jesus. That is not to suggest that exorcisms did not occur; they did and Luke records this in Acts 8.7 and 19.12. Paul also is aware of demonic malevolence (Eph. 2.2; 6.12) and the one incident in the book of Acts need not be taken to indicate a rare example of exorcism in the early Church. On the contrary, principles identifying the malevolence of evil spirits may be gleaned from it.

Although the exorcism is recorded in one verse (Acts 16.18), the following twenty-two verses record the consequences. This is not a story recording the

---

exorcists and provided an unhelpful context for his description of Jesus as the Son of God; also, insofar as John does not concentrate on the Kingdom of God, it is understandable that the clearest sign of the Kingdom (exorcisms) are omitted; as exorcisms in the Synoptics demonstrate the demise of Satan, in John, this is achieved in the cross; E. Plumer ('The Absence of Exorcisms in the Fourth Gospel', *Biblica* 78.3 (1997), pp. 350–368) also understands them as being inadequate vehicles of the Johannine kerygma; G.W. Gilpin, 'Demon Possession', *Elim Committee*, pp. 1–2.

demise of one evil spirit; it is a story recording the potential death of the Apostles and the demise of their mission in Philippi. The focus of the story is not on the authority of Paul to cast out a demon but on the authority of God to overcome all obstacles placed before the mission of his delegated messenger, whether they be demons (16.18), mobs (16.19), rulers (16.20–21), physical abuse (16.22–24) or prison (16.24). The supremacy of God over these obstacles is demonstrated in the expulsion of the demon, the occurrence of an earthquake which shakes all the doors off their hinges and unfastens the fetters of the prisoners (16.26), the expression of faith by the jailors (16.31–34), the apologies of the rulers to the apostles (16.39) and the encouragement of the believers (16.40).

Although questions are raised by the narrative, including the length of time that passed before Paul exorcized the demon and his motivation for doing so, the central message must not be overlooked. This is less a story of an exorcism of a spirit; more a record of the malevolent mastermind which seeks to destroy the mission of Paul; but of much greater importance is the confirmation that Paul is guarded by a superior power. Any lessons to be gleaned from this narrative of relevance for exorcistic procedures must be sourced after first exploring the purpose of the author in recording the narrative in the first place. Luke is less interested in the former and more interested in demonstrating the authority of the Lord who guides Paul and who supervises the mission to the Gentiles. Luke presents the subtlety of the opposition force against Paul and his potential dilemma. If he ignores the demonic intrusion, it will act as a constant irritant; if he exorcises it, it may result in the truncation of his mission in Philippi. The exorcism appears to have indicated that the spirit had won a decisive battle in its intrusion in Paul's mission for in removing the girl from bondage, the Apostles are themselves bound in prison. However, the story ends with the jailer's family becoming believers and being baptized. Although the opposition forces seem to have won the battle, Luke is desirous of demonstrating that they are pawns in the hands of the one who is supervising the destiny of Paul.

What may be concluded from this brief overview of the biblical text is that demonic activity is not a central focus of its message. That is not to say it did not occur much then nor that it is marginal today. But neither should one assume, in the light of the limited information available, that the Bible was intended to provide comprehensive guidance for responding to demonic activity when one experiences it. Paul refers to the possibility of Satan functioning in the guise of an angel of light (2 Cor. 11.14) armed with an array of schemes and plots (2 Cor. 2.11). Such a foe may not be guarded against on the basis of a predetermined battle plan but in cooperation with the Spirit who is aware of the changing strategies of the enemy and can influence the outcome by guiding believers in their fight.

It is possible that Pentecostals have been too reliant on the information provided in the Bible as if it was the only guidance available to them for identifying demonic activity and responding to it. Instead, believers are to be aware of the potential intrusion of evil and to combat it while simultaneously developing their reliance on the Spirit. It is in this regard that the role of the Spirit and the readiness of believers to listen to him individually and through the Church is crucial.

Also, although the Pentecostal church in the West, which exists in the context of a post-Enlightenment perspective, may not need to change its demonology, it does need to be open to the beliefs and practices of Pentecostals and others elsewhere who function with more regular exposure to overt demonic intrusion.[171] An African Pentecostal may view demonic activity differently to a Western Pentecostal. The prevalence of ancestor worship, for example, in an Asian setting may affect how one interprets the text and relates to demonic manifestations and similarly, confrontation with the demonic may differ from that in Western societies. To determine which is the most appropriate on the basis of the NT may be less helpful and even inappropriate as it is not clear that the latter was intended to function as a textbook for correct exorcistic practice. Furthermore, the experiences of those in Africa, South America and Asia who are aware of these issues, partly as a result of their religious and cultural contexts but also because of their experience in demonic and exorcistic activity, are valuable to Western believers whose exposure to the latter is different, often less overt and less frequent.[172] At the same time, the contextualization of some of those experiences and practices will help guard against an inappropriate and presumptuous ministry that may be less valuable in settings where the demonic presents itself in a different guise.

It is possible that the role of the demonic in many Western contexts is more subtle and disguised than elsewhere. Rather than assume that the limited number of exorcisms indicates an absence of the demonic, it may be more appropriate to acknowledge the opposite and to be led by the Spirit in considering other ways in which it may be functioning. It is probable that demonic activity in the West is even more dangerous by its devious nature and believers need to be aware that the battle is not always overt but also subliminal and no less undermining. However, listening to the Spirit and exploring the contemporary experience and praxis of others, even where it may differ from one's own, in a context of comment and reflection by mature colleagues, are all necessary elements in the developing of a practical strategy with regard to demonic issues.

---

[171] See for example A.S. Moreau (ed.), *Deliver Us from Evil. An Uneasy Frontier in Christian Mission* (Monrovia: Marc, 2002).

[172] O. Onyinah, 'Deliverance as a Way of Confronting Witchcraft in Modern Africa: Ghana as a Case History', *AJPS* 5.1 (2002), pp. 107–34.

Suffering

The concept of suffering has largely been neglected by Pentecostals though there are exceptions.[173] This has risen largely as a result of the fact that many believe that God has enabled believers to be supernaturally rescued from suffering (especially sickness) through prayer. It may also be adduced that for Western (Pentecostal) Christianity, the experience of suffering is a relatively infrequent one and that may also have resulted in a limited consideration of suffering by Western Pentecostals. However, the NT paints a different picture. Nevertheless, rather than concentrate on the suffering of the cross, Pentecostals have preferred to move quickly to the glory associated with it. The weakness associated with the cross has been reserved largely for the purposes of remembering the sufferings of Jesus rather than it being understood as representing a central component for his followers. Consequently, the theology of the cross including its emphasis on crucially important themes including victory through suffering, strength through weakness, light through darkness and salvation through death have been largely overlooked. Instead, the victory and glory associated with the cross have been understood in triumphalistic terms. The recognition of the place of suffering in Pentecostal theology needs to be redeemed as an integral aspect of an authentic spirituality that acknowledges the value of suffering in the life of the believer and does not simply attempt to exclude it or assume that its presence is intrinsically illegitimate.

Furthermore, many Pentecostals have concentrated on the Spirit in the context of enabling believers to function powerfully as God's representatives and to fulfil his will in their lives while being less appreciative of the fact that the Spirit also dynamically supports believers in their suffering. While the former is a valid exploration, it has resulted in the association of suffering and the Spirit to be marginalized. Thus, the association of the Spirit with prophecy, empowering for ministry and mission or for the purpose of

---

[173] For exceptions, see K. Warrington, *Healing and Suffering: Biblical and Pastoral Reflections* (Carlisle: Paternoster Press, 2005); idem, 'Healing and Suffering in the Bible', *IRM* 95. 376/377 (Jan.–April 2006), pp. 154–64; idem, 'Suffering and Spirit in Luke-Acts'; idem, 'A Spirit Theology of Suffering', in H. Hunter, C.M. Robeck Jr (eds), *The Suffering Body. Responding to the Persecution of Christians* (Milton Keynes: Paternoster Press, 2006), pp. 37–61; Menzies, 'Reflections on Suffering', pp. 141–49; M.L. Dusing, 'Toward a Pentecostal Theology of Physical Suffering' (SPS conference paper, 1996); M.K. Adams, 'Hope in the Midst of Hurt: Towards a Pentecostal Theology of Suffering' (SPS conference paper, Toronto, 1996); E. Gaudion, *Braving the Storm* (Milton Keynes: Authentic, 2007); Mittelstadt, *The Spirit and Suffering*; Onyinah, 'God's Grace, Healing and Suffering', pp. 117–27.

sanctification has tended to obscure the awareness that a core role of the Spirit relates to the issue of suffering.[174]

This stance has led to numerous testimonies in which God is praised for rescuing believers from natural or man-made disasters or sickness, while little reflection is offered when others (including believers) suffer or die in similar or the same occasions. There has been a tendency to rejoice with those who have been healed of sickness and 'not to be too much worried about those who are not healed'.[175] Even though it is the experience of many Pentecostals to experience a variety of forms of suffering, the suspicion that it may be inappropriate or even illegitimate for believers who exist in relationship with a supernatural, omnipotent God lingers in the minds of many. At the same time, few refuse the benefits to be gained from the medical community. It is as if they hope God didn't notice or that he may overlook their 'lack of faith' in his provision. Even though many Pentecostal hymns reflect themes of suffering, the assumption by many is that this is nevertheless unnatural for the believer; suffering is somehow the fault of the devil, insufficient faith or limited prayer. Few dare to consider the possibility that suffering could be embraced as the path intended by God for his people, for his glory and for their good.

Consequently, few are able to look forward to death as the prelude to the eternal life for which they have been destined by God; it is too closely associated with the inaccurate concept that death has actually won the battle. This has often resulted in a sense of awkwardness with regard to preparing believers for death, for fear that such might be viewed as hastening death unnecessarily.

A recognition that suffering may be a natural prelude to death need not be viewed as a lack of faith in the power of God to restore the person to full health but a recognition that the time to move more fully into the presence of God is nigh. A recognition that suffering shapes life means that the life to come, in which there is an absence of suffering, takes on a new and anticipated perspective. To thoughtlessly pray for or claim healing may be damaging when a believer is dying. Being guided by the Spirit, one's experience and wisdom are important adjuncts to prayer at such times. It is possible that although one may be led by the Lord to pray for healing, prayer may also be offered for other aspects pertinent to the situation other than physical restoration. Thus, to pray for an infusion of God's peace and an increased sense of God's presence and comfort are appropriate. Indeed, the prayer offered should be seen in the broader context of a supportive framework

---

[174] M. Hoek, 'An Analysis of the Concepts of Suffering and Weakness in the Context of the Spirit in Romans 8' (unpublished doctoral dissertation, University of Manchester, 2006).

[175] Myung and Hong, *Charis and Charisma*, p. 60.

offered to the sufferer so that s/he can practically benefit from the corporate group of believers of which s/he is a part.

A theology of suffering is not high on the agenda of most Pentecostals even though many of them experience suffering in one way or the other. They have expended little time on developing philosophical and/or theological propositions that account for the place of evil in the world. Although the dualism of many Pentecostals does not satisfy them practically or intellectually, it is the matrix they have chosen to adhere to and they do so tenaciously. Even though such dualism makes the devil appear to own a similar level of authority as God, in terms of his manifesting evil in this world that affects believers as well as others, they have spent little time reflecting on the issue and confronting the inconsistencies of such a view.[176]

However, moves towards the development of a theology of suffering have been made in recent years. The 1989 General Presbytery of the US AoG adopted a position paper relating to the Kingdom of God in which it offered a survey of the issue in the Bible.[177] In it they declared the authority of God over creation (Pss. 22.28; 45.6; 66.7) and his rule as being everlasting (Dan. 4.34). Furthermore, the notion that suffering may not be viewed as an appropriate experience for believers was identified as erroneous and elitist.[178] The features of the present and future aspects of the Kingdom of God are particularly reflected in the teaching of Jesus. It exists as a present reality (Mt. 3.2; 4.17) and a future entity also (Mt. 24.27–31).[179] Thus although Christians may be adopted into the family of God at salvation in the present, they are not yet able to benefit from all that is their inheritance including the freedom from issues consisting of sickness, sadness, sin and its effects and death; much of the latter will be realized in the future eschaton.

At first sight, it may be assumed that a basic aspect of the ministry of Jesus was to remove suffering. However, not all suffering was remedied by Jesus, nor is there evidence to suggest that this was the most important part of his agenda. In the ministry of Jesus, there is little reference to the removal of slavery, the oppression of the Roman Empire, the crippling poverty of the people caused by the taxation burden or the many other aspects of life that called for a radical solution to establish justice. Indeed, rather than cause all

---

[176] For an interesting insight into the infiltration of Manicheanism into the Christianity, see A. Louth, 'Augustine', in C. Jones, G. Wainwright, E. Yarnold (eds), *The Study of Spirituality* (London: SPCK, 1996), pp. 134–45 (137–38).

[177] Z.J. Bicket, 'The Kingdom of God as Described in Holy Scripture. A Position Paper', *Paraclete* 24.3 (1990), pp. 13–18.

[178] Bicket, 'The Kingdom of God', p. 18.

[179] M.W. Dempster, 'A Theology of the Kingdom – A Pentecostal Contribution', in V. Samuel and C. Sugden (eds), *Mission as Transformation* (Irvine: Regnum, 1999), pp. 45–75.

suffering to flee with a flick of his fingers, he forecast suffering for his followers (Mk 10.38–45).

Similarly, although Jesus healed many people, few followed him and many
rejected him; although Jesus functioned authoritatively, he himself suffered.
The path of the Messiah was the path that commenced in the clothes of a
baby in a manger and concluded in the nakedness of a cross and the burial
clothes of a tomb. It will be surprising if the testimony of his followers is
that they lived lives of luxury and limited suffering when their Lord and
Master did not. The book of Acts and the lives of the Apostles demonstrate
that his sufferings continued in their lives. As his mission was born and
ended in suffering, so also the mission of the early Church was conducted in
the context of suffering.

Suffering is part of life; it does not sidestep the Christian. It is part of the
package of life in a world that has been harmed by sin. However, in all contexts of suffering, God has committed himself to be present. This means that
his supportive resources are available and directed to believers whenever
they are suffering. It is significant to note that Paul writes more about suffering than he does about restoration from it or its removal. Instead, he
speaks about its presence in the life of a believer as being normative, a point
echoed elsewhere in the NT (Jas 1.2–3, 12; 5.10–11; 1 Pet. 1.6; 2.19–25;
4.4, 12–19).

Suffering can have positive benefits for those suffering and their communities. Because of a physical weakness, which resulted in his not being able to
travel, Paul remained and preached the gospel to the Galatians (4.13). There
is no suggestion that the weakness resulted from personal sin or lack of
prayer. It is even possible that Paul intended his readers to recognize that, on
this occasion, suffering was a divinely ordained norm for the presentation of
the Gospel. For an envoy of a god to be weak or ill was a cultural hurdle to
be cleared by the Galatians when they were confronted with Paul; but they
achieved it (4.14). At the same time, they had the opportunity to learn an
important lesson about God's ways of working in weakness to achieve his
purposes (4.15). Whether Paul was referring to a specific bodily weakness,
such as poor eyesight, or a general form of weakness that accompanied his
ministry is not clear. That which is certain is that God chose to demonstrate
his grace and power in the context of weakness. Although not all suffering
is intended to provide lessons for suffering believers and those around them,
the testimony of Paul (2 Cor. 12.7) provides encouragement to consider
such a possibility.

The issue of suffering must not be overlooked by believers as God's way of
refining, transforming or correcting believers (1 Cor. 11.29–32; Jas 1.2–4).[180]

---

[180] Eutsler, 'Why Are Not All Christians Healed?', p. 21.

Although suffering is not to be experienced in heaven and is not intrinsically good, God nevertheless has the freedom and authority to use it, on occasions, to serve his purposes. Thus, Eutsler suggests that suffering may provide an opportunity to better contemplate God, depend on God or hear from God.[181] It also provides a context for demonstrating love for others (2 Cor. 1.3–5).

Suffering has the potential for being viewed as a valid context for reflecting God and understood as a pathway of victory as much as healing or some other supernatural restoration. This is often the case in contexts where unbelievers (and believers) have the opportunity to see a believer reflecting God in adversity as well as where a person has that adversity removed.[182]

In a world that was and still is often dominated by suffering, it is instructive to note that the NT writers often identify the role of the Spirit in contexts of weakness and suffering. Although suffering is inextricably linked to life and Christians are not immune to it, it is to be remembered that it is an earthbound condition and the Spirit's involvement in the suffering of the believer is certain, motivated by love and comprehensive wisdom.

A greater awareness of the role of the Spirit in supporting believers when they suffer and enabling that suffering to benefit them and others will result in all concerned being able to realize the significant commitment of the Spirit to believers, his aim being to enable all to achieve the destiny and potential set before them by God. Cho writes, 'God lets us go through various tiny holes of adversity . . . so that we may receive the anointing of the Holy Spirit . . . and fly into the heaven of God's grace'.[183] He is the Spirit not only of power and triumph but also of power and triumph through suffering. The power anticipated in 1.8 should be contextualized in the suffering associated with the witness to the Gospel as reflected in the rest of Acts. Praying for more power needs to be recognized as simultaneously asking for more opportunities to exhibit it while embracing challenging situations. The concept of suffering is thus redeemed by the Spirit as a valuable and integral element of the development of the mission of a believer. That the Spirit does not always remove suffering in the NT narrative is significant in that it instructs believers to be prepared to accommodate it into their lives with fortitude and joy, knowing that it was such for the prophets of the OT, the spiritual champions of the NT (including Peter, Paul and Stephen) and Jesus himself.

Although the message of Acts is that the Gospel triumphs, it is in association with the fact that it does so through suffering. More particularly, the

---

[181] Eutsler, 'Why Are Not All Christians Healed?', pp. 21–2.
[182] Katter, 'Divine Healing', p. 25.
[183] D.Y. Cho, *When I Am Weak, Then I Am Strong: A Sermon Series* (Seoul: Logos, 2003).

Spirit, who set the agenda for the development of the Church and assured that it would succeed, did so on a route often categorized by opposition and suffering (Acts 9.16; 14.22). In the book of Acts, God is not presented as removing or even lessening the suffering or removing believers from it; indeed, it appears to increase (in the form of persecution) precisely because they are believers. Luke has two messages. The one is that the Spirit is supreme and will fulfil his plans; the other is that suffering is often the normal (and, by implication, chosen) route for this to occur.[184]

It is to be expected that the Gospel will be opposed and that its witnesses will be rejected as reflected in the writings of Luke and the experiences of the early Church leaders.[185] The persecuted Church is the norm; the Church that is not suffering is therefore a cause of wonder or concern. Asking the Spirit to empower believers while removing them from suffering is thus often inappropriate. However, asking for the power of the Spirit while engaging in suffering for the Gospel is to emulate the life of Jesus and the greatest leaders of the early Church.

The Spirit-worldview offers a mature and realistic construct that also incorporates the recognition that the Spirit is supremely in control of believers. It is different to the immature perception of many believers today who assume a right to happiness and who expect God to infuse their lives with regular pleasant experiences. The notion that God could use suffering in their lives as an instructive and developmental aid is a shocking and even abhorrent notion to many. However, if it is not true, the experiences of the believers in Acts and the Majority world are cause for concern for they do not fit the mould of the contemporary Pentecostal worldview of many. What is of greater concern is that the experiences of the early believers appear to be intended to be normative and motivated according to the designs of the Spirit. Somewhere along the way, the role of the Spirit in association with suffering has got lost, to such an extent that now, rather than suffering being viewed as a channel through which the Spirit chooses to effectively empower believers, it is viewed as a channel through which the devil manifests himself and that is therefore to be resisted at all costs.

Western believers have yet another reason to consider and learn from the experiences of those believers, mainly living in non-Western countries, who are experiencing phenomenal growth in the context of suffering. Their life trajectories are more in line with those instituted by the Spirit for the believers in the early Church. Pentecostals have to remember that although the triumph of Pentecost resulted in the empowering of the disciples to witness, it also introduced a context of suffering as a result of which the power of the Spirit was particularly valuable.

---

[184] See B.R. Gaventa, 'Toward a Theology of Acts: Reading and Rereading', *Interpretation* 42 (1988), pp. 146–57.

[185] Ma, 'Asian (Classical) Pentecostal Theology', pp. 75–6.

9

ESCHATOLOGY

Introduction

Clark describes Pentecostalism as 'an apocalyptic movement, in its self-understanding and its theology'[1] while Damboriena asserts, 'eschatology belongs to the essence of Pentecostalism'.[2] Indeed, Macchia articulates the view that eschatology may be of more importance to the essence of Pentecostalism than the baptism in the Spirit[3] while Land similarly identifies it as the 'driving force and galvanising vision' of Pentecostalism.[4] Certainly, belief in the second coming of Jesus ranks as one of their most important tenets of faith. Of the seventeen fundamental truths of the AoG, no less than four relate to eschatological issues, while, by comparison, only one concentrates on the Bible or salvation.

However, many of these beliefs are shared with other, especially fundamentalist, believers. Indeed, during the earliest years of Pentecostalism, its adherents adopted the eschatological vision of Fundamentalism or Dispensationalism. Coulter demonstrates the significant influence of dispensational thought on early North American Pentecostal eschatology.[5] Although Pentecostals rejected the concept of cessationism that is associated with Dispensationalism, they imbibed its emphasis on premillennialism and a

---

[1] Clark and Lederle (eds), *What Is Distinctive*, p. 90.
[2] P. Damboriena, *Tongues as of Fire: Pentecostalism in Contemporary Christianity* (Washington: Corpus Books, 1969), p. 82; Nichol, *Pentecostalism*, p. 66; Gee, *The Pentecostal Movement*, p. 2; McClung, 'Explosion, Motivation, and Consolidation', pp. 7–10; Faupel, *The Everlasting Gospel*, pp. 20, 91–114.
[3] Macchia, *Baptized in the Spirit*, pp. 27, 38–40, 46–9.
[4] Land, *Pentecostal Spirituality*, p. 62 (also pp. 61–3, 95).
[5] Sheppard, 'Pentecostals, Globalization', pp. 5–33; Coulter, 'Pentecostal Visions of the End', 85–95; P. Prosser, 'Dispensationalism', in Burgess (ed.), *EPCC*, pp. 137–41; P. Althouse, '"Left Behind" – Fact or Fiction: Ecumenical Dilemmas of the Fundamentalist Millenarian Tensions within Pentecostalism', *JPT* 13.2 (2005), pp. 185–207.

pre-tribulation rapture.[6] Van der Laan notes the influence of the Scofield Reference Bible in the dissemination of Dispensationalism, referring to it as being 'aggressively promoted by the Assemblies of God'.[7] The majority of Pentecostals chose to ignore (or were ignorant of the fact) that much of dispensational thought was anti-Pentecostal. Increasingly, some of the emphases of dispensational thinking (including the central place of Israel in the eschaton) have been marginalized by many Pentecostals.

Millennial Views

Postmillennialism, flirted with by some Pentecostals, especially those who have been influenced by the Charismatic Renewal, advocates the belief that the millennium will be preceded by a period of church growth and the return of Jesus will be ushered in by a triumphant Church. Against the optimism of postmillennialism, others refer to texts that describe the sufferings of believers towards the end of the age that seem to undermine the postmillennial claims (2 Tim. 3.1–5; 1 Pet. 4.12–19).

Increasingly, this has been viewed as naïve optimism although the massive increase in global Pentecostalism has caused some to re-examine it. Many of the songs now sung by Pentecostals (and others) reflect such a triumphant Church.

The popularity of premillennialism among Pentecostals is largely due to the fact that it was the majority view of those who were the precursors of Pentecostalism.[8] Glass suggests that World War I, in particular, served to strengthen premillennialism because 'it appeared to demolish any remaining hopes of a kingdom established through the church'.[9] The reoccurrence of charismata in the Church was interpreted further as evidence that Jesus was soon to return. At the same time, an increase in diabolic and antichristian activity was anticipated in such a time. Indeed, by and large, premillennialism is not optimistic about the future prospects of the world.

The majority of those who hold to a premillennial position are also futurist and thus anticipate that most of the contents of the book of Revelation are yet to be fulfilled, many believing this fulfilment to be imminent. It is best

---

[6] F.L. Arrington, 'Dispensationalism', in Burgess and van der Maas (eds), *NIDPCM*, pp. 584–86; Lugo (*Spirit and Power*, p. 24) records that 91% of Pentecostals in the countries researched stated that they believed in the rapture.

[7] P. van der Laan, 'What Is Left Behind? A Pentecostal Response to Eschatological Fiction', *JEPTA* 24 (2004), pp. 49–70 (55); Plessis, 'A Proprium for Pentecostal Theology', p. 146.

[8] Dayton, *Theological Roots of Pentecostalism*, pp. 143–80.

[9] Glass, 'Eschatology', p. 135.

represented currently by the *Left Behind* Series.[10] Since the premillennial view coalesces with a readiness to, wherever possible, interpret the Bible literally, it has been the natural interpretation embraced by Pentecostals.[11] Thus, Canty concludes that to assume that the millennium is not literal undermines the literal nature of the incarnation.[12] Similarly, Menzies writes, 'The thousand years are mentioned six times in Revelation 20. That kind of repetition in the Bible indicates emphasis, which gives us every reason to take the thousand years of the Millennium literally'.[13]

In order to articulate and defend pre-tribulation premillennialism, Pentecostals have engaged in elaborate interpretations of OT and NT texts.[14] As a result of these deliberations, many individuals have been identified as the antichrist (the Pope was commonly assumed (and still is by some) to be a likely candidate). Similarly, organizations (WCC, European Common Market [European Union], UN, NATO) were believed to be forerunners of a one-world government, a pseudo-church[15] or a reconstituted form of the Roman Empire (assumed to be prophesied in Daniel and associated with Rev. 12.3; 13.1, 17), countries were identified as being likely to engage in military conflict and persecution of the Church while dates were suggested for the return of Jesus.

Although premillennialism has retained a significant following among Pentecostals, it has been challenged on a number of levels and a significant minority of Pentecostals prefer an amillennial perspective. It understands the 1000 years of Rev. 20.1–7 as symbolic of the era from the death of Jesus to his return (though its weakness is in its exposition of these verses) and does not accord to Israel as much prophetic significance, believing that Israel is no longer God's chosen nation because the Church has taken that position.

---

[10] T. LaHaye and J.B. Jenkins – www.leftbehind.com. The first, of 12 volumes, was printed in 1995, the final one, *Glorious Appearing*, in 2004, by which time they had sold more than 60 million copies, translated into 34 languages as well as presented in film.

[11] Kay, 'Assemblies of God', p. 56; W.J. Maybin, 'Bible Prophecy', in Brewster (ed.), *Pentecostal Doctrine*, pp. 211–25 (222); see the 1987 position paper titled 'Kingdom Now . . .', adopted by the General Presbytery of the US AoG in 1987 which rejected alternative views to pre-millennialism (*Paraclete*, 24.3 (1990), p. 20); S.M. Horton, 'The Last Things', in Horton (ed.), *Systematic Theology*, pp. 597–638 (619–22).

[12] Canty, *In My Father's House*, p. 126.

[13] Menzies and Horton (*Bible Doctrines*, p. 236) writes, 'The pre-millennial view is the only one that takes the Bible as literally as it is intended to be'.

[14] Ezek. 38–39; Dan. 2.1–45; 7.1–12.13; Mt. 24.3–44; Mk 13.1–31; Lk. 21.1–33; 1 Thess. 4.13–5.11; 2 Thess. 2.1–12 and throughout Revelation; Article 24 of the AoG Constitution; Pearlman, *Knowing the Doctrines*, pp. 389–90; R. Riggs, *The Path of Prophecy* (Springfield: Gospel Publishing House, 1937); Williams, *Systematic Theology*, pp. 193–95.

[15] Maybin, 'Bible Prophecy', p. 219.

Although some regard it as teaching a replacement theology (of Gentiles over Jews), most amillennialists teach that the Church is the place for the extended community of God which includes Jewish and Gentile believers. They tend to view the prophecies of Jesus' eschatological sermons as having been largely fulfilled in AD 70 when the temple was destroyed. The end is anticipated as occurring after an escalation of evil and, for some, associated with the conversion of natural Israel. The other major distinctive of amillennialism, assumes that the 'rapture' occurs after the period of tribulation (Mt. 24.29–31) and precedes not a millennium but eternity itself. Thus, the rapture will prelude the judgement of unbelievers, the punishment of the devil and the welcome of believers into heaven. In effect, instead of Jesus coming twice in the premillennial timetable (to rapture the Church and then to judge the world), he comes once and does both simultaneously in the amillennial schema.

One reason for the trend towards amillennialism is the lessening of the assumption that the return of Jesus is imminent. Baby boomers brought up with this expectation have struggled to maintain a belief that has lost its central hope. The demise of the USSR has further exacerbated this diminution of attachment to the premillennial view, given the assumption and teaching that the opposition to Jesus in the eschaton would largely come from the Soviet bloc. The increase of the Charismatic Renewal and Restorationist churches with their optimistic fervour and determination to establish the Kingdom of God meant that the Church looked increasingly less like the Laodicean church of Revelation 3 that was assumed to represent a weak and disfigured twentieth-century global Church. Instead, Christians were encouraged to make an impact in their communities and new models of church were developed to ensure that this happened. The Church was on the move and Pentecostalism itself became the most notable example of this impetus with revivals occurring throughout the world; the pessimism of premillennialism with its readiness to leave this increasingly lost realm for a better one was changing as Christians sought instead to improve the earth on which they lived with an increasing desire to effect societal change.[16] Rather than praying 'Lord come quickly . . . to take us home', Pentecostals are more likely to pray 'Lord come quickly but use us to change this world before you come'. Similarly, the assumption that a loving God would automatically rescue his people from tribulation has been increasingly critiqued, the more believers are seen to suffer in the current global community.

The replacement of the theme of the return of Jesus with the theme of the Kingdom of God has also helped to reshape Pentecostal thinking.

---

[16] Glass ('Eschatology', p. 139) notes that, for example, in Nigel Scotland's book (*Charismatics and the Next Millennium* (London: Hodder and Stoughton, 1995), there is no reference to eschatology, indicating its decreased value in Charismatic priorities.

Whereas dispensational thought associated the Kingdom of God with the future millennium, increasingly, it is viewed as the responsibility of believers to establish it now in this society through the explicit preaching of the gospel and also by facilitating those who work in secular settings to express their faith in creative ways to enable kingdom values to spread and also by becoming involved in the arts, media, politics, business and society in order to redeem people from a life without God.[17]

Finally, Pentecostals are now much more prepared to analyse and question their beliefs; that is not to suggest that they have rejected or will reject them. However, they are more able and prepared to ask questions of some of 'the eschatological shibboleths of their forefathers'[18] and in so doing, some of them have arrived at different conclusions. Although premillennialism introduced a fervent drive to evangelize the world, recent decades have seen a demise in this fervour and, perhaps coincidentally, in the adherence to premillennialism. The fact that Jesus has not come back after decades of certainty that he would and the upward mobility of many Pentecostals have resulted in a cooling of the ardour to expect the rapture at any moment. Similarly, the detailed pamphlets and books that sought to identify aspects of (especially) the books of Daniel and Revelation with modern-day countries, peoples or issues have not helped the case for premillennialism since so many of them have been proved to be wrong. Meanwhile, Dispensationalism, the modern source of premillennialism has increasingly been critiqued and thus it is no surprise that one of its favoured beliefs has also been neglected or even rejected.

The Second Coming of Jesus

The physical, literal return of Jesus to the earth is an important feature of Pentecostal spirituality, Menzies describing it as 'a key to history' as a result of which 'God will bring His plan to its glorious fulfilment' (2 Pet. 3.3–10).[19] Pentecostals have viewed the return of Jesus as a major stimulus to Christian service, holiness (1 Jn 3.3) and, in particular, evangelism (Mt. 24.14).[20] Pentecostals believe that Jesus will return personally (Jn 14.3), suddenly (1 Thess. 4.17; 5.3; 2 Pet. 3.10) and gloriously (Mt. 16.27) but also unexpectedly (Mt. 24.36–44). They also emphasize the association of the return of Jesus with the judgement of believers (Mt. 25.14–30; 1 Cor. 14.9–15).

---

[17] Glass, 'Eschatology', pp. 141–43.
[18] Glass, 'Eschatology', p. 144.
[19] Menzies and Horton, *Bible Doctrines*, pp. 213–14; Rowe, *One Lord, One Faith*, pp. 76–80.
[20] Menzies and Horton, *Bible Doctrines*, p. 215.

When Jesus returns, they expect believers to be taken (the verb 'raptured' being the term often used) to heaven, leaving behind only unbelievers (Mt. 24.36–43; 1 Thess. 4.13–17; 2 Thess. 2.6–7).[21] This is generally assumed to occur after the fulfilment of much of the eschatological discourse of Mt. 24, including a rise in famines, earthquakes, wars and religious deception. The latter is referred to in 2 Thess. 2.3 where Paul refers to something/someone who is described as restraining a lawless person (2.3); when this force is removed, the lawless person will function freely for a period before Jesus returns and destroys the lawless one. Pentecostals often identify the restraining force as the Church and believe that at the Rapture, the Church will be removed from the earth, leaving the lawless one to reign for a short time (1 Thess. 4.16–18; 5.9–11; 2 Thess. 2.1).[22] While many Pentecostals accept this view, some offer other interpretations for the restraining force including the possibility that Paul may be referring to the role of law and order which has the capacity to restrain chaos and disorder. If that is removed, tyranny reigns.

Pentecostals who follow a premillennial schema, further stipulate that after the Rapture, events in the world will initially continue as normal (Mt. 24.40–41), leading a minority to believe that the Rapture will in some way be secret. Most, however, believe that the absence of believers will be noticed and will even lead some to faith in God.

Pentecostals believe that after the Church has been raptured, a period of tribulation will occur.[23] This is to be a time when the wrath of God is to fall on the world (1 Thess. 5.9–11), believers being protected from this by way of the Rapture (Mt. 24.22, 29–31). There is a minority belief that maintains that the rapture will occur during the middle of the tribulation[24] though many more believe that it will occur before.[25] Increasing numbers of Pentecostals believe that the return of Jesus will occur after a period of tribulation (Mt. 24.20–31; 2 Thess. 2.1–8). Post-tribulationists have argued that the twofold return of Jesus (once to rapture believers, the second (occurring after the tribulation) to judge the world) is not clearly reflected in the Bible neither does the NT explicitly indicate an occasion when the Church is removed from the earth.[26] Furthermore, it is argued that the wrath referred to in 1 Thess. 5.9 does not necessarily refer to the time of tribulation, a concept that is not referred to by Paul in 1 Thessalonians, but to the initial return

---

[21] I.W. Lewis, 'The Rapture of the Church', in Brewster (ed.), *Pentecostal Doctrine*, pp. 259–71 (259–64).

[22] Lewis, 'The Rapture of the Church', pp. 264–66.

[23] Menzies and Horton, *Bible Doctrines*, pp. 218–19.

[24] Lewis, 'The Rapture of the Church', p. 267.

[25] Menzies and Anderson, 'D.W. Kerr and Eschatological Diversity', pp. 8–16.

[26] Glass, 'Eschatology', p. 130.

of Jesus which precipitates the judgement to come that will result in salvation or wrath of an eternal and spiritual nature (5.9). Instead, they believe that the tribulation forecast by Jesus will occur at the end of the age, both of which will be terminated when Jesus returns, at which point the Church is finally redeemed, Satan is judged and the new era commences.

Those premillennialists who hold to a pre-tribulation rapture believe that the tribulation will last for 7 years on the earth (Jer. 30.4–7; Rev. 7.14; 13.5) that will include a reconsitituted 'abomination of desolation' (Mt. 24.15), the persecution of 144,000 Jews who place their faith in Jesus (Rev. 7.1–17) and the martyrdom of believers (presumed to have come to faith during the tribulation (Rev. 7.13–17; 13.15).[27]

The period of 7 years is based on a reading of Dan. 9.24–27 which suggests that the first 69 of the 70 weeks referred to by Daniel end with the crucifixion of the Messiah, the seventieth week being postponed until the time when the restraining influence is removed from the earth. Given the assumption that a day is equivalent to a year, the final week is deduced to last for 7 years, a feature affirmed by reference to other verses (Rev. 11.2–3; 12.6; 13.5).

During the Tribulation, the antichrist is believed to become the world leader and to function in a context of blasphemous lawlessness (2 Thess. 2.4) and powerful signs and deceit (2 Thess. 2.9, 11).

According to the premillennial schema, after this period of extreme tribulation, Jesus is expected to return again as judge and will defeat Antichrist (2 Thess. 2.8) who will have ruled over the chaos on earth (Rev. 19.11–21) at the battle of Armageddon (Rev. 16.16), and institute a reign of 1,000 years, known as the Millennium (Rev. 20.1–3). During this period, Satan is believed to be inactive (Rev. 20.2), Israel will experience a significant change with many Jews becoming Christians (Ezek. 37.21–22; Rom. 11.24–26) and Jesus will reign over believers and unbelievers. After the 1,000 years has been completed, Satan is to be released from his bondage and will lead a final rebellion of the nations against God but almost immediately will be defeated, this time with no reprieve, being cast into the Lake of Fire (Matt. 25.41; Rev. 20.7–10).

Forces that will participate in the Battle of Armageddon against God and the Church are believed to be identified in Ezek. 38–39 and these have been interpreted (especially by Western believers) as referring to Russia (and her allies), Arab countries (especially Egypt) and China (Rev. 16.12).[28] The disintegration of the Soviet Union and the demise of communism (both viewed

---

[27] The notion of a 7 year tribulation period was initiated by J.N. Darby, the founder of the Plymouth Brethren, in the nineteenth century and thereafter popularized through the Scofield Reference Bible; see F. Gaebelin, *The Study of the Scofield Bible, 1909–1959* (New York: Oxford University Press, 1959).

[28] D.J. Wilson, 'Eschatology, Pentecostal Perspectives on' in Burgess and van der Maas (eds), *NIDPCM*, pp. 601–05 (603–04); Maybin, 'Bible Prophecy', p. 224.

for many years as the major antagonistic forces to God and the Church) have resulted in the focus now being directed to Arab countries, especially since the rise of Islamic fundamentalist and terrorist activities.

The final element of this programme is the Great Judgement (Heb. 9.27) in which God will judge all, dispatching some people to heaven and others, including the devil and his minions, to hell (Rev. 20.11–15). After this, eternity ushers in a new order for believers who will live in heaven or on a newly constituted earth (2 Pet. 3.10–13) in perfect relationship with God (Rev. 21.1–22.5).[29]

Although they stress the importance of retaining a strong eschatology, that is not to suggest that there is (or ever has been) clear unanimity.[30] Despite the strong tendency to premillennialism, many do not believe that the Bible provides a clear schedule of end-time events and premillennialism itself has inconsistencies.[31] Keener is one of a few modern Pentecostal scholars who attempts to shed some light on the issue, referring to some of the countless errors that have been made over the last century with regard to attempts to identify the date of the return of Jesus and events preceding it.[32] However, although Pentecostals have noted that it is not possible to date the return of Jesus, this has not stopped them from trying to identify such an occasion, the 'signs of the times' being a common phrase among Pentecostals, especially up until the end of the twentieth century.[33]

The many dates offered by well-meaning 'prophetic watchers' for the occurrence of the rapture that were unfulfilled have often brought the premillennial view into disrepute or at least resulted in people being much more guarded in their comments. A common suggestion was that Jesus would return in 1981. This prediction was based on Mt. 24.34 which seems to indicate that the prophecy of Jesus, concerning the end-time tribulation that precedes his return, would be fulfilled before a particular generation had passed. Many assumed this generation to refer to a period of 40 years (rather than the more likely interpretation of a people group), an era that was assumed to follow the re-establishment of the nation of Israel that took place in 1948. When the period of 7 years (for the tribulation) was removed from the 40 years in question, a date of 1981 was arrived at for the rapture. However, when this year passed without any cataclysmic events occurring,

---

[29] Menzies and Horton, *Bible Doctrines*, pp. 255–58.

[30] Anderson and Menzies, 'D. W. Kerr and Eschatological Diversity', pp. 8–16.

[31] Kay, 'Pentecostals and the Bible', p. 81. In his survey of UK Pentecostal leaders, he provides the following responses of those who agree with that perception that the Bible does not provide a clear order of end time events (Apostolic 24%, AoG 56.4%, Church of God 65.3%, Elim 55.6%).

[32] Keener, 'Rightly Understanding God's Word. Revelation', pp. 40–61.

[33] J.C. Smyth, 'The Signs of the Times', in Brewster (ed.), *Pentecostal Doctrine*, pp. 381–90.

many exponents of the second coming were forced to recalibrate their charts. Paul counsels against such speculation (1 Thess. 5.1–3) because he is more interested in encouraging believers to persevere in the faith rather than be preoccupied with dates.[34] Similarly, Jurgensen, who provides an exegesis of 1 Thess. 4.13–5.11, advises Pentecostals to cease from speculating about the date of the return of Jesus while Keener concludes that since the book of Revelation is largely symbolic, it should be interpreted through that lens.[35] Given their literalistic tendencies, this has not been easily accepted by many Pentecostals.

Heaven and Hell

Because of a belief in the endlessness of life, Pentecostals take seriously issues relating to heaven and hell though they have rarely written about either, probably in recognition of the fact that others have already done so and the Bible is limited in its exposure of both.[36] Although they rarely explore the meaning of the concept of the soul anthropologically or philosophically, fundamentally they believe that when they are using this term, they are referring to the essence of a person. They assert that this core expression of an individual does not stop existing after death (Lk. 16.19–30; 2 Cor. 5.8; Phil. 1.22–24; 1 Pet. 3.19).[37] The prospect of heaven and the danger of hell and the everlasting nature of both are therefore strong motives for their evangelism.

Because they tend to view life after death in a linear fashion, they, along with many other evangelicals, have developed a timeline for expressing life after death for believers. Thus, Hunston assumes that one does not receive one's resurrection body until the Day of Judgement and speculates that, immediately after death, believers go to Paradise before heaven (Lk. 23.43) to be in the presence of Jesus (2 Cor. 5.8), though it is less clear in what form that existence will take. Pentecostals have tended to describe life after death as initially occurring in an intermediate state where the person consciously exists in a disembodied state but with Jesus. However, while some postpone the granting of new bodies to an occasion when believers and unbelievers are judged, others believe that the new body will be granted immediately after death. The concept of soul sleep (that takes as literal the word 'sleep'

---

[34] H. Jurgensen, 'Awaiting the Return of Christ: A Re-Examination of 1 Thessalonians 4.13–5.11 from a Pentecostal Perspective', *JPT* 4 (1994), pp. 81–113.

[35] Keener, 'Rightly Understanding God's Word. Revelation', pp. 49–61.

[36] R. Hunston, 'The Future State – Heaven and Hell', in Brewster (ed.), *Pentecostal Doctrine*, pp. 149–58 (149).

[37] Hunston, 'The Future State – Heaven', p. 152.

when it is used to describe someone who has died (1 Cor. 15.6, 18, 20; 1 Thess. 4.13–15)) that assumes that people enter a period of hibernation after death, has been rejected by Pentecostals.

It may be more helpful to recognize that the NT evidence was not necessarily intended to provide a complete chronology of events from this life to the next and beyond. Rather, it contains principles intended to demonstrate the sovereign rule of God and the security of the believer. These issues should dominate one's exploration of eschatological texts rather than engaging in an exercise of defining a schedule of events. The latter leads to often contradictory and internally inconsistent frameworks that also result in dissension among believers; the former is a truer reflection of the intention of the authors and is ultimately spiritually beneficial.

Pentecostals have long believed that after death, all believers will be judged on the basis of their lives on earth, as a result of which they will receive commendation or reprimand (Mt. 25.14–46; 1 Cor. 3.11–15; 13.3; 2 Cor. 5.10). However, though they believe in such a judgement, they are less clear as to its implications; nevertheless it is viewed as entailing a serious accounting for one's actions, words and motives and will result in consequences, though the identity of the latter is not clarified.

Thereafter, believers are to go to heaven, the location of which is uncertain, though most assume that it is above the clouds because of the reference to Jesus descending at the end of time in the clouds (1 Thess. 4.17). Other terms are used for heaven or, at least, to define aspects of heaven, including the New Jerusalem (Rev. 21.10–14), the dimensions and properties of which are often taken literally (21.15–21).[38] On the basis of this literalistic perspective, Menzies suggests that the new earth will be larger than the current one.[39]

The information in Revelation concerning the reconstituted earth is taken literally by many Pentecostals. Thus, that Heaven will not need the light of the sun or the moon (Rev. 21.23) and that there will be night (Rev. 21.25) are taken to mean by many that there will be no actual sun or moon.[40] Similarly, because it identifies the absence of the sea in the new earth, it is assumed that this is a literal truth rather than the possibility that issues related to the sea, including restlessness and chaos (Ps. 65.5, 7; Jas 1.6), may be in the mind of the author. Rather than indicating that there would literally be no sea, sun or moon, John may be recording the fact that issues related to instability, fear and this present life will be absent in the superior life hereafter. More reflection on the hermeneutical methods appropriate to the interpretation of such apocalyptic writings will increasingly help expose the message

---

[38] Menzies and Horton, *Bible Doctrines*, p. 259 (it is identified as a cube, measuring nearly 1400 miles on each side).

[39] Menzies and Horton, *Bible Doctrines*, p. 259.

[40] Menzies and Horton, *Bible Doctrines*, p. 258.

of the author to modern readers. 2 Tim. 2.12 (Rev. 20.4) refers to the fact that believers will reign with Jesus in heaven while 1 Cor. 6.3 notes that believers will judge angels. However, most descriptions of life in heaven relate to worship (Rev. 4; 5; 22.3) and offer limited descriptions of other aspects of life, the tendency being to describe that which is not there, including the devil (Rev. 20.10), sin (Rev. 21. 27; 22.3), sadness (Rev. 21.4), death (Rev. 21.4), unbelievers (Rev. 21.8; 22.15), temple (Rev. 21.22) (indicating a proximity of relationship to God that excludes the need for a temple, priestly and sacrificial system), as well as that which is there (the new Jerusalem (Rev. 21.10–21), the river of the water of life (Rev. 22.1) and the tree of life for healing (Rev. 22.2). For Pentecostals, eternity is not the end of time; it is the start of endless time. Believers are ushered through this life for the purpose of eternity, for that is their destiny. Eternity is not simply the reward for life on earth; it is the reason for creation. Life does not end when eternity begins; to a very significant degree, it begins.

Many Pentecostals are uncertain as to the exact identity of their form of existence after death, largely due to the fact that the Bible is not clear about it. In Rom. 8.10–11, Paul tells his readers that although their bodies are to die as a result of sin, their resurrection is affirmed since (rather than 'if') the same Spirit who was associated with the resurrection of Jesus also guarantees to raise them from the dead. 1 Corinthians 15.45 is located towards the end of a discussion concerning the resurrection body. In seeking to expand on the nature of the new body, Paul contrasts it with the physical body and defines it as a 'spiritual body' (sōma pneumatikon) (15.44). Pentecostals accept the validity of this perspective although they have not substantially explored the concept, their assumption being that their heavenly bodies will share a marked similarity to the properties of Jesus' resurrection body (Phil. 3.21; 1 Cor. 15.49; 1 Jn 3.2) while bearing some association to the present body (1 Cor. 15.37).[41] It is thus assumed to be physical in some way and not ethereal or uncorporeal.

Hell is the term normally used by Pentecostals to identify the contrasting location to heaven. The former is a place of torment, darkness and pain (Mt. 8.12; 13.49–50; 22.13), a place 'full of remorse, bitterness, frustration, and raging lusts that cannot be fulfilled',[42] and identified with the Lake of Fire, the destiny of the devil and all demons (Rev. 20.10). The NT introduces the readers to the concept of Gehenna, originally the Aramaic name for the valley of Hinnom to the south of Jerusalem which functioned as the place where refuse was deposited and burned though was also the site of idolatry in the OT (2 Chron. 28.3). Jesus refers to Gehenna as a place of eternal punishment and thus it functions, in the minds of many, as another term for hell

[41] Hunston, 'The Future State – Heaven', p. 156.
[42] Menzies and Horton, Bible Doctrines, p. 251.

(Mt. 25.46; Mk 9.47–48). Similarly, Hades, in the NT, is identified as a place of suffering for unbelievers (Lk. 16.23–28) and may also refer to hell or a place where unbelievers go before they are dispatched there. Sheol in the OT is understood to identify the location of the dead (Ps. 6.5; Isa. 38.17–18), the opposite to heaven (Job 11.8; Ps. 139.8) or the destiny of evil people (Ps. 9.17; Prov. 15.24).

Traditionally, most Pentecostals would subscribe to the traditional Christian view that heaven and hell will last forever (Rev. 20.10), Rowe concluding that this is 'beyond question'.[43] Pentecostals do not accept arguments for annihilationism (the unbeliever is annihilated at death or after judgement) or conditional immortality (the unbeliever is sentenced to punishment that lasts for a period of time depending on the gravity of their crimes). The description of the fire of hell being unquenchable (Mt. 3.12; Lk. 3.17) is viewed as being descriptive of its endlessness and not a metaphor of its ability to purge, prior to the demise of the one experiencing punishment.[44] They also note the references to the word 'eternal' in association with the destiny of believers and unbelievers (Mt. 25.46; 2 Tim. 2.10; 2 Thess. 1.8, 9; Rev. 14.11). Because this word is also used in association with God (Rom. 16.26; Heb. 9.14), it is argued that the same characteristic of endlessness of life must be retained in all its uses. However, as with some other evangelicals, cautious explorations on the part of some Pentecostals to engage with the concept of conditional immortality have occurred.

Israel

Many Pentecostals, especially in the USA, affirm that Israel is still God's elect nation, on the basis of Rom. 11.28, and many take literally the call to pray for the peace of Jerusalem (Ps. 122.6). A consequence of this view is that most Pentecostals resist the suggestions that the Church has replaced Israel and that the promises of God to Israel in the OT are now only relevant to the Church.[45] The role of Israel in this respect is particularly significant among Pentecostals who hold to a dispensational view of eschatology which teaches that the Church and Israel are two separate peoples of God with individual divinely determined agendas. Israel has the prior claim on God, the Church only existing from the day of Pentecost and ending when Jesus returns whereupon Israel is to be readmitted into relationship with God.

---

[43] Rowe, *One Lord, One Faith*, p. 53.

[44] Menzies and Horton, *Bible Doctrines*, p. 252.

[45] Steinberg (chairman) in 1987, on behalf of the US AoG General Presbytery, adopted the position paper titled 'Kingdom Now . . .' In it, the suggestion that the Church had replaced Israel was rejected.

[46] Menzies and Horton, *Bible Doctrines*, pp. 236–39.

The Church is thus the forum for God to interact with people while Israel goes through a period of rejection of Messiah.

The emphasis on the role of Israel by Dispensationalists is partly based on the OT verses that are interpreted as being timeless and to be fulfilled literally especially where they relate to the land of Israel (Gen. 15.18–19; Ezek. 38–39) and the spiritual restoration of the Jews (Ezek. 36.24–27). Thus, while looking forward to the latter, many Pentecostals are supportive of the claim of Israel to its ancient lands as promised to Abraham. The Jews are further affirmed as a result of the references to Israel in Romans; many Pentecostals understand these texts to foretell the redemption of the nation of Israel (Rom. 11.1) added to which they note that the apostles are identified as future judges of Israel (Mt. 19.28). Furthermore, many assume a rebuilding of the temple in Jerusalem (Ezek. 9.3; 10.4, 18).[46] Du Plessis argues that there will come a time when, after the rapture of the Church, Jesus will specifically preach to the Jews again during the millennium.[47]

As part of the premillennial timetable of events, the re-establishment of Israel in 1948 and the taking of the old city of Jerusalem in 1967 have been identified as signs of the imminent return of Jesus, the former event assumed to have been prophesied in Lk. 21.32 as the end of 'the times of the Gentiles' (21.24) and partial fulfilments of Isa. 66.10–24 and Zech. 14.1–21.[48]

Many Pentecostals have thus tended to view Israel through rose-tinted prophetic spectacles and thus have refrained from criticizing the Israelis for their treatment of Palestinians in their territory. At the same time, they have applauded Israeli victories over their Arab neighbours in 1967 and 1973 (that they have often identified as miraculous) while supporting the attacks on Iraq (1981) and Lebanon (1982).[49] This support of Israel is located in the earliest period of Pentecostalism especially where the notion of British Israelism was promulgated.[50] However, there has been a significant shift in thinking in that some are prepared to criticize Israeli politics, support the many Palestinian believers, re-evaluate the belief that Israel holds a special place with God in comparison with other nations and recognize that the Church is the new Israel and 'the elect' is a term referring to Christians, not Jews (Rom. 8.33).

Some Ways Forward

- The less emphatic belief in the imminent return of Jesus has resulted in the topic of the second coming being less preached than it once was. It has

---

[47] Plessis, 'A Proprium for Pentecostal Theology', p. 146.
[48] Maybin, 'Bible Prophecy', pp. 221–22.
[49] Wilson. 'Eschatology, Pentecostal Perspectives on', pp. 601–02.
[50] Hathaway, 'The role of William Oliver Hutchinson', pp. 47–9.

been put on the shelf to become dusty, now and again being retrieved for a Bible study or a reminder that Jesus is coming again sometime in the future.[51] Pentecostals need to be careful that being less enamoured with their cherished premillennialism does not result in a limited focus on eternity. Where premillennial views still have greatest impact is among the poor and marginalized. Those who have little in terms of material benefits are most attracted to the promise of an imminent removal to a place where deprivation and loss are no more. Combined with the potential benefits of healing (and prosperity), this reaching out to a better life (in the near future) in heaven has proved to be a powerful reason for many to identify with premillennial eschatology. It will be a challenge to ensure that this enthusiasm will not be disappointed by forlorn promises and hopes. 'Pentecostals need to rediscover the original eschatological fervour' that characterized much of the dynamic of early Pentecostalism,[52] not in order to ramp up anticipation of an imminent return of Jesus but because it is a glorious hope – whenever it happens. Similarly, it is appropriate to study eschatological issues with excitement, for to do so should result in improved spirituality, increased love for Jesus and heightened determination to serve him.[53]

- The eschatology of many Pentecostals has been formed by the popular *Left Behind* books.[54] Van der Laan offers a healthy review of the phenomenon, charting its development and identifying possible initiatives that could help create balance and provide a more Biblically based setting for an eschatological paradigm.[55] Such a move has been helped by greater attention being paid to the clearer and less tangential references to the return of Jesus (Mt 24.1–35; Mk 13.1–31; Lk. 21.1–33; 1 Thess. 4.13–5.11; 2 Thess. 2.1–12); these have been increasingly viewed as providing the most helpful guidance for investigating the return of Jesus and preceding events.
- Eschatological frameworks, particularly in the early expressions of Pentecostalism in the West but also to a degree now, used to be dominated by timetables of events that would usher in the end of life as we know it. The challenge is to move away from attempts to locate such schedules in the Bible and instead to concentrate on more pressing eschatological issues. Similarly, Land advocates that 'Pentecostals should focus their attention and theological efforts on understanding God as the eschatological trinitarian presence and not on speculation concerning end-time sequences'.[56] The central message of the eschatological hope is that it will usher in the complete rule of God that is being established already in this world

---

[51] H. Cox, 'A Review of *Pentecostal Spirituality: A Passion for the Kingdom* by Steven J. Land', JPT 5 (1994), pp. 3–12 (9–10).

[52] Macchia, 'The Struggle for Global Witness', p. 23.

[53] M.K. Thompson, 'Revisioning Pentecostal Eschatology' (unpublished doctoral dissertation, Luther Seminary, 2007).

[54] T. LaHaye, J.B. Jenkins (Wheaton: Tyndale House Publishers, 1995–2003).

through the Church. Pentecostals should concentrate not just on being removed from the sin and depravity of this world but also how best to introduce the Kingdom of God and righteousness into society prior to any return of Jesus.[57] Pentecostals need to work through the tension of anticipating a new earth established by God in the eschaton with the implications that this has on attempts to care for the world and affirming the goodness of creation.[58] Whereas the belief in the imminent return of Jesus resulted in little time and energy being expended on social support being offered to people in need, now there is much more attention being paid to the alleviation of suffering of people by Pentecostals. At one time, most of their energy was dedicated to exclusively spiritual needs; now, social evils are also being addressed and a holistic approach in evangelism is much more evident.

- Furthermore, although this is not true of all Pentecostals, a greater willingness to accept other eschatological views has resulted from the awareness that the Bible does not clearly provide comprehensive evidence for a particular perspective. This is the case despite the scholarly nature of one's argument, the fervency of one's presentation or the verses offered in support of one's eschatological timetable. It is not clear that a concensus may be, or even should be, easily achieved. At least one Classical Pentecostal denomination has realized this, removing the need for its ministers to espouse a premillennial perspective, though not undermining it as a valid option.[59]
- The recognition of the possible validity of other eschatological frameworks that may be supported from Scripture will facilitate greater fellowship and undermine the need for strident voices to be raised in defence of one view against another which often results in disunity and fragmentation. Instead of attempting to identify eschatological timetables, it would be more advantageous to articulate a theology that anticipates the eschaton breaking into the present thus allowing for the possibility of an anticipation of the full revelation in the future but also providing an expectation of the latter in the present.[60]

---

[55] Van der Laan, 'What is Left Behind?', pp. 49–70; also C.C. Anderson, 'A Catholic and Ecumenical Response to the Left Behind series', JPT 13.2 (2005), pp. 209–30.

[56] Land, 'A Passion for the Kingdom', p. 28.

[57] See also van der Laan, 'What is Left Behind?', p. 69; Hollenweger, 'Pentecostalism, Past, Present and Future', pp. 42–3.

[58] M. Volf, 'On Loving with Hope: Erchatology and Social Responsibility' *Transformation* 7.3 (1990), pp. 28–31.

[59] The Elim Pentecostal Church contained the notion of pre-millennialism in its 1923 and 1934 Statements of Fundamental Beliefs but removed it in its 1993 revision after a conference in which the issue was debated by its ministers and lay leadership; it now reads, 'We believe in the personal, physical and visible return of the Lord Jesus Christ to reign in power and glory'.

[60] Althouse, 'Left Behind', pp. 201–07.

10

POSTSCRIPT

Pentecostals have embraced significant changes within their traditions in recent years and yet have also maintained continuity with the past in major areas. Practices have been retained, refined and removed; beliefs have been evaluated and sometimes amended or contextualized. Some Pentecostals have dialogued with those outside their traditions and sought to embrace all who express a faith in Jesus and a desire to see the Spirit achieving his agenda for the Church. The quest for mission has been retained and developed structurally while the pursuit of excellent training of Christian leaders has been advanced. Exploration of the Bible is now much more enlightened and mature and a consideration of the role of the Spirit and the Christian community in its interpretation and application are actively being pursued as worthy objectives.

There are significant challenges ahead especially with reference to personal spirituality and the development of a moral framework that is appropriate to the contemporary context and that embraces biblical principles. Issues relating to the identity of leadership and the role of women therein as well as the training of future leaders are also of significant importance for Pentecostals to develop; the Pentecostal revival will slow down and even implode if these aspects are not seriously examined and conclusions carefully implemented. The fragmentation of Pentecostalism is an ongoing concern as is the impact of unhelpful triumphalist emphases on believers. The tension between offering healing while simultaneously redeeming the concept of suffering is also an issue worthy of continued exploration. There is also the pressing need to ensure that personal encounters with the Spirit are not restricted to experiences that are merely determined by Pentecostal traditions rather than the purposes of the Spirit himself. His agenda for encountering believers is often much wider and more innovative than has previously been anticipated.

In a movement that has experienced rapid growth, many are determined to ensure that the tidal wave of Pentecostal expansion will not be damaging to those it impacts but that the life-giving spiritual water it brings will refresh those who are swept along in its flow. It is to be hoped that this book also will be a helpful conversational partner in the pursuit of a Pentecostal theology that is authentic, culturally relevant and best radiates the agenda of God in the development of his Church. If, as a result of this book, Jesus becomes increasingly central in one's life, the Spirit becomes more vital to one's experience and the Father is recognized as more supreme in one's assessment of his sovereignty, it will have achieved its purpose.

SUBJECT INDEX

Anabaptism 2
Anointing with oil 291–3
Apostle 138–40
Azusa Street 1

Baptism in the Spirit 4,
    95–130
Baptism in water 162–4
Bible 180–205
    Application 188–91
    Inerrancy 182–4
    Infallibility 182–4
    Inspiration 181–2

Cessationism 70–1
Charismatic Renewal 5
Church, The 131–43
    Leadership 136–43

Deliverance *see* Exorcism
Demons *see* Exorcism
Dispensationalism 2

Ecology 237–8
Ecumenism 169–79
Encounter 20–7
Eschatology 258–9, 309–23
Ethics 226–45
Evangelism *see* Mission
Evangelist 142
Exorcism 293–302
Experience 15, 26–7, 48–51, 192–4,
    255–6

Fasting 218–19

Gifts of the Spirit 69–95
God 28–9
    the Father 33

Healing 80–1, 265–308
    and evangelism 281–2
    and faith 284–7
    and forgiveness 289–90
    and Jesus 269–75
    and medicine 279–81
    and prayer 287–9
    and the atonement 270–4
    and the name of Jesus 290–1
    and the will of God 274–9
Healing evangelists 4
Heaven 317–20
Hell 319–20
Hermeneutics 184–201, 204–5
Holiness 207–14
Holy Spirit, The 44–8
    and ethics 243–5
    and evangelism 249–53
    and Jesus 51–6
    convicts people 61–2
    empowers believers 56–9
    establishes the Church 59–61
    guides believers 66–9
    transforms believers 62–6

Israel 320–1

Jesus 34
    and the Spirit 51–6

Keswick 4

Latter Rain Movement, The 4
Laying on of hands, The 293
Lord's Supper, The 164–9

Millennialism 310–13
Mission 246–64, 281–2
Music 223–6

SUBJECT INDEX

Oneness Pentecostalism 31–3
Other religions 40–4

Pacificism 236–7
Pentecostal Theology 17–20
Pentecostalism 6–16
Pietism 4
Prayer 214–19, 287–9
Preaching 201–4
Predestination 38–40
Premillennialism 4, 310–13
Prophecy 81–4
Prophet 140–2
Prosperity Gospel 238–9

Racism 233–6
Roman Catholicism 175–8

Salvation 34–8
Second Coming of Jesus, The 313–17
Signs and Wonders 252–3
Sin 35–7
Spirituality 206–45
Subsequence 99–106
Suffering 303–8

Theological Education 152–61
Tongues 84–95, 119–23
Trinity, The 29–31

Wesleyanism 4, 12
Women in Leadership 142–52
World Council of Churches,
    The 172–5
Worship 219–26

SCRIPTURE REFERENCES

Genesis
1.1 *201*
1.2 *41, 46*
2.7 *42, 106*
3.14 *294*
15.18–19 *321*

Exodus
15.26 *190*
17.1–6 *62*
19.5 *135*
19.5–6 *135*
22.20–26 *240*
33.15–16 *53*
40.13–15 *204*

Leviticus
16.29 *218*
16.31 *218*
26.15–16 *208*
27.30 *208*

Numbers
11.25 *61*
14.18 *28*

Deuteronomy
4.13 *207*
7.6 *38*
7.9 *28*
12.6 *208*
13.1–5 *81*
13.18 *81*
13.20 *81*

Judges
3.10 *69*
6.34 *53, 69*

11.29 *69*
14.19 *69*

1 Samuel
16.13 *53*
19.18–24 *61*

2 Samuel
22.36 *28*

1 Kings
8.27 *28*
18.42 *218*
19.16 *204*
21.27–29 *218*

2 Kings
2.9–14 *69*
13.14 *277*
20.6 *216*
23.27 *38*

1 Chronicles
16.37–42 *223*

2 Chronicles
7.14 *208*
16.12 *190*
28.3 *319*

Nehemiah
9.7 *38*

Esther
4.16 *218*
8.8 *115*

Job
11.8 *320*
42.7 *216*

Psalms
2.7 *54*
6.5 *320*
8.1 *29*
8.3 *29*
9.17 *320*
19.1–2 *29*
19.9 *28*
22.28 *305*
38.15 *216*
45.6 *305*
50.15 *216*
51.11 *46*
65.5 *318*
65.7 *318*
66.7 *305*
103.8 *28*
104.24 *28*
104.30 *46*
119.9–11 *66*
122.6 *320*
139.1–6 *28*
139.7–10 *41*
139.8 *320*
145.10 *29*
145.17 *28*
147.5 *28*

Proverbs
1.23 *62*
3.9 *208*
14.31 *240*
15.24 *320*
16.9 *217*
21.13 *240*

Isaiah
6.3 *35*
6.8–9 *141*

Isaiah (*Cont'd*)
20.3–5 *82*
21.11 *249*
28.11 *92*
32.15–20 *46*
38.17–18 *320*
42.9 *217*
44.3–5 *46*
53.4 *273*
53.4–5 *272*
53.7 *36*
57.15 *28*
61.1–2 *55*
66.10–24 *321*

Jeremiah
4.5 *82*
9.1 *82*
11.11 *208*
11.14 *208*
23.23 *28*
30.4–7 *315*
32.17 *28*

Ezekiel
1.24 *82*
3.17 *249*
4.1–5.4 *82*
9.3 *321*
10.4 *321*
10.18 *321*
32.10 *115*
33.7 *249*
33.30–32 *142*
36.24–27 *321*
36.26–28 *61*
36.27 *62*
37.9 *106*
37.14 *106*
37.21–22 *315*

Daniel
4.34 *305*
9.24–27 *315*
10.13 *218*

Hosea
1.2 *141*

Joel
2.12 *218*
2.28 *59, 152*
2.28–29 *115*
2.28–32 *25, 60*

Amos
4.13 *29*
9.11–12 *193*

Zechariah
4.6 *275*
14.1–21 *321*

Malachi
3.10 *208*

Matthew
1.20 *51*
1.21–28 *202*
1.29 *41*
3.2 *305*
3.11 *95, 100*
3.12 *320*
3.16 *162*
3.17 *54*
4.1 *54*
4.17 *305*
5.7 *239*
5.9 *239*
5.13–16 *239*
7.7–8 *218*
8.12 *319*
8.14–17 *272*
8.17 *273*
9.35 *283*
10.1 *117, 283*
10.6–7 *283*
10.8 *283*
11.21 *287*
12.31 *36*
13.49–50 *319*
13.54–58 *287*
16.16 *103*
16.19 *107*
16.24 *216*
16.27 *313*

19.27 *103*
19.28 *139, 321*
20.28 *36*
22.13 *319*
24.1–35 *322*
24.14 *258, 313*
24.15 *315*
24.20–31 *314*
24.22 *314*
24.27–31 *305*
24.29–31 *312, 314*
24.29–35 *242*
24.34 *316*
24.36–43 *314*
24.36–44 *313*
24.40–41 *314*
25.14–30 *313*
25.14–46 *318*
25.35–39 *245*
25.35–46 *239*
25.41 *293, 315*
25.46 *320*
26.28 *165*
26.36–44 *218*
28.19 *46, 162, 163*
28.19–20 *142,
248*

Mark
1.8 *95*
1.10 *163*
3.13–15 *139*
4.15–20 *300*
5.2 *294*
5.5 *294*
6.1–6 *287*
6.12 *283*
9.17 *294*
9.29 *191*
9.47–48 *320*
10.38–45 *306*
12.35–37 *200*
12.42–44 *208*
13.1–31 *322*
16.1–20 *191*
16.7 *84*
16.15–20 *238*

Luke
1.15 *58*
1.20 *270*
1.32–33 *54*
1.35 *46, 54, 116*
1.42 *59*
1.67–79 *59*
2.36 *141*
2.38–39 *119*
2.46–47 *53*
3.16 *95*
3.17 *320*
3.21–22 *54*
3.22 *116*
4.1 *116*
4.12 *55*
4.14 *59, 116*
4.16–30 *55, 243, 287*
4.18 *55, 59, 204*
4.18–19 *51, 59*
4.18–20 *283*
5.17 *116*
7.22 *283*
9.2 *107, 283*
9.6 *107*
10.1–2 *138*
10.20 *103, 108*
11.5–8 *217*
11.13 *98*
11.26 *294*
13.1–5 *299*
16.19–30 *317*
16.23–28 *320*
18.1–8 *217*
21.1–33 *322*
21.24 *321*
21.32 *321*
22.7–8 *164*
22.8 *165*
22.14–20 *165*
22.15 *165*
22.16 *166*
22.19 *165*
23.43 *317*
24.30–31 *166*
24.44–49 *59*
24.49 *53, 99, 108*

John
1.4 *64*
1.9 *42, 64*
1.29–34 *54*
1.33 *95*
1.48 *78*
3.3 *40*
3.3–7 *41*
3.5 *62*
3.5–6 *47*
3.6 *42, 63*
3.7 *61*
3.8 *49*
3.16 *35, 38*
4.14 *61, 62*
4.17–18 *78*
4.24 *220*
4.26 *62*
6.3–7 *138*
6.52–57 *168*
7.8–39 *62*
7.37–38 *108*
7.37–39 *106, 210*
8.5–13 *139*
8.19 *32*
8.46 *36*
9.3 *299*
10.30 *32*
11.41–42 *270*
12.45 *32*
13.34–35 *91*
14.3 *313*
14.12–14 *283*
14.12–17 *134*
14.15–18 *284*
14.16–17 *47, 67*
14.17 *42*
14.25–26 *67*
15.1–8 *134*
15.1–11 *4*
15.3 *103*
15.3–5 *108*
15.7–12 *68*
15.26 *30, 62*
15.26–27 *103*
16.7 *30, 106*
16.8–9 *61*

16.13 *42*
17.14 *108*
17.21–23 *91*
17.25 *35*
20.15–19 *211*
20.19–23 *106*
20.21 *106*
20.22 *106, 211*
20.22–23 *211*
20.26 *106*

Acts
1.4–5 *53, 104, 108, 111*
1.5 *95*
1.8 *56, 58, 59, 107, 108,*
  110, 112, 116, 117,
  250, 284, 307
1.14 *98*
1.22 *139*
2.1–39 *108*
2.2 *104*
2.4 *59, 100, 110, 126*
2.6 *93, 94*
2.11 *93*
2.17–18 *100, 141, 284*
2.17–21 *108*
2.38 *33, 100, 108, 163*
2.41 *92*
2.42 *165*
3.12 *69*
4.7 *69*
4.8 *59*
4.8–12 *117*
4.27 *55*
4.31 *98, 108, 117,*
  126
5.1–2 *78*
5.1–6 *78*
5.1–8 *290*
5.1–11 *270*
5.11 *270*
6.3 *58, 59*
6.5 *59*
7.55 *56*
8.4–12 *59*
8.7 *300*
8.9–23 *79*

Acts (*Cont'd*)
8.12 *98*
8.14–17 *108f*
8.15 *98, 112*
8.16 *163*
8.17 *98, 100, 119*
8.18 *109*
8.26–38 *110*
8.26–40 *59*
8.40 *142*
9.4–6 *100*
9.9 *100*
9.10–12 *78*
9.16 *308*
9.17 *100*
9.17–18 *56, 119*
9.17–20 *117*
9.18 *162*
10.2 *111*
10.5 *111*
10.9–23 *60*
10.19–20 *250*
10.30–33 *111*
10.32–35 *111*
10.37–38 *51*
10.38 *55*
10.43–44 *103*
10.44–46 *110f*
10.44–48 *56*
10.46 *90*
10.47 *162*
10.48 *163*
11.2 *112*
11.12 *250*
11.14 *111*
11.15 *90, 112*
11.16 *95, 100*
11.17 *111*
11.24 *59*
11.27–29 *140*
11.28 *82*
12.5 *218*
12.35–37 *58*
13.2 *250*
13.2–4 *218*
13.3 *74*
13.8–12 *270*
13.12 *270*

14.14 *139*
14.22 *308*
14.23 *218*
15.14 *135*
15.16–18 *193*
15.22 *68*
15.28 *68, 112*
15.32 *140*
16.3–5 *149*
16.6 *46*
16.6–10 *250*
16.7 *46*
16.13–15 *149*
16.15 *111*
16.16–17 *79*
16.18 *300, 301*
16.19 *301*
16.20–21 *301*
16.22–24 *301*
16.24 *301*
16.26 *301*
16.30–33 *111*
16.31–34 *301*
16.33 *162, 163*
16.39 *301*
16.40 *149, 301*
17.1–9 *111*
17.10–12 *111*
17.24–28 *41*
17.34 *111*
18.8 *162*
18.8–9 *111*
19.1–7 *112f*
19.2 *48, 300*
19.5 *163*
19.5–6 *100,*
   164
19.6 *126, 141*
20.7 *165*
20.22 *108*
20.22–28 *59*
20.28 *138*
21.8 *142*
21.8–9 *141*
21.10–11 *82,*
   140
27.10 *78*
28.25 *181*

Romans
1.4 *51*
1.11 *69, 72, 73*
1.20 *28*
2.14–15 *64*
2.28–29 *135*
2.29 *62*
5.9 *36*
5.10 *36*
5.14–21 *35*
5.19 *289*
6.1–4 *163*
6.3 *113*
6.4 *163*
7.7–11 *67*
8.1 *62*
8.1–17 *62, 210*
8.2 *61, 62*
8.4 *66*
8.9 *47, 61, 126*
8.9–11 *32, 63*
8.10–11 *319*
8.14–17 *61*
8.15 *36*
8.15–16 *47, 114, 284*
8.15–17 *36, 115*
8.17–18 *129*
8.18 *206*
8.18–27 *42*
8.19–21 *238*
8.22–23 *279*
8.23 *129*
8.26 *65, 66, 215*
8.27 *49, 65*
8.29 *38*
8.33 *38, 321*
8.35–37 *129*
8.38–39 *300*
10.4 *67*
10.17 *80*
11.1 *321*
11.24–26 *315*
11.28 *320*
11.29 *69*
11.33–34 *217*
12.4–6 *72*
12.4–9 *134*
12.6 *69, 133*

12.6–8 74, 77
12.7 70
13.1–7 240
14.17 62
15.19 59, 127
15.27 69
16.1–2 149
16.7 139, 149
16.12 150
16.13 38
16.20 300
16.26 320

1 Corinthians
1.2–3 207
1.7 71
1.12 150
1.13 113
1.15 113
1.23–24 78
1.30 78, 206, 207
2.4 116, 284
2.11 46
2.12 126
2.13 66, 69, 181
2.6–16 62
3.1–4 135
3.11–15 318
13.3 318
3.16 46, 60
3.16–17 48, 135, 284
5.2 167
5.5 70
5.7 164
5.11 167
6.3 319
6.9–11 207
6.11 210
6.12 150
6.18–19 220, 284
6.19 24
6.20 36
7.1–40 148
7.5 300
7.7 75
7.25–31 242
8.4–6 294
9.1 139

9.2 139
9.11 69
10.1–5 162
10.2 113, 162
10.13 206
10.16 165
10.16–17 166, 169
10.17 167
10.20 294
10.21 165
10.23 150
11.2–16 148, 150
11.3 149
11.3–16 149
11.5 141, 145
11.17–22 167
11.20 165
11.24 168
11.26 165, 166
11.29 167, 169
11.29–30 167, 290
11.29–32 306
11.30 279
11.31–34 167
12.1 69, 70
12.3 61, 68, 72
12.4 69, 70
12.4–6 72, 75
12.4–7 134, 151
12.4–11 71
12.4–31 59, 71
12.5 72
12.6 70, 72
12.6–7 119
12.6–8 75, 134
12.11 119, 134
12.7 72, 81, 133
12.7–11 73
12.8–10 75, 76, 77, 81, 119
12.8–11 65
12.9 69, 81, 269
12.10 70, 84, 89
12.11 72, 82, 151
12.13 95, 100, 113, 119, 163
12.14 69, 81, 135
12.20 135

12.12–31 135
12.23–26 165
12.26 166
12.27 134
12.27–28 135
12.28 77, 80, 84
12.28–29 75
12.28–31 69
12.29–30 72
12.29f 77
12.30 89, 123
12.31 70
13.1 84
13.1–3 63, 72, 75
13.8 83
13.8–10 71
13.12 71
14.1 69, 70
14.1–6 74
14.1–33 59
14.2 84, 90
14.3–5 82
14.4 90
14.5 123
14.6 75, 84
14.9–15 313
14.13–20 88
14.15 88
14.20–22 91
14.26 75, 84, 220, 224
14.27 88
14.28 88, 90, 123
14.29 68, 83
14.29–32 83
14.31 141
14.32 82
14.33–35 150
14.37 70
14.40 82
15.3 36
15.6 318
15.7 139
15.7–9 139
15.18 318
15.20 318
15.37 319
15.44 319
15.45 319

1 Corinthians (*Cont'd*)
15.49 *319*
15.54–57 *35*
16.1–2 *208*

2 Corinthians
1.3–5 *307*
1.21–22 *60, 126*
1.22 *114*
2.11 *300, 301*
2.14 *78*
3.3–18 *62*
3.6 *135*
3.16–18 *62*
3.17 *32*
3.18 *272*
4.4 *294*
4.6 *78*
4.7–11 *129*
5.5 *60*
5.8 *317*
5.10 *318*
5.17 *210*
5.18–19 *36*
6.4–10 *129*
6.17 *170*
7.1 *64*
8.23 *139*
9.7 *208*
11.2 *135*
11.3 *294*
11.14 *301*
12.4 *25*
12.7 *306*
12.7–10 *129, 270*
12.9 *269*
12.12 *139*
13.14 *48*

Galatians
1.4 *294*
1.18–19 *139*
3.2 *48, 126*
3.2–5 *67*
3.4 *219*
3.5 *116, 126*
3.10 *67*
3.14 *114, 126*

3.19–29 *67*
3.27 *113, 163*
4.4–7 *67*
4.6 *61, 114, 126*
4.13 *270, 279, 306*
4.14 *306*
4.15 *306*
4.28 *148*
5.1 *67*
5.5 *62, 67*
5.16 *64, 66, 127, 210, 245*
5.16–18 *64*
5.16–26 *62*
5.22 *210*
5.22–23 *210*
5.22–24 *63*
5.22–6.1 *48*
5.25 *64, 66*
6.16 *135*

Ephesians
1.3 *69*
1.3–14 *62*
1.4 *38, 135*
1.4–5 *36, 38*
1.11 *135*
1.13 *114*
1.14 *40, 60, 114*
1.17 *67, 78, 126*
1.22–23 *134, 135*
2.2 *294, 300*
2.4–5 *35*
2.8 *80*
2.11–18 *171*
2.12 *142*
2.18 *49, 60, 220*
2.20 *139, 140, 141*
2.21–22 *135*
2.22 *220*
3.1–4 *135*
3.5 *140*
3.7 *70*
3.20 *127*
4.1–6 *176*
4.1–6.9 *300*
4.2 *91*
4.3 *48, 171*

4.5 *163*
4.7 *70, 72*
4.8 *70, 126*
4.11 *70, 75, 77, 138, 142*
4.12 *72, 138*
4.15–16 *72, 135*
4.26–27 *300*
4.30 *47, 114*
5.15 *64*
5.16 *64*
5.17 *64*
5.17–18 *64*
5.18 *64, 66, 100, 115, 126, 127*
5.18–19 *48*
5.18–33 *150*
5.19 *69, 224*
5.19–20 *64*
5.21–6.9 *64*
5.22 *147*
6.5–9 *240*
6.10–20 *64*
6.11–12 *293*
6.12 *294, 300*
6.13 *294*

Philippians
1.22–24 *317*
1.27 *48*
2.1–2 *48*
2.7 *34*
3.3 *135*
3.10 *220*
3.21 *319*
4.2–3 *149*
4.15 *133*

Colossians
1.13 *294*
1.16 *300*
1.21 *36*
2.3 *78*
2.9 *32*
2.10 *300*
2.15 *300*
2.19 *135*
3.5 *206*

3.16 *69, 88, 224*
4.1 *240*
4.3–4 *127*
4.15 *149*

1 Thessalonians
1.4 *135*
1.5 *116*
2.6 *139*
4.7 *206*
4.8 *46, 126*
4.13–15 *318*
4.13–17 *314*
4.13–5.1 *317*
4.13–5.11 *322*
4.16–18 *314*
4.17 *313, 318*
5.1–3 *317*
5.3 *313*
5.9 *314, 315*
5.9–11 *314*

2 Thessalonians
1.8 *320*
1.9 *320*
2.1 *314*
2.1–8 *314*
2.1–12 *322*
2.3 *314*
2.4 *315*
2.6–7 *314*
2.9 *315*
2.8 *315*
2.11 *315*
2.13 *135*

1 Timothy
2.4 *49*
2.9–15 *149*
2.11–12 *150*
2.12 *141*
3.2 *143*
3.16 *56*
5.17 *138, 143*
6.15 *28*

2 Timothy
1.6 *73, 127*

1.7 *72*
2.8–15 *151*
2.10 *320*
2.12 *319*
2.21 *64*
3.1–5 *310*
3.16 *107, 181*
4.5 *142*

Titus
1.5–7 *138*
1.9 *143*
2.14 *135*
3.5 *46*
3.5–7 *115*

Philemon
1.16 *241*

Hebrews
1.9 *55*
2.9 *41*
2.16–18 *34*
4.15 *15*
4.24 *55*
6.10 *135*
8.3 *34*
8.7–12 *135*
9.12, 26–28 *34*
9.14 *51, 61, 320*
9.22 *165*
9.27 *36, 316*
9.27–28 *36*
10.1–4, 11–14 *36*
10.10 *206*
13.2 *245*
13.8 *276*

James
1.2–3 *306*
1.2–4 *306*
1.5–8 *285*
1.6 *288, 318*
1.12 *306*
1.17 *28*
1.27 *240, 245*
4.7 *300*
5.10 *290*

5.10–11 *306*
5.13–18 *268, 270*
5.14 *288, 290*
5.14–16 *292*
5.14–18 *80*
5.15 *288, 290*
5.15–16 *270*
5.16 *288, 289, 290, 291*

1 Peter
1.1–2 *207*
1.2 *210*
1.3 *28*
1.6 *306*
1.6–8 *273*
1.15–16 *28*
1.19 *36*
2.9–10 *135*
2.12 *273*
2.13–17 *240*
2.18–21 *240*
2.18–22 *273*
2.19–25 *306*
2.22 *34*
2.22–25 *274*
2.24 *36, 273, 274*
3.14–17 *273*
3.19 *317*
3.20–21 *162*
4.4 *306*
4.10 *36, 72, 133*
4.12–19 *273, 306, 310*
5.2 *143*
5.8 *300*
5.9–10 *273*

2 Peter
1.4–8 *63*
1.21 *181*
2.4 *293*
3.2 *139*
3.3–10 *313*
3.9 *35*
3.10 *313*
3.10–13 *316*

1 John
1.9 *36, 206*

1 John (*Cont'd*)
2.27 *42*
3.2 *319*
3.3 *313*
4.1–3 *68*
4.14 *41*
4.16 *28*
5.14 *217*
5.15 *216*
5.16 *217*

3 John
2 *37, 232*

Jude
6 *293*
20 *215*

Revelation
1.17 *25*
4.5 *319*
5.1–2 *114*

7.1–8 *115*
7.1–17 *315*
7.4 *114*
7.13–17 *315*
7.14 *315*
8.4 *135*
11.2–3 *315*
12.3 *311*
12.6 *315*
12.7–9 *293*
12.9–10 *294*
13.1 *311*
13.5 *315*
13.15 *315*
13.17 *311*
14.11 *320*
16.12 *315*
16.16 *315*
18.4 *175*
19.11–21 *315*
20.1–3 *315*
20.1–7 *311*

20.2 *315*
20.4 *319*
20.7–10 *315*
20.10 *319, 320*
20.11–15 *316*
21.1–22.5 *316*
21.4 *319*
21.8 *319*
21.10–14 *318*
21.10–21 *319*
21.14 *139*
21.15–21 *318*
21.22 *319*
21.23 *318*
21.25 *318*
21.27 *319*
22.1 *319*
22.2 *319*
22.3 *319*
22.15 *319*

Lightning Source UK Ltd.
Milton Keynes UK
UKHW021535110220
358535UK00004B/159